Sanctuary in the Wilderness

STANFORD STUDIES IN JEWISH HISTORY AND CULTURE

EDITED BY *Aron Rodrigue and Steven J. Zipperstein*

Sanctuary in the Wilderness

A Critical Introduction to American Hebrew Poetry

Alan Mintz

STANFORD UNIVERSITY PRESS

STANFORD, CALIFORNIA

Stanford University Press
Stanford, California

©2012 by the Board of Trustees of the Leland Stanford Junior
University. All rights reserved.

This book has been published with the assistance of the Lucius
N. Littauer Foundation.

Credits appear on p. 521.

Printed in the United States of America on acid-free, archival-
quality paper

Library of Congress Cataloging-in-Publication Data

Mintz, Alan L., author.
  Sanctuary in the wilderness : a critical introduction to
American Hebrew poetry / Alan Mintz.
    pages cm.—(Stanford studies in Jewish history and culture)
  Includes bibliographical references and index.
  ISBN 978-0-8047-6293-9 (cloth : alk. paper)
  1. Hebrew poetry, Modern—United States—History and
criticism. 2. Hebrew poetry, Modern—20th century—History
and criticism. 3. Hebrew language—United States—Revival.
I. Title. II. Series: Stanford studies in Jewish history and
culture.
  PJ5024 .M46
  892.4'1509973—dc23
                                        2011032254

Typeset by Miles B. Cohen in 10.5/14 Galliard

To Susanna, Amira, and Avital, forever

Contents

Acknowledgments

Painting a collective portrait of a broad cultural movement has been possible only through the assistance of many hands. The late Gershon Shaked, who understood much about the dialectics of Israel-Diaspora relations, gave me much encouragement in the early stages of the project. Dan Miron was unstinting in making his vast and passionate knowledge of the subject available to me and in understanding the importance of the endeavor. Arnold Band, who grew out of the soil described in these pages, was supportive in manifold ways. Avner Holtzman's erudition and generosity have come to my aid on numerous occasions.

I was privileged to meet and converse with such participants in Hebrew life and letters in America as Gabriel Preil, Haim Leaf, Milton Arfa, and Jacob Kabakoff. Ezra Spicehandler remains an important bridge to that era.

Fortunately today there is a growing body of scholarship on American Hebrew literature, and I have benefited enormously from reading the work of, and having conversations with, Michael Weingrad, Stephen Katz, Philip Hollander, Shachar Pinsker, and Jill Aizenstein.

My colleagues in Jewish literature at the Jewish Theological Seminary (JTS)—David Roskies, Raymond Scheindlin, Barbara Mann, and Anne Lapidus Lerner—together with the two provosts under whom I've served—Jack Wertheimer and Alan Cooper—have made JTS an ideal home for my work, and I am proud to be a link in the chain of scholarship at JTS.

I am grateful to many whose intellectual and emotional support have been essential to me at every step: Cynthia Ozick, Ruth Wisse, Sharona Tel-Oren, Gidi Nevo, Wendy Zierler, Moshe Pelli, Shalom Lief, Hillel Halkin, Yaron Peleg, Avraham Holtz, Hana Wirth-Nesher, Anne

Golomb Hoffman, David Stern, Anita Norich, Sarah Feinstein, Natan Shifris, Hayim Goldgraber, Chaim Milikowsky, Sidra DeKoven Ezrahi, Avidov Lipsker, Hanan Hever, Yigal Schwartz, and Ariel Hirschfeld.

This study could not have been undertaken without the gift of time provided me by a research leave from the Jewish Theological Seminary and a grant from the Posen Foundation; I am grateful particularly to Daniel Posen for his sympathetic understanding of my project. I was pleased to be chosen as a fellow in a year-long seminar on modern Jewish literature at the Katz Center for Judaic Studies at the University of Pennsylvania, and I benefited enormously from the fellowship of my colleagues there. The writing of the book was completed while I was a visiting professor in the Department of Hebrew Literature at the Hebrew University, and I thank the department and the university for their gracious hospitality.

No scholar can ask for more than to have an unparalleled resource like the Library of the Jewish Theological Seminary easily at hand, and my debt to the Library's staff can never be paid off. The Hebraic Division of the New York Public Library came to my aid on many occasions; and my searches at the National Library in Jerusalem were invariably rewarded with fresh treasures.

I am grateful to Steven Zipperstein, Norris Pope, and the staff of the Stanford University Press for believing in the importance of the book and its subject. The joint expertise of Miles Cohen and Leslie Rubin saved me from many errors and generously enforced a high standard of accuracy and elegance.

This book is dedicated to my wife Susanna Morgenthau and our daughters Amira Mintz-Morgenthau and Avital Mintz-Morgenthau. The love and grounding they have given me are hidden among the words on each page of this text.

Finally, an intellectual and spiritual debt: Hovering over my shoulder throughout the writing has been the spirit of Abraham Epstein, the outstanding critic of American Hebrew writers. I can only hope that if he were alive today, his fine discrimination and exacting judgment would find something of worth in the work he inspired.

ROSH HODESH TAMMUZ 5770
NEW YORK CITY

Preface

I have titled this study a critical introduction to indicate the two goals it aims to accomplish. It is an introduction out of simple necessity. The very existence of a substantial corpus of Hebrew writing in America, not to mention poetry in particular, is a fact that is largely unknown to American Jews, to Israeli readers, and to students of American studies and American Jewish literature generally. And if the existence of the phenomenon is known to specialists in Hebrew literature in America and Israel, in its particulars, it is known only to a tiny handful. (The reasons for this cultural forgetting are considered in due course.) Hence the need for an introduction. This volume therefore attempts to set the scene for the emergence of the Hebraist movement in America, to explore the inner world of the Hebraist and the motives for the persistence of Hebraist production in an alien environment, to provide profiles of the careers of the major American Hebrew poets, and to offer individual accounts of the key poems that deal with American history and society. (The reasons why the study is limited to American Hebrew poetry rather than fiction and drama is discussed in Chaper One.)

At the same time, this is a *critical* introduction. Even if I had not intended it to be such, there is no way to prize apart description and evaluation. I have therefore undertaken the critical task with as much responsibility and self-awareness as possible. I have not hesitated to identify what I regard as the strongest works in the body of American Hebrew poetry and to offer arguments for those judgments. In presenting an essayistic account of the careers of each of the twelve poets discussed in this study, I have given an interpretation of the *shape* of the career in artistic terms together with an assessment of its successes and failures. And although the critical discourse of the study largely hovers at the range of general interpretative description, there is also frequent use of close reading. The profile of each poet concludes with a close reading of a lyric poem to give the reader a concrete experience of the poet's work. Both within the profiles themselves and in separate thematic chapters, I offer critical readings of several important texts.

Despite the many poems presented and translated, this volume is not an anthology of American Hebrew poetry. Several projects in the works hopefully will perform that function for both English and Hebrew readers. This volume is also not a literary history. By literary history I mean an exercise in historical poetics that would trace the development from early to late of literary language, genres, and poetic strategies in relation to changing thematic engagements. I very much hope that the reader will find many insights on these subjects delivered along the way, but I have not found it feasible to attempt a full-scale literary history. The reason for this is straightforward. When I first embarked on the study of American Hebrew poetry, with the exception of the path-breaking essays of Abraham Epstein, I could not find much help in getting my bearings in what turned out to be a surprisingly vast body of material.[1] There was no easy way to survey the landscape and see the forest for the trees. My only recourse was to start with one poet, read everything he wrote and that was written about him, and then go on to the next. The plan of this book, to some degree, recapitulates this journey.

My encounter with each new poet was beset with vicissitudes. Many of the American poets wrote in a formidable Hebrew style that was elevated and difficult. In the absence of translations and any real critical literature, both signs of the long neglect of the subject, I found it challenging simply to read through the material and block out a general mapping of the poet's oeuvre. It was akin, to press the metaphor, to cutting a path through a virgin forest. At first acquaintance, if truth be told, I often found the poet's verse daunting and uninviting. With persistence, however, the veil of difficulty would lift and the poetry would become differentiated and approachable. Afforded free movement within the poetry, finally, I could locate the individual poems that spoke to me and immerse myself in them. And thus, in stages and over time and somewhat unexpectedly, I would, almost without exception, fall in love with the poet I was working on at the time. I would stay with him long enough—the duration of this fidelity was not inconsiderable—to be able to sketch his profile and place him in context. Then it was time to move on to the next of my twelve figures. Thus, through a sustained sequence of serial monogamy, I moved toward the completion of the project. These successive episodes of acquaintance and rapture and separation afforded many insights about the larger picture of American Hebrew poetry, but the process has left me sufficiently challenged by the prospect of presenting what I have learned so far, and hence the status of this volume as a critical introduction. An integrative literary history, along with more specialist studies, hopefully will be undertaken at a future point and probably by hands other than mine.

This study describes the work of twelve American Hebrew poets with substantial bodies of published verse. That number might already seem surprising to those who were formerly unaware that there existed *any* American Hebrew poets. But there are indeed many more figures than the twelve, and the inclusions and exclusions therefore require some explanation. There are a number of published poets whose work, while deserving of attention, did not have sufficiently influential careers to warrant a place in a study that is structured around key figures; these include Baruch Katznelson, Eliezer D. Freidland, and M. Sh. Ben-Meir.[2] I have excluded, for example, a number of poets— among them Reuven Avinoam-Grossman, Noah Stern, Reuven Ben-Yosef, and T. Carmi—who were either born or raised in the United States but who emigrated to Israel and pursued their literary careers there. By affiliation, Avinoam-Grossman (1905–1974), who was born in Chicago and moved to Palestine in 1928, was most closely associated with his colleagues in America; he was active in translating American literature, and he participated in the collective project of translating Shakespeare into Hebrew undertaken by the American Hebrew poets.[3] But because his career unfolded in Palestine, he has not been included. (The subject of the reception of English and American literature into the Hebrew literary system in Palestine/Israel, in which American

Hebrew poets played an important role, is an important but separate area of inquiry.)

It will certainly not go unnoticed that there are no women among the twelve poets studied here. This reflects the general state of affairs in the public culture of American Hebrew literature, especially the editorships of journals and miscellanies and the publication of collections of verse. This is not to say that women were not involved in the Hebraist activity in America, especially in Jewish education, and there are poems by women scattered among the Hebrew journals.[4] The pivotal role of female Hebraist educators is just beginning to receive the attention it deserves.[5] This is a subject that undoubtedly deserves further investigation. Late in the work on this book, I was excited to learn of the existence of Claire (Haya) Levy, who published a poetry collection titled *Kissufim* [Longings] in 1941, which was, so far as I know, the first publication of its kind by a woman in America. The Chicago-based poet Chana Kleiman published a slim volume of verse in 1947 titled *Netafim* [Droplets], which is in the process of being reissued in a bilingual edition. She is joined by Chana (Annabelle) Fermelant, who published two volumes: *Iyyim bodedim* [Solitary islands] (1960) and *Pirḥei zehut* [Flowers of identity] (1961).[6] I expect that when the Hebrew periodicals of the time are combed through, we shall find a number of women who wrote poetry and published individual poems but did not bring out a book of verse. It will be intriguing to piece together the story of women's participation in American Hebrew literature.

Very late in this study I came across the unusual and impressive poetry of Avraham Zvi Halevi (1907–1966), who published gritty and splenetic poems about New York City that are unlike anything else in the corpus of American Hebrew poetry. Although I could not manage to make him a separate focus of study—the slight amount of his production would make it hard to call him major—I was able to give attention to his fascinating verse at the end of Part Three in the context of a discussion of the problematic theme of urban life.

Finally, there is the question of period. This study plots the career of Hebrew poetry as it rose and fell with the fortunes of the modern Hebraist movement in America, with its inception in the years just before World War I, its heyday during the interwar years, and its decline—with a youthful moment of revival—in the postwar years. The death of Gabriel Preil in 1993 serves as a symbolic point of closure. But just because this coherent period comes to an end does not mean that Hebrew verse was not written in America after the early 1990s. There is the improbable but delightful case of Robert Whitehill, who was born to an assimilated Jewish family and raised in Lubbock, Texas. Whitehill, who now publishes under the name Shmuel Whitehill-Bashan, taught himself Hebrew and eventually mastered the craft of Hebrew poetry and published several volumes of verse in Israel.[7] Then there is the case of George (Chaviv) Gorin (1909–1988), a graduate of the Hebrew Gymnasium of Bialystok, who came to America in 1939 and practiced as an ophthalmologist on the Upper West Side of Manhattan; in the four years before his death he wrote six books of Hebrew verse, which were published in Israel.[8] The religious community may have other Hebrew writers who are not generally known in the literary community. Zvi Meir Steinmetz (1915–2005), who wrote under the name Zvi Yair, published a number of books of religious verse. His three-volume collected poems appeared in 1997.[9] Steinmetz was born in Budapest and, after surviving the war hidden in an insane asylum, arrived in the United States in 1952. He was close to the Lubavitcher Rebbe, who encouraged him to continue writing verse. Another category includes Israelis who are living in America, like Maya Arad, a professor at Stanford University who has published verse novels in Hebrew. Within this category are the established critic-poets Rina Lee and Lev Hakak. Sadly, not much of significant literary creativity in Hebrew has been written by the numerous Israelis who have immigrated to North America or who have lived here for extended periods.

In sum, there is no end to the story, and the rumored demise of Hebrew poetry in North America—the so-called disappearance of the last of the Mohicans—continues to be undermined by interesting exceptions and outliers. Although I have endeavored to introduce the major figures in the major period, by no means do I wish to present American Hebrew poetry as a closed canon. Nothing would please me more than to see this canon destabilized and reopened.

The plan of this study is comprised of three parts. Part One begins with a historical introduction in Chapter One to the larger Hebraist movement as a context for the study of the poetry. This introduction discusses the relationship between fiction and poetry, the phases in the development of Hebrew belles lettres, the negative assessment of American Hebrew literature on the part of the critical establishment in Palestine/Israel, and the stylistic identity of American Hebrew poetry and its major themes and genres. The introduction is followed by a chapter, titled "The Apotheosis of Hebrew," which focuses on the great anthem to the Hebrew language published by Abraham Regelson in 1945. That formidable poem is used as a touchstone to speculate about the inner experience of American Hebraists and the intimate and religious nature of their bond with the language. Regelson's anthem serves as a gateway to the inner world of Hebraism and illuminates the motives behind and beneath the poetic production that is the subject of this study.

The core of the book, Part Two, contains twelve chapters—one for each of the twelve poets. It is in these essays that the volume attempts to discharge its introductory responsibility. Each essay places its subject within the larger context of Hebrew literature and the American Hebraist scene, with some gesture in the direction of biography, and foregrounds the unique features of the poet's work. In most cases, I try to outline the shape of the poet's career as a whole; in the cases of the several poets who moved to Israel, I have emphasized the American phases of their lives. I spend considerable time discussing individual works that represent the poet's best efforts and much less time on works that do not seem now to have enduring value. The essays vary in length; some essays about important poets such as Silkiner, Efros, and Lisitzky are shorter than the essays about Silberschlag and Halkin because I discuss some of their major book-length poems elsewhere in Part Three. As mentioned above, each essay concludes with—standing as a separate unit—a textual analysis of a single lyric poem. (The reason for the emphasis on the lyric is discussed in the Introduction.) It is my hope that these brief, close readings provide the reader with the kind of tactile experience of the poetry that cannot be provided by the necessarily generalizing discourse of the essays as a whole. All translations in this volume, unless otherwise noted, are mine.

Part Three ("American Vistas") reflects closer attention to a limited number of poems, most of them of book length, that address American history and the American landscape. These include three epics about Native Americans (by Silkiner, Efros, and Lisitzky), long poems about rural New England and upstate New York in the nineteenth century (Bavli and Preil), a narrative saga about the California Gold Rush (Efros), a collection of poems based on African American folksongs and sermons (Lisitzky), and poetic sequences on New York City (Halevi). In these important works, American Hebrew poets were responding, in their own way and on their own terms and certainly at their own speed, to the demand voiced by the Hebrew literary center in Palestine early in the twentieth century that the Americans deliver *ameriqa'iyyut*, American local color. The response to this demand, if they were responses at all, came decades later in sophisticated and varied ways. The works discussed in this part constitute much of the American canon of American Hebrew poetry.

The present volume, as I have described above, is a hybrid enterprise: a critical introduction to American Hebrew poetry. It undertakes both to supply the basic information of an overview, as well as to offer critical interpretations of individual poems and whole literary careers. Given these mixed purposes, I expect that there will be several different kinds of readers who will find the book useful and therefore different ways in which the book will be used. Although I will be gratified if students of Hebrew literature read the book cover to cover, I fully realize that others might find a modular itinerary more useful. After absorbing the introductory materials of Part One, such a reader might dip selectively into the individual portraits in Part Two before examining the colorful Americana of Part Three.

There are, to be sure, other equally fascinating thematic preoccupations in American Hebrew poetry that deserve exploration. There are major responses to the Holocaust, for example, in the work of several of the poets. At a time when the ideological background of the Yishuv (the organized Zionist settlement in Palestine) introduces conflict and ambivalence into the literary responses to the murder of European Jewry, American Hebrew writers were able to address the subject more directly. The relationship to Zion and to Palestine/Israel on the part of the Americans is another absorbing topic. Although they staked their lives on being Hebrew writers, their location in America did not make it easy for them to be acknowledged and play a role in the life of Hebrew at its center; moreover, the establishment of the state of Israel accelerated their marginalization. Also, the preservation of the dignity of the Hebrew language as spoken by Israelis did not always fulfill hopes. This was a complex and fraught relationship. Both subjects, the Holocaust and Israel, which I have not dealt with in this volume, will well repay attention in the future.

Sanctuary in the Wilderness

Part I *The Hebraist World*

I present two brief collective portraits of the American Hebraists from two different periods to introduce the subject of this study.

The first comes from the pen of Zalman Shazar, a historian and man of letters who became Israel's third president. On his first visit to America in the early 1930s, he made a surprising discovery: a band of Hebrew poets about whose existence he had known nothing.

They were not exactly a group because they were not joined together but rather a scattering of proud and lonely individual writers who seemed to be prophesizing to themselves. In their isolated nobility, they attached themselves only to the intangible and absolute in the national spirit. They had complete mastery over the Hebrew language in all its depth and vitality as if they lived in the Land of Israel, and they were utterly unreconciled and even oblivious to the surroundings in which they actually lived. In their loneliness, there was the sadness of being the chosen few, and in their sadness there was a marked but unexpressed pride. Just as they were alienated from their surroundings, so were they also separated from each other "like the fixed stars in the firmament." Most of them were scattered among various cities, a few here and a few there, as if no single Jewish community in America could handle them as a group. They appeared like a phalanx of knights loyal to the Hebrew language whose pride forbad them both from admitting the least hint of their difficulties to a Jew from Palestine and from paying the least heed to the seductions of English. [. . .] In this conscious renunciation of popular attention there was something of the self-gratification that proud artists allow themselves, something of the feeling of superiority enjoyed by monks offering obeisance to a Hebrew Princess and serving her with no expectation of reward either

3

in this world or in the world to come, either in the Diaspora or in the Land of Israel.[1]

Shazar describes the American Hebrew poets with the rapt fascination of an ethnologist who has discovered a hitherto unknown tribe. The very fact that their existence was a surprise to a man like Shazar, the editor of the Histadrut's newspaper *Davar* and the editor-in-chief of Am Oved, is itself a revealing instantiation of the double marginalization of the American Hebrew poets. It is understandable they would go unacknowledged at home by a Jewry rushing to Americanize and leaving Jewish languages behind. But that their existence should have been hidden to the intelligentsia of the Yishuv (the organized Zionist settlement in Palestine) and its Hebrew literary establishment is less accountable and, for the poets themselves at the time, more dispiriting. Shazar perceptively suggests that their broad streak of pride was a reaction formation to the pain induced by this deep isolation. To a representative of the Yishuv, they would never have let on how they suffered, no more than they would to the boorish representatives of American Jewry among whom they worked and lived. They saw themselves—again Shazar's eye proves true—as members of a secret society who served a higher authority, and their confidence in their high calling was enough to shield them from the ignominy of being ignored.

I take the second introductory picture, with the reader's indulgence, from the realm of my own experience some thirty years later. I was raised in Worcester, Massachusetts, and given a supplemental Jewish education in the Hebrew school of Congregation Beth Israel. In the elementary grades, the curriculum for our studies was prescribed by a central bureau of Jewish education in Boston. During four years of high school, we were directly enrolled in the Prozdor division of the Boston Hebrew Teachers College (now called the Hebrew College); we were taught the course materials by our teachers in Worcester— five two-hour sessions per week—and then examined at the end of the year by tests sent from Boston. My recollection from this experience was less of the texts we studied than of the personalities of our instructors. By far the most distinguished personage in Boston, where we students from Worcester visited occasionally, was the College's president, the remote and aristocratic Eisig Silberschlag. Handsome and dapper despite his age, Silberschlag was known to us as a disciple of the rebellious poet Saul Tchernichovsky and as the eminent translator of Aristophanes' comedies into Hebrew. We had little idea at the time that he was a remarkable lyric Hebrew poet with a broad erotic streak and a jaundiced eye for social satire. Of the teachers with whom we had everyday contact, some were scholars who published learned articles in Hebrew, and others were simply dedicated pedagogues.

What was common to all was a passionate and steadfast devotion to the Hebrew language. This was not merely a principled commitment but something on the order of a fierce and burning idée fixe that made Hebrew into the cornerstone of national and personal existence. These Hebraist teachers seemed old to us, and few were American; and although their monomania had the force to inspire awe, they often seemed to us alien and obsessed. We were American students in the 1960s, and the changes that were roiling our world seemed unrelated to the one thing that was all-consuming for our teachers, who, in turn, must have viewed us as distracted and unserious. The sovereignty of Hebrew had the curious effect of reordering other priorities. To our teachers, whether you were a believer and observed the commandments was far less important than the depth of your Hebrew literacy. About Israel and the imperative to make aliyah, there was much confusion and unspoken ambivalence. It goes without saying that the American Hebraists were enthralled by the creation of the state of Israel; the map of the new state, as well as all the crooked alleyways of Jerusalem, was etched in their brains, even if they had visited only briefly or had never been there at all. Yet, to them, Israel was only a manifestation of the great national Hebrew ideal; this was an ideal that remained larger than the state and enfolded within it the "pioneering" educational work (in the nationalist sense, *halutsiyyut*) that they themselves were carrying out.

In our eyes, the fine madness of our teachers seemed curious, eccentric, and out of touch. When it came to Hebrew, everything that seemed vital and attractive to us at the time came from Israel: the latest songs, the folk dances, slang and the ring of real speech, and even the new poetry, which eschewed florid classical diction for the lilt of a conversational register. So it was not surprising that when we moved on in life and looked back at this chapter in our education, though grateful for a firm grounding in Hebrew, we viewed our Hebraist teachers under the aspect of a benign dottiness and thought little more about them. In my case, that changed only many years later when, after a tortuous educational path, I found myself teaching Hebrew language and literature in a number of American universities. Experiencing the exhilaration and frustration of my job, I began to ask myself fundamental questions about what it means to teach Hebrew in America, to speak Hebrew in America, and generally to be involved with Hebrew as an American in relation to Israeli colleagues both here and in Israel. I was exercised by the deficient state of Hebrew knowledge not only among my students but also among supposedly literate Jewish professionals and by the general sense in the community that all essential Jewish knowledge can be conveyed in English.

In seeking answers to these questions, I sought out writers and thinkers from the earlier decades of the twentieth century who had also struggled with the mission of teaching Hebrew in an indifferent American environment. Even though I had known something about the manifold expressions of the *tarbut ʿivrit* [Hebrew culture] idea in America, I had filed away this knowledge together with the memories of the quaint fanatics who had taught me in high school. Yet, suddenly there unrolled before my eyes a vast and vigorous drama of many dozens of poets and writers and educational revolutionaries who had attempted to foment an ambitious Hebrew cultural program for American Jewry. I quickly realized that the aging eccentrics I met in the 1960s looked quite different thirty years earlier, when they had indeed resembled the romantic knights serving the Hebrew Princess whom Shazar had observed on his visit to America. I and my fellow students had had no idea that the tattered tail we had experienced belonged to a once vigorous beast. To corral and describe that beast is the goal of this study.

✳

Any discussion of Hebrew in America must begin by locating itself in reference to Christian Hebraism, which was responsible for the knowledge of Hebrew becoming a necessary attainment for the elite of Protestant clergy in the colonial period. The fact that Hebrew was the original language of the Bible counted for a great deal in a post-Reformation world in which that sacred text was regarded as the sole source of God's word. Moreover, as the language of Creation and as the tongue from which all others must therefore have been derived, Hebrew was accorded the power to explain the origins of peoples; it even led to a proposed linkage between the Jews and Native Americans, which, as will be observed later on, was a connection fertile to Hebrew poets in the twentieth century. The young men of Harvard College through its first century were required to learn Hebrew along with Greek and Latin. In the first half of the eighteenth century, they were instructed by one Judah Monis, who was born in 1683 in Italy into a family of Portuguese conversos and eventually became the first full-time instructor of Hebrew in 1722. Monis was the author of the first Hebrew textbook in the Americas, *A Grammar of the Hebrew Tongue* (1735). The price of his appointment to the Harvard faculty was his conversion to Christianity, and this requirement illustrates the fact that there was no connection between the prestige of Hebrew and sympathy for the Jews as Jews. "Some Christian Humanists," writes Shalom Goldman, "though they demonstrated the 'Christian Truth' through their study of Hebrew, were most vocal and active in their anti-Judaism."[2] Thus, quite apart from being a language employed by living Jews, Hebrew has been taught in Christian seminaries from the earliest European settlement until today. It forms a separate branch of Hebrew in America that Arnold Band has aptly called Divinity School Hebrew.[3]

As for the Jews themselves, there were no more than fifteen hundred of them in the thirteen colonies, and their use of Hebrew was reserved for the synagogue and home rituals. During the first half of the nineteenth century, Jews arriving from German-speaking lands were accompanied by rabbis trained in Reform seminaries. Later in that century, with the beginnings of mass immigration from Eastern Europe, a trickle of maskilim began to arrive in America. These were writers and men of letters who identified with the Haskalah, the Jewish Enlightenment movement that had begun in Berlin in the eighteenth century and then moved eastward into Russia. As part of a broad program for the modernization of Jewish life, the maskilim took Hebrew from being a medium of religious scholarship and made it into a modern literary language for use in belles lettres (lyric, epic, and dramatic genres, and the novel), as well as in social criticism and satire. Just like the masses of non-literary immigrants, the maskilim came in hopes of a better life, and this they most assuredly did not find. Hebrew journals, which were their natural medium, were slow to take root in America, and the maskilim were accorded no honor by their fellow immigrants, who were absorbed in the struggle for economic survival and remained indifferent to Hebrew culture. Some of these writers were far from being unknown commodities when they came to America. Naftali Herz Imber (1856–1909), whose poem "Hatikvah" became the anthem of the Zionist movement and later the state of Israel, came to the United States in 1887 after living for extensive periods in Palestine and London and publishing several collections of poetry. He floundered in America, and despite writing for the Yiddish press, he remained sunk in poverty and alcoholism. He died in New York, known principally at the end of his life for his love of the bottle and his embittered, scabrous witticisms. When he arrived in America in 1892, Menachem Mendel Dolitsky (1856–1931) was perhaps the best known poet of Hibbat Zion, the romantic proto-Zionist movement that arose following the pogroms of 1881 in Russia. (His lyric "Tsiyyon tamati, tsiyyon ḥemdati" is still sung today.) He too was resentful and abject over the absence of recognition and income; he was forced to resort to what these proud Hebrew maskilim regarded as a form of prostitution: writing serialized sensationalist novels [*shund*] in Yiddish. Living much longer than Imber, he spent forty years of wandering and unhappiness in America before dying and being buried in Los Angeles. This was also the fate of Yitzhak Rabinowitz, a Haskalah poet who was born in Kovno in 1846 and arrived in America in 1893. This disciple of Avraham Mapu and friend of Y. L. Gordon, who come to America with several published volumes of Hebrew verse to his credit, was unrecognized when he died seven years after his immigration.

There is one figure among this company who seems not to have been miserable—Gershon Rosenzweig (1861–1914). He was singular in a number of other ways as well. He came to America somewhat earlier (1888); he began his literary work only after leaving Europe; he supported himself through various shops and businesses; and, most importantly, he had a sense of humor. He was a poet, among other things, and his *Shirim, meshalim umikhtamim* [Poems, fables, and epigrams] appeared in 1898. But his genius lay in satire and parody, genres with a rich tradition in Haskalah literature. He conceived a series of talmudic parodies, complete with mishnah and gemara, on different aspects of immigrant Jewish life, under the general title *'Amireiqa*. At first glance, *'Amireiqa* simply looks like a variant spelling of America; but when pronounced carefully, the title turns out to be two words run together: *'ami* [my people] and *reiqa* [empty, boorish]. Rosenzweig was the kind of parodist whose humor is prankish and bemused rather than saturnine and caustic. As in the case of many satirists, his depiction of human foibles implied the existence of an ideal against which imperfections were judged, and this basic optimism underlies his work. His talmudic satires were collected in *Talmud yanqi* [Yankee Talmud] (1898). The same year he published a pamphlet containing his Hebrew translations of "My Country 'Tis of Thee," "The Star Spangled Banner," and "Columbia, the Gem of the Ocean." Rosenzweig can truly be said to be an American original, and his work deserves to be better known.[4]

Maskilic Hebraist activity continued into the first decade of the new century. There were dozens of periodicals in which poetry, essays, and learned discourses were published. (The maskilim also published in Hebrew in the Yiddish press.) Many were one-man operations with irregular publication schedules and content of very uneven quality. The two most important and most sustained efforts were *Ha'ivri*, which was edited by Rosenzweig, and Zeev Schor's *Hapisgah*.[5] Other avenues of maskilic engagement that emerged at this time were associations and committees to advance the knowledge of Hebrew and disseminate its literature. A New York group, founded in 1903, was called Mefitsei Sefat Ever (Sefat Ever is a classical locution for the Hebrew language). Around this time, there were approximately twenty Hebrew clubs and societies not only in New York but also in Chicago, Montreal, Milwaukee, and Cincinnati, as well as in Kansas City, Missouri, Bayonne, New Jersey, and San Antonio, Texas.[6]

In the decade before World War I, this scene was transformed by the arrival in America of young people who brought with them very different notions about what Hebrew literature should be. They were part of a second wave of mass immigration from Eastern Europe that was impelled by the Kishinev pogrom and the pogroms that followed it, the failed October Revolution, and a rapidly deteriorating economic situation. It was this influx that brought to these shores most of the poets discussed in this study. The dates of arrival and the ages upon arrival provide a profile of this cohort: Benjamin Silkiner came in 1904 at age 22, Ephraim Lisitzky in 1900 at 15, Israel Efros in 1905 at 14, Simon Halkin in 1913 at 15, Abraham Regelson in 1905 at 9, Hillel Bavli in 1912 at 20, Abraham Schwartz in 1901 at 14, A. H. Friedland in 1903 at 14, Moshe Feinstein in 1912 at 14, Shimon Ginzburg in 1912 at 22, Eisig Silberschlag in 1920 at 17, and Gabriel Preil in 1922 at 11. We shall have occasion to draw a number of conclusions from this data, especially regarding the timing of the exposure of these young people to cultural currents in America. But for the moment what is important is not what they found in America, but what they brought with them from Europe. Because most came as adolescents, their Jewish education had gone through a process of formation in Eastern Europe before they arrived.

In most cases—the individual variants can be found in the essays on each of the poets—this education had two dimensions. The first was a traditional regimen that began in the heder (sometimes the *ḥeder metuqan*, the reformed heder based on modern educational principles) and progressed to intensive talmudic studies with private teachers. The second was a less formal dimension that often reflected a limited openness on the part of parents to reading Haskalah literature; learning non-Jewish languages; and acquiring utilitarian knowledge in arithmetic, geography, and history. Thus equipped, these teenagers were perfect candidates for enlistment in the Jewish national movement and the new Hebrew literature. (Admittedly, there was nothing necessary about their turn in this direction; certainly many youths with similar backgrounds went in the direction of socialism and Yiddish literature or left it all behind in favor of an accelerated American identity. The turn toward Hebrew must be explained as a combination of parental attitudes, the cultural and ideological currents in the towns in which they grew up, and, in the end, personal temperament.) What seemed most vital, exciting, and important to them within the world of Hebrew letters was not the literature of the Haskalah or even Hibbat Zion but the new developments of the 1890s and the turn of the century, especially the late romanticism and early modernism associated with the poetry of Chaim Nachman Bialik and Tchernichovsky.

This is the period of Hebrew literature generally known as the *tehiyyah* or the revival period, although the upbeat connotation of this title refers more to the aspirations of the nationalist movement than to the bleak lives of its best writers. In the public realm after the pogroms of 1881, the optimistic outlook of the Haskalah, which had been based on the belief that Jews who modernized themselves would be accepted within Russian civil society, collapsed. The collapse was accompanied by the gathering momentum of the new Zionist movement and the ascendance of the Jewish national idea within the world of Hebrew letters. In the private realm, especially as reflected in Hebrew poetry, the collapse was less political than metaphysical. For young people raised within the piety of the beit midrash, the confident theism of the Haskalah offered only meager support when their faith crumbled in the face of modernity and exposure to European culture. The collapse of faith, which became a nearly inevitable rite of passage for this generation, was experienced not as a liberation but as a necessary fall. The crisis led to an inward turn and an exploration of the subjectivity of the self and a search for meaning in the vacuum left by traditional religion. Achieving a rapport with the *anima mundi*, the soul of the world, through an intimate connection to nature was one avenue offered by European romanticism. Another was a more vitalistic connection to nature based on a construction of the Hellenic contribution to European culture. But in few cases, despite the general approbation of the Jewish national ideal, did ideological engagement serve as a replacement for the world of faith that had been lost. The Hebrew poet remained a soul in extremis for whom writing in Hebrew, the old-new language, was an existential choice.

The new world of Hebrew literature was a rich and complex field of cultural production. On the conservative side, there were the evolutionary views of Ahad Ha'am, the august editor of *Hashiloah*, who endowed Hebrew with the capacity to provide continuity in the shift from a religious to a modern Jewish culture. On the radical side, there were M. Y. Berdichevsky and Yosef Hayyim Brenner, who argued that the old order had to be wholly extirpated before a Jewish culture sensitive to the needs of the modern individual could be constructed; for them, Hebrew was the subversive tool of Jewish modernity. In between, there were the poets Bialik and Tchernichovsky, whose powerful bodies of work expressed the losses and the aspirations of a generation caught in the twilight between the setting of the old order and rise of the new. These were the new winds that the young immigrants brought with them, and they were a far cry from the atmosphere of the maskilim in America. Their difference was inscribed in the terms they used to refer to themselves; they were *'ivrim* and *le'ummiyyim*, participants in a new Hebrew, nationalist regime.[7]

An anecdote from 1906–7 illustrates the way in which the common banner of Hebrew began to be stretched thin over the two camps. On his way to America in 1906, a fervent young Hebraist from Minsk named Daniel Persky sought out Brenner in London's East End, where he was living in poverty and struggling to produce a new Hebrew literary journal called *Hame'orer*. Brenner was already acknowledged to be one of the brightest lights among the new Hebrew writers. (Persky soon became one of the most active personalities on the Hebraist scene in New York and the author of a feuilleton that appeared for decades in *Hado'ar*.) When Brenner ask who he was upon meeting him in London, Persky said he was a reader of Hebrew and a lover of Hebrew from Minsk; Brenner replied by remarking drolly that it was the first time he had met a Hebrew reader who was *not* a writer! Brenner entrusted Persky with a letter to the Mefitsei Sefat Ever society in New York requesting financial support for his journal; the support was given and the aid greatly appreciated by Brenner.[8] Yet, when issues of the journal began to arrive in New York containing, among other provocations, the realism in Brenner's own fiction and the sensuality in Zalman Shneour's poetry, there were second thoughts. Writing eight years later in the pages of *Hatoren*, the first successful journal of the American Hebraists, E. R. Malachi recalls the furor.

Many of the members of Mefitsei Sefat Ever were Hebrew maskilim who came of age in the sixties and seventies and were used to thinking of literature as glosses on difficult verses from Scripture.[. . .] They were shocked at the ferment in our midst engendered by *Hame'orer*, which they regarded as a sullying of our high-mindedness, and they considered the style of the journal to be itself an affront to their esteemed Holy Tongue. They were joined by the conservative Yiddish press, which made a great fuss and issued a "stern warning" to the society "under no circumstances" to support *Hame'orer* because of "immorality" [*zenut*] it contained.[9]

What was at stake was not merely a generational difference in literary taste but a deeper conflict over the relationship of Hebrew to experience. For the maskilim described by Malachi, Hebrew was a venerated classical medium to be used for commentary and satire or for the sort of neo-biblical verse that lamented the sad persecutions of the nation. For the younger Hebraists, however, Hebrew served as a very existential and direct medium for representing the anguished birth pangs of the newly emerging Jewish life. The subsidy to *Hame'orer* was cancelled the next year, but it would not be long before the maskilim were pushed to the margins by the growing self-assurance of the younger writers.

In 1908 they founded their own society called Ahiever, among whose goals it was to create venues for publishing the works of young writers. Thus began a series of short-lived endeavors that eventually led to the creation of *Hatoren*. *Shibolim* was a biweekly that lasted for seven issues in 1908. In the same year, a literary miscellany called *Senunit* appeared, edited by Reuven Brainin, a veteran Hebrew writer who had recently settled in New York. Brainin also edited *Haderor*, which lasted for fifteen issues in 1911. Both *senunit* and *deror* are terms for the swallow, and their choice as titles suggests the combination of self-assurance and tentativeness that characterized the cultural moment. Although their accomplishments were still slight, they were a harbinger of things to come. In 1910 Ahiever published *Mul ohel Timurah*, Silkiner's Indian epic, which was hailed as the first great work of American Hebrew literature. Finally, *Hatoren* appeared in

The third issue of *Hatoren* [The mast] (August 1913). Image provided by the Library of the Jewish Theological Seminary.

1913 and continued, mostly as a weekly, until 1925.[10] The word *toren* means the mast of a ship, and as the part of an arriving ship first seen over the horizon, it was similar in its portent to the image of the swallow. Ginzburg and Silkiner, two of the poets discussed later in the study, were among the first editors, together with Persky, mentioned in connection with Brenner. Although the journal in part relied for editorial guidance on older and more experienced European Hebrew writers (Y. D. Berkovitz, Brainin, and Shmarya Levin), *Hatoren* was very much the expression of an increasingly active native community of Hebraists. *Hatoren* carried editorials that expressed their views, cultural criticism that engaged the issues of the day, and in addition to publishing aesthetically refined poetry and prose (again, mostly local), the journal published newsy reports of the activities of various Hebrew clubs from around the metropolis and beyond.

A more European-centric model was embodied by *Miqlat* [Refuge], the other major journal of the time, which appeared in New York for twenty-five monthly issues during 1920–21. Far from being a collective endeavor, the journal was financed entirely by A. Y. Shtibel, the great Russian-Jewish patron of Hebrew letters, who appointed Berkowitz to the editorship. Berkowitz (1885–1967) was already an established short-story writer and dramatist when he arrived in New York as part of the family entourage of Shalom Aleichem, whose daughter he had married in 1906. America was never more than a way station for Berkowitz, and he did not think much of the prospects for Jewish culture there. He emigrated to Palestine in 1928, where he became a much honored member of the literary establishment. A substantial portion of his literary energies were devoted to translating his father-in-law's work into Hebrew, and it was indeed the serialization of these translations that filled up the fiction columns of *Hatoren* because narrative prose in Hebrew developed much later than poetry in America, and there was not much to go around at the time. In editing *Miqlat*, Berkowitz used "local talent" only sparingly; he insisted on upholding the highest literary standards and made only limited allowances for the necessarily jejune nature of the young American Hebraists whose literary careers were just coming into focus. In the elegant and orderly volumes of the journal, one can find the earliest version of *Hakhnasat kallah* [The bridal canopy], S. Y. Agnon's magisterial evocation of Galician Jewry in the early nineteenth century, or *Vilna*, Shneour's epic ode to the capital of Lithuanian Jewish life, or on a vastly different scale, the miniature modernist poems of David Fogel. Because it had no intrinsic roots in the Hebraist community in New York, *Miqlat* ceased publication when Shtibel did not renew its funding. But for the Americans who had served as assistants to Berkowitz or observed his work as an editor, the lessons of literary seriousness and professionalism were not lost.

Miqlat is another journal name that is redolent with meaning. The concept of refuge or shelter had a very specific resonance during World War I within the context of Hebrew culture. The greatest centers of the revival of Hebrew culture—Odessa, Warsaw, Vilna, among them—were within the bounds of the Russian Empire. With the chaos and economic breakdown of the world war and then the cultural repression of the Revolution and the ensuing civil war, the main institutions of Hebrew culture were shut down, and the great majority of writers, publishing houses, and journals had to go into hiding or flee. Similarly, during World War I, the nascent cultural center in Palestine, which was far smaller but symbolically critical, was closed by the Ottoman rulers and its leaders exiled to Egypt and elsewhere. America remained the only Jewish population center in which civil order and economic stability prevailed. It was indeed in New York that none other than David Ben-Gurion, Yitzhak Ben-Zvi, Eliezer Ben-Yehuda, Meyer Berlin (Bar-Ilan), Levin, and other Zionist leaders waited out the war years. For some, America was a refuge and nothing more, a place to hunker down and organize and raise funds until the coast was clear to return to Palestine. But no one knew what the world would look like after the war and how successful the Yishuv would be in realizing its ambitions. In the eye of that moment, it was not unreasonable to think of America as a refuge for Hebrew culture in a more constructive and long-term sense: as a place where, alongside the Yishuv, the Hebrew creativity that had begun in Europe could gather its strength and spring forward to new accomplishments. America had great masses of Jews, relative prosperity and the absence of outright anti-Semitism, and great universities and museums; whereas the

Yishuv possessed not one of those resources. Without the benefit of hindsight and a knowledge of the subsequent success enjoyed by the cultural institutions of the Yishuv, it was a rationally optimistic stand rather than a delusional one to hope that America could proceed from being merely a shelter for Hebrew culture to become one of its true homes. It was in that buoyant spirit that the main institutions of the Hebraist movement were founded: the Histadrut Ivrit in 1917, the daily *Hado'ar* in 1921, and Hebrew teachers colleges in many major cities in the early 1920s.

※

Whence, after all, this consuming passion for Hebrew? It is worth stepping back for a moment from the story of the writers, the journals, and the organizations to inquire into the origins of the phenomenon. For many Jews today, the Hebrew language is identified with Israel— as the everyday language of Israelis and the medium of its newspapers and cultures. The revival of Hebrew as a modern, spoken tongue is often associated with the establishment of the state and with the *ulpanim*, the Hebrew-language immersion programs created to accelerate the absorption of great waves of refugees and immigrants. Now, any student of Jewish history knows that modern Hebrew has a rich history that far predates 1948. Nevertheless, the runaway success of Hebrew as the contemporary language of a contemporary state makes it difficult for anyone to visualize a time when Hebrew was very much its own idea, which, though connected to territorial Zionism, stood separately from it.

Born out of the ferment of romantic nationalism in Europe, the Zionist idea always contained two components: territory and language. For many decades after the conception of the Zionist idea in the mid-nineteenth century, its territorial realization remained largely an imaginative-literary construct, with only the tiniest number of Jews settling in Palestine out of Zionist motives. On the other hand, decades *before* the Zionist idea came into being, Hebrew was being reinvented as a modern literary language. The same Haskalah, which appeared as a hidebound old guard in America at the end of the nineteenth century, earlier in that century was an aggressively modernizing movement in

HADOAR

הַדֹּאַר

HADOAR

שבועון יוצא על־ידי
ההסתדרות העברית באמריקה
הכתובת:
HADOAR, 96 Fith Ave., New York, N. Y.

תנאי החתימה:
לשנה:
באמריקה, $5.00; בקנדה, $6.00; באירופה, $4.00
לחצי שנה:
באמריקה, $2.50; בקנדה, $3.00; באירופה, $2.00

Published weekly (except weeks of Jewish holidays) by
HISTADRUTH IVRITH OF AMERICA
96 Fifth Avenue, New York, N. Y.
Tel. Watkins 0465

Entered at the New York Post Office as Second Class Mail Matter.

SUBSCRIPTION PRICE: One Year: America, $5.00; Canada, $6.00; Europe, $4.00.
Half Year: America, $2.50; Canada, $3.00; Europe, $2.00. Single copies, 10 cents.

PRICE 10 CENTS

שנה שלישית. גליון כה (רפג). ניו־יורק, כה בסיון, תרפ"ד.

Vol. IV. No. 28 (283). New York, June 27, 1924.

התוכן

לועידה הדימוקראטית
בשעת סכנה
הועידה הציונית בפיטסבורג
פסוקים: הכשר
נצחון שלא מדעת . . . . י. מ. חלמאן
לועידה בפיטסבורג . . . . מ. שיינקין
קיסמים . . . . מ. ד. בראנדשטטר
דמים — תרתי... . . . . י. לווינבוק
מכתבים מארץ־ישראל . . . . . . ק. י. סילמאן
בבואות . . . . בר־לבב
תפילה לנער . . . . אברהם רגלסון
רסיסים . . . . י. צ. רמון
בשר . . . . ש. ל. בלאנק
סופרים וספרים:
משפחת סופרים . . . . בר־טוביה
„המורה" . . . . ג. יקותיאל
הועידה העברית באטלאנטיק סיטי
ועידת „בני־ציון" בנורפולק, ווא.
אל המורים העברים בארצות־הברית
הרשות ספרותיות
בתרבות העברית

לועידה הדימוקראטית

בשעה שהדברים האלה נכתבים, הועידה הדימוקראטית רק עומדת להפתח, וברחובות ניו־יורק ההומיה מצלצלים עוד ה„שמות" הגדולים: דז'פרסון, קליוולאנד, ווילסון, ומצטרפים אליהם עוד כמה תריסרים של שמות חדשים של מועמדים. יש בהם בתוך המועמדים האלה אנשים, שאחרים רוצים בהם, ויש כאלה, שהם רוצים בעצמם, יש שמות ידועים ושמות של „סוסים שחורים". צלילי שמות בעיר.

ומתוך הרעש הגדול והערבוביה המסובכת בוקעת ועולה גם שדרת התכנית העתידה להקרא, ואפשר גם: להתקבל, בועידה. חוק־וולסטיד והיחס לקו־קלוקס־קלן כלפי פנים, משפט־העמים וחבר־הלאומים כלפי חוץ, אלה הם הסעיפים היותר חשובים, שנמנים עליהם צירי הועידה ושדברי המפלגה נחלקים עליהם. הודאה גלויה בזכות קיומו של ה„קלן" לא נשמעה אף מפי אחד, ובימים רעים כימינו — גם זו לטובה. אולם ב„שתיקה כהודאה" מונים את מיקאדו, המועמד היותר חזק בשעה זו, שטרם מצא שעת הכושר להשמיע את דעתו עליהם. אולם לעומת זאת הוא „יבש בחרם", ומבטיח לקבל ולקיים את כל חומרותיו של חוק־וולסטיד. מזהירים לעומתו פניו של „אל. סמית", החשוד ב„לחלוחית מועטת" וכולו — כתור קתולי, מחאה נגד הקלן. יתר המועמדים, שהם לעת־עתה בבחינת „סוסים שחורים", נוטים לכאן ולכאן. הצד השוה שבכולם, שהם טוענים בשם ההתקדמות, ה„פרוגרסיביות" והדימוקראטיות, ושוב נשאים על שפתי כל „השמות הקדושים" של דז'פרסון, ווילסון וגו'.

מיקאדו „חתן המלך", הכריז עוד בדרך, שאין מקום בארצות־הברית לשתי מפלגות קונסרבאטיביות, ומבין שהועידה הריפובּ־ליקאית בקליוולאנד קדמה והחזיקה בריאקציה, מוכרחת היא הועידה הדימוקראטית לדגול בהתקדמות. הודעה זו, שגילתה הבנה פוליטית ישרה, היה בה כדי לחזק את התקוה, שהמפלגה הגדולה השניה תצעד סוף־סוף את הצעד הראשון בדרך ההתחדשות, כל עוד ידענו את שמות המועמדים הראשיים ולא ראינו את מלחמתם. סוף־סוף גם סמית, גם מיקאדו פרוגרסיביים הם כנגד קולדיז' ודאוס. אולם משהתחילה המלחמה האישית והתקיפו האיומים לצאת מן המחנה: אלה מאיימים ביציאה אם יתקבל סעיף נגד ה„קלן" ואלה — אם לא יתקבל, מצד זה — חסידי היבשה ומעבר מזה — המתפללים על „טפה מרה" אחת, — משהתחילו האיומים ופקעה המשמעת, הרימה ראש ה„פשרה" תחיה, המעמידה בסכנה את כל הועידה. ולא רק אישיותו של הנבחר מוטלת עכשיו בספק, כי אם כל התכנית כולה. מי יתן אמון לתכנית מטולאת, שתכתב כדי לצאת ידי חובת כל הדעות, ודעה אחת אין, ואין יושר ואין אמונה בלב. וכבר מזדקרת קומתו הכפופה של בריין ו„סעיף" כתוב מוכן בכיסו עוד מימים עברו, שסגולה בו להשביע גם את ה„קלן"־הזאבי, גם את כבשת העמים הנרדפים.

והכל. כל אזרחי אמריקה, בני העמים הנעלבים, הרי נכונים היו ונכונים הם גם עכשיו להטיל את אחריות כל העלבונות הגסים, שעלב בהם הקונגרס האחרון, על המפלגה המושלת, אף־על־פי שלמעשה היו גם הדימוקראטים שותפים לחטא. העלימו כל בני העמים האלה בכוונה את עינם מ„שותפות" זו ואמרו: בין כך ובין כך אין האופוזיציה אחראית על מעשיה. ראשית היא זו ליצור „חוקים לא טובים" גם מדעת, כדי להכשיל בהם את הרוב. רבים מבני העמים האלה, חברי המפלגה המושלת, היו נכונים לעזוב את מחנם ולהתנפל לזרועותיה הפתוחות של הדימוקראטיה, הנשבעת בשמו של דז'פרסון. הריאקציה החוגגת בקליוולאנד ונצחונו המכוסה של ה„קלן" עוד הגבירה נטיה זו. יד הריפובליקאים זרעה, והדימוקראטים עמדו לקצור רב־קציר. אישיות מזהירה אחת אילו הופיעה בחוגם, איש במות באמתו, כווילסון, ונכון להלחם עליה, כי אז ריכז מסביבו את כל אשר יושר בלבבו ושם אלהים על שפתיו, כל הנענים והנעלבים המחכים לגואלם, והרים אל גבהו גם את האמריקאי הממוצע, בעל ה„חשבונות" הקטנים והריוח הפעוט, והתחדשותה של אמריקה, ואתה יחד כל העולם כולו, היתה בטוחה. אולם אישיות בהירה כזו — גורה על האמת — לא נמצאה בתוכם. המנהיגים עצמם נעשו למחשבי חשבונות פעוטים וכל דאגתם ל„מספר הדעות". הן לא לחנם שותק מיקאדו הפרוגרסיבי מבלי דבר דבר על החבריה הקדושה של ה„קלן", המחזיקה גם בו מתוך שתיקה.

הבינוניי[illegible] את חגה. היא שנצחה בקליוולאנד [illegible] גם בניו־יורק. אירופה שקדמה לחטא המלחמה, קדמה למצוא גם דרך תשובה. אנגליה וצרפת עומדות שוב לנס עמים. אולם, כמו אז, בשעת החטא, ככה גם עתה, בשעת התשובה, הן זקוקות לעזרת אמריקה. ולא רק להשתתפותה בחבר־הלאומים או במשפט־העמים, כי אם, בעיקר, לשאיפתה לטהרה עצמית, להזדככותה. לכבד ולקרב את כל הנברא

Hado'ar (June 27, 1924). Image provided by the Library of the Jewish Theological Seminary.

East European society. It was this pre-Zionist cultural program that pushed Hebrew from its status as the language of liturgy and religious scholarship into its new role as a vehicle for modern literature and social controversy. One by one, the components of a modern literary system were filled in: lyric, epic, drama, autobiography, historical narrative, and the novel. By the time that dreams and schemes about Zion took center stage, a modern Hebrew literature already existed that could be retroactively enlisted on behalf of the Zionist idea. Yet despite that appropriation and despite the fact that many writers were active in the Zionist movement, Hebrew literature at the turn of the century and for quite some time afterward remained a separate enterprise. Writers like Berdichevsky, Shneour, Fogel, Uri Nissan Gnessin, and Gershon Schoffman, all living in Europe with no intention of settling in Palestine, were important actors in a kind of autonomous republic of Hebrew letters. Anita Shapira has demonstrated that even Brenner, who was venerated after his death as a martyr of the cause, remained always ambivalent and skeptical about Zionism despite having settled in Palestine.[11]

The point is not that Hebrew literature was non-Zionist but rather that even *within* the binomial conception of Zionism (territory + language), Hebrew was by far the advanced component. Characters were conversing volubly in Hebrew in novels long before a ragged assortment of pioneers attempted to do the same in the hills of the Galilee. Hebrew had the outstanding advantage of being both portable and immediate. One did not have to live in the Land, a privilege given to very few, to participate in the rebirth of the nation. Modern Hebrew, in its many manifestations, was already at hand to be read and written and even spoken. These modes of participation could be packed up when the East European centers were no longer tenable and transported to more hospitable climes, such as the one provided by America. Hebrew was immediate in the sense that it was a cultural practice that was experienced concretely in the here and now. The Zionist who is wholly focused on the settlement of Eretz Yisrael, even though his life takes on meaning from his work on behalf of the cause, is always striving on behalf of a deferred and distant goal. By contrast, the Hebraist, who may be thought of as a Zionist/Jewish nationalist for whom

Hebrew is a priority, possesses something now, in the moment, that can be enjoyed, enhanced, and exchanged. Moreover, for the majority of the Hebraists, who were no longer religiously observant, Hebrew functioned as an everyday practice that allowed them intercourse with the *sancta* of the nation. (The spiritual and libidinal satisfactions that Hebrew provided in the life of the Hebraist are the subject of the next chapter.) Persky, the genial spirit of American Hebraism, expressed it very simply in an open letter he wrote to his comrades in the pages of *Hatoren* (March–April 1915):[12]

> An ordinary Jew like myself who does not believe in religion and who does not keep the commandments, who does not stand on the soil of his national homeland, and for whom abstract conceptions of Judaism hold no appeal—for an ordinary Jew such as this, what can remain *real and palpable* for him of all the achievements of this people if it is not the extraordinary and eternal Hebrew language? For such an ordinary Jew, nationalism· is embodied by the language, which fills his entire being and to which he will devote his entire life.

As the only salvageable component of the tradition, Hebrew becomes invested with all the sanctity and ultimate importance that inhered in the total system of which it was once a part.

The primacy of Hebrew was buttressed by several powerful philosophical and ideological arguments that arose out of the culture turmoil at the turn of the century. The growing assertiveness of Yiddish as a modern national Jewish language, which was highlighted by the Czernovitz Conference of 1908, required the proponents of Hebrew to go on the offensive and explain to others what they took for granted among themselves. The writings of Ahad Ha'am were highly influential in the nationalist camp and gave a high cultural gloss to the partisan positions.[13] In the United States, the case for Hebrew was even more fraught because, however much Yiddish was a competitor, English and its blandishments presented the far greater threat. The convictions and assumptions of the American Hebraists within this debate can be summarized under several heads. First and foremost was the belief that every nation has its own genius or spirit and that its language is the embodiment of this inner life. This was a core tenet of romantic nationalism following the ideas of Johann Gottfried Herder and Wilhelm von Humbolt, and it was easily absorbed into Zionism because the Jewish people, after all, already possessed a language of hoary pedigree that reflected its national life during its classic heroic age in the Bible. The Hebrew language therefore was not simply an ornament of the Jewish people or even a great creation or treasure. It was no more and no less than the very map of the nation's being in its best self, and it was by using this map that the nation could understand its own spirit and realize that best self.

A second argument concerns the power of the Hebrew language to guarantee the continuity of Jewish culture. In contrast to the political Zionists, who saw anti-Semitism as the greatest threat to the Jewish people, the cultural Zionists saw the crisis of Judaism as the greatest threat. What would be left of the "national spirit" of the Jewish people after the great complex of the Torah and the commandments collapsed under the twin pressures of enlightenment and emancipation? In a post-religious age, what could guide the people in negotiating modernity without losing an essential connection to the Jewish national genius? In proposing Hebrew for this redemptive role, the Hebraists were making a claim about the nature of language in general. Above all else, a national language is conservative in its nature. As new meanings arise, the old meanings are not discarded but rather retained and repositioned within the deeper recesses of the language. Like a great river moving toward the sea, language accumulates vast alluvial deposits that it moves over great distances. The Hebrew language, whose antiquity and continuous employment sets it apart from other great tongues, has seen the Jewish people through periods of great disruption; it has succeeded in doing so because of the treasure house of meanings it enfolds within it. Now that the Jewish people are facing their greatest challenge, identity-annihilating absorption into the stream of general culture, it is only the protean resources of the Hebrew language that can be counted on to enable the nation to remain authentically Jewish in the new order.

Third, Hebrew has the capacity to constitute a cultural matrix for the nation. Culture as a word and a concept was a late arrival within the discourse of Hebrew literature. The term for literature itself [*sifrut*] was a nineteenth-century neologism; literature per se as we know it did not exist previously. It was the same with culture. Classical Hebrew had no equivalent to the German *Kultur* or the French *civilisation*; Hebrew writers therefore took the word *tarbut*, which appeared in the Bible and Talmud in obscure contexts, and pressed it into service as the name for the general enterprise that defined their work: *tarbut 'ivrit*, Hebrew culture.[14] It was crucial for the Hebraists to invent or refurbish these terms to stake a claim for the legitimacy of a space within Jewish intellectual and spiritual life that lay outside the traditional realm of Torah study but at the same time partook of some of its prestige. Here is where Hebrew enters the picture. Although the literature and culture they made were indeed modern departures, the fact that they made them in Hebrew provided a connection to the great chain of tradition. This was not a sleight of hand in their minds but a genuine succession; they were indeed the rightful heirs to this patrimony because, as devotees and virtuosos of Hebrew, they too were part of the same sacred métier. The Hebraists could then proceed to create the retrospective construct of "Hebrew civilization," which was an unbroken line of spiritual creativity that reached from the Hebrew Bible through the Mishnah onto the Golden Age of Spain and finally into the flowering of modern Hebrew literature and letters. The Aramaic of the Talmud and the Judeo-Arabic of *The Guide of the Perplexed* and even the abundance of Yiddish texts were explained as necessary accommodations to their times that did not blur the clarity of the direct line of Hebrew emanation.

Fourth, within the American context, culture was put forward as a mediating term between religion and politics. The Hebraists believed that *tarbut 'ivrit* could rescue the elite of American Jewry from the Scylla and Charybdis of reductive conceptions of Judaism. On the one hand lay the religious traditionalists, who claimed that the only true fulfillment of Judaism is accomplished by observing the commandments and believing in an eternal and unchanging Torah. Although this camp was far feebler in the first decades of the twentieth century than it is today, it still exercised a kind of monopoly over what could be considered authentic forms of Jewish expression. If it was perceived that the only *real* way to be Jewish is to be a believer, then the Hebraists understood that most modern Jews would simply write themselves out of the picture. On the other hand, a far more actively seductive threat between the two world wars came from the politics of the Left. If the essence of Judaism was reduced to the aspiration toward social justice, then there was no reason why idealistic young people should not bypass Judaism altogether and move directly into the embrace of socialism and communism, which was indeed exactly what took place. Because of the very fact that it *was* a nationalism, Hebrew culture would never be respectable in the eyes of Jews on the Left. Yet for young Jews with traditional sympathies and social ideals, Hebrew culture was presented as a modern way to be Jewish in America. On the one hand, although it did not require theological fidelity, it did keep faith through Hebrew with the great chain of tradition. On the other, although it did not espouse a particular politics—beyond the Zionist cause—it did put forward a humanistic understanding of Judaism that was based on human creativity and on that most social of constructs, language.

The idea of Hebrew, finally, served as a moral center from which to launch a comprehensive critique of American Jewish life. As an enlightened and educated elite in the midst of the tumult of immigrant society, it was not difficult for the Hebraists to find groups and institutions that came up short in their estimation. Orthodoxy was criticized for its obscurantism and its indifference to modern Hebrew literature. Jews on the Left were criticized for their hostility to the Zionist cause. The great majority of Jewish immigrants who evinced no religious or ideological passions and were absorbed in establishing themselves economically were criticized for doing just that. The Hebraists were most acutely incensed by those closest to them, by those who, according to them, should have known better. They were provoked especially by the Judaic and Hebrew illiteracy of American-trained rabbis with their comfortable salaries and their mellifluous English oratory. Although they respected the serious writers who were their counterparts in Yiddish literature, they despised the vulgarity of the Yiddish tabloid press and the Second Avenue Yiddish theater. The fruits of philological and biblical scholarship in America were discounted because Hebrew had been rejected as the medium of scholarly exchange. Two events of 1916–17, the completion of the Jewish Publication Society's translation of the Bible into English and the founding of the Schiff Library of Jewish Classics, which were widely celebrated as the sign of an American Jewish renaissance, struck the Hebraists as a colossal misuse of communal resources and a capitulation to the tragic necessity of translation. They gladly assumed the role of mourners at the self-congratulatory feast of American Jewry. And even when it came to the American Zionist movement, with which they shared the Jewish national idea, there was no pleasure taken; the Brandeisian emphasis on Palestine as a refuge for the persecuted excluded serious attention to cultural work and gave little honor to Hebrew and to the Hebraists themselves, who perceived their commitment to Hebrew to be the true Zionism.

Taken together, these manifold critiques display much spleen, exasperation, and self-righteousness. But at the same time, they reveal something deeper and more interesting: the emergence of Hebrew as a coherent worldview.

✻

Judging from the world-historical seriousness of these deliberations about the place of Hebrew in the life of the Jewish people, it might not be immediately evident that the Hebraists were in fact a drop in the Yiddishist bucket. There were millions of Jewish immigrants to America for whom Yiddish was their first language and the primary medium for fulfilling their cultural needs. But there were virtually none when it came to Hebrew. The young people who later became Hebrew poets in America, moved by romantic nationalist ideals, chose Hebrew and worked hard to naturalize themselves within it. Their readership was always very small and huddled around the Hebrew teacher colleges, Hebrew clubs, and a cadre of elite educators. Never did they have anything resembling the mass audience potentially available to their counterparts through the Yiddish press. There were hundreds of serious Yiddish writers and only dozens in Hebrew.

The disproportion was not merely numerical. The Yiddish poetry written in America between the two world wars—not to mention afterward—was in no sense ancillary or marginal to a center located elsewhere. It was itself the great flourishing and the main drama.[15]

Jewish cultural activity in the Soviet Union had been suppressed. While prose fiction was preeminent in Warsaw, the other great Jewish metropolis, New York, reigned as the capital of Yiddish poetry. Its great poets were second to none. It was quite otherwise for the Hebraists. During World War I, they entertained not unrealistic hopes of a strong center for Hebrew literature in America; but soon after, as the pace of cultural life in Palestine recovered from the war and gathered force, the Americans had to settle for the status of remote corresponding members. Even if they were not happy with what they deemed as the modernist excesses of the Hebrew poetry being written there, their Zionist outlook could authorize nothing other than official joy at the success of the Yishuv. Given their secondariness, the most they could hope for—and most often did not receive—was the recognition of their contribution.

For this study, which is wholly devoted to the Hebrew literature written in America, it is therefore important at the outset to acknowledge the modesty of its subject in relation to the huge presence and achievement of Yiddish literature on these shores. That disproportion having been acknowledged, however, the relationship between the two literatures remains to be investigated. Yiddish and Hebrew were, after all, both modern Jewish languages that had emancipated themselves from the religious culture of Eastern Europe and striven against the currents of acculturation to retain a place in the lives of American Jews. Were Yiddish and Hebrew writers influenced by each other's work? Did they compete with each other? Did they consider themselves part of the same enterprise? Was there a competition over readership?

"No" is the general answer to these questions. For unsurprising reasons that will be presented shortly, these two literary communities had little to do with each other. Both, to be sure, were aware of the other. All Hebrew writers read Yiddish, and most Yiddish writers knew Hebrew. Yiddish writers viewed their Hebrew counterparts with sympathetic admiration. They could not help acknowledging—and resenting—the aristocratic prerogatives of Hebrew at the same time as they pitied its poets for their miniscule audiences. For their part, Hebrew writers related to Yiddish writing with indulgent condescension, all the while envying their readership and the availability of mass outlets for their work. There were very occasional joint publishing ventures.[16] At least two of the Hebrew poets in this volume, Regelson and Preil, wrote Yiddish verse as well. Alone of this group, Preil was significantly influenced by the modernist Yiddish poetry being written around him as he came of age as a poet. In the final analysis, it must be concluded that these were parallel but separate literary communities.

They were separate because they unfolded in cultural spheres that were separated by literary tradition, ideology, politics, and social framework, in addition to the obvious factor of language. The Yiddish poets, to begin with, were much less encumbered by the weight of literary authority. The emergence of modern artistic writing in Yiddish came late relative to Hebrew. Modern Hebrew literature was already a high literature from the moment of its birth at the end of the eighteenth century; it saw itself as the lineal descendent of the Hebrew Scriptures and represented that distinction in its elevated, biblically pure register. When Yiddish began to present itself as a modern literature fully a century later, it entered the scene with a chip on its shoulder. Rather than having the Bible as its provenance, Yiddish had served as the language of personal prayer, moral instruction, and entertainment for women, servants, and uneducated men. Its authority—and authenticity—derived from the folk rather than the classical tradition. Poetry, moreover, was even more belated in its arrival than prose. The stories of Mendele (S. Y. Abramovitch), Shalom Aleichem, and Y. L. Peretz so dominated the scene of Yiddish writing that when Mani Leib and the other Yunge poets began to publish in New York in the first decade of the twentieth century they were, in a significant sense, initiating the enterprise of modern Yiddish poetry and fashioning it as they went along. By contrast, before the American Hebrew poets could put pen to paper they had to confront the heritage of M. H. Luzzatto, Micha Joseph (Michal) Lebensohn, Y. L. Gordon, Tchernichovsky, and, most of all, Bialik, not to mention Isaiah, Job, Solomon Ibn Gabirol and Judah Halevi.

The anxiety of influence was hardly equally distributed. This had the effect of freeing the Yiddish poets to respond freely to the stimuli of modern life and literature around them at the same time as it constricted the Hebrew poets by underscoring their distance from the creative center and the weight of the tradition that had preceded them.

Ideology and politics played an important role in this separation. Some American Yiddish poets were more political than others in their literary and extra-literary activity. But most all were located somewhere between the democratic socialism of the *Forvits* and the communism of the *Morgen Freiheit*. Their writing took place within a broad political-cultural space that encompassed the majority of the immigrant community, especially those whose work identified them with the labor unions. This was the territory of the Left that had its origins in the Bund, the Jewish socialist movement in Eastern Europe that was committed to Yiddish as the language of the Jewish masses; and like all imported European movements, the ideological legacy of the Bund had been dispersed and redistributed in America in unprecedented ways according to how Jews lived and worked in the new civic climate.

The Hebrew poets, on the other hand, moved in very different circles. They were by and large cultural Zionists who believed in what they regarded as the Hebrew revolution in modern Jewish culture. Like other nineteenth-century ideologies, as we have seen above, this Hebrew nationalism was put forward as a solution to the crisis of Jewish religion and society. The new Hebrew culture would span the abyss left by the collapse of traditional faith by providing cultural continuity, as well as national distinctiveness. Although the creative center of this program had passed from Europe to Palestine, the message remained urgently relevant for American Jews embarked on a course of accelerated acculturation. To the bitter disappointment of the Hebrew writers and educators, their Hebrew culturalist position received only token recognition within the larger encampment of American Zionism, which was founded upon Brandeisian ideas of Palestine as a shelter from persecution. It was within this corner that the Hebraists remained with their direct, Hebrew-language connection to the cultural life of Palestine and their patronizing disdain for the prevarications of the organizational world of the Zionist mainstream. As a group, the American Hebrew poets were not politically active beyond the confines of their own institutions, such as the Histadrut Ivrit and did not view poetry as a proper medium for political passions.

Divergent, too, were the social and economic milieus of the two literatures. The Yiddish poets generally wrote from within the proletarian circumstances of their immigrant brethren. Leib was a boot maker, H. Leyvik, a paper hanger, Zisho Landoy, a house painter, and Moshe Leib Halpern, a jack of all trades. Their identity as skilled workers was a badge of honor and integrity rather than a sign of their having failed to become bosses and owners. Their vocation was poetry and their livelihood, their trades. They were widely read in world literature even though they lacked university degrees. Even though publishing poetry in the Yiddish press was desirable to all, taking a job working for a newspaper, an option open to some, was viewed with suspicion by many. Jacob Glatstein eventually made a point of demonstrating that it was possible to maintain a separation between journalistic work and poetry writing.

The situation of the Hebraists was quite otherwise. A glimpse into that difference is provided by Efros in his attempt to explain to an Israeli readership in 1952 something of the atmosphere of the literary circles in which he had participated in America decades earlier.

> What about the yearnings for the faraway shtetl in which they were born, the anguish of immigrant adjustment, the anxieties of making a living? There were none of these, and they played no role in the thematics of their poetry. It was their brethren the Yiddish poets who underwent this long and difficult process; and something of the bitter afflictions of the sweat shop entered their blood stream and seasoned their verse. The young Hebraists, in contrast, knew nothing of factories. Because they arrived with their leaning already in hand, they began right away to give private lessons in Hebrew or to teach Hebrew school while they prepared for entrance to universities on their way to becoming doctors and professors. The immigrant experience? They put it behind them in one running leap.[17]

If we take Efros's generalizations with a grain of salt and keep in mind that he is talking about poetry and not prose, his observations about the *sitz im leben* of American Hebrew poetry are very acute. The Hebraists were far from being proletarians. Although they arrived on these shores as penniless as other immigrants, they brought with them an intangible asset whose value could be realized immediately. What I have translated as their having come "with their learning already in hand" is more trenchant in Efros's original: *betoratam betokh mei'ehem*, with their Torah in their bellies.

To a one, the American Hebraists had received a superior traditional, classical Jewish education beginning as young children before they set out or were brought to America and before they opened their horizons to modern literature. This explains something not only about their pride but also about their circumstances. They discovered what came to be known by generations of countless Jewish university students in America: knowing Hebrew can be converted into a source of supplemental income and used to subsidize studying something else. While often demeaning and exasperating, giving Hebrew lessons and teaching Hebrew school did not entail the crushing and exhausting alienation of the sweatshop. Their early success as learners in the old country gave them the confidence to scale the obstacles set by their belated arrival in the new one. The rapidity with which they conquered English was astonishing; in many cases, the high school curriculum was dispatched in two or three years on the way to matriculation at the City University of New York or Columbia or New York University (NYU).

Efros himself is a star example. He arrived in America at the age of fourteen and attended public school in the morning and the yeshivah of Rabbi Isaac Elchanan in the afternoon, from which he received ordination at the age of eighteen. After undergraduate studies at NYU, Efros simultaneously pursued rabbinical studies at the Jewish Theological Seminary and doctoral studies in philosophy at Columbia University, receiving both his ordination and Ph.D. in 1915 at the age of twenty-four. To be sure, not all became doctors and professors; many pursued careers in Jewish education (discussed below). Regelson was an impecunious journalist when he worked, and Preil did not work at all. Yet if the accomplishments of all the members of the group were not as prodigious as those of Efros, there was generally little to apologize for.

When it comes to comparing the poetry itself—the influences, themes, and genres—there are also few points of contact. American Yiddish poetry is usually understood as a succession of three trends:

the Sweatshop Poets, the Young Generation [*Di Yunge*], and the introspectivists [*In Zich*]. Of the social protest poems of the Sweatshop Poets, there is no parallel in Hebrew poetry, although some of the later maskilic Hebrew poets in America cultivated, although along very different lines, poetry's public and parodic voice. It is only in the case of *Di Yunge* can there be said to be something of an affinity, or perhaps only a homology, with the American Hebrew poets. The Yiddish poets of this trend sought to detach poetry from its harness to political purposes—to liberate it from its role as "the rhyme department of the labor movement," in Landoy's famous phrase—and return it to the experiences of the individual. Similarly, the Hebrew poets declared the freedom of their verse from the obligation to enlighten, instruct, and entertain, as well as from the burden to make the love of Zion their compulsory theme. Both groups, moreover, were influenced by late- or neo-romanticism in European literature. For the Hebrew poets, however, these influences were largely internal and mediated through the work of earlier Hebrew poets (especially Bialik), who had absorbed the European trends along with a century of Haskalah poetry. With the exception of Peretz, the Yiddish poets lacked this internal tradition and drew more directly from Europe.

Even with these parallels, the timing is out of phase. The influence of *Di Yunge* was at its height from 1907 through World War I, a period when American Hebrew poetry was still in an inchoate state. It was only during the 1920s and 1930s that Hebrew poetry gathered confidence and sophistication, both in its institutions and its creative vision. It is this later period that parallels the rise of *In Zich* or introspectivism, the trend in Yiddish verse that includes the work of A. Leyeles, Glatstein, Leyvik, Y. L. Teller, the later Halpern, Malka Heifetz-Tussman, and Barysh Vaynshteyn. The introspectivists were squarely part of the revolution of modernism, although they stood conspicuously apart from the noisy and assertive rebelliousness of Russian symbolism and German expressionism. The latter were in fact precisely the movements that had taken Hebrew poetry in Palestine by storm in the 1920s, which in turn became the set of subversive poetics against which the American Hebrew poets defined their own identity. The rejection of the Hebraists, however, was undertaken in favor of refining the Hebrew romanticism they had received and domesticating it to the American scene, whereas the rejection of the introspectivists was undertaken in favor of a different and more refined kind of modernism. It was a modernism on the Anglo-American model that featured the use of irony, distanced dramatic situations, personae, and understatement. Meter, rhyme, and stanzaic structure were put aside in favor of free verse. Events in the world were seen through the prism of the poet's deepest self; the poet's unconscious became the touchstone of reality. Aside, again, from Preil, this was a more rigorously modern poetic world than the one inhabited by their Hebraist counterparts.

New York City was the cradle of American Hebraism—all but Lisitzky spent their earliest years in America there—and it remained the major center. Yet in the early 1920s, a number of the major figures moved to cities around America: Efros to Baltimore and then Buffalo, Friedland to Cleveland, Silberschlag to Boston, and Lisitzky to Milwaukee and Buffalo and then, New Orleans. They moved for good jobs in Jewish education. Of the twelve poets discussed in this study, all but three of them counted on some kind of teaching or administration in institutions of Jewish education for their livelihood. (Regelson failed in the classroom and became a Yiddish and Hebrew journalist; Schwartz was a family physician in Brooklyn; and Preil really did not work at all.) The linkage between the profession of Jewish education and the calling of Hebrew letters was negotiated differently by each poet. Friedland, for example, was a master educationalist whose active supervision of the Jewish schools in Cleveland left him little time for his own verse until he reached the brink of an early death. Feinstein was similarly productive only late in life because earlier he had been wholly invested in founding and running the Herzliah Teachers Institute in New York. For Lisitzky, a poet whose muse never seems to have left his side, his calling as a Hebrew educator in a remote Jewish community remained as important to him as his role as a poet. For others, the component of mission in their educational work was far less prominent. In no case, however, was there any confusion about the boundary between

Hebrew Writers in America, 1915. The photograph features a number of leaders of Palestinian Jewry who were spending the war years in America, as well as American Hebrew writers. Figures discussed in this book are in boldface. 1. Z. Urbach, 2. D. Ben-Gurion, 3. **Y. Ben-Zvi**, 4. Sh. Levin, 5. **R. Brainin**, 6. **E. Ben-Yehuda**, 7. H. Ben-Yehuda, 8. I. Ben-Avi, 9. **P. Ginsburg**, 10. Sh. B. Maximon, 11. A. Frankel, 12. **E. E. Lisitzky**, 13. **B. N. Silkiner**, 14. M. Levin, 15. **I. Efros**, 16. **D. Persky**, 17. K. Whiteman, 18. **S. Ginzburg**, 19. Sh. M. Melamed, 20. M. Z. Reisen, 21. **Y. D. Berkovitz**, 22. A. Goldberg, 23. M. Leiberman, 24. **H. Bavli**, 25. A. N. Pearlberg, 26. A. Dominitz, 27. **E. R. Malachi**, 28. **H. A. Friedland**, 29. A. Fleischman, 30. Y. Z. Frischberg, 31. M. Lipson. SOURCE: From *Hado'ar* (May 23, 1947), p. 854, 25th Jubilee Volume. Courtesy of the National Library of Israel.

Hebrew Writers in America, 1927. Figures discussed in this book are in boldface. 1. **S. Halkin**, 2. I. Rivkind, 3. Y. Twersky, 4. **E. R. Malachi**, 5. **R. Avinoam-Grossman**, 6. **P. Churgin**, 7. **M. Ribalow**, 8. Sh. Bernstein, 9. **Z. Scharfstein**, 10. **M. Feinstein**, 11. **D. Persky**, 12. K. Whiteman, 13. **H. Bavli**, 14. **B. N. Silkiner**, 15. Y. Y. Wohl, 16. Sh. B. Maximon, 17. Y. Z. Frischberg, 18. A. Shuer, 19. M. Z. Reisen, 20. **S. Ginzburg**, 21. A. Goldberg.
SOURCE: *Ketuvim*, Vol. 1, No. 41 (June 6, 1927), p. 1. Courtesy of the National Library of Israel.

education and poetry, which remained inviolate. The American Hebrew poets observed a complete separation of modes, and none would have considered—regrettably, one might perhaps opine in retrospect, for the results would have been fascinating—including within the themes of their poetry the challenges that faced them in the classroom.

The map of Hebrew culture in the United States roughly follows a similar distribution. New York remained the hub, the center that contained many Hebraists institutions of different stripes. There were three Hebrew teachers colleges there: the Teachers Institute of the Jewish Theological Seminary; the Teachers Institute of Yeshiva University; and Herzliah, which was independent. The Histadrut Ivrit was headquartered in New York, as was the publication it founded, the stalwart weekly *Hado'ar*. New York had enough of a critical mass so that clubs and associations could sponsor frequent activities in

A gathering of Hebrew writers attending a banquet to honor H. A. Friedland on his election as president of the Histadrut Ivrit, New York, 1939. Figures discussed in this book are in boldface. Sitting, from right to left: **H. Bavli**, A. Goldberg, **H. A. Friedland**, **Z. Shneour**, **M. Ribalow**, **A. S. Schwartz**. Standing: **D. Persky**, Y. Z. Frischberg, A. Spicehandler, **M. Feinstein**, I. Levinthal, E. M. Edelstein, M. Maisels. SOURCE: From the Moshe Amishai (Maisels) papers at the National Library in Jerusalem. The photograph appeared in *Hado'ar*, Vol. 20, No. 30 (May 30, 1941), p. 523. Courtesy of the National Library of Israel.

different parts of the city. When a Hebrew writer from Europe or Palestine visited the city, a banquet would be organized in his honor and the proceedings reported in the Hebrew and Yiddish press. But it would be a mistake not to look beyond New York. Most all major Jewish communities in America between the two world wars had Hebraist circles or clubs, and this was true not only in the Northeast but especially in the cities of the Ohio and Mississippi River valleys. This was a large and widely dispersed network. In a poem that will be discussed later in this volume, Ginzburg reflects on the paradox of interconnectedness and dispersion of these scattered cells by comparing them to lit-up train stations that pop into view and then fade away as he sits on a speeding train: "Like a sparse string of lights, scattered but connected / belonging to a strange and darkly snowy train station / that suddenly pops up among the winter fields, / forgotten somewhere between New York and Cleveland, / I have imagined you, Hebraists in the expanses of America."[18] To be sure, the anchors of these groups were the Hebraist educators who had branched out and colonized the Jewish communities of America; but the groups also attracted non-professionals called *shoharei 'ivrit* or *hovevei 'ivrit*, amateurs in the wider and romantic sense of the term, who were attracted to the Jewish national idea in its Hebraist garb.

The network of Hebraists in America can best be thought of in terms of a virtual or invisible community. Even in New York there was little day-to-day and face-to-face interaction. There may have been a Hebrew table at the Café Royal on the Lower East Side, but Hebraist culture had nothing of the contentious, lived density of its vastly larger Yiddish counterpart. Hebraism was an elite undertaking from the very beginning by self-definition and not just by force of circumstance. How, then, was a sense of interconnection and communication achieved among the scattered flock of the Hebrew faithful? Certainly, there were conferences and conclaves and gatherings, but the most significant mode of connection was newspapers and journals. The role of the periodical in creating community in modern Jewish life in general has been vastly understudied.[19] For the Hebraist world, the periodical was its life blood. *Hatoren* and *Miqlat* from the early period have already been mentioned; there were also *Bitzaron, Shevilei haḥinukh* and *Niv* later on, as well as a number short-lived efforts. But by far and away it was *Hado'ar* that was responsible for the circulation of Hebraists energies within this far-flung network. *Hado'ar* was launched with much fanfare and many expectations on November 1, 1921, and at its height had a print run of nine to twelve thousand copies. The circulation, however, simply could not be maintained, and the paper stopped appearing as a daily eight months later. It was soon reorganized as a weekly under the editorship of Menachem Ribalow, a journalist and critic who had recently arrived from Europe. Ribalow remained at the helm of the paper until his death in 1953. (Ribalow was the closest thing the Hebraist movement had to a central personality or even a commissar of culture.[20]) *Hado'ar* became a biweekly in 1992 and ceased publication altogether in 2005). *Hado'ar* remained the most significant achievement of the Histadrut Ivrit, the central Hebraist organization in America.[21]

It was in the pages of *Hado'ar*, which was a high-minded general newspaper/miscellany rather than an exclusively literary journal, that the official business of the Hebraist movement in America was conducted. A typical issue of *Hado'ar* would offer a rich mix of articles: the latest news from the Yishuv; *publitsistika* (a free genre of writing about public affairs based on a European model, similar to today's op-ed columns); feuilletons (light and humorous essays, almost always by Persky); cultural occasions and the marking of literary jubilees or *yovelot* (e.g., twenty or thirty years since the beginning of a writer's literary career); poems, short stories, and serialized novels (with an emphasis on American material); and reviews of new books. There was a more intimate and parochial side as well. Each issue would carry news of the activities of the Hebrew clubs and societies from around the country and a listing of upcoming events in the New York area. Engagements and marriages were announced, and every September a special and larger-than-usual issue would appear before Rosh Hashanah that was wholly taken up by paid holiday greetings from individuals, groups, and institutions. It was a fund-raiser for *Hado'ar*, but it was also a way for Hebraists to greet one another in such a manner that their node in the Hebraist network would briefly light up and reconfirm their presence and participation in this otherwise invisible community. About three thousand copies were printed for much of the journal's existence, a number roughly equal to the membership of the Histadrut Ivrit. It is difficult to know how that number translates into readership. Some subscribers took the journal out of loyalty to the Hebrew cause but did not—or could not—read it. In other cases, a copy from an individual or institutional subscription would be circulated among several hands. For many it was a flag with symbolic importance. The late scholar Gershon Cohen, who was extremely active in his youth in the Histadrut Hanoar Haivri [Federation of Hebrew Youth], relates an evocative image from the life of his father, an insurance salesman and a devotee of Hebrew.[22] He remembers that his father would fall asleep on Shabbat afternoons with a copy of *Hado'ar* open on his chest. There is much to contemplate in that image.

Any discussion of the impact of Hebraism on the larger American Jewish community must begin by separating the achievements of the two interrelated but distinct components of the movement: belles lettres and education. I mentioned that this was a separation that the writers for their own interests were keen on insisting upon. It is now worth putting the focus on the education side because it is only here, in the end, that the influence of Hebraism can be meaningfully talked about. Consider the differential circumstances. At the same time as immigrant Jewish parents wanted their children to take advantage of all that America had to offer, they were anxious about assimilation and sought to be assured that their children would maintain their ties to the community and its religion. The Jewish education supplied to children in the afternoon after public school became an important commodity. To accommodate this demand, Hebrew educators had to find ways to make Hebrew, their precious but difficult treasure, accessible, inviting, and even fun. When it came to belles lettres, however, not only was there no inherent demand, but the treasure remained accessible to the few that were in the process of becoming fewer. Whereas in the case of education, the resources of Hebrew were spun centrifugally out toward the community, in the case of belles lettres, Hebrew was moved closer and closer to the center.

Still, there was nothing necessary or even predictable about the success of Hebrew in Jewish education. The desire to impart to Jewish children some knowledge of their heritage in no way required the kind of enthusiastic focus on the Hebrew language that the Hebraist educators brought to the task. In fact, just the opposite could have been the case. When it came to teaching children what Jews believe, Hebrew was often not only unhelpful but obfuscating, and one would have expected the dominance of a Sunday school model in which Bible stories and religious doctrines would have been conveyed in English. And when it came to teaching children the rudimentary liturgical skills that were sentimentally important to American Jews—singing the kiddush over the wine Friday evenings, reciting the mourner's kaddish, and chanting the bar mitzvah portions—there was no compelling reason why the Hebrew could not be learned by rote rather than being pressed into a whole cultural program. Yet what should have been the most likely outcome did not take place. All sizeable Jewish communities had several-day-a-week Hebrew schools rather than, or in addition to, Sunday religious schools. These schools were run along recognizable Hebraist principles. Hebrew and Bible (rather than rabbinic texts) stood at the core of the curriculum; subjects were taught *'ivrit be'ivrit*, that is with Hebrew as the language of instruction in the classroom; the rudiments of Hebrew as a modern spoken language were conveyed; Zionism was imbued practically through songs, folkdances, and holiday celebrations that mirrored the culture of the Yishuv; the commandments were subsumed within the rubric of "customs and ceremonies"; and the rudiments of Jewish history were presented as a narrative that moved toward its consummation in the return to Zion. It was for a very good reason, it should be quite clear, that these supplemental educational programs were called *Hebrew* schools.

How Jewish education in America was captured by the Hebraists is a story that has not yet been fully understood or told. The spring of the drama begins with the Safed-born educator Samson Benderly, who struck a deal with Judah Magnes, the head of the short-lived New York Kehillah (1908–22), to train modern Jewish educators in progressive methods at the Teachers College of Columbia University and in Hebraic subjects at the Teachers Institute of the Jewish Theological Seminary, under the leadership of Mordecai Kaplan. The graduates of this program were known as Benderly Boys, and they spread out over

America and assumed the leadership of the central boards of Jewish education that controlled the curricula of the afternoon schools and the hiring of teachers. The Hebraist agenda was often at odds with the values of the lay leaders in a community; and it was not for nothing that these professional educators often likened their work, in the stubbornness and forcefulness it required, to the contemporaneous struggles of the pioneers in Palestine to drain the swamps and subdue the land. Religion was a potential flashpoint. Symbolic piety in relationship to the commandments of Judaism was the educational outcome sought by most synagogue leaders; yet this was not an uppermost value for the majority of Hebraist educators either in the conduct of their personal lives or in their educational philosophy. Because the schools and the Hebrew colleges were supported by communal funds, the Hebraists accommodated to the norms of religious observance in the public culture of their institutions and integrated religious materials into their curricula.

It was not, after all, a difficult or unpalatably compromising adjustment, because most Hebraists were not provocatively anti-religious like members of Jewish movements on the Left; rather, they embraced an Ahad Haamist perspective that saw religion as integral to the *longue durée* of Jewish civilization, even if they believed that its time had passed. The Zionism of these educators and their intimate connection to the Yishuv made an enormous and largely unrecognized contribution to the Zionization of American Jewry. This was a process that took place from the bottom up, that is, in schools where the bonds to Eretz Yisrael had been braided with many strands, and not only from the top down, through the national Jewish organizations and the response of public opinion to the Holocaust and the struggle for statehood.

Although the influence of Hebraist education continued well into the postwar years, there were signs already in the 1930s that its dominance was beginning to wane. As Jews moved to the suburbs from dense ethnic neighborhoods in city centers, control of Jewish education shifted to new, large synagogues—this was the golden age of the Conservative Movement—and away from centralized bureaus of Jewish education, where the Hebraist norm had held sway. Although the synagogues were in tune with a portion of the Hebraist agenda, they understandably wanted issues of faith and observance to take a larger part of the curriculum. After the war especially, the existential meaning of Judaism as a religion became an urgent matter for public discussion, and this was a topic that the Hebraists were disinclined to engage and about which, in any case, they had little to say. It was a time of soul-searching and second thoughts for Hebraist educators, who were coming to terms with the fact that they had not succeeded in producing a new, American-born generation of young people committed to Hebrew and at home in its uses.

The fault lay not in the design of the Hebrew-saturated curriculum and its robust implementation but rather in the larger American environment, over which they had no control. Under the influence of the powerful ideas of Horace Kallen on pluralism and John Dewey on democracy, the young protégés of Samson Benderly like Isaac Berkson had envisioned an ideal complementarity between the American public school and the supplementary Hebrew school; each would provide a necessary and integral component in the formation of the new generation. It was a principled decision *not* to pursue the path of the kind of separate or separatist Jewish education we now call day schools. But the vision that had been exuberantly formulated and embraced during World War I looked different twenty-five years later. In the absence of a Hebrew *sevivah*, a linguistically intensive educational environment, supplemental Jewish education had turned out to be truly no more than supplemental. The idea that vigorous and vital knowledge of Hebrew could exist *within* the dominance of English had to be abandoned.[23]

The mixed outcomes in education had a withering effect on literature as well. Not only were there likely to be few if any members of the new generation who would themselves become Hebrew writers, but the prospects also seemed bleak for the continued existence of competent readers who could at least consume Hebrew literature if not produce it. (That they would not be read at home was less of a surprise than the fact that many received little attention from the main community of Hebrew readers, writers, and critics in Palestine.) The timing is ironic, even tragic in its own way, because it was during the 1940s that the best works in American Hebrew literature were produced: Halkin's *'Ad mashber* [The crash] (1945), Efros's *Zahav* [Gold] (1942), Regelson's *Ḥaquqot otiyyotayikh* [Engraved are thy letters] (1946), Reuven Wallenrod's *Ki fanah yom* [Twilight in the Catskills] (1946), Lisitzky's *Eleh toledot adam* [In the grip of crosscurrents] (1949), and others. American Hebrew writers had entered a mature stage in their careers and found their voices; but this was a late harvest that could be enjoyed mostly by other Hebrew writers in America and by the few critics in Palestine who were alert to the work of the Americans. A number of the poets—Halkin, Regelson, and Efros—moved to Palestine/Israel during these years. Halkin and Regelson had lived there in the 1930s, returned to the States during the war years, and afterward finally settled in Israel. These decisions to move were complicated by the availability of jobs, family considerations, and the disruption of the war. In the face of the waning reception of Hebrew literature in America, it is in some ways easier to understand the motives of those who departed for the cultural center of Hebrew than to plumb the hearts and minds of those who stayed on. Each case was different, and the essays on the individual poets in this volume attempt to sketch something of the mental world of each poet. But there remains much work to be done in understanding how these "prophets without honor" understood their place as time went on. The establishment of the State of Israel was the occasion for transcendent celebration in the Hebraist world; yet one wonders what mixed emotions the Hebraists experienced at a private, unspoken level about being left behind in the shadows. Moreover, the language they loved and the language whose august purity they had labored so long to protect was now moving on to a vernacular incarnation whose rough-and-tumble vulgarity was often distant from their spirit.

It was in the late 1930s that a generational shift took place that introduced fresh energies into the world of Hebrew culture and sought to change the very definition of what that culture was about. These energies flowed through the channel of the Histadrut Hanoar Haivri, which was founded in 1936. Although the name of the organization sounded like the Histadrut Ivrit, it was its own entity and independent from the older body. It was begun by American-born students in their twenties who had acquired their Hebrew not "from the cradle," like the older Hebraists, but rather in the institutions, the Hebrew colleges, that the latter had founded. Among the founders and active members were young people who would go on to become significant figures in Jewish life: Moshe Davis, Gershon Cohen, T. Carmi, Jacob Kabakoff, Haim Leaf, Shlomo Shulsinger, Preil, and Milton Arfa. One of the most significant achievements of the Histadrut Hanoar Haivri was the publishing of a journal titled *Niv* [Expression], which appeared with different degrees of regularity for the next twenty years. Here, for all intents and purposes, was a counterculture that was organized under the banner of Hebrew but defined itself not so much in opposition to the older generation of Hebraists but in contradistinction to it. What was the new message it was announcing?

The novelty of their assertion centered on the question of what culture means. For the older generation, it was argued, *tarbut 'ivrit* [Hebrew culture], the grand banner that had been carried to America from Odessa of the 1890s, had never meant anything more than *sifrut 'ivrit* [Hebrew literature]. When the Hebraists talked about culture, what they really meant was the world of letters, namely, poetry, stories, essays, plays, reviews, memoirs, biographical profiles, and so on, in addition to publishing houses and the all-important journals. In this observation, the younger Hebraists were undoubtedly correct. But why was this necessarily a bad thing? Although literature and letters obviously remained highly significant activities in their eyes, they asserted that Hebrew culture should express the totality of the modern Jew's creativity. This meant not only literature and letters but also music, dance, and theater. Indeed, in New York City in the 1940s there was a Hebrew Arts Committee, chaired by Moshe Davis, which coordinated the activities of Pargod Hebrew theater, the Simfonetta Ivrit, a dance troupe, and various Hebrew choruses. At the age of twenty, Davis had been the first president of the Histadrut Hanoar Haivri, and later, as the young dean of the Teachers Institute of the Jewish Theological Seminary, he used his office to help promote the Hebrew arts. (A historian of American Jewry, Davis later moved to Israel and founded the Institute for Contemporary Jewry at the Hebrew University.) This impatience with the hegemony of literature may have had its roots in part in feelings of inadequacy on the part of young American Jews, whose Hebrew formation, though thorough and enthusiastic in its own way, did not adequately equip them to become Hebrew writers and literary artists and thus participate on an equal footing in the hallowed precincts of literature. Those who persisted in making that their goal, like Carmi, did not tarry in New York and made their way to Palestine as soon as they could. It was the manifold creative life of the Yishuv in Palestine, in fact, that served as a model for the ambitions of the young American Hebraists to open up Hebrew culture to the arts. They wanted a culture that was diverse, alive, and performed and not bound to the written page.

The place of religion and the Diaspora in a revitalized American Hebraism were topics that were intensively debated in the pages of *Niv* and at the meetings of the Histadrut Hanoar Haivri. Sweeping the issue of religion under the rug was not acceptable to the younger Hebraists. They had been educated in institutions that publicly conformed to Orthodox practice but were staffed by teachers who were largely non-observant, and they wished to see this contradiction explored openly rather than avoided. Davis, Cohen, Shulsinger, and others sought to shake up the complacency of the Ahad Haamist/culturalist position, whose adherents were satisfied to respect religious practices and institutions but unwilling to go much beyond respect. Especially when it came to observance of the Jewish holidays, this group advocated to their comrades a fuller integration of the resources of religious ritual. The same kind of dialectical honesty was sought when it came to conceptualizing the relationship between Eretz Yisrael and the Diaspora. The arguments put forward earlier in the century on behalf of building a Hebrew cultural center in America had been buttressed by Aḥad Ha'am's contention that spiritual work in the Diaspora had to be undertaken before and alongside the building of a successful national center in Eretz Yisrael. It was the subservience of this relationship that now came under question. As American Jewry established itself and shook off its immigrant awkwardness, it became evident that the culture it was potentially capable of producing had to have a value *beyond* making a contribution to the "upbuilding" of Eretz Yisrael. In an effort to explore new models of thinking, Davis introduced his young comrades to the thinking of Simon Rawidowicz, a European Hebraist, historian of philosophy, and thinker who advocated a dual-center model of Diaspora-Eretz Yisrael relations based on the image of the dialectic between Babylonian and Palestinian Jewries during the talmudic period.[24]

Finally, the frustration with the restrictiveness of the older Hebraism found its most influential outlet in the creation of a Hebrew camping movement. Veteran educators had come to realize, as has been mentioned, that afternoon Hebrew schools would never be able to compete with the dominance of the English-language environment in which their students lived their everyday lives. Younger Hebrew educators, led by Shulsinger, proposed using the students' long summer vacations to create a counter environment in which Hebrew would function as the dominant norm rather than a burdensome add-on. Within this laboratory environment, it would be possible to experiment with fashioning a synthesis among the dynamic, new Hebrew-based culture of the Yishuv, a fidelity to religious observance, and an embrace of the positive elements of American society. Camp Massad, which later grew into a number of camps in the Poconos and Canada, was founded by Shulsinger in 1941 and benefited from the wider popularity of summer camping in American Jewish life.

It was only here and only under these special conditions that the dream of Hebrew becoming a vernacular for American Jewry was briefly and partially realized. Baseball, the quintessential American pastime, was played at Massad using Hebrew terms for ball, strike, and run, all of which could be found in the camp's own paperback dictionary of Hebrew equivalents for the terms in which American Jews lived their lives. The original Massad camps were dissolved in 1981, and the sad story of their final years tells us much about the waning power of Hebrew to serve as a trans-denominational ideal. The modern Orthodoxy of Massad's official culture had been sustained by the passions of religious Zionism, although in the excitement of camp life, Torah study and the commandments had always played a correct but secondary role to Hebrew and Israel. In 1947 under the aegis of the Jewish Theological Seminary, Davis and Sylvia Cutler Ettenberg founded the first Ramah camp, which aimed to retain the Hebrew

norms of Massad but to add an emphasis on the contemporary meaning of religious practice and on the relevance of general social values.
Camp Moshava was later started by the Bnei Akiva movement and
Camp Morasha by Yeshiva University. All of these efforts drew their
inspiration from Massad but took the model in the direction of each
movement's priorities. Despite a professed commitment in each case to
keeping Hebrew as the language of daily camp life, the fact is that, for
many reasons, over time the role of Hebrew became more symbolic
than real.

✳

מְשׁוֹרֵר שֶׁל יִשְׂרָאֵל וְלֹא בְּאֶרֶץ יִשְׂרָאֵל

לוּ חָיִיתִי בְּיִשְׂרָאֵל, הָיִיתִי
מְשׁוֹרֵר שֶׁל יִשְׂרָאֵל
מֻדְפָּס עַל יְדֵי מוֹ"לִים מַמְלְכְתִּיִּים
בְּלֹא תְּמִיכָה מִצְדִּי,
בִּשְׂכַר סוֹפְרִים סָבִיר
מִצִּדָּם,
מְקֻבָּל עַל הָעָם,
מְצֻטָּט עַל יְדֵי פְּקִידִים
בַּחֲנֻכּוֹת בָּתֵּי תַּרְבּוּת מְנֻדָּבִים
עַל יְדֵי לֹא־יִשְׂרְאֵלִים.

מְשׁוֹרֵר שֶׁל יִשְׂרָאֵל וְלֹא בְּאֶרֶץ יִשְׂרָאֵל:
זֶה יְצוּר תָּמוּהַּ, אַךְ לִפְנֵי כִּבּוּשׁ יְהוֹשֻׁעַ
כְּבָר הָיוּ כְּמוֹתוֹ, כְּבָר סָלְלוּ מְסִלּוֹת הַשִּׁיר הָעִבְרִיּוֹת
בַּיָּם וְלֹא צָלְלוּ בְּמֵימָיו.
כְּבָר הָיוּ כְּמוֹתוֹ, עוֹד יִהְיוּ כְּמוֹתוֹ
סוֹלְלֵי מְסִלּוֹת הַשִּׁיר הָעִבְרִיּוֹת
מִחוּץ לִתְחוּם עַמָּם.

A Poet of Israel But Not in the Land of Israel

If I were in Israel, I would be
a poet of Israel,
published by state presses

and not at my own expense,
paid a reasonable writer's wage,
read by the public,
quoted by officials
at the inaugurations of cultural institutions funded
by non-Israelis.

A poet of Israel but not in the Land of Israel:
a strange creature. Yet before Joshua's conquest
there were already others like him,
paving the Hebrew paths of song
on the sea but without falling into the waters.
There were others like him, and there will be more,
paving the Hebrew paths of song
beyond the bourn of their people.[25]

Published in 1981 when he was in his late seventies, this poem by
Silberschlag is a wistful fantasy by an American Hebrew poet about
what it would be like to have the disabilities of marginality removed.
The first stanza is a fantasy—one that I think is aware of its own
plaintive tone—because it imagines the lives of Israeli poets to be a
bed of roses cushioned by state subsidies and public acclaim. By way
of ancient precedent, the second stanza asserts the proud legitimacy of
being a Hebrew poet, a poet of the people Israel, outside of the state
of Israel. The balance between envious complaint and proud assertion
nicely suggests the fraught situation of the American Hebrew poet.

The neglect of their work was a source of distress to Hebrew writers
in America. Responding to a belittling of the Americans on the part
of writers in the Yishuv, Halkin deplored the want of empathy implied
by the criticism.

Bereft and parched in the heartless environment of the Jewish street
with its clamor and commotion and false personal relations, [the Hebrew
writer] creates what he creates without anyone paying the slightest
attention. He is forlorn in his isolation. And the readers for whom he
writes? Does he ever come across them the way a Palestinian writer
does from time to time? Where are his critics? Do they even know his
name? Huddled in secret without colleagues or recognition from any
source, the American Hebrew writer, the poet especially, lives his pain;

and when he seeks solace by creating, no one bothers to look at his creations. The American Hebrew writer therefore creates for its own sake [*lishmah*], but no good comes of it. His reward, if there will be any at all, will come only in the world to come.[26]

The neglect at home—except for attention the writers gave one another—was eventually taken for granted as American Jews moved farther and farther away from a connection to Hebrew. Yet the neglect abroad, in the burgeoning Hebrew literary culture of Palestine/Israel, was more hurtful. There was no question of competition; the Americans had long acknowledged, and rejoiced in, the ascendancy of Tel Aviv. Nevertheless, they viewed themselves as full-fledged members of the larger enterprise of Hebrew literature who manned a remote but significant cultural outpost. Especially when they dealt with American themes, the Americans saw their writings as dispatches aimed at contributing to the enrichment of the center. The indifference to gifts so sincerely offered was indeed difficult to endure. Now, this would be a matter of merely historical interest if the situation were different today, that is to say, if the work of the Americans were better appreciated or understood. But that is not the case. What was a kind of intentional snub during the lifetimes of the American writers created a situation in later decades in Israel in which the very existence of this group lapsed into oblivion. Succeeding generations of Israeli readers and writers could not even choose to ignore American Hebrew writers because they did not know that such creatures had ever walked the earth.

To undertake a reconsideration of American Hebrew literature, it is first necessary to understand the reasons why American Hebrew literature was ignored in the Yishuv.[27] A key factor, to begin with, was the necessary self-absorption of the Yishuv in its own formation. After world war, revolution, and civil war had caused horrific upheavals in Jewish life and put the very existence of the Yishuv in question, it was astonishing how quickly the Hebrew cultural center in Palestine was reconstituted and expanded. A steady stream of writers, editors, and publishers arrived in the 1920s. They were drawn in part by their identification with the Jewish national idea and in part by a desire to connect with an active audience for Hebrew writing. Many had been living in Germany and Austria after departing Eastern Europe, but the extreme fluctuations of the German economy (hyperinflation, deflation, depression) made residence there increasingly difficult. The gathering strength and confidence of the Yishuv as a literary center were supercharged by the ideological mystique of the pioneering ethos, as reflected especially in the early poetry of Avraham Shlonsky, Yitzhak Lamdan, and Uri Zvi Greenberg. Europe was burning and its Jews murdered in pogroms, and the only chance for young Jews to transform their lives was to throw themselves into the task of settling the land. Compared to Europe and America, only a tiny fraction of the world's Jews lived in Palestine, yet for the cultural leaders of the Yishuv, the entire drama of thousands of years of Jewish history rested on the fate of this small community.

Given this degree of perceived self-importance then, it was difficult to give serious attention to the cultural products of American Jewry, even those in Hebrew. America was widely viewed as the land of "bluff" and the "dollar," the terms used in Hebrew to dismiss immigrant culture on the grounds of its materialism, ignorance, and vulgarity. American Jewry was a degraded, superficial version of the European *galut* [exile], which Zionism had arisen to replace. What could there be in this dim and far-off Diaspora that might possibly be relevant to the revolutionary actuality unfolding in Palestine? It was also a case of very unfortunate timing. These stereotypes were fixed in the early 1920s, when American Hebrew writers did not yet have much to show for themselves beyond sensitive and depressive lyric poems scattered among journals scarce in the Yishuv. The published poetry collections came later, and the serious work in Hebrew fiction even later. Moreover, the best efforts of the poets to engage American culture and history—the works discussed in Part Three of this volume—only began to appear in the mid-1930s and continued into the 1950s. Very, very few critics in the Yishuv had the prescience of Yaakov Rabinowitz to make the crucial distinction between the America of vulgar Jewish immigrant culture and the America of Emerson, Longfellow, Thoreau, and Whitman. Despite the belated labors of the Americans to translate the classical American authors and convey their significance to the Hebrew literary community, the case had been lost and the Americans consigned to irrelevance.

The culture war that raged throughout the 1920s, which involved a bitter struggle over control of journals and publishing outlets, was decided in favor of the modernist poets, who progressively strengthened their connection with the new generation of readers. In this battle, the Americans were attached to the vanquished forces, and they paid the price for being on the wrong side. The crushingly dismissive argument lodged at the Americans was that their poetry never developed. It was a provincial offshoot, it was claimed, of the poetics of the *teḥiyyah* practiced in Eastern Europe by Bialik and Tchernichovsky, and it had never declared its independence and struck out in new directions. So, while the revolution was taking place in Palestine, American Hebrew poetry appeared to remain in thrall to the conservative forces that were holding Hebrew literature back from engaging modernity and coming to terms with the events that were violently transforming Jewish existence. While the Jewish nation and the Jewish individual were in a state of cataclysm, the Americans wrote quiet Hebrew poems about melancholy and the changing of the seasons. Worse still was the fact that they did so in an elevated classical Hebrew idiom that seemed frozen in amber from an earlier time and remained blissfully unsullied by the raucous growth of spoken Hebrew in Palestine. The fact that the path of American Jewry—and the poetry that might give it literary representation—followed quite other lines of development was not factored into this judgment. Although Shlonsky and Greenberg were chronologically of the exact same generation as Lisitzky and Efros, in the eyes of the former the latter were dinosaurs that wandered an alien planet.

This dismissal, which was born out of the dialectics of cultural conflict in the interwar years, hardened into a critical consensus, and this judgment remained in place long after the hotly contended issues that produced it had faded from the scene.[28] As a result, with the exception of Preil, American Hebrew poetry disappeared from the map of twentieth-century Hebrew poetry, and its major figures remained known, and then only dimly, to a few academic experts. What is true in Israel is all the more so in the United States, where the knowledge of literary Hebrew is scant and academics in the field of Hebrew literature, whether American- or Israeli-born, are often trained according to norms set by the Israeli center. There is no conspiracy in this erasure, only the prolonged and unexamined afterlife of a dialectic relevant many decades ago. In the intervening periods, several more revolutions in taste have taken place that make the original motives for the rejection even more remote. Therefore the time has come for a reevaluation of the claims of American Hebrew literature that would attempt to understand the Americans from their own point of view rather than seeing them through the eyes of the Yishuv. Such a reevaluation would necessarily move along two axes: reconstructing how the Americans experienced their own endeavor in its own time and reassessing it from the point of view of our own.

To begin with, we are now in possession of a broader picture of the workings of Hebrew literature in the first decades of the twentieth century. A republic of Hebrew literature is the model that Dan Miron has usefully developed to describe this period.[29] Lacking a single center but possessing many smaller centers, Hebrew literature was a kind of virtual community of writers and readers who communicated with each other across borders through a network of periodicals and through correspondence. Brenner, for example, moved from Russia to England and then on to Galicia and finally to Palestine, writing and publishing all the while; his citizenship in this republic of Hebrew letters, although colored by the places he was writing from, was not determined by it. This was not a community, moreover, that was Zionist in the conventional sense of seeing settlement in Palestine as an overarching goal. Rather, they saw Hebrew literature and culture—rather than territory per se—as the concrete and immediate ground upon which a national revival could arise; and for the hundred years before World War I, they were unquestionably correct. It was as full members—or at the very least, corresponding members—of this republic that the American Hebrew poets saw themselves and expected to be treated. Yet as the center consolidated in Tel Aviv between the wars along the lines discussed above, a Zionist template was retroactively placed upon the historiography of Hebrew literature. In this reading of the recent past, Hebrew literary activity in Europe and elsewhere had *always* been moving toward its fulfillment in the Land of Israel. The isolated Hebrew writers still left in Poland,

Austria, France, and the Soviet Union were anachronisms or curiosities that had not yet been "ingathered." The American Hebrew writers were the largest concentration of these holdouts; in their own eyes, they were playing in good faith according to the rules of the republic of Hebrew letters, which for them still existed, and making a valuable contribution to it. But in the eyes of the literary establishment of the Yishuv, their persistence represented only an inexplicable obtuseness. Now that the grip of Zionist historiography has been relaxed, we are in a much better position to understand how Hebrew literature was constituted in the first half of the twentieth century as an interplay, admittedly not symmetrical, among a number of centers. On this new map, America deserves a refurbished place.

Second, the failure of the Americans to be enlisted in the moderna, the new wave of modernism in Hebrew poetry between the two world wars, was in their own eyes a principled stance rather than a failure of nerve. They saw symbolism and expressionism as barbarisms that perpetrated an unwelcome violence upon the body of Hebrew literature. No good Hebrew poetry, they argued, could result from violating the native purity and beauty of the Hebrew language. Although they were surely conservative, the Americans were not interested in preserving Bialik in amber, and, as will be discussed shortly, there were significant ways in which they revised the poetics they inherited. Their rejection, moreover, was motivated as well by the very simple, positive fact that they lived in America and in the midst of American literary traditions. It was not so much that they repudiated German and Russian influences as they affirmed ones closer to home. Many had come as impressionable early adolescents whose tastes in general literature were shaped by the authors who were read at the time in the public schools. These were not Ezra Pound, T. S. Eliot, and Amy Lowell but rather Emerson, Longfellow, and William Cullen Bryant. When they went on to becoming more adventurous and independent readers during their university years, the poets that they most likely would have been reading included Emily Dickinson, Walt Whitman, Edward Arlington Robinson, Robert Frost, and Carl Sandburg. For some of the more metaphysically minded, like Halkin and Regelson, the great discovery was English romantic poetry, especially Shelley and

Keats. Not to be underestimated, as well, was the collective impact of reading Shakespeare, whom the Americans (unlike their colleagues in Palestine) read in English and whom they translated into Hebrew as a collaborative project. Now, the Americans may be vulnerable to the charge of not taking full advantage of the Anglo-American literature that stood at their disposal, but they should be judged within the terms of its sphere of influence rather than being condemned for declining to adopt German and Russian models.

Third, the case of American Hebrew poetry raises provocative theoretical questions about the relationship between modernism and neoclassicism. The latter is the term I propose below to describe the revisions made by the Americans in the late-romanticism of the Hebrew poets who preceded them. Theirs was not a revolution but a kind of winnowing. They sought to simplify the voice of Hebrew poetry, to disencumber it from the weighty burden of classical allusion and Jewish prophetic pathos, and to impose restraints on the amplitude of sentiment. The result they hoped for was a classic distillation of a modern Hebrew idiom. Theirs was therefore not an instance of a reactionary resistance to modernism but rather a positive aspiration toward a modernized classical model. In literary studies in general and in the history of Hebrew literature in particular, do we ignore serious works of art that are not located on the cutting edge of the period? What criteria have we developed to assess works that eschew the avant-garde for the classical? American Hebrew poetry is just one among many cases of so-called byways (*tsidei derakhim* in Halkin's terminology) in Hebrew literature, which are not easily assimilable into the major narrative or direction of a literary period. A study of American Hebrew literature on its own terms will undoubtedly contribute to this task.

Fourth, the significance accorded American Hebrew literature naturally depends on who is asking the question. What was a matter of no account to critics and readers in the Yishuv might become a matter of great moment to readers and critics in America seeking to understand their own culture. It is a story that has repeated itself often enough in contemporary times. Scholars and intellectuals who are members of a minority or an oppressed group discover cultural artifacts that have been ignored by the majority culture; they find these objects interesting and enriching because they shed light on aspects of experience left unaddressed by the acknowledged works of the canon; they develop an alternative set of criteria for interpreting and evaluating these objects; and then, at some later stage, the broader critical community finds interest in these new questions and new works and makes room for them in a newly enlarged mainstream. Now, it may seem strange to see the case of American Hebrew literature mentioned together with the literatures of women, African Americans, Native Americans, and Hispanics, and indeed the differences, it need not be said, are enormous. Nevertheless, there is potentially a similar dynamic at work. If students of American Jewish literature come to find American Hebrew literature interesting and enriching, there is every reason to believe that the Israeli literary community will as well. My own path, as I indicated at the beginning of this introduction, has brought me around in this circuit. What once seemed quaint and irrelevant became fascinating and compelling once I felt the urgency to understand the meaning of Hebrew in America. And even if it is only a small group whose rest is disturbed by this particular quest, it is likely to be a larger group that seeks to comprehend the full complexity of American Jewry's history. We are a community known for dulling the edge of ideologies and accommodating our distinctiveness to the ambient culture. It is therefore not a small matter to discover the existence of an elite cultural project, to add it to our communal memory, and to readjust our self-esteem even by that little amount.

Gaining a place in the canon of Hebrew literature, in the end, is not a matter of justice but of merit. Fogel, Devorah Baron, and a number of women poets became important because they were read and found compelling, even if they were first placed before the attention of readers by an extra-literary advocacy. So it might be in the instance of American Hebrew literature. Acknowledging the injustice of the initial dismissal is merely a step preliminary to encountering the material itself, which will have to stand on its own and be found compelling—or not. And if and when American Hebrew literature is read, the degree and nature of interest it generates is likely to depend on the subject-position of the readers, whether they are reading from Israel or America, and the nature of the linguistic tools they are equipped with. The case for American Hebrew literature, finally, can be made only by the hard work of annotating, interpreting, anthologizing, and translating. The present work is an effort to advance that endeavor.

✳

Since this drama of insult and injury unfolded, several revolutions in aesthetic taste have come and gone. That distance puts us in a better position to appreciate the differences between Hebrew poetry in America and Hebrew poetry in Palestine, not only in their relationship to one another but especially in their separate lines of development. It is crucial, moreover, to see each literary community as being shaped along two axes: its response to its poetic predecessors and its response to present, local imperatives.

Let us take, to begin with, the stance toward the state of Hebrew poetry in the first quarter of the twentieth century. Although Bialik was nearly universally admired, he essentially stopped writing poetry around 1911 when he was only thirty-eight years old. While he maintained his position as the great mandarin of Hebrew letters, he acknowledged a group of slightly younger poets as his successors. Known under the collective term of *shiratenu hatse'irah* [our young poetry], the group included Shneour, Jacob Kahan, David Shimonowitz (Shimoni), Jacob Fichman, and Jacob Steinman. In the eyes of Shlonsky and Greenberg (and joined by Lamdan and Avigdor Hameiri), this was a group of epigones who did not deserve to inherit Bialik's mantle. For Greenberg, Bialik

> was and remains the glorious First Temple in the kingdom of Hebrew poetry. But those of his contemporaries who came later are gently flowing poetry in the Hebrew tongue . . . for lack of other possibilities, they want to share between themselves the heavy crown, to parcel out the crown of literature into smaller crowns, and to fashion ostrich-feathered hats for each one—priests of "the blessed Hebrew tongue"— and to live thus, just so . . . they live frugally, spiritually and physically, and create frugally and modestly.[30]

Even though their revolutionary poetics turned Bialik on his head, they saw themselves as Bialik's true *spiritual* successors and sought to deny that status to a group of poets they regarded at middling and derivative. The stance of the Americans was quite different. Slightly younger than the *shiratenu hatse'irah* poets, the Americans saw themselves as allied with the members of this group in continuing and developing Bialik's patrimony. Their mission was to conserve, protect, and extend that inheritance. Leaving aside the question of spiritual succession, on the face of things, their poetic practice was certainly closer to that of the master's than the radical modernism introduced by Shlonsky and Greenberg. But no matter which group was the "truer" inheritor of the mantle, each, according to its own lights, was struggling to preserve the soul of Hebrew poetry.

Each group, moreover, framed its poetics in response to what it perceived to be a clear and present cultural emergency. For the young poets in Palestine, the crisis was nothing less than the violent upheaval of their lives within the chaos of war and revolution. They had experienced within their short lifetimes the utter breakdown of the Jewish society into which they had been born, and they had made their way across a bleeding and ideologically riven Europe to foment another revolution in Palestine. That Hebrew poetry should gently flow on, failing to represent the violent contradictions in the lives of the pioneers and thereby rendering itself irrelevant—this was the real danger. The Americans, for their part, were also immigrants, and they had been thrust out of Europe for similar reasons. Yet their experience of immigration, as difficult and dislocating as it was, bore little resemblance to their counterparts in Palestine. They were plunged into an immigrant culture whose enormous energies were wholly harnessed to the project of Americanization. Even if the image of America in the Yishuv as the land of bluff and the dollar was an unfair caricature, it did not miss the mark when it came to the meager fortunes of religion, ideology, and culture. At every turn, the young aspiring Hebrew poets were confronted with an immigrant society preoccupied with material success, diminished by the abandonment or the brute ignorance of Jewish learning, and stultified by the vulgar mass entertainments of the Yiddish tabloid press and the Second Avenue theater. The quietly heroic mission of Hebrew poetry would be the creation of a "sanctuary in the wilderness," a literature that privileged and instantiated beauty, love, the awe of nature, and the quest for the divine. As a response to this American emergency, the goal of the new literature would be to preserve and protect these spiritual values against the forces of impurity and materialism that assailed them from all sides.

The vastly different missions taken on by each literature assumed vastly different conceptions of the role of art and the artist. Revolutions require revolutionaries, and, indeed, the pre-state poets saw themselves as manning the barricades of culture. Poetry had to be engaged, militant, and public for it to remain not only relevant but to lead the struggle. This was a collective poetry in which the personality of the individual poet came into play as a dramatization of the ordeals of the generation. As in Bialik's poetry, the poet was a prophet whose heroic suffering both represented and reproached the people's struggles. All aspects of the poetic system were mobilized to give expression to the radical transformation of young lives and to the electrifying consciousness of the unprecedented present hour. For the Americans, the task of literature was just the opposite: to extract the timeless from the chaos of the present. To do so meant to insulate poetry from the public realm and protect its autonomy. The goal of poetry was to penetrate the embroiled world of historical contingency and to illuminate the universal and the sublime in human experience. The truth they sought was not the mystique of Jewish existence forged in the blood of the burning present moment. Instead, they sought to create a lyric Hebrew humanism in which the particularistic resources of the Hebrew language could be used to cultivate the soul's capacity for wonderment. The role of the individual poet in this conception is modest and untheatrical; the poet serves as a transparent lens through which the intimate experience of humanity becomes visible.

The consequences for the poetic text are equally dichotomous. For the young poets in Palestine, the convulsive realities of the present hour demanded the composing of a *shir parua‘* ["wild poem"], which would throw off the fetters of convention and restraint. This began with the rejection of meter and rhyme and went on to include the very organization of the poem into stanzas. The differentiated genres of poetry—lyric, epic, ode, and so forth—which had served poets for so long were also abandoned. The "wild poem" evolved its own, counter logic. In the place of all of these regulative norms,

the modernists developed new ways of making the wildness intelli-
gible, such as stamping the extremely long poetic line with alternating
rhythmic emphases or gathering groups of texts into poem cycles.
Turning to the Americans, by now it should not be surprising that
they were devoted to conserving and refining poetic traditions rather
than tossing them aside. Aside from the work of Preil and some poems
by Regelson, which are written in free verse, the Americans wrote in
established poetic meters and generally employed rhyme. Lyric poems
were organized into regular stanzas, with preference often given to the
quatrain. Distinctions were further observed between the short, lyric
poem and such longer forms as the *poema*, the epic, the idyll, and the
dramatic monologue. A *poema* is a Russian term current in Hebrew
poetry at the turn of the twentieth century for a long poem on a serious topic. The Americans took special pride in the form that was the
most preciously rule bound: the sonnet. Nearly the whole of the poetic
career, albeit short, of Friedland was devoted to writing sonnets. Most
of the Americans wrote them, and an outstanding example is Halkin's
extensive Shakespearean sonnet cycle *Beyamim shishah veleilot shiv'ah*
[In six days and seven nights]. The music of Hebrew poems composed
in America was indelibly—and, in light of later history, fatefully—
marked by allegiance to the Ashkenazic accent in the pronunciation
of the language.[31] (Here again the exceptions are Regelson and Preil.)
By the early 1920s, Hebrew poetry written in Palestine had made the
transition to the so-called Sephardic pronunciation, with its accent on
the ultimate syllable of words and its vocalizing the letter *tav/sav* [ת]
always as a "t" sound (dental plosive). The difference was fundamental
for the susceptibility of Hebrew to various meters and rhyme schemes;
and, at the level of ideological sensibilities, it became an important
marker of the divergence between Palestine/Israel and the Diaspora.
The Ashkenazic scansion of American Hebrew poetry was not an
insignificant factor in making this body of verse sound superannuated
to the ears of readers at the literary center.

   The two poetic communities were the products not only of their
divergent collective biographies but also of the influences of very different national literatures. The impact of Russian, German, and French
modernist poetry on the new Hebrew verse written in the Yishuv in

the 1920s was evident for all to see. But the sources of influence and emulation that stood behind American Hebrew poetry were less conspicuous and certainly less familiar to readers and critics abroad. Moreover, with the exception of Silkiner's *Mul ohel Timurah*, the explicitly American works—on Indians, the West, New England, Negroes, and so forth—did not begin to appear until the 1930s. Therefore it was natural for the Americans to be perceived as mere epigones of Bialik through the *shirateinu hatse'irah* poets in his camp. By the 1920s, when the debate over the work of the Americans took place, their measure had already been taken and their critical fate sealed. It was within that debate that Halkin argued that this characterization was fundamentally in error because it failed to appreciate the fact that the Americans were motivated by a parallel but different set of literary precursors. Just in the same way, he asserted, that the influences of Whitman, Baudelaire, Verlaine, Hofmannshtal, Rilke, Andrei Bely, and Alexander Blok were evident in the verse of the Palestinian modernists, one can turn to the Americans and identify the influences of Wordsworth, Shelley, Keats, Emerson, Tennyson, and Browning.[32] This Anglo-American tradition, which stood behind the work of the Americans, was invisible to the Hebrew critics of Tel Aviv because it descended from a cultural sphere alien to them. Halkin was likely reflecting his own affinities, and later American observers would add more American names to his roster, such as Robinson, Edna St. Vincent Millay, Sandburg, and Frost. But the overall argument and the general lines of connection it points to are clear. Yet how fully this argument can be endorsed as an empirical description of the historical poetics of American poetry, and not just as a counter-slogan in a tense polemical exchange, remains to be established by close and systematic reading of this literature. The literature in question, as will become evident in the individual studies that follow in this volume, is very variegated. One of the rawest sources of umbrage for Halkin was the tendency of the Palestinian critics to lump all the Americans, with their diverse poetic worlds, into a single monstrous creature.[33] The absorption of Anglo-American models, moreover, was a process rather than an event. The poets were young and new to America, and they came across English and American writers unevenly. Some influences were swallowed whole and imitated derivatively only to be returned to more subtlety and less evidently in later years, while other English-language writers might remain remote and unfamiliar until a poet's intellectual journey made his verse open to their sway. In modern theory, moreover, the very concept of influence has been interrogated and has undergone several thorough revisions. For all these reasons, the thesis put forward by Halkin, and seconded by Ribalow and Epstein, remains a heuristic rubric within which fundamental work remains to be done.

When the Americans looked inward and took stock of themselves, they saw their poetry as distinguished by two chief characteristics: seriousness and simplicity. Seriousness is a term that Halkin drew from the Victorians with deliberate provocation. He knew that Victorian poetry (especially Tennyson, Browning, Arnold) was reputed to be the old regime in opposition to which modern verse had to define itself. Yet, he nevertheless saw in the "earnestness" of the Victorians an admirable focus on the essential questions of human existence, and this was precisely the focus that had been lost in the furious engagement of Palestinian Hebrew poetry with the politics of the moment. In clamoring to attach themselves to the avant-garde, the Hebrew modernists had ironically made Hebrew into a provincial poetry, a poetry limited in time and place and cut off from the deepest springs of human feeling. There can be no great lyric poetry, Halkin avers, without the poet's striving to unite "the moments of vision that appear like isolated bubbling streams that come from a common source." The fact that the poet's quest for *sheleimut hanefesh* [wholeness of the soul], the deepest drama of true poetry, is an embarrassment to the modernists is an indication of an ultimate want of ultimate seriousness.[34] Taking care not to evoke a specifically Judaic frame of reference, Halkin formulated this quest in universal religious terms. Unsurprisingly, these were terms that were particularly well fitted to Halkin's own poetic project. Although his outlook is shared by a number of poets, a more representative and broader-spectrum characterization of the humanistic enterprise of American Hebrew poetry is given by the critic Epstein: American Hebrew poetry is "largely lyrical and individual in nature, yet it strives toward truth through a connection to the other. It is distinguished by an aspiration to beauty, to the majesty in vision, to the mysteries of nature and to the wonders of love. It is further accompanied by a romantic meditation on divine mystery, on the enigma of existence, and on the tragic fate of man. Does not all eternal poetry place man—man in the face of God and man in the face of fate—at its center?"[35] In the view of Epstein and others, it was left to the Americans to rescue Hebrew poetry from the dereliction of the modernists, who had violated the essential humanist integrity of the national literature.

These are rather large claims, and they could not be put forward if the vocation of American Hebrew literature was *only* to preserve and curate the literary practice of the generation that preceded them. And indeed, although they avoided direct criticism of the Bialik-Tchernichovsky poetic canon that they admired on many scores, the Americans did have their own revision to offer, and they cast it as an evolution on the British model rather than as a revolution. Schematically put, they sought to winnow this tradition from its excessively romantic and excessively Judaic elements. The goal was to create a classic literature. By disciplining romantic expressiveness, it would be possible to refocus Hebrew poetry on the modal human experiences at the core of human existence, as described above. Standing in the way of this project of universalization was the hermetic knot of classical allusion at the center of Bialikian poetics. As a literary device, the allusion took advantage of the transitional nature of both the writers and the readers during the national revival at the turn of the twentieth century. The male members of this generation had been raised in the beit midrash on the classics of the religious tradition; and although they parted with the ways of their fathers, this shared literacy allowed for the use of fraught, complex, and usually ironic coded references to the sources. One of the conspicuous shifts introduced by the Americans was a radical reduction in the use of classical allusion. Rather than being part of the fabric of literary texts, allusions were deployed very sparely, and then always for a focused tactical purpose. (See Efros's "'Inbol qatan" [Little clapper] and the accompanying analysis at the end of Chapter Four for an example.) There are two reasons, I would suggest, for this change. Although the poets undoubtedly possessed the erudition to fashion these coded references, the capacity to understand them was rapidly lessening among their readers both in America and abroad. But it was not only the force of circumstance, and the renunciation was not involuntary. The Americans found the allusive apparatus a cumbersome weight that interfered with the streamlining and lightening they were trying to achieve. It also pulled in the wrong direction. While they were attempting to reorient Hebrew poetry toward the universal categories of human experience, Judaic allusions pulled in the other direction.

The regime of simplification extended to the intelligibility of the poetic text, its linguistic register, and the proportions of its composition. A number of descriptive terms recur in the critical discourse of the American poets and critics, and all of them are taken up as a way of distinguishing the American project from the newly dominant norms being promulgated from Palestine. For example, *tselilut*, clarity, is the American value that is set in opposition to *'irpul*, obfuscation, the tendency of modernist poetry to wrap its subject in conflicting messages and to set up obstacles and detours to the communication of identifiable feelings. *Tohar*, purity, is proposed as the antonym to a wild linguistic miscegenation in which the exquisite and the crass cohabit the same poetic lines and ugly foreign words are allowed to sully the classical elegance of the Hebrew language. *Tsini'ut*, modesty, is the quality that holds the line against outsized prophetic pronouncements and the presumption that the poetic text can be stretched and contorted at will to serve the grandiosity of the poet.

Yet this self-portrait of American Hebrew poetry is not as demure and innocent as it first appears. In a 1927 poem "Tsimtsum" [Frugality], Feinstein reflects on the duality at the heart of this vaunted ethic of self-restraint.

שַׁלְהֲבוֹת קֶסֶם יֵשׁ בַּצִּמְצוּם וְרִמְזֵי רָז,
אֲשֶׁר אִם יִגְּעוּ בְּךָ וְהָיוּ כְּיַיִן עַז
הַיּוֹצֵק אוֹן בַּדָּם וְדוֹרֵךְ אֶת הָעוֹרְקִים וּמְגָרֶה
לְהַבְקִיעַ מִבִּצְרֵי־עַד וּלְהַעְפִּיל הָהָרָה.

וְסוֹד־הַחַיִּים יֵשׁ בַּצִּמְצוּם וּמִשְׂגָּב לַמַּחֲשָׁבָה;
שׁוּר, נִיצוֹץ אֵשׁ הֵן יַהֲרֶה לְהָבָה,
וּבְגַרְעִין קָטָן זֶה מְקֻפָּלִים כָּל הַפֵּרוֹת אֲשֶׁר יִהְיוּ תַּחַת הַשָּׁמָיִם,
וּבְאֶגֶל חֵשֶׁק אֶחָד מְפַרְכְּסִים דּוֹרוֹת בָּאִים.

There are magical flames and hidden secrets in frugality
That become strong wine if they touch you
Infusing your blood with strength, surging through your veins
To assault the fortresses and run the blockade up the mountain.

The secret of life and refuge for thought are in frugality;
Behold: a spark of fire will indeed give birth to a flame,
In this small seed all the fruit that will ever be are enfolded,
In this one drop of desire quiver all coming generations.[36]

In translating the poem's title as "Frugality," Naomi Seidman wisely opted for the homely and everyday meaning of a term that has profound and recondite associations. *Tsimtsum* is of course the term in Lurianic Kabbalah for God's voluntary self-containment that allows creation to take place, and the theologically loaded meaning of the term is made explicit in the second half of the poem, which is not quoted above. (Later Feinstein wrote a verse drama on the thirteenth-century mystic Abraham Abulafia; see in Chapter Ten.) Sparks and seeds are humble and simple things, and they are ostensibly signs of thriftiness and self-denial. Yet despite their modest garb, once activated they have Superman-like potential. This frugality unbound can intoxicate the senses, storm fortresses, and engender a bounty of living things. The paradox is no more acutely felt than in the *egel ḥesheq eḥad*, the single drop of seminal fluid, which, in contrast to its appearance in Mishnah *Avot* (3:1) as a putrid excretion, here holds *in potentia* the whole future of the race. Feinstein's poem allows us to savor something of the tone of the American Hebraists' self-perception, which moves between pride and *resentiment*. The clarity, purity, and modesty that distinguish their works, they would strongly argue, were the result of choice, not incapacity. They renounced theatrical self-indulgence in favor of classic economy and restraint, and they did so in the hope of acceding to a poetic discourse made the more concentrated by these renunciations.

The truth of this argument must be judged by the reader in the course of encountering the many different voices of American Hebrew poetry. It is essential to be reminded continually of the fact that the issues that shaped the debate between the Hebrew poets in America and their counterparts in Palestine took place early—in many senses, too early—in the formation of each community. In the 1920s, the Americans had only their sensitive lyric poems to show and poets like Shlonsky, in the Yishuv, were at their most provocative. Already by the 1930s, however, the ascendancy of Natan Alterman had softened the radical edges of modernism, and the Americans were seriously engaging the American milieu. Yet, by that time, as has been said, the perceptions of the other had been fixed.

Simplicity retains its usefulness as a heuristic concept for us today in part to draw our attention to the streams in American Hebrew poetry that *cannot* be comfortably accommodated by that rubric. When Halkin was writing his polemical defenses of the Americans, he held up the poetry of Efros as the embodiment of the ideal of simplicity, and that description did in fact stand up, in various nuances and guises, throughout Efros's long career. It also loosely fits the verse of Silkiner (in his lyrics, not his Indian epic), Bavli, Schwartz, Friedland, Silberschlag, and even Preil. But when it comes to the poetry of Halkin himself and to that of Regelson, the usefulness of the concept breaks down altogether. Both, in their different ways, use high and complex registers of Hebrew to grapple with immense mystical and philosophical questions, and both took as precursors Shelley and Keats and more ecstatic traditions of English romanticism. (Interestingly, the verse of both underwent a process of simplification when, later in life, each settled in Israel.) In sum, therefore it would be more accurate to speak of two majors styles of American Hebrew poetry: the simple style and the metaphysical style. These terms are admittedly constructs, and their utility will be explored as further work in the field is done.

Although each of the poets in this study evolved along his own path, it is possible to identify one important line of development that deserves to be singled out because of its relevance to the Americanness of American Hebrew poetry. This is the movement from the brief lyric to longer, narrative compositions. Even though it cannot be said to

characterize the majority of the American poets, this line of development does describe the careers of Lisitzky and Efros, and it is these
two poets who are responsible for the most important works about
America in the American Hebrew canon, which form the subject for
the third part of this study. (The generalization applies in significant
but lesser ways to the work of Bavli, Schwartz, and Feinstein.) The
short lyric poem, which is so ubiquitous in modern verse that we
often unthinkingly equate it with poetry itself, was famously and
aptly defined by Northrop Frye as the "overheard speech" of the self.
The poem itself is the intimate speech or articulated thoughts of the
implied poet or the speaker of the poem that we, the readers, overhear,
as it were. We are of course meant to overhear it because the poem
is published and put before us, yet we are not the addressees of the
poem's discourse. As staged by the poet, the lyric poem is a self-reflexive event in which the poet responds to stimuli in the outside world or
in his own world and then often responds to his own response to these
stimuli. In any event, the lyric poem encapsulates a one-time experience that takes place within the orbit of the self.

For the young immigrant poet, the lyric was both an opportunity
and a temptation. It enabled him to begin writing poetry long before
he mastered the particulars, both historical and actual, of the new
world he had entered. All he needed was the truth of his own feelings and the literary language of Hebrew that had been developed
in Eastern Europe. For the young poet whose experience revolved
around loneliness, displacement, the search for love, and the wonders
of nature, the lyric was the only toolkit he needed. At the same time,
the lyric by its nature could become an invitation to solipsism, an
enclave to which the sensitive soul turns to escape that which is distasteful, frightening, or overwhelming in the environment *outside* him.
Some of the American Hebrew poets stayed with the lyric throughout
their careers and, in the best instances, learned to impose the kind
of internal controls necessary to keep their poems from becoming
precious and self-involved. Without abandoning the lyric, Efros and
Lisitzky began in the 1930s to use larger poetic forms to address issues
in American history. Lisitzky's *Medurot do'akhot* [Dying campfires]
(1937), like Silkiner's earlier massive Indian poem, is written on the

model of a great epic. In his book of poems inspired by observations of African American life in the south (*Be'oholei Khush* [In the tents of Cush] 1953), Lisitzky used a more flexible repertoire of forms that emulated the folk songs and sung sermons that inspired him. When Efros wrote his Indian poem, *Vigvamim shoteqim* [Silent wigwams] (1933), he avoided the machinery of the epic in favor of a free form of the long historical poem, a version of the *poema*, as it was known in Hebrew from the Russian. Efros followed this model as well when he composed his book-length narrative poem on the California gold rush, *Zahav*. Even Preil, a master of the short lyric, experimented with the long romantic poem when he was exploring his relationship to the New England landscape and to American history. In all of these examples, the turn toward America represented two achievements that came to be one: a genuine engagement with the new world in which Hebrew had planted itself and a rescue of the American Hebrew poet from the toils of his own inwardness.

Two   The Apotheosis of Hebrew

What compelled these poets to persist in singing their Hebrew song in a strange land? Around World War I, to be sure, all the circumstances were in place to encourage visions of a creative center for Hebrew culture in America. The centers in Russia and Palestine had been shut down by revolution and war; romantic Zionism transfixed the imaginations of a new generation; and the waves of new immigrants contained sufficient numbers of young people with the learning and idealism to champion the cause of Hebrew. But then the gates of immigration were shut, and the recent arrivals devoted themselves to mastering English and becoming Americans. The displaced Hebrew writers and publishers who had spent the war years in the United States or Western Europe regrouped in Tel Aviv and made the Yishuv into the world center of Hebrew literature. Although Hebrew educators continued to make expansive strides in America, it was acknowledged early on that the ambitious visions for a Hebrew literature on these shores would never be realized. Yet the American Hebrew poets persisted in producing a rich and substantial body of verse well into the middle of the twentieth century, even as they were ignored by the center in Palestine and their readership evaporated at home.

A portion of this perseverance can of course be understood as an outgrowth of a fervent commitment to advancing the Jewish national cause. All of the American Hebrew poets believed that the flowering of Hebrew culture was the key to the revival of the Jewish people, and nearly all of them worked in educational institutions established by the movement based on this idea. There were those, as we have noted, who were not willing to reconcile themselves to a dwindling readership and

66

a community in which they enjoyed no standing; they found their way to Palestine/Israel, usually after several attempts. Those who stayed on, when encountered later in life by younger people such as myself, often seemed to have a fanatical glint in their eyes and an unapologetic dismissal of American Jewish life for its boorishness, materialism, and abandonment of Hebrew.

Yet indignation and ideological commitment are not sufficient to explain the phenomenon this study documents. Instead, I propose we understand Hebrew in the lives of the poets as an essentially religious and sensual experience that flooded their daily lives and provided them with direct access to the object of their desire. This may seem like a perverse claim given their professed secularism and the Puritanism of much of their verse; but this is only because we underestimate the wealth of personal meaning they derived from their private relationship to the Hebrew language. Yes, they were marginalized, ignored, and provoked. Yet rather than being long-suffering martyrs, the American Hebrew poets possessed creative lives marked by a kind of linguistic jouissance that came from the intimate daily experience of kneading the language, reshaping it, and being enriched by it in return. The dimension of sensual pleasure was matched by the unofficial but tangible gratifications of a kind of religious experience. It is easy to see the transcendental authority provided by participation in and service to the Jewish nation and its historical tongue. Less evident are the benefits that accrued from the devoted daily praxis of the Hebraist, who lived within the rules and conventions of Hebrew even as he picked and chose from the language's vast resources to fashion his individual path. It is not an exaggeration to say that next to the world of the true *ish hahalakhah*, the practitioner of Jewish law, the Hebraist's practice of Hebrew was a key variety of Jewish identity that was genuinely transportable into the Diaspora in modern times, specifically because of the daily tangible discipline it provided.

This profound religious-libidinal attachment to Hebrew is the secret spring of American Hebraism precisely because it played such a small role in the public rhetoric of the movement. It was a passion that could not speak its name, and this not because it was an embarrassing admission but simply because it was knowledge that was unconscious and entirely alien to the discourse of Hebraist circles. Yet without predicating this motor of desire, it would be difficult indeed to understand the pertinacity and profusion of American Hebrew poetry. Were it not for the existence of an extraordinary exception to the general lack of self-awareness on this score, it would be presumptuous to "psychoanalyze" a cultural phenomenon and claim to point to a hidden motivation unseen by all but an astute observer who speaks well after the facts. But the exception is very much there, and its existence places a privileged hermeneutical key in our hands.

The exception in question is Regelson's epic hymn to the Hebrew language, titled "Ḥaquqot otiyyotayikh" [Engraved are thy letters], which appeared in 1946.[1] Regelson (1896–1981) was a poet, journalist, and writer on philosophy and literature. He was born in the town of Hlusk near Minsk and brought to America with his family at the age of nine. Regelson, who was the uncle of the American Jewish writer Cynthia Ozick, began publishing Hebrew poetry in the early 1920s and lived in Tel Aviv between 1933 and 1936 before returning to New York, where, after a prolonged period of unemployment, he eked out a living for his large family as a journalist for the *Morgen Freiheit*. He settled permanently in Israel in 1949. (More information about Regelson's life is supplied in the chapter devoted to him in this study.)

Regelson's hymn to Hebrew is a dazzling work that is unlike any other poem in the corpus of modern Hebrew literature. It is an extravagant ode to a language offered by a lover in thrall to the object of his desire, which is figured as a beautiful woman. It is a classic anatomy, a literary form that exhaustively inventories the categories and components of its subject. It is a theological treatise on the divinity of Hebrew that advances an argument for linguistic pantheism. Written at the great hinge of the twentieth century, it is a historiosophical work that uses Hebrew as a marker for both the murder of European Jewry and the struggle for Jewish statehood. It is a polemic about the course of the revival of Hebrew and an attack on the purported guardians of its purity. It is an apologia for the life of a poet who, at the time of the writing, was stranded far from Zion. Above all else, the poem is a performance of virtuosity that, in its maximalist poetics, seeks to conjure up and demonstrate the full plastic and arcane resources of the Hebrew language.[2]

Not only is "Ḥaquqot otiyyotayikh" an extraordinary work on its own, but its explanatory power is crucial for an understanding of the project of American Hebraism as a whole. For that reason, the discussion of the poem is positioned between the historical introduction and the essays about individual poets, of whom Regelson is one. Regelson's hymn to Hebrew provides us a way into the inner spiritual and psychological world of American Hebrew poetry.

The opening two lines of "Ḥaquqot otiyyotayikh" provide a good introduction to the spirit of Regelson's hymn to Hebrew.

חֲקוּקוֹת אוֹתִיּוֹתַיִךְ בְּתַבְנִית עוֹלָמִי, רְחִימָה בַּלְּשׁוֹנוֹת!
חַרְצָן בְּזַג, עִנְבָּל בְּזוֹג, רָזֵךְ רָחַשְׁתִּי, הוֹ עִבְרִית.

> Engraved are thy letters in the structure of my world, beloved
>   among languages!
> The seed in the grape, the clapper in the bell, thy secret I have
>   expressed, O Hebrew.

It is immediately apparent from this opening that the poem is written in the mode of an ode that is addressed to an inanimate object, the Hebrew language. The object of address is not only feminized but also, as quickly becomes evident as the poem proceeds, thoroughly eroticized. The fact that the name of the language [*'ivrit*] and the nouns for tongue and language [*lashon, safah*] are feminine in gender is merely an enabling condition in the systematic construction of the Hebrew language as a woman exalted and installed in the role of goddess, mistress, and lover. Her distinction and authority are beyond compare, for she is the *most* beloved among tongues; this is a superlative exceptionality that is wholly taken for granted and requires no demonstration. Because the male speaker of the poem is so in thrall to his object of desire, an ode is indeed the poetic form best suited to his situation. By definition, the ode is a non-dialogical utterance; it is speech that flows in one direction only, from the speaker to the object of address. Because there is no expectation of response, moreover, the ode provides safe cover for the speaker to indulge himself in expressing the fullness, and indeed the fulsomeness, of his extravagant feelings of adoration and devotion. With its hoary lineage, the ode authorizes the high pathos that Regelson brings to his grand subject.

Beyond its rhetorical function as a gesture of obeisance, the first line lays bare the fateful impress of Hebrew upon the speaker's life: the very letters of Hebrew have been carved into him. The root of *ḥaquqot* connotes the act of incising letters on stone, a kind of writing that is as difficult as it is permanent.[3] The same root in its *pi'el* form means to make law [*ḥoq*], to legislate. This act of forceful and norm-setting writing is inscribed not on the speaker's soul or flesh in some kind of romantic or martyrological stigma but rather on the deep structure of his world [*tavnit 'olami*]. It is not just world in the sense of a total worldview but the form or pattern [*tavnit*] that structures that world and undergirds it. This act of inscription, then, resembles the imprinting of a circuit onto a silicon chip or the encoding of a genetic sequence within an organism. Let it be clear, however, that the world that is thus inscribed is individual and personal: *'olami, my* world. This is not the ideological sphere of Zionist discourse that supposes that every "I" speaks for the collective. The "I" of "Ḥaquqot otiyyotayikh" is not allegorical or representative as in the manner of Haskalah odes to Hebrew but the distinct voice of a poet-speaker whose passionate affair with the Hebrew language is *experienced* as an exclusive encounter, even if he may know that his devotions are not the only ones being laid at the feet of his beloved. Finally, it should be noted that the agents of the act of inscription are letters and not words. Although Regelson's poem is obsessed with words, its most fervent veneration is reserved for the letters of the Hebrew alphabet because they are the tangible and tactile atomic units out of which all meaning is constructed. Regelson's belief in the world-shaping power of the Hebrew letters is a lineal descendent of Abulafia's *Sprachmystik* and the vivid combinatorial imagination of the kabbalists, whose work he knew well.

In the second line, the seed in the grape and the clapper in the bell are presented as instances of the "secret" of Hebrew that the speaker undertakes to express. (The verb *r.ḥ.sh.* can mean both to articulate and to feel.) Yet the relevance of these examples is hardly apparent, and their homeliness represents a deflation of the exalted tone of the opening. Sudden shifts from the grand to the humble and back again, to begin with, are constant features of the poem, and they illustrate the simultaneous immanence and transcendence Regelson accords to Hebrew. A proposed identity between microcosm and macrocosm would seem to motivate the choice of the grape and its pip. The *zag* is specifically the skin of the grape, the thin membrane that encloses the flesh, which in turn contains at its center the *ḥartsan*, the seed, which then possesses the potential to recreate and replenish the life of the plant. From its seemingly arbitrary specificity, the figure of the grape makes a gesture toward the totality of living things and the mystery of how forms of life can possess a discreet existence while at the same time containing within themselves the seeds of their own regeneration. Although the figure of the bell and the clapper is taken from the realm of man-made artifacts, it is a different aspect of the same mystery of the interdependent relationship between inside and outside; for neither the bell nor the clapper can produce sound on its own.[4] The notion of secrets that lie inside is taken in a deliberately erotic direction by Regelson himself in comments he made about the poem some sixteen years after its publication. In parsing this line, he says that the poet "is discovering the mysteries of the woman, like the discovery of the seed in the fruit and the clapper in the bell, for the womb [referred to by the adjective *reḥimah* in the first line] is the woman's most secret place."[5]

Why are these two figures, among so many other possible choices, chosen to convey this sense of wonder? The fact that *zag* [grape skin] and *zog* [the outside of the bell] are words that sound almost the same is not inconsequential, and it is of a piece with the language play that pervades Regelson's poem. But Regelson's pairing of the two is motivated by something more concrete: the appearance of the two figures together in a classical source. The terms *zagim* and *ḥartsanim* first appear in Numbers 5:4 as parts of the grape used in the wine-making process; the Torah takes pains to indicate that even these are strictly forbidden to the nazarite. For the Rabbis at a later remove in time, however, the meaning of these technical terms was not entirely clear. The Mishnah (*Nazir* 6:2) records a disagreement between two tannaim; R. Yossi states that the *ḥartsanim* are the seeds and the *zagim* are the skin—this has become the conventionally accepted meaning—whereas R. Yehudah states that the terms mean exactly the opposite.[6] As a way of remembering which is which, R. Yossi recommends thinking about the bell worn by domesticated animals when they go out to pasture, in which the external shell is called the *zog* (thus resembling the *zag*, the skin) and the clapper, the *'inbal*. However, would Regelson's readers have been likely to grasp this connection? Although some may have had the necessary erudition to do so—the Mishnah is far from a recondite source—there is so much going on in these lines, so many big effects, that catching the allusion and thereby rationalizing the yoking of grape and bell were not essential to the dizzying and intoxicating impact of the poem. Nevertheless, *knowing* that a motivated link is present encourages us to trust Regelson and extend credit to the applied erudition of his compositional practices when it comes to the many, many times when our learning comes up short.

The grape and the bell are also emblems for wine and music, the venerated and customary accompaniments to poetry everywhere and always, and nowhere more so than in the Hebrew poetry of the Golden Age Spanish Hebrew that echoes so frequently in the lines of "Ḥaquqot otiyyotayikh." It is no wonder, then, that at the outset of his great hymn to Hebrew, Regelson should evoke, however obliquely, these two handmaidens of grand poetry. Yet the celebratory mood is leavened by the reference to the ascetic rigors of the nazarite, who is forbidden wine or any product of the vine for the duration of his oath. The scriptural and tannaitic passages delineating these strictures remain the one, unavoidable semantic anchor for all the Hebrew terms in use here. The connection with the nazarite therefore focuses our attention on the following. At the same time as the poet allies himself with the grand tradition at the outset of his epic poem, he signals his willingness to accept the renunciations and privations necessary to pursue his high purpose. The role and standing of the poet—is he an unacknowledged national laureate or a humble pioneer worker?—are questions that preoccupy the closing sections of the poem.

Before finally being let go, our grape and bell can testify to one more essential feature of Regelson's poem: its semantic difficulty. "Ḥaquqot otiyyotayikh" is full to the brim with Hebrew words that are rare, obscure, and archaic. Instead of the disputed *zag* for grape, the common term *ʿeinav/ʿanavim* would have served; instead of the rare *zog* for bell, the universally recognized *paʿamon* would have enabled the reader to grasp the intended meaning. *Reḥimah* for beloved, in the first line, is an Aramaicism; although its use does abet Regelson's theme of knowing the innermost secrets of the woman—*reḥem* means womb—it also tweaks the nose of the uninitiated reader, who is likely to mistake the word for the more common *raḥamim/raḥum*, "mercy/merciful." It is not, after all, as if Hebrew did not easily possess a dozen recognizable terms for beloved, some of great elegance and sensuality. Regelson also delights in the use of what linguists call domain-specific lexicons, that is, lists of technical terms that belong to a circumscribed field of study. For example, the remainder of the poem's first section, following the lines quoted above, contains a list of the principle heavenly constellations followed by catalogues of field grasses and trees. To be sure, the inclusion of these catalogues is eminently justifiable on thematic grounds. Regelson is seeking to establish nothing less than an identity between the cosmos and Hebrew as Logos, as well to demonstrate the linguistic immanence of Hebrew from the most supernal realms to the lowliest shrubs in the meadow. Yet in pursuit of these exalted goals, Regelson lays down a raft of nouns that would be transparently comprehensible only to a Semitic philologist or a specialist in biblical and talmudic flora.

The issue is not intelligibility per se. Regelson's obscurities are not difficult in the sense that the term is used in literary theory to describe works of art in which surface gaps of meaning and coherence generate stubborn challenges to interpretation, such as *The Cantos* of Ezra Pound. With a good dictionary and a concordance in hand, intrepid readers can solve most problems that come their way and be assured of revealing the patterns of coherence beneath the apparent occlusion. Indeed, there is a crossword-puzzle kind of ingenuity that is piqued by the poem. Alternatively, readers can adopt the less rigorous—and arguably more pleasurable—course of allowing the meaning of unfamiliar words to be inferred from their voluminous context. In any event, reading strategies can be found to surmount the poem's challenges. But the question still remains why Regelson places them there to begin with. What is gained by creating semantic obstacles that can be removed with some lexical diligence, however tiresome?

The maximalist semantics of "Ḥaquqot otiyyotayikh" can best be understood in relationship to our experience of the poem as a performance of language. At the center of the aesthetic experience of the poem are several related concepts: virtuosity, plasticity, sensuousness, and playfulness. The two closing lines of the poem's first section provide an illustration.

בְּכָל אֲגַשֵּׁשְׁךָ אוֹר מִתְגַּשֵּׁם,
בְּכָל אַשִּׂיגֵךְ שֵׂכֶל מִתְנוֹצֵץ.

In all things I will seek you, light that becomes embodied,
In all things I will grasp you, sparkling reason.

These lines bring the epic sweep of the first section to a conclusion. After embracing the antipodes of Creation, from the galaxies to the grasses, and after demonstrating how Hebrew both names and embodies this totality, the poet returns to his own position and mission. He consecrates himself to searching out the light of Hebrew and showing how it sparkles in all things. Now, while the sense of these lines is clear enough, the true drama resides in the *performance* of their meaning as language. Notice first that the two lines are presented as a couplet with syntactical and grammatical symmetry that is nearly exact: *baqol* + a future verb in the first person singular with a dative suffix in the second person singular + an epithet for Hebrew using a present-tense reflexive verb [*hitpa'el*]. This doubling is underscored by the fact that a single Hebrew consonant dominates both lines: the *shin/sin*. This is the paradoxical twenty-first letter of the Hebrew alphabet, which is pronounced as *sh* when the dot is on the right side (*shin yemanit*) and as *s* when the dot is on the left (*sin semolit*). To stage a mirror-image symmetry in which left and right reverse their sidedness, Regelson makes the first line a riff on the *shin* and the second a riff on the *sin*. To both lines he adds a sprinkling of repeating *gimel, mem,* and *khaf* sounds. The result is a carnival of assonance that encourages the proliferation of other words based on the permutation of these letters, as Regelson himself proposes in his commentary: *sig vesiaḥ* [business exchange], *sagseg* [to thrive], *siaḥ* [shrubbery], *siḥah* [conversation], and *tsemiḥah* [growth].

These antic possibilities cloak an errand that is fraught with devotion yet uncertain of success. The verb indicating the central action in the first line (*agashesheikh*) is based on a word used only one time in the Hebrew Bible, in Isaiah 59:10, where it describes the behavior of unrepentant sinners who grope—literally, feeling their way—like blind men along a wall searching for the light that has deserted them. In the second line, the precariousness of this quest is turned into a triumph—at least a triumph imagined in the future—when the precious object is finally acquired. The duality of that object is nicely conveyed by the verb in the second line, *asigeikh*, which means both to obtain hold of something or acquire it in a physical sense, as well as—in a meaning added by medieval Jewish philosophers—to succeed in the act of intellection, the grasping of an abstract or metaphysical truth. Indeed, throughout "Ḥaquqot otiyyotayikh," Hebrew is construed as being two things at once: a material object in the graphic impress of its letters and the words kneaded in the mouths of its speakers like their daily bread *and* a transcendent Idea, a spiritual essence existing above and behind all phenomena. One is not privileged over the other, and each is in a constant process of turning back into the other. This metamorphosis is represented in the chiastic presentation of the epithets for Hebrew in these two lines. In the first, Hebrew is called *or mitgashem*, light that is in the process of becoming material. (Surely Regelson knew the definition of light in modern physics as particles without mass.) In the second, Hebrew is called *sekhel mitnotsets*, an idea that is in the process of dematerializing into sparks of light. Whether coming or going, this way or that, Hebrew is *bakol*, in all things.

This small example provides a glimpse into the crucial performative axis of the poem. To say that all good poems enact their meaning through their language is to state the obvious. Yet there are some in which the theatrical demonstration of the poet's uncanny abilities in manipulating language creates a powerful performance effect. Regelson's poem, whose grand subject is language itself, is surely one of these. Is Regelson merely showing off? Is he indulging in poetic grandiosity? I think not, although these are fair questions that must be reckoned with. This issue can best be approached by first observing that there are two dimensions to the performativity let loose in "Ḥaquqot otiyyotayikh." The more evident of the two is the performance of the poet's virtuosity: his encyclopedic mastery of the historical lexicon of the Hebrew language, his erudition in classical sources, and, most of all, his ability to take the language not just as given but rather to invent and proliferate provocative new words and dazzling new constructions by using and extending the existing templates for Hebrew word formation. The less evident dimension of performativity resides in the inherent resources of Hebrew that Regelson sets about to exploit. Regelson could not stage his pyrotechnics if the language had not already in its long history been witness in many periods to the grafting of new forms onto old. The very fact that Hebrew is built upon tri-consonantal roots or word stems means that the system of verb paradigms called *binyanim* (explained below) and noun paradigms called *mishqalim* can potentially generate hundreds of possible permutations for each root. Although only a fraction of these are alive in the language at any one time, the latent possibilities are huge, and they are there awaiting activation.

This is Hebrew's famous plasticity, and it is the quality that Regelson prizes above all others. It is also the quality that authorizes and even encourages his own demonstration of mastery over the language. "Ḥaquqot otiyyotayikh" is the site for a creative synergy between the plasticity of Hebrew and the virtuosity of the individual talent. In its historical development, Hebrew has already demonstrated dramatic metamorphoses and extraordinary adaptations to new cultural climates. Regelson takes upon himself to advertise the creative malleability of Hebrew that is already part of the historical record by performing his own improvised-for-the-moment high jinks. His is a virtuosity that is undertaken, as he sees it, *in the service of* the honor of Hebrew. The word virtuoso, it is worth considering, comes to us via Italian and Late Latin from the Latin *virtus*, virtuous. In Hebrew's plasticity, Regelson finds license for his linguistic cartwheels. He is indeed—or at the very least, in his own eyes—performing for the greater glory.

He is also a poet at play in the fields of the Lord. The virtuosity on display on every page of "Ḥaquqot otiyyotayikh" is only occasionally of the striving and over-strenuous kind. In the main, Regelson's catalogues, word plays, neologisms, and all manner of linguistic entertainments seem like the natural expression of a Hebrew *homo ludens*, a grown-up for whom play is a creative—one might say, seriously creative—endeavor that can accomplish goals unreachable by other means. In addition to being a sacred trust and the venerated beloved, Hebrew for Regelson is also a game-like reservoir of nearly inexhaustible linguistic permutations, a treasure chest of moves opened for the delectation of the energetic poet-gymnast.

Finally, this first sampling of "Ḥaquqot otiyyotayikh" should confirm an inevitable consequence of the poem's genius: its untranslatability. This is a statement made with no triumphalism, because it is also an admission of defeat. If Regelson's poem were a true classic, it would possess a dimension of universal import that transcended its linguistic integuments. That dimension could be captured in a translation that provided both pleasure and sense, despite the many necessary losses and renunciations. I suspect that this cannot be done, although I know of no one who has tried. Yet the untranslatability of "Ḥaquqot otiyyotayikh" is less a diminishment of the work's value than a testament to Regelson's swashbuckling Hebraism. The intended readers for this poem were other passionate and highly initiated Hebraists— already an elite within an elite—and when it came to others, well, there was little purpose or hope.

✳

Illuminating the passion for Hebrew that consumed Regelson and other American Hebraists is one of the poem's chief achievements. "Ḥaquqot otiyyotayikh", we have seen, is cast as an ode, a genre that had had great currency in an Enlightenment age when poets sought to express their devotion to Liberty or Truth or other capitalized abstractions. The hypostasized value or ideal could be addressed with ardor *as if* it were God or a sovereign or a beloved to whom fealty could be pledged. These are the same conventions that Regelson is making use of, to be sure, but there is nothing abstractly allegorical about the object of *his* address. The Hebrew language, to which every utterance in the poem is directed, is represented in a variety of guises that range from goddess to Great Mother to mistress; and in all of these cases, rather than being a trope or figuration, Hebrew is embodied, and the body Hebrew is given is unmistakably that of a woman. Hebrew is incarnated, feminized, and eroticized, in addition to being elevated and deified. It is only by understanding Hebrew as an eroticized object of desire that we can make sense out of the intoxicated tone in which the whole of "Ḥaquqot otiyyotayikh" is composed.

Of the many reasons why Hebrew should be addressed as a sexualized woman, the most fundamental is the most obvious. The fact that all Hebrew nouns are either masculine or feminine means that gender is inescapable. This fact of life about Hebrew can be taken in two ways. One approach, a functionalist linguistic view, is to see gender as an arbitrary marker that is dictated by the morphology of words and the sounds they end with and not by any inherent characteristics. Thus, the word for a woman's breast, *shad*, is masculine simply because it ends in a hard closed consonant. The other approach, which is based on romantic nationalist and Whorfian views of language, would see the particular features of a given language as expressive of a unique view of the world; the presence of gender as a grammatical phenomenon would therefore be indicative of sexual difference as a real rather than constructed or arbitrary feature of the speech community of that language. It is to this latter party that Regelson belongs; he experiences Hebrew as a language that is continually dividing the world into male and female components and making these assignments of gender in conformance to deep and essential truths about existence. Rather than working against gender and its bifurcation of the world in the name of human freedom, Regelson takes the opposite course. He gives himself up wholly to gender, renouncing his individual liberty and gratefully taking his place as a masculine subject under the dominion of Hebrew.

So, it indeed makes a great deal of difference that it is a male poet who is composing a hymn to the Hebrew language. It is of a piece with American Hebrew poetry specifically, which, with few exceptions, was a wholly male undertaking.[7] It was also the case with modern Hebrew poetry generally before voices like that of Rahel (Blaustein) began to be heard in the 1920s. The case of Rahel's poetry provides an instructive analogy. As a woman among male pioneers in Palestine, Rahel wrote several poems that were addressed to the Land of Israel in which the relationship of the speaker to the addressee is that of a daughter, rather than a son, to a (step-) mother(land).[8] Qualities of humility, compassion, and empathy are among those brought into play in the pioneer-land relationship enacted in the poems in ways quite different from the practice of male poets. The analogy is significant because the Land of Israel and the Hebrew language were the two closely joined axes of the Zionist revolution; one was the adopted motherland and the other was the adopted mother tongue. For partisans of this national awakening who lived in America, it was only the language axis that could be fully appropriated, known in all its particulars, and creatively manipulated. Yet in America there was no true counterpart to Rahel in Palestine, a female poet who might have configured the relationship between the Hebrew poet and the Hebrew language otherwise: as a relationship between a daughter and a mother or between two women or, turning the nationalist gender code around, between the female poet and the Hebrew language pictured as a stronghold of *masculine* culture.[9]

The premise of the poem remains unshakably rooted in the reality of gender difference writ large. The poet is a suitor, a perennial troubadour, who is forever extolling the virtues of his beloved even as he basks in the aura of her graces.[10] The main challenge faced by the poet is, therefore, how to offer right and proper praise. Praise performs two functions. It registers the awestruck experience of the Hebrew user-speaker before and in the midst of the wonders of the language, and it also renders the tribute due to an object of veneration by its worshiper. The strategy for meeting this challenge lies in the chief organizing principle of the poem that was mentioned at the outset: the anatomy as a literary form. The beloved is praised by systematically cataloguing her qualities. Indeed, the core of "Ḥaquqot otiyyotayikh" (sections 4–15, out of twenty altogether) is taken up with discharging this task. The poet lays out in turn each of the key features of the Hebrew language, luxuriating all the while in an abundance of clever and delightful examples.

But offering right and proper praise, it turns out, is no simple matter. Before the poem launches into its grand catalogue, it pauses to meditate on the high errand the poet has assumed. Section 3, which serves as a prologue to the great undertaking, considers the Scylla and Charybdis that lie in the waters ahead. It opens thus:

כְּאוֹהֵב, מוֹנֶה שְׁבָחֵי גְבִרְתּוֹ, וּבִטּוּיוֹ קָצֵר מֵרִגְשׁוֹ,

כֵּן דַּחַף־לִי לָאֱרוֹשׁ מַעֲלוֹתַיִךְ, וְאִם אֲמַסְכְּנֵךְ בִּתְהִלָּתִי.

Like a lover who lists the praises of his lady only to discover that
    the power of his expression pales before the power of his
    feeling,
so am I constrained to utter your merits even
    if I diminish you by virtue of my praise.

The poet, who explicitly compares himself to a troubadour or chevalier in thrall to his lady [*gevirto*], finds himself thrown onto the horns of a dilemma. On the one hand, he is so smitten in his thralldom and so obligated in his obeisance that he is incapable of *not* offering fulsome praise of his beloved. On the other, he has taken on a mission that is by definition not only impossible to achieve but also likely to give offense. His winking, paradoxical solution to the problem is a kind of transparent discretion.

הֵן הַבּוֹלְטוֹת וְהַשִּׁלְדִּיּוֹת בְּגֵוֵךְ אֲרַמֵּז,

וְאָדֹם מִן הַקְּמָטִיּוֹת וְהַבֵּין־פִּרְקִיּוֹת,

הַדָּם וְהַלֵּחַ וְהַמֵּחַ עַל תַּעֲלוֹת־זְרִימוֹתֵיהֶם.

Therefore I will allude only to the protruding and skeletal qualities
    of your body,
and I will remain silent about those in the creases and between the
    joints, the blood, the marrow, and the rich tissue in all their
    oozing channels.

The awkwardness of these lines, as pronounced in Hebrew as in English paraphrase, signals the wriggling discomfiture of a man faced with an impossible task. Rather than praise improperly, either by saying too much or too little, the poet commits himself to a path of knowing and coy discretion. He will foreswear full frontal description of his beloved and instead only hint at the features grossly visible when she is turned around. All of the irksomely cumbersome adjectives in these two lines (*boltot, shildiyot, qimtiyot, bein-pirqiyot*) are feminine plural and refer back to the same *ma'alot*, the fine merits and attributes of the beloved (in the second line above) that he could not desist from listing. What kind of praise is this? Tortured and tortuous, the poet's language writhes in its fetters and acts out against its constraints by undercutting them: he ends up exposing the most intimate parts of the beloved, the vital fluids that flow in her innermost folds, under the guise of delineating the secrets that as a matter of principle he would never reveal.

The dilemma of telling or not telling is familiar to us from another realm of Jewish discourse: medieval theology. Maimonides famously argued that open discussion of the positive attributes of God compromised the integrity of God's bodiless infinity. His opponents, the kabbalists, encouraged the proliferating of metaphoric imaginings of the sacred drama that takes place within the godhead. Although it may at first seem farfetched to posit a linkage between the poet's praise of his Hebrew beloved and the philosopher's description of the Divine, "Ḥaquqot otiyyotayikh" in fact encourages the connection. Hebrew as Logos, as I discuss below, shares many of the same characteristics that God possesses, especially when it comes to the mystery of the coexistence of transcendence and immanence. It is sufficient at this stage to point out that although the poet makes noises like a rationalist who dares do nothing more than hint at the secrets of his beloved, he *behaves* like a mystic who is happy to make use of the indulgence to imagine, vividly and exhaustively, the manifold glories of the object of his adoration.

These manifold glories are nothing more than Hebrew grammar and morphology, and it is the dizzying achievement of Regelson's poem—generations of students can testify to the true enormity of the accomplishment!—to make grammar sexy. The remainder of Section 3 is a sensuous, even humid, savoring of sentences, styles, letters, vowels, and the *ta'amim* [cantillation marks]. Regelson's essential strategy for eroticizing Hebrew is to materialize the language as a body. Sometimes it is the oceanic body of Hebrew as the great mother; at other times, the hewn limbs of the Hebrew goddess; and still others, the tangled appurtenances of a coy mistress. This is not the same method as the conceit, the figure used by the English metaphysical poets for a witty systematic analogy, as, for example, when Donne compares the Church to a cow in which the teats, the tail, and head all correspond to recognizable offices and institutions. In "Ḥaquqot otiyyotayikh," although there no lack of wit, there is no one-to-one correspondence between the parts of the body and the parts of speech. The endless formations and features of Hebrew that are catalogued in the next twelve sections of the poem are marvelously non-metaphorical; they are, simply and concretely, the *disjecta membra* that, sorted out and put together, comprise the body of Hebrew.

Regelson's depiction of Hebrew as a woman is informed by two important medieval models. The first is Yehudah Alḥarizi's *Sefer taḥkemoni*, the masterpiece of Hebrew *maqama* [rhymed prose interspersed with verse] from the turn of the thirteenth century in Spain. Before proceeding to relate the picaresque adventure of the work's protagonist and narrator, Hever the Kenite, in his introduction, Alḥarizi describes the prophetic experience that, quite literally, gave birth to the work. Dejected by the downtrodden fate of Hebrew amid the triumphalism of Arabic, the poet determines to raise the fortunes of the Holy Tongue. In return for his consecration to this mission, he is vouchsafed a visitation from none other than the Hebrew language herself, who appears to him as a beautiful maiden. "Before I could speak, her lips were on mine and I tasted wondrous wine. Drink deep my thoughts, she whispered—ah, her touch was silk!—seek 'neath my tongue my honey and my milk.'" Pressed to tell her story, she reveals that although she is of royal birth she has been reviled and defiled. She turns to the poet to reveal her true self: "I am your Mistress, the Holy Tongue: if I find favor in your sight, I will be your heart's delight— only be zealous for God's name: sanctify me, who am put to shame. Be you my redeemer from every slanderer, renegade, blasphemer."[11] The poet loses no time betrothing the maiden, and "Straightway I lay with the prophetess and from this union sprang one who godly sang."

The offspring can be parsed as either the composition itself, *Sefer taḥkemoni*, or Hever the Kenite, its protagonist-narrator.[12]

Although *Sefer taḥkemoni* furnishes precedent and license for an eroticized image of Hebrew, the differences between Alḥarizi's and Regelson's poems are especially instructive. In *Sefer taḥkemoni*, the betrothal of Hebrew is only the introductory premise of the work, which then proceeds at considerable length to delight us with its stories about tricksters and mistaken identities. To be sure, the whole work is, in a sense, a compendious defense and demonstration of the honor of Hebrew in the face of Arabic virtuosity, but that theme is consciously invoked only at the outset. In contrast, "Ḥaquqot otiyyotayikh" is about nothing other than the attributes of Hebrew from beginning to end. Yet when it comes to the relations between the poet and his fair mistress Hebrew, the medieval poet is far more precipitous and forward than his belated descendant. The persona of the poet-author in *Sefer taḥkemoni* would seem to have more business than pleasure on his mind in his encounters with Hebrew; he meets, kisses, betroths, and sleeps with his beloved in very short order, and he does so for the purpose of giving birth to his book and providing it with a pedigree beyond reproach. When it comes to the poet-speaker of "Ḥaquqot otiyyotayikh," however, one could never imagine his presuming so much. On the one hand, his whole delight is to touch and handle all of the polymorphous manifestations of Hebrew all the time. Yet on the other, he is a supplicant and a servant whose boundless adoration for Hebrew would never allow him to imagine perpetrating the ultimate intimacy. This is not because he is self-effacing or servile but because it is not mastery or ownership that he seeks. What he seeks instead is to dwell in the illuminating and fertile presence of the beloved and to admire, explore, stroke, handle, and play with all of her variegated charms. This is the jouissance of perpetual, tactile intimacy rather than the satisfaction of conquest and consummation.

One of the other medieval voices heard in this section of "Ḥaquqot otiyyotayikh" is that of Halevi in his great ode to Zion, "Tsiyyon, halo tish'ali." Halevi's ode was one of the best known medieval poems not only because it was integral to the morning liturgy on the summer fast day of the Ninth of Av but also because in modern times, it became a key text in the grafting of Zionist aspirations onto traditional religious sentiments.[13] Like Regelson's ode to Hebrew, Halevi's ode to Zion is a sustained and fervent address to an exalted female object in which the unremitting use of feminine pronominal and verbal suffixes makes the presence of gender inescapable. Moreover, both poems anatomize their subjects, with Halevi's taking the form of an imaginary travelogue in which the poet visits the holy sites of biblical repute. His longing to be given the ability to make the journey is expressed in lines that will be echoed by Regelson.

מִי יִתְּנֵנִי מְשׁוֹטֵט בַּמְּקוֹמוֹת אֲשֶׁר
נִגְלוּ אֱלֹהִים לְחוֹזַיִךְ וְצִירָיִךְ!
מִי יַעֲשֶׂה לִי כְנָפַיִם וְאַרְחִיק נְדוֹד,
אָנִיד לְבִתְרֵי לְבָבִי בֵּין בְּתָרָיִךְ!

Would I were a-wandering in the places where
God had been revealed unto thy seers and messengers.
Would I had wings that I might fly afar
And move the breakage of heart over thy mountain-breaks.[14]

On the verge of embarking upon his own extensive travelogue, Regelson's speaker poses a series of similar questions in the concluding lines to Section 3.

וּמִי יְשַׁחֵר סִתְרֵי תְמוּנַת אוֹתִיּוֹתַיִךְ, חֲטוּב־צַלְעוֹתֵיהֶן
וְאׇהֱלִיאָבוּת־חֲלוּלֵיהֶן,
וּמִי יִסַּק אֶל גֹּבַהּ תְּנוּעוֹתַיִךְ, מַזָּלוֹת מַנְהִיגִים לָאוֹתִיּוֹת,
וְכַמַּזָּלוֹת בָּרָקִיעַ זְעֵרוּ לָעַיִן, גַּם כִּי עָצְמוּ בִּמְאֹד־מְאֹד?
וּמִי יִרְגַּל עַד חֶבְיוֹן טְעָמַיִךְ,
וְהֵם נְשָׁמוֹת לַתְּנוּעוֹת, מַנְגִּינוֹת לַכּוֹכָבִים?

Who will gain admittance to the secrets of the forms of your
    letters, their well-hewn planes and their well-crafted
    hollows?[15]
Who will soar to the heights of your vowels, the signs [*mazzalot*]
    that guide the letters,
Which, like the constellations [*mazzalot*] in the heavens, appear
    minuscule to eye but are colossal in fact?

Who will spy out the hiding places of your *te'amim*,
For they are the souls of the vowels, the melody of the stars?

The differences between these two sets of questions tell us something essential about the nature of these two projects. Halevi's questions are formulated in the optative mood; they express a wish and a desire that cannot be fulfilled. Although his heart is in the East, he is stuck in the West, and the only kind of wings upon which he can tour the Holy Land are the wings of poesy. Regelson's questions, by contrast, are mock-rhetorical in tone and express a paradoxical amalgam of humility and boastfulness. It is only the true lover and devotee of Hebrew who will be permitted to tour the language's precious secrets. The implied good news, however, is that the poet is just such a worthy person and that the grand tour is exactly what he is about to embark upon. This is the fateful difference between the Holy Land and the Holy Tongue, and for American Hebraists it was a saving difference indeed. In Halevi's time, access to the Land was nearly impossible, and the poet perished in a perilous attempt to reach it. In Regelson's time, even though the dream of return to Zion had begun to be realized, world war and conflict with the British and the Arabs also made approach difficult— "Ḥaquqot otiyyotayikh" appeared in 1946—and Regelson himself was stuck in America. Yet if one could not inhabit the Land, or could do so only through the imagination, the Tongue, in its infinite and perfect portability, presented no such obstacle. Nothing prevents the Diaspora-stranded poet from caressing the planes and hollows of the Hebrew letters and hearing the music of the spheres in its vowels and musical notations.

The great catalogue, which begins in Section 4 and occupies the central twelve sections of the poem, is at once a recitation and a demonstration of the features of the Hebrew language. This anatomy is not presented as a general disquisition; rather, in line with the rhetorical premise of the composition as a whole, the anatomy is declaimed as a communication from the speaker of the poem, the lover, to Hebrew, his beloved. The purpose of the utterance is both to pay tribute to the beloved and to make manifest to others, we the readers who are "over-hearing" this declaration, the richness and sweep of her attributes. The topics according to their numbers are as follows: (4) the *binya-nim*; (5) tenses of the verb; (6) the conjugation of verbs with weak stem letters; (7) the *gezarot* [paradigms for noun formation]; (8) verbs with four-letter stems; (9) words with paradoxical or contradictory mean-ings; (10) the interlocking economy of the language; (11) conjunctions and prepositions; (12) the vagaries of gender assignments; (13) proper names; (14) metaphors taken from nature; and (15) Aramaic, Greek, Arabic, and Yiddish elements in Hebrew.

Regelson takes upon himself a considerable challenge in this core of the poem. As a literary tactic, the catalogue-anatomy enables an author to conduct a systematic inventory of an abundance of detailed information. The corresponding danger, however, is tedium and pre-dictability. In satiric forms, where this tactic most commonly appears, the hazard is neutralized by comic effects that grow in hilarity as more features of the satiric analogy are enumerated, for example, the parts of the cow corresponding to the parts of the Church in the previous example from Donne. Derisive humor is obviously not the response Regelson is seeking to elicit in his litany of praise for Hebrew, although humor of a different kind, in the form of wit, is hardly lack-ing. Regelson counteracts the cumbersome weight of the catalogue-anatomy in two ways. Each new item in the inventory is intended to provoke a redoubled sense of amazement at the polymorphous plasticity of the language, as well as the poet's dazzling resourceful-ness in bringing this to life on the page. The other way is rooted in the gendered rhetorical premise of the poem. Each new item on the list is presented by the poet to his beloved as an example of yet another kind of pleasure that he receives from her. Each of the dozen sections is introduced by a synonym for "I desired," in the sense of, "I have found pleasure" in the particular attribute discussed in that sec-tion: *ratsiti, ḥashaqti, hitrapaqti 'al, shafru 'alai, ḥanoti, sha'ashu'ai, sha'afti, yafyafti li, aviti, naftu li, 'idanti.*[16] There are many more additional synonyms for the same concept scattered within the body of the various sections. (Section 10, interestingly, lacks this introduc-tory term.) In his intoxicated, dithyrambic mood, the poet discovers yet another reason to praise Hebrew and be enchanted by her, and it is this perennially renewed amazement that carries his project aloft and enables it to resist the force of gravity exerted by the catalogue form.

There is a great deal going on in each of these twelve sections. For the reader, the experience is something akin to watching a three-ring circus in which one's attention is riveted for a time on the action in one ring while remaining peripherally aware of what is going on in the other two, until the configuration shifts and another ring becomes the main focus. In these core sections of "Ḥaquqot otiyyotayikh," there are three main axes of meaning. The most evident is the thematic axis, which bears the expository burden of setting out and demonstrating the main features of Hebrew (as listed above), some of which are common to most languages and some of which are peculiar to Hebrew. The second is the axis of performativity and virtuosity. The manifold ways of forming words by applying various templates to the verb stem, what we have called the plasticity of Hebrew, constitute a potentiality that is intrinsic to the language; this is the main subject of the thematic exposition. (This is also the quality that moves the poet to shout out in amazement in the last line of Section 7: "O the creative geometry of your spaces!") The *realization* of this potentiality in the hands of the poet is the arena of individual virtuosity. The plasticity resides in the deep structures of the language; its actualization takes place along the axis of performativity in the poem. Regelson takes on the challenge of instantiating the heterogeneous riches of Hebrew and making each line a bravura performance. He marshals obscure words and coins new ones, he contorts the language to show its elasticity, and he composes whole sentences that are variations of two or three letters. In short, he makes the language jump through hoops and sets off linguistic firecrackers. Although he does all this to demonstrate the greater glory of his beloved Hebrew, it is to the brilliance of his own performance that his high jinks inevitably draw us.

This focus diverts us from the presence of a third axis of meaning in the poem, which is a serious drama taking place in an adjacent ring of the circus. In this drama, Hebrew is identified with the soul of the Jewish people, which has long been downtrodden and is now being healed and revitalized by the flowering of its national language. This narrative relies heavily on a secularized and nationalized interpretation of the drama of cosmic exile in Lurianic Kabbalah, especially as it is echoed in the Sabbath hymn to the Shekhinah, *Lekha dodi*, with its abundance of feminine word endings. Because of this reach toward mystical transfigurations, I call this the anagogic axis. In each of the sections in the catalogue core of "Ḥaquqot otiyyotayikh," the movement is toward redemption. The purpose of this praise, so lovingly addressed to Hebrew, is to restore her own sense of her dignity and high calling and to move her toward a kind of *unio mystic*—transposed into earthy nationalist terms—with the Jewish people. But unlike redemption in classical Jewish theology, which is deferred and patiently awaited, the redemption embodied by a revived Hebrew is a present fact; it has happened and it is happening, and it is experienced every time we write, speak, read, or hear the language. This is yet another dimension of the cleavage between territory and language in the Zionist vision that we have noted all along. This helps to explain the ecstatic tone of the poem, which should be understood not as the result of delusional inebriation or nationalistic zeal but as a warranted response to something extraordinary that has indeed taken place in the world.

A good example of how these three levels of meaning function together is the first section in this sequence, Section 4, whose subject is the Hebrew *binyanim*.

רָצִיתִי בְּנְיָנֶיךָ,

קַלְךָ הָעוֹשֶׂה בְּפַשְׁטוּת, לוֹקֶה בְחֶטְאוֹ וְקָם בְּצִדְקוֹ,

וְהוּא בֶּן וְכוֹתֵב מַה פָּעַל אֵל;

נִפְעָלְךָ הַנִּכְנָע לַסֵּבֶל, וְנִשְׁבָּר, וְנִשְׁאָר בֶּאֱמוּנָתוֹ, וְסוֹפוֹ – נוֹשָׁע;

פִּעֶלְךָ הַמְחַזֵּק יָדַיִם, הַמְעַשֶּׂה לְמִצְווֹת וַחֲסָדִים,

יְסַקְּלְךָ מִנְּגָפִים וִימַלְאֶךָ טוּבִים;

פָּעֶלְךָ הַמְלֻמָּד, מְקֻטָּר, וּמְעֻטָּר בְּיוֹם יְדֻבַּר בּוֹ, וּבִכְרָמָיו יָרֹנּוּ וְיִרְעָע;

הִפְעִילְךָ הַמַּשְׂכִּיל וְהַמֵּיטִיב,

אֵין כָּמוֹהוּ מַנְעִיל יָחֵף וּמַלְבִּישׁ עֵרוֹם וּמַאֲכִיל רָעֵב,

וְהוּא מַרְנִין בְּגְוָנָיו:

עָלָיו מוֹרִיקִים, נִצָּנָיו מַלְבִּינִים וּמוֹרִידִים, וּפֵרוֹתָיו מַאֲדִימִים;

הָפְעֲלֵךְ, מָשְׁזָר בַּמּוּחָשׁ וּבַמּוּכָח, וּבוֹ הַמֻּחְלָט יָבַע;
הִתְפַּעֲלֵךְ – מַה־מְּאֹד אֶשְׁתּוֹמֵם עָלָיו, כִּי רֶכֶב וָשֵׁכֶב בּוֹ הִתְאַחֲדוּ,
בְּצוּרוֹ יִדָּבֵק וְעוֹלָמִית לֹא יִטַּמֵּא, בֵּין תְּמִימִים יִתַּמָּם,
בּוֹ יִכּוֹנֵן מִקְדָּשׁ, וּבְמִקְרָאָיו, נְשָׁמָה,
הִזְדַּכְּכִי, הִסְתַּכְּלִי לְאַחֲרִיתֵךְ, הִצְטַעֲרִי עַל זְדוֹנוֹתַיִךְ וְהִשְׁתַּלְּמִי
בַּזְכֻיּוֹת,
הֵן רַק פָּעֳלֵךְ תִּשְׂתַּכָּרִי.

I have desired your *binyanim*, your *qal*, which acts with simplicity,
is punished for its sin and rises in its justice, and it perceives
and records what God has wrought;

Your *nif'al*, which has submitted to suffering and been humbled
but remained faithful and in the end redeemed;

Your *pi'el*, which fortifies the hands and enables fulfillment of
the commandments and acts of kindness, may it rid you of
obstacles and fill you with good things;

Your *pu'al*, erudite, fragrant with incense, and crowned as on a day
of betrothal, will be sung and serenaded in its vineyards;

Your *hif'il*, so enlightened and benevolent, there is none like it
for shodding the barefoot, clothing the naked, and feeding
the hungry, and it joyfully sings in its colors: its leaves turn
green, its buds turn white and then pink, and its fruits
redden;

Your *huf'al*, in which are intertwined both the concrete and
cerebral and the absolute is expressed;

Regarding your *hitpa'el*, how amazed am I for it unites the upper
and lower millstones, for to its Rock will it cleave and never
become impure; among the innocent it will be most perfect,
in it the Sanctuary will be established, and in its sacred
festival,

O Soul, become purified, look to your End, regret your sins, and
perfect yourself in your merits, and then you shall surely
come to your proper reward.

This topic is eminently appropriate as a starting point for the core
exposition of "Ḥaquqot otiyyotayikh" because the *binyanim* are the
most fundamental and recognizable feature of Hebrew grammar and
the frontline obstacle with which all students of the language must

contend. A *binyan* (singular) literally means a construction; it is a pattern or form that "constructs" the Hebrew verb by imposing various configurations upon the three-letter root. There are seven *binyanim*; three are active (*qal, pi'el, hiph'il*), three are passive (*nif'al, pu'al, huf'al*), and one is reflexive (*hitpa'el*). The names of the *binyanim* are taken from the third-person masculine singular in the past tense of the verb stem *p.'.l.*, a verb that means, appropriately, "to do or act." This terminology was borrowed from Arab scholars by Jewish grammarians in ninth-century Spain, and this provenance is useful in reminding us of the status of grammar as an empirical science. As an idealized set of norms that govern the use of language, grammar is constructed by inductive observation; in the case of Hebrew, grammarians examined the language of the Hebrew Bible in order to abstract patterns and rules that explain the regularized use of nouns and verbs. As a form of human knowledge, then, grammar is a theorized model rather than a formulation of properties organically inherent in language.

The constructed nature of grammar provides a margin of creative freedom that Regelson fully exploits. The vast corpus of Hebrew literature, from the Bible to Bialik, includes only a fraction of the possible inventory of words that could be generated by applying the rules of the *binyanim* to a verb stem. So, while a root like *b.t.ḥ.* exists in the *qal binyan* in the Bible in the sense of "to trust in" [*bataḥ*], it is no obstacle for the Rabbis to actualize the root in the *hif'il binyan* to mean "to promise" [*hivtiaḥ*] or for twentieth-century shapers of the language to use the *pi'el* form to mean "to insure, to underwrite" [*biteaḥ*], and so on. It is precisely the "and so on" that is the point, for this is a process, which once set in motion, can potentially keep on propagating riotously. Should the production of new words on this model take place conservatively, based on textual attestation and authorized usage? Or should this propagation remain uncontrolled so that the individual poetic genius can actualize all the potential forms of the language necessary for the expression of the imagination? The issue has been in contention throughout the long history of Hebrew poetry. Yose b. Yose, Yannai, and the Qalir, the great masters of synagogue poetry from the classic period of the piyyut in seventh- and eighth-century Palestine, were radical practitioners of free innovation. The dialectic swung the other way when it came to poets of the Spanish Golden Age, who saw the text of the Hebrew Bible as enrobed in a sacred purity that should not be lightly tampered with. The most casual glance at Regelson's hymn to Hebrew will leave no doubt as to with which party he stands. Like the ancient synagogue poets, Regelson delights in the paradox of a language that is highly regulated and rule driven and at the very same time opens the door to nearly endless artistic virtuosity.

The thematic axis of Section 4, then, could not be clearer. The subject is the *binyanim*, which are given pride of place among the chief topics of Hebrew grammar and laid out in their traditional order. However, the manner in which this orderly duty is performed—its actualization along the performative axis—provides an occasion for the display of wit and virtuosity. The trick Regelson pulls off is this: Each of the seven *binyanim* is presented using verbs inflected exclusively in that *binyan*. In each of these instances, which range from one to five lines, the poet describes the essential "personality" of the *binyan*—the simplicity of *qal*, the submissiveness of *nif'al*, the activism of *hif'il*, and so on—all the while working within the constraints of the *binyan*. It is a gross effect that can be appreciated by anyone with a modicum of familiarity with Hebrew grammar. For the connoisseur, there are an abundance of clever and amusing subtleties that are often variations on the theme of exceptions to the rule. *Qal* is an active *binyan*, but Regelson delights in adducing *loqeh* in line 2, which is a verb in the *qal* form that has a passive meaning [to be punished]. *Ban* [understands], also in line 2, is the rare *qal* form of the root *b.y.n.* that is in common usage in the *hif'il* form [*hevin*], which means the same thing.

When it comes to *hif'il* proper, Regelson devotes a whole line (11) to one of the great anomalies in Hebrew grammar. All verbs that denote turning a color (turning red, turning green, etc.) are conjugated in the *hif'il binyan* despite that fact that they possess none of the active and transitive meanings that mark nearly all verbs in that *binyan*. Morphology proves Regelson's playground in the final line of the section when he focuses on the reflexive *binyan hitpa'el*. Normally, the letter *tav*, which is the hallmark of this *binyan*, is followed by the first letter of the verb stem. But in a case when the first letter is a *samekh, shin, sin,* or *zayin,* it changes place with the *tav* to make it easier for the mouth to pronounce a combination containing a dental consonant. When the first letter is a *tsadi,* it causes the *tav* not only to change places but to change itself entirely into another letter, a *tet.* Suffice it to say that at the close of this section, Regelson marshals an example of *each* of these exceptions.

There is a profound game that Regelson is playing here and in other, similar sections. (The fifth, e.g., refers to verbs in the future tense using that tense and to the imperative using only the imperative; in the sixth, the irregular verb stems, the *gizrot hashoresh,* are similarly discussed using instantiations of these paradigms.) In their important study of the poem, Gideon Katz and Gideon Nevo have made the case, based on the structural poetics of Girard Genette, that in these sections Regelson is deploying a particularly acute form of the rhetorical figure called metalepsis. A sign usually refers to something in the world, its referent. We understand words not as things in themselves as much as signs that represent objects and ideas. In Regelson's poem, however, "in front of our very eyes," Katz and Nevo argue, "the sign turns into a referent, and that which represents turns into the represented."[17] So, for example, when a verb that refers to the *binyan* of *pi'el* as a subject is itself set in the *pi'el,* then it makes itself into the thing represented. Although this crossing of the boundary between a sign and its referent can be used to subversive effect in some works of literature, in Regelson's poem it works mainly to "thicken and materialize" the sign and make us feel that the words of the Hebrew language are tangible and animate objects in themselves. In their apt and piquant formulation, Katz and Nevo present "Ḥaquqot otiyyotayikh" as "the supreme example of this semiotic trickery, and Regelson is revealed in it as the maestro of this rhetorical tool, the Yasha Heifetz of the grammatical-semiotic metalepsis. He utilizes it with incomparable panache and inventiveness. The sign reacts like a tame bear—when the wand is raised it dances a dance that is not its own, cajoled into doing that which it is not meant to do."[18]

With Hebrew being made to turn cartwheels and jump through hoops, it is only natural that our attention is not drawn to what is taking place simultaneously in the other rings of Regelson's circus. What is taking place there is less brilliant but more ambitious. We can grab hold of that story line by looking to translation. One can argue that for obvious reasons "Ḥaquqot otiyyotayikh" is an untranslatable text; yet paradoxically, any translation, even the prose translation of the section I offer above, performs an important service. For the very fact that translation cannot hope to convey the language games Regelson is playing, it effectively squashes the performative axis and exposes a plainer narrative armature that has been there all along. This narrative, however, is not easily transparent because it speaks of higher things. To gain our bearings, let us first observe the rhetorical arrangements. When the speaker opens by declaring, "I have desired your *binyanim* [*binyanayikh*]," he is addressing the Hebrew language and referring to the *binyanim* as her possessions. So throughout, as each *binyan* is taken up in turn, it is not referred to as "the *nif'al*," for example, as it would be in ordinary discussions of grammar, but as *nif'aleikh*, **your** *nif'al*. The *binyanim* here, like all the features of the language throughout the poem, are presented as appurtenances, appendages, aspects, or emanations of Hebrew conceived of as a great female Thou.

It is thus the behavior of *her binyanim* that form the action of Section 4. This is a "story" that begins modestly with each *binyan* simply acting out its own inscribed character but soon reaches for greater heights. As the *binyan* of simple, direct action, *qal* sins and repents and records God's actions. Although *nif'al* is subjected to suffering and brought low, it remains faithful and in the end is redeemed. As the enabling *binyan*, *pi'el* strengthens the hands of the doers of good deeds and clears away obstacles. *Pu'al* is presented as the *binyan* of perfection and ennoblement, and it is here for the first time that the wedding theme is sounded with the allusion to Song of Songs (8:8): "What shall we do for our sister when she is spoken for?" *Hif'il* puts into practice the good deeds mentioned earlier by shodding the barefoot, clothing the naked, and feeding the hungry, a process that thereby triggers the blooming of spring in its hues of green, pink, and red. *Hof'al* puts in a brief appearance as the medium in which the concrete and the abstract are integrated. The greatest attention, finally, is lavished on the *hitpaʿel*, the reflexive *binyan*, because it is through this *binyan* that the marriage metaphor can be brought to its final realization. The English term "conjugation" cannot be far from Regelson's mind when he imagines the *hitpaʿel* as a consummation of inner male and female principles. *Rekhev* and *shekhev* [literally, the rider and the ridden] (line 13) are the terms for the upper and lower millstones, and the unification that is brought about by their interlocked grinding is unmistakably sexual.[19] Although the sexual act is concrete in its earthiness, this most heroic and redemptive of the *binyanim* remains unsullied and faithful and moves toward a consummation that is of cosmic import. Employing the language used by the biblical prophets to exhort Israel, the poet in conclusion turns toward the soul and urges her to remain pure in anticipation of her final reward.

The *binyanim* are animated and personified and pressed into service as representations of the Jewish people. Because the *binyanim* are verbal paradigms, each is a different mode of acting in the world, and altogether they enact a collective narrative. Through the agency of the *binyanim*, then, the Jewish people is presented as striving to do God's will, falling into sin, climbing back onto the right path, enduring persecution and remaining faithful, doing good works, and moving toward the fulfillment of the Covenant, which returns Israel to the bosom of God. This unification, in turn, prepares the ground for the Redemption that is to come. This movement toward redemption, which is so clearly evident in Section 4, is in fact the anagogic pattern that is repeated with variations in each of the core sections of the poem. The intoxicated spirit of "Ḥaquqot otiyyotayikh" is not simply the reflection of an idiosyncratic obsession but the assertion of a mystical theological truth about the present moment in the millennial fortunes of the Jewish people. The metaphysical and eschatological import of the revival of the Hebrew language in the poet's own lifetime cannot be underestimated.

✳

For a poem by a secular Hebrew poet, "Ḥaquqot otiyyotayikh" contains an extraordinary amount of God talk, and it is rarely easy to make out when it is the God of Israel that is being referred to or when it is the Hebrew language. Katz and Nevo have made a signal contribution to understanding the philosophical-theological frameworks Regelson is deploying. Using Regelson's own philosophical and literary essays as guideposts, they identify the two main positions that underlie the poem. The first is pantheism, the idea that God is not distinct from Creation but entirely identified with it. This is an idea that Regelson attributed to American literature in his essay, "The God of Nature in American Poetry":

> This pantheistic thought—recognition of the divinity of every inanimate object, everything growing and living, and each and every human being—permeates the corpus of American poetry wherever it took off its Old World coverings and became independent.[20]

Whereas Halkin, Regelson's close contemporary American Hebrew poet, draws on Habad Hasidism to reach a similar conclusion, Regelson prefers to stand on native ground. The other idea is that language becomes "that which reflects the deep order of the universe and therefore becomes the main key with which to unlock the mysteries of the universe."[21] Basing himself on Heraclitus's identification of cosmic truth with the Logos and on Ernst Cassirer's analysis of the historical development of language, Regelson pushes the function of language far beyond communication and representation into the sphere of ultimate being. Rather than being a creation of human culture, language as Logos precedes Creation and resides behind it and guarantees its meaning.

In his hymn to Hebrew, Regelson fuses these two ideas. In pantheism, God is the universe; in Heraclitus's Logos, the language is God. It follows then, that within the context of the Jewish people and its history, God is Hebrew. For Regelson, however, this is not a logical syllogism or a rhetorical trope or an allegorical type; rather, it is a deeply experienced truth about the ground of being. Indeed, this pantheistic conception of Hebrew as divinity helps us to make sense of many passages in "Ḥaquqot otiyyotayikh." In the opening section of the poem, for example, the poet first lists the heavenly constellations and exclaims that You are in every one of them and then turns to the lowly grasses and bushes and declares the same truth. In both cases, high and low, the drama is lodged not simply in the act of bearing witness to the omnipresence of the divine in nature but also in the act of *naming*, specifically, giving Hebrew names, in all of their exotic, obscure, and recherché glory, to the astral bodies and the terrestrial flora. It is as if it is through their Hebrew names that the divinity in these entities is unlocked and revealed. What is true in space is true in time. Section 2 of the poem delineates the stations of the sacred history of Israel from the Creation through Revelation and on to the future Redemption. At each stage, the refrain is: "with You" I went down to Egypt, "with You" I fashioned the tablets of the Law, and so on. Hebrew is presented as the medium through which Jewish historical time is enacted.

The theological radicalism of Regelson's poem can easily be missed amid the barrage of bravura linguistic effects. The elevation of Hebrew might seem like the profligate enthusiasm of a besotted Hebraist who should be viewed indulgently as writing poetry "under the influence." Katz and Nevo's work saves us from this mistake. They demonstrate that Regelson is proceeding along considered philosophical lines when he collapses God into Hebrew as Logos and that he fully intends to go as far as he goes. The considerable implications of such a national linguistic theology are considered below.

But Regelson goes farther still. His greatest provocation concerns the matter of gender, although he would certainly never have characterized it as such. In the various anagogic schemes in Jewish thought, the ultimate cosmic principle is always male, whether this is the God of Israel in relation to the people Israel as bride in the Bible, or the Holy One Blessed Be He in relationship to *keneset yisra'el* in rabbinic discourse, God in relation to the soul in Maimonides, or the Ein-Sof in relationship to the Shekhinah in Kabbalah. Yet the ultimate divine principle created by Regelson's fusing of God and Hebrew is flagrantly and unremittingly female. There can be no other major poem in the Hebrew language, Halevi's ode to Zion notwithstanding, that is so thoroughly suffused with feminine grammatical forms, especially the second-person feminine imperative and the feminine possessive suffixes of nouns and adjectives. This "poetry of grammar," in Roman Jakobson's phrase, is inescapably present in every single line of the poem. It is perhaps because of the very fact of this omnipresence that we may not see how extraordinary this practice is. Or, again, we are distracted by the virtuoso high jinks taking place at the same time. Or, knowing the poem is an ode addressed to an entity that happens to be grammatically feminine, we assume that this is a practice that simply goes with the territory. To Hebraist ears, moreover, encomia for Hebrew are easily assimilated into the Haskalah genre of allegorical figurations of the language as a fair maiden representing clarity of expression and purity of linguistic lineage.

Regelson's poem constructs a far more primordial and transgressive divinity: the Hebrew goddess, who is who She is. I use this fraught term with some care. As a term used by such writers as Raphael Patai and Tikva Frymer-Kensky, the Hebrew goddess connotes traces of the survival of Canaanite female deities within the faith of ancient Israel.[22] These were *Hebrew* goddesses only in the sense that they were figures in pagan myths that were appropriated in altered and weakened form by the Hebrews in their own language. By using the term in connection with "Ḥaquqot otiyyotayikh," my intent is to underscore the way in which the Hebrew language itself has been elevated into a deified female form. This apotheosis of language is surely an outgrowth of nineteenth-century romantic nationalism on the Herderian model, which identified a true nation by its possession of its historical tongue. Seized by adherents of cultural Zionism who had no easy access to the historic national territory, Hebrew was the principle of national existence that could be made into a ground of ultimate being.

Now, while Regelson's deification of Hebrew owes its main motivation to the currents of modern nationalism, it acquires its unique force and coloration from the vital residuum of paganism. Hebrew is manifest in "Ḥaquqot otiyyotayikh" as both the Great Mother and the Great Beloved. As Great Mother, her beneficences wash over the Jewish people and fertilize them with the gracious and life-bestowing gift of language. In its omnipresence, this gift of language resembles the theological position that later philosophers demythologize and call pantheism. As Great Beloved, Hebrew is the object of the worshiper-poet's undying love and longing. On the one hand, she is transcendent in her majesty, and, throughout the poem, the poet can address her

only in an exaltation of wonder and yearning but never with the hope
of being addressed by her in return. On the other hand, her bounty is
immediately present and available. Not just the poet but any speaker
and writer of Hebrew can touch the language, caress it, play with it,
and manipulate it. This easy availability of the numinous, the ability
to find the sensuous embrace of the divine "upon every high hill and
under every green tree," is precisely what the classical prophets of the
Hebrew Bible inveighed against. And this is precisely what, in the
form of language, Regelson sees as restored to the Jewish people with
the revival of Hebrew. Revival or, in truth, renaissance? The very idea
of death and rebirth, it is well to recall, belongs only to the realm of
the gods.[23] Tchernichovsky and Berdichevsky were hardly shy, after
all, in seeking to recover for the nation the primordial energies forced
underground as the edifice of official Judaism that was built brick by
brick.

It is not my intention to make Regelson into a neo-pagan as much
as it is to use his example to illuminate an important truth about the
Hebraist temper in general. The American Hebraists were by and
large secular men who had broken with the intensive religious educa-
tions they were given as children. The break was not the traumatic
ordeal experienced by earlier European Hebrew writers but rather an
evolution into a world of Hebrew letters that was part of the broader
cultural Zionist milieu. The Americans were not shrilly anti-religious;
they were followers of Aḥad Ha'am and shared his sympathy for the
role of religion in the preservation of Jewish culture. Moreover, many
of them worked within educational institutions of the Jewish community that needed to find modes of accommodation with synagogues
and rabbis in order to survive. But when it came to the construction of
their personal worlds, halakhic practice and Orthodox belief were very
distant from most of them.

One of the great underreported truths about the Zionist revolution
is that the need for religious experience as a human constant did not
disappear because the well of Orthodox Judaism had been poisoned.
The ways in which traditional belief were displaced within Zionist
culture and the ways in which Hebrew writers grappled with religious
experience that had nothing whatever to do with Judaism are threads

in a story we are just beginning to understand. Within this account, the case of the American Hebraists should play an important role. Living in America cut off from the national homeland was, as it were, a mixed curse. The wrenching turmoil over acquiring Jewish space and creating a Jewish state was far more embroiled than the revival of the Hebrew language, which was well under way long before the institutions of Hebrew culture moved to Palestine. The Americans had the privilege of seizing the term in the Zionist formula (land + language) that could be cultivated without external political resistance. As is the case with passionate ideological commitments of many sorts, the embrace of Hebrew served needs that had been fulfilled by the religious regime it had replaced: an ordering and orienting of existence, an ultimate value that elicited faithful allegiance, and a validating community, even if it was invisible and its members scattered. But the case of Hebrew, as revealed by the pagan substratum in Regelson's poem, goes beyond the function of religion as a substitute. For the Hebraist, the intimate engagement with Hebrew brought together the numinous with the erotic. Close at hand in his daily life and despite his vast distance from the national center and despite his deep isolation from other communicants, the Hebraist had a source of pleasure that went far beyond consolation for his losses: the ability to sport with and caress the tangled limbs of the Hebrew goddess.

It is perhaps inevitable that a poem so lavishly focused on an exalted object of worship should at some point double back to reflect on the role of the worshiper. In "Ḥaquqot otiyyotayikh," that point comes in Section 16 after the core sequence of the twelve sections (sections 4–15) enumerating the grammatical and semantic glories of the Hebrew language. Section 16 is a paean to the light Hebrew shone on the experience of the Jewish people from its beginnings until its return to its homeland. (In true Regelsonian fashion, the poem is a tour de force of ingenuity in adducing dozens of synonyms for illumination.) This section functions as a hinge between the main body of the composition, whose subject is the glories of Hebrew, and the concluding four sections (17–20), which turn toward the fate of Hebrew in the present moment and the vocation of the Hebrew poet. This is a shift in more than subject matter. Hebrew is portrayed in the core sections as a perfect and magnificent cosmic force whose effulgence permeates all existence while remaining pristine. In the concluding sections, in contrast, Hebrew becomes embroiled in history and exposed to the depredations of external and internal enemies. Without minimizing this shift, Katz and Nevo argue that Regelson's pantheism can sustain this redirection of focus.[24] For if Hebrew is coequal with the coming-into-being of the Jewish people, then surely its fortunes are dependent on the fate of the nation in the maelstrom of the twentieth century. I would add a less philosophical component to this explanation: the anxiety of self. The merging of the poem with the present exerts pressure on the fit between the poet's own situation and the grand conception of the vocation of the Hebrew poet that he himself proposes.

As the poem enters the historical arena, it is worth recalling the circumstances of its creator. Regelson was fifty years old, living in New York, and making a subsistence salary as a Yiddish-language journalist at the time "Ḥaquqot otiyyotayikh" was published in 1946. He had settled in Palestine with his growing family in 1933, but the family came back to America three years later because of an infant's death and major illnesses. Thirteen years later he managed to return to what was by then the State of Israel and live there until his death in 1981. But that return was far off and uncertain when he was writing "Ḥaquqot otiyyotayikh" at the end of World War II. Exile from the Land and exile from Hebrew (in the form of servitude to Yiddish for the purposes of economic survival) are the twin sources of shame that define Regelson's subject position in the final sections of the poem.

Regelson's intoxicated hymn to Hebrew was likely being composed while the Final Solution was being carried out. The relationship between these two facts cannot be easily interrogated. When Regelson steers his vast poem in the direction of the signal events of his century—Holocaust and Homeland—he approaches them obliquely. He ponders the impact of these events on the fate of Hebrew; or, conversely, he uses Hebrew as a metonymy for the fate of the Jewish people. Section 17 is a deeply affecting evocation of the Jewish schoolchildren of Europe whose sweet breath will no longer discover the shapes of the letters of the *alef-bet* and pronounce the "Four Questions" on Passover.

> The delightful mouths that were born to chirp your vowels were
>   contorted in death throes,
> Strangled were the slender throats that had sung your melodies.

With their death perished future generations of Hebrew writers ("The Mendeles of the future, the Ahad Ha-Ams of tomorrow"), together with masses of speakers and readers. In keeping with the conventions of the ode, the poet alludes to these calamities as part of his address to Hebrew:

> Indeed, it is your own image that has been diminished, a breach
>   has been opened.[25]

But if it is the language that has sustained a catastrophic blow, it is also the language that harbors within it the resources to promote national recovery. As the poet exhorts Hebrew to provide comfort to the broken and support for reconstruction, he offers none other than himself as a partner in this endeavor. Hebrew will redouble *her* constructive energies, he proposes, and he, the poet, will recommit himself to *his* mission to "enumerate the traces of your beauty and give witness to your righteousness."

With these, the concluding words of Section 17, the subject of the poem shifts wholly to the vocation of the Hebrew poet, or more precisely, to an apologia for Regelson's own mission as Hebrew poet. The contours of that mission turn out to be a surprising mixture of grandiosity and humility. The grandiosity comes from Regelson's presenting himself as the true acolyte of Hebrew, whose loyalty and erudition empower him to participate in Hebrew's redemptive self-unfolding. The humility comes from his willingness to demystify the office of Hebrew poet by moving it downward away from the high prerogatives of the prophet-priest in the direction of the pioneer worker.

Whether humble or grandiose, Regelson admittedly brings the poem around to himself, and this noticeable shift in the tenor of the poem has been the object of both criticism and justification. While admiring the poem as a whole, Epstein, the greatest critic of American Hebrew literature, took Regelson to task for compromising the elevation of his grand theme by introducing self-interested polemical concerns and using the poem to settle scores and defend his reputation.[26] Katz and Nevo defend the shift by arguing that it is part and parcel of the embeddedness of Hebrew in contemporary history. Regelson could not *not* confront the fragile contingency of Hebrew and its dependence on human agency while remaining in the majestic precincts of Hebrew as Eternal Language. As an actor in the drama of Hebrew's coming-into-being, then, the poet is justified in reflecting on his visions and ambitions.

There is merit in both these positions. The reader who has been caught up in the celebratory, dithyrambic mood of the poem certainly senses the loss of brilliancy and sparkle as the subject veers toward the questions of the day and the poet's place in them. Moreover, even if taking on this challenge means an inevitable loss of majesty, the polemical texture of these sections remains problematic. In Section 19, which is perhaps the least satisfying chapter in the poem from the point of view of organization and economy, the poet cites three different groups of "enemies" of Hebrew's continued evolution in a winking manner that assumes we know of whom he speaks. Yet it is likely that the shift was more wrenching for contemporary readers at the midpoint of the twentieth century than it is for us today. Regelson's very willingness to introduce a personal, confessional voice and expose his anguish over his exile from Hebrew and from the Yishuv gives the poem an existential mooring that encourages us, the poem's belated readers, to trust its declarations all the more. And the matter of trust is crucial here. We can take the delineation of the ideal qualities of the Hebrew poet (section 18) and the perfidies of his enemies (section 19) as an attempt to construct an exemplary picture frame in which Regelson will place his own portrait. Or, we can take the poet's efforts as deployed on behalf of the grandeur of Hebrew rather than on behalf of his own grandiosity. What is at stake is nothing less than the future of the Hebrew language and the future of Hebrew poetry and in the pursuit of their defense, he assigns himself a role that is true but modest.

It is little wonder then that when Regelson sets about to describe the ideal exemplar of Hebrew in Section 18, it is a prayerful psalm that serves as his vehicle. The section is explicitly modeled on the famous processional coronation Psalm 24, which begins, "The earth is the Lord's and fullness thereof," and continues with the question, "Who may ascend the mountain of the Lord?" to which the answer is, "He who has clean hands and a pure heart." In Regelson's version, it is the majesty of the Hebrew language that is the holy precincts to which admittance must be gained. The successful supplicant will have to meet three high standards: ethical conduct, Judaic erudition, and an adventurous spirit. For the true aspirant, "the hurt of humankind is his hurt, and he delights in the blossoming of the human image and marches through darkness and thorns to the light of the torch of freedom." The national language has not only been the Holy Tongue but also the tribune of the downtrodden: "Indeed from antiquity, Hebrew, you have been the voice and shield of humanity torn from the earth."

This passion for justice must be matched by the hard work of acquiring an intimate knowledge of the progress of Hebraic learning through the successive periods of Jewish civilization: Bible, Mishnah, midrash, Rashi, and Maimonides on through to Nachman Krochmal and Isaac Hirsh Weiss (author of *Dor dor vedorshav*) in the nineteenth century. Hebrew does not divulge her hidden treasures easily, states the poet, as he goes about employing terms from both military campaigning and mountaineering to describe the assault on classic Hebraic sources that must be undertaken by the Hebrew writer who aspires to enjoy some of those treasures. Over and above the cultural ballast of the past, finally, the aspirant must be equipped with an adventurous yet discriminating taste for the new. He must be open to the new and native linguistic produce that appears in the marketplace stalls of the new society, and he must know how to select among them those that not only taste good but provide sustenance for the nation. In sum, turning toward Hebrew at the conclusion of his secular psalm, the poet avers that it is only he who is graced with all three of these disparate endowments who "will repose in your bosom, selah."

From the worshipful tones of Psalms, Regelson turns in Section 19 to the excoriating rhetoric of biblical prophecy to condemn Hebrew's three antagonists. In the first category are the fakers and exploiters who use tired clichés and sensational language to appeal to the masses. The second includes those who would freeze the dynamism of Hebrew by arguing that the language has already reached its full measure of development. In the third group are those who falsely believe they are preserving the purity and sanctity of Hebrew when they protect her from the rough-and-tumble vulgarity of real everyday life. Although as readers we may be intrigued by the whiff of controversy that wafts through these lines, we also feel we are belatedly joining a conversation whose polemical contours have faded with time. From this distance, it is only the second censured group, the freezers of Hebrew, which provides an occasion for Regelson to dramatize fully his arguments rather than merely state them. This passion is evident in the disproportionate division of the section's fifty-one lines. The fakers of the first group are covered in six lines and the false protectors of the third in twelve lines, whereas the freezers of Hebrew get twenty-three. This bulge in the middle is the result of the peculiar refutation Regelson puts forward against this position. Rather than offering reasons and arguments, the poet summons as a witness the "candelabrum of existence" [*menorat hayequm 'al qol peraqeha*]. This turns out to be a miniature anatomy-catalogue full of exotic Hebrew nouns in the spirit of the earlier sections of "Ḥaquqot otiyyotayikh"; it begins with the tiniest ocean creatures and proceeds through the fauna of the dry land and the air before reaching to the stars, the meteors, and the farthest swirling galaxies. This vast swell of language concludes with a crescendo reminiscent of God's answer to Job out of the whirlwind:

אִם יֵשׁ קִצְבָה לְהַדְרַת אֱלֹהֵינוּ?
גַּם לְהַדְרַת לְשׁוֹנֵנוּ יְהוּ קִצְבָה וּגְבוּל!

Can there be any limit to God's majesty?
So to our language can there be limit or bound!

The identification of the wonder of the cosmos with God and the identification of God with the Hebrew language—and therefore the cosmos—are the familiar postulates upon which the edifice of "Ḥaquqot otiyyotayikh" rests. The reprise of this argument so late in the poem indicates how little taste Regelson has for true polemic. To make the case for the unfettered continued evolution of Hebrew, he can more successfully point us to the infinite starry heavens than give us reasons.

Having told us what the poet exemplar of Hebrew should and should not be, we might expect Regelson to install himself on that throne. But in the stirring last section of "Ḥaquqot otiyyotayikh," this is precisely what he declines to do. To be sure, the spotlight remains trained on himself, but the burden he undertakes is to reconceptualize his own role as Hebrew poet in a manner that moves it *away* from preening and grandiosity. Regelson opens Section 20 with a bold and contrarian assertion of his status:

וַאֲנִי, חָרָשׁ בְּמָכוֹן, סַתָּת חֶזְיוֹנִים וְנַגָּר דִּמְיוֹנוֹת,

As for me, an artisan of foundations,[27] a quarryman[28] of visions
    and a carpenter of imaginings,

He is not the writer as magus or a Jewish version of Stephen Daedalus's priest of the imagination turning bread into wine. He does not aspire to the sacred song or the prophetic office of Ibn Gabirol and Bialik, the two Hebrew poets mentioned later in the section. And he certainly claims no portion in the holy megalomania of Uri Zvi Greenberg, the great and wrathful poet-prophet of the twentieth century. Commenting on this section of the poem in a 1956 newspaper article, Regelson declares that in his lineage there are no rabbis, merchants, or scholars. "I regard myself as a worker-writer who does not approach the rank of Bialik, who saw himself as a 'cutter of lumber in the forests of antiquity.' I am the son of a carpenter, and it is sufficient for me to take already-cut planks, plane them and make a nice table or a book case, or in rare instances, an ark [*aron qodesh*]."

What at first looks like a simple gesture of humility quickly turns into a searing confession. As an artisan who has renounced pretensions to greatness, the poet might be expected to be allowed quietly to pursue his craft. But not even this is given him. He has been cast out of the Land and made into a "dray horse, a galley slave" that labors in other languages (Yiddish and English) and, as a result, has betrayed his "high mission" to uncover the majesty of Divinity through Hebrew. But even though this fate has been thrust upon him by circumstance, the poet takes great pains to protest before his beloved Hebrew that he has never forgotten her, that he has used every surreptitious opportunity to disseminate her glories in the languages in which he has been forced to write, and that whatever of value he has found in the cultures of England and America he has been sure to transplant and naturalize for the greater enrichment of Hebrew. Turning from confession to supplication, the final lines of the section, which conclude the poem as a whole, return to the theme of the artist as worker, but with a difference. Whereas earlier the poet presented himself as an artisan of celestial spheres; here at the end, the tone of desperation has intensified, and the acceptable "occupational spectrum" has considerably widened. If he would only be allowed to return to the Land and to the Language—"for you and your land are one!"—he would be perfectly contented to be inscribed alongside "drillers of wells, layers of pipes, . . . the tillers and the sowers" and all the other pioneering occupations embedded in the rhetoric of the settlement period decades earlier.

When he finally was able to settle in Israel and gain employment as a journalist for a Hebrew daily, Regelson wrote an article on the tenth anniversary of the appearance of "Ḥaquqot otiyyotayikh," recalling his motives for writing it. It opens thus:

> Out of forced banishment, out of the need to write in a language other than Hebrew in order to eke out a living, and out of feelings of guilt for having left the Hebrew Land, the poem "Ḥaquqot otiyyotayikh" was born. It was because of that same distance that the Hebrew language could reveal itself to me in its allure [beḥemdatah] as a complete phenomenon in a way that allowed me to see what could be seen by no one who lives within it and feels as if he swims in the blood of its veins.

Regelson's belated reflection tells us a great deal about the moral balance of his poem. The "secret" of the shame and guilt that served as the spring for the poem is placed at the beginning of his article but at the end of his long poem. For it is only after he has discharged the monumental task of describing and praising the Hebrew language and defending her from enemies that the poet allows himself to mention his own situation. He does so not to uncover the motives for composing the poem but to garner sympathy for his abjection in exile, to defend the constancy of his loyalty to Hebrew in the depths of his ordeal, and, on the strength of this faithfulness, to pray for his being taken back into the bosom of Hebrew in the land of Hebrew. In the last analysis, the real spring of "Ḥaquqot otiyyotayikh" is disclosed in the second sentence of Regelson's reflection. The poem is not about shame and guilt but rather about adoration and celebration. But it was paradoxically only by virtue of being banished from the lifeblood of Hebrew that the poet could be vouchsafed a vision of Hebrew as an erotically charged totality and the poem could come into being.

The final lines of Regelson's hymn to Hebrew, which register the worker-poet's plea to be allowed to take his place among all the other pioneer laborers, point the poem at its conclusion toward the great mystery of materialization and embodiment. "Through which," here at the beginning of the line, refers to paths to heaven that are being paved by all the laborers on the Land.

[בָּהֶן] אֱלֹהַּ מִתְגַּלֵּם־מִתְעַלֵּם וְעוֹלָם מִתְעַלֶּה־מִתְאַלֵּהַּ.

[Through which] God is embodied and en-worlds[29] himself and
    the world is elevated and turns into divinity.

For Regelson, reality is ultimately a series of simultaneous reciprocal processes whereby God is being turned into the world and the world is being turned into God. Because the God is Logos, everyone who uses the Hebrew language, however mundanely, becomes an active participant in this mystery. Each of the verbs in the line is in the *hitpaʿel*, the reflexive *binyan*, upon which the poem had earlier lavished so much attention. Making the name of God into a reflexive verb is an instance of seriously playful provocation that is a fitting conclusion to his masterwork.

✳

In this introductory study of American Hebrew poetry, "Ḥaquqot otiyyotayikh" is the only individual text to be given extended treatment because it is the only major work that makes the enterprise of

Hebrew its theme. Although the poem is marked by many distinctively Regelsonian practices, some of them maddeningly idiosyncratic, this ambitious and passionate attempt to seize the great subject of Hebrew contains within it many of the ideas and assumptions that underlay the Hebraist activity in America generally. Some of these ideas and assumptions are articulated within the poetry that will be discussed in the body of this study; yet many lie beneath the surface of the texts themselves, and it is only by making them explicit can we understand the *mentalité* that made the creation of these works possible.

First, Hebrew is the deep structure of Jewish civilization from its very beginnings and the truest and most authentic expression of the spirit of the nation. In the many shifts in Jewish religious belief and historical experience over the ages, Hebrew has not only been the carrier of those changes, but it has also provided the deep-flowing continuity among them. Second, Hebrew is a miraculously beautiful language that is gorgeous, rich, precise, supple, and dazzling in its resourcefulness. Anyone who knows Hebrew cannot help being smitten by its charms and venerating it. Third, the way words are formed based on a verb stem makes Hebrew into a flexible, open system. The language's rules of grammar and its lexical reservoir guarantee order and the preservation of wisdom while at the same time inviting the creativity of the individual talent. Fourth, Hebrew supersedes and absorbs "religion" narrowly understood as Orthodox belief and halakhic practice, and in so doing, Hebrew itself becomes a ground for religious experience and fulfillment. Through Hebrew, Creation becomes language; Hebrew names the world. It follows then that Hebrew leads to a radical amazement at the wonder of the world. Fifth, although the life of the Hebraist in America often entailed loneliness and isolation, the pleasure provided by the connection with Hebrew should not be underestimated. By becoming an active "practitioner" of Hebrew, the Hebraist tapped into an unstinting and nurturing source of quasi-erotic stimulation and enjoyment. Sixth, although virtually all American Hebraists were Zionists and some eventually settled in Israel, they regarded Hebrew language and culture as a "portable homeland" that could be colonized without access to concrete territory. Seventh, the Americans regarded themselves as citizens of a catholic republic of Hebrew letters, and their location in America gave them the privileged position, as well as the duty, to take the best of English-language culture and import it into Hebrew. Finally, a true appreciation and understanding of Hebrew as a totality could be reached, ironically, only by those, like the American Hebraists, who lived outside the daily "bloodstream" of Hebrew in Palestine/Israel.

Keeping in mind these manifold assumptions about the meaning of Hebrew will prepare us for examining the world of the twelve poets whose works are discussed in this volume.

Part II *Profiles and Readings*

Three   Benjamin Nahum Silkiner

Among the new Hebrew poets who appeared in America at the beginning of the twentieth century, the career of Benjamin Silkiner was exceptional. His fellow poets wrote lyric poetry for many years before taking on longer narrative and epic forms. The discreetness of the lyric poem afforded an opportunity for the expression of a single moment of feeling or perception that need not be integrated into a more imposing framework of meaning; and this form of composition comported well with the experiments of young men finding their way in life and in the poetic vocation.

Silkiner, by contrast, made his debut as a poet in 1910 at the age of twenty-eight with *Mul ohel Timurah* [Before the tent of Timurah], a hundred-page epic about the struggle of Native Americans against their Spanish conquerors. And what an ambitious work it is! In a powerfully elevated Hebrew style, the poem addresses such large and noble themes as heroic suffering and renunciation, native myths, the fate of nations, and the grandeur of the American landscape. Silkiner's Indian epic is a difficult work, and we shall have occasion to analyze the poem and its mixed reception in Europe and Palestine in a later chapter.[1] Yet despite the work's difficulty, its symbolic value was huge. As the major inaugural work of Hebrew poetry in America, *Mul ohel Timurah* functioned like a broadside, announcing the ambitions of this new cultural outpost to the international republic of Hebrew letters. The new Hebrew enterprise in America, it announced, would be   113
about America, and the America it would be about would not be the teeming streets of the immigrant neighborhoods but a more remote and aboriginal American landscape.

His epic written and published, Silkiner walked away from the genre and returned to it only at the end of his life and then, in a fragmentary and modest way.[2] He began his career over again as a lyric poet and served as a mentor for a group of younger poets who were starting out in *their* writing lives as lyric poets without the benefit or burden of a major epic poem behind them.

Silkiner was born in 1882 in Vilkija, near Kovno, in Lithuania, the son of a merchant who allowed him some elements of a Western education alongside the immersion in traditional Jewish studies. At the age of eighteen, Silkiner moved to Odessa and spent several years in the circles of Hebrew renaissance writers dominated by Bialik and Aḥad Ha'am. He married there and emigrated to the United States in 1904. Although he earned a law degree, he devoted his work life to Hebrew education as the principal of the Uptown Talmud Torah in New York and as a faculty member of the Teachers Institute of the Jewish Theological Seminary, where he taught Hebrew literature and Bible. His early death in 1933 was widely mourned in the Hebraist community.

The group of poets who gathered around Silkiner's mentorship included Lisitzky, Bavli, Ginzburg, and Halkin. Although they were on average only ten years younger than Silkiner, they viewed him—with much esteem and affection—as their elder. He had been in America longer and had a large published work to his name; and he was conversant with the great figures of Hebrew literature in Europe. He corresponded with Bialik, who referred to him as *rosh haḥavurah*, the leader of the group of Hebrew writers in America.[3] Silkiner began to provide this leadership at a time when the prospects for modern Hebrew literature in America remained extremely fragile. Although modern Hebrew novels and poems had been produced in great profusion in Russia in the second half of the nineteenth century, precious little of this spirit infiltrated into America in the mass immigrations that began in the 1880s. Here and there the odd maskil or Hibbat Zion poet found his way to these shores and wrote bitterly of his crushing isolation.[4] Efforts at publishing Hebrew newspapers or journals were mounted and abandoned.

The turning point came in 1910. That year saw, in addition to the appearance of Silkiner's Indian epic, the publication of *Senunit*

[Swallow], edited by Brainin, a miscellany that included poems by Silkiner, Lisitzky, Schwartz, and other recently arrived Hebrew poets. The volume was the result of Silkiner's enterprise. Brainin was an older man of Hebrew letters who was active in Eastern Europe as an editor and critic; Silkiner contacted him several years earlier, before his arrival in America, with the purpose of persuading him to use his experience and prestige to draw together the inchoate Hebrew talents in the New World. The next year Brainin started a Hebrew weekly called *Haderor* [another word for swallow], which failed after a few issues. The fire finally caught with the launching in 1913 of the monthly *Hatoren* [The mast], which appeared, although not always regularly, over the course of about eight years.[5] *Hatoren* was not the work of one man but of a group of Hebrew enthusiasts called Ahiever; and it was Silkiner who served as the editor of the belles lettres section of the journal.

Silkiner's efforts on behalf of Hebrew publishing in America were unflagging. He established a series of imprints that sought partners in Palestine for printing new works by American Hebrew writers and reprinting classics. The first of these imprints was called Asaf, which published works by Brainin, Levin, and David Neumark during the World War I period. Asaf was succeeded in the 1920s by the Haverim publishing agency, which was responsible for two volumes of an important literary miscellany called *Nimim* [Strings]. After Bialik's visit to America in 1926, the Haverim group reached an agreement to co-publish with Bialik's Dvir Publishing Company, and it was under this imprint that Silkiner published his collected poetry, including a revision of *Mul ohel Timurah* in 1926. The arrangement with Dvir was succeeded by a partnership with Mitspeh that resulted in the publishing of two additional and important collective volumes called *Massad*. Silkiner was the impresario for one of the most intriguing projects in American Hebrew letters: translating Shakespeare into Hebrew. Who better than Hebrew poets working in an English-speaking land, argued Silkiner, to take on the high task of rendering the Bard into Hebrew? Silkiner conceived of the plan in 1911 and toiled until his death in 1933 to bring the project along and persuade poets to accept their noble assignments. Eventually, all the major plays of Shakespeare were translated by such American figures as Avinoam-Grossman, Bavli, Carmi, Efros, Halkin, and Lisitzky. Silkiner's own Hebrew *Macbeth* appeared only after his death in 1939.[6]

Silkiner's lyric voice is in evidence in the slender 1926 volume of his collected poems *Shirim*, which also includes a revised version of *Mul ohel Timurah*.[7] Already ill, Silkiner records his debt of gratitude in a front note to Bavli, Halkin, and Ginzburg for their editorial assistance in his hour of need. Although there are some Zion poems scattered throughout the volume, Silkiner generally insists on observing a kind of separation of styles that calls for the lyric voice to speak without regard for fixed time or place.[8]

The first poem in the volume is a motto poem titled "Bat Shiri" [My muse], which is unusual in a body of verse that does not otherwise reflect on its craft.

בַּת־שִׁירִי

בַּת־שִׁירִי — הֲמוֹן חוּטֵי נֹגַהּ
לְכָל רוּחַ נִשָּׂאִים בַּחֲרָדָה,
וּקְצוֹתָם בְּמָקוֹם רַק אֶחָד:
בְּמָקוֹם שָׁם הַדִּמְעָה רָעֵדָה.
עֵת אֶשָּׂא אֶת עֵינַי לַמָּרוֹם,
הֵם מְרַחֲפִים עַל פְּנֵי הָאֲדָמָה;
בַּשִּׁפְלָה כִּי אֶתֵּן אֶת עֵינִי,
נִיד רַחֲפָם אַאֲזִינָה בָרָמָה.

My Muse

My muse—an abundance of filaments of light
Scatter agitatedly in all directions,
They lead only to one place:
The place where the tear trembles.
When I lift up my eyes to the heavens,
They hover over the surface of the ground;
When I look downward,
I hear the rustle of their vibrations on high.

The poet identifies his muse as a myriad of skittish filaments of light that shine and vibrate all around him and emanate from a single source: his own tremulous tear. The solipsism of this premise proves a reliable overture to Silkiner's verse. The suffering is there all the time; it is the medium in which the poet lives his life. But it is also the inspiration for the refinement of suffering, for moments of beauty that erupt in the face of suffering, and for the respite from suffering afforded by the warmth of human regard.

✳ כִּי גְבוּל שָׂם לְבָבִי לִיגוֹנִי
   "For my heart has set a limit to my anguish"

Analysis

As an example of these contradictions, we consider the poem "Ki gevul sam levavi ligoni" [For my heart has set a limit to my anguish . . .].[9] Although the poem is not dated, from its placement in his chronologically ordered collected verse, the poem belongs to the year 1916. It is one of a number of poems—the best of his verse, in my estimation—that deal with the romantic relations between the speaker and a woman or women.

. . . כִּי גְבוּל שָׂם לְבָבִי לִיגוֹנִי

וְלֹא יַעֲבֹר אֶת חֻקּוֹ – אַנְחָתִי;

וּמְקוֹר דַּאֲבוֹנִי הָאִלֵּם

לֹא יַעֲרֶה לָךְ שִׂיחַ תְּלוּנָתִי.

אַל נָא תִשְׁאָלִינִי לִנְדוּדַי,

וְכֹחִי בַדֶּרֶךְ מָה עָנָה,

וּמָה הִיא הַשּׁוֹאָה חָרַדְתִּי

מִמֶּנָּה לְמַחְסֶה בַּפִּנָּה

הַבְּרוּכָה, בָּהּ תִּשְׁרִי . . . – הַיִּי לִי

כַּכּוֹכָב בַּנְּשִׁיָּה: דּוֹמֵמָה

בִּי שִׁפְעֵי אוֹר־נֹחַם וְדַבְּרִי

בְּלִי אֹמֶר עַל נַפְשִׁי שׁוֹמֵמָה.

אָז אֶרְצֶה בְּתוֹדָה אֶת חַסְדֵּךְ

וּבְצִלֵּךְ אֶתְלוֹנֵן, יַלְדָּתִי,

וְעֵיֵף בְּחֵיקֵךְ אָנוּחַ

מְדוֹבֵב לָךְ לַחַשׁ־בִּרְכָתִי.

וְאוֹר־יוֹמִי הֶעָכוּר כִּי יִדְעַךְ
וְסָגַר הַלֵּיל בְּעַד נִשְׁמָתִי,
אַתְּ תִּירְשִׁי הַהוֹן שֶׁרָכַשְׁתִּי
וְאֶחְשֹׁךְ מֵעוֹדִי – דִּמְעָתִי . . .

. . . For my heart has set a limit to my anguish
and it will not exceed that measure—my sigh;
and the complaint of my lips
will not disclose the silent source of my misery.
Ask me not about my wanderings
and the injury my strength has dealt along the way,
or about the calamity I feared
that made me seek refuge in the blessed corner
in which you dwell . . . Be for me
like a star in the oblivion: silently
radiate consoling light and wordlessly assuage
my devastated soul.
Then shall I accept with gratitude your gracious help, my daughter,
and abide in your shade and rest exhausted in your bosom,
murmuring the whisper of my blessing.
Then, when the pallid light of my day darkens and night closes in
    on my soul,
you will inherit the wealth I have gathered
and saved this long time—my tear. . . .

A first reading of the poem readily identifies it as an address by a male speaker to a women within the context of a relationship whose nature is not easily defined but we imagine to be romantic. The abundance of references to suffering in the first half of the poem draws our attention to the pathos of the speaker's ordeal, which he seeks *not* to impose on the woman. The second half of the poem focuses on the consolation he will find in her arms and on the blessings he will bequeath to her when he dies in return for the solicitude she has shown him. The conventionality, even banality, of these sentiments, might lead us to read this poem within the traditions of romantic poetry and to approach it as essentially a tender communication between a man and a beloved.

A closer look at the rhetoric of the poem should lead us to think otherwise. The first two lines of the poem—before there is any indication that this is a speech addressed to a woman (which comes with *lakh* in line 4)—describe a willed act of restraint and containment. He has set a boundary that the expression [*anḥati*] of his suffering will not be allowed to cross.[10] What first may have seemed like a heroic renunciation turns into quite a different kind of utterance in the context of the relationship with the woman. The determination not to complain becomes a stance of withholding and self-concealment. He will not disclose to her the source of his anguish, the hurt he caused others, and, most importantly, the crisis that led him to seek refuge in the blessed corner in which she dwells. That corner may indeed be blessed for him, but the characterization of their relationship as a temporary resting place may not be very consoling to her. The three dots in the middle of line 9, in addition to breaking the poem in half, reinforce the sense of something missing or deleted: a painful history of lost loves that could be told—that is, shared—but will not.

The exhortation to the woman to shine like a star in the oblivion, which begins the second half of the poem, is a romantic gesture that, once offered, immediately rings hollow. He will bask in her healing radiance, but only if that radiance is silent and non-inquisitive. The *'az* [then] that begins line 13 indicates the paratactic structure of the poem as an utterance and the negotiated, conditional nature of the relationship he is proposing ("*If* you will do so and so for me, *then* I will do so and so for you."). The speaker is laying down a set of terms on which the relationship, at least from his point of view, can proceed. If she agrees not to contest his reticence, then he will gratefully accept her ministrations. Furthermore, in return for her compliance and for the respite from travail he will enjoy in her arms, he is willing to be generous, at least rhetorically. He not only murmurs blessings to her, but he ennobles the refuge he finds with her [*uvetsilekh etlonen*] (line 14) by invoking the shelter of God described in the familiar opening line of Psalm 91: *betsel shadai yitlonan* [he will abide in the protection of Shaddai (= God)].

The real reciprocation, however, will come later on. When the darkness finally brings his ordeal to an end, she will become the recipient of the fortune he has patiently amassed. Then, he will make up for what he cannot, or will not, bestow upon her now. The speaker's sole capital [*hon*], however, turns out to be his tear, the metonym for the sum of anguish and suffering that has been distilled through the burden of his experience.

Is this tear a precious legacy or a fool's prize? The answer is not unambiguous. The sophistication of Silkiner's poem lies in its playing off romantic topoi against a desperate rhetoric of self-interest. The sigh, the desolate soul, the tragic resignation, the radiant star, the refuge in the embrace of the female other—all these staples of the romantic tradition lead the reader to expect the poem to be about great-souled expressions of ideal love and devotion. Instead, the speaker appropriates these gestures and exploits them to mount an argument aimed at persuading the female addressee to take him in and minister to his wounds without offering in return the self-disclosure that intimacy requires. Is the speaker wrong to want what he wants? Our acceptance of his intentions depends, I think, on the exigency of his suffering. If his past ordeals have been as horrendous as he claims, then we may grant him the unreciprocated refuge he seeks as a necessity of psychic survival. But here the plausibility of that extremity is limited by the same limitation he presents to the woman. Just as he will say nothing to her about the substance of his travails, he will say nothing to us as well, and so these afflictions remain merely announced and postulated. The redemptive tear that he has distilled from his suffering and bequeathed to her similarly remains vague and elusive.

Although the poem is a single instance in small body of work, it can serve to underscore some of the patterns we shall see in the lyric poetry of Silkiner's younger contemporaries. To begin with, this is a poetry written out of a great deal of pain and loneliness. While there may be moments of mitigation in nature, fellow feeling, or art itself, this anguished modal state is always returned to. The source of this pain, to be sure, is rooted within the human condition that affects all people; but its special pathos surely derives from the redoubled isolation of being a Hebrew poet on American soil, that most invisible and freakish of figures in the teeming immigrant milieu. Second is the stunted capacity for love. The speaker in Silkiner's poem seeks a refuge in the bosom of the female addressee, but it is unlikely that he seeks anything more there. Like many of the male heroes in the literature of the Hebrew Renaissance [teḥiyyah], the poem's speaker presents himself as so damaged that he cannot give of himself to another.[11] The fact that he addresses her as *yaldati* [my daughter] (line 14) is not insignificant; while this is a standard term of endearment, it also implies that it is non-sexual tenderness that will characterize the relations he is inviting her to partake in.[12]

Third is the question of style. Readers of such contemporary poets as Yehuda Amichai and Natan Zach, whose verse attempts to represent the simplicity of direct speech, may find the Hebrew of Silkiner's poem ornate and difficult. But it is really no more so than the norms of other Hebrew poetry written during the Renaissance period that began in the 1880s. A poem of 1916, to be sure, is already located on the later verge of that period and looks forward to the aggressively modernizing trends of symbolism and expressionism, which will dominate Hebrew poetry in the interwar period in Palestine. In relation to the avant-garde waiting in the wings, the conservatism of Silkiner's poem signals the position of principled resistance that will be assumed by American Hebrew poetry.

As a preliminary generalization, we may fairly say that although American Hebrew poets created within the poetic paradigm of the Hebrew Renaissance, they sought to simplify that norm into a refined classicism. We will point out developments and variations in the formation of this American style in the works of the individual poets as we proceed. For now it is enough to notice the modified biblicism of Silkiner's poem. He has done away with the biblical tense signature that converts future into past and vice-versa, but he has availed himself of the elliptical concision of biblical syntax. There is none of the ornate periphrasis of Haskalah poetry, yet the lexical register remains high, although an educated reader familiar with the Hebrew Bible would encounter few obstacles. The poem is not, however, without its lexical rarities. The use of *ya'areh* in line 4 for "reveals" is uncommon though not obscure. The same is true for *neshiyah* [oblivion], which occurs in the construction *erets neshiyah* in Psalms (88:13), where it is an epithet for the grave or Sheol. Yet it is crucial to point out that, despite the erudition of Silkiner and his implied reader, this learning is not activated in a chain of complex allusions to classical sources as is so famously the case in Bialik's poetry. Because Silkiner's language is essentially biblical, there are naturally biblical echoes throughout the poem. Yet aside from the single reference to Psalms 91 in line 14, none of these echoes becomes a focused signal to the reader to make meaning out of a phrase in the poem by playing it off, ironically or non-ironically, against a specific passage in a classical source. In this restraint, or, one may say, in this revision of Bialikian practice, Silkiner set a tone for the American Hebrew poets who followed him.

Finally, there is the dynamics of the lyric situation. Lyric poetry, as was discussed in the introduction, is a kind of "overheard speech." In expressing feelings, describing an interaction between the self and the natural world, addressing inanimate objects, or painting a verbal picture of nature, the poet is engaging in a kind of reflexive utterance or sending a message for which there is no concrete addressee. By the act of publication, the poet puts the reader in the situation of being allowed, even invited or solicited, to overhear and be witness to this utterance, although the reader per se is not its targeted recipient. In Silkiner's "Ki gevul sam levavi ligoni" the recipient is clearly the woman whom he is trying to persuade to accept him on the terms he is offering. Yet the fact that she is addressed in the poem does not necessarily mean that she is addressed in real life. Unless we visualize the poem as a text that is actually given to the woman or read before her, we would be led more naturally to take the poem as a *substitute* for that event. So despite the presence of an addressee, the poem remains a reflexive utterance and a linguistic event within the self-system of the poet. As readers we are called upon to imagine the existential and emotional situation of the speaker that would result in the lyric discourse of the poem.

Four Israel Efros

When they arrived in America as youngsters, all of the Hebrew writers considered in this volume hungered for general education. They quickly conquered English, excelled in high school, read the great English and American poets, and applied themselves to their studies in the public universities. But it was Israel Efros, alone of this company, who became an academic scholar writing in English, as well as a practicing Hebrew poet. His training and publications allowed him to pursue a teaching career at American universities rather than at the newly established Hebrew teachers colleges, like the rest of his fellow writers. When a branch of the Hebrew University was established in Tel Aviv in the years after the founding of the State of Israel, Efros was invited to come from America to serve as its head. The gift of longevity enabled Efros to finish his life as the honorary president of what had become in the meantime Tel Aviv University and as an American Hebrew poet who had been rescued from obscurity by the chance to reconnect with the dynamic center of contemporary Hebrew literature.

Efros was born in 1891 in Poland in the town of Ostrog to a father who was both a traditional scholar and a maskil and who took in advanced students for board and instruction. The boy was moved quickly through the heder system and was then educated by his father at home. In 1905, two years after establishing himself in America, Efros's father brought the family to New York. In the mornings, Efros attended the public schools and in the afternoon, he studied at the Rabbi Isaac Elchanan yeshivah, from which he received rabbinical ordination at the age of eighteen. Persky remembers him as part of the "Hebrew Gang" of youths, together with him and Friedland on East Broadway on the Lower East Side during these years and, shortly thereafter, as head of the Yovel youth group in Harlem. After studying at New York University, Efros simultaneously pursued rabbinical studies at the Jewish Theological Seminary and doctoral studies in philosophy at Columbia University, receiving both his ordination and a Ph.D. in 1915 at the age of twenty-four. The next year Efros moved to Baltimore to become principal of its talmud torah, and shortly thereafter he founded the Baltimore Hebrew College, which, together with similar institutions in Boston, New York, Chicago, and other cities, became one of the key venues of American Hebrew culture and a chief employer of its literary figures. In 1929 Efros was given the chance to do something that was very rare at the time: to teach Jewish studies in an American university. He joined the faculty of the University of Buffalo, where he taught Hebrew and Jewish philosophy. During the 1940s, Efros returned to New York to teach at Hunter College; in 1954 he was called to head the nascent Tel Aviv University. He continued to be a productive poet during his years in Israel and found new lines of development that connected his work to the newer Israeli poetry. He was the recipient of many literary prizes before his death in 1981.[1]

Efros's specialty in Jewish philosophy was the medieval rationalist tradition. His first book, *The Problem of Space in Jewish Medieval Philosophy*, was published in 1917 in a distinguished series edited by the Columbia Semitist Richard Gottheil. He was an expert in the nuances of technical philosophical terminology and in how Greek terms were first expressed in Arabic and then adapted into Hebrew. In 1924 he published *Philosophical Terms in the Moreh Nebukim*[2] and several years later *Studies in Pre-Tibbonian Philosophical Terminology*. Among the many other subjects of Efros's research were the thought of Judah Halevi, Maimonides's writings on logic, and a synthetic study (in Hebrew) of medieval Jewish thought as a whole.

Among the Hebrew poets in America, in short, Efros was unique in his formidable knowledge of the philosophical tradition and the technicalities of its abstract terminology. At the same time, however, of all the American Hebrew poets, Efros's verse is the least abstract and conceptual. His poetry is distinguished by its search for radical simplicity, by a striving toward a stripped down classical idiom, and by a principled disinclination to make use of the weight of erudition. There are, to be sure, pronounced metaphysical concerns to be found in Efros's lyric verse; yet in mode of conception and expression, this is a poetry that is as distant from abstraction as can be imagined, and if one did not know it was written by an expert in medieval philosophical terminology, it would be exceedingly difficult to guess the nature of the writer's "day job."

Simplicity as a realized poetic norm in Efros's poetry had in fact attained a kind of iconic status in American Hebraist circles in the early 1920s. In Halkin's famous defense of American Hebrew poetry against its detractors abroad, Efros is presented as the exemplar of the lucidity and serenity that are the hallmark of the American style. The poets of Eretz Yisrael, Halkin argues, have fallen for the barbarisms of the European avant-garde such as symbolism and expressionism; and as a result, their poetry is permeated with "neurosis, stylistic unevenness, obscurantist content, and a striving toward the outlandish." American Hebrew poetry, on the other hand, "is straightforward, speaks simply, and tries to crystallize and refine emotions rather than befog them."[3] Efros is singled out for his simplicity and musicality and for his striving to compose verse (*shirah*) that approaches *song* in the English sense of the term. In short, Halkin saw Efros as an essential figure in the move to rescue Hebrew verse and "return man to poetry and poetry to man."

The components of Efros's simplicity in the first two decades of his poetic production are not hard to describe. He typically makes full use of the regularities of the Ashkenazic stress on the penultimate syllable to fashion a sonorous trochaic line, while making sparing but tactical use of words with a *milra'* stress. Most poems are organized in quatrains with the second and fourth lines rhyming. There is a distinct preference for short words over long words and for simple words over complex words. Although the lexical register is biblical, Efros avoids the grandiloquent dimension of biblical language.[4] For a Hebraist and lexicographer who controlled the language in all its esoteric coruscations—he co-edited a well-known English-Hebrew dictionary—Efros takes a principled stance of semantic renunciation; he knows all the words in the dictionary, but, as Amichai was later famously to remark about his own poetry, he uses very few of them, and on purpose.[5]

A similar purposeful minimalism is displayed in Efros's reluctance to allude to classical texts. One of the hallmarks of the great age of Bialik was the advantage taken of the classical literacy of contemporary readers, who could be counted on to recognize references to biblical and rabbinic texts and grasp their ironic, often subversive, import. Efros's readers were not much less literate, yet despite his enormous admiration for Bialik, Efros generally declined to exercise this poetic option. This was a choice made, it is important to stress, by most of the American Hebrew poets, not just Efros, and, as has been pointed out earlier, this constitutes a critical distinction between their poetic practice and that of the great poets of the *tehiyyah* [revival] period, their powerful precursors. In Efros's case, the absence of allusiveness serves the forward flow of the poetic line; the poetry seeks to avoid the kind of impedance that results from the ramifying subtexts and associations released when a reader comes across a reference that, like a pop-up toy or a land mine, scatters attention in many directions. Efros wants to rein in his language to protect the simple integrity of the mood, emotion, or image he is floating in the lyric moment of the poem. Most of all, he wants his song sung.

The ideal of simplicity, most conspicuously felt in the early lyric verse, abides in Efros's poetry through significant changes in his writing. In the 1930s and 1940s, he turned away from the lyric to compose a series of long, narrative poems on themes of American history and landscape (*Vigvamim shoteqim* [Silent wigwams] (1933) and *Zahav* [Gold] (1942) that became his most successful and best known contributions to American Hebrew letters. Here, too, the commitment to a disentangled and unimpeded poetic line enabled Efros to create an effective sense of narrative momentum. When Efros arrived in Israel in the early years of the state, his poetry again took a different turn. He went over to the Israeli accent from the Ashkenazic, which, needless to say, had profound implications for how his poetry scans and sings. For the most part, he abandoned rhyme and fixed-stanzaic structure and moved toward free verse. Efros's poetic range was also expanded by translating *Hamlet* and *Timon of Athens*, undertaken as part of the Silkiner-Bialik American Hebrew Shakespeare project.[6] Writing deep into old age—his last book of poetry appeared in 1978 when he was eighty-eight, and his collected writings in five volumes appeared in 1980, the year before his death—Efros was reborn as an Israeli poet. His longevity made him lucky in another way. The trademark simplicity and minimalism that Efros had developed in the earlier part of the century and hued to in the decades following was now precisely the quality celebrated in the new poetry of Amichai, Zach, and Dan Pagis. Efros had persevered during the stormy revolutions of Shlonsky and Greenberg and come out on the other side, and if he was not adopted as a precursor by the younger poets quite in the same way that Fogel was, he nevertheless finished his career esteemed as a hoary bearer of a fresh and relevant wisdom.

It is in *Shirim 5611–5628* [Poems 1911–1928] that Efros first established his poetic voice.[7] At the center of these poems is a lyric subject who responds to the phenomenal world around him. Night descends, a fall storm threatens, the first flowers of spring bloom, a fresh snowfall sparkles in the moonlight. Although the poems' climes are those of the American Northeast and they are signed with such place names as the Catskill Mountains and Asbury Park on the Jersey shore, there is nothing local about these locations. There are no place names within the poems, no local lore, and no effort spent in evoking the unique and indelible genius of place. Nature here is essentialized and one might go on to say refined and classicized. An engagement with the palpable Americanness of American vistas is something that would come later, and come abundantly, in Efros's long narrative poems about Native Americans and the California gold rush. Yet in Efros's earlier lyric phase, a natural scene like the aftermath of a great storm serves as a momentary expression of cosmic forces that can configure themselves differently in another mood or another moment.

"Leil ḥoref" [Winter night] (1917, pp. 41–46), one of Efros's finest nature poems, exemplifies the kind of imaginative experience triggered by the encounter with the world. The poems opens with a Frost-like consideration of whether the winter woods are more beautiful by day or by night, a question the speaker decides in favor of the possibilities of nocturnal enchantment. He explains the sparkling of the moonlight on the snow by imagining that stars above have been plundered from the heavens and installed below.

טוֹב הֱיוֹת בְּלֵיל זֶה יֶלֶד!
תּוֹךְ הַשֶּׁלֶג אֶתְגַּלְגָּלָה
עַד כָּל גּוּפִי רְצוּץ־כּוֹכָבִים
יַז נְגוֹהוֹת בָּאֲפֵלָה.

How good to be a child on a night like this!
I roll in the snow until my whole body is star crushed
And sprinkles radiance into the darkness. (p. 42)

Pondering this blessed act of cosmic naughtiness puts him in an antic mood, and—with the cry "How good to be a child on a night like this!"—he rolls in the snow and imagines that he is churning up the stars as the white sparkles cascade off of him. This regressive reverie of mingling with the snow and stars is brought to a halt when he encounters the great trees in the depths of the wood. In the eyes of these great trees, he imagines, he is a provocation: a nosy intruder dressed in black who violates the utter whiteness of their kingdom. Their anger is communicated by a fierce wind that blows the snow into a blinding swirl. Yet instead of being ejected from this wintry Eden, the speaker is vouchsafed a vision. Three white creatures emerge from the snowy wind and sing a song that announces that they are snow maidens, who, despite their icy appearance, enfold within their warm hearts the flowers that died the preceding spring and will yet be brought back to life. The infinite cycle of life is assured. The wind dies down, and the revelation from within the storm departs with it. Yet whether from afar or from within him, the poem concludes, the song of the snow maidens still resonates.[8]

Even read in paraphrase, "Leil ḥoref" shows how squarely Efros's lyric verse falls within the conventions of the romantic tradition. The poetry lives *inside* the pathetic fallacy rather than making a pretense of resisting it. There exists a soul of the world, the *anima mundi*, which the lyric subject encounters in heightened moments of experience. Does the speaker/subject originate his own fantasies and project them onto the *anima mundi*, or are the visions he sees revealed to him from a realm beyond his imagination? In "Leil ḥoref," the speaker begins by projecting and ends by receiving. His little story about the anonymous thief who stole the stars of heaven and scattered them on the moonlit snow is wholly of his own confection. But the spectacle of the snow maidens is disclosed to him from the soul of the winter forest. How does he merit this revelation? Between the fantasy of the stolen stars and this gift of vision, the speaker first allows himself to regress into a childlike state of abandonment (the rolling in the snow) and then takes courage and penetrates the darker, stormy depths of the forest. The profundity of this arrival, however, does mark his earlier fantasy as shallow and insignificant. The exercise of his imagination, though projective, was the trigger or the necessary first step in the encounter. "Leil ḥoref" presents itself as a poem about what it takes to make a genuine connection with the soul of the world.[9]

From out of the frozen depths of winter, the snow maidens deliver a consoling message about the continuity of life. Concerning many of the encounters with nature enacted in Efros's poetry, it would be fair to say the results are, like these, beneficent. Beauty is discovered, and a quickening of life won from the world. But it is not always so, and Efros has sometimes been done a disservice by such sympathetic critics as Ribalow, who recommended his poetry to those who "wish to return [. . .] to those good days when poets dreamt happy dreams and poems, joy-filled and pleasant, were carried aloft like a bird on the field."[10] Another poem set during a stormy night ("Beleil sho'ah" [On a night of destruction], pp. 30–31) ends with the speaker's being unhinged and mortified by the "wild derisive laughter that thunders from the distance." In still another poem ("Paḥad 'erev" [Night dread], pp. 66–67), the romantic expectations associated with twilight are replaced by the perception that with night "a strange fear descends / upon each hill and valley." The poem ends with the speaker wandering the rain-swept fields, his heart silently clutched in anxiety.

Whether surprised by joy or by dread, the lyric subject is most often alone in the world and with the world. Yet there are times when the encounter is shared with a female companion, but only fleetingly. The poems in which women appear always transpire on the eve of separation.[11] She is leaving him or he is leaving her, but the atmosphere is never one of abandonment, longing, or anguish. Rather, the leave taking, regardless of who is departing, is marked by a mood of melancholy resignation, as if to say that aloneness in the world is the modal state of the lyric subject, and from this situation there can be, almost by definition, only moments of reprieve marked by miss-matched expectations. In Efros's lyric poetry, as is the case with much of American Hebrew poetry in general—Silberschlag and Regelson are the exception—the erotic register is set low. The subject husbands his subjectivity for the encounter with the world rather than with others.

In one of the earliest of the collected poems "Uvemoti . . ." [And when I die . . .] (pp. 12–13, dated Av 5672/1912), the speaker invites his beloved to put her head in his lap, and he promises to tell her the secret of life. "There is an ambient veil," he reveals to her, "that covers being / and interposes itself before our eyes." This may not be welcome news to the beloved, but it nicely epitomizes the dilemma at the heart of Efros's poetry. When the veil is not entirely opaque, the world can be glimpsed and refractions of beauty collected. But when access is denied, the poet is worn down by ennui and assailed by doubt. What surprises us in the poem "'Ayafti. . . ." [I am exhausted. . . .] (pp. 61–62) is that this Kohelet-like complaint of futility and dashed hopes is addressed to the god Pluto, whose subterranean realm he presumes to disturb. After Tchernichovsky's pagan poems of a generation earlier, there is no necessary scandal in addressing a Hebrew poem to a Greek god, and the gesture seems more rhetorical than sincerely provocative. ("'Ayafti. . . ." is in fact followed directly by "Hellas," pp. 65–77, an ambitious *poema* on the high themes of art and truth. Those ambitions prompted Ribalow to remark that Efros should stick to the short lyric and leave the *poema* as a genre to Shneour.[12])

When Efros's speakers expostulate with Heaven, it is more naturally the God of Israel whom they address. In the second decade of this poetry, in the 1920s, poems directed to God become more frequent. This is not the God of history or the God of the Bible or the God of Jewish suffering, but rather, simply, the personal God of the universe. The speaker of "'Et kokhav emunah yid'akh . . ." [When the star of faith dims] (5693/1923, pp. 119–20) describes to God in a quiet, elegiac tone—so markedly different from Bialik's stormy apostasies!—how his sincere childhood faith lost its compass and drifted away. There remain, however, moments of exaltation. When the veil of the cosmos is parted, the sparks of beauty are reignited, and Efros's speakers do not hesitate to address their thanks to God. "Odkha" [I shall thank you] (Iyyar, 5684/1924, pp. 137–38) is such a poem, and it would not be out place in the liturgy, although it characteristically resists classical Jewish allusiveness and associations. "Would I could be the paintbrush, Lord, / with which you color the wide world!" is the opening (and title) of a disarming invocation that touches on the ontological sources of Efros's mission as an artist.

This discussion of Efros's poetry has focused on the lyric poems contained in his first collection, which appeared in 1932. Efros's long career had many phases. In the 1930s, he turned from the lyric to narrative poetry about American historical themes. Extended attention will be given in Chapters 15 and 17 of Part Three of this study to his book-length poems *Vigvamim shoteqim* and *Zahav*. The Holocaust had a profound impact on Efros, and his 1944 volume responding to the murder of European Jewry *Anaḥnu hador* [We are the generation] signaled a turn toward a new commitment to engaged poetry that is influenced by expressionism. This trend is continued in his 1954 book *Goral ufit'om* [Destiny and suddenly], which reflects on the postwar years and the establishment of Israel. During its final phase over the next twenty years, Efros's verse turned in the direction of modernism while at the same time harking back to an earlier attachment to romanticism. Clearly, Efros is an artist embarked on an ongoing quest to connect his poetics to changing personal and collective experience. The shape of that career and its many achievements deserve to be explored and better known.

✳ עִנְבּוֹל קָטָן
Little Clapper

Analysis

This bittersweet and complex little poem is taken from the middle of *Shirim 5611–5628* (p. 91), and, by placement in the volume, appears to have been written in 1921, although it is not dated.

עִנְבּוֹל קָטָן

גְּלִין־גְּלַן! עִנְבּוֹל קָטָן
מִתְרוֹצֵץ וָשָׁר:
הַפַּעֲמוֹן עוֹלָמִי,
עוֹלָמִי מַה צָּר.

וְעֵת כִּי אֲקַלַּע
מִקִּיר אֱלֵי קִיר,
עֵת רֹאשִׁי אֲרוֹצֵץ –
גְּלִין־גְּלַן! נִשְׁמָע שִׁיר . . .

אִישׁ עוֹבֵר וּמַאֲזִין,
וְלִבּוֹ מָלֵא גִיל, –
גְּלִין־גְּלַן! כָּכָה אוֹבֵד
מַכְאוֹבִי בְּצָלִיל . . .

Little Clapper

Ding-dong! A little clapper
dashes back and forth and sings out:
My world is a bell
my world is so narrow.

And when I'm flung
from wall to wall,
when I batter my head—
Ding-dong! A song is heard . . .

Someone passes by and listens
and his heart is filled with joy.
Ding-dong! Thus is lost
my pain in the ringing sound.

"'Inbol qatan" [Little clapper] turns on the contradiction between the clarion tones of the bell, which bring delight to listeners, and the hidden violence and self-sacrifice necessary to their production.[13] This is, admittedly, a very large theme for so slight a poem, yet the severity of Efros's lyric discipline succeeds in pulling it off. Not only are the features of Efros's signature simplicity in evidence here, but they have been wound tighter to compensate for the poem's purposeful slenderness. Efros's characteristic quatrains have been squeezed and compressed into lines with no more than two or three stresses. The language, with one key exception, is classically biblical and composed of short words. The rhymes at the ends of the second and fourth lines are strictly deployed to convey the poem's central paradox. In the first stanza, *shar* [sings] is played off against *tsar* [narrow], and the second, *qir* [wall] rebuts *shir* [song]; while in the third, *gil* [joy] is closely synonymous with *tselil* [sound], although the doubling by this time is palpably ironic.

The poem opens with the tinkling and ringing of the bell, and this onomatopoeia not only enacts the poem's preoccupation with the making of sound but also draws us toward a charmed series of associations with bells, which has already been initiated by the poem's title. Bells and clappers generally evoke beneficent images of delightful sounds announcing glad tidings. (We may also hear an echo of the more ominous bells of Edgar Allen Poe.) This is a *little* clapper and one that not only tirelessly races back and forth within the hollow of the bell but also talks, and this fact takes us a step further toward the world of animate objects in children's literature, where teapots sing and brooms dance. This progress into fantasy is complicated by the words the little clapper utters when it speaks. "My world is a bell" is an analogy that invites us to think about the conditions under which this proposition could be true, and it recalls the world of Lafontaine's rationalist fables and their personified objects. The concluding line of the stanza ("My world is so narrow.") introduces a discordant, plaintive note for the first time. There is no necessary alarm here; however, for it is in the nature of bells to be circumscribed.

After this resonant scene of happy bells and talking clappers, the middle stanza comes as a shock. We are suddenly thrust inside the bell and exposed to the infernal mechanism that produces the sounds that delight the ears of listeners outside. The violence is encapsulated in the word *aqula'* ["I am/will be flung"] in line 5. In this poem as in most of his verse, as has been observed, Efros writes in a concise and limpid biblical idiom. The morphology of *aqulla'* is a conspicuous violation of that norm. Hebrew readers would likely identify the biblical use of this root in the David narratives in the book of Samuel: first, when David flings [*vayqalla'*] one of his five smooth stones to fell Goliath (1 Sam. 17:49), and then when Abigail declares to David that he will be protected as God's chosen one and that God "will fling away [*yeqalle'enah*] the lives of your enemies as from the hollow of a sling [*qaf haqela'*] (1 Sam. 25:29). For sensitive ears, the use of this verb invokes a well-known piyyut from the Yom Kippur morning liturgy in which, following the Talmud's exegesis of 1 Samuel 25, the soul of evildoers is flung away [*tequlla'*].[14] The picture drawn in the Talmud is superbly to the point here. In a baraita, Rabbi Eliezer contemplates the differential fate of the righteous and the wicked. While the souls of the righteous in the World to Come are ensconced beneath the heavenly throne, the souls of the wicked undergo a horrific ordeal: "An angel stands at one end of the universe and another angel stands at the other end of the universe, and they sling the souls of the wicked back and forth between them."

This might be considered a morbid and overwrought piece of erudition if it were not for the fact of Efros's general deliberate avoidance of allusions to classical sources. For, despite his project to liberate Hebrew verse from the laden allusiveness of Bialik's poetry—while, of course, preserving many other of the master's practices—Efros is willing to violate his principles for the right opportunity. Here, at the beginning of the second stanza of "'Inbol qatan," he seizes his chance and positions the word *aqula'* as if it were a land mine. The back-and-forth movement of the clapper inside the bell suddenly switches from being a service happily performed to being an involuntary punishment, to which the forlorn speaker, like the feckless souls of the wicked, will be condemned for all eternity. The suddenness of the switch is also conveyed by the word *arotsets* ["I will batter," line 7], which describes the concussing of the speaker's head with each clap of the bell, whereas the happy scurrying back and forth of the little clapper in line 2 is conveyed by the word *mitrotsets*. Although the two terms look and sound similar, they derive from completely different word stems, and this semantic sleight of hand further heightens the turning inside-out of the initial situation.[15]

Yet it is toward that initial situation that the poem returns. After glimpsing the unremitting punishment necessary to the production of song, the poem moves us back toward the reified object, the song itself, as well as outside the bell, where the song sings. The onomatopoetic *glin-glan* is heard twice (lines 8 and 11), reinforcing the song's "thereness" and its success in detaching itself from its origins and entering the world. The passerby whose heart is filled with joy when he listens to the song is supremely innocent of what went into its making. The speaker, the voice of the little clapper, which returns now at the conclusion of the poem, does not protest: ". . . thus is lost / my pain in the ringing sound." The vague and bland conjunction *kakhah* ["so," "thus," "in this way," line 11] conveys in its minimalism a reservoir of resignation. Yet the submission is not without its secret consolation. The clapper's final utterance is conspicuously ambiguous. The fact that the clapper's pain is lost in the peels of the bell can mean two things. Either the clapper's pain disappears from view so that his suffering is all the more painful for being unacknowledged. Or, this pain is absorbed by or subsumed in the song and thus mitigated or at least sublimated. Because the poem as a whole documents two truths—the truth of the sung song and the truth of the battered head—it is fitting that Efros allows his poem to rest on a statement that can underscore the truth of one or another, or, perhaps more likely, both at the same time.

"'Inbol qatan" at once describes Efros's *ars poetica* and embodies it. As an artifact, this crystalline little poem displays all the characteristics of Efros's vaunted simplicity and the limpid tonality. At the same time, it brilliantly reveals the fact that this is a simplicity that is constructed, fabricated, made. And at what cost, the overly sensitive reader may not wish to know.

Five   Ephraim E. Lisitzky

We know more about the life of Ephraim E. Lisitzky, or at least some parts of it, than we do about the lives of any of the other American Hebrew poets because he alone of them wrote an autobiography. This volume, called *Eleh toldot adam* [These are the generations of Adam] (1949); published in an English translation as *In the Grip of Cross-Currents* (1959), is one of the best prose works in American Hebrew literature and a jewel in the canon of Hebrew autobiography.[1] It begins with Lisitzky's birth in Minsk in 1888 and the death of his mother seven years later. His father remarried and moved the family to Slutzk before emigrating on his own to the United States. The boy was a prized Talmud student in the yeshivot of a city that prided itself on its Lithuanian traditions of learning. After a separation of over eight years, he joined his father in Boston, Massachusetts, and was dispatched to study for rabbinic ordination at the Rabbi Isaac Elchanan Yeshiva in New York. After attending for a brief period, he left the school with certification as a shohet [ritual slaughterer] and took a job as a teacher and shohet for a small, rural Jewish community in upstate New York. Lisitzky had encountered the new Hebrew literature for the first time when he arrived in Boston, and, recapitulating a process that had already been undergone by many yeshivah students before him, he became enthusiastic about Hebrew literature at the same time as his religious worldview lost coherence and collapsed. After working in upstate New York, he returned to Boston, but he failed to find a simple trade from which to make a living and accepted a position as a private teacher for a Jewish family in a remote village in northern Ontario called Ahmic Harbor. There he met many delightful

136

and idiosyncratic people, fell in love with a gentile girl, encountered the awesome beauty of the forests and rivers, wrote his first Hebrew poems, and, after several years, made the fateful decision to return to civilization and devote himself to the vocation of Hebrew teaching.[2]

The metamorphosis of the tempest-tossed immigrant into an impassioned exemplar of Hebraism in the New World should have made a rousing and revealing conclusion to Lisitzky's autobiography. But, alas, it does not come off. The inner emotional logic that allows the young man to seize his new vocation is declared rather than dramatized. In the concluding sections of the volume, the author makes the argument that teaching Hebrew in the inhospitable climate of the New World partakes of the same ethos of backbreaking pioneering [*halutsiyyut*] enacted at the same period by the pioneer settlers [*halutsim*] of the Land of Israel. The claim, as Shaked has pointed out, serves an apologia directed at the work's primary audience, Hebrew readers in Israel who, although they may be delighted by the exotic landscapes Lisitzky has painted for them, remain perplexed as to why a Hebrew writer would choose to remain so isolated from his readers.[3] The author is twenty years old when *Eleh toldot adam* concludes, yet Lisitzky did not publish it until he was sixty-one. The impetus to write it may indeed have come from the fact that in these years the State of Israel was being established, and several of the key figures in American Hebrew literature—among them Halkin, Efros, and Regelson—were "abandoning" the struggle for Hebrew in America and taking up new careers in the new state. Lisitzky may have meant his autobiography to serve not only as a self-justification but also as a compensation. Lisitzky strives—successfully, to my mind—to persuade the Israeli reader of the fascination of America, its vistas and personalities, Jewish and gentile. He has transformed America into Hebrew. As he had already done with Indian legends and Negro spirituals, Lisitzky is widening the thematic bounds of Hebrew literature, bringing America within its reach, and, in a sense, capturing it for Hebrew. This accomplishment represents both a service and a self-sacrifice, and it could only be undertaken by remaining behind.

Aside from occasional critical essays, the autobiography is Lisitzky's only sustained work of prose in a long career that was devoted to poetry. Unsurprisingly, there is something in the artistic achievement of the autobiography that reflects back on Lisitzky's relative strengths as a poet. He was, in the end, more successful as a storyteller, whether in prose or verse, than he was as a lyric poet. He published his first poems around 1907 and produced lyric poetry in great profusion for two decades until he hit on a new mode of writing. *Medurot do'akhot* [Dying campfires], Lisitzky's great American Indian epic that appeared in 1937, displayed an unexpected gift for verse narrative on a large scale. Summoned to tell the larger-than-life story of others, Lisitzky managed to extricate himself from the toils of lyric self-involvement. He extended this new direction in *Be'oholei Khush* [In the tents of Cush] (1953), which endeavors to capture within Hebrew poetry the cadences and rhythms of jazz, Negro spirituals, and the sermons of the great black preachers.[4] The breakthrough to the Indian epic was hard won and was not the first time that Lisitzky had attempted to write big. In 1934 he published a 500–page allegorical-philosophical verse drama called *Naftulei elohim* [Struggles of the Lord], which was ostensibly set against the background of the pogroms of World War I but soon took off into the ether of avenging angels and murky explorations of the sources of good and evil. Truth be told, Lisitzky wrote too much, and the daunting task of winnowing this imposing oeuvre to arrive at a slimmer but vital canon of his work is a task that remains to be undertaken.

Lisitzky was known as the Hebrew sage of New Orleans, and it was his symbolic location within the small international republic of Hebrew letters, rather than any individual literary accomplishment, that gave uniqueness to his role. After leaving Canada and after sojourns in Milwaukee and Buffalo, Lisitzky settled in New Orleans in 1918 and worked there as a Hebrew educator until his death in 1962. From his post in New Orleans, Lisitzky participated in print in all the periodicals, miscellanies, and projects of his New York-based colleagues. Although he traveled often and made long journeys by boat to visit his friends Bavli and Halkin—he made only two trips to Israel—his enduring identification with the most colorful city of the Deep South marked a kind of outer western boundary point on the map of Hebrew literature. As that map took shape between the two world wars and after the suppression of Hebrew culture in the Soviet Union, the centrality of Eretz Yisrael became indisputable. But the productive margins of the map were far-flung. In the East, there were the Hebrew writers of Warsaw, Vilna, Vienna, and Paris; in the West, there were the Americans whom we have been describing. And in the farthest verges of America was Lisitzky of New Orleans, that staunch beacon unflaggingly sending out his poetic signals to the far-away center.

More than any other American Hebrew poet, the arc of Lisitzky's career illustrates the artistic gains realized by engaging American themes and the American landscape. The first collection of his poetry, which covers the years 1907 to 1927, reveals a poet who would use the lyric as a vehicle for expressing his rage and insult.[5] In an early manifesto poem ("Shirati" [My poetry/song], signed "Milwaukee, 1909"), Lisitzky sounds very much like Bialik wearing his prophetic mask in his poems of wrath, except for the fact that in Lisitzky's case there is no public political context.[6]

שִׁירָתִי

I

לֹא צְוָחַת נְשָׁרִים, לֹא רְנָנַת זְמִירִים,
לֹא סַעֲרַת סוּפוֹת, לֹא רַחַשׁ זְפִירִים,
לֹא נַהֲמַת יַמִּים, לֹא לַחַשׁ יְבָלִים,
לֹא אִוְשַׁת אֲרָזִים, לֹא זִמְזוּם שִׁבֳּלִים —

לֹא אֵלֶּה יִשְׁתַּפְּכוּ בְּצִלְלֵי מִזְמוֹרִי.

מֶרְחַקִּים, הָרִים, עֲמָקִים, מִישׁוֹרִים,
עֲרָבוֹת, יְעָרִים, שְׂדוֹת־בַּר, אֲחִים פּוֹרִים,
שַׁפְרִירֵי שְׁמֵי־זֹךְ, שֶׁמֶשׁ, סַהַר, כּוֹכָבִים,
צִפֳּרִים, שׁוֹשַׁנִּים, עֲלָמוֹת, אֲהָבִים —

לֹא אֵלֶּה יַרְעִידוּ אֶת נִימֵי כִנּוֹרִי.

II

תִּפָּשָׂה נַפְשִׁי קוּרֵי־שְׁחוֹרָה
וַתִּתְכַּנֵּס בָּם כִּבְשִׁרְיָה;

נִסְגְּרָה עִם זַעֲמָה, מֶרְיָהּ
תּוֹךְ מַסֶּכֶת קוּרֵי־שְׁחוֹרָהּ.

וּמִסְגֶּרֶת שְׁחוֹר־קוּרֶיהָ
יָנֹק תִּינַק מֶרְיָהּ, זַעֲמָהּ;
יָפִי, נֹעַם בַּל יְפַעֲמָהּ
בְּסֵגוֹר טְוִיָּה שְׁחוֹר־קוּרֶיהָ.

וּכְשׁוֹרְרִי שִׁירָתִי —
וְהַפְּרִישָׁה מִשֶּׁלָּהּ לָהּ:
אֵיבַת־עַד, נְאָצָה, קְלָלָה,
מִדֵּי שׁוֹרְרִי שִׁירָתִי.

מילבוקי, תרס"ט

My Song

I

Not the screech of owls, not the trilling of nightingales,
Not the roar of storms, not the whisper of zephyrs,
Not the wail of oceans, not the murmur of brooks,
Not the rustle of pines, not the hum of sheaves.

None of these pours forth in the notes of my song.

Distances, mountains, valleys, planes,
Savannas, forests, wild fields, wetlands,
Domed azure skies, sun, moon, stars,
Birds, roses, maidens, love—

None of these vibrates the strings of my harp.

II

My soul has grasped the web of its darkness
And withdrawn itself within its armor;
It has become enclosed within its rage and revolt
Within the plated web of its darkness.

Closed tight within the blackness of its web
It will suckle its revolt and rage;
Beauty and loveliness will not move it
Within the woven web of its blackness.

And when I sing my song,
It will take and set aside from itself:
eternal enmity, antagonism, and curse,
Each time I sing my song.

The speaker of that poem declares that his poetry has nothing to do with the standard repertoire of romantic topoi: the murmuring of brooks, the screeching of eagles, the roar of the ocean, and so forth. His inspiration is drawn instead from sources of revolt and *resentiment*. In images that draw strength from the prophetic discourse of Jeremiah and Bialik, the soul of the poet is imagined as a combustion chamber where rage is nurtured until it blazes forth as propulsive and corrosive verse. It is as if, spider-like, the darkness of the poet's soul has spun its own web, which now served as the poet's redoubt. Lisitzky, then, serves notice to his readers early on that poesy will not be his stock in trade. This very early poem also adumbrates the challenges in both style and content that confronted Lisitzky's poetry throughout his career. The barely contained anger that fuels the poem creates a grossly binary tension: *either* the saccharine banalities of romantic poetry *or* the blackness of hostility and imprecation. Rather than signaling revolt, moreover, the blackness turns out to be merely Sturm und Drang, the other side of the romantic coin. In terms of the craft of poetry, the poem is overwritten. The seemingly endless catalogues of romantic markers and the nearly synonymous repetition of ideas in the opening stanzas attenuate the force of the idea rather than strengthening it, and repetitions mar the closing stanzas. The temptation toward unnecessary elaboration was a continual problem for Lisitzky. This applies also to the temptation to semantic display; there are too many instances of using rare and archaic words that contribute little beyond their own preciousness.

The rage, as it turns out, is turned back upon himself more often than it is hurled at others. The ultimately self-reflexive nature of the lyric as a genre is hardly unrelated to this boomerang effect. Feelings of unworthiness, self-loathing, weariness, and doom suffuse these poems. Silkiner, too, wrote from a place of pain; but Lisitzky's pain has nothing about it of the older poet's high sense of resignation, nor does he believe that anguish can be transubstantiated into beauty.[7] What are the sources of this pain beyond the vulnerability of all humanity to which some temperaments are more mercilessly exposed than others? The autobiography, written decades later, helps us here, although we must use it with the awareness that the contemporary readers of the poems could not so avail themselves. During the phase of his life before he came to America, the young Lisitzky was deeply scarred by the early death of his mother, by the long separation from his father, and by the grinding poverty of his family. These are losses from which he never recovered.

Layered on top of this personal ordeal is a collective narrative of injury. Like the heroes of Berdichevsky's and Brenner's fiction, Lisitzky is a Talmud prodigy who loses his ontological moorings in the world when he loses his faith. Deprived of the coherence of belief and at the same time refusing to become a typical immigrant striver, the young man is thrown upon a self that is impoverished, insulted, and self-lacerating. Finally, the vocation of secular Hebrew poet, which provides something of a way out of this dilemma, carries with it a redoubled exile when that craft is practiced in America. In a 1913 poem based on Hibbat Zion topos that goes back to Judah Halevi, the speaker undertakes an imaginary tour of the Land of Israel only to conclude that he, like Moses on Nebo, will see but never arrive. Playing on the concluding verses of the synagogue hymn Adon Olam, the unreconciled speaker faces the truth: *Beyad el zar et ruḥi afkid / uveḥeik adamah zarah—et geviyati* [In the hand of an alien god I commend my soul / in the bosom of alien soil my body].[8]

In the following decades, Lisitzky turned his considerable energies to American themes. His huge Indian epic *Medurot do'akhot* was the last of the three long poems written about Native Americans in Hebrew; it attempted an encyclopedic synthesis of Indian legends and folktales based on the conflicts between two tribes in the face of European conquest. He traveled throughout the American South listening to black preachers and collecting folktales and songs, which he recast in Hebrew in his volume *Be'oholei Khush*. Both of these works will be discussed in Part Three of this study. Lisitzky participated in the American Shakespeare translation project by translating *The*

Tempest and *Julius Caesar*. Lisitzky's production was prodigious, and the true shape of his career has not yet been charted.

✳ "כְּחַיָּל שֶׁנִּתְרוֹקְנָה אַשְׁפַּת חִצָּיו"
"Like a soldier whose quiver has been emptied"

Analysis

An untitled poem from 1916 (signed "Milwaukee, Tishrei, 5677") affords us an opportunity to examine this self-myth of heroic suffering bound in tightly controlled rhetorical integuments.[9]

כְּחַיָּל שֶׁנִּתְרוֹקְנָה אַשְׁפַּת חִצָּיו
וּבְפִיק בִּרְכַּיִם שָׁב מִשְּׂדֵה-הַקְרָב —
עַל חוֹפָךְ, מִישִׁיגַן, אָנֹכִי נִצָּב,
לְבֶן תַּלְתַּלִּים
כָּמוֹךְ, מְרֻתַּח-גַּלִּים
זֶה תַּלְבִּין עַתָּה, מִקָּלַע סַעֲרַת-סִתָוֹ.

מִנְּדוּדַי בַּמֶּרְחַקִּים, אֵל כִּי הִתְעָה
מֵחוֹפָךְ אָרְחִי, מִנִּי נֵכַר-נוֹף,
אֵלַיִךְ, חוֹלַת כֶּסֶף, נַפְשִׁי נִשְׂאָה
שָׁמֹעַ שָׁמְעָה
בִּסְעָרָה וּבִדְמָמָה
בִּקְרוֹא לָהּ דָּכְיֵךְ מִקְצְוֵי-חוֹף.

עִם הַעֲרִיב חַיַּי שַׁבְתִּי, יְגַע עָנִי,
כִּי אֶטֶּה לִי עַל חוֹפָךְ אֹהֶל דָּל;
הוֹי, הַעַל מְמְצוּלָתֵךְ לִי פִּקְדוֹנִי:
חֲלוֹמוֹת, רְעָנִים,
מִשְׁכְּבָר בַּשָּׁנִים
זָרַעְתִּי קִרְבֵּךְ עַל גַּל וָגָל — — —

מילבוקי, תשרי, תרע"ז

Like a soldier returning from the battlefield,
his quiver emptied of arrows and his knees trembling,
I stand on your shores, Oh Michigan,

white haired
like you, who grow white with agitated waves,
cast about in the fall storm.

From wandering in distant lands and foreign climes—
God has diverted my path from your shores—
my soul is carried back to you sick with longing
and listens intently
in the tempest and the silence
as the breakers call to it from the far shore.

As my life sets, I sat, spent by misery,
in a rude tent I have planted on your shore;
oh dredge up from your depth my deposit:
the dreams and melodies
I long ago
sowed in you on wave after wave — — —

This is a poem of return to the shores of Lake Michigan, and it indeed hangs on an autobiographical peg. Lisitzky had studied pharmacy in Milwaukee from 1909 to 1912 before changing his vocation to Hebrew teaching and moving to Buffalo; this poem marks his return at the beginning of the new school year to Milwaukee, where he spent two more years before settling in New Orleans. (The previous poem in the volume is a poem of leave-taking from Bavli, his fellow Hebrew poet in Buffalo.)

The poem opens with an epic martial simile of a soldier returning from battle, and the decorum of that image finds an equivalent in the classical formal organization of the poem. The rhyme scheme for this poem of three six-line stanzas is ABACCB. The two proximate rhymed lines (CC= lines 4 and 5 of each stanza) are also half the length of the other lines; this couplet has a song-like quality within the rigor of the poem and provides a momentary reprieve from the onrushing rigors of destiny.

The first stanza is based on a two-part comparison. In lines 1–3, the speaker compares himself to a warrior exhausted from battle who is returning to his home grounds on the shores of Lake Michigan; in lines 4–6, the speaker compares himself to the lake itself, whose storm-tossed white caps correspond to his own prematurely whitened locks. The epic register of the first comparison is curious. Not only is he a returning warrior but an antique figure wielding a bow and arrow who might have walked off the pages of the Iliad or the book of Judges, or, closer to home, he might be an Indian brave returning to his native shores, and this at the exact time when warfare of a very different kind was raging on the plains of France. The nature and purpose of the good fight he has been fighting, moreover, remain elusive.[10] We are left with a figure of self-importance, which is augmented in the second half of the stanza when the speaker compares himself to the Great Lake. The whiteness of the frothing waves, whipped up by an autumn storm, is yoked to the whiteness of the speaker's curls. The phrase *levan taltalim* (with white curls [literally, white of curls], line 6) is a striking usage. Curls are associated with youth and sensuality, and the one time the word *taltalim* is used in the Bible (Song of Songs 5:11) the color is unmistakable: "His [= my beloved's] locks are curled and black as a raven." The speaker's hair, we must conclude, has been shocked into whiteness by early turmoil and suffering.

Whiteness, the speaker asserts, is his commonality with the lake, and the enjambment of *kamokha* [like you] at the beginning of line 5 forcefully, or perhaps forcibly, makes that point. The comparison underscores our awareness that in genre, the poem is an ode, an address to an inanimate object. The two parties in the world of the poem occupy two different ontological realms: one is a speaking human subject, and the other is both a place and a force of nature. It is the conceit of the poem—perhaps of all odes—that the two are conjoined at some essential level. This presumed communality, that shared whiteness, serves as a point of departure that is progressively undermined in the course of the poem. Here, at the outset of Lisitzky's poem, man and lake share the same storm-battered toughness; but the resilience and profundity that will attach to one will fall far beyond the lot of the other.[11]

The beginning of the second stanza stresses the speaker's wanderings. In contrast to the lake, which is a quintessentially unmovable spirit of place, the speaker has roamed far afield, and his travels have not been guided by some purposeful quest but by the hand of God or Fate working to keep him far from these shores. Now he is home. The intimate, even passionate, address to the lake as Thou is stressed by the word order to line 9, which reads, in a literal rendering: "To you, sick with longing, my soul is carried." Is this longing reciprocated? The speaker imagines it is. The second half of the stanza, with those two foreshortened lines (10 and 11) and their hypnotically sonorous feminine rhymes, describes a stance of intent listening that discerns, whether in tempest or stillness, the call of the breaking waves to his soul. He has been forced to wander far, but now the waves have called him back.

The final stanza finds him encamped on the shore, where he mounts a desperate plea to the Great Lake. The battle fatigue of the first stanza has turned into a more permanent decline; exhausted by deprivation, his day is done and his life is turning to evening. The poor tent that is now his final dwelling is a sign that he has renounced all else except for the lake and the mercies it might show him. The desperation behind the voiced appeal to the lake that concludes the poem is not immediately apparent. The speaker is ostensibly asking for the return of something that is rightfully his; this is something that has been "deposited" in the lake's depths. (The word *piqqadon* at the end of line 15 is the term in Jewish law for the property that an owner places with another person for temporary safekeeping.) What the speaker wants returned to him are the dreams and joyful songs of his youth; he once sowed (or scattered) them upon the waves, and they descended into the depths to be stored for him in this watery depository. In his reduced state, the speaker is very much in need of the renewal that contact with his earlier aspirations might give him, and he has now come to make his withdrawal.

The fact that this is a doomed transaction is indicated in any one of a number of ways. The rhyme scheme takes the hopeful term *piqdoni* [my deposit] (line 15), rhymes it with *'oni* [affliction] (line 13), and then rhymes *gal* [wave] (line 18) with *dal* [rude, poor] (line 14). The three dashes that conclude the poem—in the orthographic conventions of the period, this has the same function as the use of three dots in our own—indicates that his appeal peters out unanswered. The most significant signal is the dramatic situation of the poem itself. From the outset, the speaker has addressed Lake Michigan as if it were a sentient being. He posited a shared storm-battered strength in the first stanza and presented himself as being beckoned home by the lake's waves in the second. The desperate and unanswered plea of the final stanza, which appeals to the lake to do something it cannot, reveals the truth of the disbelief that has been "suspended" so far: the lake is a lake, an inanimate body of nature, and the human wishes projected onto it can never be anything more than that.

Does the poem's speaker own up to this truth? Beyond his growing desperation, there is no sign that he does. But Lisitzky, the poet behind the poem, brings us, the readers, to this conclusion. That is why it is crucial to observe the distinction between the poet, the author of the poem, and the speaker, the dramatized voice speaking the poem, even if the continual reference to "the speaker" sometimes seems tedious. For the success of this poem turns on the gap between the pathos of this constructed lyric "I," with its needs and illusions, and the ironic awareness of the poet/author, who knows, and brings us to know, that nature is indifferent to our fate and serves as a screen upon which we project our wishes.

There is much in this poem that is of a piece with Lisitzky's lyric poetry as a whole. The speakers of Lisitzky's poems generally complain about the pain of existence and the burden of their sorrow; they struggle to deal with the hand fate has unfairly dealt them; they experience their ordeal isolated from the consolations of community with nature as their only companion; and though still young in biological terms, they feel that their vital life has already effectively ended. Indeed, as Epstein has pointed out, it is most often very difficult for Lisitzky's poetic craft to master the stormy emotions and rankling *resentiment* that seethe in his verse.[12] I've chosen "Keḥayal shenitroqnah . . ." [Like a soldier . . .] for analysis because it succeeds, I believe, in holding those forces in check. Lisitzky achieves some distance from complaint and self-pity by focusing on an externalized dramatic situation: a battle-weary soldier who returns to the lake that nurtured his youthful dreams. The "narrative" of the poem concerns the intimacy of this encounter—as it is construed in the imagination of the speaker—during its progress from rough equality to despairing prostration. By insisting on the distinction between the poet and his speaker, we can see the poem as a kind of deconstruction of the swagger inherent in a grand address to Lake Michigan. It is an ironic perspective that defends the poem against romantic bathos.

Six   Abraham Samuel Schwartz

Abraham Samuel Schwartz was an anomaly among American Hebrew poets. Almost all the members of this group depended upon a professional involvement in Hebrew education for their livelihood, even though they scrupulously protected the purity of their poetry from their pedagogic work and ideological commitments. Schwartz, by contrast, was a medical doctor with a busy general practice in the Jewish neighborhoods of Brooklyn, and he could write his Hebrew verse only in isolated moments stolen from his attending he sick.

In 1953, when Schwartz was seventy-seven and long retired from his practice, he moved to Jerusalem to be near his only daughter. (She was Shulamit Schwartz Nardi, who worked for a number of Israeli presidents.) He settled in the neighborhood of Zalman Shazar, a historian and man of letters who became Israel's third president. Shazar had first met Schwartz in New York in the early 1930s—his startled discovery of the defiant band of American Hebraists was described in the beginning of the introduction to this volume—and the two men now re-encountered one another and became close companions. In the interval since they first met, Schwartz's poetic production had blossomed; he had written twice as much verse after he turned sixty than in all the preceding years. Shazar, meanwhile, had been elected to the first Knesset, served as the first Minister of Education and Culture, and joined the Jewish Agency Executive while remaining a member of the Knesset. It was natural that Shazar would use his connections to open doors for this Hebrew poet who had brought with him to Jerusalem a large sheath of unpublished verse and whose poems had never appeared in Israeli literary journals. Yet, although the entrée was provided and Schwartz's poems were considered by various editors, in the end they were not accepted for publication. It is of course not hard to imagine how, despite Shazar's patronage, poems written in a by now antique style by an unknown elderly poet would not make a compelling claim upon the literary editors of the time. But Schwartz, who had not been eager to expose himself to rejection, felt stung, and when moved back to America three years later for medical reasons, the sheath of poems returned with him.

In 1959, two years after Schwartz's death, the first and only collection of his poems, spanning the years 1909–1957, was published in Israel.[1] The volume included a preface by Shazar, to which I referred at the beginning of this volume (Part One, Chapter One), and a substantial and appreciative afterword by Halkin, the renown professor of Hebrew literature at the Hebrew University. It is not hard to surmise that it took their combined eminence finally to make Schwartz's poetic oeuvre available to us.

About Schwartz's life before Shazar's glimpse of the poet in old age, his own poetry tells us almost nothing. Halkin correctly stresses in his afterword that Schwartz's poetry is supremely impersonal or supra-personal and rigorously avoids autobiographical reflection and the use of materials recognizably taken from life. Little can be gleaned from his verse—either at the level of biographical information or at the level of emotional identity—about Schwartz as son, husband, father, physician (with one famous exception), or Hebraist. This elusiveness must also have characterized his relations with other Hebrew men of letters in the social realm beyond the written word, for he was asked toward the end of his life for an autobiographical statement that was subsequently included in the volume of his collected verse. The essay tells us a great deal in a factual way about Schwartz's early education and comparatively little about his later life.

Schwartz was born in Zismir, a town near Vilna in Lithuania, in 1876. His mother gave birth to ten children, five of whom survived to adulthood. His father was not only learned in traditional Torah studies but was also conversant with midrash and medieval Jewish philosophy; he also read modern Hebrew literature, with a particular interest in science. By the time Schwartz was eleven, he was expert in a number of tractates of the Talmud and capable of solving complex scholarly problems. During the next several years, he was sent to board at *yeshivot* in Lithuania run by relatives. He ended up learning on his own in a *kloyz* in Kovno for much of the 1890s, and it was during this period that Schwartz, after the manner of Brenner, Gnessin, and many other Talmud prodigies of his generation, set out on a course of illicit reading that led to a break with the traditional trajectory of his life. He learned Russian, read the Hebrew press, devoured the literature of the Haskalah, read widely in the sciences and world history, became a devoted disciple first of Herzl and then of Aḥad Haʿam, attended Zionist meetings in Kovno, and, swept up in the heady events of the time, began to write Hebrew and Yiddish poetry.

Early in the fall of 1901, Schwartz arrived in New York with the hopes of making a living as a literary editor for a Yiddish newspaper, a career option that he quickly realized was far from being practicable. Together with a friend who had preceded him to America by several years, Schwartz set up a private Hebrew school, a talmud torah, acquired pupils and used the meager proceeds to support himself while he attained the equivalent of a high school education. Shortly afterward, he obtained a regular position in a Hebrew school on the strength of a letter from Aḥad Haʿam praising his poems and promising to publish them in *Hashiloah*, the most prestigious journal of the era, although their publication never in fact came about. While continuing to teach to support himself, Schwartz gained admission to medical school and worked under conditions of privation and exhaustion to complete his education. Amidst the vulgarity and ignorance of immigrant Jewish life, Schwartz found an island of sanity in the stirrings of Hebraist activity connected to the founding of the Agudat Mefitsei Sefat Ever, the association for the dissemination of the Hebrew language. It was in the lectures and outings of these "Hebrew" youth that he most came alive.

After obtaining his medical degree in 1906, Schwartz settled in the Borough Park neighborhood in Brooklyn, which was then far from being the seat of the ultra-Orthodox that it is today, and developed a busy general practice. In 1908 he married the daughter of the famous Zionist orator Rabbi Zvi Hirsch Mazliansky. In his spare hours, he read literature, some in English and a great deal in Hebrew, and pursued glimmers of ideas for poems when they presented themselves in his rushing from patient to patient. When the Hebraist activity heated up in New York during World War I, Schwartz became a regular contributor of poems to *Hatoren*, *Miqlat*, and *Hado'ar* and a participant on the boards of various Hebrew educational and cultural institutions.

After settling into his steady work as a physician and his occasional work as a Hebrew poet, Schwartz's brief chronicle comes to an end, even though the next forty years were to see his poetic production increase several fold. It is a chronicle that is generous, if conventionalized, in its account of a young Talmudist's attraction to the new Hebrew literature yet reticent about what it meant to heed the calling of Hebrew poetry in the New World. There are also significant omissions. Schwartz does not mention Israel Jacob Schwartz, his younger brother by nine years who followed him to America in 1906. The younger Schwartz was a prominent member of the Di Yunge, the circle of Yiddish modernists in New York. He translated voluminously from Hebrew to Yiddish, especially the works of Bialik, and is best known for his *Kentucky*, an important epic poem in Yiddish about the adaptation of Lithuanian Jews to rural America.[2]

Now, while it is difficult to discover anything of Schwartz's lived life in his poetry, it is not impossible to discover there something of his spiritual life, if only obliquely. Scattered throughout Schwartz's poetic oeuvre are poems about biblical figures apprehended in a moment of heightened awareness. It is not farfetched to see in these highlighted experiences points of projection and identification that reflect on Schwartz's own sense of what, at root, defines existence. Consider, for example, Schwartz's 1916 poem "Moshe bamidbar" [Moses in the desert], which imagines Moses' thoughts in the moments before he comes upon the burning bush.[3] Reflecting on the magnificence of the desert sunset, Moses wonders about the purpose of this natural beauty if evil and oppression reign in the world and stormy emotions and ambitions rage in his heart. The wondrous fire that alights on the bush comes, in this telling, not as an unbidden spur to Moses' curiosity but as a direct response to his urgent appeal to God to reveal Himself and give some sign of the meaning of existence.

The biblical Ruth, in a poem of that name from 1918 (pp. 43–46), is apprehended by Schwartz at the lowest ebb in her fortunes. Widowed and impoverished, she gleans amid the alien corn at the moment when the Judean landscape blushes with its greatest splendor and abundance. As she stoops to scrounge for forgotten stalks, her mind is flooded with memories of the beauty of her native Moab and the warm embrace of her lost family. In the frozen frame of the poet, there is no redeemer yet in sight, and Ruth's loneliness is unremitting; it is the speaker of the poem, vouchsafed a retrospective knowledge of what is to come, who addresses Ruth and urges her to remain constant, assuring her that her ordeal will not be for naught. In "Biktseh ha'areimah" [By the edge of the haystack] (pp. 175–78), a companion piece written twenty-five years later, Schwartz returns to the same fields but shifts the focus to Boaz. After having awakened him from his sleep and to his responsibilities, Ruth is now asleep at his feet while he remains wakefully alert and agitated as he contemplates the sudden prospect of his life being transformed. Boaz is a middle-aged man of substance whose passions and ambitions are behind him, and in the presence of Ruth's Moabite beauty, he wonders whether he is capable of reentering the life of the senses, becoming again a husband and a father and thereby seizing his new destiny.

There are many others. There is a tormented Jeremiah in the pit (1908, pp. 47–49) struggling between his rage against the people's iniquities and the empathic awareness of the calamitous suffering that will soon be their fate. There is Abraham at the end of the three-day journey to Moriah, pausing in a moment of tenderness to take the burden of the wood from Isaac's shoulders onto his own before marching on to the terrible conclusion of his mission (1937, pp. 97–99). Against the stillness of the night after the holiday festivities have died down, Hannah's roiled heart rages before she pleads before God in Eli's presence (1939, p. 117). In her death throes, Rachel regains consciousness just long enough to glimpse the beauty of the boy she has just given birth to (1940, pp. 122–23). We encounter Joseph and his thoughts about his uncertain destiny at the moment a rope is thrown to him and he is pulled up from the pit (n.d., pp. 298–300).

Each of these poems enacts a kind of midrashic intervention in which an otherwise unmarked or unnarrated moment in the biblical story is selected and dilated. In the introspective space opened by these moments, we are shown men and women in the grips of a radical opposition between the resplendent beauty of the natural world and the experience of injustice and suffering. These biblical figures, in Schwartz's reframing of them, become a junction at which the irreconcilable codes of nature and morality meet and collide.[4]

This conflict is the matrix of Schwartz's poetry. This duality was pointed out by Halkin in his generous afterword to the collected poems, and he offers it as a rubric for understanding the development of Schwartz's poetry from early to late.[5] During the first third of Schwartz's career, in Halkin's argument, the poetry is open to embracing the transient beauty of the created world, although the tragic awareness of suffering is always present. The latter becomes prominent from the 1930s onward, although the appreciative responsiveness to nature never entirely disappears. There is much to recommend in Halkin's approach to the shape of Schwartz's poetic career, and in the following analysis I try to sharpen and deepen the terms he proposed and advance a complimentary argument. Not only was Schwartz increasingly overwhelmed by the pathos of history but this awareness forced him to abandon the lyric for the ballad, in a manner that parallels the trajectory of many other American Hebrew poets.

Schwartz's lyrical moment is epitomized in his use of the word *yif'ah*, a term for splendor or beauty that occurs in the Hebrew Bible only in chapter 28 of Ezekiel (vv. 7 and 17).[6] Schwartz was not alone among the poets of his generation in his attraction to this term and to the elongated guttural sensuality that set it apart from *yofi*, the everyday word for prettiness, and gave it a nuance of symbolist exoticism. When in the poem discussed just above, Moses is confused by the contradiction between the magnificent desert sunset and his internal turmoil, he asks God "What is the purpose of all this splendor [*yif'ah*]?" (p. 14), as if *yif'ah* stood for the entire category of natural beauty. The term also appears in "Nahar dinur" [River of light] (1916, pp. 16–17), a key early poem whose declamatory tone makes its something of an anthem. In tones that dance between neo-platonic Kabbalah and Walt Whitman, the poem proclaims that we are born out of the effulgence of divine light and the symphonic thunder of creation. Until "we die in song"—we are mortal in the face of the eternity of the beautiful—our senses are intoxicated and exalted by the splendor [*yif'ah*] of the world. "Nahar dinur" is written in an ecstatic register, and it is only the plastic resourcefulness of Schwartz's high Hebrew that keeps the poem from imploding under the pressure of so much exaltation.

The register is considerably modulated in the best of Schwartz's nature poems, such as "Beharim" [In the mountains] (1923, 1925; pp. 52–57), a suite of four poems on the theme of sunset. Unlike other American Hebrew poets, who are drawn to genius of a particular place such as the Catskill Mountains, Schwartz presents a generalized landscape that serves chiefly as the occasion for sensuous experience and philosophical contemplation. The third and fourth poems of the sequence provide a sharp illustration of the fundamental duality in Schwartz's poetry. The third poem (pp. 54–56), whose first line begins "'*anugah veyafah*," presents the setting sun as if it were a fabulous diva whose prolonged death throes are the stuff of the greatest drama. The poem is unabashedly romantic in portraying the sun as a majestic queen and unabashedly, though unprovocatively, Hellenic after the manner of Tchernichovsky's aesthetic paganism, in revering this heavenly body without any pretense of adopting the accoutrements of Judaic piety.[7]

The premise of the poem is the infinite generosity of the sun toward man at the moment of its death, which, as the cold loneliness of night approaches, is a moment of maximum anxiety. Rather than wanly expiring, the sun in her decline bestows her most magnificent gifts. (The feminine gender of *shemesh* [sun] is crucial to the poem.) Her rays caress rather than scorch; her visible outline at the horizon is a visage that radiates serenity and comfort. The blues and purples of the sunset are the royal vestments she voluntarily relinquishes, along with her jewels, to delight and console man at this point of difficult transition when the world is *mityatem mezivah*, "orphaned of her splendor." In an act of sacrificial suicide, she breaks herself down into radiant particles so that she can offer a final burst of illumination even after she drops over the horizon. The poem concludes with an *ars poetica* gesture. The sun's departing rays not only sweeten the sadness of the oncoming night, but they also perform an act on insemination: They enter the receptive soul of the poet like "seeds of golden dreams."

Surely this anthropomorphized picture of the munificence of nature risks verging over into honeyed pedanticism. Yet, remarkably, the rich resourcefulness of Schwartz's literary language keeps the poem just on this side of parody and succeeds in luxuriating in the conceit and maintaining an elegiac tone of sacrificial grandeur. It is an example of the kind of classical poetic practice that the American Hebrew poets were capable of in their best moments. The beneficence exuded by the poem, however, is a mood that, by any real accounting of existence, cannot stand alone. In "Bein hashemashot" [Twilight] (1925, pp. 56–57), a poem written two years later but placed immediately following in the collected poems, Schwartz lays open the contradiction between the human and the natural. After savoring the interplay of colors in the sunset as the mountains repose into serenity, the poem turns on a dime and declares:

וַאֲנִי – בְּלְבָבִי צוֹעֲקִים מַכְאוֹבַי הַיְשָׁנִים
עַל חֲלוֹמוֹת-נַעַר, תִּקְווֹת זֹהַר שֶׁהִכְזִיבוּ שָׁנִים,
עַל אַפְסוּת חַיֵּי-רִיק מִתְנַדְּפִים וְעַל תְּפִלּוֹת-תֹּם
שֶׁשָּׁוְא הִתְפַּלֵּל בִּי הַלֵּב אֶל קֹדֶשׁ וְאֶל רוֹם.

But as for me, in my heart scream the old pains
of youthful dreams and golden hopes that the years have
    disappointed,
of the nothingness of wasted life and of the innocent prayers
that my heart vainly prayed to the holy and the exalted. (p. 57)

The poem concludes with an address to the sunset, imploring it to vouchsafe to his turbulent soul something of its sacred serenity.

The appeal is moving and authentically felt, but the very fact of its being voiced acknowledges the persistence of an unbridgeable distance. Here we approach the hinge described by Halkin, which swings backward in time in the direction of the jouissance of nature and aesthetic experience and forward toward an absorption in the tragic facticity of history. In "Bein hashemashot," to be sure, the turmoil is still located within the individual soul. But as time goes on, the conflict inside will be externalized and fused with the pathos of history. For a decade after the mid-1920s, when the two poems just discussed were written, Schwartz continued to write some of his finest nature poems, including "Hatsevi" [The deer] (1933, pp. 70–71), which will be analyzed below; "Dagah qetanah" [Little fish] (1934, pp. 75–77); and "Hayofi ha'aharon" [The last beauty] (1936, pp. 83–85).

The turn toward the pathos of history requires a new form of poetic writing, and Schwartz finds the objective correlative he needs in the ballad and in other forms of verse that tell a story. Although Schwartz wrote lyric poems until his death, the narrative poem became the dominant vehicle for his most successful poems from the 1940s forward, a period during which, as Halkin pointed out, Schwartz's poetic production far exceeded that of his earlier years. One of the best texts in which to see this process taking shape is "Bein holim" [Among the sick] (1941, pp. 134–35).

בֵּין חוֹלִים

בֵּין חוֹלִים בְּהִתְהַלְּכִי כְּתמוֹל שִׁלְשׁוֹם: כּוֹאֵב
עַל סוּזִי הַשַּׁתְקָנִית הָעֲדִינָה,
שֶׁמִּתּוֹךְ רְזוֹן פָּנֶיהָ חֵן יַלְדוּתִי רוֹעֵף,
אַךְ לְבֶן־דָּמָהּ חָתַם אֶת גְּזַר־דִּינָהּ;

שָׂמֵחַ מְאֹד בְּבַת הַצְּחוֹק עַל שִׂפְתֵי לֵאָה
שֶׁנִּרְדְּמָה מֵחֹם שָׁבוּעַ תָּמִים,
וְאִם מַחֲלַת לִבָּהּ מַחֲלַת־תָּמִיד וְאֵין גֵּהָה,
אִם רַק תִּזָּהֵר אוּלַי תַּאֲרִיךְ יָמִים;

שְׂבַע רָצוֹן, כִּי כְבָר חָדַל שְׁפִיגֶל בֶּן הַשִּׁבְעִים
מֵהָקִיא דָם וְתֵאָבוֹן־אֹכֶל שָׁב לוֹ,
כִּי אֵין כָּל גָּדוֹל בִּיש בַּקֵּבָה לוֹ, רַק כִּיבִים,
שֶׁלְּהַגְלִידָם כֹּחַ רוֹפֵא רַב לוֹ;

מִתְעַכֵּב אֵצֶל שָׁנוּר, הַבָּחוּר עֲמֹק הָעַיִן,
חַחוֹלֵם אוֹר, אַךְ נִרְפַּשׁ דַּם לְבָבוֹ,
הַשּׁוֹאֵל: "דַּק', הַלָּקוּם לִי לֹא בָּא עֲדַיִן
הַתּוֹר?" אֲנִי מְשַׁקֵּר: "עוֹד מְעַט וְיָבוֹא!" —

יֵשׁ פִּתְאֹם אֲשֶׁר אֶעֱמֹד אֶשְׁמַע הִרְהוּר כָּלוּא,
הַלּוֹחֵשׁ לִי בַּלֵּב וְכֻלּוֹ לוֹעֵג:
"בַּחוּט הַשְּׂעָרָה כָּל הָעוֹלָם כֻּלּוֹ תָּלוּי
עַל עֶבְרֵי תְהוֹם אֲבַדּוֹן שׁוֹאֵג —

וְאַתָּה פֹּה כְּמְנַחֵשׁ גּוֹרָל שׁ"י עוֹלָמוֹת,
בֵּין פַּחַד וּבֵין תִּקְוָה רַבָּה מְרַחֵף,
בְּמֹאזְנֵי רוֹפְאִים תִּשְׁקֹל: הַיִחְי אוֹ יָמוּת
שְׁבַע יָמִים, עֵיֵף חַיִּים שֶׁנִּסְתַּתֵּף.

וְתִשְׂמַח מְאֹד אִם חַרְסֵי-אָדָם הָעֲזוּבִים
תֵּאָחֶה בְּרֹב עָמָל עוֹד לִכְלִי,
הַטּוֹב לְהָכִיל מִסְפַּר נִטְפֵי חַיִּים גְּנוּבִים
בְּטֶרֶם יְנַפְּצֵהוּ גּוֹרָל פֶּלְאִי,

וּמַה לְּמַכְאוֹב לְבָרְךָ פְּנִימָה, מַה לַּדִּמְעָה
עַל חוֹלֵם אוֹר שֶׁעוֹד מְעַט וְנָדָם,
עַל יַלְדַּת חֵן שֶׁעוֹד מְעַט תֹּאכְלֶנָּה רִמָּה,
אִם עוֹד מְעַט וְאָבַד כָּל הָאָדָם?

Among the Sick

I walk among the sick as I have in the past:
Quiet and delicate Susie is in pain.
Her emaciated face exudes childlike grace,
But her white blood cells have sealed her fate.

I am cheered by the smile on the lips of Leah,
Who has been dozing with fever for an entire week,
Although her heart disease is chronic and incurable,
If she only takes care she may perhaps live long.

I'm satisfied with seventy-year-old Speigel, who has already stopped
Spitting up blood and recovered his appetite,
The growths in his stomach are not malignant but only ulcers,
Which medicine can treat.

I pause beside Schnur, a deep-eyed youth,
Who dreams of light although his blood is occluded,
Asking me, "Doc, Isn't it already my turn to get up?"
I lie: "In a little while you will."

Sometimes suddenly I stop and hear a repressed thought
That mockingly whispers in my heart:
"The whole world hangs by a hair
Over the screaming depths of the abyss—"

You are here like someone who is divining the fate of hidden
        worlds
And fluttering between dread and great hope,
In the physician's balance you weigh out whether one will live
        or die
Full of days, tired of life that has been swept away.

And you are pleased if, with great effort,
You can piece back together again
The scattered shards of the human vessel
So that it is capable of containing some stolen drops of life
Before the mystery of fate shatters it?

And what about the pain inside your heart, what about the tear
For the dreamer of light who will soon be extinguished,
For the charming girl who will soon be eaten by worms,
If soon all mankind will perish?

This poem is distinctive because it is the only poem in the whole of
Schwartz's canon in which he reflects on, or even alludes to, his vocation as a medical doctor. The premise is patient rounds in the hospital
of the sort made day in and day out by the speaker-physician of the
poem. The first four of the poem's eight quatrains register both the
medical situation of the patients and the speaker's empathic relation to
them. He is pained by Susie's pallor, which is a sign that her prospects
are not good; he is cheered by the smile on Leah's lips and thinks that,
despite her heart condition, she may have a chance at long life if she
takes care; he is satisfied that Spiegel has stopped coughing blood and
does not have a malignancy; and pausing by the bed of Schnur, whose
blood disease is incurable, he lies and assures the patient that soon he
will be getting well.

    In the midst of this daily routine, the speaker is suddenly brought
up short by a mocking voice within him that coolly declares: "The
whole world hangs by a hair over the screaming depths of the abyss."
At a stroke, the whole edifice that was built up in the first four

stanzas—a world of sagely informed empathy for patients with proper names and individual histories—is brought down by a piercing skepticism. The very solidness of the speaker's identity as a physician begins to melt away as he realizes how flimsy is his art compared with the intractable forces of corruption and death. Tossed between dread and hope, he acknowledges that the most he can hope for is "with great effort, / You can piece back together again / The scattered shards of the human vessel / So that it is capable of containing some stolen drops of life / Before the mystery of fate shatters it?" (p. 135). Whereas the first four quatrains of the poem are written in the first person, in the concluding set the speaker addresses himself as "you," as if the self that is being addressed is slipping away over an unbridgeable distance. The final stanza asks the question: "And what of the pain inside your heart?" What is he to do with his feelings about a lovely girl who, despite the application of his craft, is about to die, or "even if soon every man should perish?"

The strained tether between the two halves of "Ben holim" is a good introduction to the late major phase of Schwartz's poetry. The vignettes of the individual patients in the first half are related with empathy and restraint, whereas the inward reflection in the second half initiates a cascading movement of doubt that opens onto an endless vista of pessimism. In the important later poems, the former is contained and the latter developed and elaborated. In what amounts to an act of poetic *tsimtsum*, Schwartz asserts control over his corrosive doubts and self-vitiating pessimism to make room for the stories of others. These fiercely chaotic thoughts are neither renounced nor dissipated but rather kept behind the scenes or at the margins where they are harnessed to provide narrative energy and urgency. The vignettes of the patients function in the poem as kernels of fuller narratives that are suggested but remain untold. It is these kernels that Schwartz will germinate in his ballads and narrative poems.

In the turn from lyric to narrative, Schwartz joins a general movement in American Hebrew poetry. Yet for Schwartz—like Ginzburg—the American dimension of this shift is minor. Indian myths, Negro spirituals, and rural types do not interest him, nor does the evocation of place. Several of the longer poems do in fact deal with America, but America of a very different sort. "Avraham megahets kutnot" [Abraham the clothes presser] (1938, pp. 100–104), for example, is an effectively tender poem that describes the quiet dignity of an aging garment worker who decides to live by himself after his wife dies rather than move in with his Americanized children. "Matayim veḥamishim" [Two hundred and fifty] (1945, pp. 179–82) describes the send-off of a group of young men from the speaker's neighborhood, Jews and non-Jews and many known to him, who are being drafted into the U.S. army during the last year of World War II. These are rare glimpses into the pathos of first- and second-generation urban immigrant Jewish life of the sort one expects more from the American Hebrew fiction of Reuven Wallenrod than from American Hebrew poetry with its pastoral bias.

The main subject of Schwartz's best narrative poems is the Holocaust. Lisitzky, Efros, and Bavli, among other American Hebrew poets, wrote voluminously about the destruction of European Jewry. Many of their counterparts in Eretz Yisrael, Uri Zvi Greenberg excepted, had a conflicted relationship to this subject because of the dialectics of Zionist ideology and the focus on the fate of the Yishuv. The American Hebrew poets experienced no such ambivalence, and the channels of both empathy and rage flowed without impedance. Two of the finest examples of Schwartz's endeavors in this area are "Qol ḥatan veqol kallah" [The voice of the bridegroom and the voice of the bride] (1947, pp. 193–200) and "Harav vehadayan" [The Rabbi and the dayan] (1949, pp. 222–28).

"Qol ḥatan veqol kallah" is the story of a wedding that takes place shortly after the war in a displaced persons (DP) camp near Nuremberg. Yehuda Balaban of Lodz is marrying Hanna Stein of Warsaw, the younger sister of Yehuda's wife Rivka, who perished together with his children. The community of survivors toils to give the couple their moment of joy amid the general emotional wreckage, although their efforts nearly fail when the memories of loss can no longer be held at bay. Now, this is a dramatic premise that is inherently fraught with sentiment, and Schwartz uses a number of means to maintain the intensity without giving way to mawkishness. The narrative mood of the ballad, to begin with, subsumes the scene within the gestures of storytelling. The events are told by an anonymous chronicler, who, though clearly sympathetic, maintains an objective reportorial distance. The poem is cast in long lines of rhymed couplets with each couplet standing as a separate stanza. The rhymed couplets have the effect not only of poeticizing the drama and marking it as a literary rendering but also of creating a regular rhythm that works against the swelling of feeling. Moreover, the semantic register of the poem's language is far lower than much of Schwartz's earlier verse, especially his biblical poems and nature poems. The language is familiar, spare, and communicative as if the least eloquence would break the pressure seal containing these heartrending events.

The emotional spring of "Qol ḥatan veqol kallah" is wound very tight and after it bursts, the poem is set onto a different track. The opening exposition describes the personal circumstances of the bride and groom and the diligent labors of the survivor community in the DP camp, patching their clothes and scrounging for wine and candles. At each stage of preparation, the gap grows between the present cause for celebration and the unspeakable losses that loom in the background. The memories from Yehuda's first wedding, celebrated in unalloyed joy and naturalness, threaten to overwhelm him. The bride is grateful for her veil so that her abundant tears are not visible. While maintaining the restrained tone of the chronicler, the poem's narrator notes the situation of other characters as well. Regarding Rabbi David, the prayer leader from Plotsk, who conducts the ceremony under the improvised ḥuppah, it is said as an aside, in passing: "a playful breeze frolics with the ashes of his wife and daughter on the fields of Majdanek."[8]

The spring is finally sprung when Yehuda hears the words of the blessing that compares the joy of the wedding couple to the joy of Adam and Eve in the Garden of Eden. He hears the comparison as an absurd mockery of his fate, and he can no longer hold back his tears. For a few crucial moments, his breakdown triggers a general collapse into weeping until the final liturgical moment of the ceremony, the breaking of the glass, returns the assembled to the present moment and induces them to throw themselves into the celebration. The final turn in the poem's narrative is subtle but unexpected. We are suddenly introduced to a Lieutenant Herbert Ploster of the Bronx from a neighboring U.S. army base, who has brought for the wedding guests kosher salami and brandy sent to him by his mother. He ministers to the celebrants and joins their dances. The figure of Lt. Ploster serves no apparent function in the story, but he provides Schwartz with an American lens through which to focalize the drama and place the American Hebrew reader inside the frame of the picture.

"Qol ḥatan veqol kallah" ends with an emotionally charged moment of recoupment: "Happy is the eye that saw that rejoicing and dancing" (p. 200). The happy eye [*ashrei 'ayin shera'atah*] invokes no less an image than that of the high priest emerging unscathed from the Holy of Holies in the Yom Kippur liturgy. "Harav vehadayan," in contrast, is forbiddingly devoid of comfort. There is no American moment to frame the narrative, which Schwartz provocatively locates within the evil center of the Holocaust kingdom. The setting, which is the *Selektion* of Jews of the Lithuanian town of Slonim—whether before deportation or upon arrival at a camp is not clear—serves only as a backdrop for a theological dialogue between Rabbi David Hakohen, the town's distinguished rabbi, and Noah, his former student and now its *dayan*. This is a poem of theodicy that partakes in the tradition associated with Rabbi Levi Yitzhak of Berditchev and taken up during the same years—the poem is dated 1949—in the Holocaust poetry of Uri Zvi Greenberg and in some of the Yiddish fiction of Chaim Grade. In contrast to the modest and deflated linguistic register of the poem set in the DP camp, here the language of Rabbi David's speeches represents the rich Hebrew of a scholar speaking in passionate extremity. The poem is also composed in rhymed couplets, although the lines are shorter and the couplets do not stand on their own but are absorbed in long stanzaic paragraphs.

The armature of the poem is the traditional scholarly practice of posing a question and formulating an answer. In the eye of the atrocity, Rabbi Noah turns to his beloved and esteemed teacher in Torah asks him to make sense of the spectacle unfolding before him: the torture and annihilation of the learned and pious. Have we sinned so perfidiously, he asks, that we have been so punished? Must we therefore not make confession and pray to the Lord? In responding to his cherished student, Rabbi David is faced with the prospect of offering soothing words of consolation that he, Rabbi David, knows to be false. He decides that, despite the spiritual pain he will cause, he cannot in this hour of truth on the brink of death withhold the truth (p. 224). He proceeds to explain to Rabbi Noah how he has been transformed. He is no longer the paragon of faith who interceded for his flock before heaven on the Day of Atonement but rather a man with a lacerated soul who now better resembles Elisha ben Abuya, the famous first-century apostate rabbi who declared: "hefker ha'olam!" signifying that the world is a moral chaos with no divine supervision (p. 225).

The poem is unsparing on many counts. Rabbi David takes the idea of punishment for sin raised by Rabbi Noah and subjects it to unremitting scorn. He catalogues the piety and modesty of his flock in comparison with the excesses of the gentile culture in which they live and concludes scornfully, "I cannot believe that Israel has sinned / such that it should be torn by the claws of Samael!" (p. 227). The rhyming of *yisra'el* and *sama'el* provides the provocative closure for this section. There is no temporizing either theologically or rhetorically. Schwartz could have allowed Rabbi David to encounter a God who had hidden his face from Israel and burrowed deep within the mystery of *hester panim*; he could have authorized the appeal to such a God, even rage against divine injustice. But there can be no dialogue, however one-sided, because God has been erased. In place of spiritual resistance, Rabbi David experiences only disillusion: "We have been mistaken together with our forefathers! There is no Judge and no moral law!" (p. 227). The pathos of the negation is generated by the fact that this is a statement that is not directed toward heaven but uttered within the relationship between the two rabbis, in which the disappointing of the younger colleague by the older is perhaps the saddest thing of all.

Although this is the only one of Schwartz's longer poems to ingress upon the concentrationary universe, most of the others register echoes of the calamity. "Ḥagigat nitsaḥon" [Victory celebration] (1946, pp. 186–87) describes how the celebration of the war's end among American Jews is subverted by the unspoken knowledge of the enormity of the loss. "Be'irati ein ḥogegim" [In my town there is no celebrating] (1946, pp. 191–92) renders that loss palpable by cataloguing all of the preparations for the Sukkot holiday that are *no longer* being made in the speaker's native town. In "Ba'avor nezirah" [A nun passes by] (1947, pp.203–7), the sight of a nun recalls to the speaker's mind the presence of Christianity in his Lithuanian childhood. "Sefer torah misham" [A Torah scroll from over there] (1951, pp. 235–39) describes the mixture of joy and mourning that attend the installation of a Torah scroll saved from the European destruction. All of these are strong and controlled poems that reward attention.

Of all the figures in this volume, Schwartz, for a variety of reasons, is perhaps the most buried. He is an example of a figure who, despite his resistance of modernism, produced no small number of highly affecting poems. His work deserves to be better known.

❋ הַצְּבִי
The Deer

Analysis

הַצְּבִי

עַל שְׂפַת הַבִּקְעָה, אֵצֶל חֹרֶשׁ יָרֹק־כֵּהֶה,
הוּא עָמַד, סוֹקֵר אֶת הַנּוֹף וְעֵר וְגֵאֶה,
וְקַל, וְנָכוֹן לְהִנָּתֵק בְּכָל שָׁעָה
מִמְּקוֹמוֹ, לָשׁוּב לִרְעוֹת חָפְשִׁי בַּאֲשֶׁר רָעָה . . .

אֲדַמְדַּם־זְהוּב הַגֵּו, — בְּלֹבֶן אַחַר שְׁקִיעָה
שַׁלְהֶבֶת־שַׁחַר חַיָּה נָעֲצָה אֶת אִיָּהּ;
בְּכָל עַצְמוֹתָיו רַעַד־חַיִּים תּוֹסֵס עָצוּר, —
כְּרַעַד קוֹפֵא לְנִגְהוֹת־סוֹף־הַבָּצִיר;

צַוָּארוֹ הַמְחֻטָּב — קֶשֶׁת רוֹמָה דְרוּכָה,
וְרֹאשׁוֹ — מִגְדָּל מַקְרִין רַב עִם שְׁמֵי הַמְּנוּחָה . . .
וְלִי — מְשִׁיבַת עוֹלָם כַּאֲשֶׁר עָלַי נִגְלָה,
וְעֵינִי אֶת תִּפְאַרְתּוֹ הַקְּלִילָה רָגְלָה, —

בִּלְבָבִי הָיוּ מִלִּים לוֹ: הַצְּבִי, מַחֲמַדִּי,
עֲמֹד, אַל תִּירָא, צְבִי! אָנֹכִי פֹּה לְבַדִּי,
וַאֲנִי אֵינֶנִּי רוֹבֶה קַשָּׁת, וְלֹא צַיָּד . . .
יָצָאתִי רַק לִרְאוֹת אֶת נִפְלְאוֹת הַסַּיָּד,

הַסָּד אֶת כָּל הָעוֹלָם כֻּלּוֹ בְּמִכְחוֹלוֹ,
הַמְזָרֶה רְשָׁתוֹת לְבָנוֹת עַל מִשְׁעוֹלוֹ . . .
יָצָאתִי עִם הָעֶרֶב נִכְסָף לִרְאוֹת אוֹתְךָ,
וְחֻלְדַּת־סְנָאִים מְאַחֶרֶת צֵאת כְּמוֹתְךָ . . .

אַךְ הוּא, הַצְּבִי, הוּא שָׁמַע רַק אֶת קוֹל הַצְּעָדָה,
הוּא רָאָה לְעֵינַיִם, רָאָה, – וּבִרְעָדָה
אֶת רֹאשׁוֹ הֵסֵב אָחוֹר, וּבְקַלֵּי־קַלּוֹת
הִזְדַּקֵּר אֶל הַיַּעַר בִּקְפִיצוֹת עֲקַלְקַלּוֹת . . .

The Deer

At the edge of the valley by the dark green wood,
He stood surveying the landscape, alert and proud,
Fleet and ready in a moment to cut and run
From his place to return to where he grazed freely . . .

The red-gold of his back! Against the whiteness of the sunset
A vital dawn flare inserted its lone self;
All his limbs are aquiver, at once bristling and held in check,
Like goose bumps from the end-of-harvest cold.

His sculpted neck, a taut Roman arch,
His head, a great tower radiating in the tranquil heavens . . .
Yet as for me, grey-headed when he was revealed to me,
and my eye espying his lithe magnificence,

These words were in my heart: Oh deer, my delightful one,
Stay still, fear not, oh deer! I am here alone,
I carry no bow nor am I a hunter . . .
I have come outside only to see the glories of the Painter,

Who paints the whole world with his brush,
And scatters white netting upon its path. . . .
I have come outside at evening time longing to see you,
You little late-arriving squirrel . . .

But that one, the deer, he heard only the sound of my footfall,
He saw into my eyes, and seeing, with a shudder
Turned his head backward, and with the nimblest motion
Dove into the woods with lurching leaps . . .

"Hatsevi" (pp. 71–72) was written in 1933 around the time of what we have called the hinge of Schwartz's poetic career. Stylistically, it occupies a medial position between the extravagance of the nature poems of the 1920s and the lower register of the narrative poems from the late 1930s and forward. The poem realizes, and usefully recalls to our attention, many of the elements of what we think of as the lyric experience. It attempts to render a concentrated verbal representation of the emotional and aesthetic impact of a unique occurrence. The occurrence is an encounter with the natural world that brings into play—both thematizing and problematizing—the rapport between the "soul of the world" [*anima mundi*] and the soul of the poet. The poem is constituted, in a deliberately tautological sense, by the speech of the speaker. This is speech which, even if it is addressed to a human or non-human subject, is essentially solitary and reflexive; it is the privileged position of the reader to "overhear" this speech of the self.

A regularly organized poem of six quatrains, "Hatsevi" would seem at first glance to divide its attention evenly between, first, the figure of the deer, and, second, the affective response of the speaker-observer. The presumption of symmetry is tampered with slightly but significantly when the speaker suddenly and emphatically turns the attention to himself in line 11, just before the poem's midpoint, thereby revealing an urgency that cannot quite restrain itself.

Just as the speech of the lyric poem is overheard, so the deer that appears in the clearing in the poem's opening lines is observed in a stolen moment without knowing it is being observed. The picture of the deer drawn by the unseen observer, who is presumably the poem's speaker, tells us as much about what the observer finds fascinating as about the "objective" features of the animal. This fascination flows from the privilege of glimpsing a shy wild creature close up. The deer pauses to survey the countryside before loping off to graze at its liberty in reaches beyond human gaze. Everything about the deer—the exquisite alertness, the suppleness of movement, the hair-trigger readiness to bolt and run—underscores the privileged and unnatural nature of this momentary stasis. Here at the opening of the poem, the experience of glimpsing something extraordinary is marked positively as a source of simple wonderment. By the close of the poem, however, when the deer does in fact bolt and run, leaving an acute feeling of abandonment in his wake, the experience will be marked quite otherwise.

The description of the deer in lines 5–10 emphasizes three sources of admiration. The first (lines 5–6) is ostensibly concerned with color; the red-gold of the deer's back stands out against the white haze of twilight like a "dawn flare." But the scene is transformed from being a decorative tableau by the assertiveness, even violence, of the verb *na'atsah* [insert, stick into]. The deer inserts or sticks his inflammatory colorfulness into the haze as if he were a vivid lone island on a drab sea. The second quality (lines 7–8) is the equipoise between power and restraint. The quivering the speaker notices throughout the deer's body is taken as a sign of a powerfully operating organism that is idling and voluntarily holding itself, at least for the moment, in abeyance. The third quality (lines 9–10) is the sculptural beauty of the deer's form, but here again a connection is made to the phenomenon of latent power. The tense arc of the deer's chiseled neck resembles a Roman arch in the sense that that architectural invention found an elegant way to keep the forces of gravity in check. The comparison of the proud head held aloft to a tower beaming messages in the tranquil skies establishes a noble and superior communion between this creature and Creation. This seemingly humble animal is connected to the cosmos in ways man can never hope to be.

Taken on its own terms as a sharply etched poetic rendering of an encounter with the natural world, Schwartz's description of the deer is very accomplished and a fine example of the craft of poetry. Yet for the Hebrew reader, there is another dimension. In the elegant Hebrew poetry composed during the Golden Age in Spain, the *tsevi*, often translated more romantically as the "gazelle," is a standard epithet for the ephebe, the beautiful boy who arouses the (male) observer's admiration and unrequited desire. Whether the *tsevi* is merely a literary topos or a figure that reflects actual homosexual relations is a question debated by scholars; but there is no doubt that within this genre of medieval Hebrew poems, there are strong homoerotic currents of feeling.[9] Schwartz's deer is, first and foremost, of the common American variety glimpsed most likely in the foothills of the Catskills rather than in Andalus, the native habitat of Golden Age Hebrew poets and their gazelles. Yet an awareness of the topos of the *tsevi* points to the fact that the speaker's fascination with the deer has inescapable erotic currents. The animal, we are reminded, is a *tsevi* and not a *tseviyah*, a buck and not a doe. The speaker is captivated by the spectacle of grace fused with power in its carnal embodiment. He is attracted not only to the beauty of the animal's form but also to the enormous force held in check in the animal's quivering muscles.

The abrupt shift in perspective that takes place with line 11—again, slightly before the poem's midpoint—is palpable in several ways. At the level of the poem's rhetoric, to begin with, the moment initiates eight lines (13–20) of direct address as opposed to the discursive description of the invisible speaker of the poem. Although these are words that are not voiced aloud but remain in the heart, the speaker is emphatic about the words in fact being uttered and directed to the animal as addressee. The content of the speech reveals a rush of agitated feelings that takes the form of an apologia. He labors to assure the deer that, unlike other human forms the animal is likely to encounter in these parts, he is not a hunter—he carries no weapons, he poses no threat. He asserts two reasons for his presence, and the order in which they are presented reveals something about his state of mind. The first explanation is religious awe. The speaker has come out to the countryside at twilight to glimpse the wonders of God's creation, which are presented in aesthetic garb according to the familiar analogy from rabbinic literature comparing God to an artist.[10] Referring to the white haze of sunset in line 5, the speaker goes on to describe the work of the God/artist in scattering "white netting on the path." The three dots that end that line (18) in the Hebrew indicate, I would argue, that this is the kind of overwrought, even banal, poesy that could be continued ad infinitum or ad nausea.

After that line trails off, what comes in its place is perceptibly more urgent and sincere. The speaker admits that the real reason he has come out in the evening is his longing to behold this glorious animal, which he addresses with intimate affection. Here, too, the line ends with three dots, which served as an orthographic convention for indicating an unresolved or ongoing state of affairs. But in this case, the termination comes from the outside. Alerted by the step of the human intruder, the deer, in a nimble volte-face that demonstrates his unsurpassed grace, bolts and darts off. Ironically, it is only the gross human footfall that triggers the flight, not the fulsome confession that the agitated speaker has been intoning to himself.

The poem begins with a wondrous chance encounter between man and animal that at first seems to surpass the speaker's desire simply to imbibe the inspiring beauty of nature. The connection to the deer is immediate and reveals not just an aesthetic appreciation but a kind of erotic longing. In a desperate, silent soliloquy, the speaker endeavors to persuade the deer of his benevolent intentions only to see the animal dart back into the woods. The desolation that follows is Schwartz's canny take on romantic expectations. Man yearns to believe in the mutuality of his encounter with nature and to believe that in his passionate appreciation of the world, he is met by the *anima mundi*. When the deer skits off into the glade, indifferent to his needs, he is left alone with his expectations.

Seven   Hillel Bavli

Hillel Bavli (1892/3–1962) was a quiet presence in American Hebrew letters who wrote affecting lyric poetry and developed a gift later in his career for dramatic monologue and portraiture. As an editor and essayist, Bavli played an important role in promoting Hebrew literary activity in America and establishing relations with literary centers in Eretz Yisrael and Europe. As a much beloved teacher of Hebrew literature at the Teachers Institute of the Jewish Theological Seminary over many decades, Bavli instilled an appreciation of the Hebrew renaissance in several generations of Jewish educators and lay leaders.

Bavli was born in Pilvishok (now Pilviskiai), Lithuania in 1892 or 1893.[1] His father, a merchant who had studied at the Voloshin yeshivah and received rabbinic ordination, was interested both in the Haskalah and Hibbat Zion. When Bavli was sent to study in the yeshivah in Kovno after his bar mitzvah, his father requested that his son be tutored in Hebrew one hour each day. In 1909 Bavli began a three-year stay in Vilna; he supported himself by working as a secretary to a Zionist official but spent all the time he could at the Strashun Library reading modern Hebrew literature and putting himself through a self-directed program of acquiring European culture. Here he met and mingled with other displaced Jewish youths with literary ambitions and attended gatherings with Y. L. Peretz and other Hebrew and Yiddish writers. It was during these years that Bavli published his first poems in such journals as *Ha'olam* and *Ha'ivri*.

Bavli arrived in the United States in the summer of 1912. He came on his own; his parents emigrated after World War I. After stints teaching Hebrew in Buffalo, New York City, and New Britain, Connecticut,

Bavli returned to Buffalo and lived there for three years. He came to Buffalo at the invitation of Lisitzky, who was principal of a Hebrew school there. For Lisitzky, Bavli was a kindred spirit whom he wished to encourage; and for Bavli, his position in Lisitzky's school allowed him to pursue his object of acquiring a secular education and obtaining a degree from an American college. The college in question was Canisius College, a Jesuit school; Bavli felt himself both alienated from this environment and fascinated by it, and very much alone.[2]

It was around this time that Bavli adopted his name. His family name in Lithuania had been Rashgolin or Rashgolsky. The family had a tradition that they were descended from the *rosh golah*, the head of the Jewish community in Babylonia [*bavel*] during the time of the Talmud and geonim. Hence the Hebraicized name Bavli.[3]

His return to New York City in 1917, where he lived the remainder of his life, coincided with an explosion of Hebraist activity. A number of important Zionist leaders—Eliezer Ben-Yehuda, David Ben-Gurion, and Yitzhak Ben-Zvi among them—had spent the war years in New York; two major Hebrew journals, *Hatoren*[4] and *Miqlat*, were in full swing; and plans for a daily Hebrew newspaper were being discussed. If there can be said to have been a golden age of American Hebraism, it was in the six or seven years that followed. Bavli threw himself into these enterprises and became a central participant in most all of the Hebrew literary projects in America; and he stayed in for the duration, even after the fervor and high expectations had retreated. Although he was central, his modesty rarely led him to make himself the center. Under Berkovitz's tutelage at *Miqlat*, Bavli branched out from poetry and developed as a literary critic and essayist. As a critic, his sensibility was that of a sympathetic reader who prefers to appreciate rather than to denigrate; he relates to other writers as fellow communicants in the sanctuary of Hebrew literature and honors them as such.[5] Over the years, Bavli labored to mitigate the isolation of Hebrew writers in America by building bridges with the other centers of Hebrew writing. In 1923 he edited a volume called *Nimim*, which brought together the work of Hebrew writers both in America and Germany.[6] A similar collection called *Massad* attempted to create connections with writers in Palestine,[7] as did Bavli's participation in the journal *Hedim*, which was published there under the editorship of Asher Barash and Yaakov Rabinowitz.

All these years Bavli made his home at the Jewish Theological Seminary. Soon after returning to New York in 1917, Kaplan, the dean of the Seminary's Teachers Institute, recruited him to teach Hebrew language and literature; and Bavli grew with the institution as it moved from the Lower East Side to Morningside Heights. He communicated his love for Hebrew literature to several generations of students who became lay and professional leaders in the American Jewish community. The bibliography of Bavli's works, edited by E. R. Malachi after his death, was underwritten by subscription from several hundred of his students.[8]

Among the Hebrew poets in America, Bavli was assiduous in his devotion to the lyric. Unlike Lisitzky and Efros, he did not seek out epic narrative forms of poetry to express his embrace of the American vistas. He eventually grew more at home in America, and his long poem "Mrs. Woods" (1924), which is a monologue by a Yankee matriarch with bright eyes and sturdy values, justifiably became one of the best known pieces in the American Hebrew repertoire (see Part 3, Chapter 16 for a discussion of this poem). When Bavli's poetry was imbued with a sense of place, it was most likely to be the Land of Israel rather than his adopted native grounds, or as became the case later in his life, the Lithuanian shtetls of his childhood. His first journey to Palestine in 1926–27 resulted in the moving poem sequence *Neginot arets* [Melodies of the land].[9] Two later journeys furnished much material for what is a kind of contemporary continuation of the Hibbat Zion tradition. The numbered poem cycle, like *Neginot arets*, became a favorite mode of composition; this enabled Bavli to remain within the lyric while linking his poems together thematically and sequentially.[10] His main venture outside the lyric was the dramatic monologue, in the manner of Edward Arlington Robinson, who was much admired by Bavli and other American Hebrew poets. During the 1920s, in addition to "Mrs. Woods," Bavli wrote several other extended monologues;[11] and then twenty years later, he burst forth with a series of monologues spoken by figures who inhabited the Lithuanian village in which he grew up. These were gathered together in the section "Benei Lita," at the end of Bavli's second and last collection of poetry, *Aderet hashanim* [The cloak of years].[12] Although he stood and worked on American soil for most of his life, Bavli's imagination was most nurtured by his remembrance of "Lita" and his desire for Eretz Yisrael.

The debut of Bavli's autobiographical persona in fact turns on the rupture of emigration. Although a number of his poems had already appeared in periodicals, when it came to shaping his collected poems, he put those aside and made the leap from Lithuania to America into the literal point of departure for his poetic self.[13] The reader turns from the poem on page 3, which is signed "Pilvishok, 1912," to the poem on the following page, which is signed "New York, Av, 1912," and suddenly the deed has been done, the ocean traversed, as if by sleight of hand. But how wrenching is the change for the young speaker of these poems! The poem on page 3, titled "Biḥidut" [Solitary] and written in his hometown, is a poem composed on the eve of emigration. It plays on the meanings of the root *y.ḥ.d.* The speaker begins by stating that he has set apart [*yiḥadeti*] a corner of his self where his soul can dwell protected. He next commands his heart to cease its agitation and begin drawing its strength from its own resources rather than from the outside. The fateful hour of self-reckoning and self-communing [*yiḥud*] has come, and from now on the speaker will build his world on his own and from within himself [*biḥidut*]. On the eve of the great change in his life, the speaker steels himself for imminent loss by fitting out a kind of creative bunker where his essential self can survive the coming ordeal.

And there, on the next page ("Banekhar" [In a foreign land], p. 4), just arrived in New York, the onslaught of alienation hits him. One simile follows another with a pathos that seems uncontrollable: He is like a sapling that has been uprooted, like a young bird with a broken wing that has been stolen from its nest, like a man forgotten by God who is alone in the world. The fortified bunker he had so resourcefully put in place has been blown away like so much chaff, and his soul now wanders exposed and without prospect of refuge. The panic is suddenly reined in by the last stanza, when, without preparation, he makes this assertion:

וַאֲנִי יוֹדֵעַ: יָבוֹאוּ הַיָּמִים
וְשִׁירַת עַם נֵכָר עוֹד תִּשְׁבְּ גַּם לְבָבִי,
אַךְ נֶצַח יְפַעֵם וִיחִי בִי עוֹלָמִים
שִׁיר אֶרֶץ־מוֹלֶדֶת, שִׁיר אֶל אֱלֹהֵי אָבִי!

This I know: the day will come
When the song of this alien people will capture my heart.
Yet forever and always will beat within me
The song of my native land, the song of the God of my father!

The speaker's reason is mobilized to control his alarm. He knows that eventually he will reconcile himself with his new surroundings and even be drawn to their charm. But he also knows that his heart will never cease resonating with the song of his homeland and the God of his father.

The meaning of this stirring profession, seemingly so sincere and unambiguous, is not so simple. By homeland [*erets moledet*], does the speaker mean Lithuania or Erets Yisrael? Yes, he has just left the former, but for Hebrew writers in an age of Jewish nationalism, the term often denotes the new *adoptive* homeland, the birthplace of the poet's spirit rather than his body. Yet Bavli has just arrived in New York rather than Jaffa, and he cannot proceed to compare the sylvan glades of Europe with the harsh Mediterranean sun, as was the wont with newly arrived litterateurs in the Holy Land. Moreover, in contrast to those freethinking pioneers, the speaker of this poem declares his allegiance to the God of his father. Yet even this credo is not uncomplicated. His loyalty is given not to his God but to his father's God, and while this distinction does not necessarily mean that the two are different, it does underscore the mediation of the father, to whom, in fact, the poem is offered in dedication. The language complicates here as well. The Hebrew reads literally: "the God of the Gods of my father" [*el elohei avi*]. The locution, with its echoes of the liturgy and the patriarchal narratives, subtly implies a plurality of perspectives with the attending problems in the transmission of authority. Taken together, these are the ambiguities and contradictions that set the parameters of Bavli's poetic identity.[14]

The Lithuanian pole of Bavli's imagination was profoundly shaken by World War I. By 1917, five years after his arrival in America, Bavli was completing college in Buffalo and about to return to New York when he received news of the destruction of his hometown in the great waves of anti-Jewish violence that swept through Eastern Europe. The fate of his mother and father in these massacres was not yet known to him, although it turned out that they did survive and eventually joined him in America. In a pair of poems, "'Al ḥurban 'ir moledet" [On the destruction of my native town] (pp. 26–27) and "'Al gedot hasheshupe" [On the banks of the Sheshupe] (pp. 28–29), he registers the impact of the harsh news. "'Al ḥurban 'ir moledet " is framed as an ode to his town, which is at once "so far away and so close." After Bialik's extraordinary poem on the Kishinev pogrom of 1903, no Hebrew poet had an easy time finding his own approach to this theme, and Bavli was no exception.[15] Unlike Bialik, Bavli could not visit the scene of destruction, and he is left belatedly to envision in his mind's eye the acts of atrocity, the broken limbs, and the scattered corpses. The imagined catalogue of horrors, which forms the substance of the poem, is thrown off course when the speaker sees the figure of his father among the victims. The tide of blood engulfs him, his eyes darken, and, in fear for his own life, he is forced to bring his project of high mourning to a halt. Begun as a eulogy for his town, the poem circles back to become a kind of eulogy for himself. God's cruelty, he declares at the conclusion of the poem, "has exiled me far away and my nest, / my nest He has consumed upon the pyre!" As was the case with many other Hebrew writers, Bavli had now to contend in his imagination with a childhood home in Eastern Europe whose status has been suddenly and problematically transformed. The place he had *chosen* to leave behind no longer exists as a place either to abandon or to be nurtured by. The nest has been destroyed.

Bavli's relationship to Jewish tradition in his poetry was more textured and engaged than that of most of the other American Hebrew poets, and yet, in its own way, it was emblematic of a collective attitude. It is important, first of all, to identify and separate the different strands in this skein. Although more elaborate taxonomies would give us a finer-grained picture, let us for now note six general lines of relationship. The first is the realm of the *mitsvot*, Sabbath and holidays, and ritual practice, gestures, and symbols. The second is the culture of the beit midrash as famously summoned up in many of Bialik's major poems (e.g., "Hamatmid" [The Talmud student], "Lifnei aron hasefarim" [Before the bookcase], and "'Al saf beit midrash" [On the doorstep of the beit midrash]). The third is the multilayered language of allusion to biblical and rabbinic sources that characterized the poetry of the *tehiyyah* period. The fourth is the world of East European Jewry, whether city or shtetl, as a social reality that lies in the background of all of all the American Hebrew poets. The fifth is the relationship to God either as the God of history or the God of nature. The sixth is the relationship to the poet's father and mother as figures from the world of tradition.

As a group, it is fair to say as a general statement—for reasons discussed in the introduction to this study—that the American Hebrew poets generally did not engage the first four of these subjects. Bavli is exceptional in his preoccupation with the last three. The human landscape of his native Lithuania becomes a focus of his work during his mature years as a poet. God as a dialogical partner is a constant throughout his verse. And the figure of his parents, especially his father, remained a vital presence, neither wholly idealized nor wholly ironized. Like his Hebraist brethren, Bavli disburdened himself in his literary work from the weight and the claims of the culture of the beit midrash with its dense Jewish symbolism, theological struggle, and allusive language. Yet he did find a way to God that both cast a contrastive light on the path of some of his colleagues and marked out a direction of his own.

A twinned pair of poems from 1919 cast a revealing light on this process of loss and retrieval. The first of these, "Mi yiten uteso'ar nafshi" [Oh that my soul be roiled] (p. 50), is a severe and unrelenting plea for the utter eradication of the bond between the speaker's self and the burden of ancestral tradition. In language that unmistakably invokes Berdichevsky's Nietzschean declarations from the end of the previous century, the poem's speaker longs for the obliteration of all the sanctuaries where his heart once worshiped and all the doctrines

and teachings that have hung upon him from the very beginnings
of his existence "like a congregation of frightful spirits / cast out of
dark realms." Like Berdichevsky, again, this is a revolt in the name of
radical freedom and new life. If the "shackles of ancestral tradition"
can be sundered, the self can then proudly range over the primordial
secrets of creation in search of vitality and renewal. Taken as a whole,
however, these radical assertions are blunted by the rhetorical organization of the poem as an utterance that is wholly cast in the optative
mode. Each of its three stanzas begins with the formula "Mi yiten,"
which in biblical Hebrew introduces a wish or a desire for an unattain-
able outcome. So, while the radical negations of the poem are boldly
put forward, the prospect of their execution seems to remain within
the realm of powerless fantasy.

In the companion poem that follows directly (pp. 51–52), this transgressive wish is at once granted and taken back. The opening lines
declare that "Yes, indeed, the foundations of my sanctuary were destroyed / and God's glory was exiled from me." It is as if between
the end of one poem and the beginning of the next the metaphysical
revolution that seemed beyond reach has been suddenly and conclu-
sively enacted. Yet the reader is not left to ponder the mystery of this
transformation before the poem, after only two lines, turns about face
and moves in the direction of affirmation. There are times, the speaker
explains, when his heart is filled with emotions and suddenly a prayer
wells up inside him despite all of his theological renunciations. The
discovery is likened in one figure to the bursting forth of a mountain
spring from an unknown underground source. In another, the prayer
is compared to an ember that has survived a great, destructive confla-
gration; the ember is revived when a strong twilight wind blows across
it. In the rekindled fire, the speaker glimpses an image of God in His
primal light and the destroyed sanctuaries of his youth. How has this
recurrence taken place? What has transpired in his soul to make it possible? The speaker is astonished but shows no introspective inclination
to look for reasons and origins. We are left to wonder whether the
resurgence of prayer is an instance of recidivism or restoration.

The question is answered in many of Bavli's poems that show him
to be a Hebrew poetic practitioner of a kind of romantic religion,

a panentheism without historical Jewish pathos and with roots in American Transcendentalism. (This was a sensibility shared by many of the other American Hebrew poets, although the experience of prayer, expressed in many poems titled as such, is rather special to Bavli.[16]) One of the best poems for understanding this stance is "Bimsibbat allonei gan ḥolem" [At a gathering of oaks in the dreaming garden] (pp. 45–46). Sitting alone in the woods at night with the stars above him and a brook at his feet, the speaker is all alertness and sensitivity to the sounds around him. He hears the brook babble about the day's events to the willow on its banks; he overhears the murmuring of flowers and grasses wafted by the breeze. Are they intoning a prayer to their Maker, or are they telling each other tales of love? This whimsical conjecture leads to a confession and an affirmation. As a human, these communications among natural objects are, in truth, unintelligible to him. Yet this language, despite its mystery, reveals more light to his soul than the human communication so familiar to him. The poem concludes with the wish—again introduced by the optative formula, "mi yiten . . . ," which we saw above—that the remainder of the speaker's life be spent just so, sitting among the trees and listening to the sounds of the plants and winds. For this language, which is God's language [sefat el], is what captivates his soul. "Then I will know," the poem ends, "that I have heard the sound of Eternity's pulse / and I will acknowledge my Creator in the silence."[17]

This poems gives us some important insights into Bavli's natural religion, and, by extension, that of many of his colleagues. If the divine is to be found in the world, to begin with, it is to be discovered in the bosom of nature rather than in the breast of man. There is little in the social constructions of humankind or in the feelings of one person for another that can contain the signals of eternity found in nature. As a communicant in those mysteries, moreover, the poet's place is standing, or in this case, sitting *alongside* nature; he is an outsider who is more than content to overhear the hum and buzz of a language he does not presume to penetrate or decipher. Finally, the noisy mystery of nature is not the final stop but rather a station along the way to acknowledging, out of a profound silence, God as creator.

The first line of the poem we have been discussing contains a telling semantic joke. The line reads: *bimsibbat allonei gan ḥolem yashavti.* *Ḥolem* [dreaming] is a participle that, in principle, can modify either the garden or the speaker. One option would yield: "At the gathering of the oaks in the dreaming garden I sat"; the other would yield: "At the gathering of the oaks in the garden I sat dreaming." By the second line of the poem, we realize that the first option is preferred; the speaker is sitting up at night alert and open-eyed; and, after all, the poem's title, with its omission of "I sat," requires attaching the dreaming to the garden. Nevertheless, the speaker's motionless posture of active listening, which he longs to be allowed to maintain forever, has a Zen-like dreaminess about it that remains in the background of the poem. Dreaming, not in the conventional sense of the term but in the sense of meditative observation and imaginative reverie, is an activity that pervades Bavli's poetry as the essential attribute of the poet. Bavli's verse abounds in self-referential poems about himself as the poet and the dreamer. At times the terms are used interchangeably; at other times dreaming denotes the act of imaginative engagement and observation, while poetry denotes the craft of turning these impressions into the verbal artifact of the poem.

One need only add the activity of prayer to those of dreaming and making poetry to attain a full view of Bavli's self-portrait. In a poem that reads like an anthem and sounds like a marching song ("Beshir vaḥalom" [In poem and dream] (p. 111), the speaker declares: "In poem and dream and innocent prayer / I have spent most of my days." Despite periods of black despair, a voice inside him has always bidden him to remain loyal to his calling. The poem indeed becomes an act of self-exhortation. "March on!" the speaker tells himself; "Pursue, aspire, love, / sing, cry, and pray; / For without these / there is nothing in the world to praise!" For Bavli, the vocation of the poet is to be a *homo viator*, an existential pilgrim who is not free to remain at rest; he must march on to engage the secrets of the world. At its best, this is a quest undertaken with exuberance and with the solidarity of other poets. Bavli dedicates the conclusion of one of his most beautiful poems ("'Al Lake George" [On Lake George], pp. 125–27) to his fellow American Hebrew poet Halkin, to whom he appeals: "Arise, my brother, and let us go out to encounter all of the wonders: / Our souls are bound up in the veil of faraway places."[18]

Because of the thinness of the membrane that separates the soul of the poet from the soul of the world, there is more occasion for the opposite of exuberance. The poet is exquisitely and inexorably exposed to baseness and iniquity and despair both in the world and in himself. But what oppresses him most is the adumbration of death, for in death his song will be extinguished. Before he dies, he prays to be given a moment of grace when all the forces of his life's poetry coalesce and ignite in a clarifying consummation ("'Od lo nadamah" [Not yet silent], p. 77). And he is bitterly anguished at the thought that his end will follow another course and fade away unremembered like the breaking wave whose fury is spent on the rocky shore ("Kegal adirim" [Like a mighty wave], p. 80).

תְּפִלָּה ✳
Prayer

Analysis

תְּפִלָּה

הָהּ אֵלִי, אֵלִי,
אֲבִיר חֶלְדִּי,
חֲמָל־נָא עֲלֵי בִנְךָ נִדָּחֶךָ
אֲשֶׁר תָּעָה מִנִּי אֹרַח־אָבוֹת
וְגָלָה לְמֶרְחַקִּים זָרִים, קָרִים
לְבַקֵּשׁ קֻרְבָתֶךָ –
וַעֲדֶן לֹא מְצָאָךְ!

יָדַעְתִּי,
מָרוֹם אַתָּה מֶנִּי
וְנִשְׂגָּב מֵעֵין שִׂכְלִי.
הִנְּךָ, אֵלִי.
אַךְ זֹאת גַּם זֹאת יָדַעְתִּי:

בְּמָקוֹם־מָה,
בַּמִּסְתָּרִים
תֵּשֵׁב, תִּחַכֶּה מְנִי עוֹלָם
אֶל הָאַחֲרוֹן בַּעֲבָדֶיךָ
הַחוֹתֵר לָבוֹא שְׁעָרֶיךָ
בֶּאֱמוּנָה.

חָנֵּנִי וְרַחֲמֵנִי־נָא,
אֱלֹהֵי הָרוּחוֹת,
וּקְרַע הַמָּסְוֶה מֵעַל עֵינַי
לִרְאוֹת אֶת צֵל כְּבוֹדֶךָ!
כִּי הִנֵּה נָבוֹךְ אֲנִי, נִתְעֶה
בְּאֶרֶץ גְּדוֹלָה
וְנָכְרִיָּה
וְלֹא יָדַעְתִּי מָה.
כָּעַכְבִּישׁ שְׁתוּם־הָעַיִן
כֵּן אֶתְלַבֵּט בְּקוּרֵי־אֶמֶשׁ
אָרַגְתִּי לִי אָנֹכִי;
אֲפַרְפֵּר, אָתוּר דֶּרֶךְ,
אֲבַקֵּשׁ מִפְלָט —
וּמִפְלָט אָיִן.

הָהּ, אֵלִי, אֵלִי,
הוֹשֵׁט לִי יָדֶךָ
וִינַהֲלוּנִי רַחֲמֶיךָ!

Prayer

Oh my God, my God,
Mighty One of my existence,
have mercy on Your lost son
who has wandered from the ancestral path
and, exiled to cold and unfamiliar climes,
sought to be close to You,
but has not yet found You.

I know
that You are far beyond me;

elevated above my ken,
are You, my Lord.
Yet this I know too:
Somewhere,
in the hidden places,
You sit, waiting eternally
for the last of Your servants,
who strives,
faithfully,
to come into Your gates.

Favor me and have mercy on me,
Lord of the Winds,
and rip the veil from my eyes
so that I may see the shadow of Your glory!
For lost am I, wandering
in a vast and
alien land
and I know naught.
Like a sharp-eyed spider,
I struggle in the web of darkness
I have woven for myself;
I flail, I scout out the path,
I seek escape,
but there is no escape.

Oh, my God, my God,
extend Your hand to me
and let Your mercy grant me safe passage!

Prayers are rarities in modern Hebrew poetry, a literature founded, after all, on an emancipation from traditional texts and beliefs. Bavli is an exception in this regard, and not only among American Hebrew poets; his corpus is sprinkled with poems that are addressed to God and recognized by their formulaic language as prayers, and, moreover, usually titled as such.[19] In the instance before us, the poem "Tefillah" [Prayer] (1923, pp. 112–13)[20] uses the conventional terminology of individual, supplicatory prayer in the Jewish tradition. Whereas most Jewish liturgy is collective and statutory—it is expressed in the "we" form and recited at fixed times—supplicatory prayer is the expression of an individual voice and uttered in moments of extreme gratitude or extreme distress. The poem's use of this recognizably traditional vocabulary—*hamol-na 'alai, haneni, rahameni-na*—also sets off this poem from the great majority of poems that come before and after it, which the reader naturalizes simply as "poetry" rather than as a religious utterance. The high biblical stylistic register of the poem also serves to mark it as different from the rest of Bavli's verse. It is further set apart by the fact that it is composed in free verse in short lines and without formal stanzas. At the same time, however, if this poem and others like it in Bavli's oeuvre are presented as prayers, they are prayers of a peculiar sort. For despite the traditional terms, there is almost no Judaic reference here. God is not appealed to as the God of Abraham, Isaac, and Jacob; none of the events of sacred history (exodus, redemption, etc.) are mentioned; and the language, though biblical in origin, alludes very little to verses or contexts that are meaningfully actualized in the text. In short, then, Bavli's poem plays with our generic expectations in two ways. In a book of modern poems, it is a heartfelt address to God in the language of Jewish prayer. Yet as a Jewish prayer, it jettisons most of the markers of tradition.

At first glance, the speaker's dilemma in this poem is familiar to us from both confessional poetry and personal prayer. He is lost in an alien world, and his efforts to move toward God are undermined by his own bad faith, which further distances him from his objective; it is only God's grace that can rescue him. On closer inspection, the dilemma becomes less generic and more poignant. The first stanza invokes the collective autobiography of the "Twilight Generation" in Hebrew literature; this is the generation of Mordecai Ze'ev Feierberg and Brenner, whose star-crossed members came of age after the collapse of religious faith yet before the rise of secular forms of national existence.[21] The speaker of Bavli's poem introduces his own twist on this theme. He has left the way of the fathers and wandered in cold and alien climes for a purpose: he has journeyed to seek closeness to God. The subversive implication is that he left the ancestral way *because God was not there*, or at least he could not find Him there. That old way is not romanticized in retrospect or privileged in any way. His departure was not a forced flight but a voluntary banishment that was the prelude to a noble endeavor. The pathos of his dilemma derives from the fact that despite his high purpose, he has so far failed to attain his objective and experienced only the privations of his lonely quest.

Although the dilemma sounds universal and paradigmatic, the poem's context makes it very specific. As a poem written in Hebrew and published in America, the identity of the cold and foreign climes—the association is strengthened by reference to the vastness of this alien land in the third stanza—is not in doubt. This is a poem about coming to America on a religious search that could no longer be nurtured in the old land and by the old way. The venture is, truly, an errand in the wilderness whose outcome, so far, has been loneliness and futility.

There is a striking exception to the general conventionality of the poem's language: *avir ḥeldi* as an epithet for God in the second line. Elsewhere in the poem—with the exception of one other epithet, *elohei haruḥot*, in line 20—God is addressed, simply and personally, as *eli*. In *avir ḥeldi*, a phrase that is original to Bavli so far as I know, two rare biblical words are joined together. *Avir* [mighty one] appears in the Bible only a few times and always in the bound phrase *avir-ya'aqov* [Mighty one of Jacob] in Genesis 49:24, Isaiah 49:26, 60:16, Psalms 132:2, 5 or *avir yisra'el* [Mighty one of Israel] in Isaiah 1:24; it resonates with later uses of the term to indicate a champion, a hero, or a knight. The second term, *ḥeled*, which is related to words for dirt, rust, and earth, is understood in a figurative sense to denote the limited, earthbound span of a human's life, as in its locus classicus, Psalm 39:6: "You have made my life just handbreadths long; its span [*veḥeldi*] is as nothing in your sight." By yoking together *avir* and *ḥeled*, Bavli underscores the gulf between God's heroic power and the speaker's fragile mortality. Yet by invoking the possessive and making God into the "Mighty one of *my* existence [*ḥeldi*]," the speaker, in a sense, also binds God to him and to the exigent dilemma he finds himself in.

The gulf between God and the speaker is the point of departure for the second stanza, which ends, however, with this gap being undercut. After piously professing God's utter transcendence in the first four lines of the stanza (lines 8–11), the speaker asserts a counter-knowledge he possesses of God's immanent empathy. He knows for a certainty that somewhere God waits with abiding patience for his arrival. Al-though he may be the most belated of God's servants, the concluding image of the stanza highlights the sincere efforts he is making to ad-vance toward his goal. The notorious plasticity of the term *be'emunah*, which stands alone as the last word in the stanza (line 18), allows the speaker to bestow upon his efforts a variety of compliments. He moves forward steadfastly, faithfully, and with conviction.

This self-regard collapses in the third stanza. Whereas the key image in the second stanza is determined, incremental movement toward a goal—the verb *ḥoter* (line 17) is also the word for rowing—the key image in the third is confused wandering and futile struggle. After renewing his plea for mercy, the speaker underscores his helplessness when he implores God to do what he cannot do for himself: to strip off the veil that prevents him from seeing God's glory. His description of himself in lines 23–26 as lost and perplexed represents a desultory deflection of the quest proclaimed in the first stanza. There he had presented himself as enduring the privations of exile in a new land to seek a God who was no longer to be found in the ways of the ancestors. The cold climes of America, which were described as for-eign [*zarim*] at the beginning of the poem when they were new and unknown, are now, after the experience of familiarity, marked more chillingly as alien [*nokhriyyah*] (line 25). The vastness of America only provides more scope for wandering farther afield and becoming more profoundly lost. *Velo yad'ati mah* [I knew nothing] (line 26) is a delib-erately awkward construction in Hebrew that expresses a bankruptcy of knowledge. In the spider simile in the final section of stanza three, the wandering over the vast plain is arrested. The speaker has been in motion, even if that motion had only been a directionless groping; now he is ensnared. The more desperately he flails and thrashes, the more tightly he becomes entangled. The pathetic irony is that the trap is of his own making, a web of bad faith and false expectations he has spun himself.

Bavli's prayer poem began with the privations of exile and the high errand of seeking God in new places. In its middle, the speaker pre-sented himself more modestly as a faithful servant toiling to reach his goal. By the poem's conclusion, his quest has turned into a shambles.

He wanders lost and perplexed before succumbing to his own destructive schemes. The vicissitudes of his relationship to the God he is addressing follow a similar trajectory. The relationship moves from a closeness assumed though not yet achieved and a confidence of divine favor to a receding horizon of distance and banishment. The poem begins and ends with nearly identical pleas for mercy, yet between them stretches a gap of acute desperation. The speaker is farther away at the end than at the beginning, and his closing entreaty is intoned from a place where it is very unlikely that it can ever be heard.

Although, in closing, the poem would seem to be simply a deeply felt personal prayer, it shares a great deal with the other lyric poems we have analyzed. The loneliness of the Hebrew voice in America is legitimately the subject of prayer as well as poetry. If in his prayer-poem Bavli seeks to escape from the solipsism of the lyric voice by addressing the Divine Other, in the end, he is left sadly only with echoes of his own voice.

Eight   Shimon Ginzburg

Although none of the American Hebrew poets ever felt truly at home in America, most eventually found here something to love, or at least be fascinated by. Not so Shimon Ginzburg. Neither Indian sagas nor transcendental vistas captivated his imagination, while his spirit remained brutalized by the coarseness of urban life and by the ignorance of American Jews. This righteous disdain was made electric in some of the best-known poems on New York City in the American Hebrew canon. He suffered America for over twenty years before emigrating to Tel Aviv only to return here several years later to travel from one Jewish community to another to raise funds for cultural institutions in Palestine. In his wanderings and struggles, Ginzburg was sustained by a vision that came from elsewhere. He carried aloft the standard of Hebrew poetic seriousness he had taken from Bialik in Odessa, and, on a more primordial level, he remained grounded in the Ukrainian village in which he grew up and in his profound connection to his mother, father, and sister there.

Ginzburg was born in Lipniki in the Vohlin region of the Ukraine in 1890.[1] After receiving a traditional education in heder, Ginzburg studied Hebrew and general subjects as an *ekstern* in Zhitomir, where his family had moved when he was seven. He spent 1909–1912 in Hebrew literary circles in Odessa, which served at the time as the world capital of the small republic of Hebrew letters. There he was greeted as a talented young poet who had come from the provinces; he was befriended by Bialik and became the secretary to Abramovitch (Mendele). His fist poem was published in the prestigious *Hashiloah* in 1910 at the age of twenty. After emigrating to the United States in 1912, he studied at Columbia University and the University of Saskatchewan before obtaining a doctorate from Dropsie College in Philadelphia for a study of the life and works of Moshe Hayyim Luzzatto, the Italian Hebrew dramatist and kabbalist.

At the same time, he directed Hebrew schools and participated in Hebraist projects. He served as one of the earliest editors of *Hatoren* and assisted Berkovitz in the editing of *Miqlat*; he was one of the founders of the Histadrut Ivrit and directed its Tarbut school. In 1933 he left America for Palestine, where he worked as an editor and edited a five-volume edition of Luzzatto's writings and was active in the affairs of Hebrew writers associations. The economic crisis that came in the wake of the Arab riots in the late 1930s severely curtailed Hebrew publishing activities in Palestine, and Ginzburg was asked to go to America to raise funds.[2] So, after only a few years of residence in Tel Aviv, Ginzburg returned to America as an emissary for Hebrew cultural institutions in Palestine. In pursuit of this goal, he traveled tirelessly from one Jewish community to another searching for Hebraists who would be sympathetic to his urgent appeals. The modest success he achieved took many years and incessant application. He died at the age of fifty-four while still on his mission in America. In the foreword to a posthumous collection of his later works, which had been long delayed because of lack of funds, his son David writes from Haifa with undisguised bitterness about his father's fate. Although Ginzburg devoted years to making it possible for other writers to publish their works—and died in this quest—his fellow authors did not bother themselves to see to the publication of his writings after his death. Many of his poems remained scribbled on hotel stationary during brief stops on his far-flung travels throughout America on behalf of Hebrew literature.

Ginzburg was a figure of considerable authority in the world of Hebrew letters in America. His familiarity with Bialik and the literary lions of Odessa gave him the aura of a man who, already at a young age, had been to the mountain. He was a thinker and a critic in addition to a poet, and his high-toned indictments of the ignorant vulgarity of immigrant Jewish life helped to define the Hebraist worldview in America.[3] His organizational abilities were considerable, as well, and he inevitably became the head of whatever endeavor he involved himself in. Yet despite his preeminence, and perhaps precisely because of the gravity of his ideals and passions, Ginzburg's poetry never truly took off into the ether of the imagination. His adoration of Bialik often condemned his writing to epigonic status; the motifs and language of his lyric poems are often too familiar to practiced ears. Yet there were certain powerfully personal experiences—the connection to his village and family, bereavement and desire—which sometimes endowed Ginzburg's verse with the ache of originality. Furthermore, when it came to big themes, the poetics of Bialik served him well by giving prophetic volume to his voice and allowing him to write works of moral eloquence if not cunning grace. He was a pupil of Tchernichovsky as well, and the teaching of this master came to his stead in the composition of a series of idylls, both contemporary and biblical, which were widely noted.

As a young writer, Ginzburg's reputation was made by a series of poems about New York that mounted a prophetic rejection of urban life. The years 1916–17, when these poems appeared, were a key moment in the development of the gathering Hebraist movement in America. The waves of immigration had sufficiently broadened the ranks of Hebraists to sustain new undertakings: journals, publishing ventures, and the founding of the Histadrut Ivrit. Because of revolution and war, Jewish cultural production was in a shambles in both Russia and Palestine, and many leading Zionist figures had come to New York to wait out the war years. The possible emergence of America, and New York in particular, as the next great center for Hebrew culture, and not just a temporary one, was much talked about. The young Hebraists, many of whom were both educators and writers, were busy formulating a thorough-going critique of American Jewish life from a Hebraist perspective. In the thick of this activity, Ginzburg undertook one of the most forbidding challenges: staking out a stance toward the city, the defining phenomenon of modern life and the defining milieu of immigrant life. If his achievement did not garner universal concurrence, it remained a very strong vision that represented a broad strain of Hebraist sentiment.

The challenge of New York was not one that Ginzburg was by nature inclined to take on. Several poems that he wrote before his massive composition "New York" reveal how difficult it is for him keep his gaze trained on the actualities of the metropolis. In one of these shorter poems, "'Al nahar Hudson" [By the Hudson] (1916),[4] the speaker is located in a medial position on the western shore of the river, with Manhattan to his back and the wooded stretches of New Jersey before him. The grey, overcast dome of the sky mirrors the dullness of his spirit. The clamorous din of the commercial life of the city, like a pounding remorseless song, reaches him from behind. This is the whine of great machines in giant factories with their imprisoned masses of worn-down workers. As he sits silently, his gaze wanders eastward to the opposite shore, in whose forests he imagines the Indians once hunted, and he further imagines the exotic rhythms of their native songs. His reverie is broken by a different sound: the shrieking horn of a busy ferry boat that rebukes him for the idleness of his reverie and startles him into the sad rumination that he is, indeed, a dreamer out of place in this land of spirit-wasting business.

In "Behar bet Columbia" [On the heights of Columbia] (1916, pp. 94–101), the poem that follows directly in *Shirim ufo'emot*, the speaker evinces a similar desire to escape from the urban reality that he has taken on as the subject of his poem. Here the subject is a more rarefied aspect of city life: an imposing university with its students from many backgrounds. The tone is jaunty rather than solemn, and the august university, perched on Morningside Heights with its domed capitol rising from within its walls, is presented as a temple of learning where acolytes from all nations come to worship. Yet even in this heady atmosphere, there are discordant strains. The speaker has been "swallowed by the sea of books," but even amid all this learning, he has not yet heard his soul's voice. He notes the busts of Byron and Pestalozzi and other great writers and thinkers, and it pains him deeply that the likes of Hillel and Ben-Zakkai have no place in this pantheon. Among the foreign students he encounters is a Japanese named Yokanama, who speaks proudly about his country's bold march to join the league of advanced nations. He overhears a conversation between two Jewish students about whether America and its language have now become their motherland and mother tongue. All these stimuli come together in a dream the speaker dreams that night in Riverside Park overlooking the Hudson near Columbia. He is transported to Palestine, where he disembarks in Jaffa and is vouchsafed an Isaian vision of Eretz Yisrael transformed into a radiant spiritual center and a light to the nations. The dream departs when a policeman gives his shoulder a shake and points out that he is drowsing in a public park at midnight.

The escape routes taken in these two poems are telling. The myths of the Native Americans, on one side, and the Hibbat Zion / Ahad Haamist vision of Eretz Yisrael, on the other, are the two paradigmatic "alternative universes" of American Hebrew poetry. These are spaces where the Hebrew imagination would *prefer* to roam rather than being forced to grapple with the urban dystopia of the here and now. Yet, as a morally responsible poet, Ginzburg could not decline the challenge. The year following these two brief poems, Ginzburg unveiled a major long poem titled, simply and ambitiously, "New York," which aimed to discharge this poetic burden. The poem was placed in the lead position in the literary section of *Luaḥ ahi'ever*, a miscellany published by the newly formed Histadrut Ivrit—Ginzburg served as one of the three editors—as an important step in its cultural program.[5]

Ginzburg faced the challenge by relying on the precedent of his great mentor Bialik. "New York" is modeled on *Be'ir haharegah* [In the city of slaughter], Bialik's magisterial examination of political passivity in the Kishinev massacre of 1903.[6] In Bialik's poem, a poet-prophet is instructed by God to visit each site of slaughter within the city and allow his rage against the victims' cowardice to build up inside him; Bialik makes the ordeal of the poet's mission a theme as important as the behavior of the victims. Now, New York is not Kishinev, and the depravity and alienation of the great metropolis have little to do with the pathos of Jewish history. Nonetheless, Ginzburg drew heavily upon Bialik's text to organize his own and to establish the rhetorical strategies for his endeavor. The prophetic focus is the key adoption. If Bialik's speaker is Ezekiel-like, Ginzburg's is Jonah-like, and his mission is, appropriately to his subject, to preach to the gentile city of New York, the new Nineveh. The prophetic premise elevates the poetry to the status of an oracle and authorizes Ginzburg to unleash the full armamentarium of high prophetic rage: parody, hyperbole, ridicule, epic simile.[7] It further authorizes the adopting of an absolute moral stance with no room for nuance and contextual justification.

Where the poem does indeed make provision for complexity is not in the object of the prophet's condemnation, the city of sin, but in the internal ordeal of the prophet's struggle to fulfill his calling.

Ginzburg's contestation with New York draws him into a productive aesthetic contradiction. On the one hand, there is the deployment of the high classical prophetic-Bialikian mode to attack the core experience of urban modernity. On the other, there is a palpable fascination with the evil being condemned that cannot but destabilize this classicist mode. In the very attempt to describe the chaotic rhythms and moral abandon of the metropolis and to subordinate them to poetic representation, something of the city's subversive anarchy seeps into Ginzburg's verse and changes it. Consider, for example, this description late in the poem of the reflection of the sun's last rays as it sets in the canyons of Manhattan.

וְרַד, חֲלַל־קְרָב, שַׂר־הַשֶּׁמֶשׁ
וְצָנַח לָאָרֶץ מִתְבּוֹסֵס בְּדָמוֹ –
וְהִזָּה הַדָּם עֲלֵי אַלְפֵי הַשְּׁמָשׁוֹת בְּחַלּוֹנוֹת־עֲפָלִים.
וְהֶאְדִּימוּ עַל קִירוֹת הַמִּגְדָּל כְּכִתְמֵי דָם שָׁפוּךְ:

A battle victim, the sun fell to the earth
Wallowing in its blood—
And sprinkled blood on the thousands of suns in the darkening
    windows
Which turned crimson on the walls of the skyscraper like blood
    stains. (p. 277)

Although there may be hints here of Bialik's pogrom poetry, the splattered blood on the trees and the bedding, there are also the discordant tones of a more contemporary sensibility. In describing that distinctively urban experience of the one sun being infinitely repeated and refracted in the windows of tall buildings, Ginzburg is drawing on one of the central techniques of cubism. And in saturating his image in blood he is approaching the effects of expressionism, with an especially transgressive Jewish twist. For in the splattering of blood, which is conveyed by the word *hizzah*, the Hebrew reader would recognize the biblical descriptions of the Temple priests as they splashed the blood of the sacrificial animals on the altar. I do not wish to make claims for Ginzburg as an expressionist; he had no aspirations to the avant-garde of his time. Yet in reaching for imaginative resources adequate to capturing the urban reality that so disturbed him, this, at least for this purpose, is where he had to go.

The aesthetic contradiction becomes a programmatic declaration at the very opening of the poem. The poet's initial proposal is that we see New York itself as a poem, more specifically, as a *poema*, a Russian term current in Hebrew poetry at the turn of the twentieth century for a long poem on a serious topic.[8] The tall office towers with their heads in the clouds alternate with dwarf buildings to form a pattern of radically jagged poetic lines. When it comes to rhythm of the city-as-poem, there is undeniably a beat but no discernable meter; sometimes the city explodes, sometimes it flows, and sometimes it shrieks. The words of the poem are a babble of tongues from the Irish, German, and Jewish immigrants who crowd the streets. Yet in the face of this subversively chaotic art work, the poet-speaker declares himself capable of discerning a poem with meter and the rhythm of the ocean. This is a poem that is both divine and satanic, and it is played on an enormous harp whose strings are the souls of the city's inhabitants and whose vastness even the "Wagnerian ear" could never imagine.[9]

To make good on this declaration, the poet-speaker proceeds to organize his resistant subject into categories and catalogues. He will comprehend the city within the cycle of a single day, and he launches his exposition with a description of the escapist entertainments the urban masses seek out after the grinding alienation of the work day. The music hall and the cinema, each described in a severely defam-liarized Hebrew, are presented as the key sites where the sensibilities of the crowds are both stimulated and narcotized. But as he girds himself to push on with his poetic burden, the speaker undergoes something of a crisis. Wandering the labyrinthine streets at midnight, he feels himself sinking into the darkness of the city just as the prophet Jonah must have been enveloped and unmanned by Nineveh. The engine of prophetic castigation has been silenced by the dark, unfathomable vastness of the city.

נוּ־יוֹרְק הֲמָמַנִי, בְּלָעַנִי,
וָאֱהִי מְהַלֵּךְ בּוֹ עָיֵף וְסַר יָמִים רַבִּים,
כָּבוּשׁ גָּדְלוֹ, מְשֻׁעְבָּד, מְבֻלְבָּל.

New York has stunned me and swallowed me,
I walk around for days exhausted and angry and rattled,
Conquered by its size, subjugated, confused. (p. 267)

Neither a "prophet nor the son of a prophet," the speaker nevertheless owns to having sparks of their ire in his blood, and, in a way more than reminiscent of the ordeal of the prophet in Bialik's Kishinev poem, it is the ghost of this vocation that is overwhelmed and neutralized by the metropolis. Later on in "New York," undone by the monstrousness of Wall Street, Ginzburg's speaker will admit, "The desire to curse took hold of me, but the imprecation fell silent on my lips" (p. 271).

Regaining his voice after his first crisis, the poet-speaker returns to his unremitting depiction of the pursuit of vice (p. 268). It is after midnight, and the general pursuit of diversion has gone underground and become more debauched. First there are the pool halls and billiard parlors, then the off-hours night clubs and the erotic gyrations of their performers, and then the houses of prostitution. Uptown in the mansions along Riverside Drive, the decadent rich gather secretly to perform acts in the style of Sodom and France, while downtown in the warren of narrow streets in Chinatown, men and women of a different class huddle in dens to offer smoking obeisance to the god of opium. Yet for all their depravity, these are vices practiced from time immemorial. The modern embodiment of sin, which is also the essential embodiment of the city itself, is revealed in the encounter with Wall Street. In the silent canyons of the financial district long after midnight, the poet-speaker discovers the lair of a contemporary Moloch. This blood-thirsty god of business and speculation spreads its monstrous, sinuous limbs (the great bridges of Lower Manhattan) throughout the metropolis to seize its inhabitants and feed them to its ever-hungry maw.

"New York," the *poema*, is a formidable text, and there is much more to say about Ginzburg's use of myth to bring his composition to a conclusion of a kind. But as a strong statement about New York City, the poem's formidableness needs some contextualization. It is at once representative and exceptional. It is representative of a broad turning away from the city in American Hebrew poetry in favor of the uninhabited landscapes of America and the vistas of the American past. In a generic division of labor, the exploration of urban life was taken up in Hebrew fiction rather than poetry, especially in the prose of Halkin and Wallenrod.[10] And if even here the city was not exactly celebrated, the saga of its Jews and their struggles with acculturation were deemed topics worthy of steady exploration. Ginzburg's "New York" is exceptional in the ferocity of its moralism. Finding urban life distasteful and dispiriting is one thing; depicting it as the mother of all depravity is quite another. If New York is a poem, why cannot it not be *Rhapsody in Blue* rather than the "Inferno"? What about the museums, the universities, the coffeehouses, the artists, the bustling immigrant energies? Ginzburg's stance is a variety of Hebraist Puritanism that brings to the New World an Ahad Haamist disdain for the sensuous and the diverting. Ginzburg was an active cultural critic who approached Hebraism as a moral worldview, as well as a language-based cultural program. In advancing this agenda, the choice of the prophetic mode of utterance was understandably attractive. For in this mode, alas, there are no half-measures or nuances or justifications, only turpitude, and no ironic modulations, only ringing denunciation.

The high prophetic register, curiously, turned out to be a one-time improvisation. Because of its topicality and strong effects and because of the intensity of the Hebraist scene in New York during World War I, Ginzburg's *poema* was a sensation. Yet it does not represent the general run of his verse, which tends to be lyric and short. True, he did have an aspiration for long forms, but these are more narrative in technique and often identified as idylls. His estimable book-length poem *Ahavat Hoshea'* [The love of Hosea], although it is set in the time of the prophet, focuses more on the theme of disappointed love than on moral and social castigation.[11] Ginzburg, in fact, did not see himself as a poet of big themes and brilliant effects; he was a poet in a silver age in the aftermath of Bialik. His lyrics are meditative and gloomy and in a revealing little poem, Ginzburg knowingly characterizes his verse as *qoder*, dark ("Lo sileq el . . ." [God did not banish . . .], p. 135). "I was afflicted," he writes in the same poem, "therefore I don't speak in the high style [*gevohah-gevohah*] / And my verse lacks brilliancy of form."

Ginzburg's lyric poetry emerges from darkness and ponderousness when it establishes a connection with the home he left behind in the Ukraine. This connection is rarely sought out; it erupts suddenly unbidden and provides the speaker of the poem with a complex rush of feelings. He is nourished by the near-clairvoyant channel opened up to this primal source, at the same time as he is anguished by the vulnerability of his loved ones and their unbridgeable remove from him. The "over there" remains in soft focus, and the texture of the place is never evoked with any detail or ethnographic thickness, even though the poet opines, "When I die bury me in the valley / On the slope at the verge of the wood" ("Bemoti qivruni bagai . . . [When I die bury me in the valley . . .], p. 65).[12]

One of Ginzburg's strongest poems in this vein is "Beveit-haperaḥim" [In the flower shop] (1913, pp. 53–54). The poem opens with a contrast between the brilliant, blue coldness of a winter's day, which freezes mercy and separates people from each other, and the slumbering contentment of the plants and flowers protected by the glass panes of the shop. As the poem's speaker spreads his arms to wonder at the sheltered beauty of the flowers, he experiences a visitation. His sister appears to him as a blue bird with tremulous wings. In a gesture we would now call magic realism, the speaker does not find this supernatural event at all odd. He is simply grateful and delighted and moved to a meditation about his sister and the cold. Despite her love for the winter landscape, she resembles, in his imagining, a violin whose taut strings become ruined in the cold. The meditation turns into a prayer that God protect this rare creature and all others like her from harsh storms and from captivity.

It is curious, I think, that the speaker does not try to establish communication or contact with the bird or press for news from home or express sadness upon parting. The encounter with the bird-sister functions primarily to trigger a release of empathy and a prayerful invocation of divine protection. It is a breakthrough for him in which the object that caused the breakthrough recedes from attention. This mechanism is even more pronounced in another complex poem on this theme: "Beleil nisan" [On a spring night] (1915, pp. 81–82). Here the connection to home does not come through the apparition of a family member but through the sudden lifting of a veil that enables the speaker to see in his mind's eye the village and its houses "sleeping in the pure night." Before this channel is opened, the speaker has been walking in the night air contemplating the moon, ruminating about his divided nature, and sinking into a kind of slough of despond. The vision of his village has the magical effect of slipping the "burden of afflictions and sins" from his shoulders. He is lightened and repurified.

Ginzburg is no more solipsistic than most writers of lyric poetry, and we should not be surprised that the glow of the connection made to his family and village casts its nurturing light more on the speakers of the poems than on these faraway objects. From the mid-1920s onward, however, there is a discernable shift toward an empathic bond with others. In a heartfelt poem dedicated to his fellow American Hebrew poet Halkin, for example, the speaker attempts to assuage his friend's feelings of isolation and neglect ("LeSh. Halkin" [To S. Halkin] 1924, pp. 150–51). The poems "Levayah" [Funeral] (1925, p. 159) and "Pirḥei mavet" [Death flowers] (1925, pp. 161–67) describe the death of a spouse and the ensuing grief with controlled eloquence.[13] Yet nothing prepares the reader for the enormity of the loss Ginzburg experiences upon the death of Bialik in 1934. Just the year before, Ginzburg had left the United States and settled in Palestine, where he was gratified to renew face-to-face contact with his hero and spiritual mentor. The torrent of poems eulogizing Bialik and working through the loss—not only in the intermediate aftermath but also at different removes of time—reveal how deeply rooted was Ginzburg's entire poetic enterprise in the spiritual soil of the master.[14]

✳ לָעִבְרִים בַּאֲמֶרִיקָה מִזְמוֹר
In Praise of the Hebraists in America

Analysis

לָעִבְרִים בַּאֲמֶרִיקָה מִזְמוֹר

כְּשַׁלְשְׁלוֹת־הָאוֹרוֹת הַסְּפוּרוֹת, הַבּוֹדְדוֹת־קְשׁוּרוֹת
בְּתַחֲנַת־רַכֶּבֶת אֲפְלוּלִית־מָשְׁלֶגֶת, מוּזָרָה.
תְּבַצְבֵּץ לְפֶתַע מִבֵּין שְׂדוֹת הָרְפִיִּים
שֶׁכּוּחָה אִי־שָׁם בֵּין נְיוּ־יוֹרְק וּבֵין קְלִיבְלַנְדְ –
דְּמֻיתְכֶם, הָעִבְרִים, בְּרַחֲבֵי אֲמֶרִיקָה.
אֵין יוֹדֵעַ מִי זַרְעֲכֶם פֹּה בָּאָרֶץ הַזֹּאת, זֶרַע קֹדֶשׁ,
וּמִי אָב אוֹבֵד וְאֵם אוֹבֶדֶת שְׁכָחוּכֶם
לְבַדְּכֶם פֹּה בְּלֵיל חֹרֶף, כּוֹכָבִים וְשָׁלֶג –
אוּלָם חַי זֶה הָרַחַב כִּי מֵחֹם נְשִׁימַתְכֶם
עֲגְמָתוֹ הַטְּמִירָה תָּפוּג,
וְחֶשְׁכַת לֵילוֹ תֵאוֹר, תִּמְתַּק.
זָרִים לַאֲחֵיכֶם, עַצְמְכֶם וּבְשַׂרְכֶם, וְלֹא־מוּבָנִים לְיַלְדֵיכֶם
תִּנָּצְרוּ בְרִיתְכֶם קֹדֶשׁ עִם פֶּרֶץ סְמוֹלֶנְסְקִין,
תִּשָּׁאוּהָ בְּחֶרֶף־נֶפֶשׁ דֶּרֶךְ אַלְפֵי הַמּוּלוֹת־הַחַיִּים
וּבְמֵ"ם טי"ת שַׁעֲרֵי טָמְאָה כְּשִׁירַת־עֵדֶן תַּעֲבִירוּהָ.
מִדֵּי תִצְעָדוּ בְּדֶרֶךְ־חַיֵּיכֶם לְתֻמְּכֶם
וּמִזְמוֹר תְּהִלִּים אוֹ בְּיַאלִיק מִתְנַגֵּן בְּחֶבְיוֹן־נַפְשְׁכֶם,
יַאֲזִין לָכֶם נְהַר פּוֹטוֹמַק, מִסְסִפִּי יִשְׁתָּאֶה:
כִּי רָחַף עָלָיו צֵל מַשֶּׁהוּ נָאֶה, לְאֵין עֲרוֹךְ נָאֶה
וְעָצוּב וְנַעֲלֶה,
לוֹ אֵין דֻּגְמָה, וְלֹא תִהְיֶה, בָּעוֹלָם.
וִי'וֹהָן, חָנְנִי יַנְקִי, בַּעַל בְּעַמָּיו
יוֹשֵׁב בַּכֻּרְסָה וּמְסַלְסֵל סְלְסוּלִים בַּמִּקְטֶרֶת,
מַקְשִׁיב בָּרַדְיוֹ, מְבֻלְבָּל, לַנֶּבַח
שֶׁל הִיטְלֶר מְבֹרָךְ עַל זֶבַח,
וְשׁוֹקֵל בְּדַעְתּוֹ, מְהַסֵּס, לְהַכְרִיעַ הַכָּף –
כִּי אֶחָד מִכֶּם לְפָנָיו יִקְרֶה וְחָלַף
בַּמָּאוֹר שֶׁבְּעֵינָיו וּבְעֶגְנוֹת־מִצְעָדוֹ,

וְהִפְנָה יוֹהָן פִּתְאֹם, מֵאִיר פָּנִים וּמַבָּט, כְּלַפֵּי מַעֲלָה
אֶת עֲשַׁן מִקְטַרְתּוֹ,
כְּמַרְגִּישׁ בְּחוּשׁ בַּחֲלוֹף לְפָנָיו דְּמוּת מְקוֹר־הַקְּדוּמִים
מִמֶּנּוּ שָׁתוּ אֲבוֹתָיו . . .

אוּלָם אַתֶּם,

אַנְשֵׁי־מַעֲשֶׂה וּנְסִיכֵי־חֲלוֹמוֹת גַּם יַחַד,
לֹא לָכֶם שַׁלְוַת יוֹהָן,
וְלֹא לָכֶם הֲדְרַת קִפָּאוֹן הַשָּׂדוֹת הַלָּלוּ
וּמְנוּחַת־הַחֹרֶף הַגְּדוֹלָה לְשָׁרוֹ שֶׁל יַעַר.
יוֹם־יוֹם וְלַיְלָה־לַיְלָה, בַּאֲשֶׁר תַּעַבְדוּ אוֹ תְּנַפֵּשׁוּ,
כְּנָחָשׁ מִמְּאוּרָתוֹ תִּרְדְּפְכֶם, תִּשְׂכְּכֶם לְאֵין מַרְפֵּא
זַעֲוַת קִלְלַת הַגָּלוּת וְצַעֲקַת אֲחֵיכֶם מִקַּצְוֵי־הָעוֹלָם,
וִיעַנְּכֶם גַּם עֲנֵה חֲלוֹם גְּאֻלָּה לֹא־בָאָה
וְחֶזְיוֹן הַמָּשִׁיחַ
הַתָּלוּי וְעוֹמֵד עַל סִפָּהּ שֶׁל תְּהוֹם . . .
אָז יָבוֹא לְרֶגַע קוֹל מַשָּׁק, כְּקוֹל כַּנְפֵי נֶשֶׁר
צוֹרֵחַ, פָּצוּעַ וְגֵא, מֵעַל תּוֹעֲפוֹת הָרֵי־יְהוּדָה —
וַעֲמַדְתֶּם רֶגַע קְסוּמִים, כִּבְנֵי נֶשֶׁר רְחוֹקִים, גַּם אַתֶּם,
וְנַפְשְׁכֶם יוֹצְאָה לָאוֹת, אוֹת־הַפְּלָאוֹת
שֶׁנִּתַּן לַדּוֹר, לָעוֹלָם — וְהִנֵּה שׁוּב נִגְנַז . . .
לִבְּכֶם שׁוֹתֵת דָּם עִם אֲחֵיכֶם בְּיַד קַיִן־הָמָן מְנַדֵּיהֶם
וְעֵינְכֶם — מִקְוֵה דִּמְעָה עֲצוּרָה,
בָּהּ לְעוֹלְמֵי־עַד קָדוֹשׁ, מְרַטֵּט, אֱלֹהִי,
חֲלוֹם־שֶׁמֶשׁ נְבוּאֵי זֹרוּחַ.

In Praise of the Hebraists in America[15]

[1–5] Like a sparse string of lights, scattered but connected
      belonging to a strange and darkly snowy train station
that suddenly pops up among the winter fields,
forgotten somewhere between New York and Cleveland,
I have imagined you, Hebraists in the expanses of America.

[6–11] No one knows who planted your seed, a holy seed, here in
      this land

or who is the lost father and the lost mother who left you
on your own here in this winter night of snow and stars.
Yet—I swear by this vastness—the warmth of your breath
will dispel its secret melancholy
and light up and sweeten the darkness of the night.

[11–21] Alien to your brethren, to yourselves and your families and
          misunderstood by your children,
you keep a holy compact with Peretz Smolenskin
and you carry this covenant with you at your peril through the din
          of life,
and through the forty-nine gates of impurity you bear it like the
          song of Eden.
As you march to your own lights on the road of life,
with a psalm or Bialik singing hidden in your souls,
the Potomac River will give heed to you and the Mississippi will
          look on astonished:
For passing before them is something surpassingly handsome
and sad and exalted,
which has no match and will remain unique forever.

[22–32] John, the Yankee shopkeeper, settled among his people,
sits in his easy chair blowing smoke rings with his pipe
and, confused, listens to the barking
of Hitler giving his blessings to the slaughter,
and, sorting things out in his mind, he hesitates to take a stand.
Yet when one of you happens to pass by him,
with the light in your eyes and your modest gait,
John, with a radiant look, suddenly directs
the smoke of his pipe aloft,
like one who has intuitively sensed the presence of a figure drawn
          from the same ancient sources
from which his own ancestors drank.

[33–43] But you, alike men of action and princes of dreams,
John's complacency is not for you,
and not for you either is the frozen majesty of these fields
or the Lord of the Forest's great wintry tranquility.
Every day and every night, whether at work or leisure,
the horrid curse of Exile and the cry of your brethren from the
          corners of the earth mortally wound you,

like the venomous bite of the snake that darts out from its lair to
    pursue its prey.
Answering you are the frustrated dream of redemption
and the messianic vision that hangs arrested on the brink of the
    abyss.

[44–48] Then will come the sound of the beating wings of an
    eagle, screeching, wounded, proud, above the Judean Hills.
You stand there momentarily dazed, as if you yourselves were eagle
    offspring, though far removed,
and your soul goes out to this wondrous sign
given to the generation and the world, and, behold, it is again
    hidden away.

[49–52] Your heart drips blood with your brethren caught in the
    grip of Cain/Haman, your oppressor,
yet in your eye, that reservoir of pent-up tears,
there will forever shine, trembling and divine,
the sun-drenched prophetic dream.

Ginzburg spent only a few years in Palestine before returning to
America to crisscross the land in search of contributions for Hebrew
writers in the Yishuv. Yet despite the brevity of his stay in the Holy
Land, his identity had been altered, and he now moved among his fellow Hebraists in America not as one of them but as a visitor from the
teeming center of Hebrew culture in Eretz Yisrael. He had, in a profound sense, passed over. "La'ivrim ba'ameriqah mizmor" [In praise
of the Hebraists in America] (signed "31.1.39"), is an ode addressed to
the Hebraists in America from one who is located on the other side.
Because of this newly attained subject position, the poem's speaker is
vouchsafed the necessary distance to appreciate the nobility of his former brethren and comprehend the tragic pathos of their situation, and
to do so without taint of self-regard. The poem, we shall see, also carries on a polemical conversation with the essential themes of American
Hebrew poetry and presents a belated apologia for Ginzburg's failure
to engage the American landscape and its mythic formations.

The tone of the poem is set by its title and the epic simile with
which it opens. A literal translation of the title, which would yield:
"To the Hebraists in America: A Psalm of Praise," gestures to the

book of Psalms and the enigmatic superscriptions that dedicate individual psalms to individuals and groups. The title conveys the speaker's intention to compose an encomium that will not only be sounded in the high biblical register but will also confer upon his subjects something of the Bible's authority, an authority which, at least on linguistic grounds, the American Hebraists sought for themselves. The intention to see them in a heroic light is further conveyed by the simile that fully occupies the poem's first five lines and unashamedly declares its filiation with the classical epic.

In the elaborate image of the strung-out lights of rural train stations, the poet works with focused determination to corral into a single figure the essential markers of the Hebraists' situation. Like the far-flung stations that rush in and out of view from the window of the hurtling train, the Hebraists find themselves stranded in communities widely distant one from the other. Even when they are clustered together in the same locality, they remain, like the lampposts, isolated though connected. Yes, they are points of light, but their illumination is dwarfed and enveloped by the great frigid night of the Exile and the profound depths of ignorance that surround them.

It is not until line 5, with the word *dimitikhem* [I imagined you], that our attention is drawn to the poem's speaker as the agency that conjures up this ambitious comparison. This is not a speaker who becomes dramatized in the poem, nor does his mental experience become its subject. Nevertheless, the poem is spoken from a position and from within a relationship. The poem is an ode addressed to the Hebraists in America, and what is revealed in the progress of the poem is not only the plight of those determined pioneers but also the speaker's stance toward them. So, when the speaker declares that no one knows how the scattered sacred seed got sown in these unlikely climes (lines 6–8), he is inviting us, to be sure, to join his wonderment over the very fact of their existence. But he is also playing dumb. For who knows better than someone like Ginzburg—let us conflate the speaker with the poet for a moment—the story of exactly how the Hebraists got to America and settled in its provincial cities? He parlays his feigned ignorance into a rhetorical tactic of defamliarization. Yes, the reasons may be known, but he seeks to make his readers—most of whom, after all, are the same species of which he writes—experience what is familiar to them as radically wondrous. This is the position that he in fact now occupies. Having once been one of them, he has now returned as other, and what he beholds before him now seems strange and unexplainable.

If these provincial Hebraists are marvelously strange in the speaker's eyes, in the non-Hebraic eyes of those that surround them, their strangeness is far less sympathetic. The saddest part of their fate is that their Hebraist passions make them alien, not only to other Jews, who have no conception of the ideals that inspire them, but also to the members of their own families, whose own acculturation into America makes loyalty to Hebrew seem like a highly peculiar endeavor. Yet despite their being forgotten in the darkest wintry reaches of impurity, they remain undaunted. Theirs is a *berit*, a sacred compact with the Hebrew revival of the Jewish people. Their pride is their consolation; with unshakable certainty they march through the impure wilderness around them holding the redemptive banner of Hebrew high and humming a poem from Bialik or Psalms in their heart. So impressive is their dedication that America itself, represented by two of its great rivers, cannot help admiring the uniqueness of this tragic nobility. The poem continues with its preoccupation with perception and perspective. If to their fellow Jews the Hebraists may seem peculiar and self-righteous, they can appear quite otherwise to their gentile neighbors. Although John, the storekeeper, may be confused by contemporary events and not know what to make of Hitler's intentions, when he meets one of the Hebraists, he senses the aura of an ancient sanctity that emanates from the common heritage of the Old Testament.

In the second stanza, the poem turns away from the strangeness of the image of the Hebraists to their turbulent inner experience. In contrast to John's imperturbability and the inert majesty of the wintry fields, the conscience of the Hebraists is wholly exposed to the cries of their European brethren. Because of both their empathic connection *and* their powerlessness, they, alone among their fellow American Jews, have been stung with a venom of rage and despair for which there is no antidote. This inward extremity also enables them to glimpse what is not vouchsafed to others: the blaze of redemptive promise that flares from over the Judean Hills. It is their particular fate to be fully alive to the magnitude of the opportunity granted their generation yet barred by their remoteness from Zion in taking part in its splendor. The speaker of the poem, once, like them, a noble champion of Hebrew in America, took steps to remove from himself the disability of exile. As one who has passed over, he has purchased the right to address them with a combination of admiration and condescension, although he is here and not there and is left to pen the lines of the poem as his train hurtles through the snowy fields of late January on its way from Cleveland to New York.

Nine H. A. Friedland

By all accounts, H. A. Friedland was the very emblem of the *'ivri*, the Hebraist, in America. In its original designation, an *'ivri* was one of the descendents of Abraham, Isaac, and Jacob, the primordial Jews long before the name Jews or *yehudim* [= Judaeans] came into use. The proponents of Zionism and Jewish national revival at the end of the nineteen century seized on the term *'ivri* to indicate their difference from the dominant exilic religious culture. By naming themselves *'ivrim*, they were appropriating the image of the biblical Hebrew, returning to the land of their forefathers, and reviving *'ivrit*, the language of the *'ivrim*. For the *'ivrim* who landed on the shores of America rather than Eretz Yisrael, the centrality of Hebrew as a "portable homeland" was intensified even further. Being an *'ivri* in America was a militant calling that required not only facing down Yiddish and resisting English but also actively creating a living Hebrew culture on the inhospitable shores of the New World.

Friedland embodied the many-sidedness of the ideal of the *'ivri*. He founded and led a large network of progressive Hebrew schools. He created the field of children's literature in Hebrew in America with his vast output of pedagogic stories and songs. He was active in Zionist affairs and served as president of the Histadrut Ivrit. He was deeply erudite in Jewish classical learning; he read literature in many languages, not just Hebrew, and amassed a huge private library of modern writing. And he was a poet and short storywriter in his own 205 right. He was a rarity in the expanse of modern Hebrew literature: a poet who devoted himself almost exclusively to the classical sonnet.

I have placed poet and short storywriter in the last position in this list of accomplishments not to fix its value but to indicate Friedland's own ambivalence toward his own "serious" writing. During his lifetime, Friedland was renowned for the stories, poems, and songs he wrote in Hebrew for children as an integral part of his creative approach to Jewish education; and these gained great currency because of their practical usefulness in the classroom. Yet when it came to the poems and short stories he wrote for grown-ups, which were sophisticated in their literary ambitions and decidedly adult in their themes, Friedland was often indifferent to their publication and dissemination. Some he published in the periodicals and annuals of the times, and others were kept in the drawer of his desk. It was only after receiving a diagnosis of cancer four years before he succumbed to the disease that Friedland overcame his ambivalence and rapidly put together three substantial volumes—two collections of poetry and one of short stories—two of which he was able to hold in his hands in published form before he died. Many of these writings, moreover, were themselves composed during Friedland's final years rather than being culled from previous appearances in journals or taken from the drawer. Because the books include no publication dates for individual stories and poems or any other notation, it is not easy to determine precisely how many were composed during his final illness; yet the impression remains of these years as a time of urgent and heightened creativity.

Friedland's death at the age of forty-eight in 1939 had the paradoxical effect of depriving the world of Hebraist education of one of its great figures and at the same time making Friedland into a Hebrew writer to be reckoned with. This he had not been before that moment. His occasional stories and poems had been accounted as an expression of his robust cultural appetites—an avocation of the well-rounded Hebraist, so to speak—rather than as a bid for recognition as a writer among other writers. In Friedland's day as in ours, the publication of a book of poems made a series of claims. It entitled the author to be regarded as a poet and not just a writer of poems. And it required the critical community to notice a new poetic enterprise, to locate it relative to other poetic voices, and to evaluate its achievement. The simultaneity of Friedland's death and the delivery of his books of poetry to the Hebrew-reading public created a special need to take notice. Yet this critical duty, which might ordinarily have been discharged with solemn encomia on the late departed poet, in Friedland's case presented an exasperating challenge. As a body of work, Friedland's sonnets turned out to be, in the expression used by many, a tough nut to crack. The sonnet form was archaic and unsympathetic, the syntax tortured, the vocabulary arcane, and the subjects death-ridden and unpoetical. The difficulty and darkness of the sonnets did not square with the optimistic exuberance of Friedland's activities as a Hebrew educator and with his large figure as an *'ivri* for all seasons. Although the contradictions of Friedland's career may never be neatly resolved, the starting point must be a basic, critical understanding of the sonnets, and this has yet to be undertaken.

First, some words about Friedland's life.[1] He was born in 1891 in the village of Horodok, near Vilna in Lithuania. His father was a scribe [*sofer stam*]. After displaying precocious talents in his studies, he was sent away to the yeshivah in Radoshkovitz at the age of eight, where he gained a reputation as an *'illuy*, a prodigy. It was here, as well, that Friedland was first exposed to Haskalah literature and began to write Hebrew verse. In 1903, when he was twelve, the family emigrated to New York.[2] After a brief period in school, Friedland was obliged to go to work in a garter factory to help support the family. At his parents' request, he studied at the Isaac Elchanan Yeshiva (later part of Yeshiva University) but later enrolled at Columbia University, where he studied with Dewey, Thorndike, and Kilpatrick, the great progressive educators of the time. All this time, Friedland had another life on the Lower East Side among the young Hebraists who were active in the Dr. Herzl Zion Club, Ahiever, Habimah, and other Zionist-Hebraists groups. The figure he cut in these circles, as recalled fondly by his friend the Hebrew feuilletonist Persky, was distinguished by two traits that would figure in his later career: a capacity for wit that verged on sardonic mimicry and a talent for improvisation and spontaneous composition of poems and songs.[3]

Friedland's ascendancy in the world of Jewish education in America was fueled by his devotion to the education of girls. In 1910, at the age of nineteen, he founded the National Hebrew School (Beit Sefer Le'umi) in Manhattan, an afternoon school for girls run on nationalist-Hebraist principles. In seeking a setting in which to put his vision to work, a fusion of progressive education and Hebraism, Friedland understood that he would not be trusted with the education of boys, for whom only a traditionalist curriculum would do. Yet there was little precedent for the Jewish schooling of girls, with few other institutions offering the opportunity. Friedland's school filled a void, and the girls' parents did not much mind the kind of curriculum that was put in place. Friedland therefore had a free hand and created a school centered on Hebrew Bible, Hebrew language, and Hebrew literature. The school was alive with singing, dramatics, and clubs and drew over four hundred students within a few years of its inception. Between the forbidding and highly regimented public school classrooms, on the one hand, and small, overcrowded family apartments that allowed no private space, on the other, the afternoon Hebrew school became a zone of freedom and interest. Friedland also had a flair for public relations. He made the final examinations of the graduating classes a public event and invited Zionist dignitaries and the likes of Ben-Yehuda and his son Itamar, who were spending the war years in New York. The school quickly became the darling of the Jewish nationalist movement in America and an exemplary national institution frequently visited by outside educators.

After ten years at the school, Friedland abruptly left for Cleveland. Even though he was educating girls, the school's board began to pressure him to devote more time to teaching religious subjects. He was unwilling to make the accommodation, and after traveling to Boston to view opportunities there, he accepted an invitation to teach in Cleveland in 1920. What Friedland accomplished in Cleveland became the paradigm for the transformation in Jewish education that was taking place in most large Jewish communities between the two world wars. When Friedland arrived, he found a variety of afternoon Jewish schools, each connected to either a Reform, Conservative, or Orthodox synagogue. During his first years in Cleveland, Friedland used all his charisma and political savvy to wrest the schools from their denominational sponsorship, bring them under the authority of a central "board of Jewish education," standardize their hours and curricula, and infuse them with the Hebraist spirit. Within two years, his school system had twelve branches teaching 2,200 students, four times the number enrolled before his arrival. He went on to establish a teachers institute that, like many of its counterparts founded in the 1920s such as the Boston Hebrew Teachers College and Herzliah in New York, served not only to train teachers but also to offer Judaic instruction to young people long before Jewish studies gained a foothold in the universities.[4] By force of Friedland's will, Cleveland became a site on the world map of Hebrew. Hebrew writers would be invited to Cleveland by Friedland, and the whole educational system would prepare for their coming by studying their writings. No less an eminence than Bialik made the trip to Cleveland on his 1926 journey to America, and his visit was the happy climax of months of preparation. It was on a train ride returning from Cleveland that Ginzburg wrote his poem "La'ivrim ba'ameriqah mizmor" [In praise of the Hebraists of America], which is analyzed in Chapter 8.

Beyond his work in Cleveland, Friedland became known as the creator of a Hebrew pedagogical literature for children. *For* children, it should be stressed, rather than *about* children. Teachers would come to Friedland's office and ask for something they could use for a holiday or pageant; and, exploiting his improvisational talents, on the spot Friedland would dash off a Hebrew playlet for Hanukkah or a Hebrew folk song about the Sabbath. There were many hundreds of these that circulated in mimeographed form and were sent from one teacher to another, amounting to a kind of Hebrew educational samizdat of children's literature. A small sampling of these was published in his lifetime in his *Shiron levatei sefer* [A song book for schools][5] and, after his death, in *Shirei 'am: me'izvono* [Folk songs][6]. The underlying goal of all of Friedland's writing for children was to make the learning of Hebrew a matter of pleasure rather than punishment. He was grimly aware of the hostility of the American environment to acquisition of foreign languages and the particular difficulty of mastering the Hebrew verb system; and he had no illusions about the desire of

Jewish children to spend their after-school hours and Sunday mornings in supplementary schooling.

To accomplish the task, there was no lack of Hebrew primers; however, they were all stilted and removed from the life of children, and they required rote learning of the grammar rules. With his original songs and stories, Friedland set himself the task of achieving this formidable goal by appealing to the child's faculties of humor, wit, imagination, and delight. Friedland became known far and wide for ditties that made it fun, mirabile dictu, to learn the constructions of Hebrew grammar. Consider the following example that aims to teach the infinitive and try imagining how it might sound in Hebrew with rhyming lines and sung to a tune: "To run is easy, every man says / but to walk is easier still. / To walk is easy, every man says, / but to stand is easier still. / To stand is easy, every man says, / but to sit is easier still. / To sit is easy, every man says / but to lie down is easier still. / To lie down is easy, every man says, / But to sleep is easier still."[7]

Friedland's stories for children were published in a series of pamphlets, first mimeographed and later printed, called *Sipurim yafim*. One would be hard pressed to give a suitable English equivalent for the simple modifier *yafim*: nice, pretty, beautiful, pleasant? The terms seem precious or vapid and fail to convey Friedland's desire to wrap language learning around childlike pleasure. The pleasure Friedland has in mind is of a distinctly universal cast. Looking at Friedland's stories today, especially in light of the current practice in Jewish education, one is struck by how utterly non-Jewish is the imaginative world in which they take place. Consider, for example, the story "Zemirim" [Nightingales], which tells of David, who plays the violin while he is spending the summer in a country cottage with his sister and mother. Through the open window, a nightingale hears David's playing and remarks on the fineness of the sound to other nightingales, who fly from the forest to the roof of the house to listen. When David is finished, they begin to sing and continue throughout the night. When they are finished, David leans out the window and says admiringly, "I need a violin, and without it I cannot play. But you have no need for a violin. Your little throat is your violin, and your little heart is the source of your song."[8]

It is a thoroughly beguiling story, whose charm could be easily analyzed to disclose the romantic underpinnings in the assumed rapport between the nascent artistry of the child and the organic artistry of the natural world. Such an analysis would not be beside the point, but it is not necessary to make the case that in this story, and in most of the others in this series, there is no manifest Jewish content. There are many Hasidic tales that Friedland could have availed himself of if his intention had been to teach a similar lesson in Jewish garb. But the garb, in fact, is of a normal American family of the time with no yarmulkes or Sabbath candles; and even though the illustrations (by Anita Rogoff) give us children and grown-ups dressed in the style of the 1950s, twenty-five years after Friedland wrote the stories, they are very much in the spirit of the author's intent. Furthermore, there is no mention of the Yishuv in Palestine, whose emerging Zionist and Hebrew-speaking culture might have served as an alternative to Jewish observance. The point of these children's stories, we must conclude, is not to serve as a vehicle for conveying Jewish values and commandments or Zionist culture but simply to teach Hebrew as a natural whole language, a language that might, however farfetched it seems to us now, be fully at home in America.

A final observation about the Hebrew of these stories. They are written with a watchful eye to the word lists that children could be expected to know in the first several years of their Jewish schooling. And who would know better than Friedland, the overseer of the centralized curriculum of the Bureau of Jewish Education, which words the students in his system were supposed to know in any given year, or, for that matter, in this Napoleonic-like system, in any given week? This is the challenge that Friedland met in these tales: to tell an engrossing story that delights rather than instructs using only the fifty or a hundred Hebrew words possessed by the child in the early years. In regard to his serious poetry, as we see below, Friedland was one of the most erudite users of Hebrew in his age. His active vocabulary effortlessly drew upon hapax legomena from the Bible and arcane realia from the Mishnah. His *Sipurim yafim*, then, constitute a kind of imperial act of *tsimtsum* in which the master voluntarily divests himself of his vast wealth of words and contracts himself into the tiniest linguistic space so that an American child might read a slight but charming story in Hebrew.

In now turning to Friedland's preoccupation with the sonnet, we would do well to keep in mind, mutatis mutandis, the spectacle of voluntary self-contraction. The famous brevity and formal constraints of the sonnet did not demand lexical renunciation, as did the pedagogical tales, but the form required an acute artistic contortionism all the same. Aside from narrative and lyric poems of little account, Friedland was indeed wedded to the sonnet. In this he was unique in American Hebrew poetry; others, like the prolific Lisitzky, dabbled in sonnets, but only Friedland took the vow. The book of poems he saw through to publication before his death is called *Sonetot* and contains one hundred and twenty-five of them[9]; the posthumously published *Shirim* contains forty more.[10] This was a loyalty that was not universally admired. Despite the high esteem in which Friedland was held as a cultural and educational figure and despite the pathos of his prolonged illness and early death, many found this allegiance irksome and the sonnets themselves off-putting.[11] What was found unappealing about Friedland's sonnets can be put under several heads. The syntax is tortuous and leads the reader into false directions before it arrives at a final destination. The semantic density is too high; the poet reaches unnecessarily for rare words and piles them atop one another in cumbersomely inflected forms. The themes of the sonnets, which tend to the morbid and melodramatic, are not what poetry should be about. The sonnet form is too constraining for the life stories Friedland is trying to tell; and the result is fragments that are more frustrating than suggestive. The sonnets as a body of work do not dispose themselves into obvious categories, groupings, or themes, and their ordering and interconnections remain elusive.

Are Friedland's sonnets in fact deeply flawed, or are they merely difficult in the way that some good poems have to be worked at to be understood? My impressions as a reader, which I will endeavor to present as a critical argument, lead me to see a composite picture. I find some of the sonnets impossible to make sense of after several readings and others either trivial or leaden. At the same time, I find that nearly half of the sonnets handsomely repay the necessary effort of multiple readings and yield access to a compellingly different poetic voice. It is this difference, I would argue, that explains the begrudging reception of Friedland's poetry. The sonnets are indeed difficult in form and dark in theme, and on both these counts they went against the grain of American Hebrew poetry as conceived of by some of its major practitioners.

Hebrew poetry in America saw itself as keeping faith with the simple classicism of Hebrew verse as opposed to the barbarisms of the avant-guard that had disfigured Hebrew poetry in Europe and the Yishuv. Friedland's poetic practice sinned against this norm of simplicity. Furthermore, the darkness of the sonnets and the despairing extremity of the human predicaments described in them did not comport well with the robust optimism of American Hebraism, at least in its early years. There of course existed, as has been pointed out, an accepted separation of modes between educational and cultural writing and the prerogatives of literature, which was freed from ideological burdens and given license to express feelings of loneliness and doubt. Nonetheless, Friedland's case seemed different. The weight of his poetry, sporadically published, had not been much felt during his lifetime so that the concerted picture that arose all at once from the two books, coming just before and just after his death, came as a surprise. Within the general celebration of Friedland as an expansive and successful educator, the paradigmatic *'ivri* for all seasons, it was not easy to assimilate the poetic world of the sonnets. It was easier for a critic like Ribalow to expatiate on Immanuel of Rome's importation of the sonnet into Hebrew and Tchernichovsky's revival of the form as Friedland's lineage than to elucidate the sonnets themselves.[12]

The impatience of his friends and readers did not escape Friedland's notice. He baldly opens "Sonetah" [Sonnet] (*Shirim*, p. 172)[13] with a rejoinder.

סוֹנֶטָה

שְׁאֵלוּנִי בְּשֶׁל מָה נֶאֱרְשָׂה בַּת־שִׁירָתִי
אֶל גִּזְרַת שִׁירָה אַחַת. אֶל תַּבְנִית הַסּוֹנֶטָה?
וָאַעַן כִּי עִבְרִי אָנֹכִי וּבְמֵצָרֵי הַגֶּטָה
לַחֲלוֹם עַל מֶרְחָבִים אוֹרִים לִמְּדַתְנִי אֻמָּתִי.

וְעוֹד לִמְּדַתְנִי, לְהַרְבּוֹת גְּדָרִים, סְיָגֵי־שְׁמִירָה:
הַחַי עַל פִּי הַהֲלָכָה לְכָל פְּרָטֶיהָ,לְכָל סְיָגֶהָ,
בַּת־חוֹרִין תְּהִי נַפְשׁוֹ מִצֵּל סָפֵק וּדְאָגָה,
שְׁכִינַת שַׁבָּת תִּשְׁרֶה עָלֶיהָ וּתְעַמֵּמֶנָּה הַיְצִירָה.

וּמָה אַרְצִי הַנֶּאֱהָבָה, הַקְּטַנְטַנָּה עַד לִדְמָעוֹת
אִם לֹא סוֹנֶטָה מְרֻכֶּזֶת, שִׁיר־זָהָב נֶחְמָד?
בִּגְבוּלוֹתֶיהָ הַצָּרִים הִנֵּה יַחֲלֹם עַם נָע וָנָד
לְגֹל מַסֶּכֶת חִזָּיוֹן לִמְלֹא תֵבֵל בָּהּ תּוֹצָאוֹת.

עִבְרִי אָנֹכִי וְרָגִיל לְהִתְכַּוֵּץ לְמַרְאִית עַיִן,
אַךְ שׁוּרוּ נָא אֶל תְּהוֹם נַפְשִׁי – שָׁם קֵצֶה אָיִן.

Sonnet

I have been asked why I have married my muse
To a single poetic frame, to the form of the sonnet.
I respond that I am an *'ivri* and that from within the constraints of
  the ghetto
I have been taught by my people to think of illuminated expanses.

I have also been taught to multiply fences and cordons of
  protection:
For he who lives according to all of the provisions and precautions
  of the *halakhah*,
his soul will elude suspicion or concern,
The Sabbath *shekhinah* will descend upon it and creativity will
  quicken it.

And what is my beloved land, so achingly tiny
If not a concentrated sonnet, a lovely *shir-zahav*?[14]
Within its narrow boarders, a wandering nation will aspire
To unroll the scroll of its vision to the edges of the whole world.

An *'ivri* I am and used to contracting myself for purposes of
   propriety,
But be sure to gaze into the depth of my soul—where there are no
   bounds.

Although the date of the poem cannot be fixed, its placement at
the very end of the posthumous volume would argue for its being a
belated and perhaps reluctantly offered response to his critics. In contrast to many others, this sonnet about sonnets is light, discursive, and
intently communicative; it means to shape an argument. In light of
the aesthetic questions at issue, that argument turns out, rather unexpectedly, to be about religion and nation. Concerning the riddle of
his allegiance to the sonnet, the speaker of Friedland's sonnet explains
that history has taught Jews to accommodate themselves to the physical constraints that have been imposed on them at the very same time
as they dream of expansive vistas of enlightenment. The speaker goes
on to evoke the rabbinic idea of *seyag latorah*, the fences erected by
Jewish law as a hedge against the violation of core commandments. If
he abides scrupulously by these precautionary restrictions, as he has
been taught, then his soul will be free and quickened by creativity and
the Sabbath Shekhinah will descend upon it. Finally, the argument is
extended to the territory of the nation. What is the Land of Israel after
all, the speaker asks, if not a concentrated sonnet? Within that tiny
and cramped land, a nation of wanderers will settle down and dream a
vision that will embrace the whole world.

Friedland's sonnet's sonnet makes a disarming rejoinder to his critics. You may say, so the sonnet argues, that my choice of the sonnet is
self-indulgent and idiosyncratic, a mere occasion for virtuoso performance and the preening of a difficult style. But the truth is that my
choice has been shaped by the seeming contradiction at the heart of
our history as a people. By virtue of having accommodated ourselves
to the restrictions that hedged us in on all sides, we were granted
unlimited spiritual and imaginative freedom. Now, whether or not
one finds Friedland's argument persuasive, it cannot be denied that
it is rhetorically astute. With an eye to his Hebraist readers, Friedland
grounds his rationale on the bedrock of *'ivriyyut*. Highlighting the

process whereby constriction is transformed into transcendence, he moves from the instance of the ghetto to the instance of religion and finally to the instance of Zion, whose present constraints and future promise no Hebraist could deny. Thus, far from being a humble apologia for his art, Friedland's "Sonetah" turns out to be a forceful bid to appropriate the wellsprings of national genius in support of his, at least in the eyes of others, perplexing betrothal.

There is a touch of irony in Friedland's evocation of these hallowed sources of authority because the sonnets are almost entirely free of any reference to the Jewish people, its history and homeland. There was no greater Zionist than Friedland, yet his poetry, or perhaps his conception of poetry, made it the wrong venue for engaging these matters, no matter how significant they were. We have observed that there is a general separation of modes in American Hebrew poetry that protected the literariness of literature. Even so, almost all of the poets were moved at times to react to historical emergencies, and most all of them, as belated heirs to the Hibbat Zion tradition, wrote poems occasioned by visits to Palestine and their subsequent separation from the Land. Friedland preferred not to cross this partition. The exclusion from his poetry of a set of concerns dear to him is connected to another important exclusion. He keeps himself out of his verse. Here and there one finds poems in which the lyrical "I" is dramatized yet rarely exposed, and there is an oblique disclosure of the imminence of death in a moving sequence of sonnets addressed to his daughter (*Shirim*, pp. 159–61). But by and large, Friedland's poetry avoids the reflexive and the confessional and prefers instead to observe the world and to tell stories of others. One stunning exception proves the rule and offers us a tantalizingly fleeting glimpse of the poet's *sitz-im-leben*. In "Shekheni hayehudi" [My Jewish neighbor] (*Shirim*, p. 142), on a perfect summer day, the speaker sits on his porch in a suburban neighborhood reading about the persecutions of the Jews in the newspaper. His neighbors cannot understand his long face, which he covers with the newspaper when he begins to cry. Meanwhile, his Jewish neighbor, wearing a felt yarmulke, is serenely watering his plants under the bright blueness of the sky. The sonnet concludes with the admission:

"I did not know whether to curse his serenity or bless it." There is Friedland, the *'ivri*—so he identifies himself in the poem—under the blue skies of suburban America in the later 1930s convulsed by the looming fate of European Jewry far away and caught between the obliviousness of his neighbors and the serenity of the believing Jew next door. It is a moment of self-portraiture that does not return.

In fact it was the very impersonality of the sonnet, as well as its brevity, that attracted Friedland. There was something in his temperament that found a deep affinity with a discrete, brief, and rule-governed poetic act, and the attraction came not from the discipline of the *halakhah* alone. Sustained exposition was of no interest to him. He did not wish for the scope, which many writers seek to supply the variations to their themes or to give adequate representation to a sequence of emotions or to elaborate an idea. The discrete and momentary nature of the sonnet served Friedland in two different ways in accord with the two general uses to which he put the sonnet. The greatest number of sonnets tell a story—or, more accurately, the end of a story—and are based on observations of the lives of other people. A smaller but significant number are performances of wit that showcase the audacious powers of the linguistic imagination.[15]

Let us look first at the case of wit. In reminiscing about their youth on the Lower East Side, it may be recalled, Persky singled out Friedland's gift for satire, mimicry, and extemporaneous invention. This complex of energies served Friedland throughout his career in various ways. The songs and playlets he composed for his students drew innocently on his quick-fire imagination. In the circle of his friends, his amusing parodies of familiar communal figures drew less innocently on his talents for mimicry. When it came to his serious poetry, this gift took the form of wit, as understood by Aristotle in the *Rhetoric* and by the English metaphysical poets, as the ability to make unexpected but illuminating comparisons. Under the sign of wit, the poet makes sustained and artificial comparison between two comically disparate objects. The comparison is artificial in the sense that the communality between the two exists only by virtue of the poet's ingenuity, and its life is coterminous with the poem as artifact.

Although there may be an earnest moral to be conveyed, the balance of attention inclines toward acknowledgement of the poet's powers of invention.

A good example of Friedland's practice of wit is his sonnet "Ke'anqor qatan" [As a little sparrow] (*Shirim*, p. 139). Thirteen of the sonnet's fourteen lines describe the resourceful but fragile life of a sparrow. This tiny bird sojourns amidst the hoofs and jowls of the big barnyard animals picking a meager repast from the odd kernels of feed dropped on the ground. Although at times it can hop on the back of a bull and happily see beyond ground level, there are other times when the dangerous clomp of a horse's hoof reminds the sparrow that it is a winged creature that properly belongs in the heavens, and it then takes flight into the blue and realizes his freedom. Now line fourteen: "Oh, my friend, such was my soul until yesterday." The moral, then, is something like this: I was immersed in a state of self-involvement and small-mindedness until a threat to my wellbeing reminded me that my soul was made for higher things and I raised myself up. The success of the poem depends on the power of the key given in the concluding line to realize the intent of the analogy and allow us to rethink—to reexperience, really—the picture of the sparrow's life as an allegory of the soul. To my mind, Friedland succeeds in pulling this off in "Ke'anqor qatan"; yet there remains a fundamental disproportion in the workings of the poem. The serious point is indeed made, and it is made with a kind of *frisson* of recognition when the two levels of the poem suddenly come together at the very end. In the last analysis, however, what remains most remarkable for the reader in this poem is its brilliance as a *performance*. The poet has succeeded, with evident profit, in yoking together radically dissimilar entities.[16]

Friedland takes as a particular challenge investing everyday objects with metaphysical import. In the very clever "'Amudei hatelegraf" [Telegraph poles] (p. 5), the telegraph poles are apostrophized as the steady upholders of a giant unseen harp that plays the song of man. In "Ḥallonot" [Windows] (p. 17), the window is made the subject of a series of portentous epigrams ("The window is the visage," "The window is the bosom of loneliness," "The window is the confession of the individual"), until the window becomes the very portal to eternity. In

"Hotel" (p. 44), the speaker stands as a humble supplicant before the grandeur and authority of a great hotel only to be visited by a nightmarish vision of an earthquake that demolished not the great edifice but him, the speaker, the hotel's "pale brother."

The compression of the sonnet works well for these exercises in wit. The fourteen-line Procrustean bed is world enough for an ingenious idea or a flash of brilliance, and the poet gains credit for achieving his desired effects within the demanding rules of the game. When it comes to telling a story, however, the self-assumed limits would seem to be intolerable. While such another poet as Bavli adopts the leisurely and capacious dramatic monologue for presenting the life of a figure like Mrs. Woods, Friedland chooses another path for himself. He wants what he wants: He wants to tell a story about people *and* to remain within the magic box of the sonnet. His strategy for having his way involves several techniques. First, he isolates and privileges a single heightened moment of realization or crystallization in the story line. He then places this moment within the context of a longer-term set of events, which can only be suggested in a few gestures. Finally, there is a *pointe*, a jarring and quickly reported conclusion, which usually involves death.

Friedland's story sonnets are like nothing else in Hebrew poetry, and not just in America. They stand very much apart from the lyric, confessional, and symbolist tendencies that energize Hebrew verse in the first half of the twentieth century. The source of this innovation is not difficult to find in the case of a poet so well read in American literature as was Friedland. It is the poetry of Edwin Arlington Robinson (1869–1935), the New England poet whose popularity was at its zenith when Friedland was writing his sonnets. Robinson was known both for the long Arthurian narrative poems of his later years and for the short poems, many of them sonnets, of his early years. In this latter group, each short poem or sonnet chronicled the life of a different solitary figure taken from the Yankee types in Robinson's native Gardiner, Maine, which he called Tilbury Town in his poems. (See the pilgrimage to Gardiner made by the speaker of Preil's poem "Maine" in Chapter 12.) Many of these poems, such as "Richard Cory," the story of a rich man who puts a bullet through his head, and "Miniver

Cheevy," the story of a man who cannot reconcile himself to the uncourtliness of contemporary life, were widely anthologized. Most of these vignettes are tales of disillusionment and decline and amount to an "embellished poetry of regret."[17] Robinson also was the first, according to Irving Howe, to give voice to the experience of ordinary people in American verse.[18]

Now, Friedland's borrowing from Robinson is clear. Robinson provided the model and sanction for the ambition to incorporate a life story within the circumscribed compass of the sonnet. Robinson further endorsed the idea that the lives of ordinary people are a legitimate subject for poetry and that the telling of these individual stories need not be integrated into a coherent group portrait. Upon this armature, Friedland added materials of his own. In contrast to Robinson's plain, even conversational, diction, Friedland deployed a style of imposing syntactical and lexical difficulty. The melodramatic and sometimes lurid subjects of Friedland's sonnets were his own, too; with the exception of Richard Cory's bullet in the head, the disillusionment of Robinson's subjects is finely attenuated.

Like Robinson's, Friedland's story poems are anti-lyrical in the sense that they are about others, not the self. In these poems, Friedland assumes the role of chronicler and observer. Yet there is one sonnet that vouchsafes us one of those rare reflexive glimpses and may serve as a picture of the *ursprung* of Friedland's commitment to his posture as observer. "Anaḥah" [Groan] (p. 66), one of the best sonnets to my mind, is told by a first-person speaker who is in bed trying to go to sleep.

אֲנָחָה

עַל מִשְׁכָּבִי בַּלַּיְלָה הִגִּיעַתְנִי אֲנָחָה,
פְּלֵטַת חַלּוֹן, בְּבֵית־שְׁכֵנִים פָּתוּחַ,
וְאוּלַי נִשְׂאָה אֶל תְּנוּךְ אָזְנִי עַל כַּנְפֵי־רוּחַ
מִבֵּית שֵׁנִי, שְׁלִישִׁי. לֹא בְכִי וְלֹא צְוָחָה,
כִּי אַנְחַת־עֱנוּת עַרְטִילָאִית, הֵד־מַכְאוֹב —
וַיִּשְׁתַּתֵּק כָּל יַעַר־הֲגִיגַי עַל רֹחַב־תְּשׁוּאָתוֹ.
הִבְהִין הַלַּיְלָה סְבִיב חַדְרִי, כָּבַשׁ נְשִׁימָתוֹ,

וַתְּהִי אָזְנִי מִכְמֹרֶת לְכָל רַחֲשֵׁי־הָרְחוֹב.
אַךְ כָּל הַלַּיְלָה הֵן קָטֹן הוּא מֵהָכִיל
אַנְחַת אָדָם סוֹבֵל! לְהֵד הָאֲנָחָה הַנַּעֲלֶמֶת
הָגְתָה נַפְשִׁי הָגוּת קָשָׁה, נַפְשִׁי הַמִּתְפָּעֲמֶת:
הֵן כֹּה רַכִּים נִימֵי־הַלֵּב, הֵן כֹּה עָדִין הַדָּם –
תֵּבֵל, תֵּבֵל! הוֹי, מָה עוֹלַלְתְּ לְיֵצֶר לֵב אָדָם?
וַיִּמְצָאֵנִי שַׁחַר קַר לְבֶן חָרוֹן וָחִיל.

Groan

On my bed at night a groan reached me,
Which escaped through the open window of the neighbors' house,
Or perhaps it was born to my ear on the wings of the wind,
From a second house or a third. It was neither weeping nor an
    outcry,
But rather a naked sigh of misery, an echo of pain—
And the forest of my thoughts in the breadth of their commotion
    fell silent.
The night tiptoed around my room, holding its breath,
And my ear became a net for all the sounds of the street.
Yet the whole night is surely too paltry to contain
the sigh of suffering man! To the echo of the silent sigh
My soul, my agitated soul, entertained a difficult thought:
The strings of the heart are so very sensitive, blood is so very
    frail—
Oh world, world! What have you done to the inclination of man's
    heart? Dawn found me white with cold anger and dread.

Through the open window, the sound of a groan, which comes from
an unidentifiable house somewhere in the neighborhood, steals into
his room. The sound is not that of weeping or a piercing outcry but
a sigh that bespeaks naked misery. The speaker is now wide awake;
his ears have become antennae for the sounds of the neighborhood,
and suddenly the night seems too short to contain the full chorus of
anguish that is now irrevocably audible to him. If we take "Anaḥah"
as an instance of self-portraiture, Friedland is portraying himself as
an ordinary person going through the daily business of waking and
sleeping who is suddenly assailed by the suffering of others and who

just as suddenly becomes involuntarily supersensitive to that suffering. Vulnerable and set upon by this free-floating cry of misery that comes from the outside, the speaker is robbed of the companionable company of his own thoughts and forced to reckon with the pain that stalks human existence. The experience resembles, if the comparison can be forgiven, the foundational myth about how a superhero first acquired his super powers.[19]

What are the moments of anguish that are represented in the story sonnets? The heterogeneity of these poems proscribes holding up any one of them as a paradigm or typical dramatic situation. The truest way to suggest the contours of this material is simply to offer a summary sampling of these plots. Amidst the bright lights on the way to the theater, a woman becomes deeply confused about whether she wants to be with the man who escorts her ("Baderekh late'atron" [On the way to the theater], p. 14). A visitor enters the room, and a deeply insecure man suddenly realizes from the reactions of his wife and children that this man in his wife's lover, and he has become the outsider ("Oreaḥ" [Visitor], p. 34). Ten years after his death, a father appears in a dream to his youngest and least loved son, who is plunged into a nightmare vision of fighting with his father's bones ("Sheled" [Skeleton], p. 42). A woman is brutally raped by a friend of her husband's, yet the husband, who knows of the deed despite his wife's silence, timidly greets the friend the next day as if nothing had happened ("Melqeḥei-ratson" [Tongs of will], p. 50). To solve his midlife malaise, a loving wife gives her own money to her husband to build his dream house, but once it is built and the celebrations fade, he jumps from the roof ("Missi haḥalom" [From the height of the dream], p. 63). A beautiful seventeen-year-old is wedded to a wealthy older man the same age as the girl's widowed mother; as the girl lapses into illness and dies, the two adults fuse into a parental unit ("Abba-Ima" [Father-mother], p. 86). A composer's wife surprises her husband late in his career by gathering together into a book his many unpublished compositions, but she fails to please because a mistakenly placed pause ruins the sound of a line ("Pause" [Comma], p. 88). A woman considers her fears and fantasies as she prepares to meet the man who once abandoned her into the disappointing arms of her current husband ("Rondeivu" [Rendezvous], p. 113).

Many more story sonnets could be adduced, but not a small number of them are opaque and overwrought. Inherent in the very conception of the story sonnets is the need to evoke the background events that have led to the moment dramatized in the poem. Often enough Friedland falls into the trap of excessive allusiveness; his gestures toward the explanatory context and situation are so fragmentary and murky that the thread is easily lost. There are times, however, when Friedland handles the challenge with efficient economy, and sufficient space is cleared for the turning point he wishes to illuminate. When that happens, as it does in "Baderekh late'atron" and "Rondeivu," Friedland succeeds in tapping the revelatory potential of the sonnet's concision and in creating a vivid tang of the human condition. That condition, with its regrets and missed opportunities, often ends in death. Death, of course, is the ultimate *pointe*, the ultimate closure. It is foreshortened and melodramatic and, one might say, too easy. Yet to a man like Friedland, who for a long time was well acquainted with the prospect of personal annihilation, it is not too much to ask to believe in his sincerity on this subject.

✳ גֵז
  Shearing

Analysis

גֵז

לֹא בִנְוֵה־רוֹעִים וּבֵין גְּדֵרוֹת הַצֹּאן
חָלְפוּ אֲבֵי־חֶלְדִּי, יְמֵי הַיְרָקִים:
כְּזִכְרוֹנוֹת־יַלְדוּת חַוְרָינִים, רְחוֹקִים,
יַלְבִּינוּ עֶדְרַי עַל פְּנֵי מִרְעֵי־דִמְיוֹן;

כִּי לֹא כָוִירְגִּיל וּכְוֶרְדְסְווֹרְתְ וְכְפַרְנָסֵס זַ'ם,
שְׁבִילְם הַשַּׁאֲנָן בְּחֵיק כָּרִים וַאֲחוּ הִשְׁתַּלְשֵׁל,
גָּדַלְתִּי אֲנִי הַדַּל: מִבֵּית־הָאָב עַד בֵּית־הָאֵל
נָתִיב קָצָר נִמְשָׁךְ, עָגוּם וּמְרוֹמֶם.

אַךְ זֵכֶר־כְּפָר אֶחָד גָּנוּז בְּמוֹ לִבִּי:
דְּמוּת כֶּבֶשׂ צַח, מִן הַגִּזָּה עֵת שָׁב,

חָרֵד וָבוֹשׁ יֵלֵךְ מוֹרִיד בְּמַעֲרָמָיו.
מִדֵּי זָכְרִי אוֹתוֹ, רַחֲמַי יִכָּמְרוּ בִּי;
מִדֵּי זָכְרִי אוֹתוֹ, אֶזְכֹּר אַף זֹאת: יֵשׁ יוֹם
וְגַם אֲנִי אָשׁוּב גָּזוּז, חָרֵד, עֵירֹם.

Shearing

Neither in shepherds' encampments nor among the sheep stiles
Did the flower of my youth, my green days pass:
Like the pale, fading memories of childhood,
My flocks turn white upon the pastures of my imagination.

For unlike Virgil, Wordsworth and Francis Jammes,
Whose tranquil path wound through fields and rushes,
I grew up poor: from my father's house to God's house
There stretched only a short lane, gloomy but exalted.

Yet there remains one village memory stored away in my heart:
The image of a gleaming lamb just come from the shearing,
    Trembling and abashed and turning pink in its nakedness.
As I recall it, empathy stirs within me;
Every time I recall it, I remember this too: there will come a day
When I too will return shorn, trembling, and naked.[20]

The first two stanzas set out, in declamatory and polemical tones, the fundamental difference between the speaker's childhood—and, by extension perhaps, Hebrew poetry as a whole—and the very origins of the Western literary tradition. That great tradition is rooted in a pastoral vision in which the child is nurtured by the natural world. Virgil wrote the *Eclogues* before he went on to the epic. For Wordsworth, the child raised in the bosom of nature is, famously, the father to the man. The French poet Francis Jammes (1868–1938), who grew up in the Pyrenees, was wildly popular among youth at the beginning of the twentieth century, who found the simplicity and artlessness of his pastoral poetry a fresh alternative to the esotericism of the symbolists.[21] There are two entwined themes here: the role of childhood memories in the formation of the poetic self and the role of nature as the necessary font of poetry. On both counts, the speaker of Friedland's sonnet allies himself with an exceptional, minority position. His childhood memories are meager and fading, and rather than richly unfolding in the lap of nature, his early life was impoverished and circumscribed by the gloomy path that led from home to synagogue. Yet despite all the protests and disavowals, which take up the sonnet's octet, the sestet offers the kernel of just such a pastoral memory.

Each of the first two quatrains is similarly divided in half, with the first half declaring what the speaker's childhood has *not* been and the second half stipulating what it *has* been. The ruling rhetorical trope is litotes, an affirmation given in the form of a negation. When it comes to describing the lyric-pastoral tradition that is not his patrimony, the stylistic pitch is fulsome to the point of caricature. The shepherds' oases [*nevei-ro'im*] and the flower of his youth [*ibei-ḥeldi*] are instances of periphrasis, in which ornate substitutes are used for plain substantives. The path that winds its way through fields and rushes evokes the idealized biblicism of Avraham Mapu's nineteenth-century novels set in the time of the book of Kings, in addition to the lions of world literature such as Wordsworth, the transcription of whose name in Hebrew has about it an almost comic implausibility. It is all too lush and beneficent to bear any meaningful connection to a childhood like that of the poem's speaker.

What can be affirmed of the past is far more elusive. The simile in lines 3–4 is surprisingly complex and turns on the question of the presence or absence of color. In contrast to the green days of the heralded pastoral childhood among the sheepfolds, the speaker's "flocks" turn white upon the "pastures" of his imagination. For him, the flocks and the pastures are only ironic figures of speech that bear no correspondence to the real things of nature. The whitening of these flocks is not so much a matter of purity as of the draining of color, as conveyed by analogy to the way childhood memories fade as they become increasingly distant. The depletion of the visual reservoir of childhood is extended to the impoverishment described in lines 7–8. The impoverishment is not so much material as imaginative. There may have been an abundance of spiritual sustenance—the exalted [*meromam*] quality of the circumscribed path—of the sort offered by the short tether between the synagogue and a God-fearing home.

But when it comes to the sort of green vales and rushing streams that nurtured the imaginations of the world's great poets, his deprivation was total.[22]

When all the protestations are over, however, a childhood memory is proffered after all. But only one, as if to say that it alone survived the impoverishment and amnesia. It has been stored away [*ganuz*] after the manner of sacred texts that have outlived their usefulness. (Notice the play of *ganuz* with *gizah* [shearing].) The shorn lamb is an image with powerful symbolic associations of innocence and sacrifice in the iconography of both Christianity and Judaism, as well as within folk literature and nursery rhymes. The fact that the speaker's one memory concerns a lamb is directly connected to the flocks and pastures of the first two stanzas; it is as if the speaker is saying, "If the pastoral setting has been the cradle of great poetry, I too have something to offer, however meager." Friedland's shorn lamb, whose description takes up all of two lines, is an intensely ambiguous and unstable figure. Again, color plays a key role. The lamb returns from the shearing dazzlingly white only to turn pink in its nakedness.[23] (*Mavrid bemaʿarumav* is a stroke of assonantal genius.) This is a reversal of the draining of color that the speaker claims governs his remembrance of childhood. The lamb is disoriented and ashamed; robbed of its plush coat, the skin become pellucid to reveal the blood and bone beneath the surface.

In the concluding lines of the sonnet, the second half of the sestet, the focus shifts to the feelings that are aroused by the memory of the lamb. The language is unmistakably modeled on Jeremiah 31:20, in which God admits that even though he had condemned Ephraim, the northern kingdom of Israel, to destruction for its sins, He cannot help thinking about Ephraim, and these memories move Him to feelings of tenderness and mercy. The bridge between Jeremiah and Friedland's sonnet is the involuntary experience of empathy that comes through memory. Now, there is nothing unnatural about being moved to pity by the memory of the poor shorn lamb. But with the repeating of the phrase "*midei zokhri oto*" [every time I recall it] in line 13, the focus shifts again from the feelings about the lamb evoked by the memory of the lamb to the feelings evoked by the memory of the lamb about the *speaker*'s own fate. Recalling that lamb from the depths of his child-hood, he is recalled to an awareness of what ultimately lies in store for him. Through his childhood eyes, he identified with the lamb's humiliation without knowing that its abashment would be temporary. As an adult, the identification with the lamb has changed. A day will come, he knows, when he too will be returned "shorn, trembling and naked." The import of where he will be returned *to* is clear enough, and we know that unlike the mortified lamb, which will eventually grow another coat of wool, for him there will be no second chance.

The proud dissociation from a pastoral childhood connects Fried-land to a prominent theme in modern Hebrew literature: growing up in the muddy shtetls of Eastern Europe and being taught by rote in the one-room heder was in fact *no* childhood and certainly not a sacred font from which inspiration could be drawn later in life. This is perhaps the reason why Friedland's verse eludes autobiographical reflection and focuses so resolutely on the adult behavior of others. And when Friedland does dip into the largely forgotten recesses of childhood, as he does in this poem, should we be surprised that what he finds there is there an emblem of death?

Ten   Moshe Feinstein

During the heyday of the Hebrew colleges, Herzliah Teachers Institute stood apart on two counts. It was independent and freestanding, unlike its two counterparts in New York City, the Teachers Institute of the Jewish Theological Seminary (JTS) and the Teachers Institute of Yeshiva University, which were units within larger institutions; and it was unlike its sister institutions in Boston, Baltimore, Philadelphia, and Chicago, each of which enjoyed a degree of community-wide sponsorship. Herzliah was also unique because it was wholly identified with one man, Moshe Feinstein, who founded the school and headed it until he died, when the institution effectively died with him. There were other dominant personalities in the Hebrew college world: Nissan Touroff in Boston, Mordecai Kaplan at JTS, Pinkhos Churgin at Yeshiva University; yet, there was none in which the man and the institution were nearly identical as with Feinstein and Herzliah.

Feinstein was born in 1898 in Pinsk, in what is today Belarus. His father was a Hebrew teacher and writer who gave his son a religious-national education. Feinstein attended the Russian gymnasium in Pinsk before emigrating to America in 1912. Two years later he began teaching in H. A. Friedland's National Hebrew School (Beit Sefer Le'umi), the innovative institution for girls that introduced Hebrew-language study, as well as extra-curricular activities. In 1920 Friedland resigned from the school over differences with its board and accepted a position as director of the Hebrew schools of Cleveland, where he remained until his premature death twenty years later. In that same year, Feinstein married Friedland's sister Esther and shortly afterward started a new Hebrew high school for girls with forty-five devoted graduates from the National Hebrew School. The new school, called the

228

Herzliah Hebrew Academy, soon opened to boys as well as girls; classes were held 6–10 p.m., Monday through Thursday and on Sunday, 10 a.m.–2:15 p.m. A few years later, courses on pedagogy were introduced, and Herzliah became a teachers seminary in addition to being a high school.[1]

The school changed addresses on the Lower East Side many times during the 1920s and 1930s. Lacking institutional patronage and lacking connections to Uptown Jews, Herzliah struggled from one financial crisis to another, often bailed out on the brink of collapse by the likes of Israel Metz, the Ex-Lax magnate, who supported many Hebraist endeavors. During the depths of the Depression, the total school budget declined from $11,756 in 1926 to $6,581 in 1934. The highest teacher salary was $1800, less than half the compensation received by counterparts at the Teachers Institute of JTS.[2] Finally, a permanent home for Herzliah, a four-story building located at 314 West 91st Street on the Upper West Side, was acquired for the school, to which it moved in March of 1944.

Despite these vicissitudes, Herzliah was a great educational success. Its spirit was held aloft by a common commitment on the part of the students and the faculty to the national revival of the Jewish people through the Hebrew language and the connection to Palestine. Most of the students in the upper division of the school studied full-time at branches of the City University of New York and came to Herzliah evenings and Sundays. In the 1940s about four hundred students enrolled for the year, about 35 percent in the Teachers Institute and the remainder in the high school. For only a limited percentage of the students—mostly the young women, some of whom were training to become Hebrew school teachers—did the long hours of Hebrew studies contribute to a vocational goal. Most were members of the Zionist youth movements, each of which had its own ideological emphasis and location on the political map. At Herzliah they came together to take on the cultural ballast that youth movement activities—with their songs and folkdances and stirring rhetoric—could not provide and to acquire the tools for life in Eretz Yisrael or for leadership in America.

Chief among these tools was the Hebrew language itself, and in none of the Hebrew colleges in America was its study taken more seriously than at Herzliah. Whole semesters were devoted to mastering the intricacies of certain *binyanim*, verb conjugations with endless variants occasioned by weak letters in the verb stem. (The Hebrew master of Herzliah was the inimitable Persky, an abiding and genial chronicler of the Hebraist movement and author of a weekly feuilleton in *Hado'ar*.) The classics of modern Hebrew literature were another main focus, taught by Feinstein himself. Serious attention was given to Mendele, Bialik, Berdichevsky, Tchernichovsky, and others in the first years of the college program; in the later years of the program, the courses went backward in time to the more difficult texts of the Haskalah and the poetry of the Middle Ages. (The five hours Bialik spent at Herzliah on May 28, 1926, speaking to students and autographing his books, served as a sublime recognition of the school's Hebraic achievement; nowhere among young people in America could he have been better appreciated and more sincerely lionized.)

Herzliah prided itself on the fact that its teaching of Hebrew writers was "monographic rather than anthological," as was the case in other institutions, where snippets and selections were the norm.[3] Bible, especially the classical prophets and the wisdom books, was also a key attainment; this subject was taught by the austere and erudite Epstein, who was the most astute literary critic of American Hebrew literature. Avraham Zvi Halevi, whose harrowing urban poetry is discussed in Chapter 19, was also a teacher at the school. Finally, Jewish history and Talmud rounded out the curriculum. Students in the college division attended classes at least thirteen hours per week, in addition, of course, to their full-time university programs. Feinstein was proud of the fact that even at a time when the quality of the talmud torah school was declining, Herzliah was raising its standards by adding more hours—up from nine at the outset—and more demanding and intensive courses.[4]

Herzliah distinguished itself from the other Hebraist colleges in New York in its relationship to religion and Zionism. Many students came to Herzliah because they did not want to undertake their studies within religious institutions with their implied norms and demands. Herzliah was, in a sense that is not easy to define but characteristic of the Hebraist movement in America, religion neutral. Although most of the faculty were not religious, religion was not criticized or ridiculed, observant students felt comfortable in the institution, and rabbinic texts, including Talmud, *Shulḥan Arukh*, and siddur were conspicuous elements of the curriculum. The complexity of this stance is nicely expressed in an anecdote related by Avraham Holtz, a professor emeritus of Hebrew literature at JTS, who in the early 1950s was one such observant student at Herzliah. The curriculum required four hours per week of Talmud study in the advanced years, and many of the students, activists in various Zionist youth movements, bridled at such a heavy demand in a subject that lacked paramount importance in their minds. They got together and asked Holtz to present their case to Feinstein, which Holtz agreed to do. The interview proved to be a short one. With trepidation, Holtz entered the dean's office and delivered his commission. Feinstein listened and declared, "*Kakh pasak Aḥad Ha'am!*" [Thus has Aḥad Ha'am ordained!], and the meeting was over.[5] Aḥad Ha'am had been dead for more than a quarter century, and even when he was alive, it was unlikely that he had rendered peremptory judgments about the curricular regimes of educational institutions in America. But he was still alive for Feinstein, who not incorrectly interpreted the master's catholic approach to the historical arc of Hebrew culture with its roots in religious literature. One need not accept the force of rabbinic law and its theological assumptions to see basic competence in Talmud study as a prerequisite for Jewish literacy and leadership.

The Zionist ethos of Herzliah was all encompassing but not ideological or partisan. Students from Beitar on the Right may have engaged in heated debate with students from Hashomer Hatzair on the Left in the cafeteria and in the hallways; but in the classroom, they were conjointly absorbed in mastering difficult passages in Jeremiah or a short story by Brenner or the *nif'al* future of *peh-yod* verbs. If Hebrew nationalism served as a kind of civil religion, it was one that was most characteristically celebrated in the communal singing at school-wide assemblies, marking key moments in the Jewish year. During the critical weeks of the 1948 War of Independence, classes ceased to meet because both students and faculty were too preoccupied and too filled with emotion. To gauge the depth of this unambivalent national fervor, it is worth contrasting the mood of Herzliah at this hour with the atmosphere at JTS, some thirty blocks farther up Broadway. At the same time that business as usual was disrupted by the events in Israel, Bavli, professor of Hebrew literature at JTS, wrote a searing poem indicting the aloofness of the institution where he taught. The opening lines suggest the tenor of the critique: "Vain and barren you tread / On hushed carpets in sealed-off halls of learning, / Sporting your crown of complacency / And cloaked in your mantle of self-importance."[6] Surely there were many students and faculty at the Teachers Institute of JTS who were as agitated by anxiety and anticipation as their counterparts somewhat farther downtown. However, the Rabbinical School of JTS, which dominated the institution, was exposed by Bavli for its removal from wholehearted identification with the Zionist movement and the jubilation that erupted elsewhere when the Jewish state was established.

Herzliah was Feinstein's dominion, and Feinstein was Herzliah. But that world of enthusiastic and earnest students, devoted and obsessed teachers, and an uplifting cultural vision is completely absent from Feinstein the poet. His poetry is personal, inward and romantic, and entirely detached from the thematics of Judaic pathos and national struggle. In this split, Feinstein embodied the cleavage we have seen in the careers of other Hebrew poets between Hebraist educational work and a commitment to the purity of poetry. For others, this insistence on the separate modes was modulated with time. American Hebrew poets did not begin writing about Hebrew schools, but, realizing the impasse of lyric self-involvement, they did reach out to engage America in its vistas and history. Feinstein resisted this movement outward and insisted on remaining within the precincts of the self. Feinstein also differed from others in the modesty of his poetic output. Until the late 1930s, Feinstein rarely published more than one poem a year. Epstein explains that because he *was* Herzliah, the duties imposed by the headship of Herzliah gave him no rest.[7] Yet surely it was also a matter of temperament. Lisitzky in New Orleans, for example, ran a Hebrew school and still managed to turn out many hundreds of lyric poems and the occasional epic. For Feinstein, writing poetry seems to have required a complete removal from the sphere of Herzliah and even from the ken of his family; he often found this disengagement from the public and domestic self on ocean voyages, and one of these voyages itself became the setting for his best composition, the long poem *Ḥalom vegoral* [Dream and fate] (1937). Later in life, after the death of his wife and a daughter, he found the impersonality of hotel lobbies along the Tel Aviv shore suitable for this purpose.[8]

A good introduction to Feinstein's poetic preoccupations is provided by the 1919 poem "Shenayim li milaylah" [Two from the night].[9]

שְׁנַיִם לִי מֵלַיְלָה

שְׁנַיִם לִי מֵלַיְלָה:
עָלֶה כָּמוּשׁ, פְּתַקְת־דָּקָב שְׁדוּפָה,
אֲשֶׁר יֶרֶק־חַיָּיו פָּרַח עִם הַסּוּפָה
הַמְּטַיְּלָה,
נָפַל בְּחִיל־מָוֶת אֶל חַלּוֹנִי,
עַל תַּכְרִיכֵי עַרְשִׂי סְפוּגַת שִׁמָּמוֹנִי
וְדוֹבֵב : קַר מִתַּחַת קַרְשֵׁי גּוֹלָל,
קַר וְטָחוּב . . .
וְחָה, חָה, חָה בְּחַלּוֹנִי דָּפַק כִּמְבַשֵּׂר בְּשׂוֹרָה,
צְחוֹק־גִּיל, בֶּן חָזֶה חַם שֶׁל עַלְמָה,
הָרוֹמֵז סוֹדֵי לֵיל וְקִמְטֵי שַׂלְמָה
שְׁחוֹרָה,
כִּרְכֵּר כָּאַיָּלָה דֶּרֶךְ דָּמִי,
עוֹרֵר עַל שִׂפְתוֹתַי רַעַד צָמֵא
וְקָרָא: חֵשֶׁק, חֵשֶׁק,
קָרָא וְאֶל הַלַּיְלָה גָּלָה,
כִּגְלוֹת צְלִילֵי פַּעֲמוֹן־שַׁלְגִּית זַכִּים
אֶל שַׁחֲרוּרִית הַמֶּרְחַקִּים.

עַל תַּכְרִיכֵי עַרְשִׂי פִּרְכֵּס עוֹד הֶעָלֶה.

Two from the Night

Two from the night:
A shriveled leaf, rotted and blasted,
Drained of its green vitality
By the passing storm,
Fell in its death throes upon my window,

On the desolate shrouds of my bed,
And spoke: "Cold it is under the planks of the grave,
Cold and damp . . .
Hey, hey, hey! Like someone announcing great news, on my
        window knocked
A cry of joy from the warm breast of a young woman,
Suggesting night secrets and the folds
Of a black dress,
Cavorting like a gazelle in my blood
Arousing on my lips a thirsty trembling,
And crying: Desire, desire,
Before it went off banished into the night,
As the pure pealing of a snowy bell
Is carried off into the blackening distance.

On the shrouds of my bed the leaf still shuddered.

While the speaker lies desolate in his bed, two visitors knock on his window. The first is a shriveled leaf that has been knocked about in the storm and drained of its color. Landing on the speaker's window sill, it intones: "It is cold under the planks of the grave, / Cold and damp. . . ."[10] The second is the sound of a young woman's laughter that hints at nocturnal pleasures and the folds of a black dress. The sound agitates the speaker, coursing through his blood "like the cavorting of a gazelle" and calling to him with the words: "Desire, desire," before it recedes into the dark reaches of the night like the peals of a bell getting lost in the distance. In its brief closing line, the poem cuts back to the driven leaf: "On the shrouds of my bed the leaf still shudders." The stasis and analytic distance of the poem's speaker are conspicuous. Desolate and enshrouded on his bed, the things of the night come to him, and he counts and observes them. Here the count is two: Thanatos in the form of the shriveled leaf and Eros in the form of the erotic laughter, and although Feinstein entertains multiple classifications in others poems, as we see below, binarism remains his modal way of seeing. The poem puts us squarely in the world of Edgar Allen Poe and the ambience of the grotesque. The night is a realm beyond our control in which the border between life and death, inside and outside, is easily crossed and disembodied cries of desire can float free of their source and colonize where they may. The poem's drama comes from the flare of desire that momentarily lights up the speaker's morbid state. While the desiccated leaf is all-too-familiar a confirmation of being-unto-death, the surprise visitation of erotic laughter is the very possibility of arousal, which provides unexpected evidence that the speaker's parched soul has not yet become dead to desire. When the moment falls away, however, the speaker is not left enriched by the experience. The dour leaf, which at the outset of the poem had knocked at his window, shudders on his bed. It has come inside.

During the next several years, Feinstein's poetry probed in unexpected ways each pole of the essential romantic nexus between the soul and the world. "Kamah minei 'etsev yesh" [How many kinds of sorrow are there?] (1921, pp. 15–18) is ostensibly another counting poem whose title proposes a taxonomic project. But the rational-analytical rhetorical framework of the poem is eventually overwhelmed by a wild natural malevolence that refuses to be investigated. The poem begins by answering its own question with a list of diverse sorrows. There is the sadness of love, which is dispatched in a few banal lines; then there is the sadness of parting, similarly polished off with a few conventional phrases, as if to say that these two are obvious and commonplace. Next is the sadness of death, which begins in a similarly conventional vein but soon modulates into an elaborate and grotesque image of a dying butterfly and its spasmodic sounds and wing beatings before it finally expires.

The butterfly's death throes are the bridge to the poem's real subject, which cannot easily be guessed by extrapolating from the series of sadnesses (love, parting, and death) already given. The sadness of the forest, and its delineation, arrived at only indirectly, takes up two-thirds of the poem's sixty-six lines. It begins with the reveries of a poet who is walking through the fields in the countryside and communing with the silent sounds of nature that only his poetic faculty can perceive. (The entire sequence is spoken in the second-person singular in a kind of progressive future tense as in, "You will incline your ear to the silence. . . ." The person and the tense create a compulsive, hypnotic aura of an experience destined to be repeated yet viewed from a distance.) As the poet leaves the cleared fields for the forest, he is assailed by the stinging needles of the pine trees, which declare that man and his destructive ways are not wanted in the forest and warn him threateningly to leave the forest and return to the city. Unheeding, the poet penetrates further into the forest, past hideous gnarled roots, until he is suddenly overcome by the desire to prostrate himself before these "ancient priests of the forest," to expose the wounds he has brought from the city and beg for healing. But the great ones of the forest will have none of it. "Raise not your voice," they rebuke him. "For here silence is prayer." Pushing onward aimlessly, the poet comes across a stand of birches, slender and white against the shadows, whose sorrow reminds him of the bodies of seventeen-year-old girls pining away in captivity. It is finally at this point that the poet experiences the sorrow of the forest, which he equates with 'etsev-qedushah, a holy sorrow. Lying on the cold earth, he feels purified, and hears the sound of God walking among the trees.

In contrast to other sorrows, which are either sentimental, banal, or morbid, the experience in the forest radiates an autochthonous awe. The pine trees guard some essential mystery, which, to judge from the wretched servitude of the birch trees, is no Edenic state of nature. The poet-protagonist, the second-person addressee of the poem, becomes a kind of Prometheus in his intrepid penetration of the forest after having been so menacingly warned off. Yet, although he does not steal the forest's secret to bring back to humankind, he purchases his own purgation by virtue of his very presence, however unwanted, close to these awesome forces. "Kamah minei 'etsev yesh" presents the poet as an existential pilgrim in a landscape of uncertain mystery.

The mysteries that reside within the self rather than in nature are the subject of "El nafshi" [To my soul] (1922), the poem that follows next in Feinstein's collected poetry. At once playful and serious, the poem utilizes the conventions of the ode to undertake a sustained address to the speaker's soul. Its subject introduces Feinstein as a poet with an abiding interest in metaphysical concerns and an attraction to the concepts of Kabbalah, and this at a time long before Gershom Scholem's work made Jewish mysticism a matter of general currency. Years later, Feinstein would go on to write an epic drama about

Abulafia, the thirteenth-century Spanish mystic who was obsessed with the esoteric power of the letters of the Hebrew alphabet.[11] As to the depths of Feinstein's learning in this area, academic or otherwise, one cannot be certain; he seems to be genuinely intrigued by these notions, which he then adopts and makes his own. Metaphysics also functions for Feinstein as a strategy of impersonality; it allows him to address and explore the inward dimension of existence without calling upon him to be confessional. He can write about the soul, or even about his own soul, as he does in the poem at hand, without obligation to expose the specific struggles and shortcomings he contends with in the living of his daily life. Feinstein's poetry is in love with a kind of personally appropriated generality.

The central conceit of the poem is the eternality of the soul and its temporary, even accidental, sojourn in the speaker's body. The soul, addressed throughout familiarly in the second person, was created at the time of God's Creation, and it wanders the unfathomable reaches of eternity awaiting, in a sense, its next assignment. The soul is the object of the speaker's wonderment because of its reticulated complexity. Like the strata of ancient snow at the polar icecap, it is composed of a myriad of layers accumulated from past incarnations that are continually being added to and are never taken away. The soul thus functions as a racial unconscious that is annealed to the speaker's body. It is this knowledge, arrived at through a series of meditative investigations, which enables the speaker to understand the strange promptings of his inner experience and outward behavior. He hears within himself, for example, the murmur of whispered utterances groaning from pain and affliction, and he now realizes that these are the unanswered appeals of his lost ancestors, to whom, alas, he is incapable of bringing solace. At other times, when his blood rises and he is overcome with the desire to act with wild aggression, he knows that he is impelled by the same primal fear of survival that seized his primordial ancestor among the rocks and caves. Finally, when he cries at night with a heart broken over the desolate state of the world and kneels in prayer, he is really channeling the supplication of his forefathers, dressed in talit and tefillin. This, too, he knows: the day will come when all of these worlds within worlds will be torn from him, and he will be returned to a soulless one-dimensionality. At least his death will bring him rest, while his soul, on the other hand, will return to its ceaseless wandering.

Both of these longish poems display an essentially meditative habit of mind. The concretely lived world—the world of objects, emotions, and sense experiences—holds little interest. Feinstein is indeed capable of cannily shaping concrete images, as in the death throes of the butterfly and the layers of the polar icepack. But he deploys them only in the service of the metaphysical; they forever point away from this world to others. Feinstein is, simply and disconsolately, disappointed by the world as we know it, or at least as we know it now. His disappointment is plangently recorded in a brief poem that follows directly after "El nafshi" in the collected poems but is dated four years later. This is a poem of profound complaint, whose opening line is a quotation from Isaiah 24:16 expressing dismay and panic in the midst of prophesied destruction. The catastrophe the speaker laments is nothing less than his belated birth. He has been born in the modern age rather than in antiquity, when the world was new. In that hypostasized age, men were clear of eye, perfect of soul, and pure of blood. The mystery of Creation still clung to nature, and man lived in sympathetic vibration with the newly born soul of the world. What saves the poem from being a whining grievance is the rhapsodic evocation of departed wonder, which succeeds in conveying a sense of genuine loss. The speaker's contemporary birth consigns him to a denuded, disenchanted world, and his desolation adds tragic resonance to the refrain of Ecclesiastes: "There is nothing new under the sun." The poem provides a kind of explanation for Feinstein's indifference toward the things of this world. It is not necessarily because he has the mystic's eye for eternity but because his faculty of wonder cannot be nurtured by the staleness of the daily bread placed before him. He has nowhere to look but beyond, or at least, inside.

In an early phase of his career as a poet (1917–20), Feinstein had tried his hand at writing large-scale poems with mythic figures about urban existence and about the conflict of cultures between Judaism and Hellenism.[12] These overwrought poems seem to have been produced less out of Feinstein's natural temperament than out of a notion

of the themes a responsible Hebrew poet *should* be addressing.[13]
During the 1920s, Feinstein reconciled himself with both his gifts and
limitations and acknowledged that his true domain was the reticula-
tions of the soul and the gauzy veil that separates us from the hidden
secrets of the cosmos. In the 1927 poem "Yehi lakhem hasa'ar" [You
can have the storm] (pp. 26–27), he makes this declaration and draws
his line in the poetic sand. Cast in the high prophetic mode of Bialik,
the poem castigates those who would presume to scale the peaks, float
aloft great dreams of humanity, force their visions upon others, and
relentlessly pursue their appetites. The speaker, for his part, renounces
these great and noisy desires. Leaping off his fiery chariot, he sets his
course for the quiet valley.

אֲנִי בַּדְּמָמָה אֶשְׁלוֹ רָחוֹק מֵהֲמוֹן בְּצֶעְכֶם וּמִזְמַתְכֶם,
וְאֶקְשֹׁר כִּתְרֵי־דְמָעוֹת־כְּאֵבִי לְרֹאשׁ כָּל נִצָּן שַׁלְוָה,
וּפָרַח עֵמֶק הַדְּמָמָה וְהָיָה מִקְלָט לְכָל כְּמַה־אֱמֶת אֲשֶׁר יִיעַף מִן הַסַּעַר.

In silence I will be tranquil far from the clamor of your schemes
and designs,
I will tie the crowns of my tears onto the tops of every bud of
tranquility,
And the valley of silence will blossom and become a refuge to all
who sincerely flee here from the storm.

Although the identity of these aggressive and coercive world changers
is never specified, the decade of the 1920s, with its fiercely contending ideologies, offers a raft of choices. It would not be out of place,
however, to take the poem reflexively and to see the agitators that
Feinstein's speaker is addressing—perhaps entirely unconsciously—as
representing the overreaching and inauthentic part of himself that,
until now, has kept him from turning his poetic chariot toward the
tranquility of the valley.

The promise that lay on the far side of that turning point was fulfilled in *Ḥalom vegoral*, an eighty-page poem that Feinstein published
in 1937. It is the finest poem Feinstein wrote, and it is the contribution
to American Hebrew poetry that rescues Feinstein from the marginality to which his slight production otherwise would have condemned
him. Although its shortcomings do not qualify it as a masterpiece,

Ḥalom vegoral remains a serious work of art that is unique in interwar Hebrew poetry. The poem describes a love affair between a man and a woman who have met on an Atlantic-Mediterranean ocean voyage. While shipboard romances might seem like the standard stuff of American and English cinema at the time, this was far from the case in Hebrew poetry, especially in the literary center in Palestine. The symbolism of Shlonsky and Alterman and the expressionism of Lamdan and Uri Zvi Greenberg were shot through with erotic energy, yet one would be hard pressed to find there examples of the depiction of problematic love between mature men and women. Almost exactly contemporaneous to Feinstein's poem, for example, Alterman's path-breaking collection *Kokhavim baḥuts* [The stars outside] (1938) celebrates the poet-wanderer's perennial encounter with the world as a lifelong affair with the eternal feminine. But here, as elsewhere in the period, women and the love of women are either universalized or reduced to mythic types. Feinstein's lovers, on the other hand, are quite real and embodied, and the pathos of their hopes and renunciations all too human, even if the language they speak is figurative and philosophical.

It is the very fact of embodiment that is the breakthrough for Feinstein. The preoccupation with the soul in his earlier poetry had led to a solipsistic abstractness that made it difficult for the reader not only to follow the poems' ruminations but also to be persuaded of their consequence. In *Ḥalom vegoral*, Feinstein seizes the chance to tether his soulful meditations to the bodies of two real characters, whose anguish and chances for happiness we come to care about deeply. His poetry thereby takes on a sense of substance and urgency that it did not have before and would not have again. The very act of writing the poem must also have required a degree of moral courage. Feinstein was a married man with three children when he wrote his poetic account of an affair of the heart, which sought to give voice to a grand passion rather than a mere attraction or flirtation. Although we ardently, and correctly, insist on the distinction between the poet and the speaker of the poem, Feinstein's benighted readers read their poetry before New Criticism had warned of the error of confusing the two. In the case of a man known for his penchant for ocean voyages, the autobiographical presumption would have been a natural one. The fact that the entire work is dedicated, simply, "To Sonia," the name of the woman in the couple, does not serve as a disincentive.

The poem itself is largely comprised of dramatic speech. The pair address each other in long monologues while standing on the deck of the ship at night. All the usual paraphernalia of shipboard stories—the accidental diversity of the fellow passengers, the captain and his officers, the rituals of dining and dancing—are entirely obliterated in favor of the solemn exchanges between the star-crossed lovers. Her name is Sonia; he is given no name. The voyage is presumably from New York to the Mediterranean and back, although the details remain sketchy and unimportant. When the poem begins, the ship is somewhere between the coast of Spain and Monte Carlo, and although the couple have known each other only three days, they speak to each other with the certain intimacy of a man and a woman who have discovered the loves of their life. We are not treated to the details of how their elective affinities were galvanized; when we meet them, their bond is already a given. It is a bond that is not merely platonic. Just *how* embodied is their connection is difficult to say, but the sensuality is unmistakable. His hands are continually running through her hair; her head rests on his shoulder; their hands are entwined. Her gown, hair, and eyes are endlessly eroticized.

Despite the very modern setting and premise of *Ḥalom vegoral*, the poem's style is archaized. It is as if an English poet of the 1930s chose to write in the style of Tennyson's *Idylls of the King* or of Rosetti's pre-Raphaelite mannerism. Within the history of Hebrew literature, Feinstein's style evokes the lyric phase of Haskalah poetry a century before in the manner of Michal and Adam Hacohen. The Haskalah penchant for the use of epithets and periphrasis is also noticeable. The poem is written in a biblical syntax and lexical register with an abundance of rare words that come from later periods of Hebrew as well. Most conspicuous are the locutions of classical poetry, especially dropping conjunctions with the infinitive (e.g., *eikhah ukhal harot* for *laharot* [How could I become pregnant?], or for noun-noun constructions (e.g., *tohar-ḥom* for "warm purity" or *meshi-haberekh* for "silken knee"). The language is lushly figurative with an abandoned use of elaborately built-up metaphors. The cadence of the poetry is languid, formal, and measured. In these long lyric speeches of the woman to the man and the man to the woman, one feels something of the atmosphere of courtly poetry. Although the lovers touch and caress, the erotic charge of their encounter is most potently carried through the verdant intricacies of their language. When fate calls for the renunciation of carnal intimacies, language then becomes the bearer of consolation and reconciliation. Taken together, all of these effects create a unique stylization. Just as the writing in Feinstein's *Ḥalom vegoral* is enclosed in its own vintage world, so the poem's two lovers, separated from civilization and family and alone on the seas, form a world unto themselves.

Dream and fate, the terms that make up the poem's title, provide the existential-philosophical rubrics for the romantic dilemma at the heart of the composition. Fate is the record of blind suffering that is visited upon human beings. Our chances for happiness are ineluctably curtailed by forces beyond our control; the human condition is inescapable; and in the end it makes little difference whether one calls the force that dictates our future God or fate. Dream is longing for fulfillment and escape from the integuments of fate. Dream is fueled by desire and constituted by the very willingness to believe in the possibility of human happiness. With this belief comes the courage to seize opportunities for fulfillment when they are suddenly thrown up by the vagaries of the cosmos.

The hand of fate lies heaviest upon the shoulders of Sonia, who tells her story in the first sections of the poem. To escape her home, she married an older man, a physician, with whom she had five happy years before he suddenly died of a month-long illness. She worked as a kindergarten teacher among the poor children of New York, to whom she felt deeply connected. But her relationships with men left her empty and redoubled the sadness that engulfed her. She acquiesced to wed a man to give some pleasure to her parents; then, deciding she could not marry without love, she canceled the wedding and escaped to the cruise on which she is presently a passenger. After unhappily resigning herself to a life without love, she finds herself being overwhelmed in the course of three days by feelings that took five years of marriage to develop. Suddenly, the long-suppressed dream has been aroused in the bosom of a woman who had long experienced herself a prisoner of fate. When it comes to the man, in addition to the absence of a name, there is no corresponding profile and virtually no backstory. We do not know whether his life before he stepped onto the ship included a wife or children. Given the possible exposure to scandal, it is possible that Feinstein thought that such blankness would offer him some protection. We do know that, once on board, he is as attracted to Sonia as she is to him, their affair is mutual, and the experience of suddenly falling in love has hit him with the same explosive power.

Why can't the lovers live happily ever after? The reasons are not given—is it due to his family encumbrances?—and it is simply understood as axiomatic that their affair cannot have a life beyond the length of the journey. In the cosmic-astronomical discourse of the poem we are informed that, "Thus it happens in the pathways of the heavens / That wandering stars meet for a brief moment in the eternity of time / And extend to each other caresses of joy and pain" (p. 6). It is this brief moment in the infinity of the universe that is the duration of the poem. Given the implicit boundaries of the relationship, the drama of the poem is therefore centered on how each of the lovers deals both with the eruption of this stunning event in his or her emotional life *and* with the fact of its inscribed impossibility.

The drama in *Ḥalom vegoral* takes place through a reversal in the lovers' stance toward their fate. The man begins by confidently asserting that he can save Sonia from her resigned sorrow. It is *he*, however, who ends up needing to be saved by her; and at the conclusion of the poem, she is accorded the status of a kind of teacher of wisdom. From the outset, the man regards the sudden revelation of late love as a miraculous opportunity to be seized, a golden second chance to wrest a fragment of the dream from the hands of fate. But she, at least at this stage, presents herself as an *eshet-ʿetsev*, a woman of sorrow who is immured within the narrative of her losses and disappointments. His challenge is to convince Sonia to take the chance and believe that it is possible to be rescued. His attempts and her demurrals are conveyed through a series of elaborate figures in which nautical images, not unsurprisingly, dominate. Standing on the deck of the ship, for example, the couple glimpse an island that suddenly becomes visible in the shifting fog and vapors upon the blank reaches of the ocean. For the man, this is the exact parable to their situation. "After years of nothingness, it can happen / That isles of splendor can appear and suddenly offer us their blessing" (p. 10). Happy is the one who can adroitly set his course for the island before it disappears into the fog, and, conversely, "Woe is he whose ship wanders wildly / Without a compass to guide it in the wilderness of the waters" (p. 10). Sonia answers him by insisting that it is God or fate, in ways entirely hidden from us, who sends some boats to ruin and some to a blessed destination. Her voyage cannot avoid doom because there is no one to captain her vessel, "The rudder is broken / All the sails are in tatters, and the masts are storm wrecked" (p. 10).

It is he, of course, who gallantly offers to captain her vessel, but setting sail proves a difficult challenge. It is crucial to him as a point of departure to establish, with Sonia's full acknowledgement, that her emotional life has been brought back to life and that he is responsible for this enormous change. "You are right. My well has been opened and the stone covering its mouth / You have rolled back" (p. 14). Jacob-like, he has succeeded in enabling her to water her parched soul from within herself. Sonia admits that after the losses she suffered, like a princess in a fairy tale, she walled herself up in a figurative tower surrounded by thorns, where she was resigned to wait out her days. Now, without expectation or warning, a prince has knocked and the gates are opening. Her capacity to respond—the very conviction that what is happening to her is real—has been compromised by the depths of her disappointments. "Have the thorns truly departed," she wonders, "or am I beholding the work of some meretricious spell?" (p. 19).

What of *his* heart? The hand offered to pilot their boat to the isles of happiness is hardly disinterested. Although he tells us little about himself, in a rare confessional moment, the man admits to himself: "I abandoned the shores of despondency / With the hope in my heart to bathe in the pure distances / And be purified. For naught! There is no escape from the miseries of this world" (p. 12). Like lovers everywhere and always, he too wants to be rescued by being given leave to rescue her. It is ironically the coil of bad faith wrapped around *his* heart that proves to be the more difficult challenge. For despite all of the soulful arguments and figurative resourcefulness he expends in persuading Sonia, it is he who remains unpersuaded and the less ready to believe in the transformative power of what has happened between them.

These feelings of desperation and failure, though unvoiced, seem to stiffen and deepen as the journey nears its conclusion. At the end of the poem, recalling the bravado of his promise to steer her ship toward the dream, he fears that he has only led her deeper into trackless waters. Sonia, in contrast, now reveals a serene and centered affirmation of their relationship that is far different from the ironic skepticism she displayed at the outset. How this reversal has been effected is not entirely clear. The long-seeming middle of the poem is taken up with world-weary observations offered by the male speaker concerning the great sights and arts works encountered on their cruise, especially Pompeii and the Vatican Museums, with an aside about the death of Socrates. It may be that in contrast to the reader, whose attention tends to wander during these longueurs, Sonia has in fact been listening closely and has absorbed the lessons great art has to teach concerning the immortality of the soul. Or, perhaps she has gradually been persuaded by the truth of the arguments about the attainability of the dream given to her by the man, although he himself may not have truly believed them or uttered them in complete disinterestedness.

The magnificent speeches of Sonia reborn dominate the last movement of *Halom vegoral*. However she acquired her wisdom, she dispenses it generously and unselfishly, and her first priority is to mitigate her lover's despair. She reassures him, as perhaps all men need to be reassured, that his guidance has in fact availed her and that his strong hand on the rudder has indeed led the ship of her life to still waters. With the ocean liner about to dock at its home port, she urges him not to be agitated when they descend the passenger ramp and must go separate ways. This newly attained inner tranquility comes from the belief that true love between two souls can defeat the constraints imposed by the world. She formulates her belief using the key terms of the poem: "The strands of the Dream woven together by two souls / At the time of Creation are infinitely stronger / Than the bonds of Fate" (p. 67). Far from being a shipboard romance, their meeting has been something much larger: the primordial connection of two souls that does not depend on time or place. It has been their great good fortune to have been offered a way out of the terrors of temporality. In God's compass, she teaches him, there are movements in two directions. Like a ship foundering on the rocks of the final island, the journey toward physical death is experienced by most people as a calamity to be awaited with anxious dread. The meeting of their souls, however, has given them access to the privileged countermovement, which is "the path of peace, where the mystery-crowned waves / And the wings of the Dream beat upon the water" (p. 69). When their life's journey reaches its final port, even though they may have been separated in body, Sonia sees them in her mind's eye together descending the ramp into the infinity of the Dream.

Does the consolation console? We do not know, because the man, who was so voluble for much of the poem, does not speak again. After Sonia dispenses her higher wisdom, it is given to her to conclude the poem with the telling of a long Chinese legend about the origins of two heavenly constellations, the Shepherd and the Spinner, which the movements of the stars allow to visit each other once a year. The ending is charmingly but opaquely mysterious, and it functions to point upward away from the embroiled cycle of unfulfilled human desires toward the plane of soulful eternity where Sonia—and perhaps she alone—has found solace.

Nothing Feinstein wrote later approached the sublimity of *Ḥalom vegoral*. His later life was marked by a series of personal tragedies. His wife died in 1953 while they were traveling in Israel. His daughter Anugah died of cancer soon after. The husband of his other daughter Alita died in an industrial accident. Feinstein had never been an effective fundraiser; the burden of keeping Herzliah afloat during the postwar years when the support for Hebraist education was waning, piled on top of his personal losses, turned out to be an unsupportable burden. He drank and, finally, one day in 1964, sitting and writing in a Tel Aviv hotel lobby, he took pills and died in mid-poem. The last years of his life saw the reversal of two features of his early career as a poet. He began to write lyric poetry with a prolific abandonment entirely new to him, and, in contrast to his impersonal reticence, he held nothing back of the very personal torments that had been visited upon his life. The poems, the record of a modern-day Job dragging his bleeding heart through ocean voyages and Tel Aviv cafes, are contained in *'Al saf hasof* [Near the end], which is dedicated to the memories of wife and daughter.[14]

* מִתּוֹךְ: חֲלוֹם וְגוֹרָל   *

From *Ḥalom vegoral*

Analysis

"שָׁמַעְתִּי נְאֻם עֵינֶיךָ אֲשֶׁר לֹא גִלָּה פִּיךָ.
מִתַּחַת לִכְתֵפֶיךָ זְקוּפוֹת יִכְרַע לֵב
מִכֹּבֶד צְלָלִים. וַאֲנִי אֶת רֹאשִׁי שַׁח
עַל כְּתֵפְךָ שַׂמְתִּי, אוּלַי בְּחַסְדְּךָ תּוּכַל שְׂאֵת,
וְלוּ לְשָׁעָה הָקֵל מְעַט אֶת מַשָּׂא יְגוֹנִי.
אֶשֶׁת־עֶצֶב אֲנִי וְיַד הַגּוֹרָל נְחָתָה
עַל חַיַּי לִבְלִי חוֹס. הֵן יוּכַל יָם הַדְּוָי,

הַגּוֹרֵשׁ אֶת מִשְׁבָּרָיו אֶל בָּבוֹתֶיךָ־תְּכֵלֶת,
יְגוֹנִי אֲנִי נָשָׂא וְאִם יִגְאֶה בִּמְאֹד מְאֹד."

לֹא רָאֲתָה חִיל־הַכְּאֵב אֲשֶׁר אֶת שְׂפָתָיו אָחַז.
הִיא שָׁמְעָה: "לְיַם־נִכְאַי לְרָצוֹן יְהִי יְגוֹנֵךְ.
הוּא יִגְנְזוֹ בִּתְהוֹמוֹ, כִּי עֶצֶב־אֱמֶת הוּא,
וְנִצְנֵץ בּוֹ כְּנַצְנֵץ פְּנִינָה בְּאֶשּׁוּן צוּלָה,
וּשְׁלַל נִיצוֹצוֹת יַתִּיז אֶל פְּנֵי מִשְׁבָּרִים תּוֹעִים.
אַךְ דְּלִי נָא עוֹד מִמְּקוֹרֵךְ צְלוּל־הַכְּאֵב, יַלְדָתִי.
גָּלַלְתִּי אֶת הָאֶבֶן מֵעַל בְּאֵר אֻלְמָה,
מַעֲמַקִּים יִכְלוּ לָאוֹר וּלְחֶסֶד הַשָּׁמַיִם."

"I have understood from the speech of your eyes what your mouth
    did not reveal.
Under your upright shoulders your heart bends
From the weight of shadows. Yet I have placed my bowed head
    Upon your shoulder in the hope that your kindness would
    support it

And, even if only for a moment, ease the burden of my distress.
A woman of sorrow am I, and the hand of Fate has been imposed
    on my life without mercy. Indeed, the sea of anguish,
Which has beaten its breakers into your blue eyes,
Can contain my suffering, even if it rises mightily."
She did not notice the grimace of pain that seized his lips.
She heard him say, "Gladly will your trouble become my sea of
    sadness.
It will be deposited in its depths because it is an authentic sorrow,
And it will shine there like a pearl in the darkest depths,
Its radiance cast upon the errant waves.
Yet pray now, my child, draw from your pain-purified source.
I have rolled away the stone covering your silent well;
Its depths yearn for the light and grace of heaven."

Although it has been the practice in this study to undertake close readings of whole poems rather than excerpts from longer works, Feinstein's work warrants an exception because of the superiority of *Ḥalom vegoral* and the paucity of his general lyric output. The passage (pp. 13–14) is taken from the first section of the poem, during which the lovers, having just met, are revealing themselves to each other. She has already suggested the essential sadness of her life, and he has already admitted to himself his disappointment with having fallen in love with a woman in whom he cannot forget *his* sadness. In these lines she asks for solace, and he gallantly offers it, but with a request of his own.

These acute and subtle psychological transactions are conveyed entirely though highly charged figurative language. It is as if collapsing the metaphorical distance and calling things by their real names would constitute a vulgar violation of unspoken poetic rules of engagement. Yet it is precisely these ornate tropes, as they are burnished and reformulated and passed back and forth, that allow the lovers to disclose their wills to each other and so negotiate the heightened moment they are living through. The master trope in the poem as a whole, unsurprisingly given the maritime setting, is water in all its various states and transformations. The lovers' ship of life, jointly and separately, sails over the depths toward the last port. The passage at hand develops two filaments in this vast metaphoric network. Sonia introduces the notion of a sea of sorrows, which the man appropriates and elaborates. He then works to supplant the sea of sorrows with a different and, in his mind, more hopeful figure of the well. As the poem continues beyond the passage, Sonia accepts the idea of the well and proceeds to shape the image to her purposes. So the poem moves ahead through the creative manipulation of metaphoric proxies.

The passage opens with Sonia's claim for intuitive understanding. Although the man has not voiced his disappointment over discovering her burden of suffering, she asserts her empathic ability to read his thoughts. She sees the heavy heart disguised by the upright shoulders. Her insight is checked, however, by a parallel act of blindness; for at the conclusion of her speech, at the beginning of the next verse paragraph (line 10), the poem's narrator informs us that she simply did not see the expression of pain that had seized her interlocutor's face. As readers, we will therefore need to revise our estimation of Sonia's penetrating wisdom, which now must be seen as also being a fallible knowingness. Here, at least, at the outset of her speech, she does acknowledge the discouraging impact of her story upon him. Yet despite his distress and her awareness of it, Sonia asks him, as a matter of *ḥesed*, unrequited kindness, to support her and give her a momentary respite from her burdens. In *ve'ani* in line 3, the conjunction *vav* should be understood in the contrastive sense as "nonetheless," of "even so."

Her right to make a claim on him derives from the status she accords to herself as an *eshet-'etsev*, a kind of woman of constant sorrow. At first, we are inclined to take this as a quantitative statement that conveys a lack of symmetry between their situations. The hand of Fate has lain heavier and more unremittingly upon her life than upon his. But we shall soon see that the man is ready and even eager to grant her suffering a qualitative distinction as well. In the meantime, Sonia expands on the capacity for suffering and introduces the notion of the sea of sorrow [*yam hadevai*].[15] The tortuous syntax of her speech in lines 7–9 reflects something of the strained fluidity of the image she constructs. The sea of sorrow is capable of containing the enormity of her suffering, but at the same time it sends its white-capped waves dashing against the blue eyes of her interlocutor.

The man's response—the more poignant for following directly upon the unnoticed grimace—directly engages the question of boundaries. Sonia had spoken of an impersonal sea of sorrows that exists beyond her in the world and contains her suffering. In a subtle yet rhetorically bold gesture, the man now proposes that her suffering become, or become part of—the Hebrew can sustain both readings—*his* sea of troubles (line 11). This is an inland or internal sea of his own rather than the great ocean out there. The man not only accepts the implication of the overflow of pain that the waves cast into his blue eyes; he has willingly taken on himself the disposition of her suffering. In his sea of sorrow, moreover, Sonia's suffering will undergo a kind of transubstantiation. Formerly, it was undifferentiated lumpen pain that was simply another bucket of teardrops added to the universal reservoir. Now, through the alchemy of his empathic imagination, her pain is not only transformed into a precious object that is protected and stored in his murky depths, but it further becomes a light-emitting beacon illuminating and orienting the errant waves in his sea of sorrow (line 14), the same white-capped waves [*mishbarim*] mentioned in line 9.

How does Sonia's misery jump from being a tormenting burden to becoming a luminescent jewel? The valorization of her suffering would seem to derive from the persuasive impact of her self-presentation. When she presents herself in line 6 as a woman of sorrow [*eshet-ʿetsev*], she manages to invest this role with a nearly martyrological nobility, as if it has been her particular distinction to have been called by Fate to be sorely tested. The man, in turn, accepts the truth of her claim; for when he offers to contain her pain within his, the reason he gives is that her pain is authentic [*ki ʿetsev-emet hu*] (line 12). His suffering, by implication, is made of lesser existential stuff and thus deserves to offer obeisance to hers. Indeed, there is something self-fulfilling in his self-ascribed inferiority. Throughout the poem as a whole, the man's life story, which, for all we know, may be filled with calamities as grievous as her, is unreported save for its general sadness. Neither the poem's narrator nor the male character, perhaps like Moshe Feinstein himself, chooses to disclose the specifics of his trials.

Gallant self-abnegation, however, is certainly not the final gesture in this passage. With the word *akh* [yet] that begins line 15, the man initiates a countermovement by shifting the water image from sea to well. The change in his position is marked by his use of the term "my child" [*yaldati*] in addressing her. The conceptual difference is enormous. In contrast to the unbounded, stormy depths of the sea, the well's water is still, contained, and fresh. Her true suffering is now figured as a resource from which she can, potentially, draw strength. Until now, her access to this source has been blocked, but the soulful encounter of their romance has removed the obstruction. The man has rolled away the stone sealing the well just as Jacob did for Rachel in Genesis 29, and for this he justly takes credit. Having done this for her, he now turns to his lover and bids her to dip into herself, as it were, and to make use of her purified suffering once again to be open to life and love.

As the poem continues beyond the passage discussed above, Sonia responds to his urging by agreeing that her well has indeed been opened and by marveling how such a thing could have happened as a result of knowing someone for only a few days. And thus the back and forth between the two continues throughout the poem. Each accepts a figurative verbal construction from the other, modifies it in ways aligned with his or her interests and desires, and returns it in the hope it will accomplish its rhetorical persuasion. The play between them, however, is not a zero-sum game. As we have seen in Sonia's magnificent parting speeches at the end of the poem, the encouragement to reach inside herself and transform her suffering into hope has not fallen on deaf ears.

Eleven   Eisig Silberschlag

The Hebrew poetry that flourished in America between the two world wars of the previous century can be understood in part as a struggle to negotiate the influence of Bialik and Tchernichovsky, the two great forces in Hebrew poetry at the turn of that century. Unfolding at the same time in the emerging literary center in Palestine is a very different dynamic: an outright revolt against these two leonine precursors in the name of Russian and French symbolism and German expressionism. Yet for the Americans, who were brought up in the public schools on the flowers of late romanticism, the ascendancy of the avant-garde in Tel Aviv seemed like the triumph of barbarism, and they wanted little to do with it. To Israeli critics, this stance of principled refusal has often been taken as reactionary, as if the Americans sought to preserve in amber the norms of their predecessors.[1] A truer account, I would argue, would examine how the Americans took this inheritance apart and reassembled it in ways that domesticated it within the American milieu.

Speaking of the inheritance of Bialik and Tchernichovsky together, as we often do, presumes a symmetry that is not really there. In the case of the Americans, the influence of Bialik was preponderant, and it is not difficult to see why. They saw themselves in the autobiographical persona developed in Bialik's poetry: the banishment from nature, the benightedness of the heder, the world of faith shaken to its core, loneliness in love, rage at the failure of the people to deliver itself from ignorance and passivity. Each of these essential experiences was conveyed in poetic forms that were adopted, cultivated, and refined by the Americans.

The figure of Tchernichovsky, by contrast, offered a more robust and less conflicted model for the embrace of the possibilities opened up by a Jewish national renaissance. Transposed through the Hebrew language, the Hellenic appreciation of beauty and sensuality (the "delights of Japhet") could happily expand the ken of Jewish culture (the "tents of Shem"). The project of bringing the classics of world literature into Hebrew, rather than the "ingathering" of internal classical Judaic sources, became the essential cultural work of the new age. Tchernichovsky's poetic achievement and the wealth of his translations were widely respected by the American Hebrew poets, but among them, only Eisig Silberschlag saw Tchernichovsky as the paragon and as the way out of the sterile over-refinement in which Hebrew poetry in America had encased itself.

As a poet, to be sure, Silberschlag was his own man, and he declined to emulate his precursor in many things, especially in the writing of such long narrative poems as Tchernichovsky's famed idylls. Yet the elder poet remained a paragon. Like him, the formative moment in Silberschlag's cultural formation was decidedly not the break with religious tradition; and the movement outward toward the discovery of many non-Jewish literatures in their original languages, similarly, was not fraught with angst. When it came to some of the central themes of his poetry—erotic desire, embodied beauty, nature, and art—Silberschlag was happy to accept their Greek provenance rather than fret about their absence from classical Judaism. At the height of his career, Silberschlag heeded the Tchernichovskian imperative and devoted the lion's share of his creative energies to translating the eleven comedies of Aristophanes from Greek into Hebrew, for which he was awarded the Tchernichovsky Prize in Israel in 1951. His monograph *Saul Tchernichowsky: Poet of Revolt* (1968) has served as the major presentation of the poet's work in English.[2]

Silberschlag's biography differs from the collective portrait of American Hebrew poets in two ways. Born in 1903, he was somewhat younger than most and arrived in America later than they. And rather than hailing from Czarist Russia, he grew up in Galicia within the sphere of German cultural influences. Satri, in Eastern Galicia, where Silberschlag was born, had long been part of the Austro-Hungarian

Eisig Silberschlag. Courtesy of the Archives of the Rae and Joseph Gann
Library of the Hebrew College.

Empire. But because of war and revolution, the city changed hands
several times during Silberschlag's youth between the Austrians, Rus-
sians, Ukrainians, and Poles. In our best source of knowledge about
his life, Arnold Band posits that Silberschlag's cosmopolitanism, so
much his hallmark within the confines of American Hebrew letters,

was first shaped by the exposure to the succession of these cultures and languages in Satri well before he later strode the boulevards of Vienna and Paris.[3] The gymnasium in Satri, where Silberschlag studied, had a classical curriculum, and it was there that he began to study Greek and Latin. An important formative influence, Band argues, was Silberschlag's participation in the Hashomer Hatzair Zionist youth movement in the years before it took on a Marxist outlook. The ethos of the movement stressed the promise of youth, the importance of a connection to nature, the centrality of love and solidarity, and the goal of self-realization, in addition to the primacy of the Land of Israel, where these values could be fulfilled. All these can be recognized as themes in Silberschlag's poetic work.

Silberschlag arrived in New York City at the age of seventeen in 1920. He worked in manual labor to support himself and presumably studied at the City College of New York, although we have little information about him during these years. The early 1920s were the heyday of Hebraist activity and optimism in America: the daily *Hado'ar* was started, the Hebrew colleges were founded, and Hebrew-focused boards of Jewish education organized in major cities. In the contemporary accounts and memoirs of this time, Silberschlag's name is not mentioned; he seems to have stood apart. The matter of age and date of immigration is significant here. Most of his somewhat older fellow nascent Hebrew writers had come to America before World War I. In addition to knowing one another in the Hebrew clubs of Brooklyn and the Lower East Side, their literary tastes were often fixed by the canon of American and British literature taught to them in the public schools of those years. Silberschlag, by contrast, arrived in America already as a graduate of the Satri gymnasium whose orientation toward European literature—not to mention the classics of antiquity—was already formed. Whereas many American Hebrew poets were drawn to the American landscape, to its pre-industrial mythologies, and to the lore of its oppressed minorities, Silberschlag remained largely insensible to these attractions and used the American scene mostly as a butt of satire.

In 1925 Silberschlag returned to Europe, where he spent two years obtaining a doctorate from the University of Vienna for a thesis on economic relations between England and Russia during the reign of Catherine II. Although his academic focus may have been history, he read and studied European literature voraciously, and Vienna, as a kind of capital of continental modernism, was the ideal place for a youth from the Galician provinces—especially after a sojourn within the vulgar immigrant culture of New York—to pursue his artistic and sentimental education. His immersion in European literature is reflected in his *Tehiyyah utehiyyah bashirah* [Astonishment and renewal in poetry], a collection of essays handsomely put out by Shtibel in 1938, which includes pieces on Baudelaire, Valery, Eliot, Yeats, Hofmannsthal, and Rilke. In American Hebrew letters at the time, there was nothing like it. After several months in Paris, Silberschlag returned to New York. Between 1930 and 1932 he had teaching stints at the Teachers Institute of the Jewish Theological Seminary and at the Jewish Institute of Religion before moving to Boston to accept a position teaching Hebrew literature and Bible at the Hebrew Teachers College.

Rising to become dean and then president, Silberschlag remained at the school, which is now called the Boston Hebrew College, until his retirement in 1970. Despite his long tenure, he never struck deep roots in the Boston community and returned frequently to New York to visit family and friends. The figure Silberschlag cut at the College, according to Band, who worked under him for many years, was aristocratic and aloof. A handsome man sporting a mustache and a bow tie, he retained something of the bohemian panache of his student years. His relationship to Eretz Yisrael was complicated. He was mentioned to succeed Klausner in the chair of modern Hebrew literature at the Hebrew University in the late 1940s, but when Halkin was tapped for the position, Silberschlag stayed in America and did not join other American Hebrew writers, such as Efros and Regelson, in moving to the newly established state. Although all of Silberschlag's work as a teacher, translator, critic, and poet took place in Hebrew, he keenly felt his distance from the literary center in Tel Aviv and Jerusalem, and he remained critical of Israeli slang, linguistic innovations, and contemporary literary trends. The hallmark of his intellectual world remained the classical, whether ancient Greece or ancient Israel or the "classic" modern literary idiom forged by Hebrew writers at the turn of the twentieth century.

Silberschlag's longevity allowed his life a colorful and far from abbreviated final act. After retiring from the presidency of Hebrew College and after the death of his wife Milkah, he leaped over the barrier separating the older Hebraist institutions from the newly energized world of Jewish studies in the universities. He moved to Austin and accepted a position as professor of Hebrew literature at the University of Texas, where he taught between 1973–78 and remained until his death in 1988. Silberschlag served as president of the National Association of Professors of Hebrew, and in his seventies and eighties cut a romantic even amorous swath through the groves of academe. Although he wrote wise and witty poetry until the very end, he became best known to the non-Hebrast world, alas, for his synoptic account in English of the history of Hebrew literature *From Renaissance to Renaissance*, a work that displays great erudition and enthusiasm but remains uninformed by modern literary critical methods.[4]

Silberschlag was a lyric poet, and, unlike many other American Hebrew poets, he never reached a point at which he experienced the lyric as inadequate for his ambitions. This is not to say that those ambitions were modest or narrow but rather that his temperament was well served by a form that privileged shorter utterances expressing heightened moments of awareness. Although in mid-career he did compose a number of extended poems—dramatic monologues, narratives, folk recreation, each very different from the other—this mode never became Silberschlag's métier. In fact, as he got older, his poems became even shorter and were published in a succession of volumes whose small physical size made them resemble chapbooks. Three reasons suggest themselves for Silberschlag's allegiance to the lyric. To begin with, the epistemology of the lyric locates the source of truth and knowledge in the perception of the speaker; and the conventions of the lyric, moreover, invite the reader to make no distinction between the poet and the poem's speaker. This makes the lyric "I" that utters the poem potent and authoritative, and it would seem that this premise accorded with Silberschlag's sense of himself quite comfortably. He did not feel hemmed in by the constrictions of the lyric premise that led others to seek to escape the orbit of the ego by inhabiting other minds and imagining other climes and times.

Secondly, in this connection, Silberschlag's poetry exhibits next to no romantic attraction to the American landscape, to the lore of the American past, or to its aboriginal inhabitants. It was the largeness and extensiveness of American stories and the ample vistas in which they unfolded that drew other poets toward narrative and furnished them with a way to break out of the lyric enclosure. Although Silberschlag had much to say about America in his verse, it was decidedly not a subject that called upon him to unfurl extended wings of song. Finally, in the economy of his artistic life, the Aristophanes translations must have functioned as his epic undertaking. Throughout the 1940s, with all that was happening in the world and to the Jewish people, Silberschlag continued to devote an enormous amount of his creative energy to translating Greek classics into Hebrew. He did not turn his back on America, and he did not turn his back on the struggles taking place in Europe and Palestine; yet in his capacity as a man of Hebrew letters, he turned his fullest attention to constructing a bridge between two great classical cultures.

The appearance in 1931 of Silberschlag's first book of poetry, *Bishevilim bodedim* [On solitary paths], was a surprising arrival in the world of American Hebrew literature.[5] Most of the early work of American Hebrew poets, observes the preeminent commentator Epstein, was caught between two sources of anguish:

> As immigrants, their first steps [as poets] were fraught with uncertainty, false steps, and struggle, which resulted, on the one hand, from the burden of the patrimony they brought with them from abroad, and, on the other, from the painful adjustment to new and alien modes of behavior and thought.[6]

The poems in Silberschlag's debut volume, by contrast, evinced no signs of tortured ambivalence about Judaism nor the nervous insecurity of newcomers to America. *Bishevilim bodedim* is nothing less than a collection of ecstatic love poems, and, as such, it is indeed an astonishing and significant curiosity within American Hebrew letters, which, with some important exceptions, is notable for its absence of erotic themes. The reasons for this absence have to do with conventions of modesty inherent in the literary systems, both Hebrew and American, in which these young poets were working, as well as with the depression-inducing mix of immigrant angst delineated by Epstein.[7]

Silberschlag's preoccupation with the erotic modulates significantly throughout his long career. Here at the beginning, love is represented as a generalized state of sensual arousal rather than an exchange of feelings between differentiated objects. "It is not wine but spring / that has caused the storm in my soul," avers the lyric speaker. "I kissed every flower, / I desired every girl."[8] In the intoxication of youth, the sweetness of flowers and girls comes from the same source of wonderment. These poems are filled with the natural symbols of streams, birds, villages, trees, and stars, creating a timeless and placeless quality that approaches the world of folk tales. They take place in no recognizable locale so much as in the poetic state of young manhood. The central trope, as in the case with flowers and girls, is the correspondence between the natural world and the female object of desire.

מַה נִּפְלֵאת . . .

מַה נִּפְלֵאת מֵאָז גִּלִּיתִי
בְּטִיּוּלֵי הַבּוֹדְדִים
דִּמְיוֹן בֵּין נִשְׁמָתֵךְ וּלְבֵין
לֵילוֹת אָבִיב כְּחֻלִּים.

וְהַסַּהַר גֵּא כְרֹאשֵׁךְ,
וְהָאִילָן — כְּקוֹמָתֵךְ,
וְהַדֶּשֶׁא רַךְ כְּשָׁדֵךְ
בְּלֵילוֹת אָבִיב כְּחֻלִּים.

How Marvelous

How marvelous you are since I discovered
On my solitary rambles
The similarity between your soul
And the nights of spring.

The moon is proud like your head
The tree like your erect stature,
And the grass tender like your breast
In blue nights of spring.[9]

It is the discovery of this correspondence, dramatized as a serendipitous revelation that endows the female addressee with such wonder.

What is most surprising in this surprising volume is its opening, a sequence of seventeen short poems titled "Shirei na'arah" [Songs of a young woman]. The speaker is the beloved of an unseen man who has dressed her in silk and installed her in a palace, where she awaits him and sings of their love. She describes how her body comes into bloom—yes, flowers are everywhere here, too—in response to her lover's desire, and her songs construct imaginary realms that they traverse as a golden couple. The first line of poem 4, for example, reads: *anaḥnu ma'avirim 'alufei lehavah/ kishenei meteorim* [We take wing, suffused by flame like two meteors].[10] The word *ma'avirim* (with an *alef*) [we take wing, we take flight] is comprehensible from our familiarity with *ever* as wing; but Silberschlag, of course, had recourse to many commoner choices to convey flight. The choice of *ma'avirim*, which is attested only one place in the Hebrew Bible (Job 39:26), is another instance of Silberschlag's critical deploying of Hebraic erudition in a poetic discourse that is otherwise committed to a rich but communicative and transparent semantics. The next phrase in the line, *'alufei lehavah*, takes effective advantage of the dual meaning of *'a.l.f.* (with an *'ayin*) as both to cloak and to faint; the lovers blaze through the firmament either covered in fire or having swooned into it. Finally, the *la'az* (European loan word) of *meteorim* astutely balances the exotic biblicism of *ma'virim*.

Taken as a whole, it is a beautiful line, and it exemplifies the lyric inventiveness and lyric purity Silberschlag is capable of in his early poems. What is most astonishing is Silberschlag's choice to place in the first position in his first book a series of poems in which he ventriloquizes, quite successfully, the voice of a woman. Although it is not a subject position he returns to often, this opening move makes a strong statement about how fundamental to his poetic world is the experience of desire, whether viewed from one side of the gender divide or from the other.

There is a discernable shift in *Bishevilim bodedim*, as Epstein has pointed out, from sensual intoxication to an awareness of temporality.[11] The delirium of stars and flowers and first love gives way to an awareness of experience as finite and irretrievable. We hear of love not just as a rush of the senses but as episodes of happiness that can end with misunderstanding and disappointment ("Lydia," pp. 39–40; "Harishonah" [First love], pp. 56–60). For the first time, connection to a parent is mentioned in a poem dedicated to the speaker's mother, which contrasts love as such, the romantic love of youth that permeates these pages, with the "pure waves of grace" that emanate from a mother's love ("Ahavah ve'ahavat em" [Love and mother love], p. 85). Finally, Silberschlag is able to step outside of the enclosure of his own intense experience to consider the institution of poetry and the strong practitioners who preceded him.

His debut volume of poetry comes to a close with a wonderful ode to Ibn Gabirol, the great poet of the Judeo-Spanish Golden Age (pp. 88–91). The poem is notable for the opportunity it wisely declines to take advantage of: crudely appropriating the magisterial medieval poet for the aggrandizement of a belated offspring. In any case, Silberschlag accomplishes something of this effect—drawing a line between himself and the great precursor—simply by offering sincere praise and keeping himself, as poet, out of the poem. The poem's speaker finds many things to extol in Ibn Gabirol's verse: the wonder of a Hebrew poetry that remains engagingly fresh after so many centuries, the spiritual courage of this "wondrous eagle" to beat its wings against the Divine Throne without being burnt alive, the commitment to explore the ways of love and wisdom despite the inevitability of pain. Yet the greatest empathic admiration is reserved for Ibn Gabirol as an exemplar of the true vocation of poetry, which is nothing less than to redeem humanity through vicarious suffering. Although poor, wandering, and unrecognized by the world, Ibn Gabirol nevertheless wielded his supernal powers on behalf of the world by distilling moments of divine and human beauty from the afflictions of terrestrial experience.[12]

Bishevilim bodedim, in sum, lives up to its title of charting a singular path for American Hebrew poetry. It's worth recalling the polemical claims made by the young Halkin in the pages of *Hado'ar* in defense of American Hebrew poetry against its detractors in Palestine.[13] The Americans, Halkin argued, were saving Hebrew poetry from the

stylistic barbarism of symbolism and expressionism by remaining true
to the classical simplicity and purity of the greatest modern Hebrew
verse, while at the same time jettisoning the cumbersome intertextual
allusiveness of the previous generation. Although he adduced Efros's
poetry as his example—Silberschlag was younger and unknown at
the time—the best poems of *Bishevilim bodedim* would have in fact
served as better evidence. In these, Silberschlag achieved a pure and
limpid lyric precision, a quality missed by the similar efforts of many
other American Hebrew poets. Unburdened by some of the conflicts
that weighed down others, Silberschlag could let his verse warble plangently but within a tight register. This was the trade-off: deeper and
more serious explorations would require the exertion of greater force.

   That force, in the form of poetic authority, was gained during
the sixteen years that intervened between Silberschlag's first collection and the publication in 1947 of his next book *'Aleh, 'olam, beshir*
[Ascend, oh world, in song], which became the canonical presentation
of his poetry in the world of American Hebrew letters.[14] Although
the intoxication with love, nature, and the lush artifice of language
survives in places, this simple song has largely given way to the construction of a more formal aesthetic stance anchored in the authority
of the poet as much as in the institution of poetry. *Ascend, Oh World,
in Song*: the imperative mood of the title implies the existence of a
Shelleyan poet-legislator commanding the world to transmute itself
into the truer realm of poetry. Everything about this volume bespeaks
the consolidation of a poetic identity. In *Bishevilim bodedim*, the table
of contents, tucked away at the end of the volume, simply offered a list
of the poems; in Silberschlag's second volume, however, the table of
contents, placed directly following the title page, groups the poems
under categories according to subject and genre, as if to say that before
us is not just a collection of poetry ad quem but the presentation of
a poetic career in which deliberate choices have been made to create
poetry in the various modes appropriate to a major Hebrew poet.

   In this formal arrangement, the first section, titled "Qavim lede-
muti" [Lines of self-portrait], is a group of sixteen poems that lays out
the components of Silberschlag's mature poetic persona. In the first
place in this first section is the poem "Sevel yerushah" [Anguished

inheritance] (pp. 3–4), in which the speaker tells us from where he hails and what his origins mean to him. Prompted by its placement and its declarative tone, many readers have, not surprisingly, taken the poem as the anthem of Silberschlag's creative identity. Like the volume as a whole, this presentation of self is highly organized. The three equal sections—each nine unrhymed lines with a single-line refrain—are devoted, respectively, to the patrimony of his male ancestors, the inheritance from his female ancestors, and himself as the wayward product of these influences. His male ancestors were Jewish merchants who went about their business in the birch and pine forests of the Carpathian foothills until their life was transformed by the advent of Hasidism. The Baal Shem Tov went up into those mountains on a spiritual quest and "found his soul in the form of a pure, young bride / Who lavished her playfulness upon his days and nights." When the founder came down to propagate his teaching through the medium of melody and dance, the speaker's ancestors embraced the new truth, clung to it, and transmitted its fire to their offspring. In the refrain that distills this, the male, portion of his inheritance, the speaker states: *Raz hahasidut ran bedami, raz hasidut ran beshiri* [The secret of Hasidism sings in my blood, the secret of Hasidism sings in my song]. This line has often been taken simply as a noble homage on the part of the poet to his Galician Hasidic roots. But a shrewder understanding of the refrain would underscore the implication that in a secular age, it is the poet's verse that is the true—and perhaps the last—beneficiary of this once-great spiritual enterprise.

The mothers are the transmitters of a different and more subversive force. They were possessors of a beauty that is hidden from view in the way in which the delicate violets in the foothills are obscured by the taller grasses of the meadows. Yet the fragrance of their beauty could not be concealed, and the very repute of their beauty had the power to unleash the desires of young men and women and thereby disturb the neat boundaries of traditional society. As a boy, the speaker heard tales of a Polish grandee who seduced a Jewess with the snares of love and made her betray her religion. The refrain that distills the inheritance from the ancestral mothers is more oblique than in the case of the fathers: *Nehash hasafeq na' bedami, nehash hasafeq na' beshiri* [The serpent of doubt moves in my blood, the serpent of doubt moves in my song]. Although the precise kind of doubt that has been bequeathed is left vague, its source could not be clearer, as is the link between female sexuality and the serpent. It is the real if unintended sexual radiance of the mothers that unhinges and tampers and disturbs.

When the last third of the poem comes around to the poet-speaker himself, we encounter an unexpected disjunction rather than a programmatic synthesis of the paternal and maternal influences. The stanza is built around repetitions of two similar-sounding roots: *t.h.h*, to be amazed and bewildered, and *r.h.h.*, to be afraid and to move without self-confidence. With his blond hair and blue eyes, he is puzzled by the fact that, despite being the heir to their patrimony, he does not resemble his ancestors. He is further confused by his inner life: "My heart is the meeting place for myriads of conflicts, yet I was not provoked by them, / For myriads of desires, yet I did not seek them out. Like a stranger I have passed through the lands of my heart." The inability to abandon himself either to ideas or to desires seems to be the "anguished inheritance" of the poem's title. His forebears have ineluctably put their mark on his poetry, and it is that poetry that has opened up fissures within himself and between him and his people. As a Hebrew poet, his fate has a double knot, which returns to the gender distinctions of the first two stanzas. The women never understood my song because they never knew Hebrew, and the men, in the desolation of their troubles, forgot the language of poetry. Thus the third of the poem's refrains: *Ani sharti li et shiri tahat shahakei nekhar nugim* [I sang my song under cheerless alien skies]. (By virtue of the juxtaposition of this poem with the one that follows, which will be discussed next, the "cheerless alien skies" refers not just to the disenchantment of modernity but specifically to America.) Taken as a whole, then, "Sevel yerushah" is a self-inverting artifact. Placed at the head of the poet's new book and opening with a self-confident claim to the poetic legacy of Hasidism, the poem leads us to expect an *ars poetica* anthem celebrating the poet's vital transformation of the received wisdom of his origins. Instead, the poem regresses from the Hasidic song to doubt-provoking sexuality and finally to inner and outer alienation.

The source of that alienation for Silberschlag is close at hand. In the second poem of self-presentation in the volume, "Mipolin 'ad ameriqah" [From Poland to America] (pp. 5–8), the speaker declares that at age forty half his life has been spent in Poland and half in America. Dear to him seven-fold in the throes of its destruction—the year must be 1943—Poland nurtured him from three sources: the melodies of its inhabitants and its hills, the scientific learning that came by way of its German-speaking overlords, and the faith that flowed from Zionism and the connection to Eretz Yisrael. Despite the deprivation and constriction of Jewish life there, it was an existence grounded in a yearning for transcendental meaning. America, the scene of the second half of his life so far, would seem to promise an antidote to the disintegration and persecution of European Jewish life. Here there is room to spread out, infinite reserves of youthful energy, and the talent for pragmatic accomplishment. Yet notwithstanding these apparent riches, the opposite has taken place. "Indeed, my heart has been broken by the pangs of the move / From the culture of longing to the culture of money" (p. 6). Silberschlag builds his contrast on the near identity between *kosef,* yearning, and *kesef,* money. The abundance of the latter inevitably extinguishes the former.

The indictment of America is unsparing. Rabbis resemble peddlers whose merchandise is a debased Torah made up of vacuous, inflated homilies. Educators, who are charged with teaching Torah, lack the slightest notion of what they are about. Together they care only about their salaries and are so preoccupied with their material well-being that they are insensible to the wholesale slaughter of European Jewry. At the same time as Jewish bodies are being murdered abroad, on the free shores of America, the Jewish people is condemning itself to spiritual death and killing of all that is majestic in its soul. There is but one hope, declares the speaker in conclusion, and it lies in the Land of Israel.

"Mipolin 'ad ameriqah" is the foundational text in what becomes a broad genre in Silberschlag's poetic career: vicious, and viciously amusing, satires on American Jewish life. This is something of a singular phenomenon in the corpus of American Hebrew poetry. Although all American Hebraist writers were sharply critical of the American Jewish community, the poets generally observed a kind of separation of modes in which this kind of satirical project was left to the prose writers. (And indeed such fiction writers as Arieli-Orloff, Halkin, and Blank took up the cudgel with sardonic enthusiasm.) In the poets' romantic conception of poetry, the synagogue, the Jewish school, and the immigrant neighborhood are not fertile ground for Hebrew verse. They made their own bargain with America by turning away from what was most familiar and most fallen. They turned instead toward an idealized rural American landscape that more often than not contained no people whatsoever—whether Jews or gentiles—or at most, figures like Bavli's Mrs. Woods, who represent an older, even biblical, order of values, or American Indians and Afro-Americans, whose lore similarly stood at an exotic distance from contemporary society. None of these vistas or folkways apparently held much charm for Silberschlag, or at least not enough to be adduced as a counterweight to the savaging of American Jewish institutions.[15] Among many other purposes, poetry could serve him well as a weapon. What his satirical poems lack in nuance of feeling is made up for by a wicked and efficacious display of wit.[16]

In Silberschlag's second major book, the American polemic is part of a larger program to put behind him the image of the sensitive, lyric poetaster and instead, to inhabit the figure of a poet of substance, gravity, and range. Because the dreamy, intoxicated lover was so very much a part of his early work, there is a felt urgency in his effort to portray himself as a lover of a different sort. Silberschlag seizes his chance in a long poem about an affair with a married woman, titled "Yesh yif'ah 'atsumah beḥokhmah" [There is enormous beauty in wisdom] (pp. 27–41). The remaking of his self-conception as a lover is dramatized in the opening stanza of the poem not simply as a further station in his self-realization but rather as a crisis that challenged him to expand his poetic self.

יֵשׁ יִפְעָה עֲצוּמָה בְּחָכְמָה. יִפְעָתֵךְ בְּחָכְמָתֵךְ הָעֲצוּמָה.
וְשִׁירִי, שֶׁהָיָה יוֹדֵעַ לְקַלֵּס בְּחֶבָּה יְתֵרָה
יִתְרוֹנוֹת הַגְּוִיָּה הַנְּקֵבִית: הַשֵּׁעָר הַצַּף בְּלַבּוֹתָיו

עַל גַּב וְעַל חָזֶה כְּצָעִיף מִתְפַּלֵּג, הַשַּׁד הַחִוָּרִין
וְהַפִּטְמָה הַנּוֹצֶצֶת כַּכּוֹכָב הַוְרֹדִי בַּאֲפֵלַת הַלַּיְלָה, —
מִתְנַהֵל בִּזְהִירוּת מְתוּנָה כַּנָּהָר הָרָחָב בַּמִּישׁוֹר,
בְּפָאֲרוֹ יְפָעָתֵךְ הַנַּפְשִׁית הַמְנוֹבְבָה וּמְדוֹבְבָה גְּבִיָּתֵךְ.

There is enormous beauty in wisdom; your beauty is in your
  enormous wisdom.
And my song that with exceeding affection knew well how to extol
The charms of the female form: the hair that flows like lava
Down the back and like a parted veil down the front, the pale
  breast
And the nipple gleaming like a roseate star in the night's
  darkness,—
Proceeds with prudent caution like a wide river on the plain,
When it comes to praising your soulful beauty which animates and
  articulates your body.

Note, to begin with, the ample and solid architecture of this stanza, which, like the forty-two others in the poem, has seven unrhymed lines, each with six amphibrachs. The tone is expository; and the opening line is classificatory and almost syllogistic in tone ("There is *enormous* beauty in wisdom; your beauty is in your *enormous* wisdom."), and this opening betokens a poetry that eschews lyric expressiveness in favor of making observations and distilling wisdom. The fact that it is precisely the attribute of wisdom that proves so powerfully seductive in this poem is therefore no coincidence. Although the speaker's ostensible purpose is to praise his lover, the lion's share of the stanza is given over to a characterization—bragging, really—of his own poetry, whose distinguishing theme has been female sensuality. The speaker presents himself as part troubadour and part lothario whose *métier*, whose very stock-in-trade, has the business of praising the female body. The descriptions of hair and breast in lines 3–5 move in two directions at the same time. On the one hand, they provide a sampling of the speaker-poet's talent in producing figurative language. The nipple "gleaming like a roseate star in the night's darkness" is supposed to arrest our attention not just for its sensual daring but also for its performative achievement as metaphor making. On the other hand, these lush tropes also suggest an overripe quality of self-parody. The erotic poetry of the world abounds in such chestnuts of arousal, and even his belated contributions to the genre run the risk of labeling him as a poet who is capable of appreciating *only* the superficial charms of women's beauty.

Hence the speaker's revisionist declaration that beauty rooted in intelligence and soulfulness can carry an erotic charge and that these qualities, as he asserts in the last line of the stanza, are anterior to the body, animating and articulating it. The problem with this realization is that it unmans his confidence as a poet. Once a mountain torrent, his poetry has now been reduced to a flaccid flow that seeks a new channel. He has prided himself in being a connoisseur of women's beauty only to find himself up against a greater force that challenges his mastery and compels him to proceed with caution while he hastens to improvise a new poetics adequate to the task. The poetry that follows this opening, the procession of solid, long-lined stanzas that comprise "Yesh yif'ah 'atsumah beḥokhmah," provides strong evidence for the will to measure up to this task and write a love poetry of greater range and maturity. Yet to accomplish this, Silberschlag feels compelled to abandon the lyric entirely and to adopt a more cerebral, novelistic exposition that tells the story of the doomed affair rather than instantiating the feelings it aroused. It is a style, moreover, to which he never returned in his later poetry.

It is Silberschlag's particular charm never to have entirely outgrown his "immaturity" and suppressed the rush of desire that continues to surprise him as he ages. Far more characteristic than his treatise on the beauty of wisdom and far more wise in its own way is a short poem located in the autobiographical section of *'Aleh, 'olam, beshir* titled "Me'alumay 'ad ziqnati" [From my youth to my old age] (p. 17). In very simple language, the speaker reflects on how, when he was ten years younger, his heart would pound when he would meet his girlfriend by the edge of a pine grove. Yet now, despite the fact that his youth is over, his heart still races in the same way at the prospect of meeting his lover. But there is a difference, which is spelled out in the poem's closing lines: "Even in my old age, even in my old age /

I will silently bow down before a young woman, / But she will give her heart to the young man, / And leave me to make poems." The substitution of writing about love for the consummation of love is an old trope, but Silberschlag gives it a fresh poignancy with the artless admission that he has never truly outgrown the excited anticipation of an amorous encounter. Now, rather than waiting by the edge of the woods for his lover, he makes a courtly gesture of obeisance before a beautiful young woman, but the desire and the adoration persist. There is, moreover, something gently self-mocking in the readiness of the speaker to regard himself as having entered the zone of old age whereas we know from other poems in this autobiographical gathering that the persona of the speaker is not much past forty. The poem, then, represents a kind of arrangement that Silberschlag has arrived at with himself. Although I will not and I cannot give up desiring, I will cease striving to make my poems describe that experience from within; instead, I will write poems that *observe* myself in the act of desiring.[17] Whether in youth or old age, Silberschlag remained true to his theme.

Silberschlag was given over forty more years to write poetry after the publication of 'Aleh, 'olam, beshir, and he did not squander his chance. He published four more books of verse: *Qimron yamai* [The arc of my days] (1959),[18] *Iggerotai el dorot aherim* [Letters to other generations] (1971),[19] *Yesh reshit lekhol aharit* [Each end has a beginning] (1976),[20] and *Bein alimut uvein adishut* [Between violence and indifference] (1982).[21] In these collections, Silberschlag carries over lines of development from earlier volumes. There are many fine poems here, and this is a body of work that deserves exploration on its own terms. In the best of these, Silberschlag fashioned what might be called a wisdom lyric. Like his earliest verse, there are many very short poems that evince an aspiration toward lapidary concision and toward the appearance of simplicity. They are lyric in form in that the author and the speaker are assumed to be the same and the discourse of the poems is presented as overheard speech. What is different is the stance of the speaker, who is now positioned less within experience than at a remove observing it. He observes the world and its desires and follies, and he observes himself and his desires and follies. The goal is truth rather than expressiveness, and the essential medium is a finely honed verbal wit.

The self doing the observing is ever and always a poet, and, for that matter, a Hebrew poet living in America. Being a Hebrew poet is a great gift despite the loneliness that necessarily attends this high calling; but being a Hebrew poet in America entails a depth of exile and humiliation that are a bitter fate. It is a fate visited upon him in part by the upheavals of Jewish history and in part by the imperatives of his own temperament. He is reconciled and unreconciled. In one of the final poems in the final collection published the year before he died—the poem that is quoted in the Introduction to this volume—Silberschlag reflected on this situation.[22] If I lived in Israel, the speaker opines, I would be an Israeli poet. My books would be published without my having to pay for them and I would even receive royalties, and my poetry would be part of the civic culture of the state and quoted by officials at the dedication of public buildings. But the reality is otherwise. I am a "poet of Israel but not in the Land of Israel." This makes him a "curious creature," the speaker admits, but not an unprecedented one or one lacking a distinguished pedigree. In the history of the Jewish people, there have been others who have forged paths for Hebrew poetry in the Diaspora and across the sea, and so, the poem concludes, shall there be in the future. Of the fact that Silberschlag was a proud exemplar of this outsider tradition there is no question. Whether his prophecy for the future will come true is less certain.

✳ בְּעִקְבוֹת עַכּוּ"ם
In Pagan Footsteps

Analysis

A slight but beguilingly provocative poem is at once a gesture toward Tchernichovsky's literary paganism and an anatomy of the desire that is so central to Silberschlag's poetry.

בְּעִקְבוֹת עַכּוּ"ם

שֶׁמֶשׁ וְרוּחַ וְיָם
וְגוּפֵךְ הַלּוֹהֵט עַל הַחוֹל,
שֶׁמֶשׁ וְרוּחַ וְיָם
וְגוּפֵךְ הַתּוֹבֵעַ בְּלִי קוֹל,
שֶׁמֶשׁ וְרוּחַ וְיָם
וְגוּפֵךְ הַחוֹלֵשׁ עַל הַכֹּל,
שֶׁמֶשׁ וְרוּחַ וְיָם —
הָהּ, חַיִּים בְּלִי אֵל וּבְלִי עֹל.

In Pagan Footsteps

Sun and wind and sea
And your burning body on the sand,
Sun and wind and sea
And your body wordlessly demanding,
Sun and wind and sea
And your body overpowering everything,
Sun and wind and sea—
Ah, life without God and without yoke.[23]

The poem is built around an alternation between a fixed, mantra-like refrain (*shemesh veruah veyam* [sun and wind and sea]) and a reference in the second person to the female companion's body on the beach. The alternating lines also have fixed elements: *gufeikh* [your body] at the beginning of each line, the nearly identical end rhymes, and the repetitive syntax. Working against the lulling torpor of these repetitions is the changing state of the companion's body, which moves from burning [*lohet*] to demanding [*tove'a*] to overpowering [*holesh 'al*]. The climax of this movement in line six (*vegufeikh haholesh 'al hakol* [And your body overpowering everything]) is conveyed by the rare phrase *holesh 'al*, which is known to us only from an obscure passage in Isaiah (14:12; the reference is to overpowering the gentile nations). Using this term is a canny stroke, because even for the erudite Hebraist reader who might pick up on the meaning of *holesh 'al* as overpower, the common meaning of the verb, to become weakened, can be counted on not to vanish. And so Silberschlag has found a single word that invokes both the conquest of the speaker by the companion's body *and* his swooning submission to that conquest. One also hears in this unusual phrase, *holesh 'al hakol*, an echo of the familiar poetic introduction to the Jewish wedding service under the canopy that invokes God's blessing on the union about to be solemnized: *Mi adir 'al hakol, mi barukh 'al hakol* [Who is mighty above all, Who is blessed upon all] and so forth. The association enacts a nicely wicked contrast between sanctified wedded bliss and the carnal hunger radiating on the beach blanket in our poem.

The poem's last line is the zinger. When we think that the mounting erotic tension has nowhere to go, the poem's speaker suddenly breaks off and switches to another kind of discourse entirely. He turns away from the overheated scene of sun, sand, and desire and utters a kind of historiosophical ejaculation whose import is not so clear. *Hah, hayyim beli el uveli 'ol* [Ah, life without God and without yoke]. Is the speaker's *hah* the nonverbal sound of a man who is savoring a delicious freedom from God the Judge and from the yoke of the commandments? Is it a kind of Mediterranean erasure of moral categories under the sun on the sandy verge of the ocean? Could it be the sound made by a man who has just discovered what the pagan life of the senses must really have been like and is pulling up short before he crosses that line?

The concluding line brings us back directly to the poem's title, which, in the end, does tantalizingly little to resolve these questions. *'Akum*, an acronym for *'ovdei kokhavim umazalot*, literally, "worshipers of stars and heavenly bodies," is the familiar epithet in rabbinic literature for pagans. *Be'iqvot* can mean "in the footsteps of," or, literally, "in the footprints of"; more figuratively, the phrase denotes causality ("as a result of") or imitation ("in the manner of"). Putting the components of the title together offers a number of interpretive options. As a title, *Be'iqvot 'akum* can therefore function as a cultural frame for the experience described in the poem. The semi-naked bodies radiating desire on the shore far away from the gaze of society can be described as precipitating a pagan moment. The speaker of the poem, whom the reader will inevitably associate with the distinguished translator of Aristophanes and the proponent of Tchernichovsky, is caught in an act of discovery. The idealized classical culture that he has so long researched and admired has suddenly, if but for a moment, become flesh, and he now experiences what he has only read about. The experience, by its nature, must be evanescent, as indicated by the footprints in the sand left by the ancients that have been long washed away. Finally, the title invokes the painterly or curatorial practice of indicating that a work of art has been executed *after the manner* of a grand master or his school. Writing in Hebrew within a long Hebraic tradition, Silberschlag wishes both to label and to contain the transgressive content of his poem by offering a token of homage and belatedness to the great pagans, whose true descendent he can never be.

Simon Halkin had the good fortune to elude the marginality that was the lot of most of his fellow Hebrew poets in America. This was a good fortune to which he substantially contributed by permanently settling in Israel at the time of the establishment of the state. As the occupant of the chair of Hebrew literature at the Hebrew University of Jerusalem during the 1950s and 1960s, Halkin taught virtually every important writer and critic in the young state and remained a strong presence on the literary and academic scene until his death at the age of eighty-eight in 1987. The force of his presence compelled attention to the body of his own poetry and fiction in face of the fact that his own writing flouted almost all the norms of the new Israeli literature of the time. Where the younger poets—Amichai, Zach, and Pagis among them—sought to bring the language of poetry closer to everyday speech, Halkin wrote in a high register using extreme figuration and a rarified literary lexicon. Where they prized simplicity and the brief lyric, he championed complexity and the ambitious long poem. Where they took for granted that modern man is living in a world after faith, Halkin made the search for God a central preoccupation of his poetic endeavor. Finally, where they saw themselves as the late flowering of Anglo-American modernism, Halkin saw himself as the late flowering of Anglo-American romanticism. Yet despite these fundamental differences, Halkin's poetry was accorded respect as much for the august power of the verse itself as for the influential figure of the poet who wrote it. In paying attention to Halkin's poetry, and to his fiction as well, the Israeli literary community was forced to acknowledge, belatedly, the group of American Hebrew writers from whose midst Halkin had emerged.

Yet despite the influential Israeli phase of his career, there is no question that as a Hebrew writer Halkin's was an American life.[1] He came to America with his family at the age of fifteen; he drank deeply of American and British literature in his most impressionable years and in his youth wandered widely throughout the United States. The fusion of his identity with the Hebrew language, to be sure, belongs to his Russian childhood, which took place in small towns along the Dnieper in Belarus, where his father served as a shoḥet and a melamed. Halkin was born in 1898 into circles that combined scholarly acumen with religious devotion in the particular amalgam of Habad Hasidism. In addition to his Talmudic knowledge—he read Russian and German literature as well—Halkin's father also had an encyclopedic knowledge of the Hebrew Bible and a complete mastery of Hebrew grammar. He taught Hebrew to Simon according to progressive phonetic methods, and he would at times converse with his son in Hebrew, insisting on proper pronunciation. Simon was never a participant in classroom education; he sat on the side and observed as his father taught his pupils, and he studied on his own. The stance of the ferocious autodidact, which was rooted in both pride and shyness, was to become a dominant feature of Halkin's education in Russia and America. From age twelve until he emigrated three years later, Simon left home to become a teacher of younger children in other villages. It was an occupation that afforded little opportunity for companionship with other adolescents but much time for learning Russian and taking gymnasium courses on history by correspondence.

After arriving in America, the family settled on Webster Avenue near the Grand Concourse in the Bronx. Halkin learned English from parsing every word in Washington Irving's *Sketches* and Walter Scott's *Ivanhoe* and reading the *New York Times*. With no previous American schooling, Halkin managed to get his high school diploma in two years, during which, because of self-consciousness about his accent, he took everything in but said very little. With his friend Regelson, who also was to become an important American Hebrew poet, he conversed in Hebrew about their shared enthusiasm for English romantic poetry and German idealism. Halkin's first published poems appeared while he was still in high school, and he was known in print as a master Hebraist even before he become known in person to the society of young people in the Hebrew clubs and organizations on the Lower East Side. After the appearance of his first published poem in 1915 in *Ha'umah*, Halkin's poems appeared regularly in the American Hebrew journals *Hatoren* and *Miqlat*.

Halkin matriculated at the City College of New York in 1917. He deepened his passion for the English poets, especially Shelley, Keats, Tennyson, and Browning; although when it came to prose, he preferred Dostoyevsky and Tolstoy to their English Victorian counterparts. He paid his expenses by teaching in a progressive talmud torah and by providing the vowel markings and diacritical signs for Zvi Scharfstein's series of Hebrew readers. His life took a decisive turn when it was discovered in a government-mandated physical examination that he had a moderate case of tuberculosis, and it was recommended that he spend as much time as possible away from city life. At the same time, he had been given a monthly stipend by the Shtibel Publishing House to do literary translation into Hebrew and to work on his own writing. This income enabled Halkin to leave New York and embark on a series of travels that lasted two and half years and took him all over the United States, including Florida, Louisiana, and California. The encounter with the American landscape in its variety is exuberantly reflected in his poetry and fiction. He became at home in the outdoors and adept at climbing, riding, and sailing.

Halkin returned to New York cured in 1924 and took a job teaching Sunday school teachers at Hebrew Union College while he began a master's degree program in education at New York University. As reflected in his Café Royal poems, he mixed freely in the Jewish literary bohemia of the time. A year-long sabbatical (1928–29) proved critical for Halkin. He traveled to Europe and met with the many Hebrew writers who were sojourning in Vienna and Paris on their way to Palestine; he finished his translation of *The Merchant of Venice* in Switzerland; he traveled to Latvia to aid family members who had been stranded in their efforts to emigrate; and he spent the balance of the year moving in the literary circles of the burgeoning Hebrew culture in Tel Aviv. During that year Halkin's first novel, *Yehi'el Hahagri*, was published by Shtibel in Berlin; his long poem "'Al hof Santa Barbara" [On the coast of Santa Barbara] and a sonnet sequence "Beyamim shishah uveleilot shiv'ah" [In six days and seven nights] appeared in Palestine. He returned to New York resolved to settle permanently in Palestine. In the meantime, in addition to his teaching, he learned Arabic and Greek and studied with John Dewey and Salo Baron at Columbia. The day after his marriage to Minnie Levin in 1932, the couple sailed for Palestine; a daughter was born in 1933 and a son in 1939. After serving as an English teacher at a Tel Aviv high school, a job that demanded long hours of work, Halkin was awarded a highly competitive stipend from Salman Schocken that enabled him to devote himself to writing the extant sections of his major novel, *'Ad mashber* [The crash].

Although Halkin had intended to settle in Palestine for good, through a concatenation of circumstances, he ended up spending the years 1939–49 in America. He had been offered a one-year teaching position at the Jewish Theological Seminary and had sent his family on ahead. In the meantime, the invitation had been withdrawn, and when Halkin joined his family in New York, he found himself cut off by the outbreak of World War II. It remained a source of shame and regret for Halkin that he was absent from the Yishuv during these crucial and turbulent years. After two years of teaching in Chicago, he returned to the relative comfort of a professorship at Stephen Wise's Jewish Institute for Religion. He received his doctorate from Hebrew Union College for work that formed the basis of his English book, *Modern Hebrew Literature from the Enlightenment to the Birth of the State of Israel: Trends and Values.*[2] The final phase of Halkin's career began with his appointment to the Hebrew University and his settling in Jerusalem, where he lived for the rest of his life with the exception of several visiting appointments at American universities. His translation into Hebrew of Whitman's *Leaves of Grass* appeared in 1952, but, except for occasional poems, his poetic output was submerged by the demands of his teaching and by the heavy responsibility of introducing the youthful intelligentsia of the new state to the Hebrew creativity of the Haskalah and the Hebrew Revival and to an expansive vision of the vocation of Hebrew letters in general. Halkin was the recipient of the Israel Prize in literature in 1975.

Halkin's major poetic statement is the volume *'Al ha'i* [On the island] (1946), which gathers his poems from 1918 to 1943. Most readers have taken the island in question to be America, but the association between the two does not delimit the possibilities of what this connection means. Is the island a place of shipwreck and abandonment? A way station on the path to a wished-for destination? A realm of natural innocence? America was all these things to Halkin; most of all, it was the place where he seized his vocation and became a poet. ʿAl haʾi spans the years of Halkin's long sojourn in America. It opens with nature- and God-intoxicated verse declaimed in landscapes reminiscent of the Catskills and Adirondacks, and concludes with dour meditations on the destruction of European Jewry set in the sand dunes of Michigan. Connecting these two points is the unfolding of a rich, metaphysical consciousness that exploits the vast reticulated resources of the Hebrew language to ceaselessly invent itself.

On the basis of the first poems in this volume, written when Halkin was in his early twenties (1918–22), it is already possible to distinguish the clear outlines of the persona that he was to inhabit for most of his poetic career. (Although it is proper to insist on the difference between Halkin the poet and the persona he constructs in his poetry—and indeed the speakers of individual poems—the romantic sincerity of his verse continually invites us to disregard this proper distinction and instead to hear the voice of the Poet resounding from poem to poem.) The stance that Halkin establishes in these early poems rests on several assumptions. The first is that the writer of the poems is not simply a composer of verse but a man who has been elected by destiny, by God even, as if to a sacred office to wear the mantle of Poet. The call to this high vocation precedes the actual practice of poetry. The speaker of these poems is a young man who knows that he has been chosen and that he has been endowed with a soul that thirsts for revelation and is a worthy vessel for it, although he has not yet experienced the revelation nor does he know its content in advance.

The second assumption is that the essence of true poetry is the religious encounter between the soul of the poet and the mystery of the created world. This conviction synthesizes the two formidable traditions that contributed to Halkin's spiritual-intellectual formation: English romantic poetry and Habad Hasidism. From the romantics, especially Shelley, Halkin took the idea that the poet has inherited the mantle of the priest, prophet, and legislator all combined. The soul of the poet, in this conception, is graced with a special receptiveness to the *anima mundi*, the soul of the world; poetry is both the transcription of moments in which the impress of the world's soul is keenly felt, as well as the recollection of those moments and the anxiety over their loss. From Habad, with its roots in Lurianic Kabbalah, Halkin adopted a panentheistic theology, which posits the existence of a transcendent God who is dispersed immanently within the created world. As experienced by man, the divine reality is comprised by a dialectic between the *yesh*, the finite manifestations of God the world, and the *ayin*, the infinite unknowability of God; this is a complexity that the poet discovers in the seemingly contradictory forces of nature. Like the cosmos-shaping poetry of the romantics, contemplative prayer in Habad Hasidism posits a reciprocity of influences between man and God and the human capacity to affect the dialectic within the divine milieu.[3]

To say that Halkin synthesized romanticism and Habad Hasidism is probably an oversimplification, or at least a generalization that awaits further careful and informed scrutiny of this dimension of his poetry. (Because at some primordial level both share a common root in Neoplatonism, the correlation is not as remote as might first be imagined.[4]) At the very least, one can say that the vocabulary of Habad Hasidism was highly useful to Halkin in domesticating his romantic intensity within the Hebrew language. The appropriation of Habad's kabbalistic theosophy paradoxically further allowed Halkin's poetry to camouflage its true indifference to traditional Judaism. Although the early poetry is absorbed in the encounter between man and God through the spectacle of nature, there is next to nothing about Jewish ritual, biblical and rabbinic narratives, the disintegration of Jewish life in Europe, or the critique of Jewish law. The divine-human encounter is enthusiastically religious but only remotely Judaic. As an elite, mystical path set in its own space within, or along the margins, of Orthodoxy, the theological lexicon of Habad Hasidism, though not its practice, served Halkin very well.

The third assumption is a maximalist poetics. In contrast to such poets as Rahel (Blaustein) in Palestine, Fogel in Europe, and Efros in America, who were striving to achieve a radical simplification of

Hebrew verse during the same period, Halkin was writing large. His verse displays no epistemological doubts about the potency of poetic language and no hesitations in the frequent use of metaphors and similes, most of which are taken from the realm of organic nature. The register of Halkin's Hebrew is very high. His impressive erudition, primarily in Bible but also in rabbinic literature, permits him to exploit the widest semantic resources afforded by the Hebrew language. Reaching for the right word without regard for its currency, Halkin makes few concessions to readers less erudite than he. Finally, in a way that links him to another great contemporary maximalist Uri Zvi Greenberg, Halkin is not afraid of repetition. Passages in his poems are structured in great layers or sheets of language that fold back upon themselves to reiterate and reemphasize clarion themes. For the reader raised on the privileged concision of New Critical norms, it can take some getting used to. The fulsomeness of Halkin's poetics helps to explain why, despite the existence in his canon of some beautiful, brief lyric poems, he found himself in his most natural poetic element when he was drawing longer breaths.

Taken as a whole, the poetics of Halkin's early verse occupies what might be called a position of radical conservatism. His deep filiation with English romanticism should not be understood simply as a personal aesthetic preference or as a case of arrested aesthetic development. Rather, it was a considered critique of and protest against what he perceived to be the constrictions and soullessness of modernism. Conversely, Halkin's hypostasizing of God and Shekhinah was a departure from the way in which those concepts had been degraded in modern Hebrew literature into mere ironic or at best symbolic terms. (In this, he again resembles Uri Zvi Greenberg.) The ordeal of apostasy experienced by the previous generation, the sons "banished from their father's table," was either behind him or alien to him. The presence of the divine in his poetry constitutes a critique of the fashionable and taken-for-granted secularity of the moderna.

Halkin's early poems are shot through with the anticipation and anxiety of the young visionary who is awaiting the disclosure of his vision. In "Tsipiyah" [Expectation] (p. 14),[5] the speaker insists in the opening line that the silence he abides within himself is "not the frozenness of fall but rather the wordlessness of fields in spring," which have been turned over but not yet seeded. In the meantime, he maintains a stance of openness toward the cosmos informed by a gaze of radical amazement [*mishta'eh el hapele*]. This confidence at times turns into dread as the poet wonders whether, like a withered bud on a branch, his potent readiness will ever be called upon ("Nafshi al tir'i" [My soul, do not fear], p. 77). From where will the call issue? While the young poet looks toward the wonders of the created universe for the signals he seeks, he is painfully aware of his disabilities when he looks in the direction of humankind. "The song of humanity is sealed to me," he confesses, even though he knows that human relations are also an expression of the divine.[6] He therefore prays to be transported magically to a realm where souls have been freed of their integuments and face each other without masks or barriers ("Sa'ini, haderekh" [Road, take me], pp. 19–20).

Halkin is vouchsafed a glimmer of what he seeks in a poem called "Tefillot" [Prayers] (pp. 24–26), which is divided into three sections named for the three daily services. After a prolonged appeal to the Shekhinah in the *shaḥarit*/morning section, the hidden, emanated beauty of the *Ein-Sof* reveals itself for a fraction of a second, before vanishing and leaving the poet in a state of desolate longing. Although the moment of cosmic beauty disappears, the flash of its presence gives new fuel to the poet's longing for illumination. Even after this experience, the task facing the poet continues to be finding a mode of spiritual existence that is not consumed by the anxiety of striving. Now something very much like this is recorded in "'Ad sheyafuaḥ hayom" [Until the day declines] (pp. 80–83). The speaker is an existential wayfarer who happens upon a dense pine forest, which, in an echo of Jacob at Bet-El, turns out to be a holy place. The profound sense of welcome he experiences within this bower has an extraordinary effect on him: "I suddenly forgot all about those exhausting matters / Of wandering and wondering and anticipating the revelation of the Shekhinah" (p. 82). Even though the revelation has tarried, he not only feels freed from the anxiety of expectation, but he is given the capacity to experience a kind of metaphysical playfulness within this protected space. This is no mean achievement, and this state of unagitated visionary readiness has a strong resonance with Keats's idea of "negative capability" and notions of *disponibilité*.

Yet playfulness is the last quality one can attach to *Yoḥai* (pp. 87–108), Halkin's most ambitious poem of the period, which mixes formal features of English romantic poetry (especially the epic invocation) together with a radicalized version of the Habad mystic theology.[7] The poem is closely allied with the first of Halkin's two novels, *Yeḥi'el Hahagri*, written at approximately the same time, which deals with the mystical quest of a young immigrant intellectual in New York.[8] The title of the poem refers to Rabbi Simon ben Yohai, the second-century scholar who was the only surviving student of Rabbi Akiva after the suppression of the Bar Kochba rebellion. He reportedly hid with his son in a cave for twelve years to escape Roman persecution. The authorship of the Zohar, the foundational text of the Kabbalah, is traditionally attributed to him. Aside from the detail of the case, this rich historical context is actually of little interest to Halkin, who takes the name Simon ben Yohai and foreshortens it by removing his, Halkin's, own proper name (Simon/Simon). Yet even this tenuous tether is enough to establish some distance between Halkin the poet and the dramatic monologist of his poem and thereby to create the kind of persona absent from most all of his earlier poetry.

It's a good thing, too, because Yohai's turbulent spiritual struggles prove fatal. In terms of what is at stake in the poem, there is something of a shift from Halkin's earlier work. There, the poet yearns for an illumination that will be experienced as an answering confirmation of his capacity for wonder and his poetic vocation. Here, the issue is knowledge. Yohai demands to be told the secret wisdom that explains why the cosmos is as it is. Both the posture of waiting and the sought-after revelation have been pushed to the extreme and rendered unbearably urgent. The desperate, Promethean nature of Yohai's project is set out in the first two of the poem's five sections. The prayer to God in Yohai's own voice that opens the poem remains within the formula of similar biblical appeals: If I have proved worthy in Thine eyes, my Lord, then answer my plea. The list of spiritual distinctions that Yohai claims should "qualify" him for divine attention covers ground familiar from Halkin's earlier poems. Yohai presents his soul as a vessel supremely attuned to the variegated wonders of Creation. The poem's narrator takes up the description of Yohai in the second section and presents him as a "man of visions" for whom truth is experienced solely through a transcendent language of wonders. Because he lives in such intense sympathetic connection to the soul of the universe, it has become unbearable to him to persevere without being vouchsafed the secret of the divine purpose that makes the world inhere. He is encouraged in his demand by the stars and the heavenly bodies, which complain that they are fated to turn forever in their supernal spheres without ever knowing the reason for their movements.

Yohai takes to his cave to besiege God and insist on an answer. After a prolonged but unspecified ordeal of waiting, the militant and embittered Yohai is finally given an answer, but it is one that stuns and dispirits him. Speaking in a vision, God explains that the atoms of His being are dispersed immanently within each creature of humankind; yet because of the suffering human beings experience in their lives, these divine sparks form a vast reservoir of collective sorrow that in turn becomes God's fate and His burden. Yet, whereas humans are released from suffering upon death, God's eternality means that His suffering goes on and on. Yohai has prayed for divine truth and has been granted it, but the tragic secret of that truth has only redoubled his burden. For now, instead of praying for the redemption of human-kind, he is impelled to pray in addition for the redemption of God Himself. This is a burden that no man, however holy or visionary, can discharge, and Yohai collapses and dies in a paroxysm of impotent despair.

Because Halkin did not make Yohai an exact copy of the auto-biographical persona that speaks in most of his other poems, we have license to wonder about how Halkin wants his reader to approach this parable about the soul of the artist. On the one hand, Yohai is possessed of an admirable visionary capability and an extraordinary sensitivity to the wonder of the universe; he also owns the desire to search for hidden knowledge and the brave resolve for the solitary pursuit of that goal. On the other hand, Yohai's quest can be taken as cosmic presumption; he wants to strip away the garments that cloak the divine mysteries, and when he sees "what is above and what is below," the knowledge is too much for him. Halkin strengthens an ironic reading by ending the poem with a brief fifth section that tells the story of a kind of worm that lays eggs deep in the earth and waits underground for four years before burrowing to the surface, seeing the sun, and dying. The worm emerges just after Yohai's collapse, and in the poem's closing lines it comes to rest upon the frozen open eyelid of the dead mystic.

It is not too great an exaggeration to say that Halkin was saved from spiritual self-destruction by discovering America. The poems from his travels across the land between 1922 and 1924 are open, joyful, and expansive. He is available—in the sense of being *disponible*—to the shifting vistas, allowing each to evoke fresh dimensions of his sensibility. In "Ohio" (p. 167), for example, the ploughed, flat, open fields stir an affirmation ("How good it is that there are fields in the world!") that functions as a reassurance of the baseline solidness of the world. The great composition of this period, and in many ways the capstone of Halkin's poetic oeuvre altogether, is "'Al ḥof Santa Barbara," (pp. 179–88). Although the poem stands on its own as an ecstatic celebration of the confluence of mountains, sea, and sky, it can be fully understood only as an episode in Halkin's spiritual autobiography that directly addresses the morbid impasse arrived at in *Yohai*.

Standing on the Pacific shore at the outset of the poem, the speaker is astounded and exhilarated by the pyrotechnical spectacle of sunset that returns evening after evening. The poem is written as a dithyrambic ode, whose object of address is first the twilight fire [*esh*] and later the land [*erets, adamah*]; in Hebrew, all of these entities are marked as feminine, and the unremitting repetition of the feminine singular imperative provides the poem with its breathless, driving rhythm. The play of lights is experienced as a sensual eruption in whose explosive energy lies a gratifying though consuming danger [*magor 'ongeikh okhel*]. Yet despite this hazard, or because of it, the speaker is eager to deliver himself. In an extended simile, he compares his readiness to undo the constriction of his life to the willingness of the magnificent magnolia blossom to renounce its dewy self-enclosure and open its silken leaves to the searing light of morning. This fragile enclosure is the poet's spiritual autonomy [*ḥofesh-hanefesh*], which he has assiduously and sensitively husbanded and nurtured. He is stunned by the sudden realization that it is a slight and shabby thing compared to the vital majesty he is witnessing bursting around him. Now he wants only to be consumed, literally swallowed, by the light and the fire.

The act of surrender that is central to the poem is not simply an orgasmic moment of self-forgetting. It gains enormous resonance from the theological language into which it is translated and from the long-cultivated spiritual-poetic enterprise that it seeks to vitiate. The speaker confesses that his entire life until now has been devoted to "listening in dark mists for the rustle of the Infinite [*Ein-Sof*]" and attending to each manifestation of nature in hope of discovering "the vision of divine unity that is revealed and concealed in the array of phenomena" (p. 180). But the constant search for these elusive signals of transcendence has worn him down and emptied him out. The unrelenting search for transcendence has turned the manifest wonders of experience into mere instrumental signs. The speaker understands his situation in terms of the Habad dynamic between *yesh* and *ayin*. In his exclusive pursuit of the *ayin*, the transcendent hidden oneness of God, he has become closed off to the *yesh*, the immanent energy of the divine embodied in the phenomena of the created world. Addressing the divine unity, the speaker abjures, "In vain man seeks You in the heights of exalted Ideas torn from the earth. / You are *on* earth. The *yesh* is Your essence" (p. 180). In terms of Habad theology, the poet's rejection of the transcendent and affirmation of the immanent is less an instance of apostasy than a moment in a dialectic that is in the process of correcting an imbalance.

Amidst the poem's ringing acclamations, there is an unmistakable theme of regret. "Gazing into the redoubled darkness, I used to shut my eyes / In order to pierce more deeply the infinite night, / To dredge up from the distant depths a vision of the Godhead" (p. 184). Yet, there was never a way out of this dark journey, and the Earth, whose stunning glories are now electrifying him, remained lost and shrouded in the gloom. The poem enacts the moment of this realization: the enormous resources of spirit had been invested in a futile quest, while all along the answer was visible before his eyes. It is a poignant moment that unmistakably evokes a similar stroke of regret at the center of Bialik's great poem of 1910, "Lifnei aron hasefarim" [Before the bookcase], which he wrote in the wake of his many years of work with Revnitsky on *Sefer ha'aggadah*.[9] The autobiographically reflective speaker of Bialik's poem realizes, first, that his preoccupation with the aggadah as an adult has been motivated by a desire to rediscover the youth who had lived his early dreams among the ancient folio pages, and, then, that this endeavor had been fundamentally misguided. For while he labored underground sifting through the ruins of classical Jewish culture, the real festival of life was taking place far away from him above ground. Bialik's and Halkin's poems are joined in the sudden recognition of an enormous waste of spirit. They diverge sharply, however, in what comes next. For Bialik's speaker, it is sadly too late; by the time he realizes his error, he can no longer establish a connection with the natural world. Yet, for Halkin's speaker in "Santa Barbara," the affirmation of the world is a celebration that he can still join.

The poem's crescendo (section three, pp. 186–87) stages the sunset as an explosion of colors that leads to an erotic apotheosis. This polychrome riot brings out Halkin's most sensually figurative writing as he conjures up saffron, crimson, quicksilver hues, gold-like transparent molten honey, thrilling iridescent blues, and inflammatory reds. This extraordinary, daily experience of sunset is not pictured as a decorous and harmonious tableau but rather as a dynamic spectacle in which the changing sheets and shafts of color race in from the west over the sea and then ascend into the mountains above the Santa Barbara shore. At the height of this fervor, there is a noticeable intensification in the erotic register of the poem's discourse. Throughout the poem, the light and the land of Santa Barbara have been addressed in an ode-like mode as feminine entities to which the speaker over and over again pledges his submission. But here the equivocation of grammatical and figurative femininity gives way to a Santa Barbara that is fully incarnated as a gorgeous sea creature with rosy transparent skin in a fully developed naked body. It is as if Santa Barbara as a taken-for-granted place name had been dissolved to reveal the contours of the real Barbara underneath. Furthermore, there is no escaping the wonderfully transgressive effect in Hebrew of repeatedly turning imploringly to *Saint* Barbara. The kind of consummation he seeks is unabashed. He beseeches her to stroke his neck while he drinks in her intoxicating blood; he will bathe in her snowy breasts and catch fire from the blaze of her heart and finally be extinguished in the force of her desire.

The poignancy of the tristesse that follows is deepened by what we know of the poet's life in the sense of the autobiographical persona he has dramatized in his poetry. The poem's speaker confesses that this encounter has burst open in him a depth of desire that has been entirely unknown to him until now. Recalling the image of the magnolia that opens to receive the morning light, he wonders whether there exists a heart anywhere that is both available to him and capable of containing the "fire of his life." The ecstatic encounter on the shores of Santa Barbara, which cannot be counted on to repeat itself, has revealed an unanticipated vein of erotic longing. It is a discovery that is both a beneficent act of grace and an exigent source of anxiety. For the reader of Halkin's poetry, the sudden emergence of this intensity of longing calls stark attention to how rarely the experience of human love appears in his verse. In its solitary diffidence and pride, Halkin's poetic persona is fully absorbed in his transactions with God, nature, the cosmos. The transfiguring erotic encounter, after all, has taken place between the poet and the embodiment of a natural site, and it may turn out to be that it is *only* here or in a place like it that such an encounter is possible. Although the *quest* for human love may be conducted with grand pathos, the *experience* of love never becomes a source of either revelation or redemption. It is this aporia that gives "'Al ḥof Santa Barbara" its great strength as a work of art. The ecstatic encounter with this American vista is brilliantly realized in Halkin's cascading sheets of electrifying figurative writing. But it purchases the ring of truth by admitting the pain that is the inevitable byproduct of the poem's most central discovery.

The epiphany at Santa Barbara was a pinnacle experience in several senses. Halkin succeeded in fusing the fullness of sensory and sensual immediacy together with conceptual-theological self-understanding in a way that had thus far eluded him. But it was an achievement that cast a long shadow because never again would Halkin's poetry recapture the plenum of existence dramatized in the great poem. Many romantic poets before him, to be sure, had struggled with the same problem and developed compensatory strategies of consolation. Yet for Halkin there were no spots of time that could be recollected in tranquility. The revelatory balance between transcendence and immanence broke down in the poetry following the early 1920s when "Santa Barbara" was written. The storm of Halkin's "God intoxication" fades, and, in the important transitional poem "Mimkha elekha" [From you to you] (pp. 192–95), he soberly and ruefully reflects on the coming apart of the "awesome tripartite unity of the living God, the heart of the world and the voice of song and pain." The only leg of the tripod left standing is "song and pain," and he struggles without whining complaint to accept the sufficiency of his poetic art in the aftermath of these other, significant losses.

It is a critical moment of disenchantment. The poet's daily experience of radical amazement in the presence of the natural world and the living, sympathetic rapport of the world with God as the *animus mundi*—in short, the whole romantic complex intermixed with Habad theology—comes to an end, and we don't know why. Halkin does not explore or explain the roots of the crisis, if he indeed experiences it as a crisis or simply as an inevitability. The change does coincide with the return from his travels in the American countryside to life in New York. But then, again, Halkin's most intense God searching had taken place in the metropolis; for after all, one of the most moving scenes in the spiritual biography of Yeḥi'el Hahagri, the protagonist of Halkin's first novel of that name, had taken place in Van Cortland Park in the Bronx, New York's northern borough.

This moment can therefore be meaningfully marked as the beginning of a second major phase in the development of Halkin's poetry, which lasts some twenty years and ends in 1943 at the end of *'Al ha'i*, his major collection. What is new in this phase is Halkin's greater willingness to take notice of the lives of others and to observe the cavalcade of human folly in the cityscape around him. For a poet who had been absorbed in the formation of his soul in its rapport with God and the world, there is a new awareness of the political realm, broadly construed, and the fate of the Jewish people within the historical moment. His own sojourns in Palestine provoke reactions to the experience of exile and return to the Land. In the early 1940s, the destruction of European Jewry insinuates itself into the most intimate spaces in his consciousness. The poet's construction of his self also alters irrevocably. Once favored as the recipient of God's grace, he now experiences the contradictions of human existence without special reprieve, and he is forced to confront the tragic and shameful limitations of his own nature. This is a world we know, and there is a strong case to be made for the superior power of this later stage in Halkin's poetry precisely because it is fallen and embroiled. Despite the infectious, dithyrambic abandonment of the earlier verse, not all modern readers can easily join Halkin on his flights of spirit. In these poems, Halkin approaches closer to a gnarled and difficult modernism.

Halkin returned to New York in 1924 and remained there—except for a trip to Europe and Palestine in 1928–29—until he married and departed for Tel Aviv in 1932. The ten-poem sequence *Café Royal* (1928–29, pp. 228–45)—the title appears in English letters in the Hebrew volume—reflects Halkin's entry into the Jewish bohemia of New York and marks a turning point in the mood of his poetry. The Café Royal was a restaurant on the Lower East Side that was well known as a meeting place for the city's Jewish intelligentsia; the very name conjures up a heady mix of ideological contention as socialists, Zionists, Yiddishists, and Hebraists rubbed shoulders with one another. Playing against this reputation, however, Halkin's poem drains this site of all cultural meaning. The café is presented as merely a junction where the fallen lives of the denizens of the metropolis intersect. The café is the dystopic counter to the shores of Santa Barbara. A key difference is the location of the poet's voice. Whereas in most of Halkin's earlier poetry the speaker is the poet who speaks about himself and the formation of his soul, here the distance is palpable. A satiric, even sarcastic, speaker observes the procession of human folly and offers an urban menagerie.

The artists of the first poem (p. 229), for example, are recognizable by their bald pate and the longing for their vanished forelock. Visionaries without vision, they are condemned to live out their days marking time and scrambling for creature comforts. Escaping the desolation of their apartments, they flee to the café in the evening to stuff latkes into their waxen cheeks. Another class of denizens is the actors (pp. 232–33), who, like "hairy, blind bats," arise at night to begin their day. Sorry creatures that exist as a collection of masks propped up only by the audience's applause, they are caught between the redemptive rise of the stage curtain and a tangle of envy, recrimination, and secret desire. Nor are the practitioners of Halkin's own craft exempt from his spleen. The fifth poem parodies the Birth of the Poet as a grandiose breaking out from silence into speech, which nonetheless leaves the newborn poet clinging to his mother's apron strings. The Jew of the old style is another of the café's unprotected species. The poem's speaker patronizingly calls to unnamed bystanders to provide this man with a book of Psalms. Bearded, with gold-rimmed glasses, he hides a tear of nostalgia for the corner of the beit midrash where he once sat. Now sitting and blowing smoke rings in a very different kind of corner, no one better than he knows the exhaustion of his soul. All of these types gather together around the shallow creature comforts of the café in the seventh poem, whose title, "Ha'olam hazeh" [This world] (p. 240), emphatically denies the possibility of anything beyond.

One of the strongest poems in the sequence takes place in the city streets outside the café and posits a source of life that escapes the played-out decadence within. "Sheqiyah beNew York" [Sunset in New York] (pp. 230–31) is a taunt directed to the reddish clouds of sunset on the part of a speaker who represents his youthful urban generation. As the camel-like clouds of the evening gather over the city, extending their pall of stasis and even death, the speaker sings an anthem to the frenetic energy of youth and swears that the sunset will never overtake them. The force that beats back the threat is the carnival of sexual desire that is daily enacted on every bus and subway when lustful arms and legs jostle willing breasts and mounded thighs. The ceaseless circulation of erotic charge gives New York the power to challenge the this-worldly limitations of the café; for "Tonight the City will renew its immortality, / Tonight its sons will hitch up the horses of eternity / To the chariot of desire."

Yet whether it is the entropy of bean soup and onion rolls inside the café or the jazzy sexuality outside it, the city remains a stubborn and unseductive subject for Halkin's poetry. Ironically, what he viewed as a minor subject for poetry had a quite different valence in his prose fiction. During 1936–39 when he was settled in Tel Aviv and freed from worry by support from Salman Schocken, Halkin devoted himself to the writing of a great novel about New York and American Jewry set in the 1920s. *'Ad mashber* (1946) embraces the downtown world of the speakeasies and jazz clubs and left-wing politics, as well as the uptown lives of rabbi-professors and Jewish businessmen with traditional sympathies. The disciplined framework of the novel's demanding stream-of-consciousness-modernism is broken only in one place, when the narrator, after the manner of Thomas Wolfe's lyric monologues, undertakes a grand ode to the Jews of New York, their loves and follies and excesses. That, in personal and ideological terms, Halkin had categorically rejected American Jewish life, there was no room for doubt. He was to rationalize his rejection over the coming years in a series of Hebrew essays and tracts that offer an anatomy of the failings of the Jews of America and their communal institutions.[10] Yet despite this judgment, America remained in the forefront of Halkin's creative mind precisely during the years when he had made his break and settled in Palestine.

In a displaced and camouflaged fashion, America even becomes at this time the subject of one of the key poems in the Halkin oeuvre: "Tarshisha" [To Tarshish] (1935, pp. 300–305).[11] In the Bible, Tarshish is the name of the port city that is as far west and north from the Jaffa coast as could be imagined in ancient times. It was Jonah's destination when he sought to flee before God and avoid responsibility for his prophetic mission. Although Tarshish remains the distant double or other in relation to the Land of Israel in the poem, Halkin takes the liberty of translating it to the mountain streams and crisp air of North America. This is a poem of apology and leave-taking; the speaker, who has made many previous trips to Tarshish, is about to abandon his middle eastern motherland, and presumably his daughter, as well, to return to Tarshish, perhaps for good. Yet despite the reference to America, it would be a mistake to give the poem a biographical reading, as has often been done, or to make it into an allegory of Zionist temptations and loyalties.[12] Tarshish is used as a metonym for one pole of a cleavage within the poet's psyche, although the geographical hue Halkin chooses to give that pole is of course not insignificant.

The spiritual crisis dramatized in the poem remains exceedingly stark. Like Dante, the poem's speaker has lost his way in the wood in midlife; but unlike his poetic predecessor, he has no guide or plan. Having once considered himself God's eye and God's chosen, he now finds himself abashed and depleted and shorn. But now, "having grown distant from man, I have become orphaned of God, / And my soul knows not to whom or to what to make reparation" (p. 303). He has betrayed his promise and his gifts, given way to the seductions of sensuality, and has been caught out like a common fraud. He grotesquely compares the compulsion of his desires to the gurgling of hot blood in a horse's nostrils even after it has been slaughtered. He has sentenced his soul to death and buried it embalmed within him.

In the face of such demoralization and self-loathing, Tarshish beckons with the promise of a particular kind of deliverance. Compared to the blinding middle eastern light, the dulling winds of the *ḥamsin*, and the sickly, algae-green Mediterranean Sea in the port, Tarshish is conjured up as a zone of lakes and wooded hills with sharp, crystalline air and a feeling of purity, as if it is secretly scrubbed clean each night, or as if each day, the atoms of God's reality were dispersed and then reassembled. The summers are brief, winters snowy and long, and the *qeits hahodim*, the Indian summer, which Halkin glosses in a note, thereby establishing the North American association, becomes a sustained moment of grace.

Compared to the *moledet*, the motherland, however, Tarshish is also a realm without people, moral purpose, and historical struggle. It is for that very reason that the speaker longs to extricate himself from the place where he has striven, fallen, and compromised himself so appallingly. The living sign of his embroilment in the human milieu is his daughter, who plays with shells on the shore, innocent of her father's preparations for departure. "Your father will be gone," he says addressing her outside her hearing, "before the strangeness of his shadow frightens you, and then I will kneel down on some northern mount, an unrecognized pauper listening to a horse pass in the darkness" (p. 304). Whether these things will come to pass we do not know. The speaker brings the poem to an end by expressing admiration for the "dark moist clods of the field," which have succeeded in escaping from the cycle of pain and longing. Whether he will achieve the annihilation he seeks, whether, in short, he will ever reach Tarshish, remains hidden.

אַשְׁרֵי אִישׁ אֵין־תִּקְוָה וְאֵין־אוֹנִים גַּם מְקַוֹּות.
אַשְׁרֵי מִי רֵיק הַצַּג וְלֹא יֹאכְלֶנּוּ הַקָּלוֹן.
לִבִּי לְמֶגְרְפוֹת שָׂדֶה, הַמַּשְׁחִירוֹת רָווֹת,
נִכְאָב מִבְּרוֹחַ מִן הַכְּאֵב, מִשְּׁאוֹף לַחִדָּלוֹן,
לוּ גַם כְּחֹם הַשֶּׁמֶשׁ בָּאֲגַם אֹבַד, בַּסּוּף,
וְאֶזְכְּרָה־לֹא־אֶזְכְּרָה צְדָפִים עַל חוֹף חָשׂוּף
וּבַת תּוֹעָה וְלֹא תֵדַע דַּרְכֵי אָב נַעֲווֹת.

Happy is the man who has neither hope nor the strength to hope.
Happy is he who is empty and not consumed by shame.
My heart is with the damp, black clods of the field,
Too anguished to flee from pain or long for extinction,
If only like the sun's heat on the lake I could lose myself in
    the rushes
Recalling and not recalling the shells on the exposed shore
And the lost daughter who will not know her father's tortuous
    paths.

In "Tarshisha," Halkin is saying profound things in a manner different from how he said them in the earlier poetry. *Yoḥai* and "Santa Barbara," for example, bristle with open revelations about the poetic self and with demonstrative expositions of theological affirmations and denials. Here, the transparency of Halkin's metaphysical passions has been purposefully occluded. Although the poem appropriates the dramatic monologues of Tennyson and Browning, its dominant mode is modernist in the reliance on techniques of metonymical indirection to suggest the moral-spiritual impasse his speaker has arrived at. "Tarshisha" is a powerful and moving text because it succeeds in neutralizing the natural resistance of the Hebrew reader to the very idea of fleeing, Jonah-like, from the moral responsibility of loyalty to the motherland. The crystal streams of Tarshish's northern climes are so enticing that it is impossible to imagine that a man so weighed down by shame and remorse could not *not* set his sail toward the promise of that consummation.

The knotted coils of shame and regret that darken "Tarshisha" lead directly to the final poems of *'Al ha'i*, which are suffused with an awareness of the horrors of the Nazi era. "Seliḥot: 1943" (pp. 312–14) is a devastating theodicy that evokes Bialik and Uri Zvi Greenberg in the restrained rage against cosmic injustice. The volume concludes with an extraordinary document, the sonnet corona "Beharerei haḥolot beMishigan" [On the Michigan sand dunes] (pp. 315–31). A corona is a sequence of fifteen sonnets in which the last sonnet is constructed from the first lines of the previous sonnets. Working with the sonnet, which is already a constrained and rule-governed form, Halkin takes on the virtuoso challenge of creating an even more intricate and interdependent literary structure. And it is this formal literariness that Halkin surprisingly makes the vehicle for a series of meditations on how the poet's soul has been mortally assaulted and degraded by the spectacle of the death of European Jewry. This is a horror that can be touched and explored only within an ornate set of norms.

Although the meditations take place on the shores of a great American lake, there is nothing identifiably local in the poems, nothing of the place. This is exactly the case with Halkin's other great composition of the 1940s, and one of his last works to be composed in America, *Ya'akov Rabinovitz beYarmouth* [Yaakov Rabinowitz at Yarmouth].[13] This is another extraordinary document in a very different way. It is the transcription of the series of extended monologues spoken by a Hebrew writer who had been a friend of Halkin's and who had died in an automobile accident several months earlier in Palestine. Walking on the beach in Nova Scotia over the course of several days, Halkin telepathically experiences Rabinowitz's visitations and hurries home to transcribe them word for word. Written in a remarkable conversational idiom unlike anything in Halkin's previous work, Rabinowitz's monologues touch on all the grave topics in the life of the Yishuv between the conclusion of World War II, including the Holocaust, the struggle against the British, and the run-up to the War of Independence. Throughout all these fateful years, Halkin has been stranded in America out of contact with the great historical changes affecting the Jewish people. It is both ironic and telling that although the titles of the two great poems of these years are places in America, their contents are entirely removed from America. For Halkin, left alone on the "island," America has been drained of moral meaning and become nothing other than a vast natural backdrop upon which he can project the dilemmas of national and personal conscience.

✳ אֶל הַלְּטָאָה ✳
To the lizard

Analysis

אֶל הַלְּטָאָה

אַדְמוֹנִית, זְהִירָה, מוּגַּת־הַצַּעַר,
יֵשֵׁךְ – חַיֵּי־אֵימָה מְמֻשָּׁכִים.
בַּת יוֹם אַתְּ, בַּת יוֹמַיִם, לֹא־רֻחָמָה,
וּפַחַד־עֲדָנִים לָךְ סוֹד דְּרָכִים.

דַּקָּה וְאַדְמוֹנִית, מוּגַּת־הַצַּעַד,
קַרְעֵי־עֵינַיִךְ – קֶרַח בַּסְּדָקִים:
אֵוֶשׁ גִּבְעֹל – אַתְּ קְלִפָּה מַגְלֶדֶת,
גִּבְשׁוּשׁ כָּהָר יַחְסֹם אוֹר־אֲפָקִים.

רַגְלֵךְ מַרְאֵה־כָנָף, זְנָבֵךְ – סְנַפִּיר
וְרֹם וּתְהוֹם לֹא לָךְ: רַק פַּחַד וּזְחָל.
רוֹבֶצֶת כַּמֵּתָה, תִּצְפִּי נוֹאֶשֶׁת
מוּט אֲדָמָה, בִּנְשׁוֹר רְסִיס־הַטָּל.

פַּחְדֵּךְ מִי הוּא יָמֹד לָךְ, לְטָאָתִי,
עֵת תִּתְחַפְּשִׂי מֵתָה עַל הַדְּרָכִים?
בַּת יוֹם אַתְּ, בַּת יוֹמַיִם, לֹא־רֻחָמָה,
וְאֵלֶם בָּךְ – מְלוֹא פַחַד הַנְּצָחִים.

To the Lizard

Reddish, cautious, sorrow struck,
Your being is a prolonged life of dread.
You are only a day or two old and unpitied,

Yet the dread of ages is the secret of your ways.

Slight, reddish, fearful of step,
The slits of your eyes—ice in the cracks:
If a stalk rustles, you become a rigid husk.
A clod of earth will block the horizon's light like a mountain.

Your foot looks like a wing and your tail like a fin,
You have neither height nor depth, only fear and crawling.
Lurking like a corpse, you despairingly spy
an earthquake in the falling of a drop of dew.

Who can fathom your dread, oh, my lizard,
When you pretend to be dead on the roads?
A day or two old, unpitied,
Yet your muteness is filled with eternal dread.

Short poems do not abound in Halkin's poetry, especially short poems focused on the world rather than the poet's soulful response to it. "El haleta'ah" presents itself to the reader as a recognizable Enlightenment genre in which a poet addresses an animal to learn something edifying from its special endowments. The assumption is that the orderliness of Creation has lessons to teach us even in its slightest and most anomalous arrangements. Although the speaker of Halkin's poem learns something from the lizard, it is far from the elevating life lesson we might have expected.

The poem strongly privileges the position of the speaker in relationship to the mute natural object that he is observing. It is as if this small, luckless creature has suddenly come into a windfall of informed attention and fascination. Its lot in life, the very cards dealt it by Nature, are empathically laid out by an observer who is willing to make the effort to imagine how terrifying must be even the tiniest disturbances in the environment. The speaker's relationship to the lizard can be properly called patronizing in the sense that he absorbs the creature into his fascination and catalogues its features. Most of all, he makes the lizard the object of direct address, which not only constitutes the discourse of the poem itself but also becomes almost intimate and proprietary in tone (*lit'ati* [my lizard], line 13).

As eavesdroppers on this relationship, we the readers may well be led to our own observations of the motives for the speaker's observations. Of the many things that might be interesting about a lizard, which ones captivate the poem's speaker? It quickly becomes apparent that the lizard's abrupt, jerky movements, its body slung low to the ground, and its habit of playing dead, features that could be interpreted as adaptive in various ways, are all recouped by the speaker around a single category: fear. In each instance, moreover, when the speaker makes a gift to the lizard of his empathic imagination, it is to see and feel the terrors that must dominate the creature's daily life. In the second stanza, it is the danger bruited in the rustle of a stalk or the sun blotted out by a tiny clod; in the third stanza, it is the helpless fear of the earth moving triggered by a miniscule droplet; and in the fourth, it is the fathomless terrors that must colonize its mind while playing dead, alone and exposed, on the road.

The largest observation is the most universalized, metaphysical, and least likely to be related to the poor creature's actual experience. At the opening and closing of the poem, the speaker summarizes the wonder of the lizard's existence as consisting in the fact that the creature's extraordinarily brief life span can concentrate within itself the "fear of the ages" [*paḥad-ʿidanim, paḥad hanetsaḥim*]. So awesome a truth conveyed by so slight a creature! The fraught weight of this truth leads us to wonder where the true sources of the poem's amazement reside. Is it the tiny reptile, or rather the speaker's obsessive fascination with fear that the lizard provokes? For the reader of "To the Lizard," the experience of the poem leads in a reflexive direction, back to the self of the speaker-observer and away from the creature of the poem's title.

Unlike conventional animal poems, "To the Lizard" leaves us with neither a useful moral nor an enlarged appreciation of nature. What is revealed, perhaps not so wittingly, is the speaker's preoccupation with fear as the deep continuity of existence. In the time shortly after the pinnacle experience at Santa Barbara when "To the Lizard" was written, according to its placement in *ʿAl haʾi*, a great decentering was taking place in Halkin's spiritual life. The passionate search for the divine in the pulsing phenomena of this world lost its drive. The anxieties animating the fascination of the speaker of Halkin's poem with a frightened little monster may suggest some of the forces that invaded the vacuum left behind.

Thirteen   Abraham Regelson

In a 1974 memoir, Halkin recalls how Abraham Regelson's first poem came to be published. Fifteen years old and recently arrived with his parents in America, Halkin spent the summer of 1914 preparing for entrance exams to public high school in New York. A friend named Tully Rabinowitch, the prototype for the figure of Tully Lushkin in Halkin's great novel *'Ad mashber* [The crash], introduced him to a slightly older young man named Regelson—he was eighteen and had already lived in America for nine years—who shared Halkin's passion for Hebrew. Halkin was astonished by Regelson's control of that language. Not only could he converse fluently in Hebrew—a far from common attainment at that time—but his Hebrew speech was profoundly immersed in the language of the Bible and rabbinic sources and enriched by Bialik's poems, learned by heart. Regelson, moreover, was developing a deep knowledge of English romantic poetry and European philosophy. Daily throughout that summer and the year that followed, when Halkin was in his first year at Morris High School in the Bronx and Regelson in his last, the older boy treated the younger to erudite Hebrew disquisitions on poetry and philosophy. His native shyness making him a good listener, Halkin clung to these meetings as islands of comfort and uplift amidst the noisy and unfamiliar vulgarity around him in the basement lunchroom of Morris High.

    The two young men studied together at City College before going their separate ways. Diagnosed with tuberculosis and advised to leave the city, Halkin interrupted his studies to move to the Catskill Mountains and then travel widely throughout the American countryside.

Regelson left college and worked as an apprentice to an older relative who was a druggist with a store in the Bronx. In the letters exchanged between the two friends, Halkin saw something remarkable. For all that the older Regelson inhabited the very spirit of the poet-philosopher, Halkin had hitherto never seen one word of his in written form, whereas Halkin himself had already had his own poetry published in such journals as *Ha'umah* and *Hatoren*. Halkin's work was appearing at that time also in *Miqlat*, a new monthly Hebrew journal being edited in New York by Y. D. Berkovitz, the son-in-law of Shalom Aleichem and a distinguished man of letters who was sojourning in America during the war years. In one of his letters to Berkovitz, Halkin inserted, without permission, a letter he had received from Regelson that demonstrated the latter's formidable command of poetic Hebrew. Because the European Berkovitz was known to be sparing in his praise of the "local" American Hebrew talent, the fulsomeness of the return message stunned Halkin. "Grab this lad by the scruff of his neck," Berkovitz commanded; "take him out of the drug store and induct him into Literature."[1] Halkin showed the letter to Regelson as soon as he returned to the city from the Catskills and set about prompting and urging him to get a poem together to submit to *Miqlat*. Indeed, in between his duties in the pharmacy, Regelson succeeded in composing and polishing the four sections of his poem "Gezel ahavah" [Theft of love], which, when accepted by Berkovitz and published in the Nisan issue of the journal, marked his literary debut.[2]

The figure of the young Regelson, as conjured up by Halkin at a remove of a half-century, is prescient in several ways. While Halkin crams for exams and scrambles to catch up with the unfamiliar American curriculum, Regelson floats above these demands, having read and taken in the great writers and thinkers on his own. Halkin will, of course, catch up; he graduates from high school after only two years and goes on to advanced degrees. But Regelson's path remains that of the autodidact who insists on acquiring knowledge, however vast or deep it may be, at his own pace and according to his own lights and without the mediation of teachers or mentors. Graduation from Morris High School was Regelson's highest degree, and this fact reflects

Abraham Regelson. Courtesy of Sharona Tel-Oren.

not only the constraints of poverty, early marriage, and family burdens but also his utter aloofness from institutional requirements and the professionalized organization of knowledge. It is Regelson's Hebrew that in the end captivates Halkin. That Halkin, a prodigy in his own right, should be impressed by the classical richness of Regelson's Hebrew is testimony to the early age at which Regelson made his total commitment to Hebrew as a vocation and worldview. Halkin stresses Regelson's *love* of Hebrew, as if to imply that the latter's grand passion for Hebrew was as much a matter of his having been chosen by the language for eternal fidelity as of the young man's having exercised his own will. Halkin's description of Regelson's performance of his Hebrew knowledge carries the further, and perhaps slightly critical, implication that Regelson's profound linguistic erudition was always on display as a virtuosity that required its own due.

Also evident at this early point is the twinned nature of Regelson's immersion in both poetry and philosophy. He is presented as always being simultaneously preoccupied with the great thinkers of European philosophy and the great poets of the romantic tradition, as if these two were different receptacles between which the same spiritual fluid was being continuously poured back and forth. Although this presumed fusion or convertibility may have been the inner truth of Regelson's mind, when it comes to his writing, there would always remain a question about whether his major poems, which are heavily laden with metaphysical freight, succeed autonomously as poetry. The difficulty, even the reluctance, in translating this rich inner life into outward forms is the theme of Halkin's vignette about how Regelson's inaugural poem came to be published. It is more the story of Halkin's advocacy and midwifery—with a purloined letter to boot!—than it is a record of a novice writer's campaign to gain recognition and enter the world of letters. Regelson would forever remain ambivalent about the enterprise of publication, caught somewhere between *hauteur* and *ressentiment*. He begrudged his outsider status both as an American Hebrew poet and as a romantic-metaphysical artist in a modernist age at the same time as he deemed the world unworthy of his gifts of spirit and, in an era of impoverished literacy, incapable of reading them.

I have purposefully begun this exploration of Regelson's poetry with a portrait of the young artist drawn by Halkin because of the special affinity between the careers of these two American Hebrew poets. Both are poets for whom the metaphysical dimension of existence is paramount; Jewish mysticism—Habad Hasidism in Halkin's case and Lurianic Kabbalah in Regelson's—is drawn upon as a symbology for a common pantheistic stance before the universe. Both were deeply immersed in and influenced by English romantic poetry, especially Shelley and Keats. Both rejected the norm of simplicity embodied in the poetic practice of other American Hebrew poets, such as Efros and Bavli, in favor a style of lexical plenitude and complexity. Both succeeded, after false starts in the 1930s, in settling in the new state of Israel and making it the setting for the final, but by no means foreshortened, stages of their long careers.

Yet in a fundamental respect, they went their separate ways. Regelson remained essentially unhoused within the world of Hebrew letters. He was neither a professor nor an editor nor a convener of other writers; nor did his poetry or his essays conduct a dialogue with his contemporaries either in America or Israel.[3] His isolation and the relative obscurity it entailed were, in the end, more the fruit of his temperament than the result of willful marginalization. Halkin, on the other hand, was an active citizen of what Miron has called the republic of Hebrew letters, the transnational community of Hebrew writers and readers. In that republic, separate from his high position as the occupant of the chair of Hebrew literature in Jerusalem, Halkin served as a kind of tribune, maintaining relations in person or by letter with writers scattered across several generations and writing about the their work out of a sense of responsibility to the larger endeavor and without polemical rancor. After the moment of intimacy and mutual esteem at Morris High in the Bronx and in the years immediately following, it would seem that the relations between these two men with so much in common were not close. The brief memoir that Halkin wrote in 1974 evoking that long-ago moment is, to the best of my knowledge, the only real notice that this prolific critic gave to Regelson and his body of work.

Regelson seized his vocation as poet-philosopher at a young age and clung to it throughout his life, despite the fact that the world repaid him little for his fidelity.[4] Regelson was born in 1896 in Hlusk, a town in Belarus near Minsk, and was brought to America with his family in 1905. On New York's Lower East Side, the boy studied both at the Rabbi Jacob Joseph School (RJJ) and the new-model Hebrew school of H. A. Friedland. After the family moved to the Bronx and Regelson graduated from Morris High School, he took courses at the City College of New York and worked in a relative's drug store. An opportunity for a more welcome kind of employment came in the form of an invitation issued by Friedland to become a Hebrew school teacher in Cleveland, Ohio, where Friedland had been called to reorganize the Jewish educational system. Regelson moved to Cleveland sometime in the 1920s and embarked upon a losing struggle to adapt his dreamy temperament to the steep challenges of maintaining discipline in the afternoon Hebrew school classroom. Regelson fell in love with Friedland's secretary Ida (Chaya), a young woman with a similarly strong passion for Hebrew; the couple had a child together before getting married and having several more children.

Faced with bleak opportunities for employment during the Great Depression, these two fervent Zionists, who already spoke only Hebrew with their children and each other, decided to move to Palestine in 1933. Regelson had been offered a job by Berel Katznelson to write a column for the daily newspaper *Davar* and to contribute to the paper's children's section. The couple arrived in Tel Aviv with their four children, ages three to ten, with Chaya pregnant with their fifth. Although the family adapted to the difficult material circumstances that were the lot of many other immigrant workers, the primitive state of health care in the Yishuv at that time proved their undoing. Two of the older children contracted malaria, and Yedidya, the eight-month-old baby who had been born after their arrival, died of dysentery as a result of poor hospital care.[5] Chaya became pregnant yet again, and the couple could not reconcile themselves to the new baby's coming into the world in such uncertain circumstances. The family returned to America in 1936 and settled in the Bronx.[6]

These were the years of greatest privation. Regelson had occasional work as a translator, but he was essentially unemployed for a long period until he got a job in 1943 as a writer for the Yiddish-language Communist paper *Morgen freiheit*. (Only after America's alliance with the Soviet Union could he reconcile his Zionism with writing for the paper.) During this difficult period, the family subsisted on handouts solicited by Chaya Regelson on behalf of her poet husband and their children. One of Regelson's nieces is the writer Cynthia Ozick, who recalls the atmosphere of the Regelson household on her visits there as a girl. Amid the tumult of the five children and their friends, Regelson would be sitting apart at the dining room table next to a stack of books from the local branch of the public library and unconcernedly immersing himself in the works of great philosophers and poets.[7] After their long sojourn in America, in 1949 Regelson was able to arrange for the family's return to what was now Israel although the older boys stayed behind. Regelson obtained a position as a writer for the daily *'Al hamishmar*, where he worked until his retirement in 1962, and had a second job as an editor and translator for Am Oved publishers. Even though Regelson's literary work never became widely known, his achievement was eventually recognized by the arbiters of the cultural establishment. His collected poetry, which was published in 1964 under the title *Ḥaquqot otiyyotayikh* [Engraved are thy letters],[8] was awarded the Brenner Prize in that year, and in 1972 he was the recipient of the Bialik Prize for his life achievement on the occasion of the publication of *Shirotayim* [Two poems].[9] At the age of eighty, he was brought back to America in 1976 to receive New York University's Neuman Prize. He died in 1981.

The whole of Regelson's literary enterprise can be understood as a struggle to find poetic forms capable of accommodating his philosophical thought. Regelson eventually succeeded in bringing the two together but only after following a tortuous path. What, after all, was this philosophical thought for which he undertook such a sustained quest for poetic expression? On the one hand, Regelson was a lifelong student and interpreter of a large swath of modern philosophy, as demonstrated by a book he published late in life called *Er'elei hamaḥshavah* [Mighty ones of thought],[10] which is a serious guide for the intelligent non-specialist to the thought of Bergson, Russell, Dewey, Freud, Cassirer, Whitehead, James, Maeterlinck, Croce, Leibnitz, and Rav Kook. Yet from among these studies, it is only the Rav Kook chapter that intimates the parameters of Regelson's own convictions. Those convictions, which were formed when Regelson was a young man, remained remarkably unchanged over his long career. As early as 1920, when he was still measuring out pills in the Bronx, Regelson championed the superiority of the realm of ideas over the concrete material world. In his first published essay, which appeared in the same journal in which Halkin helped him get his first poems published, Regelson argued that what we know on the basis of the dreams and reveries that we experience within our own souls is of far greater truth and value than what we learn from empirical observation.[11]

As revealed in the poems of this period, the stance Regelson takes is that of the mystic who sees the everyday world of our sense data as a reflection of a hidden world of spiritual essences. It is the primordial forces at work in this hidden world that is what is truest in our lives. The twin portals through which mortals can connect with this primordiality are artistic creation and sexuality. Although Regelson often used the symbol system of Lurianic Kabbalah to convey his ideas, it is important to stress that his own outlook was neither Judaic in essence nor conventionally "religious" in its appeal to Torah or the commandments. (This was as true in his life as in his thought.) As is the case with many mystics and their systems, Regelson's thought oscillated between a fascination with the mythic forces that animate the spiritual realm and an allegiance to a demythified pantheism in which divinity is revealed immanently within the beauty of nature and the products of the human spirit. Regelson was as much at home in the *Sefer Yetsirah*, the Zohar, and the writings of Moses Cordovero as he was in the works of the American Transcendentalist authors about whom he wrote so eloquently in his efforts to introduce them to the Hebrew-reading audience.[12]

It was a great deal to ask for poetry to convey the sublimity of this mystical knowledge, especially in an age when the very practice of philosophical verse had been almost wholly discredited. But Regelson would not desist. He refused to decouple poetry from philosophy and resign himself to writing only in the more acceptable verse styles of lyric and narrative. Between the 1920s and 1940s, Regelson experimented with a number of approaches to achieving this synthesis, some of them grotesque and tortured and others imaginatively intense and evocative. Success came in 1946 with Regelson's great ode to the Hebrew language, *Ḥaquqot otiyyotayikh*, which was used in Chapter 2 of this study to introduce the spiritual and intellectual world of American Hebraism as a whole. In this discussion of the dynamic of Regelson's career, this great composition is used more locally—and more briefly—to illuminate the play of forces, both poetic and philosophical, that had to come into alignment for Regelson finally to reconcile the ways of art and vision that he had so long sought to achieve.

The first station in this quest was a group of three poems published in 1921 in the European journal *Hatequfah*.[13] Although the three appeared together under the heading "Ḥezyonot" [Visions], the links among them are vague. In "Yeḥi'el and Dumah" (pp. 193–96), Dumah, the mother of death and silence, undertakes an epic struggle with Yeḥi'el. Triumphant in battle, she is saddened to learn that her antagonist is a human being, and she is enveloped by cosmic loneliness in the aftermath of her victory. She is cheered by the discovery of a naked child until the child identifies himself as a reincarnation of Yeḥi'el who will return over and over again to contend with Dumah and vanquish her.

In the second poem, "Avi'el," (pp. 207–13) the eponymous hero flees the evils of the city after a crushing romantic disappointment. When he lays down and sleeps among the fallen leaves, his father appears to him in a vision from the afterlife, the *'olam shel emet* [the world of truth], as it is traditionally called, and reassures Avi'el that all suffering will cease in the next world. Avi'el beseeches his father to be taken to that world directly, but the father patiently explains to the son that he has been endowed by previous generations with two gifts that will enable him to overcome the burdens of existence: an "artist's measure" [*amat oman*], with which he can build structures that can transcend time, and the male sexual potency to produce progeny. Avi'el awakes from the vision consoled, prepared to undertake the challenge of life. Finally, "Aḥiyah veyisra'el" (pp. 219–23) is a short dramatic dialogue between the Besht, Rabbi Israel Baal Shem Tov, the founder of Hasidism, and his legendary teacher, Aḥiyah Hashiloni; the dialogue is set, according to the stage directions, in the Garden of Eden during a moment when Israel's soul has ascended to heaven during intense spiritual contemplation. Upon his arrival in the realm of celestial glory, Israel is asked by his teacher why he is dejected rather than elated. Israel replies that he is overcome by uncertainty as to whether the supernal beauty he sees about him is in fact God's handiwork or only a projection of his own perceptions. Aḥiyah reminds his former disciple of the esoteric teaching he had been vouchsafed in the past: on earth, God's effulgence is rendered opaque by the *qelipah*, the husks of primordial matter, which are paradoxically necessary to enforce the boundaries that prevent the world from lapsing into chaos. Yet by living a life of holiness and love, the *qelipah* can be rendered translucent and God's infinity glimpsed.

All three poems are evocative of classical traditions and at the same time deliberately elusive of them. Avi'el and Yeḥi'el are plucked from biblical name lists more for their suggestiveness—"God is my father" and "Let God live," respectively—than for any specific reference. The Israel who speaks with his teacher here is the same as the Besht, the Baal Shem Tov known to us from Hasidic literature, yet his portrayal here is entirely defamiliarized. Although the three poems appeared together under the shared rubric "Visions," they remain an eclectic assemblage with no inherent links among them and no effort to make them expressions of the same narrative scheme. Taken together, however, the three could be said to offer etiological myths about the human condition in which the human realm as we know it turns out to be only the manifest face of a more recondite truth. Human affairs are expressions of hidden spiritual realities and contingent upon them. Although we are allowed only flashes of insight into those transcendent purposes, the message given human beings is ultimately reassuring: There is splendor beneath the opaque lineaments of our struggles, and we have been given the powers of art and eros to work toward redemption.

This promise is dramatically withdrawn in *Qayin vehevel* [Cain and Abel] (1932), a long poem which, because it was Regelson's first published book, became his formal entrance in the world of Hebrew letters.[14] The volume is richly produced with no more than ten lines on each of its sixty pages, and the page numbers are written out in words rather than numerals (e.g. *ḥamishim ve'arba'ah* instead of 54). The poem is written in iambic hexameter in the Ashkenazic accent.[15] A note at the end of the book indicates that fifteen hundred copies were printed, of which one hundred were numbered and signed. Yet what was so evidently positioned to be a prestigious debut of a poet of large ambitions turned into a critical debacle. That the book was hardly noticed in the literary circles of Tel Aviv and Jerusalem goes without saying; this was the lot of most American Hebrew literature. But even at home, within the collegium of his fellow writers who encouraged each other and worked to advance the common Hebraist project in America, the poem was savaged, and their opinion, it must be admitted, still holds up today. But as a failure, *Qayin vehevel* is an interesting failure because of what it tells us about Regelson's aspirations as a poet, and about how he rebounded from this disappointment and eventually found new ways to combine his large ideas with his extravagant language.

The poem's plot line suggests something of the scale of those aspirations. The characters are Adam, Cain, and Abel, in addition to Abel's daughter Be'er, Regelson's invention in this poem. Despite the provenance of the names in the book of Genesis, there is nothing Judaic, biblical, or even Israelite about these figures; instead, they are presented as titans from a primordial age who move in an indistinct setting that is somewhere between heaven and earth. The poem opens with Adam in old age decrying his decrepitude and longing for a last sexual romp before his senses are no longer capable of being inflamed. He is powerless to lessen the strife between his sons. Cain is presented as the great builder who is fueled by a relentless drive to accomplish; Abel is presented as representing a principle of withdrawal from the world, inwardness, and nihilism.[16] Cain is incensed because his brother's skepticism is infecting his workers and weakening their will to construct great cities. When Abel refuses to desist and Adam fails to intervene, Cain smites Abel, who dies but not before uttering a terrible curse on Cain. Then, the fearsome Cain sets out to do nothing less than court Be'er, the beautiful daughter of the brother he has just killed. He promises her that together they will be able to "build the eternity of man up to the very rim of heaven (p. 125)."[17] Despite her scornful derision, she eventually gives in and agrees to marry him. When Cain raises a boastful toast at the wedding feast, however, he soon realizes that he has been poisoned, and as he lays dying, Be'er delights in the vengeance she has wrought for her father's murder and proclaims her plan to realize her father's nihilistic principles by reversing the creation and returning the world to nothingness.

The critique of Regelson's poem was laid out in an articulate essay by the poet Feinstein and seconded by Moshe Meislish and Epstein.[18] It was immediately apparent to Feinstein that the poem was driven by the influence of strong models from the English romantics, especially Shelley's "Prometheus Unbound" and Keats's "Hyperion," which use figures from Greek mythology to probe the roots of the soul of modern man.[19] The problem was not with the pedigree of the models themselves but with the derivative way in which they had been hoisted and installed into a pseudo-biblical Hebrew epic. The poem also showed little awareness of the fundamental divergence between the tragically fated world of the Titans and the covenantal freedom of the Hebrew Bible, or at least the willingness to take up this difference. Worst of all, there is a conceptual confusion at the heart of the poem, which is the binary confrontation of the principles represented by Cain and Abel. On the one hand, Regelson gives us little to go on, saying only that Cain is the heedless and conscienceless drive for building and creating and that Abel is the countervailing force of skepticism, nihilism, and nirvana. On the other hand, Regelson seeks to make each of these figures the primordial ancestors of two great and opposing lines of world-historical leaders. In a grandiose speech at his ill-fated wedding feast, Cain presciently toasts the great ones who will follow his line, including Prometheus, Newton, Franklin, and Einstein; and then he gestures in the direction of Be'er to praise those who will follow in the line of her father, including Moses, Ashoka, and Lenin (p. 130). These latter are the lawgivers who restrain men's impulses so that individuals can live together in groups. Feinstein correctly argues that this is a binarism that is at the same time overweening and historically questionable. While lumping the great inventors together may make some sense, putting Moses together with Ashoka and Lenin muddles rather than clarifies the lines of connection. Can these three be accused of Abel's nihilism? The vindictive destructiveness inherent in this nihilism was held to be a further source of the poem's weakness. Although a fugitive atom escapes into the future at the end of the poem, the general annihilation promised by Be'er remained an inexplicable bleakness. The poem collapses under the alienating weight of Schopenhauerian pessimism.[20]

Regelson's poem about Cain and Abel boasts big language as well as big ideas, and the problem is the relationship between the two. This is the first major instance in which what came to be known as the Regelsonian style was rolled out to full effect. This is a poetic language of extreme concision at the level of the phrase and the line, even if the compositions themselves are hefty. Regelson is fond of eliminating prepositions and other connectives, and he favors shortened verb forms whenever possible. The lexical range of the word choices in the poem is dazzling in its breadth; it reflects a polymorphous erudition in all the historical levels of Hebrew and a pronounced penchant for the rare and the alternative. The syntax rests on a kind of skewered biblicism that is forcibly extracted from its native soil and made to seem primordial without evoking specific Judaic sources. The diction is often declamatory, dithyrambic, and incantatory. Discerning contemporary readers were favorably disposed to—or perhaps, more accurately, they were impressed and intimidated by—the formidableness of Regelson's Hebrew in contrast to the ideational content of the poems. They recognized in his style a poetics of strong effects that aspired to a model very different from the quiet lyricism of many other American Hebrew poets. Just as the big philosophical schemes seemed reductively exaggerated and unsupported by a requisite density of nuance and detail, so too Regelson's dazzlingly radical style lacked an intuitive modulation that would draw it close to the felt truth of human experience.[21] When it came to Hebrew, it was acknowledged, Regelson was in possession of a fierce virtuosity, and this very gift presented him with the double challenge: finding a subject truly worthy of his rhetorical powers and tuning those powers to the range of the human heart and human ear.

Regelson took a major step in this direction with the publication in 1936 of "Shir hatiqqun" [The song of restoration].[22] Like *Qayin vehevel*, this long poem is preoccupied with the primordial origins of man in the cosmos; but in casting off the dour burden of Schopenhauer's historical schemata, Regelson registers an immediate gain. As a new mythic framework for exploring these "first things" of humankind, Regelson adopts the narrative arc of Lurianic Kabbalah with its three great movements of *tsimtsum* [contraction], *shevirat hakelim* [breaking of the vessels], and *tiqqun* [restoration].[23] Halkin was also drawn to the power of this explanatory cosmogony; yet, as Epstein has perceptively pointed out, Halkin emphasized the calamitous moment of breakage and the irretrievable loss of plenitude and connection to the universe, whereas Regelson more optimistically focused on the divine sparks dispersed among the shards of non-being and the potential for redemption afforded by their existence.[24] On the level of language, it goes without saying, the Hebrew vocabulary of Lurianic Kabbalah could be absorbed into Regelson's poetic idiom with far less contortion—but still not without a residue of strangeness—than in his account of the battle of the Titans.

Also new here is the appearance of the "I" of the poet-speaker. In the previous poems of primordial origins, the speaker had remained an assiduously impersonal entity behind the chronicled events. In "Shir hatiqqun," however, the first chapter is cast as an invocation, an introduction to an epic poem, in which the poet speaks in the first person about the task he is about to undertake. The model is undoubtedly the opening of Milton's *Paradise Lost*, a work enormously admired by Regelson, who translated into Hebrew passages from it and from other poems of Milton.[25] Regelson does not follow Milton's lead—and Virgil's before him—in using the invocation to appeal for divine help in accomplishing the great task confronting the poet; but he does emulate the other thrust of the invocation: the announcement of the nature and theme of the great task and the poet's bold intention to undertake it. Milton begins his epic by declaring that he will tell "Of Man's First Disobedience, and the Fruit / Of that Forbidden Tree" and concludes the invocation with his goal: "That to the height of this great Argument / I may assert Eternal Providence, / And justify the ways of God to men."[26] Regelson begins his poem by having its speaker proclaim: "I shall speak of mystery in the language of the revealed and I shall stamp the abstract in the coinage of vision [*adabber sod bisfat hanigleh ve'etba' mofshat bematbea' ḥazon*]" (p. 152). In cadences distinctly Miltonic, he goes on to announce that he intends to explain how the first man, exiled from his source in the primordial unity of Creation, fashioned ways to recover from his fall into chaos and alienation. The speaker's high purpose is to convert secret knowledge into language that can be understood, without special initiation, into a coin or currency useable in our imaginative transactions. The concluding line of the invocation underscores this new phenomenon in Regelson's verse, the self-referential presence of the poet-speaker: "Mystery is knitted into my thoughts and in the blood of my essence flows abstraction [*hasod mesorag besar'apai uvedam tamtsiti nozel hamofshat*]" (p. 125). Regelson's speaker is not so much boasting of his natural accession to esoteric wisdom—although there is that, too, of course—as presenting his qualifications for performing the service of revelatory translation he is about to undertake. As an epigram describing Regelson's ineluctable entanglement with abstraction, it might be pointed out, there is no better line than this.

At the root of each of the poem's three tableaux is a central trauma. For man, being created and thrown into existence means being ripped out of the primal unity of the cosmos and condemned to a life of separation and loss. In the first tableau, a caveman-like primal Adam called Enosh awakes into this nightmare of separateness amid a grim and relentless landscape of ice and snow. In panic, he howls, "Who has shorn me of the wings that bore me to the Ein-Sof, that now I fall / diminished, clipped, and weak?" (p.153). Instantly, Hubalah, twin sister to Enosh, is revealed to him, and she proceeds to comfort him and persuade him that there is a way to mitigate the anguish of his loneliness. That way leads to her womb, which she offers to Enosh not out of lust but out of maternal compassion. The middle episode takes place at some undefined further point in the volcanic formation of the earth and centers on Yuval, who, a year after the death of his beloved wife Helah, is revisiting the mountainside island cave where he had placed her body to protect it from defilement. Yuval has experienced something of the oneness of creation in his intense bond with Helah and, now in the aftermath of losing her, he is bereft and disconsolate. Communing with her remains within the darkness of the cave, Yuval hears a voice like an inner prompting that instructs him to fashion a musical instrument out of the skull and sinews of Helah's decomposed body. He obeys and plays music on this instrument that succeeds in conjuring Helah from the grave and returning her to him for as long as the music lasts. He now possesses the secret of how to scorn the ravages of time and space by "hitching evil and ugliness to the chariot of majesty / and from the bones of death and rot to build joy, grace and life" (p. 161).

The final tableau at first seems familiar: Moses has rounded up a wandering kid and is standing in the desert by a bush. But the mission thrust upon him by his experience there has little to do with his role in ending the Egyptian captivity. The affliction he bewails is primal and ahistorical. Standing amidst the rocks and sand, he is afflicted by the alienation between him and the surrounding natural world. "Is there not a single desire / hidden within me and them?" he asks; "How can a bridge be built / between me and the strangled forces of the earth?" (p. 163). The sudden irradiation of the bush at his feet offers a dramatic confirmation of his intuition. Like an antenna that both sends and receives, the bush's roots pull energy from the earth and transmit it to the world above at the same time as the bush serves as a conduit for channeling the divine force produced by man and nature above ground back into the earth. This spectacular moment of revelation passes, and the individuated entities of creation—earth, stars, Moses, the kid—lapse back into their stubborn separateness. Yet the wondrous truth of the illumination has been etched deeply in Moses' soul, and his life henceforth becomes dedicated to bringing back to his people the message of the divine oneness of all creation. The poem concludes with a dithyrambic celebration of the mystery of a divinity that is forever shattering itself into pieces and forever reunifying itself into an ever-greater oneness.

It would not be too much to say that what is restored in "Shir hatiqqun," Regelson's song of restoration, is the integrity of the poet's own career in addition to matters cosmic and mystical. After the turgid titanism of *Qayin vehevel*, this substantial poem demonstrates that Regelson has finally found a mythic-philosophical schema that fits his own metaphysical temperament. Although rooted in catastrophe, the Lurianic theosophical framework moves toward the affirmative and the hopeful. Positive human actions and devotions gather together the lost sparks scattered by the primal breakage and hasten a movement of unification within the Godhead. What could be more human than the act of sexual intercourse, which Regelson makes the first of his vehicles of transcendence? (The sexual urge, as Epstein has noted, is a many-hued theme throughout Regelson's poetry.[27]) In "Shir hatiqqun," sex is presented neither as the satisfaction of lust, nor as the consummation of soulful intimacy, nor as a gateway to Zoharic-psychedelic ecstasy. Hubalah is Enosh's twin sister, whose name is related to the Hebrew for birth pangs; allowing him into her womb is a munificent act of incestuous regression that gives Enosh refuge from the ache of individuation. The substitution of art and music for lost love, as presented in the poem's second movement, would seem to be a soothingly familiar romantic topos. But Regelson makes it new by virtue of the outrageous, necrophiliac, Paleolithic backstory he provides. Yuval's fashioning of a proto-lyre from the decomposing body parts of his beloved is a very concrete assault on the forces of melancholy and non-being that overcome us in the wake of the lost unions we make. Finally, the scene of Moses and the burning bush brings to a climax the kind of counter-midrash—in the tradition of Berdichevsky's *Mimeqor yisra'el*—Regelson has been fomenting throughout the poem. Enosh is a kind of Adam, and Yuval is fleetingly mentioned in Genesis as the inventor of music; yet their "stories" are reimagined here with a content subversively at odds with their traditional exegetical treatment. In that spirit, Moses is made into a mystic who is the first recipient of a vision of the *unio mystico*. It becomes his mission to transmit that vision, the esoteric knowledge, the *torat hasod*, rather than the Law as we know it, to the Children of Israel and to future generations of teachers who will carry on this tradition of esoteric knowledge. And unto this very day, the speaker of the poem would seem to say. Who could be a better exemplar of this tradition than the poet who opens "Shir hatiqqun" with the declaration: "I shall speak of mystery in the language of the revealed and I shall stamp the abstract in the coinage of vision"?

The currency of abstraction is Regelson's declared métier; but it remains for him as powerful a challenge as it is a powerful intention. Although "Shir hatiqqun" represents a sizable stride forward in speaking about primordial things in a viable literary language, no amount of skillfulness can enable Regelson to break through an inherent impasse. On a philosophical level, there is the classic Maimonidean dilemma of disclosing esoteric truths in exoteric settings. The deepest wisdom, which, by its nature, moves toward ever purer levels of abstraction, simply cannot—and even should not—be grasped by those who have not already progressed to higher rungs of cognition. On the aesthetic level, the predicament is no less severe. The poet who seeks to speak about higher mysteries is forced to use abstractions or allegorical symbols that may be evocative to the initiate but leave the ordinary reader with only a teasing whiff of sublimity. For what are the pleasures of poetry, after all, without the sparkle of concrete images and the play of subtle verbal nuances?

The way out, of course, lies in taking a concrete object, a leaf, for example, and seeing in its wondrous specific properties an embodiment of the divine, a tiny vessel of holy sparks. Indeed, all the systems of classical Kabbalah and Hasidism have provision for this radical, manifest immanence, which valorizes the concrete without taking away from the hidden, transcendent divine mystery. This resembles the panentheism we saw inhabited by the awe-struck speaker of Halkin's "'Al ḥof Santa Barbara" as he stands overlooking the Pacific waters. Regelson's familiarity with this option is evident from what is perhaps his best-known essay, "Elohei hateva' bashirah ha'ameriqa'it" [The God of nature in American poetry].[28] In discussions of the poetry of Walt Whitman, Robertson Jeffers, Edna St. Vincent Millay, Carl Sandburg, and Robert Frost, Regelson identifies a direct inheritance from the nineteenth-century pantheism of Thoreau, Emerson, Lanier, and the Transcendentalists. Yet there were two factors that prevented Regelson from availing himself of this sympathetic solution. He was not sufficiently intoxicated by the sublimities of the American landscape, the very genius of place, to locate it at the center of his song.

Although Regelson has some poems with American backgrounds, there is nothing of the intense fascination with native locales, either their people or natural wonders, to compare with Bavli's Mrs. Woods, Halkin's Santa Barbara, or Preil's Maine.[29] (The Land of Israel did engender this kind of enthrallment, although Regelson refrained from casting it in transcendental terms.) But the problem was not just the American landscape but nature itself. Regelson would most assuredly have affirmed the proposition that the wondrous construction of a single leaf points to the underlying mystery of Creation. By temperament, however, these microcosmic structures simply did not compel him at the most fundamental level such that he could make these discreet marvels of nature, or, in the romantic mode, the soul's response to them, the occasion for his greatest powers.

What was there in the manifest wide world that Regelson could adore with such abandon that its each and every tiniest expression would make him swoon with rapt attention? The answer, ironically, had always been there under his very eyes, on his lips, and flowing from his pen. It was the Hebrew language. Hebrew beautifully fulfilled the theological requirements for providing both transcendence and immanence. Apotheosized as Logos, Hebrew became a radiant and mysterious source of meaning whose essence, so infinite and ancient, could never be captured or comprehended. At the same time, Hebrew was polymorphously and ubiquitously incarnated in the world in the words we use, the sentences we think, and the grammatical structures we abide by. Hebrew, in short, satisfied all the criteria for a kind of pantheistic worship in an age of Jewish nationalism, and it provided Regelson with the kind of poetic subject that was at once majestic *and* representable. This breakthrough came, of course, in Regelson's 1946 poem *Ḥaquqot otiyyotayikh*, which was discussed extensively in Chapter 2 as a gateway to the world of American Hebraism. Although the same ground will not be covered here, it is important to point out just how supremely significant was this poem for Regelson's own career.

Ḥaquqot otiyyotayikh was Regelson's great breakthrough because it saved him from being crushed by a metaphysical burden that he had designated as the highest calling of his poetry. He had assigned himself the role of the singer of mysteries, yet he had never succeeded in finding a way to render the recondite palpable in poetic terms, and he never freed himself from the secondariness of borrowed schemata, whether Schopenhauerian or kabbalistic. The joyful intoxication that pulses in every line of *Ḥaquqot otiyyotayikh* is a sign of a man whose imagination has been liberated by the sudden discovery that the thing he has all along loved most in life is in fact the true subject of his art. Seizing the theme of Hebrew, moreover, allowed Regelson more scope to bring his autobiographical self into his poetry. The praise of Hebrew in *Ḥaquqot otiyyotayikh* is not aloof and abstract; rather, it is a poem about how the eroticized Hebrew language engraves itself on the world of the poetic "I," who in turn catalogues his beloved's charms. That "I" may stand for a kind of Hebrew Everyman, but this implied universalization does not diminish the role played by Regelson's autobiographical persona. That persona becomes more autobiographical and less universal toward the end of the poem, when the speaker protests his fidelity to an organic expanding Hebrew despite his distant location in an imposed exile. In terms of his own literary career, finally, the poem rescued Regelson from a marginality that would have been all the more extreme without it. Whether or not *Ḥaquqot otiyyotayikh* can be accounted a masterpiece—it certainly has my vote—it is undisputedly regarded, at the very least, as a strong and unusual work of art. Regelson himself was well aware of the salient value this uniqueness brought to his reputation. When it came to the great moment in a poet's life when he is given the chance to publish his collected verse, Regelson not only placed *Ḥaquqot otiyyotayikh* in the opening position in the volume, despite its being out of chronological order, but he named the volume for the poem, such that *Ḥaquqot otiyyotayikh* became the banner for his poetic enterprise as a whole rather than the title of a discreet work.

Regelson's great hymn to the Hebrew language marked a watershed in his poetry. Never again would he deploy the lexically lush, high style with its grandiose metaphysical ambitions. Although Regelson's writing fanned out in a number of directions after the mid-1940s, none of them attempted to scale the same heights. *'Aqedat Shelemyahu* [The binding of Shelemyahu], for example, was the large work that

Regelson must have been engaged in during the late 1940s.[30] The poem is set against the autobiographical background of the three years Regelson and his family spent in Tel Aviv in the early 1930s; the central event is the death of a baby, and the poem includes scenes of the primitive healthcare arrangements of the time and of the literary bohemia of the first Hebrew metropolis. What is most significant stylistically is the genre description Regelson affixed beneath the poem's title: "po'emah sippurit," a narrative long poem. The label is accurate. ʿAqedat Shelemyahu is eighty-five pages of poetry with long lines, and it tells a story in the sequential, event-filled way of a novel. Although no one would mistake Regelson's stylized, biblically inflected verse for a contemporary idiom, the poetry is undeniably relaxed and prosaic—not for the worse, necessarily—in relationship to the grandeur that preceded it.

It is with great pleasure that one discovers, hiding in the glades at the feet of Regelson's lofty monuments of verse, delightful pockets of lyric creativity. This is Regelson's minor chord, and although its range is limited, it often evinces a playful and plangent clarity. Nowhere is the oscillation between major and minor more evident than in the literary translations that Regelson included in his volume of collected poetry in a special section with the title "'Ivrurim." (Something of a proprietary coinage, the term comes from the Hebrew for Hebrew, ʿivrit, and can be rendered "Hebraizations." The implication is that these are not simply instances of mechanical translation, no matter how skillful, but rather transformational acts that domesticate and re-realize, as it were, the original text as a Hebrew poem. As such, Regelson presumes, they deserve a place in his Hebrew canon.[31])

This section begins with three translations from Milton (the ode to light at the opening of Book Three of *Paradise Lost*, the description of Adam and Eve's love in the Garden in Book Four (lines. 720–77), and "The Library at Cambridge") and proceeds to five poems by Robert Herrick. Here are two seventeenth-century British poets whose styles could not be more different. Milton's learned and lofty epic style gestures in the direction of Regelson's most ambitious poetry at the same time as Regelson's lyric mode is evoked in Herrick's carpe diem songs of summer afternoons and maidens gathering rosebuds as they may. The translations that follow come from the works of Blake, Wordsworth, William Cullen Bryant, Emerson, Whitman, Swinburne, Tennyson, Lazarus, Housman, Joyce Kilmer, and Conrad Aiken. (The sole non-English poet is Avraham Sutzkever.) Regelson's choices tell us something about what voices within the Anglo-American canon spoke most deeply to him, although the absence of Shelley and Keats is notable. The texts he selected may have been, after all, only those he thought could withstand the solvent test of "Hebraization." Taken as a whole, the translations favor the lyric voice, and it is likely that these canonical acts of cultural transfer served as a kind of legitimate cover under which Regelson could allow himself to sing a less solemn song.[32]

The lyric strain in Regelson's poetry is inextricably tied up with his "second career" as a children's writer. When Regelson lived in Tel Aviv during the early 1930s, he was employed as a writer for the children's supplement to the daily *Davar*, as well as for the newspaper proper. In this capacity, Regelson wrote a story in installments concerning a collection of dolls that his daughter Sharona had left behind in Cleveland when the family moved to Palestine. The story recounts the adventures of the doll family on their journey to the Promised Land. *Masa' habubot le'erets yisra'el* [The journey of the dolls to the land of Israel] was first published in 1936 and went through many editions.[33] Generations of readers who have no inkling of Regelson's credentials as an epic Hebrew poet have come to know of him through the perennial charms of this little book. Regelson published several books of retold legends that were aimed at young readers: *Sham habedolah: mar'ot ve'aggadot* [There the crystal is: Sights and legends],[34] *'Ein hasus: sipurim min hamitos hayevani* [Fountain of the horse: Tales from Greek mythology],[35] and *Beit hanitsots: mar'ot ve'aggadot* [House of the spark: Sights and legends].[36]

Writing for children loosened something in Regelson that he was able to draw on in his minor poems for adults, for example, in the two poems he wrote on the death of Bialik in 1934. He had met the great poet in Cleveland on Bialik's visit to America and kept in touch with him when he moved to Tel Aviv. "'Al ish hakokhavim" [Concerning the man of the stars][37] is a rather grand elegy on the model of Milton's *Lycidas* in which the cosmic significance of the poet's passing is dramatized in the debate between heaven and earth as to which will receive the late great man. The other poem is a brief lyric dedicated to the memory of Yedidia, the eight-month-old baby who died shortly after Bialik's death. The poem is spoken by the baby's sister, who imagines how Bialik, who was childless, greets the baby in heaven and teaches him the secrets of the universe. And more: "Of course he will also learn to write poems—/ and sometime when mother is sitting in the yard, / a poem tossed off by my little brother / will fall on her head like a glistening leaf." The two poems serve very different functions, certainly; but the more intimate gesture ventriloquized through the innocent eyes of a child is substantially more successful than the weightier public tribute. The deployment of the child's voice or perspective is realized to beguiling effect also in the poems "Hasefinah 'Vardah'" [The ship "Varda"], "Mazal," and "Marlboro."[38]

In 1972 at the age of seventy-six, Regelson received the Bialik Prize, and although his life achievement was being acknowledged, it was the late flowering of this lyric potential that was the occasion for the award. That year Regelson had published *Shirotayim*, a thirty-page booklet containing, as the title—another of Regelson's neologisms—indicates, two poems.[39] "Lesulam tsorit" [To the Sulam-Tsorith] and "Shenai barburim venahar" [Two swans and a river]. The first is the recollection of a romance between the speaker and a much younger woman against the lush pastoral landscape of the Land of Israel. The second, the longer poem, is a retold chapter from the life of William Butler Yeats. Regelson himself translated the latter into English, and the translation was read before an audience in the Liffy Theater in Dublin.[40] These are poems of great force and beauty that deserve to be better known. As was the case with Halkin and Efros, his counterparts among the American Hebrew poets who settled in Israel, Regelson's poetry in old age reached a distilled wisdom and clarity. Regelson succeeded in these last gestures in disentangling the lyric from the childlike and fusing it with the semantic richness of his major style.

֍ אֶל הַקָּטָן רְאֵם בֶּן אַבְרָהָם
To the Child Raim Son of Abraham

Because an entire chapter earlier in this book is devoted to one of Regelson's works, we do not conclude with an explication of a single, representative poem, as has been the practice with the other poets discussed so far. Instead, we end with an affecting lullaby spoken by the young father to his eldest child that serves as an informal apologia pro vita sua for his allegiance to the impecunious vocation of poetry.[41]

אֶל הַקָּטָן רְאֵם בֶּן אַבְרָהָם

אִם תִּתְאַו לַלְּבָנָה, בְּנִי,
זוֹ קַעֲרַת שָׁמַיִם,
אֶתְפַּשֵּׁטָה וְאֶתְגַּנֵּנָה לְךָ
מַמָּשׁ בְּיָדַיִם.

וְאִם לְכוֹכְבֵי נֶשֶׁף, בְּנִי,
יִתְקְפוֹךְ גַּעְגּוּעִים,
מְלוֹא חָפְנַיִם אֶצְבְּרֵם
לְךָ לְשַׁעֲשׁוּעִים.

אָבִיךָ הוּא מְשׁוֹרֵר עַז,
וּמֶנּוּ מַה יִּפָּלֵא?
יְצַו עַל שְׁקִיעָה – תּוֹרִיד לוֹ
דְּלִי אוֹר־זָהָב מָלֵא.

אַךְ אַל תְּבַקֵּשׁ לֶחֶם, בְּנִי,
וּלְחֶמְאָה אַל תִּתְפַּלֵּל,
כִּי אָז אָבִיךָ יָנוּד רֹאשׁ
וְ"לֹא" לְךָ יְמַלֵּל.

אָבִיךָ הוּא מְשׁוֹרֵר עַז,
וְכֹחוֹ רַב בַּשְּׁחָקִים:
מִנְּתִיב־הֶחָלָב פִּיךָ יַשִּׁק,
יְכַלְכְּלֵךְ בְּרָקִים.

To the Child Raim Son of Abraham

If you want the moon, my son,
That disc of the heavens,
I'll grab it for you and put it
Right into your hands.

If you are overcome with longings
For the nighttime stars, my son,
I'll gather handfuls
For you to play with.

Your father is a mighty poet,
And what could be beyond him?
At his command, the sunset will let down
A bucket full of golden light.

But, son, do not ask for bread,
Nor pray for butter.
For then your father will have to shake his head
And murmur "No."

Your father is a mighty poet,
And great is his power in the heavens:
He can give you to drink from the Milky Way
And feed you with lightning bolts.

Fourteen

Gabriel Preil

The poetry of Gabriel Preil receives pride of last place in this study; not only because, born in 1911, Preil is the youngest of the group, but also because his work represents, in many senses, the culmination of the enterprise of American Hebrew poetry. Preil is the only American whose work succeeded in garnering the kind of enthusiastic and sustained critical reception among Israeli readers that had been so sorely desired by all who preceded him. The achievement is all the more remarkable because, unlike Efros, Halkin, and Regelson, who settled in Israel around the time of the establishment of the state, Preil remained in New York and visited Israel only later in his life, albeit several times. Moreover, although others took a serious interest in British and American poetry and wrote about it for Hebrew readers abroad, only in Preil's case does the poetry itself maintain an active dialogue with developments in modern English verse. This is even truer about Preil's contacts with the "other" American Jewish writers who did not write in English, the introspectivist Yiddish poets, whose modernism exerted a formative influence on Preil's poetic practice. Finally, there is New York City itself. In contrast to the prose writers, American Hebrew poets had a general aversion to city life as a poetic subject, and when they did engage America as a place, they largely sought out the countryside and its denizens from an earlier age. Although Preil has many fine poems that are set in the landscape of his beloved New England, he remains, in the great preponderance of his work, a walker   323 in the city, observing urban life and observing his own reactions to his daily encounters with the human landscape of the metropolis.

Gabriel Preil. Photo courtesy of Chava Leaf.

The style Preil achieved in his mature poetry fulfills one of the central aspirations of American Hebrew poetry: simplicity without avant-garde vulgarity. American Hebrew poetry emerged out of the romantic turmoil of such great figures of the *tehiyyah* [revival] period as Bialik, Tchernichovsky, and Shneour. In Palestine their sway was decisively thrown over in the 1920s by the incursion of the revolutionary poetics from Russia, France, and Germany in the form of symbolism and expressionism. In America, by contrast, Hebrew poetry in its main thrust—especially in the work of Efros, Bavli, and Silberschlag—sought to simplify and domesticate the romantic inheritance by limiting its reliance on classical allusion and tamping down its pathos. It sought a way, in other words, to modernize Hebrew poetry without recourse to what was considered the barbarism of foreign trends. (This was, of course, not the only path of American Hebrew poetry, as we have just seen in the work of Halkin and Regelson, poets who leveraged the English romantics to create a supercharged American Hebrew idiom.) Yet it was not until the belated arrival of Preil on the scene of American Hebrew poetry that the aspiration toward simplicity could be said to be fulfilled. Preil accomplished this on his own terms and not without resort to the transformative resources of modernism. But from the quiver of modernism, the arrow Preil selected was the most American: the imagism of Amy Lowell and H.D. (Hilda Doolittle) as refracted through the lens of the American Yiddish poetry of Jacob Glatstein and the *In Zich* poets. This was a sympathetic strain of modernism that Preil could integrate with a highly refined Hebrew romanticism in complex and variable ways that will be described in due course.

However we might account for the complexity of Preil's achievement, the signal fact remains that it enabled the last act in the drama of American Hebrew poetry to end on a note of elegiac triumph. And, one might add, to end *in* America; at a time when many of the strongest voices had relocated to Israel, Preil stayed on. With the tottering of Hebraic educational institutions, the disappearance of readership, the aging of its writers, and the vigorous glamour of Hebrew in the new Jewish state, American Hebraism experienced a precipitous decline in the period after World War II. The Hebraists were fond of conveying the pathos of their situation by calling themselves, in a phrase that reflects their fascination and identification with American Indians, the last of the Mohicans. Preil, in this sense, was the last of the last. There may yet be Hebrew creativity in America, but Preil's death in 1993 signaled the conclusion of a coherent, century-long project. What joy, then, that this ending could come in the form of breakaway success rather than anonymous failure.

Preil was born in Dorpat, Estonia, in 1911 and raised in Krakes, Lithuania. His paternal grandfather was Joshua Joseph Preil (ca. 1850–90), a rabbinical scholar and also a man of Hebrew letters, who polemicized with Moshe Leib Lilienblum in the pages of *Hamelits*. More "enlightened" than rabbinic, Preil's father, Faivl Shraga Preil (ca. 1880–1921), was an ardent Zionist who struggled to make a living as a druggist and banker. Like her husband, Preil's mother, Clara Preil (née Matzkel, ca. 1888–1977), was well versed in Hebrew and read Russian and German literature as well. The father's early death led to the emigration of mother and son to the United States in 1922. Preil attended the Rabbi Isaac Elchanan Theological Seminary and the Teachers Institute at Yeshiva University; his extensive familiarity with English and American literature was acquired through his own reading. His mother married Helman Kushner, who taught Talmud at the Rambam Yeshiva in Brooklyn. Both were supportive of Preil's poetic vocation. Until their deaths, Preil lived with his mother and stepfather in the Bronx. He never married and, with brief exceptions, did not work.[1]

Preil's first Hebrew poem appeared in *Hado'ar* in 1936 at about the same time that he began to publish verse in Yiddish. His first book of Hebrew poems, *Nof shemesh ukhefor* [Landscape of sun and frost] was published in a small run in New York in 1944. Although the volume was noticed by critics in Tel Aviv and Jerusalem, it was not until the next two books, *Ner mul kokhavim* [Candle against stars] (1954) and *Mappat 'erev* [Map of evening] (1960) were published in Israel that his critical reputation flourished. Preil's first visit to Israel took place in 1968 around the publication of his fourth book of poetry, *Ha'esh vehademamah* [Fire and silence]. A milestone in Preil's career was the publication by Mossad Bialik of his collected poetry in 1972, *Mitokh zeman venof: shirim mequbatsim* [Of time and place: Collected poems]. He continued to write and publish prolifically; he visited Israel again in 1977 and in 1983, when he received the Bialik Prize. In 1993, the poetry Preil published in several subsequent books was gathered together in *Asfan setavim: shirim 1972–1992* [Collector of autumns: Collected poems 1972–1992]. Having come to Israel on the occasion of the book's publication, Preil died in his hotel room in Jerusalem on June 5, 1993.

Preil's future biographer will not have an easy time adducing a life fraught with incident. Perhaps the most difficult experience in Preil's life was immigration to America after the death of his father. The boy and, later, young man endured a prolonged period—some fifteen years—of learning English and becoming acquainted with American culture before he felt settled enough to present himself to the world as a poet.[2] Of these struggles, there is no record in the poetry. This is the case even though this is a poetry that is largely written in the first person and in which the lyric "I" continually identifies the speaker of the poems with their author. This is the peculiar paradox of Preil's verse: the poet provides abundant information about his changing moods and the circuit of his day and his responses to rain and snow and heat. Yet at the same time, he is exceedingly reticent about what might be called the more personal events of his life. So while many of the poems begin with feelings felt by the "I" of the speaker, the action of the poems inevitably moves away from the self toward the world.

In the 1970s, however, Preil began publishing a series of poems that endeavored to present a kind of autobiographical portrait. To be sure, the reticence about the inner, intimate life persisted, but what was new was Preil's desire to construct a family literary heritage that justified the anomalous vocation of writing Hebrew verse on American soil. This wave of self-presentation seems to have been the paradoxical result of the gathering excitement around Preil's poetry among the younger Israeli poets of the time. Israel had long been a society in which Hebrew poetry served as a central mode of national experience rather than the private preserve of sensitive readers or a literary avant-garde. The 1960s were a period of profound polemical ferment over the nature of Hebrew poetry and its role in the life of the nation. The object of attack was the poetic norms of Alterman that had long dominated the literary scene: lush, figurative language; virtuoso rhyming; elevated diction; large national themes; and an essentialized, transpersonal voice. This dominance was assailed by a group of younger poets—among them Zach, Amichai, Dahlia Ravikovitch, Pagis, Moshe Dror, and David Avidan—who began to publish in the years after the establishment of the state. The critique, which was formulated and projected by Zach, was essentially a defense of the poetic practice of this new generation: poetry must renounce its inflated eloquence and instead reflect the natural language of man; regular rhyme and metered music are inauthentic expressions of the modern situation; poetry's chief vocation is to explore the private, existential space of the individual.

It was not easy for the new poetry to make headway against the weight of what amounted to an official national poetics. To enhance the acceptability and legitimacy of this revolution, Zach and others searched for earlier poets who could be construed as precursors or forbearers of the new aesthetic and thus provide it with a respectable lineage. An obvious choice was Fogel, a poet of minimalist, imagist verse who wrote in Europe between the two world wars; another was Preil, who began publishing before World War II. The conversational tone of Preil's poems, the eschewing of all formal structures for free verse, the brevity of the poems, which were spoken by an ironic lyric "I"—all these features made Preil a perfect figure to be enlisted as a precursor whose innovations could be adduced to camouflage the subversiveness of the new poetry by making it seem less unprecedented. The timbre of Preil's poetic voice seemed so natural to Israeli ears that readers discovering him for the first time could hardly be persuaded to believe that he had never stepped foot in the Holy Land. Moreover, the fact that he, like Fogel, wrote from outside Israel, one from Vienna and one from New York, underscored the oppressiveness of the literary establishment. The new style could demonstrate its first signs of innovation only beyond the reach of this cultural hegemony before gaining recognition on native grounds.

Being taken up in this way was a mixed blessing for Preil. Writing from the extreme margins of the map of Hebrew literature and from within a culture indifferent to his work and largely incapable of reading it, how could he not rejoice to become the subject of attentive and substantive critical notices and to garner the attention of enthusiastic readers? Bavli, Lisitzky, Silberschlag, and the other American Hebrew poets senior to Preil could only have dreamt of stimulating a similar level of interest in the Israeli literary community. At the same time, however, Preil could not have been sanguine about being pressed into service as a figure in a narrative not his own. For the theorists and practitioners of the new Israeli poetry, the significance of Preil's work lay in its being a forerunner of a literary trend that came to full flower only in *their* poetry, as if it had been his good fortune to have set the scene for their work. In point of fact, Preil's poetry had come from someplace else, and although admittedly there were evident similarities and intersections, it was a mistake to assimilate him into the new developments in Israel.

There was no explicit or public way in which Preil attempted to resist this appropriation. He was not a theorist of poetry despite his occasional essays on other writers; critical statement was not his idiom. And the spotlight of adulation must not have been entirely unwelcome. When he mounted a response, it was on his own grounds, that is, through poetry, specifically a series of poems he wrote in the 1970s. Rather than taking issue with the presumptions of others, these poems make a positive assertion about the very particular identity of Preil as a poet. This is an identity that can be fathomed only in its multiple contexts. There is Preil the bearer of the romantic Hebraism of his Lithuanian ancestors; there is Preil the youngest member of the collegium of the Hebrew and Yiddish writers in America; there is Preil the Diaspora Hebrew poet who identifies with Beryl Pomerantz in Poland, Haim Lenski in the Soviet Union, David Fogel in Austria and France, and other poets writing outside of the center in Eretz Yisrael; there is Preil the citizen of the American republic of letters who resonates with the poetry of Whitman, Wallace Stevens, Edward Arlington Robinson, Conrad Aiken, and Frost; and, finally and undeniably, Preil the poet who was adopted and naturalized into postwar Israeli verse.

Of these many contexts, the Lithuanian connection is asserted with special urgency in Preil's later poetry. Lithuania, or Lita in Jewish parlance, was a region of ancient Jewish settlement within the Russian

Empire in which the sway of Hasidism was much less pronounced than in the south. The standard of rabbinic learning among males was high, and the great *yeshivot* of Lita, which drew students from all over Europe, also became underground centers for Haskalah and later Zionist ferment. Preil's grandfather was Joshua Joseph Preil, the rabbi of a small town near Kovno, who embodied many of the traits associated with Lita. He was a distinguished talmudic scholar who also was at home in European literature and the Hebrew literature of the Haskalah. In the pages of *Hamelits*, the preeminent Hebrew journal of the time, he conducted polemical correspondences with both ultra-Orthodox figures and with reformers like Lilienblum. In his essays, he argued for the legitimacy and the desirability of an Orthodox belles lettres.[3] In a poem that figures prominently at the beginning of Preil's 1975 collection *Zeman aher* [Other time], as well as at the head of the collected poems (*Asfan setavim*), Preil compares himself to his grandfather.

פִּרְקֵי זְמַן: שֶׁלִּי־שֶׁלּוֹ

רָאוּ אֶת סָבָא צָעִיר בַּעֲיָרָתוֹ הַלִּיטָאִית.
הוּא נָהַג לְהַשְׁכִּים בַּבֹּקֶר־בַּבֹּקֶר
וּלְאַחַר תְּפִלָּה רָשַׁם לוֹ חִדּוּשֵׁי תּוֹרָה
הֵכִין מַאֲמָר לְ"הַמֵּלִיץ" וְגִלָּה טִיב מָן
בְּפַת חֲרֵבָה וְכוֹס מַיִם רוֹתְחִים.
הוּא הָיָה אָדָם הַמַּעֲלָה.

רָאוּ אוֹתִי צָעִיר עַל הָאֲדָמָה הָאֲמֶרִיקָנִית.
לֹא בְּדִיּוּק אֵיזֶה יְצוּר יוֹצֵא־דֹפֶן
הַכּוֹתֵב אֶת שִׁירָיו בְּעִבְרִית. אָדָם
הַמִּתְפַּלֵּל מִתּוֹךְ אֵלֶם, שׁוֹתֶה עִם צָהֳרַיִם
סֵפֶל־בֹּקֶר פּוֹשֵׁר וּמִשֶּׁתַּכְנִעַ שֶׁמָּצָא בּוֹ
אֶת טַעַם הַנָּדִיר הֶחָלוֹם.

כָּל אִישׁ לְמַנּוּ בִּזְמַנּוּ;
זוֹ גְּלוּלָה אוֹטוֹבִּיוֹגְרָפִית
הַמִּתָּרֶת לִבְלִיעָה עַד הֶנֵּץ
הָרֶבַע הָאַחֲרוֹן לִמְאַת הָעֶשְׂרִים.

הַיָּמִים מִכָּאן וְאֵילֶךְ – מוּקְיוֹנִים
מַחֲלִיקִים בְּהֶסּוּס עַל קֶרַח־לֹא־קֶרַח.

קָשֶׁה לְשַׁעֵר מֶה הָיָה אוֹמֵר סָבָא עֲלֵיהֶם –
מִכָּל־מָקוֹם הָיִיתִי רוֹצֶה לִחְיוֹת אֶת זְמַנּוּ.

Chapters of Time: His and Mine

See Grandfather as a young man in his Lithuanian shtetl.
His habit was to rise early every morning
and after prayers he would write down his Torah insights,
prepare an article for *Hamelits* and discover the taste of manna
in a piece of dry bread and a cup of boiling water.
He was a man of distinction.

See me, a young man on American soil.
Not exactly an exceptional creature
who writes his poems in Hebrew. A man
who prays from silence, drinks at noontime
his tepid morning cup and persuades himself that he has found
       in it
the taste of something rare and dreamt of.

Each man his own manna in his own time;
this is an autobiographical tablet approved for consumption until
       the beginning of the last quarter of the twentieth century.
The time from then on: clowns
skating hesitantly on thin ice.
It is hard to imagine what Grandfather would have said about
       them.
In any event, I would have liked to live his time.[4]

The fact that Preil never knew his grandfather, who died at the age
of forty, makes the comparison of the two at the center of this poem
a willed exercise rather than an instance of recollection. Our taking
notice of the two, in fact, comes in response to a set of instructions
issued by the speaker to observe each figure. (In the body of the
poem, we see first the grandfather and then the grandson, although
the order is interestingly reversed in the poem's title.) Of the many
and diverse possible points of comparison between these two complex
lives, the poem rigorously focuses on three: place, writing, and the

routine of an everyday morning. At first sight, the distance between the Lithuanian shtetl and American soil would seem vast; yet for the Hebrew reader, for whom the natural site for Hebrew writing is Palestine/Israel, these two locations are ironically joined together in their both being Diaspora outposts of Hebrew creativity.

It is likewise Hebrew itself that is the only common denominator between the literary activities of each. The grandfather composes both *ḥidushim* and *ma'amarim*. *Ḥidushim* ["novellae"] are solutions to cruxes in the interpretation of talmudic texts; they represent the contribution of individual genius to the collective tradition. *Ma'amarim* are articles, contributions to the new Hebrew periodical press, of which *Hamelits* was the flagship publication; the grandfather was a controversialist who participated in print in the great debates of the day. The verbs associated with these endeavors, *rasham* [record] and *hekhin* [prepare], connote a businesslike seriousness of purpose. The grandson, in contrast, merely writes poems. He neither contributes to the elucidation of the sacred tradition nor takes a public stand on the grave issues confronting the Jewish people. The poems that he writes are *his* poems [*shirav*], lyric poems, which are by their nature minor and solipsistic.

Apart from their writing, their characters are revealed in the conduct of daily life. The grandfather rises very early and fits in his writing between prayers and what is undoubtedly a heavy round of rabbinical responsibilities in the community. For refreshment, he gets by on a cup of boiling water—not even tea!—and some dry bread. The grandson, who has given up prayer, or who only "prays from silence," drinks a cup that is lukewarm, which he manages to get to only in the afternoon. Whereas the grandfather succeeds in revealing a miraculous quality, the flavor of manna, in his poor fare, the grandson has to persuade himself that he has come across a taste that is rare but the product of purely human fantasy. The phrase the speaker uses to epitomize the grandfather is *adam hama'lah*, a man of distinction; the term is taken from a speech David makes to God in I Chronicles 17:17, acknowledging the honor of having his house chosen for kingship. When the speaker of Preil's poem comes around to taking his own measure in the second stanza, the diminution of dynastic expectations is palpable. Rather than being summed up with a kingly biblical epithet, the speaker uses the most mundane colloquial Hebrew to describe himself as "not exactly some exceptional creature."

Yet the contrast between the discipline of the one and the lassitude of the other, which had been so elaborately developed, is suddenly swept aside at the opening of the third stanza. The speaker observes with a kind of indulgent renunciation: "Each man his own manna in his own time." Compared to the abandoned vulgarity of contemporary culture, the pointed divergences between grandfather and grandson turn out to be beside the point. The Hebraic cultural affinity that unites them beneath the differences is a remedy—tranquilizer or stimulant?—whose effectiveness is about to expire. The dour tenor of the image of clowns skating hesitantly on thin ice is unlike anything that has preceded it in the poem. *Muqyon* [clown] is a Greek term brought into Hebrew by the sages of the Talmud from the world of pagan circus performance, which they utterly despised, and it bears with it none of the antic, childlike qualities associated with the icon of American side shows. From now on, the world is given over to fools tracing figure eights over the void. But in its two-line concluding stanza, the poem backs away from this chilling prospect and assumes a tone of conjectural indeterminacy. It is all about time, the speaker insists, time before and time after. Although he cannot be sure of what Grandfather would have said about the future, that dawning era of the cynical clowns, the grandson knows, in the spirit of a man foreordained to belatedness, that he would have preferred to have been part of his time rather than theirs.

At the deepest and most profound level, grandfather and grandson are connected by their commitment to writing in Hebrew in the alien lands of the Diaspora. One dimension of this romantic exilic Hebraism, as Yael S. Feldman calls it, is the family romance. In addition to the grandfather, whom Preil never met, there was the more immediate Hebraist family circle of Preil's parents, who valorized Hebrew poetry and encouraged his earliest attempts at verse.[5] Beyond the family lay the distinguished past of Hebrew literature in Lithuania as whole, where in the middle of the nineteenth century, the first modern Hebrew lyric poetry was composed by Micha Joseph

Lebensohn (called Michal) and the first Hebrew novel by Mapu. In both these figures, Preil sees the coexistence of a dreamy passion with a quotidian rationality, and he takes this tension as the essential patrimony of his Lithuanian lineage. It is the lineage that has shaped him, and it is now his to shape in accordance with his individual temperament and his belated circumstance. Finding this balance in both Michal and Keats, Preil writes that "Out of a storm of longing Michal planted his verses like tranquil gardens."[6] When it came to wresting beauty from unsympathetic surroundings, Preil observes in another poem addressed to Mapu, that Lithuania is not so very different from America: "I, like you, am a Lithuanian Jew, / who strove to bring forth from ordinary soil / sober trees in which the dream blazes."[7]

If, on the one hand, Preil presents himself as the last lineal descendent of the Lithuanian heritage in Hebrew writing, he also identifies himself with a broader spectrum of Hebrew poets who wrote elsewhere in Europe in the generation immediately preceding his own: Fogel in Austria and France, Pomerantz in Poland, and Lenski in the Soviet Union. Fogel and Pomerantz perished in the Holocaust, and Lenski in Stalin's camps. In a 1991 poem titled "Sheloshah qerovim li" [Three who are close to me], Preil describes how, while sitting in his room on a stifling late-summer day, "my hand in New York is turned / in the direction of Fogel, Pomerantz and Lenski"; "Strange," he muses "how they live in my room."[8] The closeness is an intimacy among peers rather than an influence exerted by precursors. These three poets, each along his own idiosyncratic path, stood apart from the fashions of interwar Hebrew poetry promulgated by the literary center in Palestine, and there, in the darkest reaches of the Diaspora "each one of them remained / with the naked branch of his verse."

America is a different Diaspora, to be sure, and Preil chose to remain there rather than attach himself to the center. Yet it would be wrong to take Preil's declared kinship with his Lithuanian forebears and his European fellow poets as a distancing of himself from Israel and the enterprise of Zionism. The demurral registered here relates to the "discovery" of Preil in Israel in the 1960s and 1970s and efforts on the part of Zach and others to make him into a forerunner of their innovative poetics. In his indirect and implicit manner, Preil protests this appropriation and writes himself into a different family tree.

Yet this redirecting of attention leaves a crucial question unanswered: What is the source of the stunning novelty of Preil's poetry? For all its romantic and personal appeal, the Lithuanian heritage had little to offer on this score. The conservative poetics of the American Hebrew poets who preceded Preil is well known. Though sympathetic to the dethroning of Shlonsky and Alterman in post-1948 Israeli poetry, Preil had not been a frontline participant in that generational conflict.

The answer comes from a direction that, at least from the point of view of all that has been said so far about the course of American Hebrew poetry, is astonishing: Yiddish literature. From its origins around World War I, American Hebraism had been caustically disdainful of the vulgarity of Yiddish popular culture as displayed in the Second Avenue theaters and in the tabloid press. Toward serious high culture in Yiddish, the attitude was of course more respectful, although the two literary communities, for many reasons, led parallel and divergent lives; and the experimental modernism of the American Yiddish poets was no more congenial to their Hebrew counterparts than the avant-garde "barbarisms" of the poets of the Hebrew moderna in Tel Aviv. Why then Yiddish? Preil entered the scene of American Hebrew literature relatively late, both in respect to his own life and in respect to the development of American Hebrew poetry. This was a body of verse that, already in the 1930s, was well beyond the flush of promise and expectation, and it is likely that what Preil found there was disappointing. At the same time, the aggressive modernisms of Hebrew poetry in the Yishuv, based on Russian and German models and embroiled in the politics of national struggle, were not true to his time and place and were too fraught for his temperament.

Ironically, it was through the modernism of the "introspectivist" Yiddish poets, such as Glatstein and Leyeles, that Preil could meet on his own terms the innovations that had taken place in Anglo-American poetry. This is a story of cultural mediations and transfers that has been lucidly presented by Feldman.[9] The aesthetic stance of the *In Zich* poets, announced in their manifestoes of the early 1920s, was based on two principles that were not always easy to reconcile in practice. On the one hand, the poem is a vehicle through which the poet explores the labyrinthine depths of his self. On the other, the poem should focus on the exact description of an object in the world or a metaphor and avoid abstract discourse on the meaning or message of the object. This second principle was an attempt to bring into the staid world of Yiddish poetry the revolutionary freshness associated with imagism in American poetry, as theorized and practiced by Ezra Pound, Amy Lowell, H. D., and others.

For the imagists, the poem was "a movement of discovery or awareness, created by effective metaphor which provides the sharp, intuitive insight that is the essence of life."[10] Being true to this moment of discovery, moreover, meant abandoning the constraints of fixed rhyme, meter, and stanzaic structure in favor of free verse. It further meant writing *short* poems that would not stretch the poem's fabric beyond that moment of discovery. It was this dimension of *In Zich* that attracted Preil rather its psychologically introspective individualism.[11] Of the many contending modernisms on the international palette of poetry from which a young poet starting out in the 1930s could choose, the disciplined moderation of imagism, together with its formal freedoms, was the best match for Preil's temperament. It was through American Yiddish poetry that this aesthetic option became plausible, and this was so not because Preil could not experience imagism through the medium of English but because Yiddish had demonstrated how a Jewish language could successfully appropriate an American modernism.

The challenge confronting Preil was how to bring this new current into Hebrew. Preil wrote both Yiddish and Hebrew verse at the beginning of his career; it was the Yiddish poet Glatstein who advised the young poet that his gift lay in Hebrew.[12] Moreover, in light of the Hebraist family romance described above, it is not difficult to understand why Preil would have resolved his bilingual dilemma in favor of Hebrew. Yet just because he had committed himself to the vocation of Hebrew poetry did not mean that Hebrew poetry, at least the tradition of *American* Hebrew poetry in which he worked, would automatically be less resistant to the new style he wished to introduce. The norms of American Hebrew poetry, to speak for a moment in large generalities, were based on the late romantic poetry of the Hebrew revival [*teḥiyyah*] in Eastern Europe; we have had numerous occasions to demonstrate how the Americans sought to streamline this inheritance while advancing its essential postulates. Although Bialik and Tchernichovsky were the great lions of revival poetry and venerated as such by most of the Americans, there was a third, younger figure in this pantheon, Shneour (1887–1959), and it was he who played a key role in Preil's own formation as a poet.[13] Shneour's was an urban poetry written under the sign of European decadence as a literary sensibility; denied fulfillment of the soul's vital needs, the individual in Shneour's verse must make his way in a world perpetually on the verge of chaos and confusion.

This was the poetic language most available to Preil when he published the poems that were eventually gathered in his first book *Nof shemesh ukhefor* in 1944; the bleak outlook of this poetry, which had been born of an earlier world war, sadly fitted the somber temper of the period in which Preil was entering the world of poetry. All the while, however, Preil had been experimenting in his Yiddish poetry with the imagism of Glatstein and Teller, in which there was no place for the pathos of the despairing poet facing the rupture of civilization. Over the course of the 1940s, Feldman argues, Preil rejects "the rhetorical poetics symbolized by his former model, Zalman Schneour," and instead begins to align himself in the map of Hebrew literature with the "minor, marginal line of Hebrew poets," such as Fogel and Pomerantz.[14]

Yet even with this new alignment, Preil's stylistic evolution was not complete. Along with the freedoms conferred by imagism, there were renunciations that did not come easily to Preil. The speaker of an imagist poem kept his or her self out of the picture in favor of the object or metaphor at center focus. As a modernism, imagism sought to disturb the resonance or correspondence between the soul of the world and the soul of the artist that was at the heart of romanticism and, instead, to make the matter of the poem an object that stands in a metonymical relationship to the world. The lyric "I," in other words, was called upon to abdicate its sovereignty and, relying on the presumption that every act of observation presupposes an observer, to disappear into the poem's web of implication. This was an act of self-abnegation that Preil declined to perform. His refusal was based not on aggrandizing claims of the self's prerogatives but on an insistence that truth requires keeping the self in the picture. Although the rapport between the poet and the cosmos no longer exists, the desire for that connection—and the struggles to accept the unfulfillment of that desire—is fundamental to the modern situation. Preil makes no secret of his wish to have been born in the age of Keats and Byron or even—mutatis mutandis—of his grandfather, the Lithuanian rabbinical controversialist.[15] But his belatedness is a stubborn fact. He lives in New York City in the middle of the twentieth century, and although he can build an occasional bridge of longing to the world that preceded him, he accepts the necessity of being an inhabitant of a disenchanted world.

The result is a poetic style that is a complex amalgam of romanticism and modernism. A fusion? A synthesis? A dialectic? The precise critical terms are not clear; the "idiolect" of Preil's poetics, with attention paid to the changes wrought in each decade of his writing, awaits a definitive description. A provisional characterization, in the most general terms, might be formulated in this way: from imagism, Preil appropriated some of the practices of modernism (especially directness of observation and metaphorical precision) and absorbed them into a chastened romantic framework freed from its metaphysical moorings.

A place to begin to examine this amalgam is "Mitsiyyurei Maine" [Sketches of Maine], the longest poem in Preil's canon, which he wrote in Bangor at the age of thirty-five in 1946.[16] Both the age and the date are significant. Dante's entry into the dark forest in the middle of his life's journey in the beginning of the *Inferno*, as Miron has suggested, is not an inappropriate way to think about Preil's quest in this ambitious poem.[17] The middle of *his* life coincided with the destruction of European Jewry, and the pressure exerted on Preil's poetry by that catastrophe is acutely reflected in the closing sections of his first book of poetry, *Nof shemesh ukhefor*. The search for cleansing and healing in the aftermath of trauma is clearly enunciated as the ulterior motive for the journey to Maine (poem 1). This quest is undertaken also against the background of the strife in Palestine among the Jews, Arabs, and British. Because Preil's poem opens in the form of an ode addressed to Maine, the speaker feels impelled to justify how a Hebrew ode—in the inevitable footsteps of Judah Halevi's ode to Zion—could be addressed to any geographical entity *other* than the Land of Israel. By adducing the biblical names of the surrounding Maine towns, as well as the names on the headstones in the cemeteries, the speaker can point to a common connection to the Hebrew Scriptures and to the aspiration of the settlers to make their New England into a New Canaan. What remains unspoiled from this time of pious origins is the astonishing beauty of the landscape itself. The question posed by the poem is what persists of the curative powers that inhere in this natural realm.

Preil's ambitious Maine poem is a central event in the American Hebrew canon because it asks two large questions: When it comes to the inheritance of modern Hebrew poetry—the poetic practice of Bialik, Tchernichovsky, and Shneour—can the beauty of the American landscape sustain or reinvigorate the romantic premise? And, is it in the power of that natural beauty to provide sustenance for the soul of the modern Jew? The poem's answers to these questions are both positive and negative in ways that are illuminating but not easily simplified. It turns out that the purity, intensity, and beauty of the natural world embodied by Maine do in fact authorize a deep correspondence between human language and the physical universe. Yet at the same time this unity proves unavailable to the poem's speaker, a Jew and Hebrew poet coming into middle life at the middle point of a violent century. The vision of Maine that Preil conjures up to serve as the test case for these questions is a construction that is decidedly natural rather than human. The denizens of Maine who occasionally appear in the poem are merely chthonic outcroppings of the landscape who enact the cycles of sleeping, waking, and eating in concert with the seasons. This is also a dehistoricized construction. This is not the

Maine contested by the French, British, and Native Americans, nor the anti-slave state that poured bodies and money into the Union struggle, nor the state dominated by logging interests and rural poverty. Untrammeled and largely untrodden, the Maine of the poem remains an emblem of what nature in America can be.

The line of organization most evident in the poem is that of the anatomy, a systematic inventory of the diverse features of the landscape that make up Preil's Maine. The sea, the islands, the shore, the rivers, the coastal towns, the rain, the snow, the seasons—each one is summoned up and brought into play. The poem's title "Mitsiyyurei Maine," literally "*From* the sketches of Maine," implies selectivity; yet the poem in fact aspires to a comprehensive embrace of its subject. Each of the elements in this totality is examined and revealed as a site of vital energies and ceaseless conflict. The figurative language that Preil uses to capture these dramas is unashamedly saturated by the pathetic fallacy. The "blushing flower wounds the rock" (poem 3), "silence entered the veins of each tree like sap" (poem 4), the wooded off-shore islands "wave their hazy locks" (poem 3), "the moon sinks like a bird from above and sits in the crown of a tree" (poem 9). Each of these discrete instances of animism is drawn into larger vignettes of the back-and-forth struggle within nature. Poem 2, for example, focuses on the roses that sprout up among the granite rocks on the shore. These "little tongues of flame," vivid against the grey stone, resemble "toy goblets" that are turned into torrents of color and eruptions of "joy and intoxication" by the afternoon light. Yet as the day declines, the sea extinguishes these tiny bonfires and their sparks as it "shuts its great weary eye." The poem ends in a truce: "The roses and the sea divided the day between them and concluded a treaty / signed in a proud delicate hue and compliant fire."

In its elemental purity, Maine is put forward as a test case for the very possibility of a rapport between the cosmos and man. At the center of "Mitsiyyurei Maine," in Poems 11 and 12, that possibility is affirmed, but yet only in ways that take back as much as they give. Poem 11 opens with the description of a singular experience: "Tonight the curtain of stars has been lowered upon the highway." The cold glitter of the aristocratic stars is answered by warm points of light from the windows in the village below and the headlights of the cars. The "forest of stars" descends low upon the groves of pine and elms and for a moment becomes their neighbor. The scene switches from night to day in Poem 12, which describes a lake in the clouds that reflects a lake on the earth below.[18] Both lakes achieve an ecstasy of solitude, but, free of noisy fishermen and boats, it is only the heavenly lake that can preserve its introspective serenity. *Its* tranquil anglers nap on the shore while, without them, their nets magically yield a catch of pure silver.

These unitary moments, so plangently evoked in the intensity of imaginary experience, are qualified by the stubborn fact that the human subject is left on the outside. The effulgence of the starry curtain is so great that the passerby must shield his eyes as he would if he were staring into the sun. Yet, in vain he searches the vastness of the illuminated heavens for some small window that would beckon to him or for a single star that would reflect his own likeness. When it comes to the picture of the lake in the clouds, moreover, it is already assumed that in the rapport between the heavenly and the earthly, there is room for the human subject only as an observer but not as a participant. Now, being vouchsafed the privilege of witnessing such moments might seem joy enough if the exclusion did not represent something more fateful: a significant station in a fundamental countermovement in "Mitsiyyurei Maine" that eventually pushes the poem's speaker into a state of tragic renunciation.

The countermovement is only implicit at the beginning of the poem and gathers momentum after its midpoint. Already in Poem 4, the cold, sapphire brilliance of Lake Sebasticook is distilled as a silence that, as noted above, enters the veins of each tree like sap. What of the observer? "But I am alone on the shore: a teaming city invaded by armies of silence." Although we first assume that the silence of this beautiful locale is the apotheosis of tranquility, this turns out to be so only for the birds and the trees that organically belong to this scene. But the human observer does not belong; he is vulnerable like a defenseless city. Like a growth that is benign in one species but hazardous when it crosses over into another, the silence that flows into *his* veins has a potentially baleful effect on a man who must eventually return to the city to live among other men.

Silence turns into solitude as Preil's Maine poem turns toward fall and winter in its second half. Snow, "heaven's envoy of solitude," becomes the consummate embodiment of fleeting silence in Poem 13.

שִׁירְךָ, הַשֶּׁלֶג, שִׁיר הַחֲלוֹף הַלָּבָן, אוּלַי קָבוּעַ וְנֶאֱמָן
מֵאִיֵּי שַׁחַם בְּיָם קְדוּר־יַיִן;
הֵן גַּלְמוּד אַתָּה מֵהֶם —
וַאֲנִי עוֹד מִמְּךָ עֲרִירִי.

Your song, snow, is the song of white transience,
perhaps more fixed and faithful
than the granite islands in the wine-dark sea;
you are indeed lonelier than they—
But I am even more barren than you.

'Ariri in the last line, which I have translated as "barren," connotes sterility. It marks an even further stage in the progressive divergence between the reality of Maine and the fate of the poem's speaker. While he descends deeper into loneliness as the frigid winter blankets the countryside, the denizens of Maine enjoy the earthy pleasures of the season as if they were permanently fixed in a Currier & Ives etching. They drink deep drafts of cider, eat hot potatoes in their jackets, and partake of the profoundest sleep. Children are immersed in their play on the village green just as were their brothers before them in the days of President McKinley (poems 16 and 17). For a moment, the speaker is brought back to his own childhood. Discovering the frilly trunks and branches etched on the window by the frost early one morning, he is suddenly back in his Lithuanian village, which "dozes upon its starry winters." It is as if, again just for a moment, "like a somnambulist I passed from one cycle of childhood to another."

Surprisingly, the recollection of his Lithuanian childhood does not lead in the direction of the recent murder of European Jewry. That calamity is registered in the opening of "Mitsiyyurei Maine" and taken for granted as one of the reasons for undertaking the journey to Maine. But Preil does not adduce it in the poem as the source of the ineluctable exclusion of the speaker from the sphere of nature. The exclusion is ontological rather than historical. The encounter with Maine has resulted in a double negation. Not only can he not partake in the pageant of nature and its constant renewal, but the deathlike cold of winter has entered his soul for good. While the merry-go-round of the seasons continues to revolve enchantingly for others, it has deposited him forever in a place where the days grow ever shorter and darker.

Again, surprisingly, there is no revolt against this fate. To the contrary, it is as if, rather than visiting upon him a cruel decree, the encounter with Maine had confirmed a deep truth that been latent all along. That truth comes in the form of an identity that has been forged in this new knowledge, and a name is given to it in the opening lines of Poem 18, which sing with a celebratory resignation:

סְתָו הַקְדִּים אֵפֶר בְּרוֹשִׁים מוּל גֶּבַע חַלּוֹנִי,
הִרְבָּה הַשְׁקִיעַ בַּנָּהָר גּוֹנֵי־צֶל שֶׁל מַתֶּכֶת,
וְלִי, הָאָדָם הַמִּקְרִי, נָע מְכֻשָּׁף בְּמַעְגְּלָיו,
דְּמוּת סְתָו בְּרֵאשִׁיתוֹ, בּוֹעֵר וְאֵינוֹ אֻכָּל.

Autumn has applied an early mask of cypresses
against the hill of my window,
it has greatly deepened the metallic shadows on the river.
As for me, the accidental man, I move bewitched in its circuits,
a figure of autumn at its outset, burning but not consumed.

Ha'adam hamiqri, accidental man, is one who observes and travels through but does not belong. He is a man who will always be fixed in the fall, the time of almost death, no matter what the season is for the rest of the world. The revelatory quality of this self-knowledge, which is indicated by the allusion to the burning bush of the Moses story, is qualified a few lines later when the speaker describes himself as a "glowing human ember" [*adam-ud mehavhev*] making crowns for the Queen of the Autumn. He is on fire, but make no mistake: this is the sustained smoldering that precedes extinction.

The contours of a self-portrait emerge more clearly in the homage to the poet Edwin Arlington Robinson (1869–1939) in the penultimate poem. The speaker travels by train through the winter countryside to the poet's home in Gardiner, Maine, to commune with a kindred spirit who becomes a kind of genius loci. The author of "Edwin Cory" and other poetic profiles of desperation and silent nobility, Robinson endured a life of family tragedies and personal renunciation to hew to his vocation. Preil expresses his admiration by floridly conjuring him up as a "poet with a hard heart who set out to conquer the winters in the seasons of thought /—and arrived in a land of song full of spring brooks" (poem 21). With the black winter visible through the train windows on his return ride in the evening, something important becomes clear: "I, the elder of all the winters that came before him or me," the speaker avers, "have become the voice of springs that sang in him and resonate in me." Those springs only exist in poetry and can be reached only through poetry. The price that must be paid for this achievement in art is being permanently stationed in winter in life. The movement of the many sections of "Mitsiyyurei Maine" is toward the clarification of this stark choice. Like Robinson, the Maine poet who spent most of his life in New York City, the speaker of Preil's poem has steeled himself to make this renunciation. He had come to Maine to seek renewal and repurification against the background of the recent European horrors. This was an errand that failed. What he learned instead was that although the ever-changing natural beauty of Maine will always remain enchanting, it belongs to an order of reality he can never be part of.

The order of reality to which he now belongs is clearly, if enigmatically, proclaimed in the concluding poem (22) of "Mitsiyyurei Maine": "I will belong to the conquered city of the Minister of Death." This is stated as a fact of life without the melodrama that would seem to be inscribed on the face of these ominous words. It is an image that has been prepared for since Poem 4, in which the speaker feels the stillness of Lake Sebasticook permeating him: "I am alone on the shore: a teaming city invaded by the armies of silence." As the seasons turn, the speaker is severed from the cycle of nature and permanently installed in the ontological zone of winter. By Poem 19, the invasion of his being is nearly completed: "The lands of my noon have been conquered by the armies of twilight, / and my path already leads to that land of night / whose boundaries will never be reddened by the

approach of dawn."[19] Yet instead of this capitulation being accompanied by agitation and anxiety, the concluding tone of Preil's Maine
poem is proud and even buoyant.

How are conquest and submission transformed into noble resignation? "Mitsiyyurei Maine" should be read as a decisive moment in the
search of Preil's poetic persona for self-definition and vocation. The
point of departure is an impasse that combines, on the one hand, the
polluting pressures upon the soul of the extinction of European Jewry,
and, on the other, the dilemma of choosing between modernism and
romanticism as an artistic direction. "Maine" is the ultimate construction of the American pastoral, and toward it the speaker turns out of
a combination of hopefulness and bad faith. The more his painterly
eye—these are sketches [*tsiyyurim*], after all—registers the stern but
vital energies of these northern climes, the more the speaker is forced
to recognize the finality of his alienation from them. He is cut off
from the cyclical renewal they bestow upon others both because he is
a Jew for whom there can be no flight from Jewish history and because
he is a modern man for whom there is similarly no escape from the city
as the new ground of being. The question has now been decided, and
the paradox of triumphal resignation at the poem's conclusion can be
understood as the result of this definitive clarification and the poetic
mission that flows from it. He knows the outcome to be true, and he
accepts his destiny.

Preil's Maine poem belongs to a grouping of longer poems on
American themes in the 1954 collection *Ner mul kokhavim*.[20] In "Beit-
qevarot ameriqani" [An American cemetery], happening upon a long-
forgotten rural cemetery provides an occasion for meditations on America as a land of "variegation and mystery" and on the absence of Jews
from the collective story told by the gravestones.[21] "Zer-shirim qatan
la'Aviyah" [A small bouquet of poems for Abijah] (pp. 183–85) carries
a note stating that the poem cycle was written in a house in Putnam
Valley, New York (in the Hudson Highlands) built in 1824 by Abijah
Lee, a pious Christian and lover of the Bible. This complex poem
considers the profound historical role of the Hebrew Scriptures in
forming American character and consciousness. (These two poems are
discussed in Chapter 16.) "Tiyulim" [Trips] (pp. 186–94) is the title of

a peculiar, long composition, half of which describes the thoughts of the young Washington Irving as he strolls through his father's plum orchards along Battery Park at the beginning of the nineteenth century, and half of which describes conversations about the metaphysical meaning of the game of chess between the poet's two grandfathers as they walk in the woods of Lithuania. In contrast to Silkiner, Efros, and Lisitzky, it is worth noting, Preil showed little interest in one of the distinguished topics in American Hebrew poetry: American Indians.[22] After the grouping of American poems in *Ner mul kokhavim*, Preil rarely returned to the landscapes and the people of rural America. For reasons implicit in the Maine poem, his poetry had to turn elsewhere, and the city, which had been a preoccupation of his verse from the outset, was the place it returned to.

Among the critical clarifications Preil brings back to the city from Maine is the notion of the *adam miqri*, the accidental man, which combines within it a poetic persona, a stance toward the world, and a conception of the mission of poetry. Rather than making an essential or general statement about poets and poetry, this position presents itself before the reader as a proprietary description of Preil as poet who, with the publication of *Mappat 'erev* in the 1960s, enters the major, middle phase of his career.[23] As poet, then, Preil comes before us as a man who has renounced expectations for a fertile rapport with world and accepted the loneliness and isolation of his existence. In the metropolis, he moves among others whose lives have been worn down by the metallic alienation of urban life. His difference from them is constituted by his awareness of his situation and by his resolve to use his poetic gifts to ameliorate this fallen reality.

Developing the insights of Eliezer Friedland, a younger contemporary poet and critic of Preil's, Miron has gone so far as to see Preil's poetry as undertaking a mission to repair the brokenness of the world.[24] This is a kind of poetic activism that makes poetry writing and poems themselves into acts of *tiqqun*, restoration and reconciliation. There is no swagger to this ambition, nor an expectation of some great transformation. To the contrary, each poem is aware of its own fragility and the temporariness of its staying power in the face of the corrosive forces arrayed against it. Nevertheless, Preil's verse remains engaged in an ongoing commitment to poetry as the everyday work of healing. The particular instances of brokenness that present themselves before the poet as candidates for treatment come precisely from his status as an accidental man. His status as an efficacious and disinterested observer of the life of the city has been purchased by renouncing the expectation of vital, emotional participation. As the solitary poet sits in his apartment, drinks coffee in a café, and walks the streets of the city, he encounters, by observation or thought, slices of the city's life that become the occasions for poetic intervention. To the reader who takes Preil's poems as discreet instances without grasping the larger vocation of his poetry, these solitary occupations can readily seem like vacant indolence or the expression of a narcissistic preoccupation with the daily rituals of life or the self-indulgence of poetic fancy. But understood within the context of the poetry's ameliorative calling, the waiting and the walking betoken something very different: a stance of moral *disponibilité*, an existential availability for what may come his way.

Yet we should not hasten to view Preil as some urban Albert Schweitzer selflessly sacrificing himself for broken humanity. Even if writing a poem lifts the lot of others, it remains an act of self-realization and even self-transcendence for the poet. And the true and correct deployment of language in that act surely yields pleasure as well as purpose. As Preil enters the major phase of his career, his poetry displays greater confidence in balancing opposing poetic intentions and effects, or at least in negotiating their difference. Although the long contest between romanticism and imagism for his creative allegiance is never definitively decided, his poems are forged through an ongoing mediation between the two. This can be observed in the typically two-part structure of many of Preil's poems. The first part is a picture or an observation of the urban landscape, the weather or some feature of life in the city that suggests disuse, unfulfillment, or alienation or discloses seemingly disparate oppositions.[25] The second part of the poem attempts to effect a temporary measure of reconciliation or restoration. The resources of imagism—precision, concreteness, and defamiliarizing metaphors—are most drawn upon to do the work of description in the poem's initial premise. When it comes to the subsequent reparative or transformative move, as is evident in the poem analyzed below, it is the resources of the romantic imagination, or even the persistence of that desire, that are most often mobilized.[26]

The work of redemption is never completed, at least in this world. Although Preil's ameliorative ambitions remain steadfast in his later poetry, the focus of attention shifts from place to time. In titling the first comprehensive collection of his verse *Mitokh zeman venof* (1972), Preil understood that these were the two fundamental terms that define his poetic world. In the poetry published before this collection, especially in the poems devoted to New England and New York, the emphasis is placed on repairing the ruptures of place. Later on, the balance shifts to time. The poet is burdened by the gap between the belated time he is living in the present and the past, which, as we have seen in the case of his grandfather, is often the nineteenth-century Hebraism of his native Lithuania. Preil is the latest and greatest Hebrew bloom on American soil, and precisely because his poems seem so slight but accomplish so much, they will preoccupy us and nurture us for some time to come.

✳ גַּנֵּי אֱמֶת וְלַבָּה לְבָנָה
Gardens of Truth and White Lava

Analysis

גַּנֵּי אֱמֶת וְלַבָּה לְבָנָה

הַחוּץ כְּאִלּוּ לָמַד חָכְמַת הַגֵּיאוֹמֶטְרִיָּה הָעֶרֶב
וְקָבַע מְשֻׁלָּשׁ־אוֹרוֹת דַּק, מְפֻנָּן, קָטְבּוּ אֶבֶן־אָדָם,
הַקּוֹרֵעַ זָוִיּוֹת בְּמַרְאוֹת־מַיִם מִלְּמַטָּה, הַמְחַיֵּג מַרְאוֹת־שָׁמַיִם מִמַּעַל.
בֵּינֵיהֶן מְכוֹנִיּוֹת – קַוֵּי לַבָּה לְבָנָה, שׁוֹטֶפֶת וְאֵינָהּ קוֹפֵאת.
וּמֵעַבָרִים שְׁנַיִם צוֹבְאִים חַלּוֹנוֹת, תּוֹפְסִים רְבוּעֵי אֹפֶל מְפֻנָּס.
אַךְ בְּחֶדְרִי, עַל הַשֻּׁלְחָן, הָאוֹתִיּוֹת שֶׁבְּסֵפֶר עִבְרִי קַדְמוֹן נוֹצְצוֹת חֲרִישִׁית:
הֵן זֶה מִכְּבָר הִגִּיעוּ לְתִכְנוּן גְּשָׁרִים רַבִּים
וּתְהוֹמוֹת הַסָּפֵק הָיוּ לְגַנֵּי הָאֱמֶת.

Gardens of Truth and White Lava

It is as if the outside has learned the science of geometry this
      evening
and set up a delicate, pearl-like triangle of light with a carnelian
      point
that rips angles in the watery reflections below and rotates heavenly
      reflections downward from above.
Between them, automobiles—lines of white lava that flow and
      never freeze.
On both sides are arrayed banks of windows that seize rectangles
      of lamp-lit darkness.
But in my room on the table, the letters in an ancient Hebrew
      book sparkle silently:
Yes, for a long time now they have succeeded in planning many
      bridges,
and abysses of doubt have turned into gardens of truth.

"Ganei emet velabah levanah" is the third of seven short poems
comprising "Tsiyyurim miNew York" [New York sketches], which
appeared in Preil's third collection *Mappat 'erev* (1960, pp. 124–27).
The title makes a gesture in the direction of "Mitsiyyurei Maine,"
discussed above, which appeared in the second collection. The formulation of the titles, close but not exact, underscores the passage
from country to city between these two volumes, as well as the acute
revision of the ratio between romanticism and imagism in Preil's verse.

The poem divides into two unequal parts. Lines 1–5 describe the
play of lights in a nighttime urban scene as glimpsed from an apartment window. (The bridge is probably the George Washington Bridge,
with its arced strings of lights, which connects upper Manhattan to
the Palisades of New Jersey and would have been visible at night from
Preil's apartment in the Bronx.) Lines 6–8 describe the effects of the
Hebrew letters in a book lying open on a table in the apartment. The
rendering of the nighttime scene in the first part reflects the imagist
aspiration to convey an objective and precise word picture of a discreet and definable aspect of the external world through a carefully
deployed and sustained metaphor. The key term is geometry. The
cityscape of boulevards, buildings, street lights, and illuminated signs

is transposed into the figural abstractions of a cubist painting, thereby undergoing a thorough process of defamiliarization. The static, banal, and familiar components of the city at night are dissolved into geometric light forms that are thrown into a dynamic, even violent relationship to one another. The delicate, luminous triangle in line 2, which is already so abstracted that we cannot truly know the specific sources of the city lights that comprise it, tears and blunts the sharply defined angles by virtue of their reflection in the river below the bridge or in the pooling water on the streets and sidewalks. It further sets the reflections in the nighttime sky spinning. In the space between these lower and upper planes, the blur of the cars' headlights—finally an easily identifiable object—becomes lines of white lava whose molten, unstoppable streaming is beautiful in its distant abstract flow at the same time as it is vaguely threatening. On either side, finally, the windows of the buildings gather for war [*tsov'im*] and seize the rectangles of lamp-lit darkness.

The ominous tone of this picture, with its swirl of aggressive forces, is counterbalanced by the frame in which it is set and by a series of peculiar word choices. The whole scene, to begin with, is founded upon an "as if" [*ke'illu*] premise that invites the reader to undertake a thought experiment that reimagines the nocturnal scene transmogrified. Preil could have simply taken the word *ke'illu* out of the line and been left with an *implied* metaphor ("The outside learned . . .") that conformed more neatly to imagist protocols. The violence of the scene is thereby qualified by virtue of being placed in a heuristic frame of reference that exists at a remove from reality. Moreover, there is an antic quality to the metaphor itself: a personified "outside" has taken up the study of geometry and, although having begun that very evening, proceeds directly to transpose all the elements of the city vista according to this new wisdom. Can we also not see something of a joke in the opposition between the seething tensions of the night scene and the science of geometry with its ideal forms and implied rationality?

At the semantic level, playful and exotic echoes further serve to mitigate the hostile potential of the night scene. *Mufnan* in line 2 is—so far as I have been able to ascertain—a neologism coined by

Preil from the word for pearl/pearls in Hebrew: *peninah/peninim*.[27]
Employing a similar technique of deriving an adjective from a noun
by using one of the passive verb conjugations (nif'al and pu'al), Preil
takes *panas* [street light] (line 5) and turns it into *mefunas* [lamp-lit]
also, presumably, his invention. It is not difficult to parse the meaning
of these new coinages, but the competent Hebrew reader must still
pause for a moment to take them in. This is also the case with *mehayeg*
in line 3, which in modern Hebrew means to dial a telephone number;
it was formed from the root *hug*, to circle, to describe the action of
rotating the phone's dial. Preil takes this very ordinary but bounded
term and applies it strangely to the reflection in the nighttime sky.
Although all these are instances of the kind of license common in
modernist Hebrew poetry, its use here creates a kind of poetry effect
that makes us aware of the poet's linguistic resourcefulness and the
constructed nature of the poem's language. *Even-odem* at the end of
line 2 is not an invented word but a rare and exotic one. It is a red
semi-precious stone that is one of the twelve gems that made up the
breastplate of the high priest (Exodus 28:17 and 39:1); the gems would
light up in special combinations to communicate God's directives in
times of national crisis.[28] Again, if Preil had simply wanted to indicate
the color red, he had numerous options that did not evoke the ancient
cult and its modes of divination. An ancient or otherworldly ambience
is also hinted at by the use in line 2 of *mar'ot*, which can mean either
mirrors or visions; although the main sense in this context—which
is impressionistic in any case—is connected to the phenomenon of
reflection, hints of visionary experience are present as well.

To summarize: the main thrust of the first part of the poem is to
heighten the alienating power of the nighttime cityscape by defamiliarizing it, "making it new," and revealing the contending forces latent
within it. It will be the job of the second part of the poem to ameliorate this picture by offering an antidote to its harshness. Yet already
in the first part, we see signs of this redemptive ambition at work in
a series of devices that serve to leaven the bleakness of the scene. The
personification of the outdoors as a wayward student, the very premise
of this section, wittingly perpetrates the pathetic fallacy so basic to the
romantic code.

With the words, "But in my room" [*akh beḥedri*] in line 6, the shift to the second part of the poem is emphatically made. The "I" embedded in the possessive pronoun is the first sign of a human presence in the poem. Its sudden appearance deepens our awareness, retrospectively, of the fact that humanness of any sort, discounting the purely figurative trope of the geometry student, is utterly absent from the nighttime scene in the poem's fist part. The difference between the two parts is also the difference between outside and inside. The room with a table and a book on it constitute a private, human space that is entirely ordinary and unheroic; it is a space that is domesticated in reference to the world outside, but it is hardly domestic. It is only a room and not a house or home, yet it nonetheless has the power to stand as a bulwark against the non-human forces in the night streets beyond the window.

Line 6 is the longest in the poem, and it moves our attention from the room to the table and finally to the letters of the open book. The room is not just a habitation but a redoubt of literacy. The sparkling of the letters answers the phantasmagoric lights of the street scene outside. The violent profusion of light and darkness beyond the window contrasts with the restrained constancy of the light emitted by the twinkling letters, which resemble stars that have been relocated indoors. The fact that this is a silent twinkling reminds us that this is a poem based wholly on the sense of sight and one in which the auditory plays no role. The colon at the end of line 6 prepares us for a summary insight. This statement is prefaced by the emphatic interjection *hen* [Yes! or Indeed!], as if what is to follow needs to be reiterated or defended for the sake of others or for the sake of the speaker's own reassurance. This insight comes in the form of a gnomic utterance comprised of two short lines: For a long time now, we are told, these Hebrew letters have succeeded in planning many bridges, and, as a result of this bridge-making activity, the "abysses of doubt have turned into the gardens of truth."

In a poem sequence about New York, bridges cannot be an arbitrary symbol. The George Washington Bridge is the title and subject of the poem that follows next in "Tsiyyurim miNew York." Bridges represent the triumph of practical human ingenuity over the disabilities of nature; they overcome separation and enable the flow of people and goods. The *planning* of bridges betokens an activist and optimistic stance toward the possibility of overcoming gigantic obstacles. This is a process of long usage, the poem implies in a tone of familiarity and reliability, as if to make a contrast with the newly constructed urban world outside the window. The agent of all this planning and endeavoring, after all, is the Hebrew letters in the ancient book. Another poet might have infused these letters with the sentimentalized aura of Jewish tradition; but Preil neutralizes this prospect by presenting the letters to us in the guise of pragmatic engineers. The stress on their being *Hebrew* letters, moreover, sounds a subtle echo of the Hebraist insistence on the endurance of culture rather than religion.

Even though the letters may be presented as a sort of industrious corps of Hebrew engineers, their achievements are nothing less than stupendous, in the same way that the marvel of the completed Brooklyn Bridge in its time overcame the technical challenges posed by its building. Abysses of Despair have been turned into gardens of Truth. Nothing less! The addition of the definite article (**ha**safeq, **ha**'emet) makes these terms into allegorical figures that would usually seem out of place in the discourse of Preil's verse. *Tehom* [abyss] carries an unsettling sense of primordial chaos because of its use in Genesis 1 to represent the state of the universe before Creation. Doubt is the disease of modernity that reverses the work of Creation by questioning the possibility of divine purpose in the world. The abysses of Despair are allied to the nighttime cityscape beyond the window, where the constructed buildings, avenues, and street lights have devolved into a violent and alienating confusion of shapes and lights. This is a fallen world that all of us know, each in his or her own way. But what of gardens of Truth? It has been commonly observed of Dante's *Divine Comedy* that it is far easier for the reader to understand the depiction of Hell then to fathom the mysteries of Paradise. A garden is an enclave of domesticated nature, all the more so when it is a city garden like Central Park, which is the title of the sixth poem in "Tsiyyurim miNew York," although a trace of the Edenic garden is never absent.

"Gardens of Truth" sounds like a pastoral version of the sweet dream of reason or a figure in an allegorical drama by Luzzatto. It points to a notional reality about which we can only dream.

The transformation, even the transubstantiation, of what is into what should be is precisely the point of the poem's conclusion. Despite its brevity, the poem multiplies oppositions: indoors versus outdoors, light versus darkness, angles versus curves, playfulness versus danger, writing versus nature. As it produces oppositions, it works to mediate, contain, or resolve them. This is Preil's own version of the redemptive work of poetry, his own attachment to the romantic code in a Hebraic key. For does not he, romanticism's most belated offspring, belong to the gap-spanning tradition of Hebrew letters? The bridges the letters have planned have indeed come into being, but that world of truth exists only in the poem, and when the poet next walks the streets of the city or gazes out his window and takes in the unredeemed world before him, he will have to start all over again.

Part III   *American Vistas*

Introduction

Would American Hebrew literature be truly American? Would it report on the struggles of millions of immigrants from Eastern Europe to gain a foothold in the new land? Would it inform the Hebrew reader in Europe and Palestine of the strange wonders of America's storied history and its vast and varied reaches? These questions were pointedly directed to the members of the tiny community of Hebrew writers, all very young and recent immigrants themselves, which began to coalesce in the United States in the decade before World War I. The very existence of this nascent community came to the attention of the world of Hebrew letters because of the publication of two literary miscellanies: *Senunit* in 1910 and *Haderor* in 1911. (Both terms mean swallow and underscore the hopeful yet tentative nature of the new enterprise.) Because the young Hebraists lacked sufficient material to sustain an ongoing journal—this would not come until the founding of *Hatoren* in 1915—the occasional collection, and even then only under the editorship of the veteran Hebrew writer Reuven Brainin, was as much as they could manage at the time.

These publications elicited virtually no response from reviewers abroad, except for one deafening exception, which was voiced by Brenner. At the time, Brenner was the most highly regarded young writer of fiction in Hebrew literature, as well as one of its most distinguished and active critics. He had long been aware of the Hebraist activity in New York and maintained an ongoing correspondence with Persky, 357 one of its central personalities. Writing from Ottoman Palestine in the pages of *Ha'ahdut*, Brenner expresses delight in the existence of these miscellanies and the potential they open up for future Hebrew writing in America, despite the harsh assessment he offers of the quality of the contributions and Brainin's bombastic editorial style. The most fundamental critique, however, concerns what is missing. "A new literary publication," Brenner asserts, "must draw upon its own source, its own surroundings, and if it fails to do so it would better off not being established."[1] In Brenner's prescient eyes, the mass immigration of Jews to America was an event that was in the process of utterly transforming the Jewish people. From his fellow Hebrew writers in America, he therefore sought a penetrating understanding of this bewildering new milieu that went beyond the stereotypes of "bluff" and the "dollar" and the pious condemnations of vulgarity and spiritual poverty. In the pages of *Senunit* and *Haderor*, however, Brenner is dispirited to discover no genuine encounter with America. "Perhaps in fact the time has come," he opines, "to minimize the platitudes about devotion to the old-new [Hebrew] language and adoration of the national renaissance and instead to pay more attention to the depths of the experience of Jews in this new diaspora. Thereby some depth might be added to their lives, lives of work and community, by a literature worthy of its name."[2]

Brenner's call to the Americans to be more American was the opening salvo in a controversy about the quality and prospects of American Hebrew literature that heated up in the early 1920s with the publication of a series of harsh and probing articles by Yaakov Rabinowitz. As was discussed in Chapter 1, the responses to this critique on the part of young American Hebrew writers, especially Halkin, helped to crystallize an emerging self-definition of the enterprise of writing Hebrew literature in the New World. Among other items in his critique, Rabinowitz called for an engagement with the "American" America of Edgar Allen Poe, Harriet Beecher Stowe, Mark Twain, and Whitman at the same time as he demanded depictions of the newly Jewish America of immigrant neighborhoods and wandering peddlers.[3] What the vocation of Hebrew writing in America should or should not be is clear to Rabinowitz. It should not be merely a recycling of the same themes of displacement and loss that can be found in the poetry of a whole generation of young Hebrew writers scattered over Europe. The vocation of the American Hebrew project should be to discover America for the Hebrew reader, probe its depths, and make it part of the new national literature. The fact that already in 1910, only six years after his immigration to America, Benjamin Silkiner had published *Mul ohel Timurah*, his epic poem on the history of American Indians, meant to Rabinowitz that such a goal could indeed be accomplished and that it did not have to wait.

Although these expectations must have weighed heavily on the shoulders of the Americans, there was very little immediate response. Most of the poems dealt with in this part—the major poetic works on the subject of the Indians, New England, the Gold Rush, and African American culture—did not appear until the 1930s and 1940s and even later. This appeal for *ameriqa'iyyut*, the appropriation of American material, moreover, was a call that a number of the poets declined to hear altogether. Silberschlag, Schwartz, Friedland, and Feinstein evinced little interest in American lore and landscapes, and even Silkiner reverted to sensitive lyric verse after his early and monumental Indian poem. Although Regelson was a devoted interpreter and translator of American poetry, only a few poems in his oeuvre have an identifiably American setting. The case of Halkin's poetry is more complex but surprisingly similar. To be sure, Halkin translated *Call of the Wild* and *Leaves of Grass* and took on Jewish New York in the 1920s in his unfinished novel *'Ad mashber*. Yet when one probes some of the great poems that bear the names of North American places—Santa Barbara, California, the Michigan dunes, Yarmouth, Nova Scotia—one discovers that these locations serve merely as settings for transcendental experiences or historiosophical speculations that are unlocked by the isolated encounter with nature but possess no specific or necessary connection to place. In the final analysis, the argument that American Hebrew poetry strove to satisfy the demand for *ameriqa'iyyut* rests essentially on a small number of longer works by three poets: Lisitzky, Efros, and Preil.[4]

There are a number of reasons for this resistance. The most important, as was pointed out at the beginning of this study, was a perceived division of labor between poetry and prose. It was the prerogative of poetry to reflect on the soul's response to nature, love, and fate, whereas it was the duty of prose to represent the actuality of the individual's embeddedness in society. This division is well illustrated in the work of Halkin and Lisitzky, the two major poets who were also major prose writers.[5] And, it should be acknowledged, writers of American Hebrew fiction did in fact step up to the challenge of supplying *ameriqa'iyyut*, even if they did so unevenly and imperfectly, and in doing so diverted pressure from their poetical brethren. Yet for the great majority of the poets, who did not write fiction, the "Jewish street," the sweatshops, the dogged pursuit of business, the vagaries of acculturation were all phenomena in a grand spectacle about which they felt revulsion or disconnection or a principled conviction that these were matters beyond the ken of poetry.

Many poets balked even when the expectation was not to engage the vulgar Jewish present but to explore more exotic and distant American themes that had nothing to do with Jews and urban life. They did not want to be made responsible for purveying material about a culture that was not—or at least had not yet been made—their own. What was unassailably their own, they passionately felt, was at once more personal and universal. They wanted to be free to carry forward those themes of their immediate predecessors in Hebrew poetry—Bialik, Tchernichovsky, and Shneour—that spoke most deeply to their hearts: loneliness in a disenchanted universe, the thirst for human connection and the impossibility of love, the moments of beauty that break through quotidian existence, and the availability of nature as a prod to reflection and a source of transcendence. Why should the higher calling of poetry be traduced by demands for gritty actuality?

The several poets who applied themselves to American themes did so very much on their own terms. With one or two key exceptions, they said no to representing present-day America; they said no to representing life in the metropolis; and they said no to representing the lives of American Jews. They said yes to an America that was distant from the present and distant from the cities and was populated instead by Indians and African Americans who appeared to be entirely "other," that is, until they were looked at in a certain complex light.

This qualified affirmation, moreover, was made in their own time; rather than complying with the urgent expectations from abroad, they waited until they became sufficiently familiar with the American past to write about it coherently in Hebrew. Finally, they did it for their own reasons. They wanted to distinguish the contribution that Americans could make to the larger republic of Hebrew letters and widen the repertoire of Hebrew literature beyond its parochial core. In contrast to the dystopian spectacle of galloping acculturation among American Jews in the present, they sought out in the cavalcade of American historical experience examples of countervailing values that could give meaning to this new and fraught phase in the unfolding of the Jewish Diaspora. For some it was a matter of creative survival. As a form, the lyric poem, which had long served as a sensitive instrument for expressing the fluctuations of individual consciousness, had come to feel like an enclosure of solipsism, and it was only the more expansive and narrative forms of verse that could deliver the poet from himself and enable his verse to make a connection with others.

The major texts, in the small but significant "American" canon of American Hebrew poetry, focus on the following topics: (1) the plight of American Indians in different historical periods under the shadow of destruction (Silkiner, Efros, and Lisitzky); (2) the lives of Christian inhabitants of nineteenth-century rural settlements in their relationship to the Old Testament (Bavli, Preil); (3) the California Gold Rush as an emblem of American ambition and unrest (Efros); (4) the experience of African Americans in the South before and after Emancipation, also in their relationship to the Hebrew Bible (Lisitzky); and (5) New York City as the embodiment of modernity (Halevi, Preil). These are undoubtedly all important themes in American history and culture, but, given the relatively small number of works in evidence, the selection must be understood as necessarily very selective. The question that therefore must be asked in every instance is what drew the Hebrew poet to this particular subject. What service did he hope to provide to the wider world of Hebrew readers? What discreet aspects of America were fascinating enough and revelatory enough to shed light on the enterprise as a whole? Should the turn to the past be read as a recoiling from the present or as an alternative way of engaging the present? Finally, there is the question of Hebrew itself. How does America look different when it is reprocessed and reconstituted through this old-new "foreign" language?

The three Indian epics written in Hebrew surely serve as the flagship curiosities of American Hebrew literature. Indeed, who would
not agree that there is something wonderfully absurd about young
Jewish immigrants, recently arrived from Tsarist Russia, undertaking
to write huge narrative poems about Native Americans in the Hebrew
language? Over time, moreover, the three epics became a kind of
emblem for the entire enterprise of American Hebrew literature. As
Hebrew literature became Israeli literature and grew in depth and volume over the course of the twentieth century, the American moment
receded into the evermore distant margins. Even for literate and erudite Hebrew readers, it was often only the remembrance of these three
exotic texts, those strange Indian epics with their amusing titles, that
remained. It is not surprising that from a distance in time and space
it eventually appeared as if the creators of the texts had merged with
their subjects: both became the last of the last of the Mohicans.[1]

The three Indian epics are Silkiner's *Mul ohel Timurah* [Before the
tent of Timurah] (1910), Efros's *Vigvamim shoteqim* [Silent wigwams]
(1933), and Lisitzky's *Medurot do'akhot* [Dying campfires] (1937). As is
often the case with exotic objects viewed from afar, these three poems
have commonly been spoken of in one breath as if they are simply different iterations of the same idée fixe. On closer inspection, however,
it turns out that the poems are extremely different from one another
in regard to the style of their composition, the historical models upon
which they are based, and the contemporary dilemmas that each projects onto the lives of Native Americans who lived long ago. These
differences are presented in what follows. Yet it would be disingenuous

362

to argue that the very subject of American Indians was only an accidental commonality. Despite the differences, in fairness, it can be said
that all of the poems are driven by two similar concerns.

To begin with, by writing about the Indians, the American Hebrew
poets were seeking to discover and connect with the bedrock of originary Americanness. The America they encountered upon immigration
was wholly the construction of European colonization, and although
few hailed from those parts of Europe responsible for the settling of
the Americas, they wanted to uncover what was primordially authentic
in this new world. Because of where they came from, they were in
search of an America, moreover, that was pre-Christian, whether the
Christianity was the Roman Catholicism of the Conquistadors (contemporaneous with the Inquisition), the Dutch Reform of the first
settlers of New York, or the Presbyterianism of the New Englanders.
They furthermore wished to imagine the American landscape before
industrialization and before the proliferation of populous cities. It
was this distilled essence of America that the American Hebrew poets
wished to bring as an offering to the Hebrew readers of Palestine,
both as a way of justifying and distinguishing their remote location
from the emerging center and, perhaps, as a monitory reflection on
the very different kind of settlement taking place there. For all of these
reasons, the aboriginal world of the first Americans exerted a powerful, attractive force.

The second large concern was connected to the tragic fate of the
Indians. The great and proud native peoples of America had been
decimated by conquest, disease, and alcohol. It should not be surprising to find a fascination with the rise and fall of nations on the part of
the American Hebrew poets, who themselves were the descendents of
a great and proud people that had survived, so far, many threats to its
existence. The nationalist fervor of the nineteenth century in Europe
encouraged peoples to think of themselves as nations and to examine
the pageant of history for answers to the question of why some nations
prosper and others disappear. The American Hebrew poets did not
seize on the fate of the Indians as an emblem for the vicissitudes
of the Jewish people or as a figurative embodiment of the biblical
Lost Tribes. Yet they remained fascinated by the spectacle of the

vulnerability of peoples that had once possessed not only rich cultural integrity and tradition but also military will and prowess. The Indian epics were written at a time of great anxiety about the continuity and survival of the Jewish people by poets whose allegiance to Hebrew placed on their shoulders the mantle of national conscience. A dark shadow had fallen over European Jewry; the new Hebrew-speaking Yishuv was struggling to establish itself; and as for American Jewry, in whose midst they lived, there were growing indications that accelerated Americanization would hollow out the people from within. In this atmosphere of intense concern about the rise and erasure of nations, the story of the Indians and the lessons inferred from it were compelling.

*

It does not take much to imagine the perplexity of the customers who frequented Jerusalem's book shops when they examined the newly arrived copies of Silkiner's *Mul ohel Timurah*, which was printed and published in that city in 1910. The form of the poem was familiar, indeed perhaps too familiar and out of fashion; it was a *poema*, a long narrative, historical poem—fifteen hundred lines in fourteen cantos—on a serious subject and written in an elevated style. Although the vehicle was recognizable from the compendious compositions of the Haskalah, the content was most assuredly not: the life of an American Indian tribe and its exploitation and slaughter at the hands of Spanish conquerors. Not only the subject of this epic poem was exotic but so was its source. *Mul ohel Timurah* was the first book-length work of serious Hebrew literary prose or poetry to be written by an American. The combination of the disused form of the *poema*, the difficulty of the language, and the strangeness of Indians in Hebrew garb proved too much for almost all readers. Speaking of one of the major booksellers in Jerusalem, Brenner reports in a letter to Persky that "many readers entered his store, opened the book and began to read it but did not buy: 'We don't understand what he's saying.'"[2]

Silkiner had purposefully arranged for the publication of the book in Jerusalem because he foresaw a productive collaboration between the existing infrastructure for Hebrew printing there and the emerging Hebrew literary community in America and its financial resources. Silkiner was the most senior among the younger Hebraists in New York who championed the nationalist cause and supported the new Hebrew literature. He was also the most visionary and ambitious when it came to making plans for the establishment of a rich and productive Hebrew literary center in America. It was he who set up various publishing houses; spearheaded the drive to create *Hatoren*, the first sustained journal; and corresponded with Bialik about a grand plan for a series of translations into Hebrew of Shakespeare's major plays by different American Hebrew poets, a plan that indeed came to fruition over the next two decades.[3] The earliness of Silkiner's Indian epic, both in terms of his own immigration to America in 1904 and in terms of the inchoate state of the Hebraist activity in New York, is a significant fact. *Mul ohel Timurah* bears the markings of a willful foundational act that was meant to show the way and to demonstrate that such a thing could be done. Silkiner intended the poem to serve as a kind of "fact on the ground" that would challenge the airy and ambitious daydreaming of the young Hebraists by presenting them with a real and accomplished cultural act upon which to build.

It is rather stunning to consider that Silkiner completed the poem only five years after his arrival in America during the same period in which he was enduring the privations and upheavals of immigration, learning English, and completing his university studies to become a lawyer. During this brief and intense interval, it would hardly have been possible for Silkiner to master the historical and anthropological background of sixteenth-century Indian life and to make the American climates and landscapes his own. Although he worked up his material from such popular accounts as William H. Prescott's *The Conquest of Peru* (1847), the most Silkiner could do was to stitch together a synthetic picture of Indian religion and culture that drew on features from different tribes, locales, and periods. The lack of authenticity and verisimilitude was criticized by none other than the young Harry Wolfson, who would later become the great Harvard professor and doyen of medieval Jewish philosophy. Writing in Hebrew in the pages of *Haderor*, Wolfson called Silkiner's poem to task for the prevalence of stereotypical characters and stock descriptions that made it impossible to locate the characters in a specific time and place.[4] This was less a literary deficiency—Wolfson acknowledged the many impressive passages in the poem—than a failure to grasp and internalize the American materials.[5]

The critique is undoubtedly valid, but it misses a main point about *Mul ohel Timurah*. In composing an ambitious poem about American Indians only five years after coming to these shores from Russia as a young Hebraist intent on cultural activism, Silkiner could not *not* make his epic into a screen upon which were projected the deepest concerns of his heart and mind. The fate of European Jewry after the pogroms in Russia, the prospect of cultural assimilation in America, the pride and loneliness of the young Hebraist, the conflict between personal fulfillment and duty to the collective—all these pressing anxieties and dilemmas could, of necessity, not be left out of any large and serious artistic project. They constituted what we would call today Silkiner's subject position. In his sincere exertions to represent the Other in the form of the experience of Native Americans and to bring that into the world of Hebrew literature, Silkiner could approach the task only out of the truth of his own identity. Silkiner's central accomplishment in *Mul ohel Timurah* is to fashion a set of central conflicts that work on both levels, as figures of the fate of the Indian peoples *and* as expressions of anxiety concerning the fate of the Jewish people.

Mul ohel Timurah is the story of the Silent Tribe, its chief Mugiral, and the tragic encounter with the Spanish conquerors. This main narrative is enclosed within a nominal frame structure (cantos I and XIV) in which an aged Indian Timurah, who gives the epic its name, relates to his daughter the story of Mugiral, now a bent and wizened old man on the brink of death, who has appeared at their tent. For generations, the Silent Tribe had lived in peace and tranquility in the rich Jacinth Valley between the sea and the mountains. They worshiped the Great Spirit, the god Elnefesh, to whom they offered a yearly sacrifice of one randomly chosen member of the tribe. The blood of the sacrifice seeped into the ground at the base of the Red Rock, and when a white flower blossoms a few days later, the tribes know that the sacrifice has been accepted and that the coming year would be one of prosperity. This harmony is disturbed by the arrival of the Spaniards, who are first greeted with innocent hospitality by the Silent Tribe. Potera, the Spanish commandant, covets a horse that belongs to one of the Indian braves, and when it comes to the annual sacrifice, Potera uses slander to persuade the tribe's chief, against the sacred custom of random selection, to designate the horse's owner as the cultic victim. The corrupted sacrifice is not accepted by the Great Spirit, and a punishing drought is visited upon the tribe. In return for bread, the members of the tribe indenture themselves to the Spaniards and agree to dig up the valley for hidden gems, which mean nothing to them but feed the insatiable greed of the Europeans.

It is at this point that Mugiral, who has been supernaturally hidden since birth, reveals himself and becomes the militant leader of the tribe. The first step in the path of resistance that he advocates is to dig up the valley again, but this time for iron to make weapons instead of for gems. In an armed conflict with the Spaniards, the tribe's temple is destroyed together with the statue of Elnefesh. The only religious artist capable of recreating the figure and its enigmatic smile is Eiztima, whose origin and mission also have a supernatural cast. He succeeds Tomiya as priest and takes up a position of purity and prayer wholly opposed to Mugiral's policy of total armed resistance. He pays with his life when he stumbles and breaks his neck at the same time as the statue of Elnefesh is toppled in anger by Mugiral. On the eve of the decisive encounter between the tribe and the Spaniards, Mugiral is lured away from the valley by a beautiful and mysterious maiden who invites him to leave with her for the Palace of Joy where they will live forever as lovers. At first he protests that he will remain and fight to the death alongside his people, but eventually he gives in and accompanies her. The woman is suddenly transformed into an ugly old hag who draws back the veil of distance to reveal the blood of his fallen countrymen beneath the uncaring snow and the spiteful rejoicing of the Spaniards in their newly constructed church. Sickened and ashamed, Mugiral draws his sword on the woman, who has escaped into the mist to sow her evil in another valley. All that is left of the Silent Tribe is the story that Timurah tells his daughter before his tent at twilight.

It should be said at the outset that Silkiner's Indian epic is not an allegory for the fate of the Jewish people. As a cosmopolitan mercantile people that has survived attempts to obliterate it, that possesses a sophisticated written tradition, and that maintained its cultural identity despite global dispersion, the Jews are emphatically not the Indians. Nevertheless, as refracted through Silkiner's contemporary Hebraic literary imagination, telling the story of the first Americans becomes a way of pondering the future of the most recent Americans and their brethren abroad. The conflicts and anxieties dramatized in the poem can be considered fraternal rather than universal in the sense that they pertain to points of connection between these two nations rather than to truths that apply to all peoples. One people is ancient and, in the course of the poem, becomes broken and decimated. The other people is ancient but surviving under adversity and striving to create shoots of new life. *Mul ohel Timurah* is at one and the same time an act of empathic understanding toward the other and an exigent attempt to gain knowledge and draw lessons for the self.

When it comes to the fate of nations, alas, the lessons drawn are unrelievedly bleak. *Mul ohel Timurah* chronicles the rise and fall of several peoples. In their possession of the blessed Jacinth Valley, the Silent Tribe succeeds the Tribe of the Rocks, which has passed out of existence. The evil witch at the end of the poem proceeds on to other valleys where she will impose her blight of defeat and erasure. Before the arms and wiles of the Spaniards, the aboriginal innocence of the Indians lies wholly exposed and defenseless. In the shadow of catastrophe, the conflict between Mugiral and Eiztima is distinctly resonant with biblical contests between kings and prophets (David and Nathan, Zedekiah and Jeremiah) and between the zealots and the Rabbis in Jerusalem at the end of the resistance to Rome. Silkiner's insistence on balancing our sympathies between the chief and the priest is one of the strongest achievements of the poem. Mugiral's call to total violent resistance seems at one moment to be the only possible self-respecting response to the crisis; yet at another moment, his demand to dismantle the stones of the temple and use them to construct a fortress goes too far and provokes us to attend to Eitzima's argument that to vitiate the tribe's communion with the Great Spirit is to concede victory to the enemy. The Hebrew reader of the day could not take in this confrontation without thinking about the contest between Herzl and Aḥad Ha'am, about the Kishinev pogrom and the pogroms that followed it, and about Bialik's famous poem "In the City of Slaughter" and the controversy it provoked. All of these contemporary associations functioned primarily not to judaize the Indians but to provide a familiar and exigent lens through which these ancient and exotic struggles could become real.

The Edenic harmony of the Silent Tribe's life in the Jacinth Valley before the entanglement with the Spaniards is presented as the essence of America ab ovo. Like the other Indian epics in the American Hebrew canon, *Mul ohel Timurah* strives to retrieve a pristine image of America before the land was degraded and before European settlement and the building of cities. The Indians work the land and live on the land and from the land, but they do not penetrate it until they are forced, first, to dig up the earth for gems to trade for food and, then, persuaded by Mugiral to excavate iron to arm themselves. The religious life of the tribe is also presented as simple, pure, and essential. The rapport with the Great Spirit and its protection is achieved by a natural faith and a minimum of ritual and ceremony. The yearly sacrifice concentrates the need for violence and propitiation into a single regulated act. For the Hebraist reader, who had disburdened himself of the heavy weight of Orthodox formalism, there must have been enormous appeal in the vision of a life imbued by spirit yet unencumbered by the minutiae of ritual. The hieratic ritualism and hypocritical triumphalism of the Spaniards' Catholicism, mutatis mutandis, was another expression of the corruption of religion. This was the same church whose inquisitorial zeal was pursuing the conversos on the Iberian Peninsula at the very same time.

One of the preeminent themes of Hebrew literature at the turn of the twentieth century is the predicament of the uprooted individual who, once released from the constraints of traditional life, must decide whether to remain true to his people or to pursue personal fulfillment

by seizing the opportunities now open to him in Western society. For
the young Hebraist in New York in the years before World War I,
those opportunities must have seemed vast; and devotion to the cause
of Hebrew culture in America, despite an abundance of ideological
enthusiasm, must have been a lonely path. It is not surprising, then,
that one of the most moving sections of *Mul ohel Timurah* is the scene
in the thirteenth canto when Mugiral allows himself to be seduced
into abandoning his tribe at the decisive hour of its fate. In its romantic and operatic realization, moreover, it is a scene that must have
originated wholly from Silkiner's imagination rather than from the
historical sources he used as an inspiration. The following exchange
takes place on the evening of the final battle with the Spaniards.
The beautiful mystery maiden has asked Mugiral to accompany her
that evening on a journey to the Temple of Happiness, where they
will elude death and she will share her love for him forever. Mugiral
responds:

"לַעֲזוֹב אֶת שִׁבְטִי אֵיךְ אוּכָל, עֵת יַחְתֹּם יוֹם נוֹלַד גּוֹרָלוֹ?"
עָנְתָה – וְקוֹלָהּ הִתְגַּבֵּר –: "כְּבָר נֶחְתַּם הַגּוֹרָל: בֵּין 'יַלְדֵי־
הַשֶּׁמֶשׁ' וְחַיְתוֹ־הַשָּׂדֶה וְעוֹף־הַשָּׁמַיִם יֵחָלְקוּ –
קוּמָה, מֻגְרָל, נֵלֵכָה!" הֱלִבִּינוּ אָז פָּנָיו וַיֹּאחַז
בְּיָדָהּ וַיִּרְעַד אֶת קוֹלוֹ: "עִמָּם – אֹבֵדָה, וְחֶרְפַּת־
עוֹלָם בַּל־תִּמָּח לַחֲרָדָה נֶעֱרָצָה בְּמוֹתִי אֲהַפֵּךְ."
הִשְׁפִּילָה אֶת קוֹלָהּ וַתִּלְחַשׁ: "כּוֹכְבֵי־הַזָּהָב לֹא יָדְעוּ
מְאוּמָה מִמּוֹתְךָ, וְאַחֲרִיתְךָ לֹא יִתַּנֶּה יָם אַדִּיר בִּשְׁאוֹנוֹ –
תֵּן לִי אֶת יָדְךָ וְנֵלֵךְ בְּטֶרֶם יוֹם נוֹרָא יוֹפִיעַ."

"How can I desert my tribe at the moment their fate is being
   sealed?"
She answered, her voice growing stronger: "Their fate is already
   sealed: Between the Children
Of the Sun [the Spaniards] and the beasts of the field and birds of
   the heavens [their bodies] will be divided—
Arise, Mugiral, and let us depart." He blanched and clutched
Her hand, his voice trembling: "With them shall I perish,
And by my death let indelible eternal shame be exchanged for
   exalted awe.

She lowered her voice and whispered: "The golden stars will know
Nothing of your death, nor will your end be mourned
by the mighty sea in its roaring.
Give me your hand and let us go before the dawn of this fateful
    day."

And he does go with her, only to discover her hideous transformation and the deceitfulness of her promise. Mugiral's first response to
the maiden's seductions is proudly to invoke the code of the warrior
and commander. He will fall with his people rather than live igno-
miniously; his commitment to the collective is seemingly unshakable.
Yet this noble renunciation is shown to rest precariously on a set of
assumptions about cosmic repute and collective memory. Once she
reveals to him—and he unquestioningly accepts—that not only will
his slaughtered tribe be unable to honor his memory but that the
very forces of the universe will be indifferent to his sacrifice, his high
resolve collapses, and he submits himself to a dispirited act of shameful betrayal. When added to the genocidal fury of the Spaniards,
Mugiral's capitulation would make *Mul ohel Timurah* a wholly bleak
work were it not for the frame story with its eponymous Timurah.
Mugiral's story and the chronicle of the Silent Tribe as a whole, as
Michael Weingrad has pointed out, are not entirely lost to memory.
They persist as a tale told by the aged Indian to his daughter, and
they are thereby granted that modicum of redemption from oblivion.
The fact that all this is ultimately a tale told by a Jewish poet in the
Hebrew language is a knot of ironies perhaps too tangled to untie.

   Although genuinely affecting in dramatic terms, the exchange between Mugiral and the sinister maiden is composed in a Hebrew that
would have already been experienced as stilted when the poem first
appeared in 1910, not to mention when it was republished in revised
form in 1927. Silkiner was a teacher of Hebrew Bible and wholly immersed in the language of Scripture; his taste and temperament drew
him to poetic models that preceded the age of national awakening in
which he lived. Bialik and Tchernichovsky, the great exemplars of the
new Hebrew poetry, had broken the classicist mold of biblical Hebrew,
which had been the Haskalah ideal, and introduced a more flexible
idiom that drew on later layers of the language.

In this regard, Silkiner was far more conservative than American Hebrew poetry in general. Whereas many of the American poets were criticized by their counterparts in Palestine for cleaving to the norms of Bialik and Tchernichovsky, Silkiner's aesthetic bond connected him to the literary generation that preceded them. He must have believed that this mode was especially suited to the writing of a *poema* with its high moral seriousness and extensive exposition. There are, to be sure, moments in *Mul ohel Timurah* when Silkiner's biblicism serves his purposes well. For example, when the seductive maiden murmurs in Mugiral's ear about the indifference of the universe to his sacrifice, the use of Haskalah conventions succeed in conveying a crisp Miltonic portentousness. Using the periphrasis-like construct *kokhvei-hazahav*, "the stars of gold," instead of "the golden stars" provides an appropriate nuance of mystery to the concept of the twinkling of stellar light. The canny use of parallelism—deployed here in its chiastic variant—underscores the atmosphere of fatefulness. The image of the mighty sea drowning out the echo of the warrior's death is not a mechanical repetition of the image of the insensibility of the stars; rather, it deepens the awful prospect of gratuitous death by extending it to a different dimension of the cosmos and to the more concrete realm of sound.

Yet there are unfortunately as many instances where the awkwardness of diction and syntax do not serve the sense of the poem. For example, when Mugiral makes his high-minded declaration that he would rather fall with his brethren than bring shame upon his name, the syntax makes parsing the idea difficult indeed. Hewing to a biblical stylistic model in modern Hebrew verse was far from being a recipe for failure. For instance, in Y. L. Gordon's *Tsidqiyahu beveit hapequdot* [Zedekiah in prison] (1879), a poem on the king-prophet conflict that likely influenced Silkiner, the biblical style is dynamic and incisively dramatic. Silkiner was, alas, not possessed of the same gift, and the language of his long poem proved an obstacle to many readers. The difficulty was acknowledged by the poet himself by his willingness to allow his younger poet colleagues, Halkin and Ginzburg, both of whom revered Silkiner, to assist him in modernizing the syntax of the poem with an eye to relieving its cumbersomeness and preparing a new text for the collected edition of his verse that appeared in 1927. The revision was helpful but not much more than cosmetic. In the final analysis, then, the reader is left with a deeply divided experience of *Mul ohel Timurah*. There is the issue of verisimilitude regarding all things Indian, which can be put aside, as I have argued, if we accept the fact that Silkiner is encountering Native Americans from within the lived crisis of Jewish culture. These contemporary anxieties in fact serve to create an empathic depth of feeling in many of the central scenes of the epic. Access to the power and truth of these moments, however, is often blocked by the difficulties of a language that is arrested in an earlier era.

Silkiner's stylistic predicament is in fact part of a larger problem that runs throughout most all of the ambitious Hebrew works about America: How does the poet neutralize the Judaic component inherent in Hebrew when representing the lives of non-Jews? It goes without saying that modern Hebrew evolved out of the language of the Hebrew Bible and the Mishnah and the midrashim. For the poets of the revival period [*tehiyyah*] like Bialik, the latent presence of these past layers offered an unparalleled opportunity for ironic reflection on the tensions and inversions in the experience of a generation of young Jews after the collapse of tradition. Yet for Hebrew writers in America who sought to write persuasively about the Indians and other American originals, the near-irrepressibility of the classical Judaic basis of Hebrew presented a stiff challenge. How could Hebrew be made strange in the ears of readers who prized its hoary familiarity? It was not desirable to have Indian braves sounding as if they were Israelite chieftains stepping out of the pages of the book of Judges. The challenge took on a particular coloration for poets like Bavli and Lisitzky, as we shall see, who wrote about American groups—the old Protestant stock of New England and the Catskills and the African Americans of the South—for whom the Hebrew Bible in its classic English translations served as a primary source for the content and cadences of preaching and prayer and self-reflection. When Lisitzky sought to re-present in Hebrew the sermon of a black minister that adapts the story of Moses, Miriam, and Tsipporah to African American life, the poet had to negotiate a thicket of problems involving the register of Hebrew in its many inflections.

✳

It was not until twenty-three years after the publication of Silkiner's Indian epic that American Hebrew poetry undertook a major engagement with American history, and, again, the object of fascination was the first Americans. Efros's *Vigvamim shoteqim* and Lisitzky's *Medurot do'akhot*, each in its own way, returned to the glory and the tragedy of the Indians, and, with Silkiner's epic, joined together to present a forceful rejoinder to the calls from abroad for *ameriqa'iyyut*. What could be more archetypally American?

A quarter century, which is the time it took for this response to crystallize, is not a small interval in the life of a young literary culture. During this time, the Hebraists put their definitive stamp on Jewish education in the large Jewish communities throughout the East and Midwest and even founded a series of Hebrew teachers colleges. Several Hebrew literary journals had been created (*Hatoren* and *Miqlat*), and *Hado'ar*, begun as a daily, had settled into its long weekly run as the flagship of the movement. Dozens of Hebrew writers were publishing their poems and stories here and abroad. Therefore, when in 1933 Efros returned to the Indian theme in *Vigvamim shoteqim*, he was writing from within a culture that had picked up considerable substance and identity and deepened its familiarity with America. Comparing Silkiner's Indian poem with Efros's makes evident just how much ground was covered.

The sense of place in *Mul ohel Timurah* is mythic and stylized. It is not important for us to read the physiognomy of the landscape, which may as likely be located in Peru as in North America. In *Vigvamim shoteqim*, by contrast, the narrator is at pains to explain to us the exact location of the action on the eastern shore of what would later become the state of Maryland near the English settlement of Talbot and the exact location of the Nanticoke Indians who lived there and formed part of the Algonquin Nation. These tranquil woodlands surrounding the Chesapeake Estuary are not an imagined historical space, as Efros reveals in a prefatory note to the poem, but a place that is invested with personal meaning. A further degree of personal proximity is conveyed by the fact that it is the English rather than the Spaniards who are the European antagonists of the Indians. The devious inquisitorial greed of the Spaniards in Silkiner's poem is equally repulsive to American and Jewish sensibilities, but it is very far in the past. In Efros's poem, however, the mother culture of the English settlers, with its bitter conflict between class privilege and artistic individuality, is much closer to the residual values in the public educational system that East European Jews found when they arrived in America as immigrants.

The newness and nativeness of *Vigvamim shoteqim* are evident in the way it is written. Whereas Silkiner was consciously emulating the ponderous Russian-inspired *poema*, Efros called his work simply "a poem." More specifically, it is a long narrative poem that gestures to the kind of story poems written by Edward Arlington Robinson, an American poet much admired by Efros. In moving the narrative along, there is no place for unnecessary decorative language and tortuous or obscure side plots. At the semantic and syntactic level, the kind of poetic line Efros is writing is so simplified and streamlined in relation to Silkiner that it is hard to imagine that only twenty-three years separate the two. Of all the Americans, Efros strove the most to lighten the poetic language of the great poets of the revival period and to disencumber it of its allusive weight. In the larger construction of Efros's narrative language, Weingrad is right to observe, there is likely the influence of the cinema, the great preoccupation of the immigrant youth culture.[6] On the other hand, one can think of the speeches of Mugiral in *Mul ohel Timurah*—and not badly—only in terms of opera.

The plot of *Vigvamim shoteqim* centers on the relationship between Tom and Lalari. Tom is an impoverished English artist who has come to the colonies to seek his fortune. But his sensitive, taciturn nature provokes some of the loutish youth of Talbot, and he is severely injured when they tie him to a horse and drag him through the woods. Found by a local Indian hunting party, he is brought before the sachem [leader] of the village, who, instead of allowing the braves to take his scalp, puts his daughter Lalari in charge of nursing him back to health. During his convalescence, he returns to his painting and produces pictures of Indian life. Viewing these visual representations of themselves is a novel, if pleasing, experience for his hosts. Gradually, Tom and Lalari fall in love. He is drawn to her beauty and her self-sufficiency; she has an unusual capacity for solitariness and is given to extended retreats in the woods. She is drawn to his extravagantly blond hair and his creativity as a painter; he evinces a capacity for wordless communion that makes him a match for her own inwardness.

Tom and Lalari go off to another village to live together and to escape the jealousy of a brave who has long been in love with Lalari. Their idyll is short lived. Not painting and at loose ends, Tom begins to drift away from Lalari as he returns in his memories to a beautiful, well-born young woman to whom he had been engaged in England. Prevented from marrying her because of his poverty, he had set off to the New World to acquire the wealth necessary to establish his worthiness. Tom remains in thrall to these memories, and once Lalari discovers the divided state of his affections, she selflessly shows him where he can obtain gold from the wreck of an old Spanish galleon and then disappears. Tom returns to England, and Lalari discovers that she is pregnant. In the meantime, the old sachem reveals to her that Lalari is in fact not his daughter but the offspring of an adulterous union between his wife and a white man who abandoned her. Lalari gives birth but the baby is stillborn. Tom has returned from London in the meantime, where he found that his intended had married another. Having dissipated his gold, he has come back to rekindle his relationship with Lalari. He returns in time to witness from a distance the funeral rites for Lalari, who has taken her own life as had her mother before her.

Some contemporary readers objected to the melodramatic conventions of *Vigvamim shoteqim*, which they saw as deriving from celluloid depictions in popular culture rather than from the historical sources of Native American life, of which there was a vast literature. Despite the poem's intimate and accurate connection to place, it displays little interest in verisimilitude when it comes to the realia of Indian daily life, and it declines to draw authentic materials from the corpus of Indian myth and storytelling. Tom and Lalari's story is made of whole cloth; there is nothing resembling it in the collections of Indian lore.

In turning away from epic toward narrative, moreover, Efros encouraged the kind of expectation of psychological realism that comes with
novelistic truth. Yet readers found some plot developments insuffi-
ciently motivated (Tom's attack by the townspeople of Talbot, the
sachem's unaccountable sparing of his life), and they felt credulity
strained by the prospect of an illiterate Indian girl with an elaborately
philosophical inner life.[7]

Some of the sharpest criticism was lodged by a fellow American
Hebrew poet Lisitzky, who was to publish the other great Hebrew
Indian epic four years later. Precisely because the Indians were so
naturally fascinating a subject for American Hebrew writers, he took
it for granted that the writer's first obligation is to accurately portray
Indian life and lore. The obligation is not only to the material itself
but to the very institution of Hebrew literature, which is counting on
the Americans to make their contribution from their outpost in the
New World. On this score, there is no doubt that Efros's poem comes
up short. The possibility that Lisitzky could not account for was this:
Efros might be mining the Indian material for very different purposes,
and perhaps opportunistically, but with no intention of being negli-
gent, he was using the Indian setting as a backdrop for dramatizing
a set of ideas about silence, language, and loss. At an important level,
Vigvamim shoteqim is much more about the aesthetic options confronting the future of Hebrew poetry in the twentieth century than it
is about the tragic fate of a brave aboriginal people.

Silence is the over-determined theme of *Vigvamim shoteqim* that
fashions its symbolic order and makes sense of its instances of awkwardness. The purest distillation of silence is embodied in Lalari's
capacity for solitary contemplation.

לִפְתֹּחַ אֶת דֶּלֶת לְבָבָהּ בַּחֲשַׁאי,
הִכָּנֵס עַל בְּהוֹנוֹת רַגְלֶיהָ וְשֶׁבֶת
לְשָׁעוֹת רְצוּפוֹת בַּחֶדֶר הַדְּמָמָה
בְּסוֹד שְׂעִפִּים וַהֲגִיגִים הַשּׁוֹתְקִים וְצוֹפִים.
גַּם יֵשׁ אֲשֶׁר עָזְבָה אֶת בֵּיתָהּ וַתִּפְרֹשׂ
לְחֻרְשׁוֹת וִיעָרִים לְיָמִים אוֹ שָׁבוּעוֹת
לְהִתְבּוֹדֵד עִם עַצְמָהּ וְעִם הָעוֹלָם הַחֲרִישִׁי.

She was long used to opening the door to her heart without a
     sound,
entering on tiptoe and sitting
for many hours in the silent chamber
in the mysterious company of thoughts and musings that remained
     wordlessly attentive.
There were also times when she left her home and lit out
for the trees and forests for days or even weeks
in order to be alone with herself and with the silent world.

Now, it was easy enough for Lisitzky to ridicule Efros for placing the sophisticated mind of a pantheist inside the body of a preliterate Indian maiden. And, indeed, Lalari sometimes comes off as a cross between a Zen master and a Buberian Hasidic rebbe. But Efros is less concerned with the dramatic credibility of his characters than with the philosophical possibilities they can dramatize. What is remarkable about Lalari's capacity for sustained communion with nature is the very fact that it is wordless, and, quite literally, preliterate. She has not worked out a philosophical position called pantheism, which she is now implementing as a spiritual practice. Rather, in Efros's imagining of primitive experience, she is already intuitively lodged in the space that a pantheist, after much speculative searching, might hope to inhabit. It is, moreover, a distinctively American space that is influenced in its conceptions less by continental thought than by the Transcendentalism of the Hudson School. It is a transcendentalism that has been purged of its Emersonian will and self and returned, purified as it were, to its first, native practitioners.

It is this secret font of silence that Tom finds restorative when he is recovering from his wounds among the Indians. In response to the quiet attention to nature he observes in Lalari and others, his long-suppressed artistic impulses are revived, and he is reborn as an artist, but with a native difference. He fabricates his pigments from local herbs and minerals; and to fashion a paint brush, he plucks hairs from his own extravagantly grown blond locks. The landscapes and scenes of Indian life that now flow unstintingly from his brush are first viewed by his hosts with suspicion but then with amusement and finally with some wonder. Even though his art has been recast by its immersion in nature, Tom is aware that the representational capacities of Western art are far different from the aboriginal sublime. The Indians appreciate the cleverness of his inventions; however, despite the fascination of seeing themselves depicted, his art remains alien to their lives.

For his part, Tom offers his art as a kind of anticipatory compensation for the destruction of Indian civilization that he sees as an inevitable fate though still in its early stages. Integral to the "secret of silence," which is the crown of the Indians' intuitive spirituality, is a receptive stance toward nature that seeks to live alongside the world rather than to dominate it. In the face of the world-shaping will of the European colonizers, however, this receptiveness becomes a life-threatening vulnerability. Even though the Indians are capable of effective organization against local threats, they have nothing in their experience that allows them truly to grasp the systemic and fundamental nature of the threat. With a kind of postcolonial foresight and guilt, Tom imagines the time when Indian life will have been so obliterated that to repair the damage "from sea to sea sanctuaries will arise / to rescue your beautiful objects, to collect them and preserve them." Yet precisely because the supreme achievements of Indian civilization are spiritual, all that will fill these belated museums are "blankets and wampum, colored feathers, / pairs of moccasins and nothing more, nothing more" (p. 37); hence, in a small but heartfelt way, the gift of representation embodied in his own paintings of Indian life.[8]

Now, given Tom's artistic vision and his empathic understanding of the Indians' situation, why can he not sustain his fidelity to Lalari? His own taciturn inwardness, which provoked the ire of his countrymen, should have made him the perfect match for Lalari, the virtuoso of silence. Observing Tom's restiveness with helpless despair after they have lived together as man and wife, Lalari homes in on the precise problem.

תָּם, אַתָּה שַׁתְקָן וַאֲנַחְנוּ שַׁתְקָנִים.
אַךְ נִדְמֶה שְׁתִיקָה לִשְׁתִיקָה לֹא דּוֹמָה.
שׁוּר! הַכֹּל שׁוֹתֵק. הַשֶּׁמֶשׁ מִמַּעַל,
הָאִילָן הַמְלַבְלֵב, הָעֵשֶׂב הַמּוֹרִיק,

הָהָר, הַצִּפֹּרֶת, הַבְּעִיר, כָּל הָעוֹלָם –
שִׁמְעוּ! הַכֹּל יַמְשִׁיךְ קִיּוּמוֹ בִּשְׁתִיקָה.
כַּךְ שׁוֹתְקִים גַּם אָנוּ אִם נִחְיֶה אִם נִגְוַע.
וְאוּלָם לֹא אַתָּה, הַשְּׁתִיקָה שֶׁלְּךָ
חוֹנֶקֶת דְּבַר־מָה שֶׁעַל אַפָּה הוּא צוֹעֵק.

Tom, you are reticent and we are both reticent people.
But these two kinds of silence are not alike.
Look! All is silent. The sun above,
the blossoming tree, the greening grass,
the mountain, the bird, the cattle, the whole world.
Hear! All things abide their existence in silence.
So shall we be silent whether we live or die.
Yet not you. Your silence
Strangles something that seeks to cry out.

Tom's silence is repression masquerading as resignation. It is a lid that has been tamped into place to cover painful memories of abasements and abjections. It is not mere personal weakness that is at the root of Tom's failure; for despite his exceptional status as an artist, he cannot escape the limits of self that have been imprinted upon him by the civilization to which he belongs. The sovereign desires of the self, the need for wealth and status, romantic love, the urge to explore, expand, invent—all these foundations of Western man cannot be extirpated and rolled back into a primeval innocence.

Lalari herself is no less a creature of the culture into which she has been born, but hers is a worldview that allows for a way out that is not open to Tom. Lalari's noble and unexamined primitivism grants her a saving communion with the physical universe. She does not view her own being as separate in kind from the trees and the animals but rather as an expression of the undifferentiated Great Spirit that animates the world. Both the suffering she endures as an individual as a result of Tom's betrayal and the defeat her people experience at the hands of the British settlers are sources of great pain, but they are not ultimate facts. Her spirit and the spirits of her people will be reabsorbed into the cosmos rather than being broken down and annihilated. The quietism that results from this belief is knowingly accepted.

When Tom gives Lalari a painting depicting the plight of her people, she examines it and says, simply: "Yes, I understand.[. . .], / Here we sit sunset facing sunset [*sheqi'ah mul sheqi'ah*], / the sunset of a people facing the setting of the sun. / Have I understood correctly?" (p. 37). *Sheqi'ah* means both sunset and decline. Lalari's resignation is wide-eyed not only because of the futility of resistance but because resistance would mean traducing her being and alienating herself from the source of life. Her suicide at the end of the poem, which was criticized as a piece of gratuitous melodrama, becomes a coherent act when construed as a return rather than a gesture of despair.

Loss and the compensations for loss are subjects that seem to have weighed heavily on Efros's mind in composing *Vigvamim shoteqim*. In the beginning of a prefatory note to the poem, Efros cryptically states: "Sunny and serene are the fields of Maryland. For someone who loved them very much but was forced by a double catastrophe to flee to a distant, cold city because the ground produced painful memories and scorched the souls of his feet, is it any wonder that he should wish to return to them at least in verse?" We know from the events of Efros's life that the double catastrophe was the death of both of his much beloved parents within a short time of each other.[9] The immigrant family had moved from New York to Baltimore and had quickly fallen in love with America and with the Chesapeake Bay area. The cold and remote city is Buffalo, New York; the actually writing of the poem took place, the introductory note goes on to relate, over two summers on the beaches of one of the New England islands. The writing of the poem becomes a means of obtaining restitution for the loss of place and the loss of love. In this quest the latter is absorbed into the former; that is to say, Maryland, as a construction, is invested with the nurturing beneficence associated with the parents. The beautiful and plangent opening lines of the poem present Maryland as a kind of *omphulus mundi*, an earthly site connecting to Heaven in which all contradictions are reconciled and transcended: north and south meet, the fierceness of winter and the scorch of summer are both tempered, ocean water and fresh water mix happily in a vast estuary, and the earth brings forth all manner of good things. That a Diaspora location of such Edenic plenitude should be extolled in a Hebrew poem in the

1930s, with the upheavals in Europe and the struggles to secure the Yishuv, should not pass unnoticed.

The preface to *Vigvamim shoteqim* has one more unwitting revelation to divulge. In justifying the devoting of a long verse narrative in Hebrew to the Indians, Efros makes a claim to the Hebrew reader about the significance of the oral lyric folk poetry of the Indian tribes in America. "It seems to me," Efros declares, "that among the folk poetry of the Pale Face it would be hard to find the equal of these poems when it comes to precision of image, the abundance of colors, and a depth of feeling that nevertheless restrains itself and silently endures." It is not too much to suggest that Efros's advocacy of Indian lyric is an advocacy for his own poetic choices and an indication of how he would like his own poetry regarded. In the strong currents of Hebrew poetry between the two world wars, Efros was seeking a course that avoided the symbolism and expressionism that prevailed in Palestine, on the one hand, and the refined and fulsome romanticism of such American colleagues as Lisitzky, Halkin, and Regelson. Efros sought to hone a lyrical voice that was unencumbered by allusion and semantic reverberations and, thus simplified, could approach an ideal of pure song. Whether or not the folk poems of American Indians sustain his claims, it is clear that in the lyric songs that are interpolated at the beginning of many chapters of *Vigvamim shoteqim* and in many of the lambent descriptive passages in the poem, Efros did not fall far from the claims he could make for himself.[10]

Lisitzky's *Medurot do'akhot* is the longest and most ambitious of the three Indian epics written in America. Its appearance as the last in this series begs a fundamental question: Why write about Indians in Hebrew in the United States of the 1930s? Immigrants and their children who were fascinated by the story of the Indians had an abundance of sources to consult in English. Since the publication of Longfellow's *Hiawatha* in 1855, which had in the meantime become a staple of the public school classroom and a much parodied icon of American culture, numerous collections of Native American folklore had appeared. As for the prospect of Hebrew readers eager to take on a book-length poem on whatever subject, it was clear by 1937 that the Hebrew literary center in America would not be graced by a younger generation of readers with such robust appetites.

The natural address for Lisitzky's epic was the literary community in Palestine, which in the years of the British Mandate following the war, had become the undisputed center of Hebrew literature. Bialik and Tchernichovsky had settled there and brought with them the publishing houses and the ambitious schemes for expanding the scope of Hebrew literature that had earlier been formulated in Europe. Lisitzky's Indian epic would have fit especially well into Tchernichovsky's program of widening the nascent national literature by importing the literary bounty of other nations through translation into Hebrew. Already in 1913 the great poet himself had translated *Hiawatha* into Hebrew—probably through the mediation of the German—as just one among many of his efforts to expose the Hebrew reader to great and exotic national epics.[11] Yet the question naturally arises: If the Hebrew readers of Palestine already had Tchernichovsky's Hebrew Longfellow in hand, should they feel an acute need for another Hebrew Indian epic? Lisitzky must have believed that they should. He must have been persuaded that the wealth of more accurate source material about Indian life that had become available in the eighty years since the publication of Longfellow's poem made a new conceptualization possible and thus justified a return to the Indians. Moreover, it was his duty and destiny as a Hebrew poet living and working in America to make his contribution to Hebrew culture and to realize the precious thematic "capital" of the New World that was entrusted to him.

Lisitzky's enthusiasm for his subject went far beyond a sense of ethnographic mission. He saw in the story of the Indians, their myths and their struggles, an imaginative power that had the capacity to revive the flagging fortunes of a central institution of Hebrew literature. He adumbrates his hopes in the beginning of his review of Efros's *Vigvamim shoteqim* in 1936 in a literary miscellany dedicated to the memory of Silkiner, who had died two years earlier.

There is no finer material for equipping an epic poem than the lives of the Indian tribes that vanished from the American scene. In these lives there were the beauty of nature, the innocence of childhood, the majesty of mystery, and the tragedy of contending tribes. Here is a wondrous encounter between two races—the Red Face and the Pale Face—so different from each other in their temperaments, their outlooks, and manners. This was an unremitting and irreconcilable contest between a primitivism wholly rooted in its own soil and an alien civilization. With vexed struggles and heroic measures the Indians sought to throw off the yoke of the White Man, but their fate was awful defeat, banishment, or annihilation under the skies of their native lands. Here you will find primitive cultural values that, though they may lack the sheen of sophistication, divulge a wealth of inner beauty, innocent naturalness that lacks all false artifice, and, above all, human integrity and unmediated religiosity that flow directly from nature and life. Their legends are marked by a heartfelt innocence, a soulful purity, and an intelligence that comes from experience, and their lyric poems are wonderful and heart-rending in their sincere simplicity. Here you find unparalleled raw material for epic poetry, clay that calls out to the artist: "Work me, shape me, and transform me into art!"[12]

One does not need to read further to know that Lisitzky is volunteering himself as willing and able to heed this call, whereas Efros, whose own Indian poem was the subject of the review, fell seriously short. What is wonderfully exposed in the gush of Lisitzky's confessional enthusiasm is the desperate need to connect with a subject that will be worthy of his aspirations and talents.

It should be recalled that at this time, Lisitzky and other American Hebrew poets were facing a crisis of direction. Having begun their careers under the ruling mood of late romanticism and decadence in European Hebrew poetry at the turn of the twentieth century, the young Americans were seeking a way out of lyric solipsism and the preoccupation with the individual's romantic longings, aloneness, and response to nature. The struggle with religious tradition was behind them; the world of the shtetl and the Old World held no interest; the electrifying events taking place in Palestine were not theirs; and the unsightly accommodations of immigrant Jews to American life in the cities in which they, the poets themselves, lived was not the stuff that poetry—poetry of the sort they wanted to write—was made of. On this score, at least for Lisitzky, the Indians came to the rescue. Their story was compellingly exciting for all the reasons described above, but also, crucially for the Americans, because it was *their own*. It was not carried over from Europe or experienced at an empathic remove from Palestine. There was no subject that could be more primordially and essentially American.

Yet Lisitzky's passion goes beyond the prize of originality. The kind of poetic realization that the Indian materials cry out for in their ripeness is specifically named: it is the epic. And who would not agree that, given as Lisitzky has framed them, all the ingredients are present for the writing of an imposing epic poem? The conflict of civilizations, doomed heroic resistance, primal innocence, exotic myth—in short, everything a poet could want for the construction of a riveting work of the broadest ambitions. The problem, however, is with the desire itself. For a poet to aspire to write a historical epic in the 1930s is to wish to resurrect a mode of writing that has long been disused. Lisitzky is not Sir Walter Scott writing *The Lay of the Last Minstrel*, a work that survived long enough to be required in my own ninth-grade English curriculum; nor Mapu in 1853, composing an epic novel of love and politics set in the time of the kings in ancient Israel; nor is he even Silkiner, recently arrived in America at the beginning of the century. In an astounding and touching way, Lisitzky's enthusiastic and energetic proposal is not clouded by the least shadow of irony. He is a believer, and he has never abandoned an intuitive belief in the romantic underpinnings necessary to make the epic a credible, even commanding genre. If the epic has been moribund within Hebrew literature, it is only for want of a truly great subject, which is now at hand. The Indians, then, come to rescue more than Lisitzky himself; they have a direct hand in saving a pillar of Hebrew literature that has lapsed into desuetude.

I have described this situation not to mock Lisitzky, whose aspirations were sincere and genuine, but to suggest what an enormous challenge he took upon himself when he harkened to the call, seized the lumpen clay, and sought to create a majestic and sublime work of art. The very size of the completed volume is a testament to Lisitzky's ambitions. *Medurot do'akhot* is over 320 pages of *double columns* of poetry. This compendiousness is the result not only of a complicated story line but an abundance of interpolated legends and tales; for the very conception of Lisitzky's project called for supplying the Hebrew reader not only with a stirring narrative but also with quantities of authentic, folkloric Indian materials. And it would seem that the reader did not feel shortchanged.

The story is built along two axes. Along the historical axis we are given the chronicle of two tribes, the Children of the Serpent [*Benei hashififon*] and the Children of the Viper [*Benei haperes*], who conspire against each other and face such common external threats as drought even before the advent of the White Man. Once the Europeans arrive, the tribes and their leaders are bitterly divided over what kind of response to mount against the intruders. The other axis connects the human and divine realms. In a kind of anticipation of magic realism— or a throwback to the Homeric epics—*Medurot do'akhot* is written as if these two realms were entirely and naturally intermixed. In the initiating incident in the epic, for example, an Indian mortal happens across a cavorting group of sisters from the spirit world who have been lowered to earth in a magic basket; he falls in love with the youngest and makes her his wife. By combining these two axes, Lisitzky intends to dramatize the porous phenomenology of the primitive mind from within rather than assuming the role of the Western, rational narrator who tells the story from the comfortable stability of defined boundaries.

The offspring of the marriage between Nanpiwati, the son of the chief of the Serpents, and Namissah, the Star Maiden who was lowered in the magic basket, is the maiden Genetaskah. To the disfavor of her father, Genetaskah frees Midaingah, the son of the chief of the Vipers, who has been imprisoned by his own father. Genetaskah's punishment is death by drowning; Midaingah has fallen in love with the dead maiden and follows her to the World of the Spirits to be with her. In his absence, his father has been killed by the White Men, and Yahahadzah, the medicine man of the Vipers, is attempting to install his son, the militant Hanuhagi, as the chief of the tribe. Midaingah returns from the Spirit World just in time to claim his rightful status as successor to his father and to oppose Hanuhagi's virulent and headstrong reprisals against the Whites. Midaingah counsels diplomacy and a cautious dialogue with the White Man rather than wholesale opposition, and he works to unite the tribes in a coordinated response. But eventually the implacable enmity of the Whites and their duplicitous dealings with the Indian overtures undermine his position. Rather than facing the forced relocation of his people away from their tribal lands, Midaingah takes his own life by steering his canoe over a waterfall. There he meets the dead Genetaskah, who is steering her own canoe to greet him and accompany him to the entrance to the World of Spirits.

Lisitzky approached the task of composing *Medurot do'akhot* from a principled position of fidelity to the Indian sources. Silkiner had written his Indian poem with only vague notions picked up from indiscriminate secondary sources; and Efros seemed not to care a whit about authenticity, basing his story on the memory of a legend he had once heard and on his knowledge of Indian realia on celluloid Westerns. Lisitzky, by contrast, immersed himself in the vast literature that had arisen, beginning with the collections assembled by Henry Rowe Schoolcraft in the middle of the nineteenth century; gathering, transcribing, and retelling the legends and folktales of American Indians.[13]

Lisitzky's problem turned out to be that he knew too much. There are many hundreds of tribes in radically separate regional cultures whose deities are not identical and whose legends, in infinite variants, overlap but remain distinct. Faced with this superabundance of material, Lisitzky made a fateful choice. Instead of selecting one tribe with the proprietary coherence of its own repertoire of folktales and religious myths and the mappable specificity of its own territory, Lisitzky chose to synthesize. He made his depiction of the Vipers and the Serpents a composite of many native peoples and their imaginative religious lives an anthology of the beliefs and tales he found most evocative. He must have reasoned that Hebrew literature had room for only one authentic Indian epic and that the presentation of the subject was best served by eclectic inclusiveness. Was this the right decision? Absent an example of the alternative, of course, we cannot judge. But one wonders, for instance, what would have been gained if Lisitzky's Indian tribes moved over a terrain of identifiable streams and mountains and around the campfire retold legends shaped by the genius of place.

Another consequential decision was to reshape the legendary materials and adapt them in a way Lisitzky intuitively felt proper for a Hebrew epic. Stephen Katz has made a signal contribution by taking the episode of the sisters that are dropped in the magic basket in Book Two of *Medurot do'akhot* (pp. 13–30) and comparing it to the original Shawnee tale of "The Celestial Sisters."[14] He demonstrates the numerous points at which Lisitzky works to blunt what might be perceived as some of the more objectionably "primitive" aspects of Nanpiwati's behavior. Observing the maidens from his hiding place, he is propelled by an appreciation of their beauty rather than the erotic arousal evident in the original. Rather than surprising the sisters and carrying off the youngest (Namissah), he politely introduces himself to the ladies like a prince with good breeding; and with verbal professions of admiration, he persuades the young lady to follow him. When Namissah longs to visit her parents in the celestial world and prepares for a protracted sojourn, Lisitzky has her returning after only one day because of her love for her husband and their child. Domestic tenderness in the poem trumps the patriarchal order in the original.

Katz's summary of Lisitzky's reworking of this tale provides a good overview of the general method employed in the poem. "In contrast to the original folktale, Lisitzky's rendition underscores the significance of words. It is by them that the plot progresses, not by actions. Characters affect others by what they say, foregrounding the value of mutual respect, communication, and, above all, logic to affect and persuade. In so doing, Lisitzky modernizes and Westernizes the Indian story, as many American and European writers have done with authentic Indian tales. [. . .] The reader, who learns to accept the Other by virtue of this account, is also presented with a sanitized version of a world purportedly unlike his own, although as human as his."[15] Lisitzky, it is important to note, was in many instances working from collections and anthologies of Indian folktales in which the job of "universalization" had already been carried out by the collectors and anthologizers.

One comes away from a reading of *Medurot do'akhot* with a mixture of admiration and regret. There are passages of elevated beauty and heroic eloquence, which, if they are not sustained throughout, nonetheless move one to appreciate the ambitiousness of what Lisitzky was attempting to achieve. At the same time, there is a sense of missed opportunities. If Lisitzky had not been so scrupulous in respecting the sensitivities of the Hebrew reader; or if he had carried through on his ethnological idealism by allowing the true primitivism of his source materials to poke through; or if he had not loaded down his narrative with the recitations of tales and legends that frustrate the forward sweep of the action, if the ornate register of the language had been dialed down several degrees, if the composition were shorter and more compact—if these many conditions had been met, then he might have breathed an irresistible excitement into his poem and created a work which, even if it could not be expected to resurrect the Hebrew epic as a genre, would have found an appreciative audience. That audience might naturally have been the audience of young adult Hebrew readers in Palestine and America. More than one generation of European boys, after all, had been transfixed by the stories of Karl May about the American Indians, and an imagined Hebrew version of a writer of such stories is unforgettably embodied by Anshel Wasserman in the third section of David Grossman's novel *'Ayen 'erekh: ahavah* [See under: love]. Reconceived in this way, Lisitzky's Indian epic might have become a classic, if not quite in the vein he had hoped.

Sixteen

New England,
the Nineteenth Century

Decimated and removed to reservations far away from Jewish communities, the Indians were a subject that was constructed by American Hebrew poets primarily from literary sources. This was an enterprise, moreover, that was programmatic and intentional. For despite the very diverse purposes to which they put the Indian materials, Silkiner, Efros, and Lisitzky were all motivated by a desire to penetrate the originary center of the American experience and make it more available to the Hebrew literary community abroad than at home. Yet there was a different and less alien kind of "authentic" America that was still readily discoverable in the first half of the twentieth century. This was the America of the farms and villages of New England and upstate New York populated by northern Europeans, the descendents of settlers who had come during colonial times.

Like most city dwellers, Jewish immigrants sought to escape the suffocating heat of summertime tenement life by spending time in the country. As soon as they could afford to, they set up bungalow colonies, boarded in farmhouses, or flocked to resort hotels from the spartan to the luxurious. One of the finest works of American Hebrew fiction is Wallenrod's novel *Ki fanah yom* [Dusk in the Catskills] (1946), which chronicles a year in the life of the Jewish owner of a small family hotel and his guests from the city. For the sensitive young intellectuals and writers ordinarily immured in the metropolis, the country was a zone of spiritual freedom where nature could properly be experienced and appreciated. The country was also a place where one could still find traces of the early years of the American nation: the intrepid, individualist Dutch and British settlers who farmed and traded in the years before and after the founding of the republic. These rural areas were already in steep decline by the time that the immigrants and their children arrived on the scene; the children of the settlers had moved westward for more fertile land or left for mill jobs in cities. It was the influx of summer visitors that brought these regions a modicum of financial relief and the possibility of a growing service economy.

But as for the American Hebrew poets, their interest lay squarely in the past. The countryside that they encountered provided a portal backward into the nineteenth century, when the rural life was imagined to have been lived in vigor and integrity and could be taken as a paragon of American values. And taking it as such, it must be stressed, was very much a choice. Physical privation, isolation, economic failure, infant mortality, mental illness, generational discontinuity, xenophobia, sectarian religious strife—all these were also integral to the picture of life on the land and in country villages. The process of idealizing rural life was already well underway in the middle of the nineteenth century itself in the popular and widely read works of John Greenleaf Whittier and the other Fireside Poets, and it was undoubtedly their verse that was encountered as a staple of the English curriculum of the New York City public schools, in which immigrant youth, the future American Hebrew poets among them, studied in the years before World War I.

The belated idealization of country life in American Hebrew poetry was a far from disinterested move. The poets were drawn to the subject out of the hope of finding there a connection to themselves, a bridge between what was natively and indelibly American and the ostensibly alien culture they had brought with them from Europe. The bridge they found was nothing other than the Hebrew Bible itself—the Old Testament or the Hebrew Scriptures—as it was most often called. They saw the sturdy farmers of New England and the rugged denizens of the Catskill Mountains in the first century of the new nation as living lives suffused with Scripture. In a Protestant revision of the spirit of early Christianity, these early Americans lived according to a simple, primitive faith that jumped off the pages of their home Bibles into their busy hands and the daunting work of clearing and working the land. The stories of the Patriarchs, their ordained wanderings, providential betrothals, fraternal rivalries, and worldly salvation were not simply edifying stories or moral lessons but the dramatic stuff of real life being realized with typological immediacy. This was a piety whose place was not a church or organized public worship but the family circle in which the Good Book, which was often the only book, was read aloud on Sundays and informed the conduct of life during the weekdays.

It was a matter of no small excitement to the American Hebrew poets that the greater part of the Book of Books was composed in Hebrew. The fact is that on a Sunday, the average householder may have at best been dimly aware of the Hebrew origins of the sacred text he was reading. But this knowledge did little to diminish the exhilarating prospect of a kind of common ground between the uncouth immigrants with their Hebraist passions and a bedrock formation of American life. It did not even matter much that this was a one-way bridge in that the contribution of Hebrew to the faith of America remained largely unacknowledged.[1] It was enough for the Hebraists, for their part, to know that Hebrew had played a central role in the new land. It gave them a way, however indirectly, of reading themselves into the narrative of America and making this new world less strange to them and making themselves, in their own eyes, less strange to it. Building this bridge required a certain willing blindness. The Book of Books was in truth two books, but the Hebraists conveniently managed to let the Gospels recede into the background to maintain the illusion of a common Hebraic biblicism. Christology was understandably elided in construing the practical faith of common Americans. This became a more considered strategy, as we shall soon see, when Lisitzky of New Orleans set about the task of casting the biblical cadences of African American preachers into modern Hebrew.

"Mrs. Woods," a 224-line poem by Bavli written in 1924, is largely responsible for consolidating the iconic status of the biblically informed country life in American Hebrew poetry.[2] The work is a monologue delivered by the ninety-two–year-old Mrs. Woods, a widow who contentedly lives by herself on a farm in the Catskills, to a group of visiting young people from the city who have come on an excursion to hear about the secrets of longevity and living on the land. Written in fluid iambic pentameter, the poem hews to the poetics of classical simplicity that Bavli shared with Efros. The fluid style and the avoidance of rare words and elevated biblical locutions made the poem accessible and widely read in the Hebraist community, which took pride in it as an estimable response to critics abroad who demanded more *ameriqa'iyyut*. Unlike Efros's and Lisitzky's Indian poems, which did not appear until the mid-1930s, "Mrs. Woods" became a standard of Hebraist culture a decade earlier and helped establish a thematic norm that had considerable sway. The interrogation of this norm came in a series of poems written by Preil in the mid-1940s and collected in *Ner mul kokhavim* [Candle against stars] (1954). In this chapter, an examination of the iconic image of Mrs. Woods is followed by a discussion of Preil's revisionary consideration of the bridge between Jews and the rural life of early America.

The eleven-line mise-en-scène that introduces Mrs. Wood's monologue creates a picture of icon-like radiance. She sits Abraham-like at the entrance to her home—*ohel*, tent in Hebrew—"bathing in the glowing and singing beauty of Sunday afternoon" (p. 136). She lifts up her eyes to the mountains in the distance to retrieve "dreams from forgotten times." One hand strokes her loyal dog curled up at her feet, and the other hand plays with the compendious Bible that rests in her lap. Shaken from her reverie, she turns to the group of young people seated in a semi-circle at her feet and, in a "hoarse, broad masculine voice," begins the monologue that will last the course of the poem.

Here at the beginning of the work, Mrs. Woods is carefully posed, illuminated by the Sunday light, as if she had undergone a process of secular beatification. One hand gestures to an endearing representative of the benign and faithful order of nature, while the other affirms the familiar authority of God's word. Mrs. Woods is a sage at whose feet sit young people who have made a pilgrimage from the city to drink in her wisdom and obtain clues to living a long and good life. She speaks with serene confidence in the self-evident truth of her message, and she concludes each section of her speech with words to the effect of "thus spake Mrs. Woods," as if to underscore the near-oracular status of her pronouncements. The masculine timbre of her voice helps to desexualize her and remove the taint of vulnerability that might attach to her being a woman alone in the world. The world of this poem, moreover, is one in which sexuality and sexual difference do not strongly figure.

The secret of life that Mrs. Woods dispenses to her listeners is, of course, no secret at all but only a testament to the power of faith, hard work, and the capacity to appreciate God's handiwork in nature. Mrs. Woods presents herself as the primary exhibit for her case. At age ninety-two, she is straight of back and keen of eye, and living alone and unaided, she keeps house, feeds the chickens, prepares the feed for the livestock, milks the eight cows, works hoeing and raking in the fields, harvests and stacks the hay, and performs many other chores that, taken together, would test the mettle of a entire field crew. Morally towering over her listeners, she heaps scorn upon their whining requests to be told about the wondrous deeds of the first settlers, as if they were not merely courageous and hard-working men and women, or to be vouchsafed the secret sources of the vigor of country people like herself, as if the abundant blessings of sky and field were not self-evident. Mrs. Woods is both gratified by the waves of curious visitors that continue to come and sit at her feet and contemptuous of their stultified city consciousness. The fact that she has been made into a paragon—even something of a side show—indicates that the life of nature and the countryside is wholly alien to these young people, the children of immigrants or young immigrants themselves, who have motored up from the city to meet her. It cannot even be a lost paradise for them because, raised in the city, they can know it only as a romance or a curiosity.

Mrs. Woods's attitude toward the city was definitively shaped by the one time she visited New York when her brother lay severely wounded in a hospital during the Civil War. The teeming streets, the army units stationed on street corners to suppress civil violence, and the screaming of the wounded in the hospitals all contributed to her conception of the metropolis as a "monster of blood" (p. 138). She has never since been tempted to leave her home. Now, at an advanced age and living alone, she reconfirms for her young listeners the plenitude of her present life and strives to open their minds to an expanded notion of what it means to be "at home" in the world. She lives among mountains and valleys and forests and fields that are not only intimately familiar to her but which *know her*. This is not a cartoonish animated world of talking trees, but it is a world that is capable, in a profound but not mystical sense, of embracing those who live in its midst. She has cared for the land, and the land has cared for her. The land in its specificity—that field by the hillside and those trees over there—is now the repository of the memories of her long life.

The central section of the poem (pp. 140–43) is taken up with Mrs. Woods's recollections of her childhood among the rambunctious gang of children who shared the three benches in the one-room schoolhouse taught by the beloved Miss Virginia Clark, who held them spellbound with her retold stories from Greek mythology and her accounts of the American Revolution and the founders of the republic. Outside the schoolhouse, every glade and hill in the countryside served as part of the children's playground, especially when they divided into competing Indian tribes and fought mock battles, only to make peace at the end of the day by the "tribal rock." A boy named Seymour leads a rival tribe, and the speaker (Mrs. Woods as a young girl) gives him a bloody wound on his head, and it was this same Seymour who, in the fullness of time, was to become her husband.

The stream of associations eventually leads her to the font of childhood memory: Sundays in her father's house. Living too far from church, the family circle, dressed in their best clothes, gathered around as the father read from the thick family Bible that had been passed down from previous generations, whose births and deaths were inscribed on the insides of its covers. The recollection of the domestic nature of that worship prompts Mrs. Wood to launch into a prolonged digression inveighing against organized religion, the proliferation of churches and denominations, and the conspicuous display of fashion and the shallow socializing that motivate most churchgoers.[3] Out of exasperation, Mrs. Woods exclaims:

לְלַוְיָה וּלְוָיָה אֶצְטָרֵף — הֵן כֹּה גַם לֹא יָדַע הַבּוֹרֵא
כָּל כִּתּוֹת וְרִיב כָּל מִפְלָגָּה וַיִּתֵּן לְכָל בְּנֵי־הָאָדָם
אֶת שָׁמָיו הַכְּחֻלִּים, אֶת שְׂדוֹתָיו וּפְלָגָיו, אֶת הָרָיו וַעֲמָקָיו
כְּאוֹמֵר: הִסְתַּכְּלוּ בָאֵלֶּה וִידַעְתֶּם הַטּוֹב וְהָאֱמֶת
וּלְמַדְתֶּם אֶת אָרְחוֹת־הַחַיִּים וּמְצָאתֶם גַּם אוֹתִי בָעוֹלָם;
אַף הֵא לָכֶם סִפְרִי הָאָהוּב, הוּא יוֹרְכֶם אֶת עֵינְכֶם לֹא תֵרֶא
וִיבִינְכֶם לְהַרְגִּישׁ אֶת רוּחִי וּלְגַלּוֹת הָאשֶׁר בָּאָרֶץ. — — —

I would attend all the funerals, for indeed the Creator does not
    recognize
sects and schismatic parties but gives to all human beings
His blue sky, His fields and streams, His hills and valleys,
as if to say: Behold these and you will know good and truth
and you will learn the way of life and find Me in the world; here
    is My beloved Book, which will teach you what your eyes
    do not see
and you will understand how to sense My spirit and to discover
    happiness on the land. — — —

Mrs. Woods's religion is a kind of homegrown panentheism that sees
God's spirit in the common wonders of the natural world. It is univer-
salist in its openness and access to all, at the same time as it is rooted
in the very local fields and streams and hills and valleys of her home
in the mountains. This natural religion does not stand by itself but is
fused with a holy text; as she proclaims in God's name shortly before
the passage above: "Only here will you find Me: in the pages of this
book and in the mountains" (p. 144). The Book *and* the mountains,
the mountains *and* the Book—these are sources of divinity that are
ineluctably conjoint. In all of Mrs. Woods's forthright convictions
about religion, one thing is clear: there is nothing that is specifically
Christian about it, and the reader will look in vain for any mention
of Christ or Christian doctrine. By constructing her religious world
in this way, Bavli smartly removed a serious obstacle that might have
impeded the identification of Hebrew readers with the admirable Mrs.
Woods.

I suspect that readers today would be impatient with the idealization within which Bavli has enfolded the figure of Mrs. Woods. The

gloss of sentiment, even if sincerely applied, deflects too many things we know to be true about the world in which the poem is set. We know that nature is not always beneficent, that Bible stories are not always uplifting, that the Jews are a vexed subject for Christian readers of Scripture, that the fate of the Indians transcends childhood games, and many other truths for which the glow of Mrs. Woods makes little affirmation. As an explanation for these exclusions, Stephen Katz has proposed that Bavli's choices were imposed in part by the genre of the idyll, in which he composed "Mrs. Woods."[4] In the European-Russian version that Tchernichovsky introduced into Hebrew literature at the end of the nineteenth century, the idyll is a simple descriptive narrative poem that deals with rustic or village life and suggests a mood of peace and contentment. If the idyll was indeed the model Bavli had adopted for himself in writing "Mrs. Woods"—although there is no explicit generic subtitle or marker to this effect—then there is implied license to exclude dimensions of discord or violence in order to preserve the conventionalized integrity of the pastoral picture. Idealization and harmonization would be part and parcel of this allegiance. Bavli was likely urged in this direction by the traditionalism and filial piety that are integral to his larger poetic endeavor, as well as by the revulsion toward the city he shared with most other American Hebrew poets. In the final analysis, however, even if the structure of idealization is abetted or even enjoined by the genre of the idyll, the adoption of that genre and the conventions attached to it remains a choice and not a fate.

Are there seeds of irony in this poem? Certainly for today's reader, there are seeds aplenty. But it is more intriguing to ask whether the possibility existed for Bavli and his contemporary readers. The argument can be made that there are a number of features of the poem that are at odds with a wholly harmonized presentation of the figure of Mrs. Woods. These include her status as a rural curiosity and tourist attraction, the extreme authority and self-confidence of her pronouncements, the absence of any reference to her children and their fates, and the sufficiency of her dog and her Bible for companionship. Irony is a very subtle quality to measure because it is a product of the interplay between the text and its readers. I at least would like to entertain the prospect that even Bavli understood the hyperbolic nature of his construction and the eddies of irony that might lap at it from around the edges.

When Bavli died at the age of sixty-eight in 1961, Preil wrote a brief reconsideration of the Americanness of Bavli's verse, whose centerpiece was the widely read "Mrs. Woods." Preil suggested that the elements of the American character that Bavli had foregrounded in his poetry were in fact those that most accorded with his sense of Jewishness. There is so much implied Jewishness in Bavli's affectionate and admiring descriptions of rural Americans "that it sometimes seems that the poet's intention was not at all so much to take the measure of America as to underscore the pure humanity that flows from the sacred truths of Judaism."[5] A Lithuanian Jew by temperament like Bavli, Preil saw the elder poet drawing an imaginative bridge between the Lithuanian village of his youth and the bygone rural settlements of the American countryside where one could find the same values of "simple goodness, sincerity, and strict sobriety." Although the spirit of Preil's observation is generous as befits memorial reflections, the critique is there nonetheless. Out of a desire to find common ground between the best of the old world and the new, Bavli declined to confront otherness and difference.

This was a confrontation that Preil himself had undertaken in a remarkable series of poems he wrote around 1945. Awed by the piercing natural beauty of the New England landscape and seascape and fascinated by the hard work, homely pleasures, and biblical mindedness of the early Americans, Preil went beyond simple appreciation to pose a set of difficult questions. What was the potential degree of belongingness and at-homeness that a Hebrew poet—and, by extension, a sensitive Jew steeped in his heritage—could expect to achieve in relationship to the American landscape and its early denizens? At a moment when the murder of European Jewry has just been completed and the struggle for a Jewish homeland in Palestine is heating up, how and in what terms is an American Hebrew poet to understand his attraction to the American landscape and his place in it? To what degree is the shared attachment to the Hebrew Bible a bridge that can bear the weight of the Hebraist desire for common ground?

In three substantial and related poems, Preil engages different aspects of this ambitious line of inquiry. The longest of these (and the first in its placement in *Ner mul kokhavim*, the collection in which it was published) is "Mitsiyurei Maine" [Sketches of Maine],[6] which was discussed in detail in Chapter 14. In this poem Preil engages the meaning of the natural landscape in its physical beauty unconnected to history and society. It is this latter question, the relationship of the belated Jew to the vestiges of the culture of nineteenth-century Americans, which is taken up in the other two poems, which follow the Maine poem: "Beit-qevarot ameriqani" [An American cemetery][7] and "Zer-shirim qatan la'Aviyah" [A small bouquet of poems for Abijah].[8] In contrast to Bavli's "Mrs. Woods," in which the American figure speaks in her own voice and the presence of the poet is nowhere to be seen, in these three Preil poems, as in almost all his verse, the lyric "I" of the poem, which is conflated with the persona of Preil the poet, is the authority that conducts the quest for the answers. In the sturdy and self-assured Mrs. Woods, Bavli has already secured an admirable American figure who he can comfortably set talking before us, and we need not see any of the trouble the poet has taken to find her. For Preil, the search itself is more fraught and indeterminate and becomes the subject of the poems themselves.

The quest is given concrete expression at the outset of "Beit-qevarot ameriqani," in which the poet, intrepidly following a disappearing path in the woods and jumping over streams and fallen fences, finally arrives at an old, untended cemetery.[9] This is not a serendipitous encounter but the fruit of a determined search for a secret portal that would allow him access to layers of American life far deeper than what he sees around him in the present. In reaching the cemetery, he has attained "the place where, fixed in a frozen dream, / are those who formerly trod / the surface of this many-hewed and musing land" (p. 178). Here, standing amidst the worn tombstones sunken into the wild overgrowth, his imagination summons up the lives of the average folk buried underneath: bearded men finishing a roof, women planting in the garden, a farmer planting seed in the last season of his life, a shopkeeper selling his last candle, a tavern keeper drawing his last ale. In the second and third of this five-part poem, the poet expands this reverie into a miniature epic of the settlement of the land with an account of the round of the seasons and the cycle of life of its energetic inhabitants.

This is a poem built on catalogues; the poet has put himself in the position of taking in a grand narrative of rural America in its early years, and he can acquit himself of covering this territory only by stringing together lists of acutely observed details: immigrant English villagers creating clearings in the virgin forests that "grow dark brown with squirrels," barn raisings in which English and Dutch settlers join together "to crown, as if with a wreath, a chimney from which smoke will curlicue like the letters of the alphabet / above the gleaming valley sunk in the torpor of snow," carefree square dances in the spring evenings with white-haired fiddlers and girls whose dresses balloon out like "buds blossoming" as they whirl. In the third section, the list is rendered in the form of the many sights seen by the mountain overlooking the cemetery during former and better times within the circuit of life from birth to death. The mountain has seen children bearing baskets of freshly picked strawberries, men gashing the trees to make maple syrup from the running sap, women strolling with "lilies placed in their rye-colored braids" after the midday meal has been cooked, swaggering young men after a day of plowing or tanning hides, and farmers and artisans "bearing middle age / with equanimity and a sort of soft, mirthless laugh" (pp. 180–81).

In this celebration of rural work and play, the central sections of "Beit-qevarot ameriqani" are as much of an idyll as Bavli's "Mrs. Woods." The Sunday sanctity and Bible reading are missing in Preil, but there is a similar sense of the plenitude that flows from a privileged moment in the past of the nation when the life of those who lived on the land and the land itself were joined in an autochthonous bond. It is a duration in which there is "no hint of sadness." Yet, whereas Mrs. Woods's vitality seems to transcend death, the working and dancing figures in Preil's poem are caught by surprise and struck dumb: "It seems as if life is a summer stream that will course forever without being dammed; / It seems as if life is a summer sky in which the lightest of clouds float. / Then suddenly the deep sleep—aha!—into which they sink without explanation, / under the grey stones standing in the shadow of the mountain" (p. 180). *Tardemah* [deep sleep] is a fraught term that is closer to suspended animation or oblivion than it is to death; for the young men and women, who were once dancing under seemingly endless summer skies and now lie under the grey stones, are still available to the poet's fancy for reanimation. Yet the proximity to death is close enough that the speaker of the poem, calling attention to himself for the first time, ponders his own end. It is twilight, and as he looks up at the first stars appearing in the heavens, his perspective abruptly jumps into a future dimension when, his own star having been extinguished, future pilgrims will make their way to this place, as he had done, to consider the "musing and many-hued land" (p. 181).

The "mystery" of America remains both compellingly fascinating and maddeningly elusive. The phrase *erets hozah-sasgonit* [musing and many-hued land], which appears in the first section and ends the third, now becomes the poem's main focus in its fourth section. A compound of a gerund and an adjective, *hozah-sasgonit* is itself an elusive and difficult-to-translate phrase of Preil's concoction. *Hozah* connotes daydreaming, musing upon something in an abstracted state of mind, or entering into a reverie or a heightened imaginative state. *Sasgonit* connotes the quality of being variegated, kaleidoscopic, colorful, alluring, shifting in aspect. The fourth section opens with a question addressed to the land: "Oh, musing and many-hued land, what form will you take then, / when the jaws of oblivion have bitten me and moss grows over me?" (p. 181). These clichés and frequent repetitions introduce a desperate and histrionic tone that carries through to the conclusion of the poem. The answer to the question of what the land will be like in the future is answered in a paradoxical way. On the one hand, the answers are uttered with complete assurance and twice introduced by the interjection *vadai* [certainly!]; on the other, the actual nature of that future American reality is elusive and inscrutable.

וַדַּאי דְּמוּת הַחָכְמָה הַמְנֻמֶּרֶת כְּעַתָּה;
חֲדוּרָה אוֹתוֹ קֶסֶם מְתַעְתֵּעַ, מְסֻנְוֶרֶת בְּמֶלַח דִּמְעוֹתֶיהָ.
וַדַּאי אוֹתָהּ מַלְכוּת גְּדוֹלָה שֶׁלָּאי־נִתְפָּס, כֻּלָּהּ רֶמֶז אֱלֹהִי,
זָהָב־מִסְתּוֹרִין לֹא יִגַּע;
אוֹתָהּ תּוֹפַעַת־מַמָּשׁוּת רַחֲבַת־הַיָּד, גּוֹנֶיהָ יִשְׁאֲגוּ עָלַי־בַּד,

יַדְלִיקוּהוּ.
לִי, כְּלָהֶם עַכְשָׁו, תִּהְיֶה רַק נֶחָמַת־הַמָּוֶת הַסְּתוּמָה —
וְרַק מַצֵּבָה קָרָה תְּסַמֵּן הַמָּקוֹם, בּוֹ שָׁקַעְתִּי עַל אִשִּׁי.
רַק מָטָר פּוֹשֵׁר מֵעָבִים יִזַּל לְבַכּוֹתֵנִי.

> Certainly this will take the form of a heterogeneous wisdom as it
>   does now,
> permeated with the same meretricious charm, blinding with the
>   salt of its tears.
> Certainly the same great kingdom of the incomprehensible,
>   infused with divine implication,
> an untrammeled golden mystery;
> the same prodigious and substantial phenomenon whose hues
>   scream onto canvas,
> igniting it.
> As for me, as for them now, there will be only the blank comfort of
>   death—
> Only a cold stone will mark the spot where I sank upon my fire.
> Only a dull rain will drip down from the clouds to mourn me.

If the speaker's predictions of the future are the fruit of all the conjuring of the rural American past that has taken place while he has stood in the graveyard, then this is a baffling wisdom indeed. Through the metonymy of the land, America is presented in three linked manifestations. America is a great, hulking enormity, a kingdom of reality, a phenomenon of substance. It is also a reality of multiple aspects, captivating and entrancing, that changes kaleidoscopically and resists containment. (The image of the colors igniting the canvas is returned to at the conclusion of the poem.) Finally, America is ultimately unknowable. It remains a mystery not because of the failure of our acumen and intelligence to decipher it but because the depths of its richness, which bear signals of the divine, cannot be plumbed or grasped.

America, in sum, exerts a streaming, open-ended fascination that moves from the past into the future. But all this elusive wonder suddenly dissipates when the speaker, gesturing to the graves at his feet, contemplates his own death. Just above, at the end of section three, this thought had spurred him to consider what future pilgrims might discover. Here, however, the extinguishing of his fire and the dull rain on his stone convey resentment and futility. The *tardemah*, the deep sleep from which he had imaginatively summoned up from the grave the figures from antique rural life in the poem's opening, has become personal and final.

The fifth and final section takes the reader by surprise. As befits the thoughts provoked by a visit to the American cemetery of its title, the poem until this point has been devoted to contemplating the lives of early Americans and their relationship to this mysterious and many-hued land. Without warning, the poem's speaker launches into a screed decrying the fact that until his belated arrival on the scene, not a single Jew had found rest from his wanderings in this valley and had been nurtured by its streams and woods. The pitch of the tirade is heightened by rhetorical repetitions and elaborations and a central confusion about who is responsible for this regrettable, infuriating absence. The fact that the early settlers cannot be held truly account-able for excluding Jews from their Edenic haven robs the speaker's fury of a clear object of address and makes it into an eruption of resentment rather than a targeted utterance. The harangue is relent-less. To this beautiful place, no Jew has come who "looked up at the book of stars open on the horizon, / and from whose heart had arisen the song of the psalms of David, praise for the grace / vouchsafed to him by a familiar God on this continent such that his alienness would be dispelled. / In vain. Here an isle of repose was not discovered by one of my brethren / to whom a dove came with leaves of redemption in its mouth" (p. 182). Is God, then, the one who is being accused of barring access to His own people, who may in fact turn out to be less His, than, judged by their good fortune, the happy denizens of these happy territories? The issue of responsibility is not pressed or clarified, but the feeling of deprivation remains. The pastoral idyll, so lavishly elaborated at the center of the poem, is brought back here at the end but turned upside down. These are the oaks and birches, the creeks and hills, and the bowers and furrows that the Jews *cannot* have the privilege of enjoying.

Although the reasons for this righteous rage are never made clear, its sudden eruption leads us to look for what has been repressed that can no longer be contained. We know nothing of the speaker's

Jewish-Hebrew identity at the beginning of the poem (except, perhaps, for the very fact that we are reading a Hebrew poem). He had
made his way to this forgotten, overgrown cemetery, after all, not to
find what he already knows but to encounter the America of yester-
year. As he discovers the "musing and many-hued land" and submits
to the fascination it exerts, we can imagine unspoken thoughts, even
unconscious thoughts, building up inside him concerning the disjunction between this beautiful land and the tempest-tossed life of
his own people. The eruption that comes in section four is as much
of a surprise to the speaker as it is to the reader, and this delirium of
expostulation signals a loss of control over the well-wrought shaping
of the poem. It should therefore not be surprising that "Beit-qevarot
ameriqani" does not achieve a sense of closure but lurches to a halt in
mid-sentence. But this sputtering ending, if far from elegant, is decidedly revealing. After inveighing against the fact that no Jewish gaze
has beheld all the goodness of this valley, the speaker, concluding the
poem, adds:

עַד שֶׁבָּאתִי אָנֹכִי וּבְמִכְחוֹלִי הַיְהוּדִי הַמֻּרְדָּף הוֹסַפְתִּי
אֶת גּוֹן הַשָּׁחוֹר, כְּמֵהָה לוֹ בְּלִי־דַעַת הַתְּכֵלֶת הַתְּמִימָה;
אֶת גּוֹן הָאָדֹם, הַמֵּבִין בְּטִיב הַיָּרֹק הָרוֹגֵעַ, מַפְרֵהוּ.
עַד שֶׁבָּאתִי אָנֹכִי — — —

Until I came and with my persecuted Jewish paintbrush added
the hue of black, which the innocent blue has been unconsciously
        longing for;
and the hue of red, which comprehends the nature of cozy green
        and fructifies it.
Until I came — — —

Echoing the heroic swagger of the Song of Deborah (Judges 5), the
speaker of Preil's poem rises to the occasion by passing beyond complaint to action. The image of painting and pigments already had been
introduced in reference to the kaleidoscope land whose "hues scream
upon the canvas / igniting it." The provocative assertion the poet is
making in this last grand gesture is that there is something in that riot
of color, and by extension, in the land itself that is deficient. The blue
of the sky and the green of the forest, the purities of this beguiling
landscape, are incomplete because they are insulated from the black

and the red that can be applied only from the palette of the Jew's experience. Rather than being an admirable and perfect totality from which the Jew has been excluded, the promise of the land can only be made real and connected to the historical world by the placement of the Jew into the picture. And this is precisely what the poet claims he has done.

The potential of the Bible as common ground is the theme of the poem that directly follows "Beit-qevarot ameriqani" in *Ner mul kokhavim*. "Zer-shirim qatan la'Aviyah" makes its subject explicit in a footnote to the poem's title: "This sequence of poems was written in a house built in 1824 in Putnam Valley in New York State by a pious Christian and lover of the Bible, Abijah Lee" (p. 183).[10] The poem, which is a dramatic monologue addressed by the poet, who is staying in the house, to its builder and first occupant, explores the spiritual and ontological climates in which these two men live. Can the Hebrew Bible, from whose depths both drank deeply, provide the basis for a connection between two men from radically different backgrounds? In pressing this question, Preil is testing a claim that could be put forward on behalf of American Hebrew literature generally. Hebraists, it could be argued, have a privileged relationship to the classic American past that is not accessible to the mass of East European immigrants. Their aristocratic lineage, through the Haskalah appropriation of biblical language and models of discourse, connects them directly to the Hebrew Scriptures and thereby, leaving aside the gap of a century or more, puts them on a kind of equal footing with the serious and biblically minded early settlers of the American nation. In Preil's poem, the grandiosity of this claim is undermined, but the challenge comes from an unexpected direction.

The first section of "Zer-shirim qatan la'Aviyah," which is divided into five sections like the preceding poem, establishes as a point of departure a profound sense of the simultaneity of past and present. Both stanzas of the first section begin with the observation, "It is as if time has not passed" and register the wonderment of sitting in a house that was erected "when Lincoln was a long-legged lad." In that charmed era, when "[t]he stars sparkled like heavenly apples upon the pickers of new apples," there was an accord between the cosmos and this new human endeavor, whose traces the poet is amazed to still

savor sitting in the house Abijah Lee built in Putnam Valley. The poet
experiences this persistence as an amiable haunting. The spirit of the
man is still about the place. Noble "like the shadow of an aristocratic
lily," Lee's shade also hovers around the house busying itself with
familiar domestic tasks. This life after life is a reward, the poet sur-
mises, for the life of faith that Lee led when he was alive. That faith
is inscribed in the name itself. Abijah succeeded his father Rehoboam
as king of Judah after dissolution of the united monarchy in the
aftermath of Solomon's death. As described in Second Chronicles 13,
Abijah was a courageous military leader whose loyalty to God was
rewarded with victory against the rebels of the Northern Kindgom.
(Although common among early Americans, Abijah is curiously not a
name often take by Jews, even in Zionist Palestine where names like
Asa, Abijah's successor on the throne of Judah, were in fashion.)

Addressing Abijah Lee, the poet savors the duality of his name.

אַתָּה, חָבֵר־לְשֵׁם לְמֶלֶךְ יְהוּדָה, עֵינָיו כַּפֶּחָם הַשָּׁחוֹר וְלוֹחֵשׁ,
אַתָּה, בֶּן אַנְגְּלִיָּה־חֲדָשָׁה, לוֹ עֵינַיִם כְּחֻלּוֹת, יוֹשְׁבוֹת עַל מְלֵאת.

> You, titular associate to a Judean king, whose eyes were like dark,
>   murmuring coal;
> You, son of New England, whose blue eyes are deeply and fitly set.

In contemplating the figure—perhaps a portrait—of the ghostly pro-
prietor of the house in which he is staying, the poet is savoring a large
paradox: that the culture of Britain and northern Europe, whose
descendents colonized New England, should have identified so intimately with the heroes and locales of the Hebrew Bible despite the obvious disparity in racial origins. Those physical racial traits, moreover,
are capable of migrating and crossing categories. While we recognize
the coal-dark eyes of the Judean king as prototypically Semitic, the
blue eyes of the scion of New England settlers are described as *yoshvot
'al mileit*, a phrase that occurs only in the Song of Songs (5:12), where
it describes the eyes of the male lover. The meaning of the phrase is
not entirely clear; it has been taken to refer either to the way in which
jewels are expertly secured within their setting or to the brimming
nature of the pools in which the doves (the eyes of the lover) bathe
themselves.[11] Tying down the specific reference is less important than

noting what Preil is accomplishing here. By making a very recognizable reference to the Song of Songs, he is establishing a romantic
biblical code, which is elaborated as the poem progresses and which is
the key to Abijah Lee's religious life. That life is lived within a direct
imaginative communion with "Mount Carmel when it still glistened
with its vineyards," and with the "cedars of Lebanon, the roses of Sha-
ron"; for him it is still possible to seek "the balm of Gilead" to apply to
his "wounds of love." Abijah Lee lives simultaneously and seamlessly
in the fertile fields of Canaan, as well as among the woods and ponds
of the New World.

Sojourning in an old country house with a benign, Bible-loving
ghost would seem to be a happy prospect. If we recall for a moment
the angry ending of Preil's poem in the American cemetery, then we
can appreciate the possibility offered here for inclusion and accord
rather than rupture and alienation. Yet, sadly, this is a bridge that the
poet cannot cross, and this time the fault is not on the gentile side.
What constrains the poet from taking advantage of this opportunity,
as is the case in so many Preil poems, is the conviction of being been
born in the wrong era. The poet fully appreciates the sincerity and
purity of Abijah Lee's feeling of at-homeness in the pages of the
Bible: "You watered your flocks in the morning, and in the evening
you reaped a harvest of truth from the fields of the Holy Scriptures"
(p. 184). This is a joy that perhaps can be understood fully *only* by
a Hebraist like Preil, who was raised in a world of faith and textual
erudition and for whom the Hebrew words of Scripture were the very
breath of life. Yet the faith that undergirded this unity of language
and scripture is no longer possible in the world in which the poet
now lives. He no longer stands on the firm ground of belief that was
the sure possession of his rabbinical ancestors in Lithuania at the very
same time in the early nineteenth century that Abijah Lee was building his house in New York State.

This is an ontological loss that manifests itself in profound and
subtle ways. Abijah Lee reads the ancient text as if the words were
young and had just been written and "there was still spaces among
them for tents of gladness." But for the poet, joy is rare. "It is as if my
body had become a book of nazariteship, bound in hard leather, and

hidden in a dark cell." Rather than taking naïve delight in the Book, he himself has *become* a book, a forbidding, ascetic tome, disused and hidden away from sight. Speaking to his apparitional host, he avers that "You had a love of God that was younger than the reviving elm tree unfurling in the spring, / fleeter than the quicksilver hooves of the deer clearing the cops." That fresh and ready faith underwrote a serene courage in the face of death and a confidence in God's salvational plans for humanity. Not so the poet. Lying awake in the middle of the night, he thinks of Abijah Lee as a burnished brass trumpet that once gleamed "like a river awakening in the morning" but is now nothing more than a silent, rusty, and disintegrated clod of earth. The poet's response to this thought is feelings of dejection, even depression. "I am saddened by the hand and the mouth that knew how to obtain an enticing, dream melody / but now sleep there in the land where song has been silenced." It is this sadness that has become a modal state for the speaker, and although he can conjure up the bright world of faith inhabited by Abijah Lee, it is a territory in which he can no longer tread.

"Zer-shirim qatan la'Aviyah," which until now has flowed forward with its plaintive and pensive music, comes to a surprisingly ironic and tragic conclusion. The poem begins with the almost giddy discovery of a place where time has stood still and with an encounter with an intriguing apparition who is at home in the Hebrew Bible. That happy accord breaks down as the poet acknowledges the fact that he has been born into an age that cannot authorize the believer's hopeful response to life. His must ultimately be "the inheritance of temporality and its sad smile." If the poem concluded here, it would end with savoring the following irony. Although I as a Jew have not been able to take advantage of the patrimony of faith bequeathed to me, you as a Christian in your age were able to reap a harvest of faith from the Scriptures given you by *my* ancestors. Yet, the poem goes on to end with a tragic *pointe*.

כֹּה קָרוֹב הָיִיתָ לְמַעְיְנוֹת־עַמִּי שׁוֹקְקִים,
עַל שְׂפָתָם גָּחַנְתָּ לִשְׁבֹּר צְמָאוֹן.
אַךְ קְרוֹבֶיךָ בְּיָמַי נִפְּצוּ כָּל פַּךְ קָטָן,
בְּעָמְדָם בִּלְבָבוֹת קֶרַח, בְּשָׁרָב מִדְבָּר זָרְעוּ.

So close were you to the gushing wellsprings of my people
at which you knelt down to slake your thirst!
But your relatives in my day smashed every little container
as they stood with hearts of ice in the desert drought they had sown.

The tables turn with the sudden introduction in the final two lines of the poem of an allusion to the murder of European Jewry.[12] Once there was a moment of rapprochement when the spiritual resources of the Jews were gratefully drawn upon by gentile Christians. But then it was the dispirited and belated modernity of the Jews themselves that barred them from slaking their thirst from the wells of their own tradition. All this is finally swept aside by inexplicable acts of gratuitous cruelty performed by "your" relations. *Qerovekha* [your relations], literally, those close to you, resonates ironically with *qarov* [close] ("so close were you . . .") in the first line of the stanza. The desert drought they have sown has now become the state of humankind, and for no one, gentile or Jew, are there any containers left whole, or any water to put in them.

Taken together with Preil's magnificent Maine poem, "Beit-qevarot ameriqani" and "Zer-shirim qatan la'Aviyah" undertake a major exploration of the connection possible between the Hebraist and the American historical landscape. That connection is ultimately dismissed, as we have seen, despite the deep attractions and historical reverberations. In terms of Preil's long career as a Hebrew poet in America, the mid-1940s were still a relatively early stage, and one in which the romantic mode of his verse had yet to make room for the modernist minimalism that was yet to come. America in its physical presence never ceased to fascinate Preil, but in the major phases of his career in the postwar decades it was the city rather than the countryside that compelled his attention.

If Preil, for the many reasons discussed, cannot make a connection with the American historical landscape, at least his construction of that landscape is clear enough: the Maine coast, the streams and valleys of the Northeast, the circuit of traditional village life, the Hebrew scriptures as a template for the blessings of life in the New World. Fixed in stability and recurrence, Preil's understanding of nineteenth-century America knows little of the great upheavals that uprooted waves of settlers and propelled them toward the western frontier. Grappling with this phenomenon is the aim of Efros's book-length, narrative poem *Zahav* [Gold] (1942), one of the masterworks of American Hebrew literature.[1] The poem traces several years in the life of Ezra Lunt, a veteran of the Mexican-American War who leaves his family and farm in Salem, Massachusetts, to travel overland to the gold fields of California.

There are a number of features common between this work and Efros's Indian poem *Vigvamim shoteqim* [Silent wigwams] published nine years earlier. Like Tom, the Englishman who falls in love with Lalari, Ezra betrays his vows to his wife for wealth and fortune, an act that leads to his own doom. The life wisdom of Native Americans is idealized. And the American landscape is vividly and passionately evoked, with the lands of the Chesapeake estuary being exchanged for the slopes of the Sierra Nevadas and Yosemite Valley. But the differences indicate how much Efros grew as an artist between the two works. The depiction of Ezra Lunt's character is vastly more complex, and his motives are organically and productively linked to essential currents in American history. Whereas Efros's grasp of the details of

Indian life and lore seemed sketchy and derivative, his control of the concrete details of the lives of the forty-niners and their primitive mining techniques is self-assured. The narrative scaffolding of both poems is melodramatic and turns on betrayal and suicide; but *Zahav* is elevated by a tragic wisdom won through loss and renunciation. Finally, there is the American landscape itself. In exile in the cold north, Efros wrote affectingly in *Vigvamim shoteqim* of the Maryland woods and waterscapes so dear to him. The remote mining camps along the American River, the jagged California mountain chains, and the magnificence of Yosemite Valley open up vistas far more rough, exotic, and varied; and Efros's poetry sounds an accord ample and resonant enough to take on this challenge.

At the center of the poem is a fundamental question about the human condition as it relates to the engine of American history. Why would a man abandon his loved ones and modest prosperity to undertake a quest for fortune that will destroy his soul? This is not the plight of immigrants who have fled grinding poverty and persecution. Ezra Lunt, his wife Abby, and son Danny live as free people on a productive farm sufficient for their needs, which they own without encumbrance. And, yet, Lunt leaves this all behind because he cannot still the urge to join the waves of men going off into the unknown to extract gold from the California soil. He is an imperfect man in many ways; he promises to return to his family after a year but fails to do so, and he falls in love with another woman and betrays his wife. But he is also a man who is brave, well intentioned, entrepreneurial, and forward looking, and the call that he heeds to put his life in danger and trek across the American continent does not come solely from the "lust for lucre."

What the call of gold means *beyond* greed and adventure is the question that troubles the poem. The answer is as complex as the restlessness of spirit that lies at the heart of the human condition, especially in its nineteenth-century American manifestation. Although *Zahav* does not offer a solution to this conundrum, it succeeds best in dramatizing the question and meditating on its profound difficulty. At every step Lunt takes, pushing higher and further and sacrificing both proximate and ultimate happiness, the poem wonders anew about the indistinct and enigmatic forces that push him from within. The stunning descriptions of the variegated vistas of California are, in a certain sense, an answer unto themselves. As readers, we are complicit with Lunt in taking in the spectacle of his quest and owing to the fact that his story might not have engaged us if he had chosen to remain on his farm in New England. There are fateful cosmic intentions, the poem implies, which we cannot fully grasp.

At the conclusion of *Zahav*, Abby has journeyed to California in search of Ezra, and, believing him dead, she has remarried and reestablished her family on a farm on the fertile California soil. Looking about her at the industrious settling of this new territory, she wonders aloud whether Americans would have ever left their homes behind to risk their chances in a remote and unknown land had it not been for the lust for gold. It is with the broaching of this historical theodicy, a version of the Rabbinic notion of *mitzvah ba'ah be'aveirah* (the fulfillment of a commandment arrived at through transgression), that the poem ends.

The Salem homestead establishes a norm at the outset of the poem. The land has been passed down to Abby from her ancestors; it is a productive farm that forms a unit in the kind of rural village society that Preil describes admiringly in his New England poems. Living on the land and working it are central to Efros's proto-Zionist, physiocratic vision of the human endeavor; this was the message that Tom preached, with little effect, to the braves of the Nanticoke Indians in *Vigvamim shoteqim*, who left sowing and planting to their women while they pursued the hunt. Ezra comes to the Salem farm as a hired hand seeking security and quiet after his army service in Mexico. He marries Abby; they have a son, and Ezra happily settles into the routines of the agricultural life until the reports begin to circulate about the discovery of gold in California, the territory that had been won for the United States in that same Mexican-American War. He is, of course, not alone is contracting gold fever. As he accurately represents to Abby, men from all walks of life and social class in the towns of New England around them are preparing to set out for the West. Indeed, in the years after 1849, approximately 300,000 Americans made their way to California on this quest.

Ezra's journey to the gold fields, which is proposed to be a sojourn of no more than one year, receives support from two sources that shed light on his motives. The first comes from Abby's father, who has lived through two great migratory spasms: the settling of the Ohio River valley and then the push on to Missouri. His failure to join the pioneers, he claims, has left him "wizened, reduced, and abashed." Espousing a version of manifest destiny, he posits a fundamental disquiet in the American body politic, which cannot be still when the nation bestrides territory unknown and unpossessed. This restlessness is made more combustible by the unpredictable changeableness of the human soul. "Perhaps man's heart is like the heart of the sea / And there is no knowing what upheavals will be produced in its depths / By the combination of moon and storm above [*tseruf sahar vesa'ar*]" (p. 14). So even though it is impossible to foresee where heeding this imperative will lead, as far as Abby's father is concerned, the consequences of turning one's back on the call have been disheartening. She steps aside and Ezra sets off.

The second perspective comes late in the poem after Ezra has been through his ordeal of arching happiness and agonizing loss among the remotest peaks of California. The poem suddenly cuts to the late-winter maple syrup festival celebrated for the whole community on Abby's farm in Salem on the eve of her departure for California (pp. 141–44). The passage is one of several tours de force of descriptive precision in *Zahav* in which Efros takes on the challenge of rendering into Hebrew a scene rooted in realities alien to the language and Jewish experience. What first appears to be a set piece belonging to the genre of the idyll—an organic, community-wide celebration of the earth's bounty—is undercut by a chorus of elders of the community, clergymen who are deaf, blind, or lame. In their ignorance, superstition, and condescension, they can understand the pull of the Gold Rush solely as the work of the devil. The sharp juxtaposition of their sneering obtuseness with the depths of Ezra's moral ordeal belatedly adds another layer of explanation. To have remained in Salem would have meant consigning one's self to a life circumscribed by a version of old Puritan values that have since degenerated into a set of soul-crushing social controls.

Lunt makes his way to Independence, Missouri, which is the staging point for the wagon trains setting off for the West. The provisioning of the expedition and the gathering of men and women from all sectors of the young nation offer Efros the opportunity to suggest the epic proportions of the drama into which Lunt's own desires have been enfolded. Like the embarking of a great ocean vessel, the wagon train departs with the exhilaration that comes from loosening the ties to the compromised past and being bound for glory. The weeks traversing the Great Plains go by in a blaze of high spirits and the singing of "Oh Susanna" around the campfires at night. But after that point, the difficulties set in. The wagon train is attacked by Indians, and Lunt is wounded in the defensive sorties. The ascent of the Rockies is grueling; every unnecessary though treasured possession must be jettisoned to lighten the wagons. Appalling starvation in the snowy high valleys recalls the grisly events of the Donner Party.

From among the collective presence of the wagon train, two figures emerge who will play a fateful role in Lunt's life once he reaches California: Thomas Logan, a master hunter and story teller, and his daughter Lola. Lola is a beautiful young woman with black eyes and black hair who is the opposite of retiring. She dances ecstatically around the campfire, rallies the defense against the Indians, and urges the pioneers onward toward their goal when their spirits have been devastated by privation. Lola's own spirits seem almost preternatural, and her fierce restlessness places her far apart from the conventions of female behavior. She is strongly linked symbolically in the poem to the primordial origins of California itself. In one of his fireside tales, Thomas Logan reminds his listeners of the ancient Spanish legend of Califia, the magnificent warrior queen who ruled a race of black Amazons inhabiting an island kingdom where the only metal was gold. For Lunt, Lola becomes a challenging and provocative muse who is finally revealed to be his true kindred spirit.[2]

There is a respite between the savage rigors of the journey west and the arrival at the gold fields that contributes to our understanding of the poem's symbolic code. Lunt recovers his strength in the presence of an old Indian named Hutslohan, who farms a plot of land overlooking the Pacific Ocean near San Francisco. A wisdom figure like the sachem in *Vigvamim shoteqim*, Hutslohan has arrived at a position of renunciation and quiescence after many hardships. Having once fought the White Man, he has come to accept the futility of resistance and has instead sought to extract what is useful from the culture of the colonizer. He has learned the importance of education, the rudiments of which he has worked painstakingly to acquire. He has further learned the importance of working the land and enriching it with human labor, a lesson that stands in stark contrast to the miners, who dig up the land and then abandon it to move on to the business of extraction elsewhere. His convictions affiliate him with the values embodied by Abby, who, at the close of the poem, reestablishes her farming life on the parcels of land near Hutslohan's that Lunt had purchased before moving on to prospect in the mountains. This was in fact the purpose for which Lunt, prompted by a resonant admiration for the Indian's tranquility, had bought the land in the first place. But the force that impels him toward the gold fields will exact a steep renunciation. Abby will indeed eventually work that plot of land, but it will not be Lunt who is at her side.[3]

The central section of *Zahav* (the third of five sections) opens with a fantastical scene. Strung out along the American River in the foothills of the Sierra Nevadas are young men with full beards, straw hats, and blue work shirts, each seemingly unaware of the others, and all of them bent with monomaniacal attention over large metal pans that they tilted and swirled incessantly. This frenzied, atomized activity becomes all the more strange when conveyed in Hebrew; Efros mobilizes the realia-laden concreteness of the mishnaic resources of the language to render a scene which, as seen through Lunt's eyes when he first rides into the encampment, seems incomprehensible. The driven, feverish movements of these men appear to him like shades in the netherworld who are compelled to repeat endlessly the deeds they performed when they were alive; the nightmarish scene looks like a "terrible game / in which the players have forgotten that they are playing" (p. 69). (Section Three is titled *Be'olam hatohu* [In the world of chaos].) But once Lunt discovers that Thomas Logan and Lola are among the miners and he settles into their company and begins to pan for gold himself, he soon finds himself wholly immersed in a world that at first had seemed so spectral and unreal.

Lunt takes to the task and quickly realizes the limitations imposed by the primitive manner of work in which each individual miner swirls the gravely water in his own pan. Lunt goes off to Sacramento to bring back large wooden cradles that allow two men to process two hundred buckets of gravel per day; he brings in Mexican workers to speed the work. His next plan is to dam and divert the river to create dry basins to get at the large veins of gold along the now-inaccessible riverbed. Nicknamed the Great God Lunt [*ha'el hagadol Lunt*], the man is everywhere at once directing, organizing, and making plans.

After months of punishing labor, the miners begin to wax nostalgic around the campfire and talk of returning home with their stakes to marry the girl who had once refused them or to buy the store that had been out of reach or set themselves up on a plantation. But Lunt will have nothing of it. Speaking like a man transfixed, he embarks on a lengthy speech in which he admonishes his brethren not to give up and go home but to redouble their resolve to pursue the track of gold intrepidly unto its ultimate source. If they march ever upwards into the mountains toward the head waters of the San Joaquin River, he promises them, they will eventually discover the fabled mother lode [*eim ha'oreqim*]. This, he continues in a state of hallucinatory fervor, is what they will find there.

אַךְ אֵי־שָׁם בְּרֹאשׁ הֶהָרִים אֵם הָעוֹרְקִים,
וּפְצַע־אֶרֶץ שָׁם לִרְחָבָה נִפְתָּח
הַמְזֻלָּף נִטְפֵי דָמוֹ הַזּוֹרֵחַ
אֶל תּוֹךְ גְּבִיעַ עָמֹק זֶה וְאָרֹךְ.
אֵי־שָׁם עַל מִטַּת הַר גָּבוֹהַּ שׁוֹכְבָה
מִתַּחַת מַרְבַד צַח וְרוּחוֹת שָׂרוֹת
הַמַּלְכָּה כָּלָּה פָּז חֲמוּדַת גֵּו.
נְחַפְּשֶׂנָּה, אַחַי, נָרִים מַרְבַד שְׁלֻגָּה
וְקֵץ לְחֵלֶק רַב שֶׁל צַעַר הָאָדָם,
עֲנִיּוּת תִּתֹּם, רָעָב בַּל יִוָּדַע,
וְחֶרֶב קְרָבוֹת תּוֹךְ נְדָנָהּ תִּישַׁן.

Somewhere at the head of the mountains there is the mother lode,
A broad earth-wound will be opened up
that showers drops of its glistening blood
into this deep and wide chalice.
Somewhere, recumbent on the bed of a high mountain,
under a pure coverlet and singing winds,
lies the beautiful queen who is all gold.
Let us seek her, my brothers, let us lift the snowy coverlet
and put an end to a great portion of man's suffering,
want will end, hunger will be unknown
and the sword of battle will be returned to slumber in its sheath.
    (p. 83)

In contrast to the other miners, ordinary men who are moved by greed and the desire for power, Lunt is launched on a quest. They long to return home to seize the prizes formerly denied them, but for him the tether to home has withered. In pursing the Gold Queen and later his love for Lola, Lunt is not in the position of a man who has turned his back on his wife and family, as much as one who has fallen under the spell of a new dispensation and been wholly delivered to it.

The passage above shows that his mania is not simple. On the one hand, his words produce a Promethean discourse about the manipulation and penetration of nature and the attainment of dominion over it. The quest is not about gold per se but about man's capacity to force the earth to yield unto humankind its most precious secrets. This language of force is, of course, not ungendered. The enterprise that Lunt is so ardently proposing comes close to rape, with its wounds and blood and stripping bare. Yet on the other hand, the quest is suddenly redirected, sublimated really, into a discourse of social redemption, as if to say that urges of such ominous and runaway potency must be harnessed to higher ends. The turnabout is not convincing, and it remains an outward sign of Lunt's failure to fathom his motives and understand the nature of the forces to which he is enthralled.

The solidarity of the mining encampment, which has until now been held together by shared greed and the force of Lunt's grand rhetoric, begins to breakdown. Thomas Logan dies an agonizing death after he is pinned under a fallen beam. With the winter approaching, the miners face diminishing returns on their labor because they have already taken most of the surface gold accessible through placer mining techniques. This time it is Lola who enters the breach. Since embarking for the West, the poem's narrator observes, she has grown from being a spirited girl to being a young woman whose figure "sent a hot current / into the hearts of miners who had deprived themselves of desire" [*nezirei ḥemdah*] (p. 97).

Sharpened in her passions by her father's death, Lola appeals to the men in terms similar to those used by Lunt. She tells them that they have only begun, literally, to scratch the surface of the vast deposits of gold that the earth conceals under the river flows. What they have touched so far is only the hem of "the petticoat of the queen / who is entirely gold" (p. 98).[4] Exploiting the sway of her femininity over these deprived men, she mocks them for their softness and their urge to cling to their mother's apron strings and assures them that their fiancées and wives will wait for them for another season. Her suasion, however, can succeed for only so long. As the winter worsens and the rain-swollen river threatens to overflow the hastily improvised levees, the miners' moods blacken, and they begin to turn on those who had given them dangerous and false encouragement. Early the next morning, Lola and Lunt escape and ride off together.

Yosemite is the place they travel to, and it is in that extraordinary valley that the two are, for a brief time, reborn. Lunt has long been in love with Lola, but she, possessed by the fierce and exalted quest for gold, has had no room in her heart for a competing passion. The departure from the mining camp somehow breaks the spell and opens up a deep reserve of tenderness. She finally responds to Lunt's overtures, and the two become lovers who find ardor and comfort in each other's arms. Cut off from human society and alone in the lap of nature, they are the world to each other. Lola regains a childlike spontaneity and innocence, and while Lunt makes expeditions to explore the water sources in the upper reaches of the valley, she spends her days sporting with the deer and the birds and roaming the valley and delighting in its wonders. Yosemite for them is an American Eden: a joining of miraculous natural beauty with erotic innocence that is experienced as existing before, or at least, beyond time and society.

Efros makes of Yosemite something far more than a picturesque backdrop for this idyll. Ever the bearer of the romantic poetic tradition, Efros makes the geological history of Yosemite into a drama of violence and restitution (pp. 118–19). He tells the story of how, many thousands of years ago, glaciers formed and proceeded in their deliberate deadly crawl to wipe out all life and tear deep gashes into the earth's surface. The eventual melting of the glaciers left behind a scene of astonishing wild beauty. Through a deep, narrow green valley flows the Merced River—*nehar harahamim* in the poem—which is fed by the snow melt of the Sierra Nevadas. Along the sides of the valley are gigantic stone monoliths punctured by waterfalls cascading down from enormous heights. Like other American Hebraists influenced by the Hudson River School and American transcendentalism, Efros cannot see grandeur in nature without feeling the awe of the Creator. The great hulking sides of the valley look like massive cathedrals whose great doors, amidst the swelling chords of the organ, are about to burst open to disgorge a crowd of worshippers. The hand that once visited an arctic death upon all forms of life repented its purpose and left an otherworldly paradise as recompense. Beneath the huge and austere rock formations runs the verdant valley "like Eden after the bonfires of Sheol." There "with supplications of forgiveness, God kisses / all that He had once afflicted" (p. 119).

For Lola, who at this moment is playing in the fields of the Lord, this geological theodicy is meant to offer an explanatory key. For hers is a character that is most assuredly in need of explanation. How otherwise can we understand her sudden transformation from a fierce, taunting man-woman to a flower child cavorting with the animals in the garden by day and falling into her lover's arms by night? The explanation, after the manner of Victorian novelistic conventions, comes in the form of a concealed story of origins. As Thomas Logan lays dying, he reveals to Lunt that Lola was placed in his hands by an Indian for safekeeping and is not his daughter; Logan's dying wish is for Lunt to watch over her. The full story does not emerge until the couple arrives at Yosemite, when Lunt observes that Lola is subject to unexplained periods of dejection. She explains to Lunt that her moods are the result of the sudden recurrence of painful memories from her childhood. When she was a child traveling west with her parents, the family was attacked by Indians; her mother, father, and younger brother were murdered before her eyes, and she was taken captive. The attack took place during a year of extreme drought; desperate for survival, the Indian tribe undertook a four-day vigil of solemn dancing and prayer. With no rain in sight, the medicine man of the tribe is seized by a holy delirium through which he is told by the gods that the evil Manitou will be propitiated only by a blood sacrifice. The white girl is the chosen one, and she is tied to a tree to await her fate the next morning. But she is rescued by an Indian from another tribe—none other than Hutslohan, the wise old Indian Lunt had met outside San Francisco—who eventually places her in the care of Thomas Logan.

Although the reader may be tempted to dismiss all of this as stereotypically melodramatic, a closer look at the poem's narrative shows that Efros is making productive use of this convention. It makes psychological sense that a girl raised without a mother and among hunters and cattlemen would seek to compensate for the frailty of her sex by becoming combative, fearless, and manly. It is only after Logan's death and the persistence of Lunt's solicitude that Lola can allow herself to loosen the grip of repression and open herself to being loved and to loving in return. It is here that the geology of Yosemite becomes a figure for the recuperation of Lola's feminine self. The catastrophic winter that shaped the valley's fierce beauty finally abated and left an Edenic garden in its stead, and it is in this special, primal place that Lola is allowed a brief but rich reprieve from the consequences of the violence that had disfigured her life. But, alas, so great a trauma can grant no lasting mitigation. The very relaxing of repression, which makes possible the exchange of tenderness with Lunt, brings back the buried memories with renewed force. Lola displays the classic symptoms of what today we would call post-traumatic stress disorder. She cannot prevent the gruesome scene of her family's massacre from being replayed repeatedly in her mind. Depressed and cut off from Lunt, whose gold mania has been reignited, Lola commits suicide without warning by galloping off the side of a mountain ledge as the two ride higher and higher above the valley in search of the mother lode.

Yet Lola would not be so fascinating a figure if it were only her psychology that is on display in the poem. And it is far too reductive to say that her playing the Amazon is merely a reaction to early trauma. Early in *Zahav*, long before we know about her origins, Lola is linked to Califia, the dark warrior queen, a figure that instills awe and fear in the minds of the pioneers when they hear tales told about her. This association imparts to Lola something of a representative, allegorical function in the poem. It is not coincidental that the wound she bears was incurred when her family was embarked on their journey westward to settle the frontier. It is a wound which, on a collective level, is a necessary and inevitable consequence of conquest and settlement. Necessary and inevitable, too, is the transformation of gender imposed by this errand. To be a woman among these men, a girl must be spirited, intrepid, and imperious. Beyond this fierce and lonely independence, there exist only the figures of the prostitute and the consort.

Except, that is, for Abby. At the very moment that Lola is sinking into depression in the High Sierras, Abby is gaining in moral stature as she organizes herself to take leave of New England. Having had no word from her husband and fearing for his safety, she undertakes to find him, even though it means uprooting her elderly parents, giving up her ancestral farm, and traveling to California by ship to Panama, through the jungle roads to the Pacific, and then on to San Francisco. After she deposits her son with her parents, Abby pushes on further to the gold fields; she becomes a singer in a saloon for the purpose of gaining information about her husband. There she meets a man named Eric, who had once worked for her on her Salem farm—and admired her—before she was married. Together they go deep into the mountain mining camps in search of Ezra, and it is there that they are told by supposedly reliable witnesses that Ezra had died in a fall from a cliff in the high mountains on his relentless search for the mother lode.

Eventually, Abby and Eric marry and establish a successful farm on the land Ezra had purchased overlooking San Francisco. But, in fact, Lunt had not died. Driven nearly mad by grief and regret, he is now an empty shell of a man who aimlessly roams the countryside. On two occasions, his wanderings put him in a position to observe Abby and Eric unbeknownst to them. The first time is in the saloon where they meet, and this one-sided encounter leaves Lunt in a state of wretchedness and remorse so consuming that he causes a disastrous fire that becomes "a metonym for the finality of things."[5] The second time coincides with the abundant first harvest on the couple's farm. In the conversation he overhears from behind a haystack, Lunt comes to understand that the two had married only after the news of his death and after Abby's mourning him. He even has a conversation with his son Danny, who has grown into a handsome and intelligent boy. With tears in his eyes, he tells the boy, who does not recognized him in his disheveled state, that his father had loved him very much. He then moves on, and the poem ends.

Although, here again, a melodramatic anagnorisis marks the poem's filiations with older modes of writing, the historical and moral messages of the narrative are heightened rather than diminished. Abby's willingness to give up her ancestral land, uproot her family, and settle in the West represents the beginning of a critical shift of balance in the life of the new nation. Although finding her husband is the immediate impetus, the move and the mobilization of fresh energy it entails reflect an intuitive awareness of the decline and even perversion—remember the deaf, lame, and blind ministers—of the New England moral heritage. (It would not be far afield to see a parallel between the move west within America and the move to America by masses of East European Jews; the immigrants came upon the fresh opportunities they found in America because they were fleeing the prejudices and persecutions, both internal and external, of their lives in the Old Country.)

Abby replants the best of those New England values in the soil of California, and rather than being a moralistic killjoy amidst California's gold frenzy, she represents the dynamic future. For it is agriculture that will become the state's great economic engine long after the gold deposits have been played out. That depletion is prefigured by the course of Lunt's life. By remaining alive, he is condemned to suffer a double loss. For Lola's death, there can of course be no reprieve; but the loss of his wife and child could have been recouped if he had revealed the fact of his survival. But chastened by the baleful consequences of his obsessions and in possession of the tragic knowledge that comes from scourging suffering, he renounces his own chance for rescue to allow Abby the measure of happiness left to her. As he glimpses Abby's golden tresses as she sits among the newly harvested golden sheaves of wheat, the folly of his search for another kind of gold comes fully home to him.

Zahav is one of the strongest works in the corpus of American Hebrew literature. Efros has created a set of complex characters whose personal dilemmas are interlocked with a transformative event in American history. The poem approaches the artistry of a successful historical novel without leaving poetry behind. An early advocate of the simple, lyric song as the ideal for American Hebrew poetry, Efros performed an impressive act of self-transcendence when he widened his lens to take on the burden of the large, historical-narrative poem. This jump also required a different way of using words. The radical simplicity of the early lyrics had to give way to a much more densely textured lexical palette, especially when it came to portraying the mining scenes and the ravishing but unfamiliar western landscape. Efros could not rely on tropes borrowed from his European Hebrew predecessors, who had adapted biblical Hebrew for the purpose of describing the lush woods and streams of the Russian countryside. The realities of California, both human and natural, emblematize the newness of America much more than either the gentle pastures of New England or the exotic practices of Native Americans. In creating such vivid tableaux in *Zahav*, Efros has, in a very real sense, brought Hebrew to America. Of all of the works discussed in this section, moreover, *Zahav* is the least Jewish, lacking even the implied national allegory that characterizes the Indian epics. True, Efros denominates the months according to their Hebrew names to signal a common cultural identity between poet and reader. But beyond that, this is an American story and one of the great achievements of American Hebrew poetry. That Efros's poem should be so profoundly unknown in both America and Israel is a great pity.

Of necessity, the lives of Native Americans and California miners could be known by American Hebrew poets only second hand. But when it came to African Americans, the opportunities for observation were as unconstrained for the Hebraists as they were for other white residents of large northern cities. The fact that these opportunities were generally not taken advantage of is part of the larger turning away from urban life that, with notable exceptions, characterized the enterprise of American Hebrew poetry. Encounters with blacks can be found here and there among the poems of Silberschlag, Halkin, and Preil and, with somewhat more intensity, in American Hebrew fiction.[1] But there is only one work that aspires wholly to engage African American experience: Lisitzky's *Be'oholei Khush* [In the tents of Cush] (1953). This is a key text in the canon of American Hebrew poetry, not only because of its singularity but also because of its insistence on going beyond observation and description toward an impersonation of the black voice. In a fiercely sincere and idiosyncratic act of identification, Lisitzky appropriates the voices of black preachers and, through the fluently ornate biblical Hebrew idiom they are made to speak, builds a poignant, if fragile, bridge between black and Jewish historical experience.

New Orleans is fundamental for understanding Lisitzky's difference. He arrived there in 1918 at the age of thirty-two after stays in Boston, upstate New York, rural Ontario, Milwaukee, and Buffalo, described in his classic autobiography *Eleh toledot adam* (1949), translated into English as *In the Grip of Cross-Currents* in 1959. The autobiography concludes with Lisitzky's settling in New Orleans, an act that

represents an end both to his wanderings and to his quest for a vocation.[2] Accepting a position as a Hebrew teacher in New Orleans—a
small Jewish community cut off from the centers of cultural dynamism
in the North—signified Lisitzky's embrace of a calling that he saw to
be pioneering work on behalf of the Jewish people that was as arduous
as the contemporary toils of the *ḥalutsim* in Palestine.

Like the autobiographies of so many men and women of achievement, *Eleh toledot adam* takes Lisitzky just to the moment when it
becomes clear to him in what field of endeavor his great contribution
will lie.[3] He seizes the challenge, and the book comes to an end, as if
to say that once the private self grasps its public role—here it is cast
in nationalist terms as service to the Jewish people—there is no further need to chronicle its vicissitudes. To be sure, many of the other
Hebrew poets in America were committed Hebrew educators. But
most attained distinguished positions heading educational systems
or teaching in Hebrew colleges, rabbinical schools, or even in secular
universities; and for some, the teaching was more on the order of a
livelihood that supported the life of letters. Lisitzky stood apart in
his willingness to stand his ground and take on the fight for Hebrew
in a small community that evinced no evident sympathy for that language or for traditional Jewish culture. He taught Hebrew and wrote
Hebrew poetry in New Orleans for fifty-four years until his death in
1962.[4]

The Hebraist vocation in America, in Lisitzky's rigorous conception
of it, presupposed a reciprocal obligation. Parallel to the struggle to
plant Hebrew within the souls of young American Jews was the duty
to take in America, to learn its history, and to absorb its otherness. If
other Hebraists in America often felt stranded in a spiritual wasteland,
Lisitzky seemed perpetually transfixed by the spectacle of America and
invigorated by the opportunities it presented for conquering new thematic frontiers on behalf of Hebrew literature. Of all the Hebrew writers in America, Lisitzky was perhaps the most American in the sense
that he did not view his life on these shores as the result of an arbitrary
decree of history, nor he did long to be transported to Eretz Yisrael.
The commitment to know America and take it seriously was most dramatically expressed, as we have seen, in the writing of his mammoth

Indian epic *Medurot do'akhot* [Dying campfires] (1937). Saturated with a super-abundance of legendary materials, that poem was the fruit of an intention that was too programmatic and too diligent, as well as being far removed from personal experience.

The case was far different when Lisitzky took on the subject of African Americans. Despite segregation, living in New Orleans in the first half of the twentieth century meant living alongside a population removed only one or two generations from slavery. Lisitzky was fascinated by the oral culture of this community, its folk songs and spirituals, as well as the sermons of preachers and the testimonies of former sinners presented at revival meetings. Although Lisitzky tried his hand at rendering these sermons into Hebrew as early as the late 1920s,[5] most of the poems were written in the 1940s during his summer holidays. The result was the collection *Be'oholei Khush*, which was published by the distinguished Israeli publishing house Mossad Bialik in 1953.

Be'oholei Khush is a mixed performance, stumbling when it tries to convey Hebrew versions of black folk songs and spirituals and brilliant when it underscores the preachers' quasi-midrashic elaborations on the biblical stories in their sung sermons. But as interesting as is the work on its own—we shall return to an analysis of it directly—even more fascinating are the very fact of its existence and the question of why Lisitzky wrote it in the first place. Lisitzky would seem to have anticipated this curiosity by providing a general preface (*Divrei petihah*, pp. 3–4) that clearly lays out his intentions and explains the origins of the volume. Many critics, as Katz has pointed out, have taken the preface at face value and offered quotations from it as a sufficient description of the book rather than analyzing the poems it contained.[6] Although the preface is undoubtedly an important statement, there is a second, far more consequential autobiographical statement that occurs in the first pages of the longest poem in the volume ("'Ezra hakohen" [Reverend Ezra], pp. 204–55) buried deep in its final section, and this statement has been largely overlooked. A comparison between these statements moves us closer to understanding the complexity and force of Lisitzky's motives for embarking on this extraordinary undertaking.[7]

The preface describes three stages in the evolution of the project. Lisitzky first sets the scene by adducing the more than thirty years he has spent living in the South that have given him a privileged point of observing African Americans, who, because of segregation, have been forced to live among themselves and have thereby maintained the integrity of their way of life. From his first encounters with them, he has been attracted to southern blacks because of several distinguishing qualities: their primitivism, their childlike innocence and guile, and the felt authenticity of their religion. What draws Lisitzky most is the unadorned simplicity of this religiosity, which is immediate, embodied, and concrete. Because of this attraction, Lisitzky is moved to the next stage, which involves undertaking a disciplined, firsthand examination of black culture and spirituality.

Describing the thoroughness of his researches, Lisitzky writes: "It is now many years that I have been entering into discussions with them concerning matters between man and man and between man and God, meeting with them at meetings, clubs, and church gatherings, attending the speeches of their leaders and the sermons of their preachers, paying attention to their prayers, and listening to their spirituals as they are sung by their congregations and choirs with the enthusiastic fervor [*behitlahavut uvidevequt*] of Hasidim." Once he had learned as much as possible for a white man to learn, it occurred to him that the phenomenon he had been investigating had within it the potential to contribute something vital to Hebrew poetry in America. He therefore set about giving this material shape [*lahatil bah tsurah*] in such a way that "its roots should be planted in the soil of America while its crown should take its place within general Hebrew literature."

There are several points to be noted here. The phrase that indicates Lisitzky's attraction to southern blacks is *laqḥu halalu et libi*, which literally means "they took my heart." The idiom can carry the implication of being beguiled or charmed, and this is a phrase that we return to later. Here the echo of desire and seduction is muted and quickly folded into a quasi-scientific discourse of description and investigation; but the case will be quite otherwise when we look at the later poetic statement. There is no escaping the colonial-ethnographic standpoint

Lisitzky establishes, which includes the assumption that, with enough exertion, the other can be known. (And this is indeed an end that Lisitzky claims his thirty years of active observation have allowed him to achieve.) It is the primitive that fascinates him, and he mobilizes the resources of reason to penetrate this mystique and comprehend it. The project of observation requires—or is it *allows?*—a sustained and multifarious incursion into the social and religious spaces of black society, which becomes a kind of reverse vaulting over the barrier set by segregation.

Black religious experience, it becomes clear, is the dominant allure for Lisitzky; yet nowhere in his expansive description of what attracts him is the word Christianity or Christ mentioned. The use of the term *datiyyut*, religiosity, is an understandable avoidance for a Hebrew writer and his audience, but it remains a critical evasion that puts in question the reliability of his account of black religion. Finally, there is the matter of the poetic use to which his researches are put. Lisitzky's preface describes a distinctly sequential set of events: he was attracted, he set about observing, and then he decided to use his observations as the basis for Hebrew poetry. This final moment is presented as the sudden realization of an opportunity. In a stroke, Lisitzky succeeds in turning the disability of his location on the remotest margins of the Hebrew literary map into an advantage for himself, as well as for Hebrew literature. The sapped vitality of Hebrew poetry in America, moreover, is in need of the reinvigoration that will be effected by bringing this subject within its bourn. And in turn, American Hebrew poetry will be able to justify itself within an Israel-centered litera-ture that often barely acknowledges its existence. Lisitzky intends to reshape the materials of Afro-American culture in such a way that, without effacing their American roots, they will make sense within the context of a Hebrew poetry, whose center is elsewhere. It is a conjur-ing act that will reward our close examination.

The second autobiographical statement is the prologue to the first-person narrative of Reverend Ezra, a biblically erudite escaped slave whom the poet interviews on the porch of an old-age home in New Orleans. The prologue is stunningly exceptional because it is the only instance in the volume's three hundred pages with its dozens of poems in which Lisitzky violates the premise of the work and speaks in his own voice. Every other poem, including the remaining forty-three pages of "'Ezra hakohen," is spoken through the personae of black speakers, whether preachers, choirs, singers, or sinners. (The complexities of this appropriation and the problems it raises will be addressed in due course.) The prologue's eight pages of blank verse, fluidly expository like the poem it introduces, manage to gather within themselves several interlocking narrative threads. The first is the poet-narrator's resolute quest to find a true native informant, a former slave who can describe to him firsthand the experience of slavery and its aftermath.

His determination comes from two sources. The spectacle of elderly blacks behaving obsequiously to whites and moving aside to make room for them on the sidewalks of New Orleans, and the persistence of the behaviors of slavery after the abolition of slavery troubles and confuses him. Since settling in New Orleans, he has fallen in love with its azure skies, the paradisiacal lushness of its plantings, and with the compelling blackness of its citizens' physiognomies and the winning sincerity of their enthusiastic prayer services. The depth of his response, he realizes, stems in part from a childhood encounter with a Hebrew translation of *Uncle Tom's Cabin* and a heartfelt early identification of the enslavement of blacks in America with the bondage of Israel in Egypt.[8] He is, therefore, deeply stirred when he meets concrete embodiments of figures from the moral imagination of his youth. His yearning [*hishtoqaqti*] to locate a living former slave who could satisfy his desire for a firsthand account of that terrible period is continually frustrated. The memories of many of his informants are too compromised by old age to be of much good, and the abundant recollections of others are too obviously reshaped by nostalgia for youth and longing for the days when they were cared for by the benevolent master.

He draws closer to his goal as a direct result of his role as a kind of participant-observer in black prayer meetings. He is strongly drawn [*ahov ahavti*] to expressions of black spirituality of all sorts, and he makes a special point of attending a series of revival meetings held in a big circus tent and led by a visiting minister. The exceptional presence of a white man who is also a descendent of "Abraham, Isaac and

Jacob" is publicly noted with approbation, and this distinction enables the poet to approach the minister and enlist him in his search for the informant he is seeking. His appeal results in the referral to Reverend Ezra.

Given the ardor of his quest, we would expect the poet to pursue this lead directly, but, surprisingly, the mission is indefinitely deferred because of troubles closer to home. The narrative turns onto another path, which illuminates the poet's "day job" as the principal of the city's Hebrew school. He is embroiled in a struggle, shared by many Hebrew educators elsewhere at this time, to establish a curriculum that is rooted in the cultural values of Hebrew nationalism, as well as in the study of classic religious texts. These efforts are fiercely opposed by most of the parents, who are perfectly happy if their children to do not proceed beyond learning some basic home and synagogue ritual skills by rote (haftorah, kiddush, and kaddish) and enough Yiddish to read a newspaper and write a letter.[9] The difficulties in advancing his program leave him dejected, exasperated, and preoccupied. His investigations of black slavery are ironically forgotten for the time being because of the enslavement that he himself had been placed in, "the Bondage of Israel / in which were cast the pitiable first Hebrew teachers / in the land of America!" (p. 208).[10]

There is one more digressive turn before the prologue can bring the reader to the poem's eponymous subject. It concerns the miserable fate of a Palestinian Jew who had disembarked in the port of New Orleans only to be placed under quarantine because he manifested early signs of leprosy. The disease took its course—drugs against leprosy were not developed until the 1930s—and he was confined to a leper hospital. A wealthy, local Jewish businessman took pity on the leper, paid him occasional visits to comfort him, and sent a monthly stipend to his wife and children in Palestine. This man, who came from modest origins and was uneducated Jewishly, was one of the poet's staunch supporters in his educational battles. When the leper's condition nears its fatal stage, the man asks the poet to go to the hospital to help the leper compose a final letter in Hebrew and Yiddish to his wife and children.

Performing this commission, despite the succor it confers, brings the poet no joy. He is mortified by the scenes of monstrous disfigurement he witnesses in the hospital, which he experiences as a defacement of the nobility of God's image in human beings. When he leaves, his whole world is darkened and embittered; the pristine skies and beautiful surrounding fields, all formerly part of the charm of this southern city for him, now seem to mock the human form and its fated breakdown. He is rescued from a descent into melancholy when he recalls that the institution where Reverend Ezra is a resident stands close by. Thus the strands of the story are gathered together. He finds Ezra to be alert, articulate, and of noble carriage; he is in possession of a fine memory, and he is unstinting in sharing his recollections. He is a man in whose soul, in contrast to the gruesome sights he has just seen, "the candle of God" burns brightly. The pall of despondency lifts as the poet attends to his words, which become the body of the poem.

A comparison of the preface to the prologue has a lot to tell us about Lisitzky's motives for writing *Be'oholei Khush*. In the preface, which is a formal prose document that introduces the whole volume, Lisitzky presents himself as a citizen of the republic of Hebrew letters who, having arrived at a remote and exotic outpost, is resolved to make something useful out of his enthusiasm for the local inhabitants. Addressing the Hebrew reading public, now located almost entirely in the new Jewish state, he explains how he worked through his enchantment and the field work it entailed, mastered his subject, and found a way to make it available as a contribution to Hebrew poetry. At the core of the preface, then, we are offered a difficult but successfully completed act of appropriation.

The prologue to "'Ezra hakohen," which, in contrast to the preface, is a confessional document in verse introducing a single poem, discloses a very different balance of power between the observer and the observed. The casual idiom in the public preface, *laqhu halalu et libi* [they took my heart, i.e., charmed me] becomes a literal truth in the confessional prologue, which is saturated with the language of desire (*ahov ahavti, hishtoqaqti*). This is not to say that the blacks of New Orleans conjoined to *take* the poet's heart—his devices and desires were his own—but the indubitable result was that it *was* taken. Religion is foregrounded as the most alluring of the aspects of black experience described in the preface; the prologue seconds that emphasis and adds the experience of slavery and its connection to the ordeals of both Jewish history and his own chosen vocation. (One suspects that there is also an aesthetic and sensuous dimension to the attraction, although this remains latent.)

The powerful attraction of the spirituality Lisitzky witnessed in black church services and revival meetings can be understood only within the context of Lisitzky's identity as a modern Hebrew writer. *Eleh toledot adam*, Lisitzky's autobiography, makes it clear that he belongs squarely among the cohort of writers like Brenner and Gnessin who were steeped in talmudic erudition and punctilious piety in their childhood, lost their faith in adolescence through reading Haskalah literature, and discovered in Hebrew writing a vehicle for conveying their post-religious sensibilities.[11] For some it was a liberation, and for others a necessary loss; but for all, there was a collapse of the plausibility of traditional Jewish faith and its power to underwrite a life of adherence to the commandments. Sincere and fervent regular worship was of course central to the theological complex that had broken down.

It is therefore exceedingly interesting that it is just this dimension of black experience that so enthralls Lisitzky and brings him to spend years traveling throughout the South to attend black church services and other religious gatherings. Both the preface and the prologue are rich in describing the qualities the poet admired in the religiosity he was observing—immediacy, sincerity, simplicity, fervor, and so on—but they are poor in any real self-reflection about *why* this should be the case. Whereas the reasons may be hidden from the writer—and indeed perhaps uninteresting to him—for the reader familiar with Lisitzky's generation in Hebrew literature, there is really nothing inexplicable about the mystery. The collapse of traditional faith and its renunciation in favor of modernity had left a vacancy in the inner lives of writers like Lisitzky who, despite their principled negations and less-principled repugnance, persisted in experiencing religious needs.

If the Jewish piety of the old world was poisoned fruit from a lost garden, how much more so the temples of American Jewish communities with their ignorant rabbis and arrogant congregants? In the ecstatic and heartfelt outpourings of the gospel choirs, Lisitzky felt the *hitlahavut* and the *devequt*, the fervent cleaving to God of the Hasidim, yet without the inconvenient presence of real Hasidim to remind him of all the reasons he had broken with the world of Jewish piety in the first place.

There is something of the same displacement at work in the poet's indefatigable search for a witness to black slavery. The urgency of this mission had its origins in the awakening of the moral imagination of a boy as he discovered a narrative of monstrous oppression. That the boy was Jewish and that he read the story of escaped slaves in Hebrew are facts that materially colored the lens through which the mature poet would view the descendents of the figures in *Uncle Tom's Cabin* when he met them in real life on the streets of New Orleans rather than in a book. It is in fact an impatience with textuality that is one of the factors that impels his quest; he demands a real person rather than a book. The other is an intimate fusing of the bondage of Israel with the enslavement of African Americans. The Exodus is of course the great trope of black folk songs and preaching in which the enslaved identify with the oppression and liberation of ancient Israel. Lisitzky works the equation in the opposite direction by making the experience of the blacks in modern times into the paradigm for historical authenticity. It is with the burning intensity of that experience that he longs to make a connection precisely because it represents a reanimation of the core historical experience of the Jewish people. It is, in short, now black history that is invested with the authentic historical charisma that was once the possession of the Jews.

For Jews, persecution is surely not just an ancient phenomenon; but what Lisitzky has in mind as its contemporary manifestation is not, amazingly enough, anti-Semitism but rather the humiliations of pioneer Hebrew teachers in their struggles with boorish communal leaders in America! This equivalence between black slavery and the uphill battles of Hebrew education seems less bizarre or offensive if we remember that Lisitzky is making an analogy to the ordeal of black experience from what is most profoundly important in his own experience. The analogy nonetheless tells us something fundamental about his temperament. The boundaries between the world and his self are weak, and he is prone to an aggrieved existential misery when his efforts to realize his lofty goals are checked or when, as in the case of the leper hospital, he is thrust into a milieu of wretchedness and despair. Exposed to adversity or affliction, Lisitzky cannot help having his whole worldview infected with gloom. He is raised from the slough of despond only by finally making contact with Ezra in the old-age home near the hospital. In the former slave's nobility of character and unstinting clarity of recollection, the poet discovers not only the elusive authenticity he has been seeking but also deliverance from his own demons.

The prologue to "'Ezra hakohen," in sum, undermines the confident programmatic posture of the volume's general preface and opens up a revealing interior space. From this inner perspective, the poet is shown to be in thrall to and dependent upon the phenomenon he is supposedly appropriating for the greater glory of Hebrew literature. He has projected on to African Americans a romance of suffering that was once the preserve of the Jews; and he is powerfully drawn to an elemental religious enthusiasm that had been one of the necessary losses of his own intellectual formation. As an educator who daily faces the Sisyphean task of implanting Hebrew within an unwilling community, he needs contact with black culture both as an alternative source of vitality and as an explanatory paradigm for his own ordeals. Regarding the songs and sermons he has collected and recast, Lisitzky states in the preface that he realized that "here is material for poetry that has the capacity to benefit Hebrew poetry in America, and it is fitting for us to be in need of it" (p. 3). In the prologue, Lisitzky discloses, despite himself, just how large and how unelected is that need.

Turning to the poetry itself, the first question that might naturally strike a reader opening *Be'oholei Khush* is, "Are these poems translations or inventions?" What did Lisitzky do with the wealth of materials he collected over many years of assiduous attendance at church services and revival meetings? One possible answer points in the direction of translation understood in a broad sense. Although not necessarily adhering to the literal sense, he "rendered" these materials into Hebrew while striving to remain loyal to their original spirit. The other option points in the direction of the autonomous poetic imagination. Lisitzky listened closely to the songs and sermons of southern blacks and then went about composing Hebrew poems that, although inspired or based on what he had heard, were his own creations. (It is important to keep in mind that both alternatives presuppose a rather large intervention: the transformation of oral performances into modern, written verse.) There is no ambiguity as to Lisitzky's own position, as he makes clear in the opening lines of the same preface to the volume discussed above. Referring to the general title "From the Songs of the Negroes," under which some of the volume's poems had previously appeared in journals, the poet declares that these poems are "not a reworking or a translation of the songs/poems of the Negroes. This title indicates only that their themes were taken from the milieu of the Negroes and that they were written in the spirit of the Negroes" (p. 3).

Despite Lisitzky's asseverations, the nature of his poetic practice in *Be'oholei Khush* remains complicated. The issue is both illuminated and made more complex by the work in the 1920s of the Harlem Renaissance poets, which undoubtedly served as a model for Lisitzky's own project. In the poetic activity of such figures as James Weldon Johnson, Countee Cullen, Langston Hughes, and Gwendolyn Bennett, there were often indistinct borders between, on the one hand, collecting and anthologizing folk materials (which were also put through various processes of transcription and conventionalization to make them stand as poems) and, on the other, composing new poems that were "based on" authentic folk models. The work of Johnson is a good illustration of this duality. He is the compiler of the *Book of American Negro Spirituals* (1925, together with J. Rosamond Johnson, who arranged the music), which presents a collection of supposedly authentic sung songs that preserve the dialect speech used in real life. Johnson is also the author of *God's Trombones: Seven Negro Sermons in Verse* (1927), a book of his own poems, which are patterned on African American folk sermons, and whose language is standard poetic diction rather than dialect.

Lisitzky most likely would have identified with the latter, which confirms the authorship by the poet of the poem despite the fact of its folk provenance. A related question concerns the source of the sermons and songs that served as the models for the poems. Were they wholly the result of Lisitzky's firsthand field experience attending southern churches, or were they also indebted to the kinds of anthologies compiled by Johnson and other figures of the Harlem Renaissance? The tangled skein of these issues cannot be sorted out in the present context, but closer attention to these texts has the potential to teach us not only about Lisitzky's practice but also the way in which translation can be used to maintain and disguise cultural barriers, as well as to surmount them.[12]

The mixed success of Lisitzky's realization of his project is a direct result of the Hebrew-language commitments he brought to the task. Like most of the American Hebrew poets, he was committed to the serious, classic norms of modern literary Hebrew of the generation of Bialik, although disencumbered of its heavier allusive apparatus. Slang, vulgarisms, dialect, and all forms of defective linguistic registers were alien to this conception of a proper literary language. This allegiance hampers Lisitzky in some sections of *Be'oholei Khush* and works to his advantage in others. An example of the former is the first of the book's three sections, which is devoted to folksongs (pp. 17–93). This includes a wide variety of genres: train songs, chain gang songs, banjo songs, gallows songs, and many spirituals, sung by lone sinners or by church choirs. Many are affecting and charming, and the variegated nature of the gathering as a whole is highly instructive to the Hebrew reader and undoubtedly constitutes a contribution of something new to the corpus of Hebrew literature. But unfortunately, they do not work well as poems. The themes and subjects pass through this stylistic filter successfully, but the distinctive voices of the poems do not. Declining to use dialect, which in any case may not have proved workable in Hebrew, is a major renunciation that forces the poems to do without the tang and the edge and the otherness of rural black speech in the age before general literacy. Lisitzky's efforts recall Bialik's attempts to transpose Yiddish folk melodies into Hebrew a half century earlier. The force of conviction is felt, but the folk has gone missing.[13]

Ironically, those same stylistic loyalties stand Lisitzky in good stead in the major, central portion of the book (pp. 96–168), which focuses on sung sermons. His goal in this section is to represent the imaginative and rhetorical eloquence of southern preachers as they elaborate on the biblical text to drive home a contemporary moral message to their congregants. In its authentic manifestations, this was a form of speech that was itself already elevated, stylized, and suffused with King James-inflected borrowings from the Bible. So, when Lisitzky sought to put these homilies in Hebrew garb, what then could be more fitting than the rich, classical, and biblically suffused style that Lisitzky and other Americans had distilled from Bialik and his contemporaries? It was, in many senses, a marriage made in heaven, with the Hebrew Bible as a common background and point of departure. The fit was based not only on language but on method as well. Nearly every Hebrew reader of the period was familiar with the techniques of midrash and aggadah, either as a textual practice in Jewish classical literature or as a mode of popular sermonizing that made the ancient text come alive to inveigh against sins in the here and now and to speak about issues of the present moment. Playing fast and loose with the Holy Writ to achieve a higher good was not a monopoly of the rabbis. This is essentially what the southern preachers were doing after their own manner and carrying it off with a virtuosity even more extravagantly imaginative.

A good example of this fit is the first sermon in the section, "Yisra'el baShittim" [Israel at Shittim] (pp. 97–104).[14] From the title, the Hebrew reader can conjure up the familiar story at the beginning of Numbers 25 that describes Israel's whoring after the Moabite god Baal Peor and the dramatic steps taken to extricate them from their infidelities. After Balak, the king of Moab, failed to vanquish Israel using Balaam's curses, which were turned into blessings, the Israelite men fall prey to the wiles of the Moabite women and are lured into idolatry. God's wrath erupts, and He commands Moses to behead and impale the leaders of the people. While Moses orders the judges to kill all who had participated in the heathen cult, an Israelite man is brazen enough to flaunt his relations with his Midianite lover in the presence of Moses and the entire camp. At this point, Pinḥas (Phineas), the son of Elazar (one of Aaron's sons), arises from within the camp, takes a javelin in hand and impales the two lovers through the genitals. God's anger abates, and the plague he has sent against the people is curtailed. In recognition of Pinḥas's zealotry, God awards him and his descendents the high priesthood in perpetuity.

There is surely no lack of sex, violence, and high drama in the original biblical episode, but the anonymous black preacher of Lisitzky's poem chooses to re-imagine the story in ways relevant to him and to his community. If in the biblical account the function of harlotry is to seduce Israelite men into idol worship, in the eyes of the reverend speaker of the sermon, it is the immorality itself that is the main focus. He expatiates broadly on the saloons, gambling dens, whorehouses, and dancing parlors, in short all the places of sin that his congregants know flourish on the outskirts of their own community and ensnare its men folk. In setting these seductions in place, the Moabites act out of material rather than religious motives. They covet the gold and silver objects and the luxurious fabrics that the Israelites had taken out of Egypt, and they aim to separate them from their possessions by guile. As the enraged figure, God's role in the biblical account is replaced in the poem by Moses, who has appointed the rhetorically gifted Aaron to minister to the people. At Moses' command, Aaron hastily assembles a revival meeting in the Tent of Assembly, complete with deacons and Levitical choirs, and there he preaches the most stirring fire-and-brimstone sermon he has ever delivered. To no avail, however; the people slide right back into the mire of turpitude. God's people are like sheep without a shepherd; the manna turns wormy, the quail go uncollected, and the cows unmilked.

It is at this point that Pinḥas approaches Moses. Pinḥas is a tall and attractive young man who wishes to be a preacher, but because he is awkward of speech, his aspirations have not been taken seriously, and he has been advised to work in the cotton fields instead. Moses is so desperate that he accedes to Pinḥas's appeal to be allowed to minister to the people. Exploiting his attractiveness to women, Pinḥas immediately assembles a battalion of wives armed with their husbands' razors, who, like a temperance army, set about demolishing all the institutions of immorality erected by the Moabites and proceed to cut gashes in their husbands' faces to serve as perpetual reminders of their sins. On the morrow, the social fabric has been knitted back together; the authority of the ministers has been restored, and the people attend frequent revival meetings to keep themselves from sin. As a reward for his initiative, Pinḥas is invested with robes of priesthood, as Moses pronounces the moral of the story:

"לֹא בְנִיב יְיֻסַּר פֶּרֶד סוֹרֵר אַךְ בְּשׁוֹט!
תַּעַר כִּי יִשָּׁלֵף לַאדֹנָי – לוֹ הָבוּ פְאֵר –
דַּם־בְּרִית הַדָּם הוּא אֲשֶׁר יָזִיב מִן הַשְּׁאֵר!
רְפָאוֹת לִמְשׁוּבַת אִישׁ בְּמוֹ הַקֶּזַת דָּם –
כֹּהֵן לִי אֲשִׂימְךָ לִכְנֵסִיָּה רַבַּת עָם!"

"Not with words but with the whip will the rebellious ass be
    chastised!
The blood drawn from the flesh by a razor unsheathed for the
    Lord, praise be to Him,
Is covenantal blood, a medicinal bloodletting for recalcitrant man!
A priest I appoint you to a great and populous church!" (p. 104)

Lisitzky's preacher is doing, after his own fashion, precisely what masters of midrash have done since late antiquity. He is taking a famously laconic passage from the Bible of some fifteen verses and exploiting the gaps and blanks in the text to spin a full-blown narrative. This new construction functions exegetically to fill in the missing details in the original account and homiletically to enlist the ancient biblical tale to address a pressing problem in the present. For the preacher and his listeners, the problem is not the temptation to alien worship; it is, simply, men—their sinful nature and their vulnerability to temptation. Certainly the instance of the flaunted sexual relation (Numbers 25:6) provides the preacher with ample license to expand his sermon in this direction.

A notable change is the fact that the figure of God, whose wrath threatens the existence of the people in the biblical account, is largely missing in the sermon. The shift of emphasis to Moses and Aaron makes one of the major themes of the sermon a crisis in the authority of the clergy and in its capacity to use its hallowed instruments of moral suasion to keep the people—or, more properly, the men—from being wholly lost to damnation. Aaron tries his best, but even the most hair-raising homily by the highest priest blows over the men's heads like so much chaff. It takes the extraordinary mobilization of the community's unrealized assets—angry women led by an inarticulate aspirant to the priesthood—to restore the community's stability, which will now return to being kept in check by the clergy at regular revival meetings. Yet while preaching regains its status as the main mode of spiritual authority, a place is made for a different model of leadership embodied by Pinḥas. Although the effectual limitations of performative language are thematized within the sermon, Pinḥas's non-verbal activism remains contained within the larger and rhetorically successful performance of the sermon itself.

Let us suppose that the preacher's fictive congregants, the implied audience for the sermon, would have reacted with awe and approbation.[15] But what about the Hebrew readers who are the true intended consumers for the poem that is the sermon?[16] My conjecture is that they would have responded with feelings of amusement and instruction. The homiletical exploitation of the biblical text would have been familiar to them from innumerable Jewish contexts, and they would have been bemused to see the same dynamic unfolding in a completely alien culture. There are also insider jokes that can be appreciated only by the Hebraically literate. The *ohel mo'ed* [tent of meeting] in the books of the Pentateuch is a structure within the enclosure of the portable desert sanctuary where Moses communes with God and key cultic events take place. Because revival meetings were often held under circus-sized pitched tents, it was perfectly natural, and very funny in a defamiliarizing way, for Lisitzky to make the *ohel mo'ed* into the site for a Christian revival meeting. Hebrew readers would have felt instructed by the entrée they were being granted into the inner life of a culture that, though exotic and far-away, was central to the history of the West because of slavery and the Civil War.

Lisitzky's challenge in this poem and many others in the volume vis-à-vis the Hebrew reader is the careful calibration of strangeness and familiarity. The biblical language, the references to biblical events, and the midrashic method draw the Hebrew reader close to the text. Yet because the religious milieu in which the speakers of the poems are immersed is wholly Christian, Lisitzky took measures to make sure that it was not *too* Christian. We do not hear much about being dipped in the blood of the lamb or Jesus dying for the sins of humanity. The biblical incidents that are midrashically expounded are taken from the *Old* Testament; the depictions of saints and sinners arriving in heaven amidst angelic choirs are decidedly folkloric rather than seriously theological. And the emphasis throughout remains on such universal experiences as slavery, persecution, and sin. In the end, it is the Hebrew vestments in which Lisitzky has enrobed his black homilists that enable the Hebrew reader to embrace these poems. They speak in a rich and resonant Hebrew, which is at times colorfully dramatic, as in the description of the razor-wielding women tearing down the sites of sin, and at times orotund and full of high moralizing, as in the peroration quoted above, but always well matched in its linguistic decorum both to the clerical setting of the sermons and to the cultural amour propre of his Hebrew readers.

There are a number of other sung sermons in the middle section of *Be'oholei Khush*, and they remain the strongest poems in the volume. The best of these is "Vatedaber Miryam beMosheh" [So Miriam spoke of Moses] (pp. 119–26), in which Moses is presented in the guise of a nineteenth-century abolitionist who invites the Cushites (= Negroes) to join the Israelites in the exodus from captivity.[17] He and Tsipporah hire a comely and innocent young Cushite woman named Ketura to be their maid, but they send her away when they discover that their son Gershom is attracted to her. Tsipporah dies suddenly. Moses, now pictured as a widowed southern preacher, does not manage well on his own, and Ketura is invited back to keep house for him. It is at this point that Moses' sister Miriam, who has long harbored envy for her brother's prerogatives and his direct access to God, puts out the rumor that Moses has taken Ketura as a mistress. Moses promptly marries Ketura, and as a punishment for slander and for the disparagement of Ketura's blackness, Miriam is stricken with the sickly whiteness of leprosy. Similar to "Yisra'el baShittim," this sermon, like all midrash, takes as its point of departure a difficulty in the biblical text. When Numbers 12 opens with, "Miriam and Aaron spoke against Moses because of the Cushite woman he had married," we are at a loss because we know nothing about this woman. The backstory provided by Lisitzky's poem is clever, charming, and affecting.

The final section of *Be'oholei Khush* contains "'Ezra hakohen," the longest poem in the volume, and several other long poems that are either first-person testimonies of reformed sinners given at revival meetings or third-person narratives of the struggles with sin and salvation. Here, as elsewhere in Lisitzky's project, linguistic register is a determining factor. Ezra's monologue takes him from slavery under several masters (one of them an ameliorating Sephardic Jew!) and a successful escape to the North to serve as an assistant to Frederick Douglass and courageous combat in the bloody battles of the Civil War and finally to the difficulties of Reconstruction. It is a riveting and moving performance that rings true because Ezra is an educated man with total command of the Bible, and the Lisitzkian Hebrew that he speaks seems perfectly natural to him. With the reformed or still-struggling sinners of the other poems, however, the raw uncouthness and the vernacular ring with which they *should* speak is unfortunately elevated by the inherent decorum of Lisitzky's diction.

Having reviewed Lisitzky's motives and assessed his achievement, there remains, finally, to step back from the book and appreciate its strangeness and its presumption. Before us is a Jewish immigrant from Lithuania, a longtime resident of New Orleans, who takes upon himself to compose a substantial book of poems in Hebrew, all of which—with the single exception of the prologue to "'Ezra hakohen"—are written as if they were spoken by African Americans. Lisitzky could have approached this project as an anthologist who collects, transcribes, and translates or produces renditions of the songs and sermons of southern blacks. Or he could have placed himself within the frame of the poems, as he did in the exceptional case of "'Ezra hakohen," thereby acknowledging his position as a Jew and a white man in relationship to the African American speakers of the poems. Instead he decided to ventriloquize black voices and write the poems *as if* they were spoken by black speakers. There are a number of possible reasons for this choice. Lisitzky may have been wary of mediation and indirection and believed that the maximum dramatic impact, as well as a mystique of authenticity, could be acquired only by sustaining the illusion of the native speaker. He may have further believed that the qualities of innocence, nobility, and religious fervor that he sought to convey to the Hebrew reader could be effectively felt only if they were presented from within, in the first person, and through the human voice. Lisitzky disappeared within his characters also for his own needs. His relationship to African American culture was suffused with fascination and attraction, but as a white man there was only so far he could approach, no matter how attentive and participatory he was as an observer. Writing through the mouths of escaped slaves, grandiloquent preachers, and tortured sinners enabled him to put on the verbal skin of these figures and to imagine from the inside what it would be like to be them.

Is Lisitzky then, we may finally ask, putting on blackface? Is he following the long tradition of minstrelsy in American culture and using a verbal equivalent of burnt cork to imitate stereotypical modes of black performance? In the wake of Al Jolson's performance in *The Jazz Singer* in 1927, the argument has been made that Jews in show business used blackface as a means of entering the American mainstream and advancing the status of their own immigrant group.[18] I think not. To be sure, speaking not on behalf of or in the name of African Americans but in their own voice is an act of appropriation, as well as one of identification. And certainly one of Lisitzky's motives is to enhance his profile as a writer burdened by "subaltern" status as an American within the Hebrew literary system. Yet the fact of Hebrew and its audience was determinative. Lisitzky could not be said to be playing to a "white" audience or using the black voice to be assimilated into American society. The kind of voice he adopted, moreover, had nothing to do with the belittling mimicry of blackface, and it spoke in utter dignity rather than in vernacular caricature. The small audience of Hebrew readers who read Lisitzky's "Cushite" poems in America and in Israel were likely fascinated and intrigued by the world of the other they opened. Of the inner drama of Lisitzky's intimate and over-determined attachment to the spiritual world of black culture, they probably had little idea.

The aversion to making city life into a subject for poetry is a phenomenon we have encountered on many occasions in this study. When the American Hebrew poets were ready to emerge from their lyric enclosures, they sought out the great natural vistas beyond the cities and the great narratives of American history. In their conception of the division of labor within the republic of Hebrew letters, the job of representing the "way we live now" as an urban people was assigned to the prose writers; and that task was in fact taken on by such writers as Lev Aryeh Arieli, Wallenrod, and Halkin himself in their short stories and novels. In poetry, to be sure, there are exceptions to this broad generalization. Ginzburg's early *New York* (1917) is a boldly mythic engagement with the satanic metropolis, and Halkin's *Café Royal* poems (1928–29) play off the dissipated ambience of Jewish bohemia against the nervous erotic energies of the city's youth.

On the face of things, American Hebrew literature would seem to have its poet laureate of the city in the figure of Preil. In a poetic tribute to Preil, Pagis famously called the poet the Grand Duke of New York and described how he travels incognito by subway each day from his "palace" in the Bronx to walk among his subjects in Manhattan.[1] Yet a close look at Preil's poetry reveals that the city serves most often as a setting for reflection rather than an object in itself. The poet walks the city observing the sunset, the changing of the seasons, or the vagaries of clouds and pigeons, which in turn become occasions for meditations on the nature of time and memory, the poet's Lithuanian ancestors, or the very act of making poems. As was evident in the analysis of "Ganei emet velavah levanah" [Gardens of truth and white lava] (see Chapter 14), the harsh geometry of the metropolis dissolves into fluid meditations that seek to repair flaws inherent in the created world.

When it comes to the true grit of the city, there remains only one Hebrew poet on the American scene: Abraham Zvi Halevi (1907–66). The sole collection of Halevi's poetry published during his lifetime, *Mitokh hasugar* [From inside the cage] (1948), contains the extraordinary poetic sequence *Manhattan*, as well as a corona of sonnets titled "Ḥadarim meruhatim" [Furnished rooms].[2] Halevi was born in Poland in 1907 and brought by his family to Palestine when he was seven. His mothered died when he was twelve years old; his father sent Halevi's four younger sisters back to his family in Poland, while he, his older sister, and younger brother remained in Palestine. After studying in the Mizrachi teachers seminary in Jerusalem, he traveled to America and settled in New York in 1924, where he lived until his death, except for two return sojourns to Palestine (1929–30 and 1935–38). He served as a sergeant in the United States Army for three years during World War II. The sisters who returned to Poland perished there in the Holocaust together with the father. In addition to teaching at the Herzliah Teachers Institute, he served as the secretary of the Hebrew PEN Club and wrote critical essays that appeared in *Bitzaron*, *Hatequfah*, and other Hebrew journals. Halkin was a mentor to Halevi, and they were involved together in founding the Hebrew publishing house Ohel.[3] Halkin is thanked for his help in the editing of *Mitokh hasugar* in a note at the end of the volume (p. 93), and it is Halkin's substantial review of the book that remains the most serious critical attention given to Halevi's work.[4]

Halkin concluded his encouraging review of *Mitokh hasugar* by expressing his confidence that the elements of self that remained inchoate in the work would come together in his future poetry. Although Halkin was only eight years older than Halevi, who was forty-two when the book appeared, Halkin had produced an enormous body of poetry and prose and was about to assume the chair of Hebrew literature in Jerusalem. The notice he gives to a slightly younger, fellow American poet who was making a late debut in the world of Hebrew letters is generous indeed.

The expectations invested in Halevi as a poet, alas, were not fulfilled. There was no second book forthcoming, and the volume (*New York*) that his brother-in-law Yaakov Rimon compiled shortly after his death contained only some dozen poems that had not appeared twenty years earlier in *Mitokh hasugar*. Several of the new poems bear witness to the acute and painful experience of silence. At no stage in his life, says the speaker of "Lo peqakadani hashir" [The poem has not come to me] (p. 59), has poetic inspiration favored him with its bounty. As he has grown older, the imaginative springs of childhood have dried up, and the integuments of his self-enclosed isolation have been pulled ever tighter. A profound sadness, whose "tongue licks the dust / of the open grave," has taken root in his being and separated him from the possibilities of song.

The sources of this impasse are transparent in *Mitokh hasugar*, and it may have been Halkin's regard for his protégé that allowed him to hope against hope that there could be a future unfolding of the poetry's promise. There is a deep divide in this volume between the lyric poems and the city poems, and these two groups, each from its own very different angle, combine to create a perfect storm of anguished poetic paralysis. The lyric poems are written in poetic meter, almost all are rhymed, and there is a preponderance of sonnets. The lyric "I" is pervasive and the point-of-view reflexive. In the city poems, by contrast, traditional poetic forms are abandoned; these poems are big blocks of text, unrhymed and undivided into stanzas, that are written in very long lines. The lyric "I" disappears into an objective lens and observes and describes the lives of the city's dispossessed. Common to both modes, in addition to their use of the Sephardic-Israeli accent, is a lush figurative language that deploys metaphor as an aggressive technique of excess.

Mitokh hasugar gains in richness because Halevi does not leave the tension between these modes unaddressed. He concludes his collection with a corona of sonnets that draws elements from both.[5] "Hadarim meruhatim" describes the daily round of desperation on the part of an unnamed man who lives alone in a furnished room in the city. Although the cycle carries over the distanced observation of the city poems about city matters, the poems are cast in the highly disciplined mold of the sonnet form, with its regulated rhyme patterns and stanza divisions. The very fact of the corona itself is a stunningly ambitious conclusion to the volume. A corona is a cycle of fifteen sonnets in which the first line of each sonnet is the last line of the preceding sonnet and the last sonnet is composed of the first lines of the preceding fourteen.[6] Halevi's twist on this romantic showpiece is to a take a poetic form that demands intricate virtuosity and make its subject the dead-end despair of a modern underground man. The lyric and the city modes are thereby drawn together and twisted into a paradoxical knot; and, as we shall see shortly, this unresolved contradiction suggests why it might have been very difficult for Halevi to continue to write poetry.

Halevi's intensely confessional lyric poems construct the autobiographical persona of a man tortured by contradictory drives. This persona is advertised in the motto poem at the front of the volume, "Mitokh hasugar," which also gives the collection its name.

בְּתוֹךְ מִקְלָט־עַצְמִי, אוֹתִי אָסַף כְּאָב,
אֲנִי רוֹנֵן וְיֵחָמְרוּ בִּי דְּמֵי הַשֵּׁבֶט.
רְעַב חוּשִׁים אֲנִי נִכְסָף אֱכוֹל שַׁלְהֶבֶת
אֱלֵי מִקְלָט־עוֹלָם קוֹרֵן בִּשְׁלַל צְבָעָיו.

מִקְלָט הוֹפֵךְ סוּגָר סוּגַר לְלֵב אֲשֶׁר נָאַף
וְלֹא יַשְׁרִישׁ, צוֹעֶה מִתְּחוּם לִתְחוּם, וְעָבֵד
יִצְרֵי אֱנוֹשׁ, נִקְלָע בֵּין שְׁתֵּי אַבְנֵי מִשְׁאֶבֶת,
שָׂבֵעַ רֵיק וְנֶכֶר קַר וְרַב חֲרִי הָאַף.

תּוֹעֶה מָבוֹךְ יוֹמִי פּוֹנֶה. יָרֵט הַדֶּרֶךְ
בִּשְׁנֵי הַמִּקְלָטִים אֲנִי אַךְ זָר, אוֹרֵחַ.
יָדַי רֵיקוֹת. עֲלֵי רֹאשִׁי הָרָם קֵרֵחַ.
סְכָסֵךְ בִּי אֵל וְיִקּוֹם. עֻוּ יְסוֹד וָעֶרֶךְ.

מִתְּהוּ סוּגְרֵי אֶקְרָא אֱלֵי שִׁירִי:
הֱיֵה אַתָּה צִיּוּן לְקֶבֶר לֵב מְרִירִי!

Into the refuge of myself it has gathered me like a father,
I sing and the blood of the tribe bubbles within me,
Starved of senses and consumed by a burning passion, I am drawn
    To the refuge of the world, radiant in its array of colors.

Refuge turns into cage for the heart that has philandered
And struck no roots, wandering from boundary to boundary,
    slave To human urges, thrust between the two poles of the
    magnet,
Sated with futility and cold estrangement and great rage.

Lost in a labyrinth, my day turns. The way is obscured,
In both refuges I am only a stranger, a sojourner.
My hands are empty. My high head is bald.
God and existence have become embroiled in me. Foundation and
    value have been corrupted.

From the abyss of my cage I call to my song:
Be a marker for the grave of a bitter heart!

The speaker of the poem is a man whose needs have deprived him of freedom and have led him to be tossed back and forth between two enclosures. The self as an enclosure is evident; but it is less immediately clear how the world, which should presumably serve as a liberation from the self, also could serves as a refuge. The speaker therefore explains that, despite himself, he is driven from the redoubt of his self into the arms of the glittering world, which is also an enclosure, by a sensual hunger he cannot control. In this binary division there remains an element that does not fit: the blood of the tribe fermenting within him. Even within his self-absorption, the visceral connection to his people pulsates and agitates, and this, too, is an involuntary experience.[7] This unintegrated or "leftover" primal feeling expresses itself throughout Halevi's verse as an irreducible attachment to the Jewish people, to the fate of the Yishuv, and to his murdered family; yet this fervent connection to a realm outside himself never has the power to break the bind of Halevi's fundamentally bifurcated situation.

Although it is possible for a refuge [*miqlat*] to turn into a haven, the first line of the second stanza asserts that the metamorphosis has gone in the other direction, and the refuge has become a cage [*sugar*], a term used in connection with penned animals. It is the speaker's own adulterous [*na'af*] heart that is responsible for his forcible confinement. He can make no sustained and rooted attachments because he is overmastered by his needs and urges. Flung back and forth between the two poles of the magnet, he inhabits a chronic state of alienation, rancor, and resentment. The third stanza, the beginning of the sonnet's sestet, adds the dimension of temporality; the oscillation between the two poles is now seen under the aspect of aging and death. From the corruption of the fundamental categories of existence that defines his life, there will be no reprieve. In a gesture of romantic pathos, the poem concludes with a desperate appeal to the speaker's poetry, which is adjured to serve as the marker for the grave of his rancorous heart.

The realization of the poem as a sonnet makes that appeal less clichéd and more credible. The sonnet is itself the ultimate cage in which the poet voluntarily constrains the expansiveness of his discourse. In Halevi's case, the content of his sonnets is conspicuously at odds, if not at war, with the provenance of the form of the sonnet. The sonnet is a remnant of the high age of poetry, when this ornate and tightly designed receptacle was used to contain meditations about love and the wisdom of life. Into this noble and exquisite chalice, Halevi has had the temerity to pour compulsion, dissolution, vexation, and spleen.[8] It is a brilliant tension that continually threatens to explode into bathos and bad taste. The brinkmanship in Halevi's transactions with the sonnet emblematizes the risks he takes as a poet who uncompromisingly lays bare his basest urges and feelings of self-loathing.

The speaker of Halevi's poems would prefer to remain husbanded within himself, but he is forced outside by sexual hunger and a fascination with the world. The need to resort to prostitutes is a pervasive theme. Intimacy that flows from a romantic connection between equals appears to be out of the question, although an erotic exchange is sometimes possible ("Yiqron besareinu" [Our flesh will radiate], p. 47).[9] Generally, he purchases his satisfaction, and it is only when his "blood is strung like a bow" that he delivers himself to the commercial transactions that inevitably unfold in the most squalid parts of the city ("Bistelol yomi" [When my day sinks], p. 17). There is no licentious pleasure in this capitulation, only compulsion and degradation.

For the Hebrew reader, this candor can be shocking. Although sexuality can be found in American Hebrew poetry, especially in Regelson and Silberschlag, it is decidedly not common and then always charged with positive erotic energy. Halevi's journeys into abasement chart new and often uncomfortable thematic ground.

The hunger is not just for the flesh but for the sights of the world. Although this curiosity would seem to be the stock-in-trade of poets, for Halevi it has the force of shamefully separating him from the fate of others. An American soldier on foreign soil in the theater of destruction, the speaker of "Ve'ani bevigdei tsava ḥamudot" [I in my smart uniform] (pp. 38–39) confesses: "The distant horizon is dissolved in blood yet I drink in the wine of sunset to my satisfaction." Even in proximity to the calamity of his own people, he cannot stay his own appetitive response to the natural world.

וַאֲנִי מִתְחַיֵּב וְנַפְשִׁי חוֹלַת עוֹלָם בְּקִסְמָיו
וַאֲנִי מִתְחַיֵּב וְלִבִּי אֶל הַנִּיר וְהַשִּׁיר.

I condemn myself, but my soul longs for the world and its charms
I condemn myself but my heart is for the furrow and the song.
(p. 39)

These, the concluding lines of the poem, play with the well-known passage in Mishnah Avot (3:4) that censures the student who breaks his concentration on his studies in order to admire a beautiful tree on the side of the road. The bound phrase in Avot is *mitḥayev benafsho*, literally, he becomes culpable in his soul. Halevi cleaves the idiom in two and separates the soul from the self. Using another familiar idiom—the state of being "love sick" [*ḥolat ahavah*] from Song of Songs (2:5)—it is then the soul that cannot help itself in its passionate attraction to the charms of the world. Even amidst the ruins of his people, the poet confesses a besotted love for nature and poetry. There is no aesthetic preening here; the attraction to the world and the attraction to women partake of the same compulsive cycle of self-abasement. In "Mipnei artsi ani boreaḥ" [From my land I am fleeing] (pp. 52–53), a letter of apology to the Land of Israel for his return to America, the speaker presents himself as a broken vessel incapable of remaining faithful to the Land despite his ultimate loyalty to her. In explanation he admits that he has been made captive by "trees and rivers and the world like a stalking woman. / Her stern beauty has seduced me." This is the confession of a man who has renounced the pretense to moral agency and accepted the self-described turpitude as his fate.

At the beginning of this study, it was noted that the lyric plays a special role in the development of American Hebrew poetry. Before the young poets attained a firm grasp of the American landscape and the history of the republic, they wrote about what they knew: themselves. They composed short expressive poems that recorded responses to the natural world and experiences of displacement and the search for love. All of the poets expanded the range of their verse as they grew in their craft and in their life experience, and quite a few reached beyond the lyric to longer narrative forms in which the "overheard speech" of the poet's self is muted. The lyric thus always had the potential to serve, on the one hand, as a sensitive setting for self-exploration, and, on the other, as a solipsistic chamber for keeping the poet enclosed within himself. The lyric poetry of Halevi brings the restrictive option to its self-vitiating consummation. The refuge hardens into a cage, and the human subject, reduced to his animal needs, resigns himself to his fate.

Halevi must have sensed this dead end in turning toward the composition of his New York poems. Aside from stating in an endnote that the poems of *Mitokh hasugar* were written between 1937 and 1948, Halevi does not date individual poems or otherwise indicate the order of composition. But he does position *Manhattan* and the sonnet corona "Hadarim meruhatim" as the final two units of the collection; we may therefore take this as the signal of a desire to be released from the prison house of lyric into a realm outside the self. That the world outside turns out to be even more base and ignoble than the world inside is the appalling discovery that would seem eventually to shut down Halevi's poetic production altogether.

In its original 1948 iteration, *Manhattan* is a tightly organized suite of twelve poems. What first strikes the reader in turning to these poems from the earlier sections of *Mitokh hasugar* is the sudden abandonment of rhyme and traditional poetic forms like the sonnet, which together had served as finely wrought but tensile containers for Halevi's despair and self-laceration. The poems are large blocks of unrhymed verse undifferentiated into stanzas and composed of very long lines. With up to twelve words per line, the poems at times seem to use the kind of "rhythm of extensivity" [*ritmus haraḥavut*] that Uri Zvi Greenberg developed for his out-sized poetry. In contrast to Halevi's lyrics, in which the persona of the poet and the speaker of the poem are one, the city poems are spoken by an anonymous and unseen narrator who observes and describes the spectacle of the city. It would be inaccurate to call this objective narration because there is a constant modulation of judgment and sympathy. Moreover, because the narrator possesses such intimate knowledge of the seamy and squalid material he describes, the poems encourage the implication that he is a participant, as well as an observer.

The first poem ("Marzeaḥ" [Bar], p. 59) opens with the declaration:

יִשְׁלָיו בָּתִּים. תַּעֲטְפֵם אַדֶּרֶת הַלַּיְלָה.

Let houses rest in peace. Let the cloak of night envelop them.

This poem and all the others after it proceed to describe bars, flop-houses, dance halls, encampments of the homeless, whorehouses, revelers in Times Square, and Harlem street scenes. The opening declaration is a conciliatory stipulation that cedes the bourgeois order to the world outside the poem. Let people with homes and families, the poet opines, sleep in their beds at night while I take leave to explore an alternative universe of human experience. This initial act of letting go makes it clear that the narrative voice is a citizen of this nighttime world rather than a voyeur or an ethnographer who is slumming downtown. Moreover, the reader of these Hebrew poems, who is a denizen of the settled, daytime realm, is thus being ushered into a journey among the unhoused. Indeed, the quality of being *unheimlich* (literally, "unhomely") in Freud's sense of the uncanny, creates a gro-tesque reality in which human agency is subordinated to the malevo-lently activated forces of the inanimate metropolis.

The exile from everything related to the concept of home is acutely felt in the description of homeless men bedding down for the night on newspapers spread on the asphalt under the arch of the Williamsburg

Bridge ("Taḥat gesher Williamsburg," p. 61). One sleepless man, suddenly remembering his parents, is tortured by memories of his lost childhood. To dull the pain of these unwished-for longings, he drains his bottle and smashes it against the pillar of the bridge out of rage; and the broken glass then metamorphoses into a "wrathful and mocking green eye" that returns to haunt him. The men in these poems live in the grip of perpetual sexual hunger, which, when mitigated, often leaves them more deeply vulnerable to loss. In "Burlesque," for example, the men in the audience individually take care of their needs after being aroused by the striptease (p. 64). But when the stripper is followed on stage by a modestly dressed young woman who sings plaintively of lost love and lost home, their defenses are undone entirely. The frenzied goal of the masses that are "disgorged by the jowls of the subway" into Times Square in the poem by that name (p. 63) is to narcotize themselves against the daily grind of work by losing themselves in the carnival of entertainment and stimulation. In "'Asarah sent hariqud" [Ten cents a dance] (pp. 68–69), men purchase the momentary illusion of gracefulness and romance to escape the burden of wives and children and making a living. Amidst the swirling smells of perfume, tobacco, sweat, and alcohol, the dancers resemble passengers on a ship of fools "making its drunken way toward an enchanting, invisible isle of oblivion, beckoning from afar."

Love for sale is a dominant theme in the poems. Women prepare for a night on the streets, or men find their way to a prostitute's room. The arousals of the burlesque performance and the purchased intimacy of the dance hall are variants of the same fundamental condition. Sexual need has become entirely disconnected from intimacy and family, and its satisfaction has become a traded commodity. The singularity of the one couple of happy lovers that wanders through the second poem ("Besimtah ne'elaḥah" [In a foul alley], p. 60) is underscored by the drunk who vomits on them and by the unnamed stranger whose climbing the stairs to a prostitute's room concludes the poem. Throughout the poems, Halevi uses the word *qedeishah* for prostitute rather than the common term *zonah*. Rather than simply being a matter of a preference for an archaic usage, the choice directly reflects the symbolic framework in which the poet understands carnal relations. In the terminology of the Hebrew Bible, *qedeishot* were cultic prostitutes connected to pagan shrines, and they are often mentioned together with idolatrous images and altars in prophetic denouncements of Israelite backsliding.

The reference to cultic prostitution is just one element in a fully elaborated arc of allusions, which is set out in the first poem of *Manhattan*. The bar in the title of this poem beckons to its patrons through a yellow light that penetrates the curtain window, which radiates like a *parokhet*, the curtain that covered the Holy Ark in both the desert tabernacle and the Jerusalem temple. The tables are *mizbaḥot*, altars upon which holy beverages are poured; "from mouths perverted like a wound incense [*qetoret*] ascends" bearing dreams and desires. In their solemn assembly [*'atseret*], the drunks prophesy [*mitnabe'im*] about their visions of God. "Allen Street" describes the waiting room of a prostitute on the Lower East Side filled with men tense with desire and anticipation.

וּמְנוֹרַת צִנּוֹר־הַגַּז, הַתְּקוּעַ בַּפִּנָּה, תַּבְלִיחַ שַׁלְהַבְתָּהּ כְּנֵר נְשָׁמָה
וַעֲשָׁנָהּ תַּקְטִיר, יִתַּמֵּר מֵעַל רָאשֵׁי הָעֵדָה, לֵרְאוֹת בָּאָה אֶת פְּנֵי
הַקְּדֵשָׁה . . .

The wick of the gas lamp stuck in the corner flickers like a
    memorial candle
Sending up smoke that wafts over the heads of the company, who
    have come to make pilgrimage to the *qedeishah* . . .

All that is missing is the blood of the sacrifices, and in due course that is provided as well. The pimp or bouncer who presides over the scene "stands at his post / To make sure that there is no cessation of the cult of blood [*'avodat hadamim*] and the giving of gifts in this, the hidden sanctuary of the city."

In Halevi's use of this master trope, there is little difference between the worship of the one God in the Jerusalem temple and the pagan rites that were its constant competitor. In either guise, it remains a primeval ceremony of blood that is used by the poet to convey several dimensions of human degradation in the metropolis. On the one hand, the evocation of the sancta of worship serves to sharpen the effect of desecration by the willful and perverse parody of what was once most holy. On the other hand, the analogy underscores that which is truly continuous between the two experiences. The men drinking in the bar or lining up to visit the prostitute are paying obeisance to an unrelenting, primordial need in a way similar to the efforts of ancient cults to propitiate cruel cosmic forces. If, then, the blood of something, or even someone, precious had to be spilled to assuage the gods, today it is debasement and the sacrifice of humanity that are the exacted payments. Yet, now as then, despoiled sacrifices are no guarantee of mitigation. The classical prophets are tireless in their indictment of a desperate and cynical reliance on the cult to cleanse inexcusable moral behavior. The transactions between the prostitute and her customers are similarly ritualized, mechanical, and impelled by need. And their fruits are similarly futile.

Is the speaker himself an officiant in these bloody rituals, or does he merely describe them from a safe distance? The stance of the speaker/ narrator of the Manhattan poems is equivocal. He often assumes the position of a Virgil who accompanies the reader on a tour of hell. The reader is assumed to be a citizen of the daytime world who is, or at least believes himself to be, "housed" in the life of families and institutions and who therefore exists at an incalculable remove from the "unhoused" souls described in the poems. The narrator tears away the veil of obtuseness and self-satisfaction and attempts to force the reader to take in the nighttime world of the dispossessed. This is a world that the narrator accepts as given and does not judge. His own relationship to that world—the question of whether he is within it or apart from it—is indicated obliquely but unmistakably by the insertion into the poems of a character who seems closely associated with the narrator: the figure of the nameless *helekh*.

There is no satisfying English equivalent for this term, which derives simply from the verb "to walk." The *helekh* is a passerby, wanderer, existential pilgrim, roamer, traveler, *flaneur*, *homo viator*. It is a figure familiar from the Hebrew poetry of the period, especially Alterman's *Kokhavim baḥuts* [Stars outside]. The *helekh* appears in three of the Manhattan poems and implicitly in several others. In each case, he enters the poem once the scene of debasement has been put in motion, and he joins in the action along with the anonymous denizens of the fallen metropolis. In the opening poem ("Marzeaḥ," p. 59), for example, the *helekh* hastens his steps toward the bar, impelled by an embittered frustration with life. Although not explicitly named in "Besimtah ne'elakhah" (p. 60), he seems to be the one who makes his way up the stairs to the prostitute at the end of the poem. In "Times Square" (p. 63), the *helekh* appears among the throng of New Yorkers seeking to lose themselves in an overload of cheap amusements. Overstimulated, his blood pounding, he is swept along with the crowd like someone who is "drowning for the rustle of silk dresses and hose," and he ends the evening swallowed up by a bar, where he tranquilizes himself by drinking a "glass of oblivion." In the next poem, "Burlesque" (p. 64), the *helekh* is among the men in the audience. "Hungry for bread and a woman," he decides to spend the last of his money on the latter, or at least on the vicarious stimulation available to him as a spectator. In a weakened state after the wished-for release, he becomes entranced along with the other men by the ingénue who sings of home, sweet home.

As the sequence progresses, the *helekh* seems to be assimilated into the narrative persona, and vice versa. The last two poems ("Lenox Avenue," p. 71, and "Tsemaḥ tsedeq," pp. 72–73) take place in a Harlem setting that whites visit only at their peril and only to satisfy their desires. The final poem takes place on 115th Street in the vicinity of the abandoned synagogue of the poem's title. (This is the only Jewish reference in the sequence.) The synagogue was built by immigrants whose eventual success allowed them to move to "Flatbush, the Bronx and Long Island," where they built palatial modern temples. A white man looking for sex, perhaps the same figure from the previous poem, is sucked into one of the adjacent houses, only to be thrown out into the street shortly afterward. Is the white man the *helekh*? How can the narrator, also a white man, report on these Harlem scenes if he himself is not a participant in the action? *Manhattan* concludes without any further elaboration of these lines of connection between the speaker of the poems and the fallen world they describe. Yet his complicity in that world is never in doubt. Although these poems remain "objective" in comparison to the confessional exposures of the lyric verse, they also present another way, if a more oblique one, of baring the self.

In its largest conception, Halevi's *Manhattan* is organized around a provocative paradox. Human existence in the poems is uniformly presented as emptied of meaning and attachment and reduced to a grinding and grimly repetitive pursuit of the satisfaction of animal-like needs. As an aesthetic correlative to this dystopian universe, we might well have expected a poetic language that was brute, scant, and impoverished. The opposite turns out to be the case. Halevi's language is lushly figurative and composed of metaphors piled one atop the other. It is operatic in its effects and brazen in its systematic practice of the pathetic fallacy. This jarring disconnect between theme and style creates a sense of unease and disorientation in the reader, which, I will argue, works in the service of Halevi's larger ambitions for his work.

Consider, for example, the description of sunset in the opening lines of "Besimtah ne'elaḥah," the second poem of the sequence.

בְּמִפְלַשׁ סִמְטָה נֶאֱלָחָה בְּלֶב־הַכְּרַךְ גָּסַס הַשֶּׁמֶשׁ.
נִצְמָד, נָשַׁק לְבָתִּים־דִּירִים, בָּם יֶהֱמֶה צֹאן־אָדָם,
נִתְלָה בְּרָאשֵׁי־גַגּוֹת, הִכְתִּירָם וְגָוַע עָלוּף־זִיו.

On the sides of a foul alleyway in the heart of the city the sun
    expires.
It kisses and clings to houses-pens in which the people-animals
    stir,
Suspended [hanged] from the tops of the roofs, it crowns them
    and then breaths its last, drained of its glow.

In an obscure and squalid passageway buried deep within the city, an extraordinary spectacle unfolds. The dying sun, which can usually be observed to be declining with unnatural rapidity when it nears the horizon, is here setting in an unnatural slow-motion sequence. It is a prolonged, melodramatic stage death. Resisting its inevitable fate, grasping onto the rooftops, the dying sun embraces the human world from which it must depart and, in a gesture of self-sacrifice, gives up the last of its light to crown the surrounding buildings with its final rays.

This swooning, operatic death, which makes the sun into a diva of the celestial world, stands in marked contrast to the urban filth and the animal-like conditions of human habitation in the midst of which this spectacle transpires. The swarming creatures, who will soon be released from their pens by the coming of night, inhabit an order of existence that is far less human than the sun's bravura performance. In a world in which human existence is brutalized and reduced to herd-like animal instincts, it is not surprising that the inanimate objects of the cityscape would be brought to life, however demonic and gro-tesque that life should be. After the swooning death of the sun, the onset of night in the opening of the next poem ("Taḥat gesher Williamsburg," p. 61) proves to be no less theatrical.

תַּחַת גֶּשֶׁר וִילְיָמְסְבּוּרְג, בַּעֲצַלְתַּיִם יִרְבַּץ כְּחַיַּת בְּרֵאשִׁית,
הִתְכַּנֵּף לַיְל אָפֵל וָלַח. גָּהַר עַל מֵי אִיסְטְ־רִיוֶר,
מַשְׁחִירִים כְּזֶפֶת קוֹפֵאת בֵּין רַפְסוֹדוֹת נִרְדָּמוֹת,
סְפִינוֹת־מַשָּׂא וּבָתֵּי־חֲרֹשֶׁת מְפֻחָמִים, מַעֲשֵׁנוֹתֵיהֶם
יִזְדַּקְּרוּ כְּצַלְלֵי־אֵימִים וְיִשְׁתַּקְּפוּ בַּמַּיִם כְּצַלְמֵי־בַלָּהוֹת.

Under the Williamsburg Bridge, lazily hulking like a prehistoric
     creature,
Night enshrouds itself, dark and wet. It spreads out upon the
     waters of the East River,
Turning black like frozen pitch among the dozing docks,
The freighters, and the sooted factories, whose smokestacks
Stand erect like horrifying shadows and are reflected in the water
     like nightmarish images.

The area on the bank under the span of the bridge before it extends over the water is a liminal space that is imagined in the poem as the lair of a primeval monster. The coming of darkness is presented as the effect brought on by the creature's bestirring itself. In an infernal parody of Genesis 1, this demiurge stretches out over the waters of the East River and undoes creation by turning all things to the color of soot and tar and making the lumpen and familiar industrial skyline into a phantasmagoria of ghastly shapes.

The poems of *Manhattan* not only open with the terrifying stag-ing of defamiliarization, but they end with them as well. It is only in between, within the unsettling embrace of these extremes, that the human activity, such as it is, takes place. In the poem above, for example, what follows the monstrous opening is the description of the tortured night spent by the homeless as they toss and turn on their newspaper beds while remembering the homes and families from which they are cut off. The poem concludes by panning cinematically away from the sleeping bodies to the street lamp nearby.

פְּנָס עֲרִירִי בְּעֶרְוַת רְחוֹבוֹת כַּעֲנָק חַד־עַיִן יַשְׁקִיף מִגָּבוֹהַּ,
יַכְהֶה עֵינוֹ כְּמִסְתַּתֵּר, יִתְעַרְפֵּל וְיִזְדַּוֵּג עִם הַלַּיְלָה . . .

Like a one-eyed giant, a barren street lamp looks out from on high
    at the nakedness of the streets,
It dims its eye like someone hiding, becomes hazy and couples
    with the night . . .

Instead of providing protective illumination, the street lamp is transformed into a perverted paradoxical creature: a voyeuristic Cyclops which, despite its sterility ['ariri], copulates with the night. The Cyclops image is evident throughout the poem sequence, especially at the end of "Times Square" (p. 63), where the Empire State Building dozes above the revelers with only its "eye aglow."

The threatening eye of the Cyclops is an example of the grotesque, even gothic, mood of Halevi's poetic language. Human characteristics are detached from humans and attributed to inanimate objects; and, thus robbed of their humanness, humans are depleted and degraded. Wandering the city unhoused, they become literalizations of Freud's figure of the *Unheimlich*. This disconnection and unnatural re-mixture are evident in one of the major paradoxes of the *Manhattan* poems: the highly wrought and highly wound figurative language that frames a human milieu that is diminished and depleted. To fashion his discourse of the city, it is as if Halevi has taken the florid language of nineteenth-century romanticism and passed it through Baudelaire's spleen and then applied it to the mid-twentieth-century cityscape. The result is a poetry that is rich, powerful, and disorienting.

The paradox is pushed to its ultimate, self-vitiating conclusion in the corona of sonnets that follows *Manhattan* and brings to a conclusion Halevi's collection of poems and, in effect, his poetic oeuvre. A corona, it will be recalled, is a cycle of fifteen sonnets in which each begins with the last line of the sonnet before it, and the final sonnet is made up of the first lines of the fourteen preceding sonnets; and the last line of the entire cycle is the same as the first line. If the sonnet is itself already a highly demanding and conventionalized poetic form, then the corona has to be one of the most baroque and virtuosic of literary constructions in existence. In "Ḥadarim meruhatim" (pp. 77–91), Halevi brings together the two disparate modes of poetry writing in his work: the rhymed short confessional lyric and the objective representation of the urban experience. In making the subject of the sonnets the life of a nameless man living alone in the city, Halevi makes a double synthesis. He takes the focus of the lyrics on the individual and shifts it from the confessional "I" to the third person. He also takes the brutal and sordid reality of the city, which had been presented in undifferentiated blocks of verse, and submits it to the filigreed constrictions of the sonnet. This aesthetic miscegenation, in which theme is constantly pulling against form, makes "Ḥadarim meruhatim" one of the most interesting achievements in modern Hebrew poetry.

The generic, impersonal connotation of the corona's title sets the tone. Furnished rooms are temporary lodgings rented by individuals without family. They are furnished by others, and their occupants live among dressers, beds, and tables not their own. The room in which the protagonist of "Ḥadarim meruhatim" lives is a spatial projection of his self, which is individuated and walled off. It is a prison built by himself but furnished by others. At the same time, the room is a "solitary, anonymous nest in the midst of the abandoned din of the city" (Sonnet 3), which, poor as it is, houses the self and places a protective membrane between it and the threatening and chaotic roar outside. The protagonist needs to leave the room to go to work, and he is impelled to leave by the hope of satisfying his inflamed hungers. But it is to the room that he always returns, not only for refuge, but also because it is there that he knows that the remainder of his life's sentence must be served.

Despite the anonymity of the protagonist, his similarity to the poet is undisguised. The early death of a mother and the murder of a grandfather as the shtetl goes up in flames are autobiographical facts that Halevi's reader learns from earlier poems. A man who has lost the faith of his youth and lives without wife or child within the teeming metropolis is a description of both the persona of the poet and the subject of the sonnets. Yet even though the reader is almost invited to conflate the two, Halevi's decision to preserve the distinction is crucial for the success of "Ḥadarim meruhatim." The poems in the earlier sections of *Mitokh hasugar* are weighed down by the pathos of the lyric "I" with its considerable burden of pain and self-contempt. Halevi gains invaluable distance and control by renouncing the freighted "I" for a nameless "he" without having to give up the intensity of his identification with an existential situation the two share so intimately.

Describing that existential situation is the main job of the sonnet cycle, which maintains an affinity with the existential literature being written in France at the same time. The definition of the protagonist's situation begins with the givenness of his orphanhood. The early death of the mother echoes throughout the work as a formative deprivation that lies at the root of his inability to form intimate connections with women. Yet, as a man with sexual hungers, he is driven out of the enclosure of his room to seek satisfaction in the streets of the city. (Like the protagonist, that city remains nameless and faceless, although its identity is no mystery.) He is impelled to rely upon "*she'er sakhur*," hired flesh, for these needs and to endure the self-abasement that results from this compulsion. To sustain himself he must work, and this is another constraint that keeps him from being walled up in his room. Like the other members of the lumpen urban army, each morning he is spit out of the subway and into an office to do meaningless work, described as *tiflut* [bullshit], only to be sucked back in at the end of the day. In making his protagonist an office drudge, Halevi chose to make him an Everyman rather than exploring the option of potentially more meaningful work, such as his own as a writer and teacher.

A man whose present life is empty might look to the world of his childhood as a source of strength or connection. But for the protagonist, alas, "Off somewhere, the enfeebled palace of childhood sinks"

(Sonnet 6). When he succeeds in retrieving from oblivion "the rustle of childhood" memories, all he can come up with is a nightmarish vision of a shtetl going up in flames and the murder of his grandfather. "Ḥadarim meruhatim" was apparently written before the Holocaust, in which Halevi's father and three of his sisters perished. (The entire volume of *Mitokh hasugar* is dedicated to their memory.) If the protagonist of the sonnets is thrust into a state of denial and alienation by the earlier calamity, one can only imagine his condition if the poem sequence were composed after the second blow. If we read "Ḥadarim meruhatim" against an autobiographical template, it is interesting to note that the ten years (ages 7–17) that Halevi spent in Palestine do not enter the emotional reckoning. Halevi's attachment to the Yishuv and the fate of Zion is evident from earlier poems, yet for the urban Everyman at the center of his sonnets, no affiliation beyond the self seems possible or relevant.

Even if the memory of childhood could be purged of its terror, the protagonist would not be available to connect with it.

אֵיכָה יָשׁוּב מֻכֵּה חַיִּים, פְּצוּעַ עִיר?
חֲזוֹן גְּדוֹלוֹת בּוֹ עוֹד תּוֹסֵס, פּוֹרֵשׂ הָרֶשֶׁת.
סָגְרוּ עָלָיו בַּרְזֶל וּמֶלֶט קַר וָעֶשֶׁת –
מִתַּעְתּוּעֵי הַקֶּרֶת מִי לִבּוֹ יָסִיר?

Struck by life, wounded by the city, how could he return?
A vision of great things still seethes within him spreading its web.
Iron, cold concrete and steel have closed in upon him—
From the illusions of the metropolis who could pull him away?
    (Sonnet 7)

This is the loop of bad faith. He has abandoned himself to the city not only because the early foundations of his life have not stood by him but also because of his own devices and desires. He came to the city with fantasies of greatness (recognition? love?), and although his aspirations have foundered against an iron and concrete wall, he persists in his secret great expectations; thus he is caught in a web of his own weaving. The rhetorical questions that begin and end this stanza from the sonnet's sestet serve to deflect responsibility. The opening word of the stanza, *eikhah*? [how?], is one of many fleeting references to the book of Lamentations throughout "Ḥadarim meruhatim." In a poetry that generally does not indulge in biblical allusion nor evince interest in national experience, the echoes of Lamentations serve to widen the cosmic import of his situation and to present it as a fate from which no simple exercise of will power can save him.

Caught in the toils of bad faith, the protagonist is condemned to an existence of unending ennui. Attempts to escape into sex or alcohol always end in a redoubled sense of futility and orphanhood. Even books, which were once his companions, have become mute and alien; "the soul of their letters has flown off" (Sonnet 9). The last sonnets of "Ḥadarim meruḥatim" describe an unrelenting process of entropy. The world has become disenchanted, its colors dimmed, its energies slowed down to a point approaching an existential absolute zero. The protagonist's response to this decline is to be engulfed by a nausea that makes the physical world into a grotesque excrescence.

יְתוֹם הָעֵלֶט

זָב מִמַּצֶּבֶת־קִיר, לָפַת אָדָם־מַפֶּלֶת,

כִּרְסֵם בְּתַאֲוָה נַפְשׁוֹ הָאֲשֵׁמָה. —

> The orphan of deepest darkness
> oozes from the gravestone-walls, grabs the human heap
> and hungrily eats away at his guilty soul. —
>   (Sonnet 13)

It is man's own awareness of his bad faith, his guilty soul, that makes him vulnerable to the depredations of noxious and malevolent forces. In images that owe not a little to Edgar Allen Poe, the room becomes a burial chamber or a cell with ever narrowing walls.

Where is the zone of human freedom in the world of these sonnets? Cannot the protagonist at least mount gestures of resistance against the forces that would entomb him? The answer is that it is simply not possible for him. The deprivations of his childhood, the hypnotic spell of the city, the incessant pressure of his needs—all these conspire to make him experience his situation as an irreversible fate. The language of ritual sacrifice that permeates the *Manhattan* poems is present here as well. Taking refuge in a bar, the protagonist takes a look at the table before him and concludes that it is a *mizbaḥ shulḥan, ʿalav adam ʿaqud, ʿazuv* [an altar upon which man is bound and abandoned] (Sonnet 5). *ʿAqud* is the unmistakable marker of the Binding of Isaac.

In Halevi's version of the story, the sacrifice is not carried through, but neither is the sacrificial victim released from the altar. He remains there, perpetually bound *and* abandoned.

The final position of Halevi's protagonist is delineated in the fifteenth sonnet. Because it is made up of the first lines of the fourteen preceding sonnets, this is by definition a summary, even a summa, of all that has gone before; yet by virtue of its ultimate position, it is also a gesture of closure. The sonnet has the same *abba abba cddc ee* rhyme scheme as all the others in the corona. The proportions of the required virtuosity should be kept in mind. Not only does the poet have to anticipate how the first lines of the sonnets will be knit together in the final poem; but he also has to make sure that these scattered lines will be able to be mobilized into the uniform rhyming pattern.

דֶּלֶת אֲטוּמָה, שֻׁלְחָן, מִטָּה מֻצַּעַת.
עֵירֹם קִירוֹת מַבְעִית. חַלּוֹן בּוֹהֶה, קָרוּעַ.
קַן אַלְמוֹנִי בּוֹדֵד תּוֹךְ נַהַם עִיר פָּרוּעַ.
בַּעֹל יִשָּׂא דוּמָם, לֹא יְאַבֵּד הַדַּעַת.

הַיּוֹם מַעְגַּל תִּפְלוּת, גַּם אֵל מָנַע הַסַּעַד.
אַרְמוֹן יַלְדוּת אֵי־שָׁם שׁוֹקֵעַ וְרָעוּעַ,
אֵלָיו שׁוּב לֹא יוּכַל לִבּוֹ מִכְּרָךְ נָגוּעַ.
יָתוֹם קַר מַצָּעוֹ; הַשִּׁמָּמוֹן אַט יַעַט.

גָּדֵר חַדְרוֹ בַּעֲדוֹ, אָסַר בּוֹ כִּבְסוּגַר.
לִפְדוּת לֹא יִשְׁאָגוּ עֲבָדֵי מִקְסַם הַקֶּרֶת.
מִפֶּגֶר יוֹם יִרְמֹץ לָהֶם אוּד הִתְפָּאֶרֶת —
יָחוּל לֵאֶה, שְׂרִיד חֲלוֹם אֲשֶׁר מָגַר.

גּוֹסֵס זִכְרוֹן יְרָקוֹת, הוֹעַם זִיו אֲדָמָה.
כְּאֵל הַחוֹף עוֹלֶה הָאִישׁ אֶל וַו בְּלִימָה.

A sealed door, a table, a made-up bed,
A frightening nakedness of the walls. A torn window gapes.
A solitary nameless nest within the wild roar of the city.
He will bear the yoke in silence, he will not lose his mind.

The day is a round of stupidity, and even God has withheld all
    succor.
Off somewhere, the enfeebled palace of childhood sinks.

Scarred by the metropolis, his heart cannot go back there.
An orphan's pallet is cold; desolation stalks him.

His room has enclosed him, he is imprisoned in it as in a cage.
The servants of the city's spell do not cry out for rescue.
From the corpse of the day an ember of majesty smolders for
    them—
Tepid hope, the trace of a dream that was toppled.

The memory of greenness expires, the gleam of the ground has
    been dulled.
As if onto the shore, the man ascends to the peg of the void.

The sonnet has the staccato pace of a drum roll. A single declarative
sentence followed by a full stop fills almost every line. It is as if the
argument of each of the preceding sonnets has been distilled and
epitomized in an authoritative judgment. The reader has the eerie feeling of reading a text that is simultaneously new and familiar. The first
stanza sets out the spatial coordinates of the bare room, which is both
a protective nest and a claustrophobic container. The second stanza
describes the destroyed world of childhood that has orphaned him
and left him defenseless before the experience of emptiness. The third
stanza returns to the room, which has now become a cage, and, in this
metamorphosed state, becomes the site in which the ember of hope
approaches total extinction. The enigmatic final gesture of ascending
to the "peg of the void" [*vav belimah*] becomes clearer against the
background of Sonnet 14; there the peg is both a physical hook on the
wall on which coats are hung and a metaphysical protuberance of the
void on which the protagonist has hung his body and soul.

But what can this final gesture possibly mean? Even in figurative
terms, how can the void have a point of stability upon which anything
can be hung? It is Halevi's achievement to make the central symbol
of this work, the room, into just such a liminal space. The room is a
cage that dangles over the face of the void, hanging by a thread, as
it were. "Ḥadarim meruhatim" concludes with the sounding of an
accord of resignation, which, though not heroic, nonetheless stirs
because it is painful and hard won. The stance is stated clearly in
line 4: "He will bear the yoke in silence, he will not lose his mind,"
with its distinct echoes of Lamentations 3:27–28. The alternatives to
not losing his mind are madness and suicide. Although everything

about the radically bleak reality of these poems would seem to lead to those ends, he does not go there. Resisting the flaming gesture of self-extinction, he hangs his body and soul on the peg and persists, resigned to living his fate.

Halevi's reputation as a poet, both during his life and after it, has had to abide existing in just such a small box. His literary production was slight, and the frank, harsh, and confessional tone of his verse, challenging. He entered the scene of American Hebrew literature two decades later than most of the major poets. This was a time when the literary community in Palestine had largely written the Americans off the map of Hebrew literature and when, with one major exception, Hebrew poets in America were devoting themselves to American vistas far beyond the metropolis. That exception is Preil, with whom Halevi shares his preoccupation with the city, and with New York City in particular.

Both were modernists with interest in, and knowledge of, American Yiddish poetry.[10] But Preil was nurtured by the minimalist and imagist strain of modernism, and this influence placed him in the purview of such Israeli poets as Pagis and Zach who came to prominence in the 1950s and were looking for precursors. Halevi drew from the maximalist, post-romantic strain of modernism, closer to Whitman and Halkin, Halevi's mentor; and there were few younger Israeli poets interested in a retrospective filiation with this path. Both Halevi and Preil were single and childless and belated practitioners of a craft for which there would be no offspring in America, where they had chosen to live. Yet Preil possessed a core of self-regard, a rich and unstinting narcissism, which bolstered and secured his vocation as the last avatar of generations of Hebrew writers and was a poet who believed that reflections on the world around him inherently deserved to be embodied in verse. Preil's confidence and productivity were fueled by the empowering adoration of a mother who lived long into the poet's life and in very near proximity. Halevi, alas, was not so embraced. The brilliant poetic gifts with which he was endowed could never surmount the deprivation into which he was born.

Afterword

It is much to be hoped that an awareness of the work of the American Hebrew writers will affect the way we think in a number of areas of study. In the context of American studies, the related yet distinct instances of Yiddish modernism and American Hebrew poetry extend and complicate what we know about multilingual American literature, that is, American literature not written in English. Each in its own way created a high literary culture, and this aspiration set them apart from other immigrant literatures, in which communication in the vernacular language remained the main focus. In the context of American Jewish literature, an awareness of creativity in Hebrew compels a triangular definition of this field of study. English, to be sure, remains at the center, and the relevance of American Yiddish literature has long been acknowledged. Hebrew should now take its place alongside Yiddish as the second of the two essential components of American Jewish literature written in Jewish languages.

It is in the context of the study of Hebrew literature, finally, that the "discovery" of American Hebrew literature should make its largest impact. If the present study proves anything, it is that the phenomenon of American Hebrew poetry was not slight or trivial. Yet despite its being the only major literary center outside of Palestine/Israel, its existence was all but erased from accounts of Hebrew literature in the twentieth century. The reasons for this erasure in its own time have been sorted out and explained. Yet there can be no justification now 467 for perpetuating this exclusion. To the contrary, it is hard to imagine anyone who cares deeply about Hebrew literature not rejoicing over this unexpected bounty and the expansion of boundaries it invites.

The most palpable presence of Hebrew in American universities is as a subject of foreign language instruction. As the tongue of contemporary Israel, Hebrew is certainly a foreign language; yet for the many American Jewish students who study Hebrew as a heritage language, it is much more. It is now, happily, an established tenet of foreign-language instructional theory that language and culture cannot be disentangled from one another and that to teach language is of necessity to teach culture. The ramifications for Hebrew have yet to be thoroughly explored. Hebrew is the language of Israel today; Hebrew is the language of historical Jewish civilization; and Hebrew is also, as this study demonstrates, a language of intense creativity on these shores over the last century. It would therefore seem unnatural and even ludicrous that American students should be studying Hebrew in America without some awareness of all that was written here in that language.

Will more Hebrew literature be written in the United States? Will new writers arise to continue the tradition described in this volume? It does not seem likely, but no possibility should be foreclosed. The American Jewish community is part of what Simon Rawidowicz famously called an ever-dying people. The example of Robert Whitehill, the assimilated Jew from Texas who learned Hebrew and began publishing books of poetry in Israel, was mentioned in the Preface. As Regelson demonstrated in his extravagant hymn to Hebrew, it is not always possible to resist the seductions of the Holy Tongue.

There is most assuredly a future for Hebrew in America—a vitally critical role, in fact—even if it lies in the domain not of creative literature but of serious cultural literacy. The state of American Jewry in regard to Hebrew can be characterized by two simultaneous and opposite processes. For the majority of identifying American Jews, Jewish identity is one element woven into a broader way of life. They have little or no familiarity with the sources of Judaism in the original Hebrew, although they will encounter some Hebrew in the synagogue and may know some Hebrew phrases current in the culture. For a minority, however, the study of these Hebrew sources—as well as the religious practice that often accompanies them—has deepened and intensified, and they are joined by other American Jews who have been deeply affected by Israel and have applied themselves to learning spoken Hebrew. The future of Hebrew in America depends on the leadership cadres, both lay and professional, that will emerge from this minority. Given the flourishing of day schools and university programs in Jewish studies, there unquestionably exists the capacity to supply a solid knowledge of Hebrew. What is in doubt is the communal and institutional will to do so.

The very notion of what it means to know Hebrew is a source of great confusion in American Jewish life. With the establishment of Israel and the reported successes of the ulpan method in the middle of the previous century, the romance of oral fluency, the capacity freely to converse in Hebrew in a contemporary idiom, took hold in the American Jewish imagination. Thus the ability to speak Hebrew became the benchmark of knowing Hebrew. Making speech the criterion for success, I would argue, has had a profoundly harmful effect. This is not because speaking Hebrew is unimportant—to the contrary!—but because speech is the specific language competence least likely to be realized in America. Knowledge of Hebrew, like any language, is comprised of four skills: reading comprehension, oral comprehension, writing, and speaking. Without being immersed in a Hebrew-speaking environment, it is almost impossible for anyone, except for those exceptionally gifted in foreign languages, to become fluent in Hebrew. Even Israel cannot be counted on to provide this immersion because English is so pervasive in the settings where most Americans spend their time. In America, such Hebrew-saturated pockets once existed in the Massad camps, the Hebrew colleges, and a few day schools, that is to say, in the world made by the Hebraists described in this volume. Yet although that world no longer exists, the expectation of oral proficiency has persisted and created a standard that, almost by definition, cannot be achieved. This one-dimensional definition of Hebrew achievement has condemned many serious American Jews to a sense of frustration and pessimism about learning the language.

There must be a general rethinking of the kind of Hebrew knowledge that is achievable and meaningful in America. This does not necessarily mean a "dumbing down" of expectations, and the current news is not all bad. Average day school graduates, for example, cannot speak Hebrew with much fluency and often have a negative self-perception in that area for this reason; yet because they have spent many years reading Hebrew texts, the passive store of knowledge they have acquired can be activated and built upon in an intensive Hebrew-speaking environment in Israel. (The fact that many of these graduates spend their time in Israel in American enclaves is an obvious instance of educational shortsightedness.) It is much more difficult to move in the other direction, that is, from spoken Hebrew to an understanding of the sources of Judaism in Hebrew. I make this point not out of partisan sentiment but to argue that when it comes to Hebrew in America, there are more assets and infrastructure than we imagine. In the case of Jewish leaders who have not had the benefit of these intensive years of schooling, it would make sense to approach Hebrew not through its formal grammar but through the concepts and values embodied in its three-letter roots. Computer-aided instruction has a vast potential for Hebrew learners of all types that has not yet been explored.

The afterword to an academic study is not the place to initiate a discussion about educational options and strategies. But in conclusion, it is worth attending to one of the essential insights of the Hebraists who populated these pages. They may have been wrong about Hebrew being the measure of all things—this was the monomania that contributed to their eclipse—but they were surely correct in seeing Hebrew as the deep structure of Jewish civilization, its DNA, as it were. They understood the unique role of Hebrew as a bridge that spans many cleavages: between classical Judaism and the present, between religious and secular Jews, and between Israel and the Diaspora. They further understood that any Jewish society that takes place largely in translation runs the risk of floating free of its tether to Jewish authenticity. It is much to be hoped that a revived interest in Hebrew in America will provide that integrity.

Reference Matter

Notes

Preface

1. Abraham Epstein, *Soferim 'ivrim ba'ameriqah* [Hebrew writers in America] (Tel Aviv: Dvir, 1952).

2. Moshe Brind, Avraham Soladar, and A. Domnitz are three poets who did not develop into significant figures that are included in Menachem Ribalow's *Antologiyah shel hashirah ha'ivrit ba'ameriqah* [Anthology of Hebrew poetry in America] (New York: Ogen, 1938).

3. His translations of *Anthony and Cleopatra*, *King Lear*, and *Romeo and Juliet* are included in William Shakespeare, *Tragediyot* (Am Hasefer: Tel Aviv, 1960).

4. The Hebrew colleges in the interwar period, especially the Teachers Institute of the Jewish Theological Seminary (alongside the all-male Rabbinical School at JTS), were places where young men and women mixed freely. The creative culture of these institutions in their heyday has yet to receive the attention it is due.

5. An important beginning is Carol K. Ingall, *The Women Who Reconstructed American Jewish Education, 1910–1965* (Waltham, MA: Brandeis University Press, 2010).

6. Kleiman and Fermelant were brought to my attention by Shachar Pinsker, who is helping to make their work more widely known. Kleiman was 99 years old in 2008.

7. On Whitehill, see Michael Weingrad, "The Last of the (Hebrew) Mohicans," *Commentary* (March 2006): pp. 45–50.

8. I found out about his work only serendipitously when his daughter Ora Kurland, a Jewish educator, participated in a summer program at the Jewish Theological Seminary. I thank her and her sister for introducing me to his work. He also published a number of poetry collections in English.

9. *Kol shirei Zvi Yair* (Jerusalem: Heichal Menachem, 1997).

Chapter One

1. From the foreword written by Shazar to A. S. Schwartz, *Shirim* [Poems] (Tel Aviv and Jerusalem: M. Newman, 1959), p. 7. Schwartz was a Brooklyn physician and Hebrew poet. He and Shazar were neighbors and became closer acquaintances during a brief time that Schwartz lived in Jerusalem before his death. See Chapter 6. All translations are mine unless otherwise noted.

2. Shalom Goldman, *God's Sacred Tongue: The Hebrew Bible and the American Imagination* (Chapel Hill: University of North Carolina Press, 2004), p. 3. See also Shalom Goldman (ed.), *Hebrew and the Bible in America* (Hanover, NH: University Press of New England, 1993). Together, these two volumes contribute greatly to our knowledge on this subject.

3. For a valuable typology of different kinds of American Hebrew, see Arnold Band, "From Sacred Tongue to Foreign Language: Hebrew in the American University" in Alan Mintz (ed.), *Hebrew in America: Perspective and Prospects* (Detroit: Wayne State University Press, 1993), pp. 171–86.

4. The best source of information about nineteenth- and early twentieth-century Hebrew writing in America is the work of Jacob Kabakoff, the finest literary historian of the subject. See his *Ḥalutsei hasifrut ha'ivrit ba'ameriqah* [Pioneers of Hebrew literature in America] (Tel Aviv: Yavneh and the Cleveland Institute for Jewish Studies, 1966) and *Shiḥarim vene'emanim: masot umeḥqarim 'al hasifrut vehatarbut ha'ivrit ba'ameriqah* [The early and the loyal: Essays and research on Hebrew literature and culture in America] (Jerusalem: Reuven Mass, 1978). For a publishing history of Hebrew books in America in the nineteenth-century, see J. K. Miklishanski, *Toledot hasifrut ha'ivrit ba'ameriqah* [The history of Hebrew literature in America] (New York: Ogen, 1967).

5. Shai Nahshoni has forty-six items in his list of Hebrew periodicals in America between 1871 and 1914. See "The American Hebrew Press 1871–1914: Themes and Trends" [in Hebrew], *Kesher* (Nov. 1988): pp. 31–49.

6. For a contemporary account of the Hebraist activity in America from 1903 to 1912, a good source is Mordecai Waxman (ed.), *Teḥiyat lashon* [Language revival] (New York, 1913), which is a collection of the papers and reports published on the occasion of the tenth anniversary of the founding of the Mefitsei Sefat Ever.

7. The shift between the old and the new orders is affectingly dramatized in Lisitzky's autobiography *Eleh toledot adam* [In the grip of cross-currents] (Jerusalem: Mossad Bialik, 1949), pp. 171–79, when in Boston, the teenager with literary ambitions meets Dolitzky, the embittered Haskalah poet.

8. The incident is recounted in Anita Shapira, *Brenner, sippur ḥayyav* [Brenner, a biography] (Tel Aviv: Am Oved, 2008), p. 94.

9. *Hatoren* 2, no. 1 (June 1915).

10. On the publishing history of the journal, as well as a general description of the enterprise and its significance, see my "A Sanctuary in the Wilderness:

The Beginnings of the Hebrew Movement in America in *Hatoren*" in Alan Mintz (ed.), *Hebrew in America: Perspective and Prospects* (Detroit: Wayne State University Press, 1993), pp. 29–67.

11. Shapira, *Brenner.*

12. Persky was the only Hebraist to have been the subject of a *New Yorker* profile. See Dwight MacDonald, Profiles, "The Slave of Hebrew," *The New Yorker*, November 28, 1959, p. 57.

13. The Hebraist movement in America can properly be thought of as one of three branches that emerged from this late nineteenth-century consensus about the bond between the Jewish nation and the Hebrew language. The Tarbut schools in Europe between the two world wars are the counterpart to the Hebraist movement in America; and of course the other is the entrenchment of Hebrew in the school system of the Yishuv. Each branch developed differently according to local conditions.

14. Ironically, the connotations of *tarbut* in the few sources in which it appears are generally negative. Numbers 32:14 speaks of the company of evil men; Talmud *Hagigah* 16a describes the apostate sage Elisha ben Abuya as having gone astray [*yatsa letarbut ra'ah*]. The term is also used in rabbinic literature to describe the domestication of animals.

15. The best sources for an understanding of American Yiddish poetry are Ruth R. Wisse, *A Little Love in Big Manhattan* (Cambridge: Harvard University Press, 1988); Benjamin Harshav, *The Meaning of Yiddish* (Berkeley and Los Angeles: California University Press, 1990); and Anita Norich, *Discovering Exile: Yiddish and Jewish American Culture during the Holocaust* (Stanford: Stanford University Press, 2007). Two important anthologies with rich introductions are Irving Howe, Ruth R. Wisse, and Khone Shmeruk (eds.), *The Penguin Anthology of Modern Yiddish Verse* (New York: Viking Press, 1987) and Benjamin and Barbara Harshav (eds.), *American Yiddish Poetry: A Bilingual Anthology* (Berkeley and Los Angeles: University of California Press, 1986).

16. One of the few joint enterprises was the literary miscellany *Ahisefer*, edited by Menachem Ribalow and Shmuel Niger (New York, 1943).

17. "Episodah ameriqanit," in Yisrael Efros, *Sefer hamasot* [Book of essays] (Tel Aviv: Dvir, 1961), p. 232; the essay appeared originally in *Davar*.

18. See Chapter 8.

19. See the special issue of *Prooftexts* devoted to this topic, "The Role of Periodicals in the Formation of Modern Jewish Identities," *Prooftexts: A Journal of Jewish Literary History* 15 (January 1995), pp. 1–4.

20. Ribalow was born in 1895 and came to America at the age of twenty-one. He is particularly significant for this volume because he compiled an influential anthology of American Hebrew poetry, which remains the only work of its kind.

21. Moshe Pelli, *Hatarbut ha'ivrit ba'ameriqah: 80 shenot hatenu'ah ha'vrit be'artsot haberit (1916–1995)* [Hebrew culture in America: Eighty years of the

Hebrew movement in the United States (1916–1995)] (Tel Aviv: Reshafim, 1998), pp. 108–10. Pelli's volume is a comprehensive account, rich with documentary evidence, of the institutional history of the Hebraist movement in America. See p. 365 for a list of the thirty national conferences that took place between 1917 and 1964.

22. Personal communication.

23. For a sensitive discussion of this decision, see Walter Ackerman, "A World Apart: Hebrew Teachers Colleges and Hebrew-Speaking Camps," in *Hebrew in America*, pp. 105–28.

24. On Rawidowicz's thought, see *The State of Israel, Diaspora, and Jewish Continuity: Essays on the "Ever-Dying People"* (Hanover, NH: Brandeis University Press, 1998); and David N. Myers, *Between Jew and Arab: The Lost Voice of Simon Rawidowicz* (Hanover, NH: Brandeis University Press, 2008).

25. Eisig Silberschlag, *Bein alimut uven adishut* [Between violence and indifference] (Jerusalem: Rubin Mass, 1981), p. 93. Translation by Michael Weingrad, with his kind permission.

26. Simon Halkin, in his masterfully polemical defense of the American poets in *Hado'ar* 4, no. 3 (1925), which was reprinted as "Paragons and Epigones in our Literature" [in Hebrew] in *Derakhim vetsidei derakhim basifrut* [Paths and byways in literature], vol. 2 (Jerusalem, 1969), pp. 82–94.

27. It is important to point out that the indifference to the activity of the American Hebraists was not absolute. Both Brenner and Yaakov Rabinowitz, two very important critics living in Palestine, reacted to Silkiner's early Indian epic *Mul ohel Timurah* (1910) by challenging the Americans to engage the American milieu more fully. On Brenner's critique, see the beginning of Chapter 3 in this volume. Rabinowitz's critique is reviewed in Spicehandler, *"Ameriqa'iyyut* in American Hebrew Literature," in *Hebrew in America*, pp. 75–77. Another kind of exception is embodied in the poet Yitzhak Lamdan (1899–1954), who, as editor of the literary journal *Gilyonot*, was hospitable to some of the American writers in his pages during the 1930s and 1940s.

28. The clearest and strongest distillation of this position was presented by Nurith Govrin, "The Demand for Americanness and its Realization in Hebrew Literature in America" [in Hebrew], in Stanley Nash (ed.), *Migvan: mehqarim basifrut ha'ivrit uvegiluyeha ha'ameriqaniyyim mugashim leYa'aqov Kabakov* [Spectrum: Studies in Hebrew literature and its American manifestations] (Lod: Haberman Institute, 1988), pp. 81–97.

29. Dan Miron, *Bodedim bemo'adam: lediyuqnah shel harepubliqah hasifrutit ha'ivrit betehilat hame'ah ha'esrim* [When lovers come together: A portrait of Hebrew literature at the turn of the twentieth century] (Tel Aviv: Am Oved, 1987).

30. Naomi Seidman, trans., *Kelapei tish'im vetish'ah* [To the ninety-nine] (Tel Aviv, 1928), pp. 12–13. The passage is quoted in Uzi Shavit, "The New Hebrew Poetry of the Twenties: Palestine and America," *Prooftexts* 12, no. 3 (September

1992): p. 215. Shavit's article is an exemplary exercise in historical poetics and has been of great use to me in preparing this section.

31. It should be noted that there were several variants of Ashkenazic pronunciation. The variables included not only the pronunciation of the *tav* consonant but also of the *qamats* vowel.

32. Halkin, p. 86. Halkin expresses extreme impatience with the influence of Russian literature on Hebrew writing. Although he honors Russian fiction, he argues that the effect of emulating modern Russian poetry has been deleterious.

33. Ibid., pp. 82–83.

34. Ibid., pp. 91, 89.

35. Epstein, *Soferim 'ivrim ba'ameriqah* [Hebrew writers in America] (Tel Aviv: Dvir, 1952), p. 12.

36. A reworking of a translation by Naomi Seidman (with her kind permission) in Uzi Shavit, "The New Hebrew Poetry of the Twenties: Palestine and America." These are the first two of four stanzas of the poem, which originally appeared in Menahem Ribalow (ed.), *Sefer hayovel shel Hado'ar* [The *Hado'ar* jubilee book] (New York, 1927), p. 69. I have taken the liberty of retranslating the second line of the second stanza in a way that makes more sense in the context of the poem. The original is "Fortification, a spark of fire and arrogant flame."

Chapter Two

An earlier version of this chapter appeared in *Prooftexts: A Journal of Jewish Literary History*, 30, no. 1 (2011), published by Indiana University Press. Reprinted with the permission of the publisher.

1. The poem first appeared in the journal *Hatequfah* 30–31 (1946). It was reprinted in Regelson's collected poems, which carried the name of the poem as the title of the collection as a whole: *Ḥaquqot otiyyotayikh* (Tel Aviv: Maḥbarot Lesifrut, 1964), pp. 7–26. The text of the poem, together with all of Regelson's poetry, is available on the Internet at www.benyehuda.org/regelson. In an article he wrote ten years after the publication of the poem (*'Al Hamishmar*, October 12, 1956), Regelson gave the following account of how the poem came to be written. After escaping the Nazis and reestablishing himself in New York, Abraham Shtibel, the publisher and patron of Hebrew letters, invited Regelson to his office to discuss his participation in *Hatequfah*, the journal whose publication had been interrupted by the war. Shtibel put a hundred dollars on the desk and said, "Write a poem." Regelson took the money but at first had no idea what would be the subject of the poem he had committed himself to write. Soon, however, his head was filled with thoughts about the Hebrew language at this most poignant moment in the life of the Jewish nation in the years before statehood. These thoughts spontaneously presented themselves as prime poetic material, and the poem was written and delivered to Shtibel within the course of several months.

2. For a work that is arguably a significant masterwork, the record of serious critical treatment is meager. The major exception to this generalization is Gideon Katz and Gideon Nevo, "Two Perspectives on Abraham Regelson's *Ḥakukot Otiyotayich*" [Engraved are thy letters], *Hebrew Studies* 48 (2007): pp. 299–320. This is an exceptional contribution that has informed my thinking and to which I shall return many times in the course of this chapter. A useful gathering of critical references to the poem can be found there in notes 23–25.

3. The choice of *ḥaquqot* is a clear echo of the opening of the mystical work *Sefer yetsirah*, which proclaims that God formed [*ḥaqaq*] the world through thirty-two mysterious paths, the twenty-two letters of the Hebrew alphabet and the ten *sefirot*. See Isidor Kalisch (ed.), *Sefer Yezirah: A Book on Creation* (New York: L. H. Frank & Co., 1877), p. 10.

4. See Efros's poem, "The Little Clapper," analyzed in Chapter 4.

5. In 1962, at the request of his daughter Sharona Tel-Oren, Regelson explained the references and difficult words in the *Ḥaquqot otiyyotayikh* on a line-by-line basis. The transcripts of these sessions, which were conducted in English, were later edited, translated into Hebrew by Sharona Tel-Oren, and posted, together with a note on their origins, on www.benyehuda.org/regelson. This is an illuminating and useful document, and as a comprehensive commentary by a poet on a major work of his own perhaps a unique instance in the annals of modern Hebrew literature. Yet for all of the reasons we speak in literature of the "poem itself," this commentary should be used as one, valuable explication rather than as an authoritative and definitive parsing of the poem.

6. My thanks to Ephraim Karnefogel for calling my attention to this passage in the Mishnah.

7. The case of Chana Kleiman from Chicago was noted in the Preface.

8. See, esp., "Hoy, artsi horati" and "El artsi," in Rahel Blaustein, *Shirat Rahel* (Tel Aviv: Davar, 1963), pp. 98, 58.

9. The most fascinating contemporary Israeli poem about Hebrew is Yona Wallach's "'Ivrit," which appears in *Tzurot* (Tel Aviv: Hakibbutz Hame'uḥad, 1985), pp. 17–19.

10. The relationship between the poet and Hebrew in Regelson's poem bears an uncanny resemblance to such signature poems of Alterman as "Pegishah le'ein qets" in his 1938 collection, *Kokhavim baḥuts*. See Natan Alterman, *Shirim shemikevar* (Tel Aviv: Hakibbutz Hame'uḥad, 1999), pp. 12–13.

11. The quotation is taken from David Simha Segal's dazzling translation and explication of *Sefer taḥkemoni*. *The Book of Taḥkemoni: Jewish Tales from Medieval Spain* (London: Littman Library of Jewish Civilization, 2001), p. 13. I am grateful to Raymond Scheindlin for suggesting this connection, as well as the link to Ibn Gabirol's *Keter malkhut* (see note 16 below).

12. Segal, pp. 13, 417–20.

13. Abraham Rosenfeld (trans. and ed.), *Seder qinot hashalem letish'ah be'av* [The authorized *qinot* for the ninth of Av] (London: C. Labworth & Co., 1965), pp. 152–53. Halevi's poem became the template for a series of dirges concerning later catastrophes; the *qinot* in this genre are called Zionides. See, esp., the *qinah* "Sh'ali, serufah ba'esh" by Meir of Rothenburg, which responds to the public burning of the Talmud in Paris in 1242. Halevi's ode to Zion was used repeatedly by American Hebrew writers. See Stephen Katz, *Red, Black, and Jew: New Frontiers in Hebrew Literature* (Austin: University of Texas Press, 2009).

14. This is Regelson's own translation of these lines, which is taken from *Israel's Sweetest Singer: Yehuda Halevi*, a long essay in English that appeared in pamphlet form. It can be viewed at www.benyehuda.org/regelson/sweetest.html.

15. In the Hebrew, Regelson makes an adjective from the name Oholiab, the assistant to Bezalel in the crafting of the desert sanctuary; see Exod. 31:6.

16. As Regelson makes clear in his 1956 article (*'Al Hamishmar*, Oct. 16, 1956), he is explicitly emulating the practice of Ibn Gabirol in his *Keter malkhut*, in which each section begins with a rhetorical question that uses synonyms for comprehension. (See Solomon ibn Gabirol, *A Crown for the King*, trans. David R. Slavitt [New York: Oxford University Press, 1998].) The dependence of Regelson's text on Ibn Gabirol's deserves greater exploration.

17. Katz and Nevo, pp. 303–4.

18. Ibid., p. 304.

19. "A reference to sexual intercourse," says Regelson himself in the glosses recorded by his daughter. See www.benyehuda.org/regelson *ad loc.*

20. Abraham Regelson, "The God of Nature in American Poetry," in his *Melo hatalit 'alim: masot vesihot* [A shawl full of leaves: Essays and talks] (New York: The Committee for the Publication of the Writings of A. Regelson, 1941), pp. 9–26.

21. Katz and Nevo, p. 308.

22. Raphael Patai, *The Hebrew Goddess* (Detroit: Wayne State University Press, 1990); Tikva Frymer-Kensky, *In the Wake of the Goddess: Women, Culture, and the Biblical Transformation of Pagan Myth* (New York: New York University Press, 1992).

23. An ideological linkage between Canaanite mythology and the creation of a new Hebrew culture in Palestine/Israel was a plank in the program of the Canaanite movement, expressed esp. in the works of Yonatan Ratosh and Aharon Amir. (See James S. Diamond, *Homeland or Holy Land? The "Canaanite" Critique of Israel* [Bloomington: Indiana University Press, 1986].) Regelson was far too committed to the continuity of Hebrew creativity in the millennia between the ancient and modern tenure of the Land of Israel to ally himself with this movement. Yet there remain intriguing points of conceptual connection.

24. Katz and Nevo, pp. 306, 314–20.

25. It should be noted that responses to the Holocaust were widespread among the American Hebrew poets, especially Lisitzky and Halkin, in contrast to Hebrew letters in the Yishuv. See my *Ḥurban: Responses to Catastrophe in Hebrew Literature* (Syracuse: Syracuse University Press, 1996), pp. 157–64.

26. *Soferim 'ivrim ba'ameriqah* [Hebrew writers in America] (Tel Aviv: Dvir, 1952), p.163.

27. *Makhon* has many meanings, including an institute of higher learning. It is also the name of one of the seven heavens in Merqavah mysticism as Regelson points out in his auto-commentary.

28. *Satat* connotes the craftsman who cuts and finishes quarried stone to make it suitable for use in building.

29. This is Regelson's own term as suggested both in the auto-commentary and the 1956 *'Al Hamishmar* article.

Chapter Three

1. See Chapter 15 below.

2. At the end of his abbreviated life, Silkiner was working on a long narrative poem on immigrant life in New York called *Shekhenim* [Neighbors]. It was an intriguing departure for him on several scores. It engaged the contemporary urban milieu; it put aside lyric self-absorption for a sustained focus on the lives of others; and it lowered the high biblical register of the Indian epic to a more flexible and utilitarian level. A long historical poem called "Manoaḥ Franco: Po'ema" [Manoah Franco: Poema] was published after his death in *Massad: Ma'asaf ledivrei sifrut 2* [Massad: A literary miscellany 2], ed. Hillel Bavli (New York and Tel Aviv: Haverim and Mitspeh, 1936), pp. 9–54; it appears in Silkiner's collected poetry, *Shirim* [Poems] (Tel Aviv and United States: Dvir/Haverim, 1927), pp. 63–67. It is unclear whether any more of the poem was written than this section.

3. For this detail and for much information about Silkiner's activities, see Jacob Kabakoff, "B. N. Silkiner and his Circle: The Genesis of the New Hebrew Literature in America," *Judaism* 39, no. 1 (Winter 1990): pp. 97–103. For other biographical information, see Menachem Ribalow (ed.), *Antologiah shel hashirah ha'ivrit ba'ameriqah* [Anthology of Hebrew poetry in America] (New York: Ogen, 1938), p. 55.

4. For a survey of these early attempts, see Jacob Kabakoff, *Ḥalutsei hasifrut ha'ivrit ba'ameriqah* [Pioneers of Hebrew literature in America] (Tel Aviv and Cleveland: Yavneh and the Cleveland Institute for Jewish Studies, 1966).

5. On the cultural world of this journal, see my "A Sanctuary in the Wilderness: The Beginnings of the Hebrew Movement in America in *Hatoren*," in Alan Mintz (ed.), *Hebrew in America: Perspective and Prospects* (Detroit: Wayne State University Press, 1993), pp. 29–67.

6. For a complete listing of the Shakespeare translations, see the appendix to Ezra Spicehandler, "*Ameriqa'iuyut* in American Hebrew Literature," in *Hebrew in America*, pp. 103–4.

7. Benjamin Silkiner, *Shirim* (New York and Tel Aviv: Haverim/Dvir, 1926).

8. An exception is the very strong poem "Bein sela'im 'ilmim" [Among silent stones], p. 6, in which the speaker on a walk in the Connecticut woods encounters a mountain once holy to the Algonquins and meditates on their lost grandeur. The poem was written around the time of the publication of *Mul ohel Timurah* and has obvious relevance to the poet's connection to that project.

9. Silkiner, *Shirim*, p. 40.

10. It is "my heart" [*levavi*] that sets this policy. Silkiner may be using "heart" in its biblical meaning as the seat of the intellect rather than its romantic connotation as the organ of emotion.

11. For a fuller treatment of the theme of erotic insufficiency in the turn-of-the-century generation, see my *Banished From Their Father's Table: Loss of Faith and Hebrew Autobiography* (Bloomington: Indiana University Press, 1989), esp. chapter 4.

12. Bialik famously implores his beloved to take him under her wing and be for him as a mother and a sister in a poem that set the tone for Silkiner's. See "Hakhnisini taḥat kenafekh," in Dan Miron et al. (ed.), *Ḥ. N. Bialik: Shirim* [Ch. N Bialik; Collected poems 1899–1934] (Tel Aviv: Makhon Katz and Dvir, 1990), p. 216.

Chapter Four

1. Sources for Efros's biography include Menachem Ribalow (ed.), *Antologyah shel hashirah ha'ivrit ba'ameriqah* [Anthology of Hebrew poetry in America] (New York: Ogen, 1938), p. 129; Efros's own note about himself in Yitzhak Orpaz, Nurith Govrin, Asa Kasher, B. Y. Michali, and Tzvi Malachi (eds.), *Yisra'el Efrat: meshorer vehogeh* [Israel Efros: Poet and thinker] (Tel Aviv: Makhon Katz Lesifrut Ivrit, Tel Aviv University, 1981), pp. 13–14; and Daniel Persky, *Yisra'el Efrat*, pp. 37–42. For an excellent time line of Efros's life, see Ilana Elkad-Lehman, *Temurot po'etiyot beshirat Yisra'el Efrat* [Poetic changes in Israel Efrat's poetry] (PhD diss., Bar-Ilan University, 1995), pp. 2–4.

2. The dedication to this English volume is written in Hebrew, and it is a moving tribute to Efros's father, upon whom he lavishes thanks for his nurturing introduction to Jewish study and to Maimonides. In an endearing play on words that unpacks the title of Maimonides's great philosophical treatise, Efros makes a gesture to his father's haskalah interests—and to his own unconventional discipleship—by saying that he implanted in the son esteem for both the guide and the perplexed (*gam lamoreh vegam lanevukhim*).

3. Simon Halkin, "Hashirah ha'ivrit ba'ameriqah," *Hado'ar*, November 28, 1924, pp. 10–12; the translations are taken from Ezra Spicehandler, *"Ameriqa'iyyut* in American Hebrew Literature," in Alan Mintz (ed.), *Hebrew in America: Perspectives and Prospects* (Detroit: Wayne State University Press, 1993), pp. 78–79.

4. For insight on Efros's poetics generally, see Elkad-Lehman, *Temurot po'etiyyot beshirat Yisra'el Efrat.*

5. Edited with Benjamin Silkiner and Yehuda Ibn-Shemuel Kaufman, Efros's English-Hebrew dictionary was first published in 1929 (Tel Aviv: Dvir) and went through several subsequent revisions.

6. *Hamlet, nesikh Denmark* (New York: Ogen, 1944) and *Timon, ish Atunah* (Tel Aviv: Dvir, 1953).

7. The volume was published in Tel Aviv in 1932 as a joint venture between the Haverim imprint in New York and the Mitspeh publishing house in Palestine. All page references are to this edition.

8. Efros has a particular affinity for winter scenes; see his delightful evocation of a winter storm in his long Indian poem *Vigvamim shoteqim* [Silent wigwams] (Tel Aviv: Mitspeh, 1933), pp. 99–102.

9. "Leil *ḥoref*" bears an evident debt to a key poem in the Bialik canon, "Tsafririm" [Morning spirits, 1901], in which the speaker summons up a recollection of the rambunctious sprites that lured him to frolic in nature as a boy. In Efros's poem as in Bialik's, these creatures are presented as real rather than merely fanciful or allegorical, and their appearance is revelatory. Efros's treatment of the scene lacks the autobiographical framing of Bialik's text, and hence the endings, though similar, have different resonances. For Bialik, the appearance of the *tsafririm* is presented as being constitutive of his developing imagination, whereas for Efros the event merely leaves a consoling echo.

10. Menachem Ribalow, "Yisra'el Efrat—Shirim" [in Hebrew], in *Yisra'el Efrat*, pp. 37–43.

11. See the poems on pp. 1, 12–13, 26–28, 40, and others.

12. Ribalow, "Yisra'el Efrat—Shirim," p. 40.

13. The bell's clapper can be either *'inbal* or *'inbol* in Hebrew. The former is more common in modern Hebrew, although the latter is closer to the original Greek *embolon* or Latin *embolus.*

14. The piyyut, which begins *Tamid titlonen beyadkha kol nefesh*, can be found in Daniel Goldschmidt (ed.), *Maḥzor leyamim nora'im* [High holiday *maḥzor*], vol. 2 (Keren Yerushalayim: Jerusalem, 1970), pp. 172–73. The talmudic reference is in Bavli *Shabbat* 152b.

15. *Mitrotsets* is the future hitpa'el of *r.u.ts.*, to run, whereas *arotsets* is the future pi'el of *r.ts.ts.*, to smash or batter.

Chapter Five

1. Ephraim Lisitzky, *Eleh toldot adam* (Jerusalem: Mossad Bialik, 1949); *In the Grip of Cross-Currents*, trans. Moshe Kohn and Jacob Sloan and revised by the author (New York: Block Publishing Co., 1959).

2. For an important study of Lisitzky's autobiography, see Jill Havi Aizenstein, *Engaging America: Immigrant Jews in American Hebrew Literature* (PhD diss., New York University, 2008), pp. 254–349.

3. *Hasiporet ha'ivrit 1880–1980*, vol. 3 (Jerusalem: Keter and Hakibbutz Hame'uḥad, 1988), pp. 135–38. Shaked also points out the work's affiliation with the tradition of Hebrew autobiography, especially Solomon Maimon and Moshe Leib Lilienblum, as well as with the immigrant novel. See my *Banished From Their Father's Table* (Bloomington: Indiana University Press, 1989), chap. 1 and conclusion.

4. Lisitzky became something of a master of the *poema*, a medium-length narrative verse genre, which he began writing in the 1930s. These are collected in *Adam 'al adamot: Po'emot* [Man on earth: Poemas] (New York: Ogen/Histadrut Ivrit, 1947).

5. Ephraim Lisitzky, *Shirim* (New York and Tel Aviv: Haverim and Dvir, 1928).

6. Lisitzky, *Shirim*, pp. 9–10.

7. See the moving sonnet sequence Lisitzky dedicates "with love" to Silkiner, titled "Minham'aqim" [De profundis], *Shirim*, pp. 219–24.

8. Lisitzky, "Banekhar," *Shirim*, pp. 48–50.

9. Lisitzky, *Shirim*, p. 112.

10. Might the autobiographical notation of the poem give us leave to conjecture that the battle the speaker has been waging has taken place inside a Hebrew school classroom, a battle on behalf of Hebrew for the hearts and minds of resistant and ungrateful children of Jewish immigrants? The reference will seem silly only to those who have not been so tested.

11. The model for this aspect of the poem, I would argue, is Bialik's 1911 poem "Tsanaḥ lo zalzal" [A twig fell], in which the speaker's decline is compared to the barrenness of a tree in winter. When spring comes, however, the tree will bloom again whereas the speaker's depletion will never be renewed.

12. Abraham Epstein, *Soferim 'ivrim ba'ameriqah* [Hebrew writers in America] (Tel Aviv: Dvir, 1952), p. 46.

Chapter Six

1. A. S. Schwartz, *Shirim* [Poems] (Tel Aviv and Jerusalem: M. Newman, 1959).

2. See his autobiographical essay, "The Path of a Bilingual Yiddish Poet" [Hebrew], *Hado'ar* 29 (1973).

3. Schwartz, *Shirim*, pp. 13–15. All references to the poems are to this volume and will be given in the body of the text in parentheses.

4. One of the cleverest and most substantial of Schwartz's biblical poems is "Behithadshut Iyov" [Job's renewal] (1950, pp. 273–82), which extrapolates from the narrative situation at the end of the book of Job and follows Job into the years after he has had all his losses restored to him; the images of loneliness and dissociation amid apparent prosperity are chilling.

5. "The Poetry of A. S. Schwartz," in Schwartz, *Shirim*, pp. 338–39.

6. Dictionaries variously relate it to *yafeh* [beautiful], or, because of the letter *ayin* in the last position, to the root of the verb *lehofiaʿ*, to appear.

7. Schwartz's "ʿAl Shaʾul" [On Saul] (1944, pp. 162–65) is one of the most successful poetic eulogies for the eminent poet. On Tchernichovsky's vitalist connection to the sun, see Alan Mintz (ed.), *Reading Hebrew Literature: Critical Discussions of Six Modern Texts* (Hanover: Brandeis University Press, 2003), pp. 64–101.

8. Schwartz makes a devastatingly ironic rhyme between *mitʿaneg* [playful] and Majdanek.

9. On this question, see Raymond Scheindlin, *Wine, Women and Death* (Philadelphia: Jewish Publication Society).

10. Bereishit Rabbah, ed. Theodore-Albeck, p. 8 ("A certain philosopher asked R. Gamaliel, saying to him: 'Your God was indeed a great artist, but surely He found good materials which assisted Him?'"). Schwartz has changed the term for the artist from the *tsayar* [painter] in the source to *sayad* [whitewasher, house painter]. He may simply have wanted a rhyme that was not too close to *tsayad* [hunter] at the end of line 15; but he also may have wanted a less grandiose register for the assertion.

Chapter Seven

1. Bavli gave his birth date as 1892, although he is listed in most reference works as having been born in 1893. The most extensive source for Bavli's biography is E. R. Malachi, "The Life of Hillel Bavli," [in Hebrew], *Bitzaron* 44, no. 7 (1961): pp. 166–73 and 45, no. 2 (1962): pp. 67–75, no. 3 (1962): pp. 137–48. I have largely drawn from Malachi's work in framing Bavli's life.

2. Later in life he wrote a memoir about this experience, Hillel Bavli, "A Catholic College in Buffalo" [in Hebrew], *Gilyonot* 31, nos. 8–10 (1954): p. 122ff.

On the fascination reflected in his poem "Beḥatsrot el nekhar" [In the precincts of an alien God], see below.

3. Malachi, "The Life of Hillel Bavli," p. 173.

4. On *Hatoren*, see Alan Mintz, "A Sanctuary in the Wilderness: The Beginnings of the Hebrew Movement in America in the Pages of *Hatoren*," in Alan Mintz (ed.), *Hebrew in America: Perspectives and Prospects* (Detroit: Wayne State University Press, 1993), pp. 29–67.

5. A selection of his essays appeared much later on. See Hillel Bavli, *Ruḥot nifgashot* (New York: Ogen, 1957).

6. Hillel Bavli, *Nimim, ma'asaf ledivrei sifrut yafah uledivrei biqoret* (Berlin: Haverim, 1923).

7. Hillel Bavli (ed.), *Massad: Ma'asaf ledivrei sifrut* [Massad: A literary miscellany], vol. 1 (Tel Aviv: Haverim/Mitspeh, 1933). A second volume, dedicated to the memory of Benjamin Silkiner, appeared in 1936.

8. E. R. Malachi, *Zekher leHillel* (New York: Alumni Association of the Teachers Institute and Seminary College, 1962). See p. 84–85 for the list of subscribers. This volume presents a full bibliography of Bavli's writings and critical articles written about him.

9. Hillel Bavli, *Neginot arets* was published separately as a booklet (Tel Aviv: Hedim, n.d.) and then included in his collected poetry, Hillel Bavli, *Shirim* [Poems] (Tel Aviv: Dvir, 1938), pp. 179–209.

10. See *Tse'if–yegonim* [A veil of sorrow], pp. 297–316; and *'Al saf hasod* [On the verge of mystery], pp. 375–91 in Bavli, *Shirim*.

11. "Bema'avarah le-New York" takes place on the Staten Island Ferry and is the speech of an immigrant reviewing his life in America (ibid., pp. 149–54); "Sergiev mehar tabor" is the self-narrated story of a Russian gentile who has come to live in Palestine (ibid., pp. 211–21).

12. Hillel Bavli, "Benei Lita," pp. 174–221, in *Aderet hashanim* (Jerusalem: Mossad Bialik, 1955).

13. The sketch of Bavli's lyric poetry that follows focuses on the first dozen or so years of writing as contained in Book One (pp. 1–171). The volume is divided into two books of *Shirim* [Poems] (Tel Aviv: Dvir, 1938). All page numbers refer to this work.

14. This phrasing is likely a conflation of *el elohei yisra'el* (in Gen. 33:20) and *elohei avi, elohei Avraham ufaḥad Yitsḥak* (in Gen. 31:42); my thanks to Samuel Bavli for making this suggestion and for his comments and suggestions on my translations of his father's poems.

15. On Bialik's poem, see the special issue of *Prooftexts* (25, nos. 1–2, 2005).

16. Also special to Bavli was a fascination with Christianity. See his long poem "Beḥatsrot el nekhar" [In the precincts of an alien God], pp. 64–76, which was begun while Bavli was studying at a Jesuit college in Buffalo.

17. The time implied by "then I will know" [*az ed'a*] is ambiguous. The access to this epiphany would seem to become available only after the speaker's wish has been granted to spend the rest of his days sitting and listening. In addition, the use in close proximity of *qol* [sound] and *demamah* [silence] in these last two lines unavoidably evokes the *qol demamah daqah* ["the soft murmuring sound"] or ["still small voice"] in 1 Kings 19:12.

18. In this quest, he joins, after a fashion, the *helekh*, the poet-wanderer, who emerges as the protagonist in the poetry of Alterman and the poets of the moderna in Palestine.

19. In *Shirim*, examples can be found on pp. 96, 112–13, 277, and 437; in *Aderet hashanim* on pp. 32, 60, 65, and 75.

20. "Tefillah" first appeared in *Hado'ar*, no. 42 (7 Tishrei 5686 [= 1925]). The date falls between Rosh Hashanah and Yom Kippur, and the appositeness of the poem's theme for the High Holiday season must certainly have been on the editors' minds.

21. On this theme, see my *Banished From Their Father's Table* (Bloomington: Indiana University Press, 1989).

Chapter Eight

1. Shimon was the middle of three brothers. The elder, Jekutiel, became a professor of mathematics first at Columbia Teachers College and then at Yeshiva University; he contributed Hebrew feuilletons to *Hado'ar* and wrote on the history of mathematics for such journals as *Hatekufah*. The younger brother Pessach—he spelled his surname with an "s" rather than a "z," i.e., Ginsburg—left America for Scandinavia but later settled in Tel Aviv, where he was an editor at *Ha'aretz*; he was a prolific translator of Scandinavian literature into Hebrew. A sister named Chaya, who became a Hebrew teacher in Miami Beach, occasionally contributed Hebrew verse to Hebrew periodicals. From Ginzburg's poetry, it would seem there was another sister in Europe, although the demographics of the family is not clear to me. Sources for Ginzburg's biography include the entry in Geztl Kressel, *Leqsiqon hasifrut ha'ivrit badorot harishonim* (Merhavya: Sifriat Po'alim, 1965–67), pp. 472–77; and Daniel Persky, *Hado'ar*, January 21, 1944. (The issue contains a number of tributes to Ginzburg.)

2. His appointment and mission are described by Shlomo Hillels in *Hado'ar*, January 21, 1944.

3. See my "A Sanctuary in the Wilderness: The Beginnings of the Hebrew Movement in America in *Hatoren*," in Alan Mintz (ed.), *Hebrew in America: Perspective and Prospects* (Detroit: Wayne State University Press, 1993).

4. Shimon Ginzburg, *Shirim ufo'emot* (Haverim/Dvir: Tel Aviv, 1931), pp. 91–92. Page references are to this edition unless otherwise noted.

5. Shimon Ginzburg, Sh. M. Melamed, Zvi Scharfstein (eds.), *Luah ahi'ever* (New York: Histadrut Ivrit, 1918), pp. 3–28. The poem is signed 1917. The poem

is reprinted in *Shirim ufo'emot*, pp. 263–85; references are given as page numbers in that edition.

6. For an interpretation of Bialik's poem, with an emphasis on the ordeal of the prophet, see my *Ḥurban: Responses to Catastrophe in Hebrew Literature* (Syracuse: Syracuse University Press, 1996), pp. 129–54; see also the special issue of *Prooftexts* (25, nos. 1–2 [2005]) on "Kishinev and the Twentieth Century."

7. Ginzburg refers to the discourse of the poem as *masa New York*, just as Bialik's poem originally appeared under the title *masa Nemirov. Masa* is a prophetic oracle often directed at a country or city-state.

8. Persky reports that for him, and the other young Hebraists starting out in writing careers, the idea of the *poema* was surrounded by an aura of hushed respect. Ginzburg, of course, had already written some.

9. For the way in which American Indians are figured in the poem, a subject I have not discussed here, see Michael Weingrad, *American Hebrew Literature: Writing Jewish National Identity in the United States* (Syracuse: Syracuse University Press, 2011).

10. Halkin's lyric ode to New York ("Betokhekhi New York") in his magisterial novel *Ad mashber* [The crash] (Tel Aviv: Am Oved, 1947) is one of the great meditations on the life of New York Jewry. It comes, it should be noted, thirty years after Ginzburg's fiery condemnation of the city.

11. See Abraham Epstein's fine pages on the poem in *Soferim 'ivrim ba'ameriqah* [Hebrew writers in America] (Tel Aviv: Dvir, 1952), pp. 98–102.

12. An exception is the long poem "Hedvigah," pp. 288–316, which describes an attraction between a Jewish boy and a Polish girl.

13. One assumes that Ginzburg is describing the passing of his wife, a figure who does not figure in his poetry until this point. I do not have biographical information about Ginzburg's wife. Ginzburg may have married again because Kressel mentions biographical memoirs written after his death by "his wife Devorah Horkenos-Ginzburg," *Leksiqon*, p. 477.

14. In *Shirim ufo'emot*, see the poems on pages 84, 85, and 130–48; see also the many essays on Bialik in Ginzburg, *Bemasekhet hasifrut* [Literary essays] (New York: Va'ad Lehotsa'at Kitvei Shimon Ginzburg, 1945), pp. 79–113.

15. I have broken the prose translation into paragraphs for easier comprehension; this division docs not reflect the Hebrew, which is divided into only two units, the first ending with line 32.

Chapter Nine

1. The best collection of biographical and critical writings about Friedland is Menachem Ribalow (ed.), *Sefer zikaron leH. A. Friedland* [Memorial volume for H. A. Friedland] (New York: Histadrut Ivrit, 1941). A useful essay with more information about his educational career is Shlomo Haramati, *Meḥankhim yehudim batefutsot* [Jewish educators of the Diaspora] (Tel Aviv: Ministry of Defense, 2003).

2. Ribalow gives different dates in the biographical note on Friedland in his *Antologiyah shel hashirah ha'ivrit ba'ameriqah* [Anthology of Hebrew poetry in America] (New York: Ogen, 1938), p. 291. He has Friedland going to yeshivah in Lithuania at the age of thirteen and arriving in America at the age of fifteen. I do not think this dating is reliable.

3. "Lezekher Friedland," in Ribalow, *Sefer zikaron*, pp. 15–17.

4. This is the revolution usually associated with the "Benderly Boys," the disciples of Samson Benderly, who was in charge of education during New York's short-lived Kehillah experiment. Educated at Columbia Teachers College and the Teachers Institute of the Jewish Theological Seminary, these educators fanned out across America, especially in the cities of the Mississippi valley, and Hebraized Jewish education. While Friedland was not one of Benderly's protégés, his work in Cleveland partakes of the same aspirations and dynamics.

5. New York: Hotsa'at Neḥemyah Lin, 1929.

6. Chaim Orland (ed.), with an introduction by Israel Efros (New York: Ogen/Histadrut Ivrit and Lishkat haḥinukh hayehudi beqlivland, 1963).

7. Haramati, *Meḥankhim yehudim batefutsot*, pp. 117–18.

8. H. A. Friedland, *Sipurim yafim 2* (Cleveland: Cleveland Bureau of Jewish Education, 1959), pp. 5–16.

9. H. A. Friedland, *Sonetot* (Tel Aviv: Ogen, 1939).

10. H. A. Friedland, *Shirim* (Tel Aviv: Ogen, 1940).

11. It is telling that Friedland is the only one of the twelve poets in this study who is ignored by the great critic of American Hebrew poetry Epstein in his classic *Soferim 'ivrim ba'ameriqah* [Hebrew writers in America] (Tel Aviv: Dvir, 1952).

12. Ribalow, "Friedland's Literary Work" [in Hebrew], pp. 83–86 in Ribalow, *Sefer zikaron leH. A. Friedland*.

13. References throughout are generally to page numbers in *Sonetot*; poems that appear in the sonnet section of the posthumous volume are referenced as *Shirim* with the page number.

14. This is the term that was used by Renaissance Hebrew poets for the sonnet. *Zahav* means gold, but the numerical equivalent of the sum of its letters (*zayin* = 7, *heh* = 5, *bet* = 2) is fourteen.

15. There is still another group that might be called lyric sonnets. These poems recount a moment of harmony or grace experienced by the lyric "I." Because they resemble the poems of other American Hebrew poets, I have chosen not to discuss them, even though there are some lovely examples here, including "Al penei haye'or" [On the surface of the river] (p. 24), "Dimdumim yerukim" [Green twilight] (p. 56), "Kesefog layofi" [Like a sponge of beauty] (p. 74), "Ein ḥalomot" [Eye of dreams] (p. 92), and "Tsiv'ei reshit haqayits" [The hues of early summer] (p. 112).

16. "Ba'esh nafalu" [Felled by fire] (p. 84) operates on a similar principle by comparing the depredations of time to the attack of a cloud of locusts.

17. The phrase is Robinson's own from his "The Glory of the Nightingale," as quote by Dennis Donoghue in Harold Bloom (ed.), *Edwin Arlington Robinson: Modern Critical Views* (New York: Chelsea House, 1988), p. 32.

18. Irving Howe in *Edwin Arlington Robinson*, p. 121.

19. A parallel figure can be found in the subject of "Zeqenah" [Elderly woman] (p. 21), who, despite the comfortable circumstances of her own life, cannot *not* be aware of the troubles of others that she glimpses in her neighborhood.

20. H. A. Friedland, *Sonetot*, p. 20.

21. A well-known reference to Jammes appears in Rahel Blaustein's poem "Ani" [I], which opens with the declaration: "Quiet as lake water—/ this is the way I am: / fond of children's eyes, daily tranquilities, / the poems of Francis Jammes." Trans. by Robert Friend with Shimon Sandbank from *Raḥel: Flowers of Perhaps* (New Milford, CT: Toby Press, 2008), p. 21.

22. There are unmistakable echoes here of Bialik's well-known autobiographical poem "Shirati" [My poetry/song], which evokes the muse of poverty. In Bialik's case, in contrast, the poverty is material and emotional.

23. For *tsaḥ* as dazzling whiteness, see Song of Songs 5:10, Isa. 18:4, Jer. 4:11, and the entry in Jastrow, *Dictionary of the Talmud Bavli*.

Chapter Ten

1. This information comes from the useful chapter on Herzliah in Isidor Margolis, *Jewish Teacher Training Schools in the United States* (New York: National Council for Torah Education of Mizrachi-Hapoel Hamizrachi, 1964), pp. 242–80.

2. Moses Feinstein, *Herzliah Hebrew Academy: Educational Survey 1921–1941* (New York: Herzliah Hebrew Academy, 1942), pp. 14–15.

3. Ibid., p. 6.

4. Ibid., p. 5.

5. Personal communication, June 22, 2006.

6. Translation mine. See my "The Divided Fate of Hebrew and Hebrew Culture at the Seminary," in Jack Wertheimer (ed.), *Tradition Renewed: A History of the Jewish Theological Seminary* (New York: Jewish Theological Seminary of America, 1997), 100–103; the poem originally appeared in *Hado'ar*.

7. Epstein's chapter on Feinstein in *Soferim 'ivrim ba'ameriqah* [Hebrew writers in America] (Tel Aviv: Dvir, 1952), pp. 125–41) is a wonder of tact and sympathetic appreciation. Although Feinstein was his employer—Epstein was the Bible instructor at Herzliah—Epstein gives an honest account of the poet's achievements and limitations. Epstein frames his assessment with the assumption that Feinstein would have been a greater poet if he had not heeded the call of the Jewish nation and devoted himself to education.

8. My thanks to Dr. Sara Feinstein for providing a rich set of recollections about her father-in-law.

9. Moshe Feinstein, *Shirim vesonetot* (New York: Ogen/Histadrut Ivrit Ba'ameri-qah, 1935), p.14. All references to poems in this section will be from this edition.

10. Given the context, for *golal* I have rendered "grave," assuming the poet is using *golel* in an end stop formation, although the usage is curious.

11. Moshe Feinstein, *Avraham Abulafia* (Jerusalem: Mossad Bialik, 1956). A section, dated 1932–35, was published in *Shirim usonetot*, pp. 79–93.

12. These include "Mishe'on krakh [Urban clamor] (1917, pp. 45–49), "Ilem gesher Williamsburg" [The Williamsburg bridge is silent] (1919, pp. 53–57), "Sinai ve'olimpus" [Sinai and Olympus] (1918, pp. 61–67), and "Hazut" [Vision] (1920, pp. 69–75).

13. Epstein is characteristically perceptive in this judgment. Epstein, *Soferim 'ivrim ba'ameriqah*, p. 130.

14. Moshe Feinstein, *'Al saf hasof* (Jerusalem/Tel Aviv: M. Newman, 1964).

15. It's worth noting that this passage contains almost an entire Hebrew lexi-con of suffering: *yagon, 'etsev, devai, ke'ev, nekha'im.*

Chapter Eleven

Some of the material in this chapter originally appeared in *Modern Jewish Literatures: Intersections and Boundaries*, (ed.) Sheila E. Jelen, Michael P. Kramer, and L. Scott Lerner (Philadelphia: University of Pennsylvania Press, 2011). Re-printed with permission.

1. See Nurith Govrin, "The Demand for 'Ameriqa'iyyut' and its Fulfillment in Hebrew Literature in America" [in Hebrew] in Stanley Nash (ed.), *Migvan: Mehqarim besifrut ha'ivrit uvegiluyeha ha'ameriqani'im le Ya'akov Kabakoff* [Spec-trum: Studies in Hebrew Literature and its American Manifestations Presented to Jacob Kabakoff] (Lod: Haberman Institute, 1988), pp. 81–98.

2. *Saul Tchernichowsky: Poet of Revolt*, trans. Shalom J. Kahn et al. (Ithaca, NY: Cornell University Press, 1968).

3. Arnold Band "The Lonely Paths of Eisig Silberschlag" [in Hebrew], *Ha-do'ar*, December 30, 1988, pp. 13–15. This thoughtful article by a scholar who taught under Silberschlag for many years at the Boston Hebrew College is the source of much of the biographical information presented here.

4. Eisig Silberschlag, *From Renaissance to Renaissance: Hebrew Literature from 1492–1970* (New York: Ktav, 1973).

5. Eisig Silberschlag, *Bishevilim bodedim* [On solitary paths] (New York: Ogen Press, 1931).

6. Abraham Epstein, *Soferim 'ivrim ba'ameriqah* (Tel Aviv: Dvir, 1952), p. 209.

7. As young Jewish intellectuals who had left the traditional world of faith in which they had been reared, the American Hebrew writers were enmeshed in the same psycho-social syndromes as such writers as Brenner and Berdichevsky, who were older than they by only half a generation. I have described these issues in

my *Banished From Their Father's Table: Loss of Faith and Hebrew Autobiography* (Bloomington: Indiana University Press, 1989), esp. chap. 4.

8. Silberschlag, *Bishevilim bodedim*, p. 18.

9. Ibid., p. 38.

10. Ibid., p. 6.

11. Epstein, *Soferim 'ivrim ba'ameriqah*, p. 211.

12. Judah Halevi is the other medieval master whom Silberschlag takes as precursor in two poems that are far more ambitious but less successful than the Ibn Gabirol poem. See "Ruho shel Halevi" [The spirit of Halevi] and "Yehudah Halevi," in Eisig Silberschlag, *'Aleh, 'olam, beshir*, [Ascend, oh world, in song] (New York: Ogen, 1947), pp. 63–81.

13. Simon Halkin, "Hashirah ha'ivrit ba'ameriqah," *Hado'ar*, November 28, 1924, pp. 10–12.

14. Silberschlag, *'Aleh, 'olam, beshir*.

15. *'Aleh, 'olam, beshir* does contain one sequence of poems ("Mipi khushim," pp. 107–22) that is devoted to African American materials, but it pales in comparison to Lisitzky's far more successful inventions.

16. In Eisig Silberschlag, *Qimron hayai* [The arc of my days] (Jerusalem: Kiryat Sefer, 1959); see poems on pp. 31 and 60–62. In *Iggerotai el dorot aherim*, [Letters to other generations] (Jerusalem: Kiryat Sefer, 1971) the first section of the book ("'Al admat ameriqah," pp. 19–46) is devoted to satirical poems about American Jewish life. The epitome of this genre, to my taste, is the poem "Sam, Sy and Sol" (pp. 24–32), whose title plays with archetypal second-generation American Jewish names.

17. Silberschlag's relationship to the representation of women and sexuality should also be examined in reference to an interesting play he wrote with a Palestinian setting titled *Shev'a panim leHavah* [Seven faces of Eve] that was published as a supplement to the journal *Gilyonot* 7, no. 2 (1938): pp. 88–107. In addition, see his translations from the Greek of the erotic verse of a fifth-century C.E. Byzantine poet named Paulus Silentarius (*Shirei ahavah* [Love poems], [Tel Aviv: Mahbarot Lesifrut, 1962]).

18. Silberschlag, *Qimron yamai*.

19. Silberschlag, *Iggerotai el dorot aherim*.

20. Eisig Silberschlag, *Yesh reshit lekhol aharit* [Each end has a beginning] (Jerusalem: Kiryat Sefer, 1976).

21. Eisig Silberschlag, *Bein alimut uvein adishut* [Between violence and indifference] (Jerusalem: Reuven Mass, 1982).

22. Silberschlag, "Meshorer shel yisra'el velo be'erets yisra'el," in *Bein alimut uvein adishut*, p. 93.

23. Silberschlag, *'Aleh, 'olam, beshir*, p. 45. It is worth noting that this poem, with its playfully erotic tone, is the poem that directly follows "Yesh yif'ah 'atsumah behokhmah" in the volume. It is also one of the poems designated with

an asterisk in the table of contents that are meant to be read in the new Eretz Yisrael accent.

Chapter Twelve

1. The best source for biographical information about Halkin is Boaz Shachevitz, *Ya'arot metuhamim: Episodot babiographiah literariyah shel Shim'on Halkin* [Forest abysses: Episodes in the *biographia literaria* of Shimon Halkin] (Tel Aviv: Hakibbutz Hame'uhad and Makhon Katz, 1982). See also, Hillel Halkin, "My Uncle Simon," *Commentary* (May, 2005): pp. 60–67 for a moving and insightful memoir by Halkin's nephew.

2. Simon Halkin, *Modern Hebrew Literature from the Enlightenment to the Birth of the State of Israel* (New York: Schocken, 1950 and 1970).

3. See Rachel Elior, *The Paradoxical Ascent to God: The Kabbalistic Theosophy of Habad Hasidism,* trans. Jeffrey M. Green (Albany: The State University of New York Press, 1993), pp.66–79.

4. See the chapter on Shelley and Neoplatonism in M. H. Abrams, *The Mirror and the Lamp: Romantic Theory and Critical Tradition* (New York and London: Oxford University Press, 1953), pp. 126–32.

5. All page numbers refer to Simon Halkin, *'Al ha'i* (Jerusalem: Mossad Bialik, 1946).

6. Belonging to this period (1922–23) is a sequence of seventy-six sonnets titled *Bayamim shishah veleilot shiv'ah* [In six days and seven nights] (pp. 117–54), which is devoted to the longing for human love and its tragic impossibility. Although the sequence demonstrates Halkin's mastery of the sonnet form, it also demonstrates his difficulty with representing intersubjectivity and making the existence of others deeply felt.

7. See the persuasive essay by Shimon Zanbank, *"Yohai* and *Alastor*: The Poet Who Chooses Negation" [Hebrew] in his *Shetei bereikhot baya'ar: Kesharim umaqbilot ben hashirah ha'ivrit vehashirah ha'eiropit* [Two pools in the woods: Connections and parallels between Hebrew poetry and European poetry] (Tel Aviv: Hakibbutz Hame'uhad and Tel Aviv University, 1967), pp. 101–21. Reprinted in Dan Laor, *Shimon Halkin: mivhar ma'amarei biqoret 'al yetsirotav* [Simon Halkin: A selection of critical articles on his work] (Tel Aviv: Am Oved, 1978), pp. 107–26.

8. The novel was published by Shtibel in Berlin in 1929.

9. On the relationship of the poem to the anthology, see my *"Sefer ha'aggadah*: Triumph or Tragedy," in William Cutter and David C. Jacobson (eds.), *History and Literature: New Readings of Jewish Texts in Honor of Arnold Band* (Providence: Brown Judaic Studies, 2002), pp. 17–26.

10. *Yehudim veyahadut ba'ameriqah* [Jews and Judaism in America] (Jerusalem and Tel Aviv: Schocken, 1947) and *Tsiyonut shelo 'al tenai: Masot verishimot*

[Zionism without condition: Essays and sketches] (Jerusalem: Hasifriyah Hatsi-yonit, 1985), which contains pieces beginning from the 1920s.

11. For a very creditable attempt to translate this most difficult poem, see Ruth Finer Mintz's translation in her *Modern Hebrew Poetry: A Bilingual Anthology* (Berkeley and Los Angeles: University of California Press, 1968), pp. 145–57.

12. In fairness, it should be pointed out that four years after settling in Tel Aviv, Halkin did make a brief trip to New York to visit his mother; his father had died two years earlier, in 1934. Halkin paid for his passage with payment he received for the translation of *The Merchant of Venice*, which was presented by Habimah in 1936.

13. The poem is included in Halkin's collected poems, *Ma'avar yabbok*. One of the poem's four sections appeared in a translation by Hillel Halkin in *Ariel* no. 73 (1988), pp. 4–20. A translation of the entire poem remains in manuscript and awaits publication.

Chapter Thirteen

1. I have rendered "by the scruff of his neck" for *betsitsit rosho*, which means literally, by the hairs on his head. The phrase comes from Ezekiel 8:3, in which a divine creature yanks the prophet by his hair and pulls him up to the space between heaven and earth to prepare him for a vision.

2. Abraham Regelson, "Gezel ahavah" [Theft of love], *Miqlat* 3 (1920): pp. 118–20.

3. Regelson did edit a journal called *Riva'on qatan lemahshavah veshirah* [A little quarterly of thought and poetry] that lasted for two issues in 1942.

4. The sources for Regelson's biography include the website www.abraham-regelson.org, maintained by his daughter Sharona Tel-Oren, her prologue and epilogue to Regelson's *The Dolls' Journey to Eretz Israel*, trans. Sharona Tel-Oren (Acco and Miami: Biblio Books, 2004), and Eisig Silberschlag's obituary for Regelson in *Hado'ar*, October 30, 1981.

5. Ten years later Regelson published *'Aqedat Shelemyahu* [The binding of Shelemyahu], an 85-page narrative poem based on this incident that evokes the bohemian circles of Tel Aviv in those years and includes confessional materials. The poem appears in *Haquqot otiyyotayikh* [Engraved are thy letters] (Tel Aviv: Mahbarot Lesifrut, 1964), pp. 29–114.

6. Berel Katznelson's angry and insulting letter to Regelson concerning his departure is contained in an appendix to Yeshayahu Peles, "Regelson: A Poet's Poet" [in Hebrew], *Moznayim* 5, nos. 5–6 (October–November, 1984).

7. Personal communication. Ozick avers that, although she was not immersed in Hebrew, she was deeply influenced in her own life choices by the very existence of a close family member who was devoted to the vocation of art and thought.

8. Regelson, *Haquqot otiyyotayikh*.

9. Abraham Regelson, *Shirotayim* [Two poems] (Tel Aviv: Sifrei Siman Qeri'ah, 1972).

10. Abraham Regelson, *Er'elei hamaḥshavah* [Mighty ones of thought] (Tel Aviv: Dvir, 1969).

11. Abraham Regelson, "The Unfettered Imagination and the Constrained Imagination" [in Hebrew], *Miqlat* 3 (1920): pp. 253–56).

12. "The God of Nature in American Poetry" in his *Melo hatalit 'alim: Masot vesiḥot* [A shawl full of leaves: Essays and talks] (New York: The Committee for the Publication of the Writings of A. Regelson, 1941), pp. 9–26.

13. *Hatequfah* 11 (1921): pp. 357–72; when these poems were included in Regelson's first poetry collection, *El ha'ayin venivqa'* [To non-being and was cleft] (Tel Aviv: Am Oved, 1943 and 1945), they were dispersed within the section labeled "Metered But Not Rhymed." This placement was carried over in *Ḥaquqot otiyyotayikh* (1964), and the page numbers here are from that edition.

14. Although printed in Jerusalem, the publisher is given as Yam, Cleveland, Ohio. (I have not seen other publications from this press, which may have been established only for the purposes of publishing this volume.) The poem was reprinted in Regelson's first collection, *El ha'ayin venivqa'* (1943, pp. 93–116), and again in *Ḥaquqot otiyyotayikh* (1964, pp. 115–34). In the latter printing, Regelson appended about 1400 words of notes explaining the philosophical roots of the poem in the thought of Schopenhauer and others.

15. Regelson abandoned the Ashkenazic accent after his sojourn in Palestine in the early 1930s.

16. Regelson derives Cain's character from its affinity to the Hebrew word *qinyan* [attainment]; Abel is allied to *hevel* from Ecclesiastes in the sense of vanity or vapor.

17. Pages are according to the version in *Ḥaquqot otiyyotayikh.*

18. Moshe Feinstein, "Cain and Abel," in *Massad: Ma'asaf ledivrei sifrut* [Massad: A literary miscellany], vol. 1, ed. Hillel Bavli (Tel Aviv: Haverim/Mitspeh, 1933), pp. 121–29. Moshe Meislish, "*Cain and Abel:* A Poem by Abraham Regelson," *Hado'ar,* February 9, 1934 (www.abrahamregelson.org); Abraham Epstein, *Soferim ivrim ba'ameriqah* [Hebrew writers in America] (Tel Aviv: Dvir, 1952), pp. 154–60.

19. It should be noted that the epigram affixed to the poem is from William Blake's *The Book of Thel;* there are also several poetic texts from Blake in the section of literary translation in *Ḥaquqot otiyyotayikh.* Regelson's filiation with Blake bears further investigation.

20. In partial answer to this critique, Regelson added several pages of endnotes when the poem was reprinted in *Ḥaquqot otiyyotayikh* that explicitly explain the Schopenhauerian underpinnings of the poem. In a parenthetical paragraph (p. 343), he explains that today—one assumes the 1960s when the collection was published—he no longer holds the views expressed in *Qayin vehevel*, having progressed to a more life-affirming philosophy of life.

21. Feinstein, "Cain and Abel," p. 229.

22. The poem first appeared in *Moznayim* 4, no. 5 (1936); it is printed in *El ha'ayin venivqaʿ*, pp. 22–49, and in *Ḥaquqot otiyyotayikh*, pp. 152–68, (page numbers are from this volume).

23. Steven P. Hudson in his *Fragmentation and Restoration: The Tikkun Ha-Olam Theme in the Metaphysical Poetry of Abraham Regelson* (Chicago: Adams Press, 1988) takes the kabbalistic notion of restoration and makes it into the key to understanding all of Regelson's major work. Although the approach is obviously very useful for "Shir hatiqqun," its mechanical application elsewhere does not ring true. The book, which originated as a dissertation at New York University, contains a great deal of useful bibliographical references.

24. Epstein, *Soferim ivrim ba'ameriqah*, p. 146.

25. These are included in the *'Ivrurim* section of *Ḥaquqot otiyyotayikh*, pp. 259–65. Regelson's own classicism made him a particularly successful translator of Milton.

26. Merritt Y. Hughes (ed.), *John Milton: Complete Poems and Major Prose* (Indianapolis and New York: Bobbs-Merrill, 1957), pp. 211–12, Book One, lines 1–2, 24–26.

27. Epstein, *Soferim ivrim ba'ameriqah*, p.151–52; see esp. the charming poem "Avi'el veḤavah" (*Ḥaquqot otiyyotayikh*, pp. 207–13).

28. *Melo' hatalit 'alim* [Shawl full of leaves] (New York: The Committee for the Publication of the Writings of A. Regelson, 1941), pp. 9–25.

29. Two poems with American Indian themes are "'Arafel bekerem Marta" [Fog in Martha's Vineyard], pp. 17–78; and "Gesher haselaʿ" [The rock bridge], pp. 179–83. A patriotic poem published in 1944 is "Hadegel ha'ameriqa'i betaḥtit" [The America flag in the subway, 184–86].

30. It first appeared in *Hatequfah* 34–35, 1946; Regelson, *Ḥaquqot otiyyotayikh*, pp. 29–114.

31. Regelson, *Ḥaquqot otiyyotayikh*, pp. 259–328.

32. A rich source for understanding Regelson's poetic world is his *Revivim vetal: siḥot ve'ollelot shir* [Spring showers and dew: Talks and poetry gleanings] (Tel Aviv: Eked, 1979).

33. The book was translated into English by Regelson's daughter Sharona Tel-Oren, who simultaneously edited a reissue of the Hebrew with drawings from previous editions by Nahum Gutman, Arey Navon, Bina Gevirtz, and others (Abraham Regelson, *Masaʿ habubot le'erets yisra'el* [The journey of the dolls to the land of Israel], trans. Sharona Tel-Oren [Acco and Miami: Biblio Books, 2004]).

34. *Sham habedolaḥ: mar'ot ve'aggadot* [There the crystal is: Sights and legends] (New York: Committee for the Publication of the Works of A. Regelson, 1942).

35. Abraham Regelson, *'Ein hasus: sipurim min hamitos hayevani* [Fountain of the horse: Tales from Greek mythology] (Tel Aviv: Dvir, 1967).

36. Abraham Regelson, *Beit hanitsots: mar'ot ve'aggadot* [House of the spark: Sights and legends] (Tel Aviv: Dvir, 1972).

37. Regelson, *Ḥaquqot otiyyotayikh*, pp. 139–46.

38. Regelson, *Ḥaquqot otiyyotayikh*, pp. 235–37, 244–43, and 248–49, respectively.

39. Regelson, *Shirotayim* [Two poems] "Lesulam tsorit" [To the Sulam-Tsorith] and "Shenai barburim venahar" [Two swans and a river].

40. According to biographical information at www.abrahamregelson.org, Regelson's auto-translation of the poem, together with notes in Hebrew, can be found at www.benyehuda.org together with many of Regelson's writings.

41. Regelson, *Ḥaquqot otiyyotayikh*, p. 227. The poem is included among the poems to be read with the Ashkenazic accent and was probably written in the late 1920s.

Chapter Fourteen

1. A useful source of biographical information is Yael S. Feldman, *Modernism and Cultural Transfer: Gabriel Preil and the Tradition of Jewish Literary Bilingualism* (Cincinnati: Hebrew Union College Press, 1986), notes to chap. 4. I am also grateful to Shalom Leaf for reminiscences of Preil in his parents' home.

2. Feldman, *Modernism and Cultural Transfer*, p. 53.

3. G. Kressel, *Leksiqon hasifrut ha'ivrit badorot ha'aḥaronim* [Lexicon of Hebrew literature in recent times], vol. 2 (Merḥavia: Sifriat Po'alim, 1967), pp. 664–65; see this entry for publication information about books authored by Joshua Joseph Preil.

4. See Feldman's translation of this poem in *Modernism and Cultural Transfer*, pp. 43–44. The poem is also translated and commented on by Ezra Spicehandler in Stanley Burnshaw, T. Carmi, Susan Glassman, Ariel Hirschfeld, and Ezra Spicehandler, *The Modern Hebrew Poem Itself* (Detroit: Wayne State University Press, 2003), pp. 201–3.

5. Feldman, *Modernism and Cultural Transfer*, p. 52.

6. Gabriel Preil, "Besiman hasha'ah haqetsarah" [Under the sign of the short hour] in *Mitokh zeman venof*, (Jerusalem: Mossad Bialik, 1972), p. 110–11.

7. Gabriel Preil, "Shurot leAvraham Mapu" [Lines for Abraham Mapu] in *Mitokh zeman venof*, p. 149–50.

8. Gabriel Preil, "Sheloshah qerovim li" [Three who are close to me], *Asfan setavim: Shirim 1972–1992* [Collector of autumn: Collected poetry 1972–1992] (Jerusalem: Mossad Bialik, 1993), p. 207.

9. Feldman, *Modernism and Cultural Transfer*, chap. 5.

10. Stanley K. Coffman describing the thought of T. E. Hulme in Alex Preminger (ed.), *Princeton Encyclopedia of Poetry and Poetics* (Princeton, NJ: Princeton University Press, 1974), p. 378.

11. Feldman makes a convincing case that it was the poet Y. L. Teller, whom Preil had known since childhood, whose Yiddish minimalism had the greatest impact on Preil. See Feldman, *Modernism and Cultural Transfer*, pp. 61–70. For Preil's poem titled "Yehudah Leib Teller," see *Asfan setavim*, pp. 72–73.

12. For poems in which Glatstein figures, see "Hartsa'ah" [Lecture] and "Elul: Nisayon autobiografi" [Elul: Autobiographical experiment] in *Asfan setavim*, pp. 42–44. Preil's important essay on Glatstein is "'Al Ya'akov Glatshtein: Bimlot lo shishim shanah" [For Jacob Glatstein's sixtieth birthday], *Hado'ar*, November 9, 1956, p. 28.

13. Feldman, *Modernism and Cultural Transfer*, pp.89–97. See the Preil poem that makes reference to Shneour's poetics, "Ein zeh ha'ed hamerafref" [Not the hovering mist] in *Bitzaron*, 40 (1949):, p. 19. Preil's essay on Shneour is "Leyovelo shel Zalman Shneour [For Zalman Shneour's jubilee], *Niv* 2, no. 1 (November, 1937): pp. 4–5. It should be noted that Shneour spent most of the 1940s in New York. He was extremely prolific, and after Bialik and Tchernichovsky had fallen silent and died, Shneour's voluminous production remained the chief representative of the sensibility of his generation.

14. Feldman, *Modernism and Cultural Transfer*, p. 146.

15. The romantic option is still alive in his mother's time. See "Bazeman hazeh, bamaqom hazeh" [In this time, in this place] and "Shir sho'el qatan" [A little interrogatory poem], *Asfan setavim*, pp. 53, 97. In each case, romanticism is paired with a modifier that denotes strangeness or vagueness (*romantiqah temuhah, romantiqah setumah*).

16. *Mitokh zeman venof*, pp. 164–77. The poem originally appeared in *Ner mul kokhavim*. References in parenthesis will be to the twenty-two numbered sections that comprise the poem.

17. See Dan Miron's essay "Bein haner lakokhavim" [Between the candle and the stars] in *Asfan setavim*, p. 327.

18. Miron explicates the rich intertextual allusions to poems of Bialik and Tchernichovsky. "Bein haner lakokhavim," pp. 330–33.

19. For the Hebrew reader, it is difficult not to think of the image of the conquered city in conjunction with Natan Alterman's famous poem cycle *Simḥat 'aniyyim* [Joy of the poor], which appeared in Palestine in 1941.

20. Preil's first collection *Nof shemesh ukhefor* [Landscape of sun and frost] (1944) also contained several poems in this vein that were carried over into the selection included in *Mitokh zeman venof*. See "Nancy Linqon ḥolemet" [Nancy Lincoln dreams] (p. 217), "Mishirei Vermont" [Vermont poems] (pp. 225–27), and "LeNew Hampshire—'iggeret qetanah" [A little letter to New Hampshire] (p. 227).

21. "Beit-qevarot amer'iqani" [An American cemetery], *Ner mul kokhavim* (1954), 178–82. The poem is noted at its end: "Woodstock, 1945." Since each of the New England states and New York have a Woodstock, it is not easy to identify

the locale. Note also that the stated date of composition precedes the Maine poem by a year, even though the latter precedes it in the collection.

22. "Iggeret qetanah miNew York" [A little letter from New York] (*Asfan setavim*, p. 75), a poem from the late 1970s dedicated to Efros, expresses skepticism about the relevance of this achievement: "Yet now what was written here / about Indians, for example, / turns into a nearly historical artifact, spent and suspect / I myself am an Indian gaping in a darkening mirror."

23. Gabriel Preil, *Mapat 'erev* [Map of evening] (Tel Aviv: Dvir, 1960).

24. Friedland's essay, "Shirat ha'ani bekhivshono shel hazeman" [The poetry of the self and the mysteries of time] appeared in response to the publication of *Mapat 'erev*. It can be found in *Bitzaron* 43, no. 1 (Tishrei–Ḥeshvan 1961), pp. 42–47. Miron, "Bein haner lakokhavim," pp. 326–48.

25. On the ways in which Preil's poems handle a series of binary oppositions, see the important essays by Menachem Perry, "*Eineha mimul*—'al shiro shel Gavriel Preil 'Pereidah' ve'al aspeqt eḥad shel shirato" [On the Gabriel Preil poem 'Parting' and one aspect of his poetry], *Siman qeri'ah* 1 (September, 1972): pp. 255–63; and "Ha'onah hame'uzenet: 'al mivneh ha'omeq shel shirei Preil" [The balanced season: On the deep structure of Preil's poems], *Siman qeri'ah* 9 (July, 1979): pp. 453–61.

26. This structure can have many variations; it can even be wholly inverted, such as when the poem begins with a totality that later deconstructed. See Miron, "Bein haner lakokhavim," pp. 341–48.

27. The revised *Even Shoshan* dictionary has the stem (*p.n.n.*) in the hif'il but not the huf'al.

28. *Odem* is variously translated as sardius or sard (King James and Revised Standard Version translations of the Bible) and carnelian in the New Jewish Publication Society version.

Part III: Introduction

1. *Kol kitvei Yosef Hayyim Brenner*, vol. 2 (Tel Aviv: Hakibbutz Ham'euḥad and Dvir, 1960), pp. 389–90.

2. Ibid. Note that Brenner is describing the potential role of an American Hebrew literature not just in its responsibilities to the world Hebrew literary community, but also as a vehicle for deepening American Jewish self-understanding.

3. Rabinowitz's critique and the responses to it are summarized and given important context in Ezra Spicehandler, "*Ameriqa'iyyut* in American Hebrew Literature," in Alan Mintz (ed.), *Hebrew in America: Perspectives and Prospects* (Detroit: Wayne State University Press, 1993), pp. 68–104; and in Nurith Govrin, "The Demand for *Ameriqa'iyyut* and its Realization in Hebrew Literature in America," in Stanley Nash (ed.), *Migvan: Mehqarim basifrut ha'ivrit uvgilluyeha ha'ameriqani'im muggashim leYa'akov Kabakoff bimlot lo shiv'im shanah*

[Spectrum: Studies in Hebrew literature and its American transformations presented to Jacob Kabakoff on his seventieth birthday] (Lod, Israel: Haberman Institute, 1988), pp. 81–98.

4. There are a number of qualifications that must be made for this generalization to be accurate. Ginzburg's early poems about New York are a notable exception, as are Halkin's *Café Royale* poems. Although Silberschlag has little interest in American locales, he does write sharply satirical poems about American Jewish leadership. In Friedland's sonnets, there are occasional insightful glimpses of suburban life.

5. This applies as well, in a more minor key, to the relationship between Friedland's sonnets and his short stories.

Chapter Fifteen

1. Although I am approaching the Indian poems within the dynamics of American Hebrew literature, I am aware of the existence of several relevant, far broader contexts. How Indians made the passage from savages to "first Americans" in the American mind is a fascinating and important process that has been explored by, among others, Walter Benn Michaels (*Our America: Nativism, Modernism, and Pluralism* [Durham, NC: Duke University Press, 1995]); and Alan Trachtenberg (*Shades of Hiawatha: Staging Indians, Making Americans 1880–1930* [New York: Hill and Wang, 2004]). Trachtenberg's study focuses particularly on the connection between two simultaneous processes: the transformation in the perception of the Indian and the creation of immigrant culture. His chapter on Yehoash's Yiddish translation of Longfellow's iconic *Hiawatha* in 1910 is especially relevant to the Hebraists' efforts. Chaim Zhitlovsky's introduction to the translation stresses the need for Yiddish speakers to be imbued with the kind of "nature and the love of nature" that they do not come by easily in the teeming immigrant neighborhoods. The appropriation of Longfellow into Yiddish would moreover give Jewish immigrants a vicarious experience of the indigenousness they missed as latecomers to the American scene. "In choosing Longfellow's text for remaking as a Yiddish poem," Trachtenberg observes, "Yehoash chose an American epic that represented itself as a translation from a seeming indigenous American text of aboriginal myth and legend. What better choice for entry into what the American immigrants experienced on the streets of New York, a fast-stepping modern world that still dreamed itself innocent by imagining origins in an imaginary Indian past?" (p. 159). Indian material in Yiddish literature was also put to less romantic purposes. In her *Members of the Tribe: Native America in the Jewish Imagination* (Detroit: Wayne State University Press, 2010), Rachel Rubinstein explores how translations into English of Indian songs and chants with their proto-imagism created a bridge, albeit a one-way bridge, between modernist Yiddish poets and the American modernism being fostered by Harriet

Monroe and the circle around the journal *Poetry* in the second decade of the twentieth century.

2. Letter 479, *Kol kitvei Yosef Hayyim Brenner*, vol. 3, pp. 357–58, as quoted and trans. in Ezra Spicehandler, "Ameriqa'iyyut in American Hebrew Literature," in *Hebrew in America: Perspectives and Prospects*, Alan Mintz (ed.) (Detroit: Wayne State University Press, 1993), p. 75.

3. For a list of plays translated by American Hebrew authors, see Spicehandler, *Hebrew in America: Perspectives and Prospects*, pp. 103–4. For more on Silkiner's centrality, see Chapter 3 above and Jacob Kabakoff, "B. N. Silkiner and his Circle: The Genesis of the New Hebrew Literature in America," *Judaism* 39, no. 1 (Winter 1990): pp. 97–103.

4. Tz. H. Wolfson, "Mul ohel Timurah (biqoret)," *Haderor* 1, no. 6 (October 6, 1911): pp. 107–8, quoted in Stephen Katz, *Red, Black and Jew: New Frontiers in Hebrew Literature* (Austin: University of Texas Press, 2009), p. 22.

5. Our understanding of Silkiner's poem has been immeasurably deepened by Michael Weingrad's "Lost Tribes: The Indian in American Hebrew Poetry" in *Prooftexts* 24 (2004): pp. 291–319, which is included in his *American Hebrew Literature: Writing National Identity in the United States* (Syracuse: Syracuse University Press, 2011). Weingrad was the first to penetrate the work's stylistic mannerisms to appreciate the effective pathos underneath. He offers a comprehensive reading of *Mul ohel Timurah* as a reflection of Silkiner's Hebraist anxieties that has been instructive to me at every turn. In a similarly helpful vein, Katz's *Red, Black and Jew* offers a learned and insightful study of all the Indian epics, as well as the other major treatments of America in American Hebrew literature. Katz offers a particularly useful overview of the critical reception of the poem. He is more reserved than Weingrad in reading the poem as an expression of Silkiner's dilemmas.

6. Weingrad, *American Hebrew Literature*, p. 95. For Weingrad, the comparison to the movies is not flattering and stresses the conventions of melodrama and stereotyping that Efros borrowed from the new medium.

7. See Abraham Epstein, *Soferim 'ivrim ba'ameriqah* [Hebrew writers in America] (Tel Aviv: Dvir, 1952), p. 75 and Lisitzky's review of the poem in *Massad: Ma'asaf ledivrei sifrut 2* [Massad: A literary miscellany 2], ed. Hillel Bavli (New York: Haverim; Tel Aviv: Mitspeh, 1936), pp. 340–45. More recently, see Michael Weingrad, *American Hebrew Literature*.

8. Tom's prescience extends to the art of survival. When he observes the low status of crop cultivation among the Indians, which is relegated to the women while the men devote themselves to hunting, he lectures to anyone who will listen about the shortsightedness of this path. In terms that sound anachronistically physiocratic and proto-Zionist in equal measures, Tom argues that only by striking roots in the land by planting and cultivating can a nation hope to hold on to its territory (pp. 58–59). Katz (n. 13 to p. 40) points out that the Zionist echoes of this section were noted by a number of reviewers and that it was this passage

that was excerpted by Zvi Scharfstein's introductory anthology of Hebrew literature *Sha'ar lasifrut* [Gateway to literature] (New York: Shilo, 1947). See also Weingrad, *American Hebrew Literature*, p. 311.

9. See Katz, *Red, Black and Jew*, pp. 31–32 for information conveyed in an expanded version of the preface in the manuscript.

10. For insight on Efros's poetics generally and on the role of this poem in his development, see Ilana Elkad-Lehman, "Temurot po'etiyot beshirat Yisra'el Efrat" [Poetic changes in Israel Efrat's poetry] (PhD diss., Bar-Ilan University, 1995).

11. On the relationship between Lisitzky's poem and *Hiawatha*, see Katz's valuable observations, *Red, Black and Jew*, pp. 241–42, n. 14.

12. *Massad*, vol. 2, 1936, p. 334.

13. For a good overview of this literature, see Katz, *Red, Black and Jew*, pp. 242–43, nn. 15–22.

14. Ibid., pp. 60–65.

15. Ibid., p. 65.

Chapter Sixteen

1. The career of Hebrew among Christian divines and professors in elite universities is another story with manifold dimensions, which has been valuably treated in Shalom Goldman, *God's Sacred Tongue: Hebrew and the American Imagination* (Chapel Hill: University of North Carolina Press, 2004) and Shalom Goldman (ed.), *Hebrew and the Bible in America: The First Two Centuries* (Hanover, NH: University Press of New England, 1993).

2. The title of the poem is of course written in Hebrew letters as "Missus Vuds"; it appears in Bavli's *Shirim* [Poems] (Tel Aviv: Dvir, 1938), pp. 136–45.

3. The only mention of Jews in the poems comes here where she includes Hebrew congregations together with Catholics, Baptists, and Presbyterians (p. 144).

4. Stephen Katz, *Red, Black and Jew: New Frontiers in Hebrew Literature* (Austin: University of Texas Press, 2009), pp. 101–2, following suggestions by Epstein and E. R. Malachi.

5. "On the Americanness of Hillel Bavli" [Hebrew], *Bitzaron*, no. 227 (Kislev–Tevet, 1961): p. 76.

6. Gabriel Preil, *Ner mul kokhavim*, pp. 164–77.

7. Ibid., pp. 178–82.

8. Ibid., pp. 183–85.

9. The poem is signed "Woodstock 5705 (= 1945)." I assume that the reference is to the town in the Catskills not far from the Hudson River in New York State. But it also could be Woodstock, Vermont.

10. Putnam Valley is located in the Hudson Highlands in Putnam County, about sixty miles north of New York City to the east of the Hudson River. Abijah Lee is mentioned in the historical records of the time as a man who had

moved north from Westchester County and built a home on one of the lakes; see William J. Blake, *The History of Putnam County, N.Y.; with an enumeration of its towns, villages, rivers, creeks, lakes, ponds, mountains, hills, and geological features; local traditions; and short biographical sketches of early settlers, etc.* (New York: Baker & Scribner, 1849).

11. The King James translation favors "fitly set," whereas the New Jewish Publication Society renders "set by a brimming pool."

12. Even though the poem is not dated, it is safe to assume that it was written at about the same time (1945–46) as the two poems ("Mitsiyyurei Maine" and "Beit-qevarot ameriqani") that precede it.

Chapter Seventeen

1. *Zahav* was printed and published in New York under the Sefarim imprint through a partnership of the Hebrew Writers Association of Palestine, the Histadrut Ivrit of America, and the Keren Letarbuth of Cincinnati.

2. See this association in Abraham Epstein, *Soferim 'ivrim ba'ameriqah* [Hebrew writers in America] (Tel Aviv: Dvir, 1952), pp. 80–81.

3. See Stephen Katz's insightful treatment of the Indian theme in *Zahav* (*Red, Black and Jew: New Frontiers in Hebrew Literature* [Austin: University of Texas Press, 2009], pp. 44–47).

4. "Petticoat" is a euphonious equivalent for *petigil*, a term that occurs only in Isaiah 50:24; in later Hebrew, it can connote the female genitals. See Even Shoshan *ad loc.*

5. Katz, *Red, Black and Jew*, p. 44.

Chapter Eighteen

1. Chapters 6–8 of Stephen Katz's *Red, Black and Jew: New Frontiers in Hebrew Literature* (Austin: University of Texas Press, 2009) offer an excellent discussion of the range of these responses.

2. Although the autobiography concludes with Lisitzky seizing his vocation as a teacher of Hebrew, the book itself does not lead up to this fateful choice. The sudden materialization of this resolution suggests a retrospective revision of events that had taken place thirty years earlier. Lisitzky's settling in New Orleans was also the result of many domestic and psychological factors that the autobiography does not delve into. A true biographical portrait of Lisitzky is a great desideratum.

3. On the poetics of autobiographies by prominent people, see my *George Eliot and the Novel of Vocation* (Cambridge, MA: Harvard University Press, 1977), ch. 2.

4. The entire project of *Be'oholei Khush* should be understood against the complex attitudes of southern Jewry toward African Americans and the civil

rights movement. A good overview can be found in chap. 1, "The Liberal Jew, the Southern Jew, and Desegregation in the South, 1845–1964" in Seth Forman, *Blacks in the Jewish Mind: A Crisis of Liberalism* (New York: New York University Press, 1998). Forman underscores the importance of the mercantile identity of southern Jewry and the strength of religious rather than ethnic identification. In his Lithuanian origins and his Hebrew literary and education vocation, Lisitzky certainly stands apart from many of his fellow southern Jews. For a good discussion of the literary relations between African American and Jewish intellectuals, see Emily Miller Budick, *Blacks and Jews in Literary Conversation* (Cambridge and New York: Cambridge University Press, 1998). There is, furthermore, a considerable literature about the American Negro in American Yiddish literature, especially in the works of Israel Jacob Schwartz (*Kentucky*), Berish Vaynsthtayn's New York poems, and Yosef Opatoshu's novel *Lyncherei*. See Merle L. Bachman, *Recovering "Yiddishland": Threshold Moments in American Literature* (Syracuse: Syracuse University Press, 2008) and her "American Yiddish Poetry's Encounter with Black America" in *Shofar: An Interdisciplinary Journal of Jewish Studies* 21, no. 1 (2002): pp. 3–24.

5. "Merivei kohanim," pp. 171–81 (in *Be'oholei Khush*).

6. Katz, *Red, Black and Jew*, p. 118.

7. In addition to the preface ("Divrei petiḥah"), which precedes the table of contents, there is an introduction ("Haqdamah," pp. 7–13) that follows it. This is a brief historical account for the Hebrew reader of the origins and institutions of American slavery. Lisitzky frames his account of the enslavement of African Americans in relation to the biblical story of Israelite enslavement.

8. As a boy, Lisitzky must have read *Ohel Tom*, the 1896 translation by Abraham Singer published in Warsaw. For more recent translations, see Katz, *Red, Black and Jew*, p. 262, n. 28. On the level of cultural reciprocity, there is something quite extraordinary taking place here. The indebtedness of black liberation narrative, as well as Harriet Beecher Stowe's novel, to the Hebrew Bible and the story of the Exodus is fundamental. Then, we have a Jewish boy in Lithuania reading a translation of Stowe's novel into Hebrew. Later in his life, which has now been transferred to the American South, he observes the real-life descendents of the characters in Stowe's fiction, and then in turn, he seeks to re-inscribe them into a kind of neo-biblical Hebrew poetry. (I'm grateful to Wendy Zierler for this observation.)

9. The contest is succinctly summed up in the seemingly abstruse difference between *'ivri* and *'ivrit*. The first, a kind of Yiddish pronunciation of the name of the Hebrew language, connotes the use of Hebrew in traditional liturgical settings, while the second connotes Hebrew as a modern language and culture.

10. The analogy between slavery and the struggles of Hebrew educators is truly outrageous, and the fact that the narrator of the poem can present it without ironic markers is an indication of the degree to which he has personalized his identification with black slavery.

11. I have described this phenomenon in my *Banished From Their Father's Table: Loss of Faith and Hebrew Autobiography* (Bloomington: Indiana University Press, 1989).

12. I am grateful to Stephen Katz for conversations on this matter. He also clarified an important point about the place names and dates that are attached to the end of each poem. These are the places where the poems were composed rather than places where Lisitzky may have heard the songs or sermons upon which they were based. Hendersonville and Silva are locations in North Carolina where Lisitzky spent summer vacations, and that is why the poems written there invariable carry summer dates.

13. Katz, *Red, Black and Jew*, pp. 124–26 provides a good example of the difficulties by comparing one of Lisitzky's poems with a poem on a similar theme that uses dialect.

14. The poem is signed, "Hendersonville, North Carolina, Av 5702 (= 1942)."

15. It should be kept in mind that Lisitzky makes no effort to represent the responses of the implied audience in any of the sermons. Answering aloud the preacher's rhetorical questions and supporting his words with shouted comments were integral parts of the event; but Lisitzky must have found these ejaculations to be a violation of the kind of poem he was writing.

16. Katz, *Red, Black and Jew*, pp. 256–57.

17. I have taken "Yisra'el beShittim" as an example for analysis rather than "Vatedaber Miryam beMosheh" because the latter has already been capably illuminated in English by Stephen Katz, who has translated the full text of the poem ("So Miriam Spoke of Moses," *CCAR Journal: The Reform Quarterly* [Fall, 2008]: pp. 55–89), and by Wendy Zierler, who has discussed the poem together with another representation of Miriam in modern Hebrew poetry ("'On Account of the Cushite Woman that Moses Took': Race and Gender in Modern Hebrew Poems about Numbers 12," *Nashim: A Journal of Jewish Women's Studies & Gender Issues,* no. 19 [Spring 2010]: pp. 34–61).

18. On this issue see Michael Rogin, *Blackface, White Noise: Jewish Immigrants in the Hollywood Melting Pot* (Berkeley and Los Angeles: University of California Press, 1996) and the cogent assessment of his argument in Joel Rosenberg, "Rogin's Noise: The Alleged Historical Crimes of *The Jazz Singer*" in *Prooftexts*, 22 (2002): pp. 221–39.

Chapter Nineteen

1. Dan Pagis, "Hadukas hagadol shel New York" [The grand duke of New York] in *Milim nirdafot* [Synonyms] (Tel Aviv: Hakibbutz Hame'uḥad, 1982), p. 58.

2. *Mitokh hasugar* (New York: Ohel, 1948). Two works were assembled from his literary estate and published after his death: *Mehashirah ha 'idit ba 'ameriqah*

[From American Yiddish poetry] (Tel Aviv: Menorah, 1967) is a selection of poems by American Yiddish poets translated into Hebrew by Halevi; and *New York: Shirim ve'iyyunim besifruteinu heḥadashah* [New York: Poems and essays about modern literature] (Tel Aviv: Menorah, 1968). The latter was edited by the poet's brother-in-law, the writer Yaakov Rimon, who in turn, is the brother of the poet Yosef Zvi Rimon. The volume contains a biographical preface by Yaakov Rimon.

3. The information on Halevi's life is taken from Yaakov Rimon's preface in *New York*, pp. 9–14.

4. Shimon Halkin, "Avraham Zvi Halevi," in *Derakhim vetsidei derakhim basifrut* [Paths and byways in literature], vol. 2 (Jerusalem, 1969), pp. 121–28. The review first appeared in *Bitzaron* in 1949. It is interesting that Halkin focuses on the lyric poems in the volume and only mentions the New York City poems in passing. There are poems dedicated to Halkin in both of Halevi's collections. See also references to Halevi in Michael Weingrad, *American Hebrew Literature: Writing Jewish National Identity in the United States* (Syracuse: Syracuse University Press, 2011), pp. 38–40, 212, and 228.

5. *Mitokh hasugar* is carefully ordered, and Halevi took care to place the Manhattan poems after the lyric poems and to conclude the volume with the corona. When Yaakov Rimon put together the posthumous volume *New York*, which includes all the poems in *Mitokh hasugar*, he took it upon himself to reorder the sections, and he placed the Manhattan poems in the first position, followed by the corona, and only then did he place the lyric sections. Although he was right in sensing that the city poems are Halevi's most distinctive achievement, it is unfortunate that he disturbed the compositional design that the poet had constructed.

6. For the role of the corona in Hebrew literature and esp. Tchernichovsky's important corona *Lashemesh* [To the sun], see the discussions of Tchernichovsky by Robert Alter, Arnold Band, and Aminadav Dykman in Alan Mintz (ed.), *Reading Hebrew Literature: Critical Discussions of Six Modern Texts* (Hanover, NH: Brandeis University Press, 2002), chap. 2.

7. *Ronen* in line 2 is ambiguous. The primary meaning of the word is to sing; but a secondary meaning, derived from Lamentations 2:9, is to shout in agony and supplication.

8. In Hebrew, the sonnet is often called a *shir zahav*, a golden poem, because the numerical value of the letters in *zahav* is fourteen, and the appellation strengthens the form's privileged lineage. See Halevi's poem, "Shir zahav," in *Mitokh hasugar*, p. 46.

9. All page numbers refer to *Mitokh hasugar*.

10. Halevi's translations of American Yiddish poetry into Hebrew were collected after his death and published as Avraham Zvi Halevi, *Mehashirah ha 'idit ba 'ameriqah* [From Yiddish American Poetry] (Tel Aviv: Menorah, 1967).

Index

Locators in italics indicate pages that include photographs.

507

Credits

Moshe Feinstein, "Tsimtsum" [Frugality] is from *Sefer hayovel shel Hado'ar*, Hahistadrut Ha'ivrit Ba'ameriqah, New York, 1927.

Benjamin Silkiner, "Bat Shiri" [My muse]. Originally published in *Shirim*, Haverim/Dvir, New York and Tel Aviv, 1927.

Simon Halkin, "To the Lizard." Originally published as "El haleta'ah" in *Shirim 1917–1973*, Mossad Bialik, Jerusalem, 1977. With the kind permission of Mossad Bialik.

Abraham Regelson, "To the Child Raim Son of Abraham." Originally published as "El haqatan Re'em ben Avraham" in *Ḥaquqot otiyyotayikh*, Maḥbarot Lesifrut, Tel Aviv, 1964; to be published in Regelson's collected works by the Bialik Institute.

Gabriel Preil, "Gardens of Truth and White Lava." Originally published as "Pirqei zeman" in *Asfan setavim*, Mossad Bialik, Jerusalem, 1993.

Israel Efros, "Little Clapper." Originally published as "'Inbol qatan" in *Shirim*, Haverim/Mitspeh, Tel Aviv, 1932.

Ephraim E. Lisitzky, "Shirati" [My poetry/song]. Originally published as "Shirati" in *Shirim*, Haverim/Dvir, New York and Tel Aviv, 1928.

Ephraim E. Lisitzky, "Like a Soldier." Originally published as "Keḥayal she-nitroqnah ashpat ḥitsav" in *Shirim*, Haverim/Dvir, New York and Tel Aviv, 1928.

Hillel Bavli, "Prayer." Originally published as "Tefillah" in *Shirim*, Dvir, Tel Aviv, 1938.

Shimon Ginsburg, "In Praise of the Hebraists in America." Originally published as "La'ivrim ba'ameriqah mizmor" in *Shirim ufo'emot*, Haverim/Dvir, Tel Aviv, 1931.

H. A. Friedland, "Sonnet" [I have been asked . . .]. Originally published as "Sonetah" in *Shirim*, Ogen, New York, 1940.

H. A. Friedland, "Groan." Originally published as "Anaḥah" in *Sonetot*, Ogen, New York, 1939.

H. A. Friedland, "Shearing." Originally published as "Gez" in *Sonetot*, Ogen, New York, 1939.

Moshe Feinstein, "Two from the night." Originally published as "Shenayim li milaylah" in *Shirim vesonetot*, Ogen, New York, 1935.

521